Operations Management

A Systems Concept

Richard A. Johnson
William T. Newell
Roger C. Vergin

University of Washington

Houghton Mifflin Company
Boston

New York / Atlanta / Geneva, Illinois
Dallas / Palo Alto

Library of Congress Catalog Card Number: 77–172024

ISBN: 0–395–04695–5

Preface

The changing nature of Operations Management has outdated much of the existing instructional material on this subject. Traditional textbooks spend time describing manufacturing facilities and layout, work procedures and measurement, and operating practices. This offers students little foundation for continued learning. What only recently was a study of the production function for a manufacturing concern is evolving into the analysis of design and operations in general, with emphasis on analysis rather than description. The change in Operations Management emerged with the development of some sophisticated techniques of analysis, grew with the application of computers, and blossomed with the introduction of systems theory.

We have used the systems approach to provide a framework or general model of analysis to which specific concepts, techniques, and tools can be related. Our framework, which is not limited to the manufacturing industry, can be used for outlining and analyzing problems, for designing and operating organizations effectively, and for accumulating knowledge in proper placement and perspective. The material in this book has application to any organization of people and machines, such as hospitals, governmental agencies, service organizations, and industrial concerns. This book does not, however, contain all of the concepts involved in the management of an organization. For example, we include only a brief discussion about the relationships among people or human resource administration, although this is obviously one of the most important subject areas in management.

We have integrated tools and techniques of management into the subject matter so that they are presented in those areas where their application has been successful and most practical. These same techniques may be used elsewhere. On the other hand, they should not be used every time a manager considers similar problems of resource allocation. Our contention is that managers should use techniques and tools when they can improve the decision-making process, and when the marginal gain resulting from their use is greater than the additional cost incurred.

Perhaps our most difficult decision in planning this book relates to its level of difficulty, particularly as it applies to some of the mathematical concepts. More and more students can comprehend and appreciate a high order of complexity and want to understand any technique which refines the decision process. We decided to include materials of various levels of difficulty so that instructors can omit the more difficult chapters without upsetting the basic concepts developed in other sections of the book. Students with little or no background and skill in mathematics can derive much from this book, although the benefit will be greater for those who have studied college algebra and can express concepts and relationships in simple equations. A general knowledge of calculus is helpful in a few chapters for evaluating relationships for maximum and minimum conditions. In the area of statistics, an understanding of trend analysis, measures of central tendency, and the basic concepts of probability will add meaning to some of the material. Finally, a student should have some exposure to beginning computer technology (hardware and software).

Throughout this book, we have attempted to present a message and a challenge. During the past few years we have heard much about our environmental problems. How, for example, the profuse garbage generated by our rich economy threatens our air, land, and water. These problems are closely related to the increasing world population. From one billion in 1850, the world population increased to two billion in 1930, to over three and a half billion today, and could increase to seven billion by 2000 if present trends continue. Even though the economic wealth of the world is expanding rapidly, an absolute shortage of resources still exists. Consequently, we must organize and develop priorities for the available resources. This is a job for well-informed and resolute decision makers.

The best way to get the flavor of this book is to read the first and last chapters. These chapters not only outline the framework of the book, but suggest the possibility of applying the systems concept of analysis to current problems. Operations Management as an analytical study of organizations is a subject which most students will find challenging and useful.

We wish to thank all of our colleagues who reviewed and criticized materials in this book. We are particularly grateful to Professors Robert C. Meier and Albert N. Schrieber for their help in outlining the project. In addition, Robert C. Meier contributed much of the material for Chapters 3 and 4. We also wish to thank Professors Fremont E. Kast and James E. Rosenzweig for allowing us to use some of the concepts developed in *The Theory and Management of Systems,* second edition. We owe much to Professors John D. Demarel, University of Colorado, Bernard E. Smith, Dartmouth College, and Wickham Skinner, Harvard University, for their reviews of the initial manuscript. Finally, we wish to express our appreciation to Kermit O. Hanson, Dean of the Graduate School of Business Administration, University of Washington, for creating the kind of academic environment where the development of new ideas is encouraged.

Richard A. Johnson
William T. Newell
Roger C. Vergin

Contents

Chapter 1
Systems and
Operations
Management

At the turn of the century, a number of Britons believed that every significant invention had already been recorded, and so they instituted a drive to close the Royal Patent Office. Their failure to envisage the countless new inventions developed since that time vividly demonstrates man's inability to foresee the future.

Perhaps this inability to look ahead results from the desire to keep things as they are—to maintain the status quo. The majority has never accepted change as an essential of life. When Richard Arkwright invented the spinning frame in 1769, hostile workmen attempted to destroy any replicas that appeared. Similarly, upon the introduction of steam power, many newspaper publishers urged mothers to cease bearing children because steam power would rob them of job possibilities. Nevertheless, advances in technology were adopted in the face of widespread resistance, with scores of new economic opportunities opening for the people.

In the United States, acceptance of new ideas and adjustment to the changes wrought by innovation have occurred more readily than in most other countries around the world. But this ability to accept and adjust will be tested more rigorously in the future than ever before. The transition which overcame American society in the 1960s was merely a foretaste of tomorrow.

The change is evident everywhere. Since the end of World War II, for example, the population has increased dramatically; in November, 1967, the number of people inhabiting the United States passed the 200 million mark. Whereas it took 35 years for the population to grow from 100 to 150 million, the next 50 million was tacked on in less than half that time, namely, 17 years.

We also experienced tremendous economic growth during the 1960s. The Gross National Product (expressed in 1958 dollars) increased from approximately $300 billion in 1950 to nearly $488 billion in 1960 and up to almost

$750 billion in 1970. This new wealth generated dramatic increases in personal income, in consumer spending, and in the value of resources allocated for education and public welfare.

The increase in the size of institutions in this country during the same period is of great significance to the function of management. The 20 largest corporations in the United States had combined sales of over $139 billion in 1970—a volume larger than the entire Gross National Product in 1940. Similarly, public organizations greatly expanded their operations. By 1967, one out of every six nonagricultural employees had a job at some level of the government. In 1967, federal, state, and local governments were by far the largest customers in the United States, buying $176.3 billion worth of goods and services, or twenty-two per cent of every dollar spent. The size of giant private and public organizations often defies comprehension, and the growth continues.

Although we are living in an age of intense social change and unrest, many of the problems in our society are not unique to this age. In the mid-nineteenth century, every major city of the United States had slums so horrible that, in comparison, our contemporary slum areas appear benign. By 1900, New York's traffic problems with the brewery drays, horse trolleys, hackney coaches, and steam locomotives had reached a crisis. Many large cities had areas where anarchy or gang rule went unchallenged. And the history of American cities is replete with accounts of epidemics caused by polluted drinking water, streets made impassable by snow or mud, strikes and riots, and operating inefficiencies and corruption in city government.[1]

In the eighteenth century, when the plight of the poor in Ireland became intolerable, Jonathan Swift suggested, in "A Modest Proposal," that if the rich would fatten and eat the children of the poor both food and population problems would be solved. With the resources and know-how available today, Jonathan Swift would be able to suggest more reasonable solutions. For the first time, we are acknowledging the existence of such problems, and we are aware of the urgent need to solve them. The situation presents us with a tremendous challenge and opportunity. Imagine the excitement in redesigning urban centers to rid them of pollution and slums, in creating new economic opportunities to reduce poverty and increase the standard of living, in designing new transportation systems to accommodate the increasing number of travelers, and in developing the knowledge and the means to explore unknown areas of the universe.

The immediate task of our society is to marshall resources to solve these problems—to create public and private institutions which can achieve social and economic goals in the most effective and efficient manner possible. We must structure organizations of the future to accommodate and adjust

[1] Raymond Vernon, *The Myth and Reality of Our Urban Problems* (Cambridge, Mass.: Harvard University Press, 1966).

to change, to work as a unit toward common goals, and to evaluate the performance of each of the various segments toward accomplishing the master plan.

Unfortunately, the typical functional organization cannot meet current or future requirements efficiently. If traditional organizations had possessed sufficient flexibility, the buggymakers of the past would have become today's automobile manufacturers, and the railroads would have used the airplane in their transportation system.

Management by system is more adaptable to change than the typical functional organization. For this reason, we have chosen management by system as a framework for the study of Operations Management. We define Operations Management as *the design and operation of systems, including the application of those tools and techniques which are useful in achieving efficient and effective systems performance.* Operations Management, as described in this text, has application to all forms of public and private organizations, those engaged in manufacturing, distribution, and service. A more detailed discussion of this field of study, and its relation to other subject areas, is included later in this chapter.

General Systems Theory

What is systems theory? What is a system? We might modify the phrase "happiness is different things to different people" and say "systems mean different things to different people." For example, some relate systems to science which they describe as a systematic body of knowledge; an array of essential principles or facts arranged in a rational dependence or connection; a complex of ideas, principles, laws, forming a coherent whole. Scientists endeavor to develop, organize, and classify material into interconnected disciplines. Two well-known works, Darwin's *The Origin of Species* and Keynes' *General Theory of Employment, Interest, and Money,* represent attempts to integrate a large amount of related material. Darwin, in his theory of evolution, integrated all life into a "system of nature" and indicated how the myriad of subsystems were interrelated. Keynes, in his work, connected the many complicated natural and man-made forces that influence an economy. Both men had a major impact on man's thinking because they were able to conceptualize interrelationships among complex phenomena and integrate them into a systematic whole. The term *systems,* when used in this context, connotes plan, method, order, and arrangement.

Similarly, general systems theory has been described as the development of a systematic, theoretical framework for describing general relationships of the empirical world. Existing similarities in the theoretical construction of various disciplines become apparent upon examination. Models can be developed that are applicable to many systems, whether physical, biological, behavioral, or social. An ultimate but distant goal of general systems theory is to develop a framework (or systems of systems of systems) that will tie all disciplines together in a meaningful relationship.

The Need for a General Systems Theory

One of the most important indications of the need for a general systems theory pertains to the problem of communication among the various disciplines. Although there is similarity in the general approach (scientific method), the results are not often communicated across discipline boundaries. Hence, the conceptualizing and hypothesizing done in one area seldom are used in other areas even though such work might contribute to a significant breakthrough. Specialists seldom communicate with one another between disciplines. Of course, the conflict of ideas and difficulties of communication are even greater between the various fields of study—the scientific, the social sciences, and the humanistic.

On the positive side, there has been some tendency toward interdisciplinary study in recent years. Areas such as social psychology, biochemistry, astro-physics, social anthropology, economic psychology, and economic sociology have been developed in order to emphasize the interrelationships of previously isolated disciplines. More recently, areas of study and research that call on numerous subfields have been advanced. For example, cybernetics, the science of communication and control, draws on electrical engineering, neurophysiology, physics, biology, and several other fields. Operations research is often pointed to as a multidisciplinary approach to problem solving. Organization theory embraces economics, sociology, engineering, psychology, physiology, and anthropology. Problem solving and decision making are also becoming focal points for analysis and research, drawing on numerous fields. Unfortunately, the "new" cross-disciplines sometimes create a jargon that tends to compound the communication problem.

With such examples of interdisciplinary approaches, it is easy to understand the surge of interest in large-scale, systematic bodies of knowledge. However, this trend calls for the development of an overall framework within which the various subparts or disciplines can be integrated but in which they still retain the type of discipline that distinguishes them. The approach of providing an overall framework (general systems theory) extracts phenomena common to many different disciplines and develops general models which include such phenomena.

Systems Defined[2]

Within the context of general system theory, we stated that a system is an assemblage or combination of things or parts forming a complex or unitary whole. In this usage it covers an extremely broad spectrum of concepts—for example, in the world around us, there are mountain systems,

[2] Richard A. Johnson, Fremont E. Kast, and James E. Rosenzweig, *The Theory and Management of Systems*, 2nd ed. (New York: McGraw-Hill Book Company, 1967).

river systems, and the solar system. The human body is a complex organism made up of a skeletal system, a circulatory system, and a nervous system. We come into daily contact with transportation systems, communication systems, and economic systems.

An obvious hierarchy of systems can be created: systems, systems of systems, and systems of systems of systems. For example, the universe is a system of heavenly bodies, which includes many subsystems of stars called galaxies. Within one such galaxy (the Milky Way) is the solar system, one of many planetary systems. Similarly, an organism is a system of mutually dependent parts, each of which might include many subsystems. The human body is, for example, comprised of organs which are themselves subsystems of the organism as a whole.

Now we can use this same framework or philosophy in the task of managing resources. If organizational units are designed and operated as a system, each segment or subsystem can be viewed as a self-contained unit and its relationship or contribution to the next level in the hierarchical structure can be programmed and measured. This means that precise identification of units and of their input and output is an essential part of management by system. Before elaborating in greater detail, however, we should offer a working definition of systems, a definition which can be used as a basis for the study, design, and operation of man-made systems.

We will define a system as *an array of components designed to accomplish a particular objective according to plan.* This definition contains three significant parts. First, the system must have a purpose or objective to perform. Secondly, components are designed (and sometimes constructed) in a meaningful arrangement. Finally, inputs of information, energy, and materials are allocated according to an operating plan. This definition may be clearer when it is considered in conjunction with Figure 1.1, a model of a basic system. Planned resource inputs of information, energy, and materials are transformed by men and/or machines to produce output of products, ideas, or service. This output, if the system is effective, achieves the purpose or goal of the system.

Figure 1.1   Model of a Basic System

Input   *Transformation*   *Output*

Types of Systems Systems may be classified in various ways—for example, natural systems, such as the solar system, as compared to man-made systems, such as a transportation system. Those relationships between objects and sequences of events observed in their natural setting which have meaning for us constitute natural systems. Such systems behave according to the laws of nature and their input-output relationships are predictable in a scientific sense. In contrast, man-made systems are those designed and operated by man. They utilize inputs from natural systems, but retain little of the scientific predictability found in nature, largely because man is somewhat unpredictable. *Our discussion will be limited to man-made systems.*

We may also distinguish between flexible and rigid systems. In a flexible system, the *structure or design* of the system is adjusting continually to maintain a balance or equilibrium between the system and its changing environment. In contrast, a rigid system is not a self-maintaining unit and its structure does not adjust, at least not in the short run. Most life forms, as well as economic, political, and social systems are examples of flexible systems. A highway is an example of a rigid system—once constructed, little could be done in the short run to adjust to a change in traffic.

Man tries to build some flexibility into every system he constructs. For example, a building might be designed so that it could be converted to some other use if the primary need for the structure changed. The reader should not confuse flexible and rigid systems (which relate to design) with open and closed systems (which relate to operations). The control of systems in operations will be discussed in Chapter 6.

Another classification of systems pertains to the degree of human involvement in relation to the machine. At one end of the spectrum we can visualize a system utilizing few, if any, machines or tools. A group of natives weaving straw hats illustrates a manual system of production. At the other extreme, an automated refinery programmed to produce petroleum products without human involvement during the transformation process is an example of an automatic-machine system. The man-machine relationship in most systems falls somewhere between the two extremes. Some industries have a high capital investment in machines (for example, the steel industry), whereas in others the human factor is more significant (for example, service industries).

The classifications natural versus man-made, flexible versus rigid, and man versus machine have all pertained to the design or structure of systems. The nature of a system's output forms another grouping: (1) systems that produce things, and (2) systems that serve clients. The manufacturing department of the Chevrolet Division of the General Motors Corporation is a subsystem of that corporation which is designed to produce automobiles. Man and machines follow predetermined instructions to achieve the operating goals outlined by the company. The essence of a producing organization or system rests in the processes by which resources are converted or transformed into output.

The fundamental purpose of other systems is to serve clients. Service may be performed by distributing products, ideas, or providing utility for people in general. For example, a retail store does not produce a product per se, but makes goods available to customers and therefore produces a service. Similarly, a doctor or lawyer produces a service by providing medical or legal assistance for the client.

The classifications which have been presented illustrate the various hierarchies or levels of systems, and also reveal the difficulty of distinct and meaningful groupings. The classifications are presented chiefly to help the reader gain some "feel" for systems and to see the relationship between this theory and the world in which we live.

Components of Systems

In many kinds of analysis the inputs and outputs of a system are more significant than the actual transformation process. We can use this "black-box" approach to demonstrate the relationship between components and systems. A component is a basic unit or "black box" which performs, or provides the facility for performing, some part of the defined transformation process. There is little or no value in subdividing or describing the component in further detail, at least not in that instance. For example, a classroom building may be considered a component in an education system when there is limited value to detail the analysis of the building according to its heating system, lighting system, and so forth. A teacher may be classified as a component in a university system, even though the same individual may be described for a medical illustration as a system with several subsystems. A component cannot satisfy the total specifications of a given system, even though the component may qualify as a system in another situation or context. Moreover, a component may be a part of more than one system— for example, we are components in our economic system, and also in parallel social and political systems. The determination of what is a system, subsystem, or component occurs when the objectives of that system are determined. The need to define the system and outline the exact boundaries, turns out to be a significant advantage of the systems approach. It also should be noted that the definition of the system determines the "total system" for the purpose of operation and analysis.

Every system includes components, some of which may qualify as systems under different circumstances, and each system in turn is a subsystem of the next higher level of abstraction. The boundaries of a system will be a function of the scope of the organization or system, the extent to which control can be exercised, and/or the nature of the problem requiring analysis. Figure 1.2 shows the relationship of components to systems in the network hierarchy; how, for example, when A is defined as the total system, sublevels A_1, A_2, and A_4 apply. Segments of A_4 are components of subsystem A_3 unless an additional level of analysis is meaningful, that is A_5.

Figure 1.2 Hierarchy of Systems

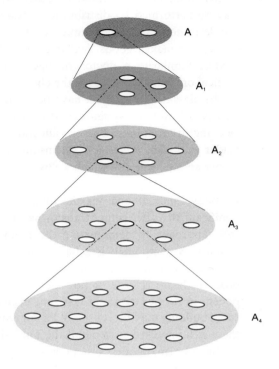

Systems and Organizations

In arranging and managing the resources of an organization as a system, the achievement of goals and optimization of the input-output relationship of the total system receive primary attention. The preparation and management of a system require a sequence of decisions, each distinct but closely related to the others:

   1. systems determination,
   2. design and creation,
   3. operation and control,
   4. review and evaluation.

First, a decision is made to create a system. An entrepreneur decides to open a corner grocery store, a large aerospace organization decides to establish a missile division, or the government decides to create an agency to help solve the problems of the cities.

After the decision is made to have a system, it must be planned—facilities are provided as required, components arranged, and people hired. This is the design stage. The grocer must find a location, build or rent a building, add facilities in some logical layout to expedite customer service, and hire and train clerical help.

...tem has been designed and created, it is ready to function. ...tore manager, for example, will buy and sell foods and notions ...ds to provide a service to the customer and, hopefully, make a

...operation by system is the premise that given certain inputs, ...will produce certain outputs, or operate within established limits. ...r, the relationship between structure and operation may not be ...ictable. A predetermined equilibrium, particularly in flexible systems, ...an seldom be forecast by equation, and will change, within limits, as the components of the system are rearranged (structure), or as the inputs are allocated (operation). In most instances, therefore, there must be control of operations, or a means of keeping the system on course in spite of unpredictable variables. Control includes a sensor for measuring output or related characteristics, a means of comparing the measurement with a standard, and an activating unit to adjust inputs to correct any indicated deficiencies. The control should regulate the variables so that the system will tend to stabilize near an established equilibrium. This objective is possible only if a meaningful standard can be determined and if such operating values can be measured. A system incorporating a control subsystem is illustrated in Figure 1.3. Note the significance of feedback. First, control measures operating information and feeds it back to be compared with an established standard. When corrective action is indicated, control releases instructional information to activate a change in input. A more detailed discussion of control is included in Chapter 6.

Figure 1.3 The Four Elements of a Control System

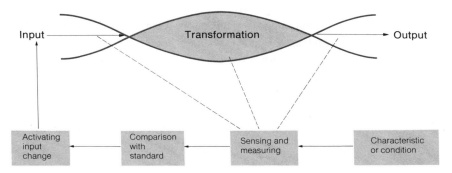

The fourth decision level pertains to how well the system has operated. Has it been effective and/or efficient? A system is *effective* if it accomplishes its objectives, while *efficiency* is the relationship of resource input to output. A system can be effective while wasting resources (inefficient), and conversly, may transform inputs efficiently without achieving the objectives as outlined (for example, more shoes per man-hour of input, but all for the

left foot, or a product few people wish to b
a balance between effectiveness and efficie
position. Obtaining such a balance becom
and we say the system is optimized. A non
extent that this balance does not occur. For e
flict between the quality of the product and the
try to achieve the greatest quality (effectiveness)
ciency) acceptable to the competitive environment.

Periodically, review and evaluation occur during the
tem, and they may lead to design changes in the present s
mendations for change which may be incorporated into f
Review and evaluation are often conducted in conjunction with
tions of a system. The feedback of operating information furnishes
of how the system is doing, that is, whether or not design change
required. Such analysis may bring changes in design, whereas control acti
causes changes in operating input.

Inputs of information, energy, and materials are basic to all systems. *Information* is needed during the design and creation stage to determine how the stated objectives can be accomplished (determination of transformation process); *energy* (effort spent designing and creating the system) exerted by people or the power to operate machines; and *materials* are transformed into the equipment and machines that will be part of the system. In operation and control, all inputs are either inputs of *information* (for example, customer data, quantities, prices, discounts, and delivery dates), inputs of *energy* (energy exerted by the workers or the energy used to operate machines), or inputs of *materials* (such as raw materials, invoice forms, and machine ribbons).

Planning or decision making takes place at all four stages. The kind and extent at each stage, however, will vary with the nature or kind of system. For example, an automated oil refinery (rigid system) must be carefully preplanned. Most operating decisions are programmed into the system. A department store (flexible system) establishes more general objectives and plans, and uses decision making at the operating level to adjust the system to various environmental influences which are bound to occur.

The Case for a Systems Approach

During the past two or three decades, several concepts and theories have been proposed as a framework for the management of organizations. A brief review of some of these approaches will illustrate why we have chosen a systems approach as the general model in this book.

Information Theory

Information theory, or the mathematical theory of communications, can be used to study various management situations. By making certain basic assumptions (ignoring semantics or meaning), a simplified set of mathematical relationships has been developed which is used primarily in the technical aspect of information transmission. Information theory has been applied as a methodology for determining the rate at which information can be transmitted under certain specified circumstances. Some of the factors affecting transmission include the nature of the signal source, whether the signal is discrete or continuous; the nature of the channel and, in particular, its capacity for transmitting information; the nature of the noise, if any, which disturbs the transmission; and the fidelity criterion by which the adequacy of the transmission is judged.

Although a wide range of applications is claimed for information theory, most are in the technical aspects of transmission. Some of the subdisciplines are filtering theory, detection theory, and the analysis of signals statistics. Information theory is cited as an integral part of such areas as the theory of communications, the theory of automata, the theory of automatic control systems, the analysis of language, and informational aspects of physics. Fields where information theory is cited as operative (applicable) and unified (integrative) are thermodynamics, statistical mechanics, photography, language, models, gambling, cryptology, pattern recognition, and computer technology.

Information flow is one of several integral systems in a business or public organization, while systems management is the overall framework within which communication or information flow fits. Communication systems, or systems of information flow, are the vehicle through which the key management functions can be integrated and administered.

Decision Making Theory

Many theorists have focused their attention on the *decision-making processes* within an organization. One group concentrates on the human problem-solving processes and decisions mechanisms as the primary forces in organizational behavior. According to this thesis, organizational participants should not be viewed as mere mechanical instrumentalities, but should be perceived as individuals with wants, motives, aspiration levels, and drives, and with limited rationality and capacity for problem solving. In other words, this theory regards people not as components but as very complex subsystems contributing to the system. The question is often raised whether the objectives of the system or those of the people participating in the system should be optimized.

Others view the field of decision making as synonymous with "managing." In this sense, decision making has three principal stages: *intelligence*—searching the environment for conditions calling for decisions; *design*—inventing, developing, and analyzing possible courses of action; and *choice*—selecting a particular course of action from the available alternatives.[3]

---

[3] Herbert A. Simon, *The New Science of Management Decision* (New York: Harper & Row Publishers, Inc., 1960), pp. 1–4.

Another group of theorists regard the quantitative aspects of decision making as the key to the selection, design, and operation of systems. These theorists have concentrated on developing and refining mathematical models and techniques.

Systems Analysis

The systems approach may be used as the general model for designing and operating organizations, but *Systems Analysis* is a technique for planning and solving problems. As such, it becomes an orderly method used to review and appraise alternative ways of using scarce resources to accomplish a particular objective. Considering the integrative nature of a problem (that is, the cause and effect relationships among the elements), the constantly changing environment in which planning must be formulated, and the limited resources and time available to complete a study, the logic of this approach can assist and refine the decision-making process.

In many ways systems analysis is very similar to the scientific method. It includes a phase in which requirements and constraints are carefully outlined, alternative methods of achieving the objectives are carefully outlined in detail, trade-off studies are made within the selection criteria for determining the best alternative, and a decision plan developed which satisfies specified objectives.

Systems analysis is problem-oriented and follows a logical process of deductive-inductive reasoning. Questions considered include:[4]

1. How many distinguishable elements are there to this seeming problem?

2. What cause-and-effect relationships exist among these elements?

3. What function needs to be performed in each case?

4. What trade-offs may be required among resources, once they are defined?

The reasoning process always goes from deductive to inductive as it progresses from general objectives to plans and then back in a cyclical, closed-loop fashion to redefining objectives and making more detailed plans. The process, illustrated in Figure 1.4, goes through several stages of development starting with general objectives and proceeding to plans, then back to refining objectives and detailing plans further, then back again, and so forth.

The four main stages—translation, analysis, trade-offs, and synthesis—are also illustrated in Figure 1.4. Translation represents the statement of the problem, including all of the constraints placed on the solution. Organizational policies prescribing general patterns of action, and time or cost

---

[4] P. G. Thome and R. G. Willard, "The Systems Approach—A Unified Concept of Planning," *Aerospace Management,* General Electric Company, Missile and Space Division, 1, no. 3 (Fall–Winter 1966): 25.

restrictions placed on the design and/or operation of the system are examples of constraints. At this stage, selection criteria, such as cost/effectiveness, timing and risk, are outlined and used to evaluate the appropriateness of various trade-offs. The practical reiteration of the cycle until refinements have sharpened the final plan or solution illustrates the feedback features of the model.

Figure 1.4 A Model of Systems Analysis

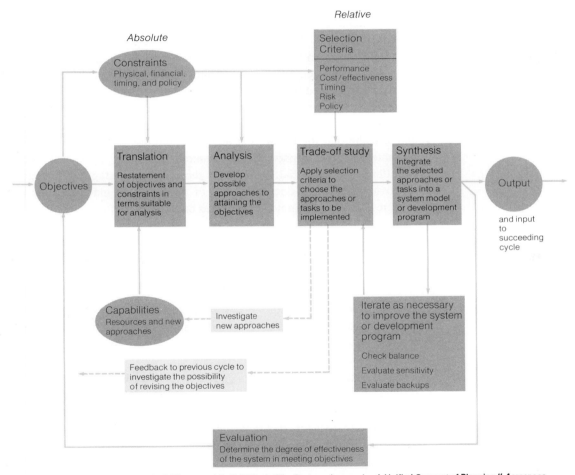

Source: P. G. Thome and R. G. Willard, "The Systems Approach—A Unified Concept of Planning," *Aerospace Management*, General Electric Company, Missile and Space Division, 1, no. 3 (Fall–Winter 1966): 31.

At some point, a practical solution or plan may not be feasible. If this occurs, the decision makers review the objectives, along with constraints and selection criteria. A slight modification or adjustment may free the decision makers to increase the alternative solutions, or to develop feasible solutions from among the current alternatives.

Material, energy, and information flow are essential elements of any given system or subsystem, although each may be developed as a flow process itself. The design of a system may highlight any one of these elements, but it must consider all three. For example, material flow could be traced through a process flow chart. A space and layout study could determine optimal arrangements of facilities and equipment in consideration of the flow of raw materials through the system. In layout analysis the human element in the man-machine system is an extremely significant factor. Decision makers can develop organizational charts as a matrix to apply to specific systems, rather than arranging them in the traditional, functional hierarchical manner. The organization, structured around the flow of material and information between decision points, would cut across traditional, functionally specialized department boundaries. This structure focuses attention on subsystem and total-system objectives and goals.

Systems analysis has been used effectively for planning advanced systems and technologies. When used with skill and common sense, it has been a valuable technique for identifying advanced requirements of complex systems, assessing the impact of environmental changes on developmental plans, identifying potential problems in the conceptual stage of a program, and providing accurate documentation of the decisions made and the supporting reasons for recommended courses of action.

The Systems Approach

The systems approach is the broad framework to which such concepts as information flow and decision theory, and techniques like systems analysis relate. These various forms of analysis should not be considered separately, but as segments of something larger where each can contribute enormously to the others for "—the integrated whole is much greater than the sum of the parts. Each produces an analog of an enterprise system or subsystem, and these analogs simulate the behavior of the system caricatured."[5]

The systems approach is not new; it is a concept borrowed from the natural sciences. Now it is being used as a philosophy for operating organizations—inputs and outputs are identified relative to stated objectives. For students of management, this philosophy is equally valuable for organizing, classifying, and simplifying knowledge which can be applied to organizations of one kind.

To summarize, and also to establish a more formal relationship among the various usages of the term systems in this chapter, we would like to suggest that there are three different ways to consider systems: (1) systems concepts or philosophy, (2) systems management, and (3) systems analysis. All three are included under the most general classification, the Systems

---

[5] Billy E. Goetz, "Synthesis of Several Techniques," *Management Science,* 15, no. 10 (June 1969): B–506.

Approach. These relationships are illustrated in Table 1.1, showing that systems can be used as a concept or philosophy, as a means of organizing and managing resources, and/or as a planning or problem solving technique. In every instance it is the systems approach.

Table 1.1. The Systems Approach

	THE SYSTEMS APPROACH		
	Systems Concepts	*Systems Management*	*Systems Analysis*
V E H I C L E	General Theory and Principles	Applications of Theory in Man— Machine Systems	Models of Analysis
E M P H A S I S	A Way to Think— A Philosophy	A Way to Organize Resources	A Way to Plan and Solve Problems

Operations Management and Systems

At the turn of the century, Frederick Taylor published his concept of Scientific Management, emphasizing the need to organize industrial production more effectively. Several techniques such as methods study, time and motion study, planning and progress charting, and pay incentives were developed in conjunction with scientific management.

Taylor's work had a great influence on production management and on the way it was taught in colleges. For many years, the typical book in this field was organized around his philosophy and also included something about every function needed to operate an industrial concern, for example, finance, forecasting, engineering design, and personnel management. Since that time, a gradual change has taken place to exclude those general management concepts which warranted a more specialized and comprehensive coverage, and to include the more sophisticated techniques which have been developed (largely mathematical), and to concentrate on certain basic ideas and techniques that apply to all organizations.

This broader application meant that the name, production, was somewhat inappropriate because production means manufacturing to most people. Therefore, a change in name is taking place—from production to operations management. Another problem relates to the difficulty of presenting a group of techniques without an adequate relationship to some general model.

Under industrial management, the manufacturing firm was this model, but with the broader application, there was a need to change the name in order to counter the arguments that manufacturing continued to be the central core of this field of study. The systems approach solves this dilemma, because it is a general model to which the operations of any organization can be related.

We defined Operations Management as the design and operation of systems, but this definition is too broad. We shall confine our discussion to those principles which relate to the analytical consideration of resources. (People are categorized as a resource of the system without emphasizing the behavioral dimension. A thorough discussion of the psychological and sociological aspects of managing people is beyond the scope of this book.)

The choice of subject matter for a text is always a difficult decision. We have included those areas which apply to all systems, such as design, the scheduling of resource inputs and transformation activities, management of various types of inventory and more generally, control of operations. A question may arise, however, about such an activity as purchasing—isn't it common to all organizations? Although this may be true, much of the significant information about purchasing is institutional, and it becomes difficult to make an effective presentation of the subject matter without lengthy review of the nature and character of the items or services to be purchased and of the environment of the organization.

Throughout the book, we present models, techniques, and tools as they apply to specific applications of management. Understanding this technical part of systems analysis is important and extremely useful when the application occurs within the philosophy of the systems approach. Decisions on what systems to design, and how to design and operate them, must be made. Chapter 2 presents a foundation for understanding and relating the application of those techniques which are included in the text.

The analysis of operations begins in Chapters 3 through 5 with the study of relatively large systems. Such systems are a composite of individual systems or nodes, linked together by various forms of communication and transportation. This total system approach involves many interesting analytical and philosophical questions of strategy and trade-offs.

The study of design and its relation to control and evaluation starts in Chapter 6. Closely related to the design function is the study of information flow (Chapter 7), and the selection and replacement of equipment (Chapter 8). There are many interesting and valuable models and techniques for analyzing control systems. These are reviewed in Chapter 9.

Chapters 10, 11, and 12 consider the management of inventory and the scheduling process for both product and service organizations. Chapter 13 presents a study of the dynamics of operating a system. Simulation and industrial dynamics are demonstrated as meaningful approaches for analyzing the impact on the operation of the system caused by a variation of input combinations. Obviously, one of the most important facets of operations relates to the management of human resources. Although this input is included in the operation model, its development is left to authors specializing in that field of study.

The final chapter relates all of the materials in the book to the systems approach. In addition, two illustrations are used to demonstrate that the study of Operations Management is of practical value for all students. Finally, the authors consider future developments and raise questions which merit additional study.

Summary

Some scholars equate systems and science. When used in this context, systems connote plan, method, order, and arrangement. General systems theory is concerned with establishing hierarchical relationships among the various disciplines, or to establish a framework where new information and knowledge can be classified in a meaningful way.

A system can be defined as an array of components designed to accomplish a particular objective according to plan. In other words, components are arranged to transform inputs into output in order to accomplish a stated objective(s) or mission(s). The allocation of inputs of information, energy, and materials into the system occur according to an operational plan.

There are different kinds of systems. Classification can be made relative to the structure or design, for example, natural or man-made, flexible or rigid, and man or machine. On the other hand, a distinction may be made in regard to the kind of output, that is, product or service.

Every system contains components—that segment of a system which performs, or provides the facility for performing, some part of the defined transformation process. A component cannot satisfy the total transformation requirement as defined, even though in another instance it may be regarded as a system. Therefore, the distinction is often a matter of definition, a matter of establishing boundaries for convenience of operations or analysis. Components serve systems, which in turn serve other systems, which serve other systems, and so on.

When the resources of an organization are arranged and managed as a system, we refer to this approach as management by systems. There are four stages to this process: (1) determination, (2) design and creation, (3) operation and control, and (4) review and evaluation. If the relationship between structure and operations were always predictable, we would not need to have control, but this seldom is the case. Control includes four elements: (1) a characteristic or condition to measure, (2) a sensor or measuring unit, (3) comparison with a standard, and (4) an activating unit for reallocating inputs.

Whereas management by system relates to the total organization, concepts like information theory and decision theory abstract something less than the total design and operation of organizations. However, the concepts developed in such theories form a solid base for the application of systems theory and are used, along with every other theory, concept, approach, model, technique and tool to improve the effectiveness or efficiency of operating organizations. One useful technique, for example, is systems analysis, a methodology for planning or problem solving in an orderly and logical manner.

Selected References

Churchman, C. West. *The Systems Approach.* New York: Delacorte Press, 1968.

This book examines the systems approach in some detail, giving examples of its development in the space sciences and its use in planning of government, business, and industry.

Johnson, Richard A., et al. *The Theory and Management of Systems,* 2nd ed. New York: McGraw-Hill Book Company, 1967.

The first section of this book presents the theory of systems and relates it to the managerial concepts of organization, planning, control, and communication. The second section provides illustrative applications and the third section reviews some of the significant factors of implementation.

Starr, Martin K. *Production Management, Systems and Synthesis.* Englewood Cliffs, N.J.: Prentice-Hall, Inc., 1964, pp. 1–42.

The introductory section of this book provides a sound theoretical relationship between the systems concept and production.

Questions

1 Trace the relationship of a local bus company to the national transportation system.

2 What advantages may be gained from having an integrative body of knowledge?

3 List and describe three different examples of a system, using the definition of a system developed in this chapter.

4 List the resource inputs, transformation components, and output of a banking institution.

5 How would you classify the following systems?
   a. a hospital
   b. a public market
   c. a guided missile
   d. a rubber plantation

6 Trace the control exercised by the driver of an automobile from the act of sensing to activation.

7 What relationship exists between the operation of a system and its design?

8 Prepare a simple model to relate information theory, decision theory, and operations management. (Use Figure 1.1 as a guide.)

Exercises

1 Diagram this country's educational system to show the various organized subsystems of private and public instruction that occur at the different levels. You may wish to illustrate by showing how the output from one subsystem becomes input to the next.

2 Describe in some detail, showing the subsystems and their relation to the total system, any one of the following:
a. a health care system,
b. a transportation system,
c. a business firm and its surrounding environment, or
d. a pollution control system.

3 Use the systems analysis technique to outline the problem of pollution caused by discarded bottles.

Chapter 2
Management
Science and
Decision
Processes

Managers make decisions about and within systems which will achieve their objectives and make efficient use of the available human and natural resources. Managers not only make decisions themselves, but also must see that effective decisions are made throughout the organizations they manage. The decision-making function of management is an intellectual task which involves choosing the right course of action at the right time.

A question of major importance is how to make better decisions. Certainly, an important aspect of decision making is the experience, judgment and intuition of decision makers. But are we limited to making decisions merely on the basis of intuition? Must we depend upon the genius of a few gifted men? Do we have available knowledge and methodology which enable us to supplement intuition and replace, to some extent, approaches based upon experience alone? Can science contribute to the managerial process?

The idea of using science to improve decisions is not a new one, but there are many to whom using science in management is an alien concept. To argue that management is an art which cannot be reduced to a science misses an important point—that the judgmental aspects of the decision process may be augmented by applying the logic and methodology of science. Science is not merely the laboratory technique of physics and chemistry; it is the systematic discovery of knowledge about the world. The management scientist is concerned with the study of the decision process.

In this chapter we will explore some of the characteristics of management decisions. We will discuss different types of decisions and their susceptibility to formal systematic analysis. We will also present some of the rudiments of decision theory and decision analysis.

Decisions and Decision Making

A decision is a choice from among alternative courses of action, for if there are no options, no alternatives, then there is no decision to be made. But decision making is more than the final choice. There is a lengthy process of exploration and analysis which precedes the moment of choice.

Executives do not follow any one procedure in arriving at decisions. Expanding on the stages of decision making mentioned in Chapter 1, we can identify several clearly defined elements in the decision process, as portrayed in Figure 2.1:

1. Problem definition.

2. Discovery of alternative courses of action.

3. Evaluation of alternatives.

4. Selection of course of action.

5. Implementation of decision.

6. Information feedback of results.

Let us examine these elements, each of which involves a set of activities.

Figure 2.1   Flow Diagram of the Decision-Making Process

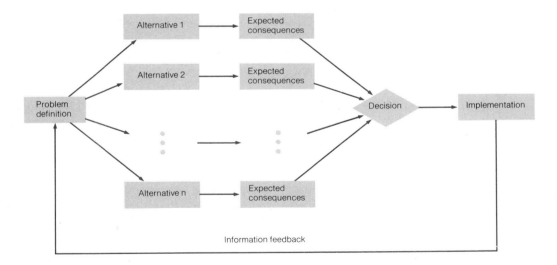

| Problem Definition | What is the problem to be solved? What are the environmental or boundary conditions it must satisfy? On what criteria is the ultimate choice to be based?—These are the kinds of questions a decision maker asks. |

Consider the following problem presented to John Walters, a production manager of Electronic Apparatus, Inc. This small west coast manufacturer of precision electronic testing equipment intended to demonstrate its new line of oscilloscopes at an engineering convention opening the following day in a city 200 miles away. Mr. Walters' schedule was crammed for the rest of the day. Following an important luncheon meeting he was to fly to Houston later in the afternoon. At 11 o'clock the sales manager phoned from the convention site to say that by morning he needed a replacement for one of the oscilloscopes that was not functioning properly. A quick check showed that another unit was available. The problem was to find the best method to ship the replacement so that it would be at the convention on time. But on what basis would the choice be made, and what conditions needed to be met?

First, Mr. Walters had to make certain that the replacement unit was functioning properly and then select the shipping method that best fitted the deadline. Cost was clearly secondary to the speed and reliability of the shipping method. Another secondary criterion was the conservation of his own time in order not to disrupt his personal travel schedule.

In attacking a problem, there always lurks the danger that the wrong problem may have been solved or that its extent may not have been fully defined. For example, in response to complaints about slow deliveries, a manufacturer installed a complex computerized inventory control and scheduling system. Yet, even though the new program functioned effectively and provided voluminous data on the location of orders and scheduling of shipments, many delivery commitments were unmet. Investigation revealed that the information supplied by the computer was the wrong kind. It dealt with part numbers and operations which facilitated in-plant work schedules, but ignored end products which would have improved customer service.

Some problem not fully defined may seem reasonable even though significant factors have been omitted. Take the European company which planned to increase its productive capacity by constructing a new plant. Management anticipated a growing demand which could easily match the additional output by the time the new facility was designed and constructed. But during the planning stage, the company decided to expand the present plant rather than build a new one. Therefore, it undertook a complete analysis of the expansion problem, including critical path network analysis of the construction, purchase, and installation of equipment, and integration of the additional capacity into the present one. However, management overlooked one critical factor: expansion of the existing plant would take six months less time than building a new one. As a result, the new facility was completed before the market had grown enough to absorb the additional capacity. Thus the company spent its money six months too soon. This outcome would have been avoided if all the relevant environmental conditions had been included in defining the problem.

The criteria for evaluating various courses of action are an important part of the decision process. In one situation, a manager may seek a satisfactory but not necessarily the best possible solution. In another situation, he may seek an optimum solution, or one which maximizes attainment of an objective, and still satisfies the constraints which limit the decision maker's choice. Thus an optimum decision requires that the objective be expressed as a value function, that is, the expected gain or loss, which can be maximized or minimized. If an objective is expressed as profit then the greatest degree of attainment of the objective would be maximization of a profit function. Conversely, if an objective is expressed in terms of cost, the maximum attainment of the objective would be the minimum cost.

Environmental or boundary conditions are constraints which place limits on the value function. Since the minimum cost of producing a product would occur when no product is produced, constraints are placed on the attainment of minimum cost. Similarly, there are limits to the attainment of maximum profits. Constraints are also necessary because we can maximize only one value function at a time.

One of the most difficult problems in the decision process is the transformation of goals into criteria for evaluating alternatives. Decision makers may not clearly define goals and, indeed, in some situations it may be desirable not to define goals too precisely. Moreover, there may be conflicts among criteria that are difficult to resolve.

The goals of subsystems which comprise a larger system are often interdependent, so that optimization of the objective of one subsystem may result in lower attainment of the goal of other subsystems and of the total system. This is referred to as *suboptimization*. It is often tempting to concentrate on optimizing parts of systems, but we must consider the impact on other parts of the system. For example, a company faced with a seasonal fluctuation in demand for a product might decide to schedule production at an even rate throughout the year in order to minimize costs of changing production rates. But unless management considers other relevant costs such as inventory carrying costs, serious suboptimization of total costs may occur.

Since a decision is optimum only for a particular point in time, it is important to specify a planning horizon when formulating objectives and criteria. The length of the planning horizon is itself a critical variable in the decision process, because of our inability to forecast the future accurately.

Discovery of Alternative Courses of Action

Finding alternative courses of action often calls for a high degree of creative imagination. In this stage, the decision maker asks: "How might the problem be solved?" "What options are available?" Mr. Walters might arrive at the following alternative solutions to his problem of getting the oscilloscope to the convention:

1. Have a local airline pick up and deliver the shipment.

2. Have Mr. Walters take the package and leave it at the airport, and have an assistant pick it up at the destination.

3. Have Mr. Walters stop at the convention with the package on his way to Houston.

4. Have an assistant take it to the convention and return to the plant.

5. Send the package by bus if weather conditions delay air shipments.

Because of limitations on time and resources, it may be impossible to explore every feasible option (options which will satisfy the boundary conditions). Part of a decision maker's skill is discovering attractive and feasible alternatives which others overlook.

An important alternative in some decision-making situations is to resolve to postpone a decision. Postponement does not suggest procrastination, which most of us are prone to occasionally, but rather a conscious decision that now is not the best time to act. For example, in those product development areas where an anticipated technological breakthrough or changes in market trends may drastically alter the decision problem or the alternatives, delaying a decision, until the outcome of such changes are known, may prevent a wrong decision.

Evaluation of Alternatives

In evaluating alternatives the decision maker gathers and weighs data on each alternative, and asks: "What are the expected outcomes?" "What will be their costs and benefits?" "What are the probabilities that those outcomes will occur?" "What is the relative importance of those outcomes?"

The evaluation phase of the decision-making process may be very complicated and time-consuming. Predicting the outcomes of an alternative may require a great deal of data collection and analysis. As a result, much of the work in management science and decision theory has been concentrated on finding ways to facilitate decision analysis.

An alternative may have not one but several possible outcomes depending upon the occurrence of external conditions over which the decision maker has little or no control. These external conditions are called *states of nature*. In the case of Mr. Walters' oscilloscope delivery problem, on-time delivery by the airline depends partly upon weather conditions. If he decides to ship by bus, he must contend with schedules and traffic conditions. Moreover, with either means of transportation a delay may occur due to breakdown or accident. His evaluation of alternatives, to be complete, must include consideration of such contingencies and an assessment of the probabilities that they will occur. Later in the chapter we will examine ways in which uncertainty and probability forecasts may be formally included in a decision analysis.

The way in which a decision maker approaches the process of searching for and evaluating alternatives depends upon such factors as his personal style of operating, his and the organization's value systems, complexity of the decision, and importance of the decision. One decision, such as designing the layout for and equipping a new hospital, may require a highly formal analysis with written reports setting forth requirements of the various functions, scale drawings, flow charts of traffic patterns within the hospital, scale models, and detailed schedules showing time completion of each part of the project. Another decision, such as Mr. Walters' oscilloscope delivery problem, may require an analysis of only the schedules and costs of alternative shipping methods.

Selection of a Course of Action

The executive comes to the moment of choice when he selects a course of action. Which alternative will meet the decision criteria and satisfy the constraints placed upon the decision? What action is to be taken? He weighs the pros and cons of each alternative, and if he is fortunate, one alternative may stand out as clearly superior to the others. However, he is not often so fortunate. Even a formal decision analysis in which careful quantitative analysis has been made will typically have factors which cannot be quantified and uncertainties which must be resolved. The decision maker must then use his judgment and intuition to solve the problem.

For example, a purchasing agent in selecting a supplier may have to choose between one supplier with a lower cost proposal and another with a better reputation for meeting delivery promises. Or, a manufacturer of high-quality stereo tape recorders may consider adding medium-quality recorders to his product line. Management must weigh the uncertain reaction of competitors, gains to the company if the new line is a success, and risks of loss to the company if it fails.

Implementation of a Decision

After an executive has selected a course of action, he must decide how to implement his choice. Who is to take action? Are they capable of doing the task? Who must be informed of the decision? A decision is not complete until someone has been given specific responsibility to carry it out.

If Mr. Walters decides to send the oscilloscope by air freight to the convention city, he must also decide who is to get the package ready for shipment, who is to take it to the airport, and who is to pick it up at its destination and deliver it to the convention site. In addition, someone should inform the sales manager at the convention about the delivery so that he can receive and install the unit in the exhibit.

Failure to inform everyone who needs to know of the decision can lead to unfortunate results. Consider the problem of a food company which decided to launch an extensive promotional campaign on one of its specialty items. Management carefully prepared the sales force and had newspaper, magazine and television advertisements ready. However, they did not properly inform the production group. As a result, sufficient amounts of the product were not available to take full advantage of the increased demand generated by the promotional campaign. By the time production rates could be increased, much of the potential benefit of the campaign was lost.

In another case an equipment manufacturer purchased component parts for equipment based upon current usage. When the company announced that it would discontinue one of its old models, many customers increased their orders for that model. Since no one informed the buyer in the purchasing department, he kept reordering parts. When production was discontinued, the company had parts enough for several years' production. These were written off later at a substantial loss.

Information Feedback

Finally, management should have a continued feedback of information which reports whether the decision is being carried out, whether it is achieving its desired purpose, and whether the forecasts and assumptions upon which the decision was based are still valid. Changing conditions necessitate new decisions and the process begins again.

We have described the decision process as though it were a discrete sequence of steps, but the cycle is much more complex. Each step in the sequence is itself a decision-making process, and there is a complex interaction among the steps. Although we have included only one explicit feedback loop in Figure 2.1, we actually have a continual feedback among the steps. Discovery and evaluation of alternatives may lead to redefinition of the problem. Evaluation of one alternative may lead to development of others.

Decision Making in a Systems Context

Managers operate and make decisions within the framework of dynamic interacting systems. An understanding of their place in the system and of their relationship to other parts of the system and to other systems can help them make more effective decisions.

An important aspect of a systems concept of management is explicit recognition that the boundaries of a decision problem are not necessarily identical to formal organizational boundaries. The system for the particular decision problem at hand encompasses all activities relevant to that decision. Recognition of this is critical in the problem-definition phase of the decision process. If the food manufacturer had considered this relationship, adequate production planning in preparation of the promotion campaign could have been made. And if the equipment manufacturer had informed the parts buyer that a particular model was to be discontinued, the loss resulting from purchasing unneeded component parts could have been avoided.

The Information Feedback System

In a systems context, decision making may be viewed as decisions and activities required to bring the state of a system into conformity with a desired state. Figure 2.2 illustrates the complex feedback process in which goal-seeking activities respond to differences between the organization's objectives and its apparent achievements. The decision maker is a part of this feedback system and, as such, acts as a regulator of the system. The implementation process, which transforms decisions into achievements, is affected by complex structural relationships within the organization, by time delays between a decision and resulting changes in the state of the system, and by noise such as random behavior in the organization. These factors affect to varying degrees how well the achievements of the organization correspond to the intention of the decision maker.

Figure 2.2 Feedback Structure of Decision Process

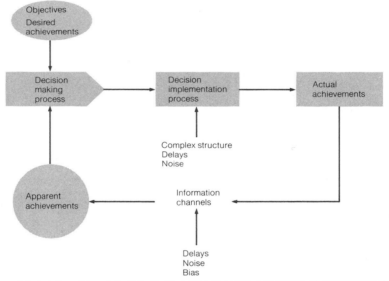

Source: Adpated from Edward B. Roberts, "Industrial Dynamics and Design of Management Control Systems," *Management Technology* 3, no. 2 (December 1963).

Recognition of these factors affects how a manager chooses to implement his decisions. Suppose a synthetic fiber manufacturer wishes to introduce a new fiber for men's suits. The manufacturer cannot expect to have the new fiber on the market at once. Many people and departments in the organization—manufacturing, distribution, marketing, finance, personnel, engineering, and so forth—must work together for a long time to bring the project to fruition. The decision must be transmitted through many levels in the organization's hierarchy. The implementation of this kind of a decision will require meetings and discussions, written reports and instructions.

In addition, there are other complications occasioned by differences between the actual achievements of the system and achievements apparent to the decision maker. The extent to which perceived achievements are representative of actual achievements depends upon the quality and timeliness of the information received through the feedback process. This information is affected by delays, noise, or bias in the information channels. There is always some time lag between an event and the time it is perceived. In an organization these time lags may be long enough to affect the decision-making process significantly. Noise in an information channel, such as errors in data and imprecise or confusing language, randomly distorts information. Bias distorts information in a particular direction.

Much of this information feedback comes to an executive in the form of written and oral reports and more recently in the form of printed output from a computer. However, even the best reporting system introduces time delays and is subject to error. To shorten delays and overcome the abstraction inherent in reports, one might wish to engage in direct observation of what is happening. Direct observation cannot replace reports, of course. For example, looking through a warehouse will give very imperfect information about the level of inventories. Therefore, both reports and direct contact contribute to better information feedback.

Hierarchies of Decisions

We can identify hierarchies of systems and subsystems, and we can also identify, in practice, hierarchies of decisions ranging from strategies to tactics. Strategies and tactics may be differentiated on the basis of the length of the planning horizon. Tactics are involved in short-range planning, whereas strategies are involved in long-range planning. In some situations, distinguishing between global and local strategies may also be useful.

Global strategies form the grand design of a system, the long-range concept of a system. For example, an airline company's global strategy may be to provide safe, reliable, fast and inexpensive air transportation for people and goods. Such strategies determine the fundamental nature and direction of the enterprise. Product and service diversification decisions are part of the global strategy of an enterprise, as are decisions to move into a new field of endeavor.

Strategy is a term taken from the military which connotes an awareness of a competitive environment. Decisions made by competitors alter the environment in which a firm operates. Strategies are important for public as well as private enterprises, because even public enterprises are in competition for resources. The library in a university system is in competition with other departments for funds and physical facilities. For private industry, competition exists on several levels. A refrigerator manufacturer is in competition not only with other refrigerator manufacturers, but also with enterprises producing other products and services which compete for consumers' funds.

Tactics are procedures for carrying out strategies. They flow from strategies. Several tactical options exist for a single strategy, and for some strategies, so many tactical alternatives may exist that it is easy to lose sight of the strategic problem. Evaluation of a strategy requires consideration of the tactics which will be used to carry it out. For some decisions, a choice of strategy has a low sensitivity to tactical considerations, because one strategy is superior to another regardless of the tactics used. In other words, if the poorest tactic for one strategy yields a result that is superior to the best tactic of another strategy, the choice of strategy is insensitive to tactical considerations. If, however, the poorer tactics of one strategy yields results that are worse than the better tactics of another strategy, the choice of strategy is sensitive to tactical alternatives. In such a situation comparison of the strategies requires careful definition of tactics and their consequences.

Managers in operations phases of an enterprise must be aware of the importance of strategy in their decisions and of their own role in strategy formulation of the firm. In manufacturing industries, managers typically concentrate on tactical considerations and company strategies, and devote insufficient time to the strategies of their competitors.

Often top management also fails to give proper consideration to operating policies in the formulation of corporate strategy. Some of the reasons for this failure relate to the historical short-sighted emphasis on short-range tactics —cost reduction for example—and the resulting failure to consider long-range strategies in planning and control of operations. Other reasons relate to top management's failure to realize the strategic long-range implications in the design and performance of operating systems. Some of this may in turn result from a tendency to regard operations management, especially in manufacturing firms, as a technical specialty. A systems approach to decision making and a recognition of a hierarchy of decisions can serve to insure that strategic considerations are made an integral part of operating decisions, and that operations policies are considered in long-range strategy formulation.

The Role of Models

When we consider the systems approach to managing and decision making, the oversimplified and traditional view that scientific methodology involves merely measurement and experimentation collapses. The traditional view is not even adequate to describe scientific activity. The concept of the so-called objective observer who carefully measures and experiments may be sound for Newtonian physics, for optics and mechanics, but it is wholly inadequate when one ventures into atomic physics. The fish and the plant can be understood only as systems. The boundaries of these systems are different from the boundaries of the physical objects, they extend to include the ecological system which comprises the environments in which the species exist. Similarly, organizations—such as businesses, hospitals, schools, and armies—industries, and economies cannot be studied and understood through classical methods of experimentation and measurement.

Managers have known right along that they operate in the context of large and complex systems. They realize the difficulties which arise from estimating and measuring decision variables without an understanding of their structural relationships within the system. Rational decision making requires not only knowing and interpreting what has happened, but also predicting what is likely to happen. Prediction is based upon a model of the system.

Definition of a Model

A model is a more or less abstract representation of a system. It is used to capture the essence, but not the detail of the system. In organizational systems, models are required because it is seldom possible to experiment with the actual system in an effort to discover preferred decision strategies. The extent to which such a model is able to predict a system's behavior depends upon how accurately it represents the underlying system structure. If we have a model which does capture the essence of a system, we can experiment on the model to discover the effect of various decision strategies.

Managers operate through models of the system, models which range from mental images to highly formalized mathematical models. These models are representations of the structure of the organization, the market, costs and prices, the work force, the production process, and the financial situation of the system. When a manager is confronted with a particular situation, he applies his experience to it—he compares his model of the present situation with models of similar situations with which he is familiar. If some of these other models sufficiently correspond to his model of the present situation they can be used as a basis for prediction because, if his memory is good, he knows their outcomes. If these models do not sufficiently correspond to the present model, then new models are required. Much of the work of management science deals with development and application of formal models to management decision problems.

Management is turning increasingly to model building because evidence shows formal models can improve decision-making performance. Model building and use are still in a formative stage. In some areas, such as important strategic decisions, model building is at a low stage of development. However, for many important tactical decisions, such as inventory control, model building is quite advanced.

Types of Models

The models used in decision analysis can be classified into three general types: iconic, analogue, and symbolic.

Iconic models, in general, represent visually the relevant aspects of a system. They are images of a system such as scale models, maps and photographs. Iconic models are useful to convey information about a system, but experimentation with them is not easy.

Analogue models use a characteristic of one system to represent some other characteristic of another system. A hydraulic system, representing an inventory system, might consist of reservoirs of water with interconnecting pipes and valves to regulate the flow through the pipes. By appropriate adjustments of the rates of flow, the model could simulate an inventory system. Such an analogue simulation, however, would be cumbersome to use and subject to measurement errors. Graphs use geometric analogues to represent interrelationships among variables. Flow charts, PERT/CPM network graphs, schedule graphs and time-series graphs are commonly used forms.

Symbolic models, which use various types of symbols to represent system variables and interrelationships, are the most general and abstract type. These models are often mathematical models which use an algebraic statement to represent the system.

The various types of models may be used alone or together to represent a system. An analysis of a decision problem may use all three types, but mathematical models are generally more desirable because they usually are easier to manipulate and tend to give more accurate results. In the discussion that follows on decision matrices and decision trees, we will observe the combination of analogue and symbolic models.

The Decision Matrix

A decision matrix is often a convenient way in which to present the components of a decision problem. A matrix, like a table, is an array of items. A decision matrix is an array in which the rows represent alternatives available to the decision maker, the columns represent states of nature or conditions which are likely to occur, and the entries in the body of the matrix represent the outcomes of the decision. An example of a decision matrix is presented in Figure 2.3 in which A's represent alternatives, N's represent states of nature, and O's represent outcomes.

Figure 2.3   Decision Matrix

Alternatives	States of Nature				
	N_1	N_2	N_3	. . .	N_j
A_1	O_{11}	O_{12}	O_{13}	. . .	O_{1j}
A_2	O_{21}	O_{22}	O_{23}	. . .	O_{2j}
$\vdots$	$\vdots$	$\vdots$	$\vdots$	$\vdots$	$\vdots$
A_i	O_{i1}	O_{i2}	O_{i3}	. . .	O_{ij}

Measurement of Outcomes   The selection of a particular alternative will result in an outcome or payoff. If we are fortunate enough to know what the payoff from a particular alternative will be, then we could choose that alternative which would result in the best outcome. An outcome O_{ij} is a function of the alternative selected A_i and the state of nature N_j which occurs (see Figure 2.3):

$$O_{ij} = f(A_i, N_j).$$

Measurement requires scales, of which there are four types: nominal, ordinal, interval, and ratio. The relationship among the various scales is summarized in Table 2.1.

Table 2.1   Types of Scales of Measurement

Scale	Basic Empirical Operations	Allowable Mathematical Transformation	Example	Statistics	Remarks
Nominal	Determination of equality	Any one to one substitution	Numbering types or classes	Mode x^2-test	
Ordinal	Determination of order	$x' = f(x)$ where $f(x)$ is any monotonic increasing function	Street numbers	Percentiles Median Rank order correlation	
Interval	Determination of equality of intervals	$x' = ax + b$ $a > 0$	Temperature Potential energy	Mean Standard deviation t-test F-test	Zero point by convention or for convenience
Ratio	Determination of equality of ratios	$x' = cx$ $c > 0$	Length Temperature (K°)	Geometric mean Harmonic mean	Actual zero point

Note: Each column is cumulative in the sense that any statement against a given scale not only applies to that scale but to all scales below it. The third column shows the mathematical transformations that leave the scale form unchanged.

Source: R. W. Shephard, "An Appraisal of the Problems of Measurement in Operational Research," *Operational Research Quarterly,* September 1961, pp. 161–166.

The only requirement for a *nominal scale* is that it is possible to distinguish between two or more categories which pertain to the attribute under consideration (for example, fat or thin; black or white; small, medium, or large). An *ordinal* scale defines the relative position of the descriptive data with respect to a characteristic, with no implication of the distance in between positions. Examples of such scales are street numbers, medians, and percentiles. Positions are not only ranked on *interval scales,* but the intervals of measurement are equal, that is, the distance between 7 and 9 is equal to the distance between 21 and 23. The centigrade scale to measure temperature is an example, and one that uses the zero point for convenience. The *ratio* scale includes those properties listed for all of the three other scales. Statistical examples of a ratio scale include geometric means and harmonic means.

As we noted earlier, some outcomes cannot be measured. For some decisions the time lag between a decision and its final outcome may be very long. The results of a decision to pursue a particular product research and development strategy may not be known for many years. Since the outcome predicted depends upon the time selected for measurement, it is important whenever possible to select a planning horizon which adequately reflects the impact of the alternative.

Since outcomes are the result of future events, they are often difficult to predict with accuracy. There may be many variables affecting the outcome in ways about which little is known. For most business decisions, we are not able to predict outcomes with certainty.

Evaluating those alternatives for which there is no obvious natural measure of outcomes presents an even more difficult problem. How are we to measure quantitatively, for example, the payoff from a management development program, or of a company's public responsibility? Even in situations in which payoffs can be quantified, they may not be measured in terms of the objectives or values which a manager wishes to optimize. Profits and costs are often inadequate to measure the utility of outcomes to the decision maker.

One may suggest ranking outcomes in terms of their utility to a decision maker. However, ranking is feasible only when there is one dimension to be compared, and many decisions involve multiple dimensions. In such situations the principle of transitivity breaks down. Transitivity refers to the property that if one prefers A to B and prefers B to C, he should prefer A to C. Measurements of height, weight, length and cost involve transitivity. The attempt to find a single quantitative measure of the state of an individual's health, or of the state of the economy, illustrates the problem of multiple dimensions. In situations such as these, many quantitative measures of different aspects of the system are available, but no one measure adequately represents the state of the system. However, if decision outcomes can be ranked, the ranks can be used as an indication of their utility to the decision maker.

Ranking has limitations as an indicator of utility, because it ignores the degree of preference for outcome over another. If we rank three outcomes in order 1, 2, and 3, we cannot tell whether the difference in preference for 1 over 2 is greater or less than for 2 over 3. Because of this we cannot use arithmetical methods of analysis based upon ranks.

Alternatives   Alternatives are the options available to the decision maker, and they are based upon the resources under his control. The number of alternatives may range from two to infinity. The decision to select a computer to perform a specific data processing task may involve several, but a finite number of alternatives. However, the decision alternatives in choosing the amount of perfume to add to the mix for a batch of soap are infinite in number. The limitations and inaccuracies in the measurement system prevent us from distinguishing infinitesimal differences in volumes and make it appear that there are a finite number of alternatives.

Many decision situations have such a vast number of alternatives which might be considered, that some must be eliminated immediately. The constant risk of eliminating some highly desirable alternatives presents a problem in decision theory, which has received a great deal of attention in the management science literature. Several techniques are available for eliminating alternatives. Some use the experience and judgment of the decision maker, others involve policy guidelines and rules. In recent years, attention has focused on heuristic methods for reducing the number of alternatives under consideration. These methods are rather formalized procedures, usually computerized, for successively applying appropriate rules to reduce alternatives to a manageable number. An example of one of these procedures is described in Chapter 5 in the solution of a plant location problem. If the number of alternatives could be reduced to one, then, of course, the problem would be solved. Optimizing techniques in operations research are algorithms for selecting the one alternative out of available alternatives which satisfies the constraints and maximizes or minimizes the objective function.

In other situations, it may be difficult to identify a sufficient number of alternatives. At this stage of the decision process, the manager needs ingenuity, creativity, and innovative approaches if he is to avoid the trap of considering only traditional alternatives. Enumeration of alternatives and their display in a decision matrix or a decision tree may help to ensure that appropriate courses of action are considered.

States of Nature

States of nature are the conditions of those variables which affect the outcome of the alternative, but over which the decision maker has little or no control. They include those environmental variables exogenous to the system under consideration. For a particular operating system a state of nature might refer to such factors as climatic conditions, the state of the economy, tariff barriers to international trade, technological innovation, social and legal conditions, availability and cost of raw materials, and availability of skilled workers. Strategies of competitors are also states of nature, but in this case the decision maker is confronted with rational opponents. An opponent's competitive strategy is not dictated by chance, and therefore, in decision theory, is often treated separately from environmental factors.

The discovery of relevant states of nature is similar to the problem of discovery of alternatives. Like the identification of options, recognition of states of nature requires creative insights, and may require reduction of the number of states to a manageable size.

Decision Making Under Certainty

In the decision theory framework, decisions may be classified according to our knowledge of the states of nature as decision making under conditions of certainty, risk, and uncertainty. These three conditions represent varying degrees of information about the states of nature. The distinction among them is important because they affect the decision process itself.

Under conditions of certainty we assume that only one state of nature exists, and we know what it will be. In addition, we assume that our prediction about future events is perfect. Such an assumption simplifies the decision process, but may lead to wrong decisions in situations where the assumption does not hold true. In the certainty situation, the decision matrix has only one column, and an alternative is chosen which yields the best outcome.

Three primary methods which may be used to select an alternative under conditions of certainty are:[1]

1. enumeration of all feasible strategies;
2. progressive improvement;
3. use of optimization techniques.

Enumeration   In the method of enumeration, we specify all the feasible solutions to the decision problem at hand and select that one which yields the optimum result of the value function. A feasible solution meets the requirements of the restraints imposed upon the decision.

Consider a decision to select a warehouse location from among four possible locations, and assume that the best location is one which minimizes annual transportation costs as depicted in Figure 2.4. In this case alternative A_3 would be chosen.

Figure 2.4   Decision Matrix Under Conditions of Certainty

Alternatives Warehouse Location	State of Nature Annual Transportation Cost
A_1	$210,000
A_2	$170,000
A_3	$110,000
A_4	$250,000

[1] Arnold Kaufman, *The Science of Decision Making* (New York: McGraw-Hill Book Company, 1968), p. 108.

Decision making under certainty may seem trivial, but problems arise because we often have a great number of possible courses of action from which to choose. The method of enumeration involves combinatorial problems in which we search for and compare all possible solutions to a problem. Decision problems under conditions of assumed certainty with an enormous number of possible alternatives often arise at tactical and strategic levels where we are dealing with short-range decisions. In these situations the process of searching through the alternatives to find the one with the highest payoff (maximum or minimum) may be impossible.

Consider a rather common sequencing problem, one variant of which is the assignment problem. In a job shop assume that we have five jobs to produce (A, B, C, D, E), that there are five machines (1, 2, 3, 4, 5) which can do the task but at different costs, and that each job must be assigned to one machine. The objective is to make the assignment at the lowest total operating cost. We can assign job A to any of the 5 machines, but then we can assign job B to any of the 4 remaining machines, job C to any of the 3 remaining machines, and so forth. There is a total of $5 \times 4 \times 3 \times 2 \times 1 = 120$ different possible assignments, which corresponds to the number of permutations of 5 things taken 5 at a time. The formula to find the number of permutations of n items taken r at a time is:[2]

$$_nP_r = \frac{n!}{(n - r)!} \tag{2.1}$$

In this illustration the number of possible assignments is

$$_5P_5 = \frac{5!}{(5 - 5)!} = 5! = 120$$

This small problem is manageable by enumeration, and with enough time and fortitude (or with the aid of a computer) one could enumerate the total cost of each schedule of assignments and select the one with the lowest cost. But the number of possible assignments increases very rapidly as the number of items increases. The number of assignments with 10 machines and 10 jobs is $10! = 3.6 \times 10^6 = 3,600,000$. And the number of assignments of 100 jobs and 100 machines is approximately 9.3×10^{157}. This is clearly more than even the fastest computer could handle. A few calculations will reveal why this is so. There are 10^9 nanoseconds (billionths of a second) in a second, and approximately 3.2×10^7 seconds in a year. If a computer could evaluate each assignment in a nanosecond, it could evaluate about 3.2×10^{16} assignments in a year. On such a computer this problem would require something on the order of 3×10^{141} years! This property is

---

[2] The symbol $n!$ is read "n factorial." The factorial of a number is the product of that number multiplied by each lower integer down to one. Thus, $4! = 4 \times 3 \times 2 \times 1 = 24$. The quantity $0!$ is defined as equal to 1.

one of the major factors which has led to the development of procedures that permit us to avoid enumeration of sequences and permutations.

Progressive Improvement

The method of progressive improvement essentially involves finding a feasible solution and then searching for another solution which has a higher payoff. It is the most widely used approach to decision making and scientific discovery. It is used when one does not have a sufficiently complete model to permit locating directly an optimum solution, and when one does not have time for enumeration. The methods suggested for taking this approach to problem solving cover a wide range of sophistication. In their simpler forms they involve study of results from known feasible solutions based upon experience, judgment, and analysis, and the search for an improved solution.

At the other end of the spectrum, there are some quite sophisticated formal heuristic methods of search, most of which require computer assistance. Some quite complex heuristic computer programs have been developed and applied to chess playing, warehouse location, physical plant layout planning, assembly-line balancing, and project scheduling. We will explain some of these applications in several later chapters.[3]

The search for improved decision strategies in dynamic systems often utilizes computer simulation techniques. Simulation refers to the operation of a mathematical model that represents the behavior of a dynamic process. A particular set of conditions is used as input for the model and a simulation is run to represent the behavior of the system over time. A simulation run is an experiment on the model. At the conclusion of the experiment, a new set of conditions may be used as input for the model and another experiment run in a search for an improved solution. This procedure is explained in greater detail later in the chapter.

The methods of progressive improvement do not necessarily yield optimum solutions. We can observe that we have achieved better solutions, but we may not be able to tell whether or not we have reached an optimum. However, an experienced decision maker using these methods may be able to achieve results that are very close to an optimum solution.

Optimization Techniques

From our previous discussion we can easily see why there has been, and continues to be, a sustained interest in applications of optimization techniques to management decision problems. A perusal of the management science and operations research literature of the past two decades reveals that many models have been developed to find optimum solutions to complex administrative problems. These methods include applications of the

---

[3] An explanation of several of these applications may be found in Robert C. Meier, William T. Newell, and Harold L. Pazer, *Simulation in Business and Economics* (Englewood Cliffs, N.J.: Prentice-Hall, Inc. 1969), Ch. 5, "Heuristic Methods."

differential and integral calculus, and computational algorithms. Most of the models and applications deal with deterministic systems, but some deal with probabilistic systems as well. More recently, we have seen developments of optimum-seeking computer programs which can be used together with simulation models to search out optimum solutions.

An algorithm is a computational procedure for solving a mathematical problem. As applied to complex decision problems of the types we have examined, it refers to a series of computations which lead to an optimum solution. Some algorithms, such as those of linear, nonlinear, and dynamic programming use an iterative procedure to arrive at an optimum solution. An iterative procedure begins with a feasible trial solution and a set of computational rules for finding an improved solution. Then the improved solution is substituted for the previous solution, and the process is repeated until the incremental improvement derived from further iterations does not justify the cost of additional calculation.

Some types of decision models permit direct calculation of an optimum solution. Consider, as an example, an elementary economic lot size model for inventory replenishment in which we wish to determine an optimum reorder quantity that will minimize total annual inventory carrying costs and reordering costs. Since our purpose at this point in the text is to illustrate an optimizing technique under conditions of assumed certainty, and not to develop a realistic model of a complex inventory problem, we will assume that demand is constant and known, and that costs are stable and known. We will discuss the difficulties of modelling and solving inventory problems in Chapter 10.

For the present illustration assume that demand for the item is 400 units per year, inventory carrying cost is \$2.00 per unit of average inventory per year, and that replenishment cost is \$100 per order placed regardless of the size of the order. We will use the following symbols in the model:

$$d = \text{annual demand for the item} = 400 \text{ units}$$
$$S = \text{replenishment cost} = \$100 \text{ per order}$$
$$iC = \text{inventory carrying cost} = \$2.00 \text{ per unit of average inventory}$$
$$Q = \text{reorder quantity}$$
$$Q^* = \text{economic reorder quantity}$$
$$TC = \text{total annual cost}$$
$$TC^* = \text{minimum total annual cost when } Q = Q^*.$$

Inventory varies from a minimum of 0 to a maximum of Q with an average of $\frac{Q}{2}$. Annual inventory carrying cost is $\frac{Q}{2}(iC)$, the product of average inventory and unit inventory carrying cost. Annual replenishment cost is $\frac{d}{Q}$ (S), the number of orders placed per year times the replenishment cost per order. Total annual cost is then

$$TC = \frac{Q}{2}(iC) + \frac{d}{Q}(S) \tag{2.2}$$

$$= \frac{Q}{2}(2.00) + \frac{400}{Q}(100)$$

These relationships may be graphed as in Figure 2.5. As depicted in the graph, the minimum total annual cost occurs at the lot size at which annual inventory carrying cost equals the annual replenishment cost or:

$$\frac{Q}{2}(iC) = \frac{d}{Q}(S)$$

We can solve this equation to determine the economic lot size:

$$Q^* = \sqrt{\frac{2\,dS}{iC}} \tag{2.3}$$

$$= \sqrt{\frac{2(400)(100)}{2.00}}$$

$$= 200 \text{ units}$$

Note that equating replenishment and carrying costs is not the general procedure to solve for minimum total costs. The procedure works here only because of the special relationship between the replenishment cost and carrying cost curves. The general procedure, as explained in Chapter 10, is to use calculus to find the minimum point of the total cost curve.

Figure 2.5 Cost as a Function of Lot Size

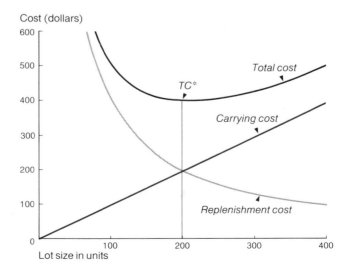

The optimum solution obtained from a deterministic model is no more than a guide to managerial action. Economic and social systems are almost always more complex than models which represent them. Since the system represented in a model is part of a larger system, we run the risk of suboptimization if we act solely on the basis of such a model. Sensitivity analysis, which provides information about the behavior of the system in the region around an optimum solution, is often desirable. This is true for all decision models, but especially so for deterministic models which have assumed away the troublesome uncertainties arising from predictions of the future.

Decision Making Under Risk

Under conditions of risk, we can identify two or more states of nature and we can predict the probability of their occurrence. Probability in this situation is the long-run relative frequency of occurrence. The decision matrix has several columns—one for each state of nature—with several payoffs for each alternative as shown in Figure 2.3, and a probability of occurrence p_j for each state of nature N_j. In a system characterized by risk, we have a stable system of chance causes at work.

In the context of operating systems many problems fit within the definition of a risk decision situation. They tend to be short-range problems involving physical systems, although there are long-range problems and behavioral systems for which risk analysis may serve as a good approximation. Examples of operating systems involving risk decisions would include failure rates for component parts of electronic equipment, breakdown rates for machinery, error rates in clerical processes, distribution of delivery lead times, traffic flow rates, telephone system utilization rates, worker productivity, games of chance, and stable consumer demand rates for certain products and services. Detailed discussions of some of the models which have been developed to analyze these problems are contained in later chapters, but an illustration of an elementary decision problem is given below.

Suppose a company is purchasing some equipment and it must decide on the quantity to order of a critical spare component part. If the company orders extra parts at the same time as the equipment, they will cost $1200 per unit. If they are ordered later, they will have to be made specially at a cost of $4500 per unit. In addition, the company estimates a cost of $5500 for having one unit of equipment out of service while a replacement part is being made. Thus, the total cost of a failure of the equipment, if no spare parts are in stock, is $10,000.

The company, if it decides not to carry spare parts, would incur no additional cost if this component does not fail over the life of the equipment. One failure would cost $10,000. Two failures would cost $20,000, and so on. If one spare unit is carried and this component does not fail, there would be a cost of $1200 for the unit purchased and not used (assume that there is a zero scrap value if the part is not used during the life of the equipment). The cost of one failure would also be $1200, but the cost of two failures would be $1200 plus $10,000 to obtain a part for the second failure. Proceeding in this same fashion, we may calculate the other conditional values of the decision matrix. Figure 2.6 shows a matrix of conditional values for alternatives of carrying 0 through 5 spare parts.

Figure 2.6 Decision Matrix of Conditional Costs Under Conditions of Risk

Alternatives	Number of Spare Parts	N_1 0	N_2 1	N_3 2	N_4 3	N_5 4	N_6 5	Expected Total Cost
		0.40	0.25	0.15	0.10	0.05	0.05	
A_1	0	$ 0	$10,000	$20,000	$30,000	$40,000	$50,000	$13,000
A_2	1	1,200	1,200	11,200	21,200	31,200	41,200	8,200
A_3	2	2,400	2,400	2,400	12,400	22,400	32,400	5,900
A_4	3	3,600	3,600	3,600	3,600	13,600	23,600	5,100
A_5	4	4,800	4,800	4,800	4,800	4,800	14,800	5,300
A_6	5	6,000	6,000	6,000	6,000	6,000	6,000	6,000

The header rows above read: States of Nature (N_1–N_6); Demand (0 1 2 3 4 5); Probability of Occurrence (0.40 0.25 0.15 0.10 0.05 0.05).

Expected Value

From a statistical analysis of similar equipment we obtain information about the probabilities of occurrence of the states of nature in the form of a distribution of the relative frequency of failures. Figure 2.6 also shows the probability distribution for this example. The distribution indicates that the probability of zero failures is 0.40, of one failure, 0.25, and so forth. Since the six states of nature include all the likely events, the sum of the six probabilities is 1.00.

Which strategy should be chosen? The decision might be based on one of several criteria. One might be inclined to select the strategy with the lowest simple average cost, but this would ignore the relative frequencies with which the states of nature are expected to occur. A rational criterion which does give weight to the probabilities is expected monetary value. Expected value is merely a weighted arithmetic average. In general, an expected value is obtained by multiplying each outcome by its probability and summing these products. In equation form, the expected value for alternative A_i is:

$$E(A_i) = p_1 O_{i1} + p_2 O_{i2} + \cdots + p_j O_{ij}. \tag{2.4}$$

For alternative A_1 (stock zero spares) in the present example the expected cost is:

$$E(A_1) = 0.40(0) + 0.25(10,000) + 0.15(20,000)$$
$$+ 0.10(30,000) + 0.05(40,000) + 0.05(50,000)$$
$$= 13,000$$

Since the outcome measure is in terms of cost, the decision criterion might be to minimize expected costs. If this were the case, we would select alternative A_4 (stock 3 spares). The expected value criterion is the most common for conditions of risk, and will produce satisfactory results in many cases.

Expected value may be criticized in some situations, because it does not give proper consideration to extreme conditions. Suppose we are faced with a choice between two strategies: A_1 with a certain payoff of $100, and A_2 with a 0.9 probability for a payoff of $120 and a 0.1 probability for a loss of $80. The expected value of alternative A_2 is $0.9(\$120) - 0.1(\$80) = \$100$. Although the expected value for each is $100, the preferred alternative may well be A_1 which has a certain payoff of $100. The issue here is not the concept of expected value, but rather the form in which the outcome measure is expressed. In cases such as this one, monetary value may not adequately measure the value or utility which the decision maker wishes to optimize. The analysis may be improved by introducing utility considerations and calculating expected utility values for alternatives rather than expected monetary values.

We could use other criteria for the spare parts decision problem presented in Figure 2.6, such as selecting the alternative for which the probability of a cost greater than $15,000 is zero. This criterion would lead to a choice of alternative A_5. Another possibility is to stock enough spares so that the probability of having the equipment shut down is 0.05, which indicates a stock of 4 spare parts. Each of these other criteria imputes other utility or cost values to the problem. Thus, although a calculated expected monetary value may often lead to a correct decision, it should not be used without careful consideration of all relevant factors in the system.

Opportunity Loss

We may also construct a decision matrix showing costs which could be avoided given perfect information about the state of nature. These costs are conditional opportunity losses. In the spare parts problem, the strategy-state of nature pairs (A_1, N_1), (A_2, N_2), (A_3, N_3), and so forth, represent the same number of spares as are on hand. The pairs (A_4, N_3), for example, involve extra costs because they represent alternatives for which cost is not minimum for the state of nature. These extra costs are opportunity losses.

We calculate opportunity losses for the decision matrix by subtracting the lowest conditional cost in each column representing a state of nature from each entry in the column. Consider state of nature N_3 in the spare parts problem illustrated in Figure 2.6. If we follow alternative A_3, we would incur an opportunity loss of zero, because the number of spare parts in stock just equals the requirement. If we follow alternative A_4, however, we have an excess unit, the extra cost for which is $1200. Similarly if we follow alternative A_5, we would have an opportunity loss of $2400. If we follow alternative A_2 the total cost is $11,200, and the opportunity loss is $11,200

less the $2400 minimum cost for the column, or $8800. This $8800 repre-
sents the extra cost which would be incurred above that for the optimum
strategy. We can then calculate the expected opportunity loss for each
alternative by using equation (2.4). The complete opportunity loss matrix
is shown in Figure 2.7.

Figure 2.7 Decision Matrix of Opportunity Losses Under Conditions of Risk

				States of Nature				
		N_1	N_2	N_3	N_4	N_5	N_6	
	Number			Demand				
	of	0	1	2	3	4	5	Expected
	Spare			Probability of Occurrence				Opportunity
Alternatives	Parts	0.40	0.25	0.15	0.10	0.05	0.05	Loss
A_1	0	$ 0	$ 8,800	$17,600	$26,400	$35,200	$44,000	$11,440
A_2	1	1,200	0	8,800	17,600	26,400	35,200	6,640
A_3	2	2,400	1,200	0	8,800	17,600	26,400	4,340
A_4	3	3,600	2,400	1,200	0	8,800	17,600	3,540
A_5	4	4,800	3,600	2,400	1,200	0	8,800	3,740
A_6	5	6,000	4,800	3,600	2,400	1,200	0	4,440

Note that the expected opportunity loss approach leads to the same choice
as the total cost approach. Expected opportunity losses for each alternative may be calculated directly as above, or the difference between expected
total cost and expected opportunity loss may be subtracted from each
expected total cost in Figure 2.6. This difference may be found by multiplying the amount subtracted from each column by the probability for that
column. Thus:

$$0.40(0) + 0.25(1200) + 0.15(2400) + 0.10(3600)$$
$$+ 0.05(4500) + 0.05(6000)$$
$$= \$1560.$$

Subtracting $1560 from each of the expected total costs in Figure 2.6 yields
the expected opportunity losses in Figure 2.7. The relative ranks for each
strategy are not affected by the subtraction of a constant amount from the
expected total costs. The same decision choice could also be achieved by
taking a marginal cost approach as explained in Chapter 10.

**Expected
Value of
Perfect
Information**

What would be the value of a perfect forecast of the future state of nature?
Complete information about the future is referred to as perfect information,
and it would remove the uncertainty from a decision problem. Let us examine an example to see how we can determine the value of perfect information. Joe, the ice cream man, sells ice cream bars at ball games. He is continuously faced with a decision of how many ice cream bars to buy for the
following day's game. We will assume that he has only two alternatives, to

buy either 120 dozen or 60 dozen, and that he will sell these quantities depending upon whether it is a sunny or rainy day. Joe knows that it is sunny about 60 per cent of the time and rainy 40 per cent of the time. Thus there is a 60 per cent probability of selling 120 dozen and a 40 per cent probability of selling 60 dozen. Figure 2.8 shows, in a decision matrix,

Figure 2.8 Decision Matrix of Conditional Profits

Alternatives	States of Nature		Expected Profit
	Sunny: Sell 120 dozen p = .6	Rain: Sell 60 dozen p = .4	
Buy 120 Dozen	$72	$22	$52
Buy 60 Dozen	$36	$36	$36

his alternatives and sales possibilities (states of nature). If Joe buys 120 dozen and sells them, he will make $72; if he buys 60 dozen and sells them he will make $36; but if he buys 120 dozen and sells only 60, he will have 60 dozen left over which he can return to the distributor with a penalty of $14. This would leave him with a net profit of $36 − 14 = $22. The expected profit of the alternative of buying 120 dozen is

$$0.6(\$72) + 0.4(\$22) = \$52,$$

and of buying 60 dozen is $36.

Now if Joe knew what the weather would be for the following day, he could order accordingly and avoid opportunity losses from not having enough ice cream bars, or return penalties from having too many. A perfect weather forecast would remove the uncertainty from his decision. This does not mean that he would always sell 120 dozen or 60 dozen, but that he would know in advance how many he would sell the following day, and order just the right amount.

Given a perfect forecast, his profits would be $72 (60 per cent of the time) and $36 (40 per cent of the time). Joe's average (or expected) profit with perfect information would then be

$$0.60(\$72) + 0.40(\$36) = \$57.60,$$

which is the maximum possible profit. Since his maximum expected profit without the perfect forecast is $52, the value of such a perfect forecast is the difference

$$\$57.60 - \$52.00 = \$5.60.$$

Note that the expected value of perfect information is equal to the expected opportunity loss, because this is the loss we would avoid if we had the perfect information. Verification of this fact is left as an exercise at the end of the chapter.

**Decision
Trees**

Decision trees, graphic models of decision problems, can be very useful in analyzing complex management decision problems. This technique enables a manager to display alternatives and their consequences, and the final results and risks associated with them. One of the major advantages of decision trees is that they can be used to introduce probabilities into a decision analysis. A decision tree shows the same type of information as a decision matrix, but a tree form is especially useful in analysis of sequential decisions. We will illustrate some aspects of the development and use of decision trees through an example.

Plant Modernization Problem. A company is faced with the problem of modernizing an existing adequate, but technologically obsolete, plant. An executive suggested that since business is expanding, this would be a good time also to expand the plant. Another executive pointed out that there is still considerable uncertainty about whether the anticipated business expansion would take place. Moreover, he asserted that the company should postpone the expansion decision for three years when the company would have a much clearer idea of the likelihood of the market expansion. The first executive agreed that this was a valid point, but that it would probably cost much more to expand later than to make the expansion at the same time as the modernization.

A review of the data from the proposed modernization or modernization and expansion alternatives revealed the following information. The plant could be modernized at a cost of $3.5 million, or modernized and expanded to provide the capacity necessary to cope with the anticipated expanded business volume at a cost of $6.0 million. If the plant were modernized now, it could be expanded at the end of three years for an additional $4.0 million. For simplicity, we will assume only two possible levels of sales —low and high—although other sales volumes could be readily introduced into the analysis. Estimates of annual after-tax net income over the next 10 years resulting from the possible outcomes are:

1. The existing modernized plant with a high sales volume would yield $600,000 per year.
2. The existing modernized plant with a low sales volume would still be an economical operation and would yield $550,000 per year.
3. An expanded and modernized plant would yield at a high sales volume $1.2 million for the first three years, and $1.5 million for the fourth through the tenth years.
4. An expanded and modernized plant with a low sales volume would yield only $300,000 per year because it would be an uneconomical operation.

Decision Tree Diagram. We may portray the decision choices and their possible outcomes in decision tree form as shown in Figure 2.9. This tree indicates the modernization and expansion choices as defined by the firm and the possible sales volumes predicted.

On the diagram the sales volumes are represented by the following symbols:

$$H_I = \text{High initial demand (first 3 years)}$$
$$H_S = \text{High subsequent demand (years 4–10)}$$
$$L_I = \text{Low initial demand (first 3 years)}$$
$$L_S = \text{Low subsequent demand (years 4–10).}$$

In addition, the tree diagram shows the cash flows resulting from the various actions and events in millions of dollars. For example, the net after-tax income in years 4 through 10 for an expanded and modernized plant with high demand is $1.5 million/year for 7 years, or a total of $10.5 million. On the diagram cash inflows are shown as positive numbers, and cash outflows as negative numbers.

The right-hand side of the diagram shows the cumulative cash flows for the entire path leading to each end point. Following the topmost branch from the initial decision fork, we find cash flows of

$$- \$3.5 + \$1.8 - \$4.0 + \$10.5 = \$4.8 \text{ million}$$

These cumulative cash flows are called conditional profits (or losses), because they are the total after-tax profit dependent upon reaching the particular end point on the tree. Examination of the tree in Figure 2.9 reveals that with the options and outcomes specified in this situation, the range of conditional profits is from a high of $8,100,000 if the plant is modernized and expanded now, and if demand is high initially and continues high, to a loss of $3,750,000 if the company modernizes now, has low initial demand, expands in three years and continues to have low demand.

Up to this point, we have defined the problem faced by the company and identified the alternatives available and the projected costs and returns which would result from each combination of decision choices and levels of sales volume. In many problems faced by management, arriving at this point in the analysis may be very difficult. The process of identifying the relevant choices to include at each decision branch, the pertinent results from them, and the sequence of the decision-event chains may require a great amount of effort. Having done this for the present problem, we next turn to the assignment of probabilities to the various outcomes and to finding expected values for the alternatives.

Probabilities and Expected Values. On the basis of a market analysis the company estimated the likelihood of achieving high or low demand in each

Figure 2.9 Decision Tree with Cash Flows (Millions of Dollars)

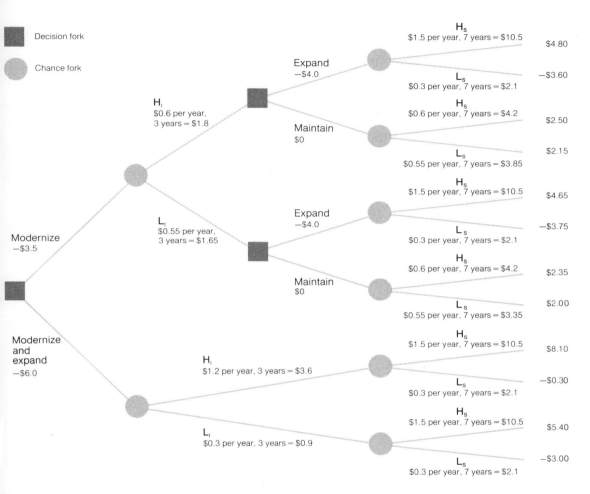

of the two time periods, as shown in Figure 2.10. The company estimates that there is a probability of .3 that sales will be low in the initial period and a probability of .7 that they will be high. Sales in the subsequent period—years 4 through 10—are believed to depend heavily upon sales in the initial period. If sales are low in the initial period, they are very likely to continue low with a probability of .9, and there is only a $(1.0 - .9) = .1$ probability of having low sales in the initial period followed by high sales in the subsequent period. On the other hand, if sales are high in the initial period, the company managers feel that there is a .85 probability that they would continue high, and only a .15 probability that they would be low in the subsequent period.

Figure 2.10   Forecast: Probabilities of Achieving Demand

Level of Demand	Years 0–3	Years 4–10	
		If years 0–3 demand is	
		Low	High
Low	.30	.90	.15
High	.70	.10	.85
Total	1.00	1.00	1.00

Figure 2.11 is the decision tree portrayed in Figure 2.9 with probabilities and expected values added. The purpose of including the probabilities and

Figure 2.11   Decision Tree with Probabilities and Expected Values

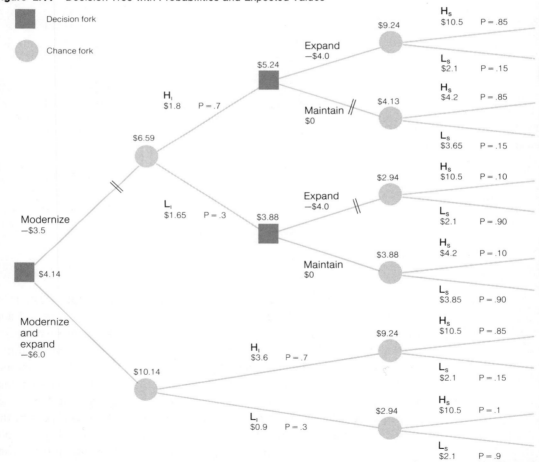

expected values is to help the company executives assess the risks associated with the various alternatives confronting them. The procedure by which we determine the expected values is called "averaging out and rolling back." We begin at the tips of the tree and work back to the immediate decision facing management.

Modernize Branch. We will begin this process by evaluating the decision choice to expand or maintain the plant which follows the event H_I on the modernize branch. Recall that following an initial period of high sales, there is a estimated probability of .85 that demand will continue high and .15 that it will be low. Using these probabilities, we find that the expected value of the net income during years 4 through 10 from a modernized and expanded plant is

$$.85(\$10.5) + .15(\$2.1) = \$9.24 \text{ million.}$$

This expected value has been entered on the diagram just above the (H_S, L_S) chance fork on the expand branch. Since an investment of \$4.0 million is required to expand the plan, that amount must be subtracted to find the expected value of the decision to expand:

$$\$9.24 - 4.0 = \$5.24 \text{ million.}$$

Looking at the chance fork leading to H_S and L_S for the alternative to maintain the plant we find that its expected value is

$$.85(\$4.2) + .15(\$3.65) = \$4.13 \text{ million.}$$

This expected value is entered just above the chance fork on the maintain branch.

Now looking at this decision choice to expand or maintain the plant size, what do we see? Looking at the expansion choice we see a risky option with an expected value of \$5.24 million. Using the criterion of maximizing expected monetary values, we would choose the expansion alternative and block off the maintain option. This is indicated on the tree diagram by the double slash.

Next we make similar computations for the options to expand or maintain following the event L_I on the modernize branch, and enter the expected values \$2.94 and \$3.88 million above the two chance forks. The expand option has an expected value of \$2.94 − \$4.0 = −\$1.06, which is clearly less than the \$3.88 million expected value for the maintain option. In this case we block off the expand option and enter \$3.88 million as the expected value at this decision fork.

The next step in the evaluation of the decision tree is to find the expected value at the (H_I, L_I) chance fork on the modernize branch. The net income anticipated from the initial period of high demand is \$1.8 million, to which we must add the expected value of the (expand, maintain) decision fork of \$5.24. Similarly, we add to the anticipated return of \$1.65 million from the initial period of low demand the expected value of the (expand, maintain) decision fork of $3.88. The expected value of the (H_I, L_I) chance fork is

$$.7(\$1.8 + \$5.24) + .3(\$1.65 + \$3.88) = \$6.59 \text{ million.}$$

This value is entered above the chance fork. Deducting the $3.5 million cost to modernize we find a net expected value for the modernize choice of

$$\$6.59 - \$3.5 = \$3.09 \text{ million.}$$

Let us review what we have done. We have gone out to the tips of the decision tree which follow from the modernize branch, and have worked our way backward to the initial decision choice by a process which uses two techniques. The first is averaging-out at each chance fork to find its expected value, and the second is to choose at each decision fork the path yielding the maximum expected value. This process is called averaging out and rolling back.

Modernize and Expand Branch. Now let us turn to the modernize and expand branch. Here we use the same basic procedure with the exception that there are no intermediate decision choices. The expected value of $9.24 million for the (H_S, L_S) chance fork following the event H_I has been computed already in the upper part of the tree and is entered here. We also enter the expected value of $2.94 for the (H_S, L_S) chance fork following the event L_I. Then the expected value of the (H_I, L_I) chance fork is

$$.7(\$3.6 + \$9.24) + .3(\$0.9 + \$2.94) = \$10.14,$$

and the expected value for the modernize and expand decision fork is

$$\$10.14 - \$6.0 = \$4.14 \text{ million.}$$

Since the value of the modernize and expand decision fork is greater than the value of the modernize decision fork, we block off the modernize decision fork and enter the expected value of $4.14 million at the initial decision fork. This means that if we were making the decision on the basis of these data and an expected value criterion, the decision would be to modernize and expand the plant rather than to modernize now and consider expanding later.

There may well be many other factors which should enter into the decision, however, and these should be considered. The decision tree as presented and evaluated here can be very valuable for certain types of management decisions—those major decisions which involve uncertainty that can be forecast with some degree of confidence. A decision tree presents a visual image of the alternatives and consequences of the whole problem, and includes the impact of future decisions upon the decision presently under consideration. It is a direct way of combining analytic techniques in the analysis of data. The example presented here does not take into account the discounted time value of money, but discounted cash flows (present values) can be readily included.

The process of analyzing a problem in order to examine it in decision tree form forces a systematic approach and a clear definition of the problem that may not be present when a less rigorous approach is used. The visual image of the problem and the interactions among components of the problem aid communication among managers and experts in the various areas included. It may also be of help in communicating the rationale for the chosen course of action, and in securing approval of it. The analysis serves to distinguish between the decision maker's assessment of uncertainties and his preferences for the consequences of risky situations.

The development and use of decision trees does not suggest that maximizing expected values is necessarily the preferred criterion. Techniques have been developed for including in the decision analysis the decision maker's own preferences for the consequences of risky situations. These techniques involve the concepts of utility theory, a discussion of which is beyond the scope of this chapter, but for interested readers references to them may be found at the end of the chapter.

In the case of decision making under uncertainty, the states of nature and their corresponding probabilities of occurrence cannot be predicted. We will not deal with the uncertainty case, because most of the decision problems with which we will be concerned can be analyzed as certainty or risk situations. Information on decision making under uncertainty may be found in the references at the end of the chapter.

Simulation Models

With the availability of large-scale digital computers, simulation has emerged as a powerful and interesting tool for analyzing management decision problems. Through simulation we can observe the behavior of systems under controlled conditions, and run experiments to predict system behavior. Simulation provides managers with a laboratory for analysis of decision problems that often cannot be solved by other means, and provides a way in which the computer can be used to improve the process of management decision making.

Physical models representing phenomena under study have been widely used in engineering and scientific studies. However, these models have not been used in management and social science studies because of the difficulties of representing administrative processes by physical models. Nevertheless, numerical simulation models run on digital computers have become widely used in both administrative studies and in scientific and engineering work.

Simulation refers to the use of a numerical model which represents the dynamic relationships in a system to predict the behavior of the system. In a simulation values which describe initial conditions of a system are used with values which describe changes in the system during a time interval to generate the behavior of the system during that time interval. The results are values of variables which describe the state of the system at the end of the time interval. This process is then repeated until the desired length of time has been represented. For example, in a simulation of an inventory system, values of beginning inventory are used with receipts and disbursements during a time interval to calculate the value of the ending inventory.

A simulation model, then, imitates reality. If the imitation is sufficiently realistic we can infer behavior of the system from observations of behavior of the simulation model. We can easily alter conditions in the model and infer what the impact of those changes would be on the system. In this way a manager may ask a series of "what if" questions about the system. An advantage of this process is that we can use simulation to analyze systems and problems that are too complex for other mathematical techniques. An example is a system in which we would like to explore the effect of the interactions of several probability distributions.

Inventory Simulation

Let us look at a simulation of an elementary inventory problem to illustrate how this one type of simulation model works. A company is faced with a problem of determining the size of orders and when to reorder, but in the face of sales that vary randomly from day to day. The company studied sales records for 500 days and found that demand varied between 17 and 26 units per day according to the frequency shown in Table 2.2. The number

Table 2.2 Probability Distribution of Daily Demand

Number of Units Demanded	Number of Occurrences	Probability of Occurrence	Cumulative Probability of Occurrence	Corresponding 2-Digit Numbers
17	5	.01	.01	01
18	65	.13	.14	02–14
19	75	.15	.29	15–29
20	140	.28	.57	30–57
21	60	.12	.69	58–69
22	50	.10	.79	70–79
23	40	.08	.87	80–87
24	40	.08	.95	88–95
25	15	.03	.98	96–98
26	10	.02	1.00	99–00
Totals	500	1.00		

Average Demand = 20.71 units/day

of days on which each level of demand occurred was converted into relative frequencies in column 3, and since management felt that this same pattern of demand would continue for the immediate future, these relative frequencies were taken to be the probabilities of occurrence. From the table we find that .15 is the probability for a demand of 19 units on any given day.

Monte Carlo Process

We can simulate sales which vary randomly according to this pattern by the Monte Carlo process. The Monte Carlo process is a technique of selecting numbers randomly from a probability distribution.[4] In the last column of Table 2.2 we assigned sets of two-digit numbers to each demand. One number (01) is assigned to a demand of 17 since it has a .01 probability of occurrence; thirteen numbers (02–14) are assigned to a demand of 18 units since it has a .13 probability of occurrence; and so forth.

We now obtain two-digit random numbers by some means such as rolling dice, drawing numbers from a hat, generating them on a computer, or selecting them from a table of uniformly distributed random numbers like the one in the appendix of tables. We use them to select demands from the distribution of demands in the table. If the number selected is 60, the demand would be 21, since 60 falls into the 57–68 set of numbers in the last column of the table. In Table 2.3 we have drawn five random numbers and use them

Table 2.3 Simulated Demand for Five Days

Day Number	Random Number	Demand (units)
1	60	21
2	18	19
2	18	19
3	10	18
4	85	23
5	55	20

to determine simulated demand for five days. If we repeat this process many times, we would have a randomly varying pattern of demands which would occur with the relative frequencies shown in Table 2.2.

Figure 2.12 shows how this might be done in a computer program using the cumulative probabilities from column 4 of Table 2.2. If the random number generated is .60 the program in effect reads across to the cumulative distribution, determines that .60 falls above the cumulative probability for 20 units and below the cumulative probability for 21 units, and selects 21 as the demand for that period.

[4] Application of the term "Monte Carlo" is attributed to John von Neumann and Ulam who used the method to study neutron diffusion problems. The method has been used to analyze nonprobabilistic problems of evaluating calculus integrals. In current usage it generally refers to randomly selecting numbers from a probability distribution. Daniel D. McCracken, "The Monte Carlo Method," *Scientific American* 192, no. 5 (May 1955).

Figure 2.12 Use of Random Numbers to Determine Daily Demand

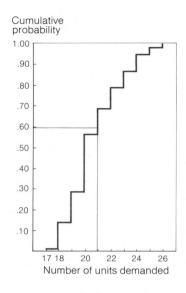

Returning to the inventory simulation problem, there is another probability distribution with which the company is concerned. That is the distribution of lead times, or the time between placing an order and receiving the goods, as indicated in Table 2.4. Mathematical analysis of this type of

Table 2.4 Probability Distribution of Lead Times

Lead Time (Days)	Probability of Occurrence	Cumulative Probability of Occurrence
6	.10	.10
7	.20	.30
8	.30	.60
9	.25	.85
10	.15	1.00

problem is difficult because of the interaction between the demand and lead time probability distributions, but we can simulate the behavior of this system using the Monte Carlo method and determine the cost of various purchasing policies.[5]

Computer Simulation

We could simulate this situation by hand using the method described above, but the amount of calculation required to simulate, say, a year's operation of the system would be rather tedious. This is the type of calculation for which a digital computer is suited. Figure 2.13 shows the output

[5] Analysis of this type of inventory problem is discussed in Chapter 10.

Figure 2.13 Computer Simulation of Probabilistic Inventory System

```
INVENTORY SIMULATION
DEMONSTRATION

RUN INPUT DATA

X =     .48
Y =    1.35
NUMBER OF TIME PERIODS = 100
INTERVAL BETWEEN REVIEWS = 1
PRICE OF ITEM =     9.50   PER UNIT
BEGINNING INVENTORY =   240   UNITS
ORDER POINT =   160   UNITS
ORDER QUANTITY =   750   UNITS
COST OF PLACING REPLENISHMENT ORDER =     15.00
COST OF RECEIVING REPLENISHMENT ORDER =     30.00
COST OF LOST DEMAND =    3.50   PER UNIT
INTEREST COST PER TIME PERIOD =   .001000


  LEAD TIME      CUMULATIVE FREQUENCY
      6                 .1000
      7                 .3000
      8                 .6000
      9                 .8500
     10                1.0000


  DEMAND         CUMULATIVE FREQUENCY
     17                 .0100
     18                 .1400
     19                 .2900
     20                 .5700
     21                 .6900
     22                 .7900
     23                 .8700
     24                 .9500
     25                 .9800
     26                1.0000
```

TRANSACTIONS

PERIOD	ON HAND	ON ORDER	ORDERED	DUE IN	RECEIVED	DEMANDED	LOST	COST
1	216	0				24		
2	193	0				23		
3	174	0				19		
4	154	0	750			20		15.00
5	154	750		11		17		
6	137	750				18		
7	119	750				19		
8	100	750				25		
9	75	750				19		
10	56	750				19		
11	37	750			750			30.00
	787							

PERIOD	ON HAND	ON ORDER	ORDERED	DUE IN	RECEIVED	DEMANDED	LOST	COST
11	764	0				23		
12	743	0				21		
13	723	0				20		
14	703	0				22		
15	681	0				20		
16	661	0				21		
17	640	0				19		
18	621	0				20		
19	601	0				20		
20	581	0				20		
21	561	0				20		
22	541	0				18		
23	521	0				21		
24	501	0				18		
25	483	0				23		
26	462	0				22		
27	444	0				20		
28	421	0				18		
29	399	0				19		
30	379	0				20		
31	359	0				18		
32	341	0				18		
33	322	0				24		
34	302	0				18		
35	284	0				19		
36	266	0				19		
37	242	0				18		
38	224	0				20		
39	205	0				19		
40	186	0				18		
41	168	0				20		
42	148	750	750	52		18		15.00
43	130	750				22		
44	108	750				18		
45	90	750				24		
46	66	750				20		
47	46	750				18		
48	28	750				24		
49	4	750				21	17	59.50
50	0	750				18	18	63.00
51	750	0			750	20		30.00
52	730	0				24		
53	706	0				20		
54	686	0				22		
55	664	0				20		
56	644	0				18		
57	626	0				19		
58	607	0				18		
59	589	0						

Period	Inventory	On Order	Receipt	Demand
60	564	0		25
61	542	0		22
62	523	0		19
63	503	0		20
64	484	0		19
65	466	0		18
66	445	0		21
67	427	0		18
68	407	0		20
69	386	0		21
70	362	0		24
71	343	0		19
72	320	0		23
73	300	0		20
74	279	0		21
75	259	0		20
76	239	0		17
77	222	0		22
78	200	0		23
79	177	0		20
80	157	750		19
81	157	750		25
82	138	750		24
83	113	750	89	19
84	89	750		21
85	70	750		20
86	49	750		21
87	29	750		21
88	8	0		19
89	0	0		20
89	750	0	750	20
90	731	0		19
91	711	0		20
92	691	0		21
93	672	0		18
94	652	0		20
95	631	0		21
96	613	0		18
97	593	0		20
98	574	0		19
99	556	0		18
100	538	0		18
	516	0		22

15.00

13   45.50
30.00

TOTAL DEMAND = 2022
AVERAGE INVENTORY = 370.41
NUMBER OF ORDERS = 3
NUMBER OF RECEIPTS = 3
DEMAND LOST = 48
SERVICE FACTOR = .98

RUN SUMMARY

CARRYING COST	= 351.89
ORDERING COST	= 45.00
RECEIVING COST	= 90.00
LOST DEMAND COST	= 168.00
TOTAL COST	= 654.89

from a computer simulation of this system for 100 days for an order point of 160 units (a purchase order is placed when inventory level falls to 160 units), an order quantity of 750 units, and a beginning inventory of 216 units.[6]

The computer printout, in the first part, shows the data used as input to the program. Stock level is reviewed every period to see whether a purchase order should be placed. The item in question costs $9.50; it costs $15.00 to place a purchase order and $30.00 to receive the order regardless of the quantity ordered. Annual cost of carrying inventory is 25 per cent of the purchase cost. If the item is not in stock, the company estimates that it will lose $3.50 per unit.

The second part of the output lists each transaction as it occurred. Tracing through these transactions, we can see the pattern of activity in the system for the 100-day period represented. The third part of the printout shows a summary of the results of the simulation run. Note that total cost of following this policy is $654.89. The program does not locate an optimum purchasing policy; it merely shows the consequences of following this particular policy. The company managers may wish to explore the results of other policies, in which case they could try them out on the model and observe their consequences. A simulation model is used in this manner essentially as a vehicle for search. The information it provides can be a valuable adjunct to the decision process.

Simulation Applications

Not all simulations involve probability distributions, as does the one illustrated here. Other models, like the industrial dynamics models presented in Chapter 13, are of deterministic (nonprobabilistic) systems. Simulation models have been applied to a wide variety of activities, such as corporate planning, distribution systems, railroad car scheduling, refinery operations, capital investment decisions, scheduling service facilities, maintenance operations, quality control systems, location of facilities, personnel planning, consumer behavior, fisheries management, and water pollution control. Some of these applications will be described throughout this book.

We have noted that simulation often permits us to analyze problems which are too complex to be analyzed by more formal mathematical techniques. It also offers some advantages over those techniques that may make it preferable in some decision situations. It permits direct observation of the dynamic behavior of systems. Where the criteria for evaluating system performance are complex or not well defined, the ability of a simulation model to give a total picture of the operating characteristics of the system is a distinct advantage.

---

[6] A detailed description of the program and its use is contained in Robert C. Meier, William T. Newell, and Harold L. Pazer, *Simulation in Business and Economics* (Englewood Cliffs, New Jersey: Prentice-Hall, Inc., 1969), Chapter 1 and Appendix B.

Simulation is not without its own limitations, however. Analyzing the system, creating a simulation model of it, and developing a computer program for the model are major difficulties in using simulation. Validation of models and interpretation of simulation results are important problems facing a simulation user. Models of complex systems are costly to create and to run on a computer. Some of these problems are being reduced by advances in computer technology.

Remote inputs, rapid access, graphic display devices, and the development of computer languages which are oriented more toward the computer user than the computer specialist are making it increasingly possible for us to test ideas and policies through simulation before applying them to an actual situation. Of all the recent advances in mathematical approaches to problem-solving, simulation probably has greater potential for aiding top-management decision making than any of the others.

Summary

A decision is a choice from among alternative courses of action. Prior to the actual choice, the decision process includes problem definition, discovery of alternative courses of action, evaluation of alternatives, selection of a course of action, implementation of the decision, and information feedback of results.

Decision making ranges from long-range planning (strategies) to short-range planning (tactics). Providing that strategies are properly formulated, tactics are procedures for carrying out strategies at the operating level. It is significant to note that information on feasible tactics is important to managers making decisions on strategy.

A model is an abstraction of the real world. It may be an iconic representation (image), an analogue (one characteristic used to represent another), or symbolic (symbols used to represent variables or relationships).

A decision matrix is an array of items or the components of a decision problem. Included are the alternatives, states of nature, and outcomes. In the decision theory framework, decisions may be classified according to information of the states of nature, that is, decision making under conditions of certainty, risk, or uncertainty.

Under conditions of certainty, only one state of nature is assumed to exist, and we know what it will be. We may choose to find a feasible solution and then continue to seek other solutions which offer a better pay off, or conduct a formal method of search (heuristic programming) to find the optimum solution.

Under conditions of risk, there are two or more states of nature which can be identified and the probability of their occurrence is known or can be predicted with a high degree of confidence. Situations of risk are common in most organizations and techniques such as expected value serve useful functions in improving the decision-making process.

One useful technique in the analysis of alternatives is a decision tree. This method provides a graphic model of what the consequences of various courses of action will be under different risk conditions. Probabilities can be included to determine the expected value in an "averaging out and rolling back" procedure.

Simulation models imitate real systems, and provide a laboratory for analysis of decision, problems which may be too complex to solve by other means. Simulation describes changes in a system over time. The Monte Carlo process is used to permit simulating probabilistic systems.

Selected References

Beer, Stafford. *Management Science: The Business Use of Operations Research.* Garden City, N.Y.: Doubleday & Co., Inc., 1967.

The author presents a non-mathematical introduction to the role and application of management science and cybernetics in business decision making.

Kaufman, Arnold. *The Science of Decision Making.* New York: McGraw-Hill Book Co., World University Library, 1968. (paperback)

This book is an introduction to scientific tools useful in decision making. Topics covered include choice of decision criterion, search for an optimal policy, dealing with chance and uncertainty, and simulation.

Magee, John F. "Decision Trees for Decision Making." *Harvard Business Review,* July–August 1964, pp. 126–134.

Magee, John F. "How to Use Decision Trees in Capital Investment." *Harvard Business Review,* September–October 1964, pp. 79–96.

The articles provide an explanation of construction and use of decision trees. The author includes several examples of applications.

Meier, Robert C., Newell, William T., and Pazer, Harold L. *Simulation in Business and Economics.* Englewood Cliffs, N.J.: Prentice-Hall Inc., 1969.

This text is an introduction to computer simulation and application to business and economic analysis. The authors include heuristic and simulation gaming methods, and technical aspects of constructing and operating simulation models.

Raiffa, Howard. *Decision Analysis.* Reading, Mass.: Addison-Wesley, 1968.

The author presents an approach to problems of choosing a course of action under conditions of uncertainty using decision trees, probabilities, and personal preferences. The emphasis is on logical analysis with minimal formal mathematics.

Schlaifer, Robert. *Analysis of Decisions Under Uncertainty.* New York: McGraw-Hill Book Co., 1969.

The book is a comprehensive treatment of decision analysis.

Miller, David W., and Starr, Martin K. *Executive Decisions and Operations Research,* 2nd ed. Englewood Cliffs, N.J.: Prentice-Hall, Inc., 1969.

This book examines management decision problems in terms of a decision theory formulation. It also describes applications of operations research in functional business areas.

Questions

1 Describe management decision making as a feedback process.

2 Under what circumstances may a manager's perception of achievements of a system differ significantly from actual achievements of the system?

3 Distinguish between optimization and suboptimization of a system. Give an example.

4 In operations management much attention is frequently given to reducing operation costs. How may this lead to significant suboptimization of a system?

5 Why is it useful to distinguish between strategies and tactics in management decision making?

6 What functions do models serve in a decision process?

7 Describe the difference between strategies and states of nature.

8 Explain the primary methods used to select a strategy under conditions of certainty.

9 Discuss the advantages and disadvantages in the use of formal decision analysis.

Problems

1 The Hard Metalworking Company has 7 jobs to produce and 7 machines that can perform the task but at different costs. Mr. Hard, owner of the company, wishes to assign one job to each machine at the lowest operating cost. If he approaches this problem by enumerating all the alternatives, how many alternatives would he have to investigate?

2 George Frank, a retailer, stocks a certain perishable item which he orders each day for sale the following day. He buys the item for $8 per case and sells it for $14 per case. Any amount not sold the first day must be discarded. An analysis of customers' demand for the past 120 days revealed the following data:

Demand per day (cases)	Number of days
30	24
40	24
50	36
60	24
70	12

Mr. Frank feels that the same pattern of demand will continue for the immediate future.

a. Calculate the expected value of sales for this distribution.

b. Prepare a decision matrix showing conditional profits and expected profits for this situation.

c. What quantity should be stocked each day in order to maximize expected profits?

d. Prepare a decision matrix showing conditional opportunity loss and expected opportunity loss for this situation.

e. Calculate the expected value of perfect information for this situation.

3 Prepare a conditional loss table for the ice cream problem in Figure 2.8; calculate the expected opportunity loss, and compare the result with the value of perfect information in the text.

4 The Leman Bakery Company has received a request from the Green Grocery Supermarket Chain to produce a private brand of bread for sale in Green stores.

The Leman managers agree that they have three alternatives:

1) Refuse the request,

2) Agree to produce the private brand, or

3) Institute a system of price differentials based upon quantity and service offered by Leman. Such price differentials would presumably result in lower prices to Green because of their expected volumes of purchases.

The managers of Leman are uncertain what will happen but their best guess is that the following outcomes are possible.

1) If they turn down the offer one of three outcomes will occur:

a. the Vaud Bakery will supply Green with a probability of .20. This would result in a net loss to Leman with a present value of −$2,000,000 over 5 years.

b. Green will establish its own bakery and reduce its purchases from Leman with a probability of .30. This would result in a net loss with a present value of −$2,000,000.

c. Green will wait and take no further immediate action with a probability of .50, and no gain or loss to Leman.

2) If Leman agrees to produce the private bread, one of these outcomes will occur:

a. Green will accept and the Vaud Bakery will retaliate by lowering the prices on its bread with a probability of .20. The present value of the resulting net loss will be −$6,000,000.

b. Green will accept and Leman will lose some share of bread sales to independent grocers because of Leman's sales to Green. Probability of .60, and present value of net loss −$200,000.

c. Green will accept and Leman will lose no sales to independents. Leman will realize a net present value of $6,000,000, with a probability of .20.

3) If Leman offers a price differential, these outcomes are possible:

a. Green will reject the offer and Vaud supplies Green with a probability of .20, and the same loss as in 1 (a).

b. Green will reject the offer and establish its own bakery with a probability of .20, and the same loss as in 1 (b).

    c. Green will reject the offer and take no further immediate action with a probability of .35. No gain or loss.

    d. Green will accept the offer with a probability of .25. Present value of net gain from added volume $6,000,000.

Draw a decision tree for this decision problem.

5 The Cleeberg Company has developed a new product. Now they are considering whether or not to construct a pilot plant at a cost of $0.3 million which is needed to investigate the feasibility and economics of manufacturing the product in large volume for commercial sale. If a pilot plant is not built, the product will be dropped.

    The managers feel that if a pilot plant is built the following outcomes are likely:

    a. There is 0.1 probability that the pilot plant trial will show that the product should be dropped. There would be no further cost if it is dropped.

    b. There is a 0.6 probability that the pilot plant trial will show that the product can be produced in large volume in a standard plant.

    c. There is a 0.3 probability that the pilot plant trial will show that the product can be produced in large volume, but will require a complex plant.

    Depending upon the outcome of the pilot plant trial, the company will then face decisions whether to build one of the large plants or to drop the product. If the product is dropped at this point, there would be no further cost.

    The company managers further estimate that if the standard plant is built it would cost $1.3 million, and would result in recovery (positive cash flow) of the following amounts:

1) $4.0 million with a probability of 0.3.

2) $2.0 million with a probability of 0.7.

If the complex plant is built it would cost $3.0 million, and would result in the same recovery as the standard plant, that is:

1) $4.0 million with a probability of 0.3.

2) $2.0 million with a probability of 0.7.

Draw a decision tree to determine the expected value of building the pilot plant.

Chapter 3
Aggregate
Systems of
Operations

The whole is often easier to understand than any of its parts. For this reason it makes sense to begin an analysis of any operation by turning attention to the total system in which it occurs. Although we are interested in analysis in general, the systems of particular interest to us either transform raw materials into finished goods, or store or move materials (or goods) at any stage in the process. These systems provide both processing and service facilities, and their operations enable a steady flow of materials, goods, or services through the appropriate channel.

For the present, the aggregate, or overall view of systems, holds the center of the stage. Here we consider aggregate, or total, characteristics of the system and over-all operating problems, while treating the operating principles of the components as fixed. Later we shall take a closer, more detailed look at the internal characteristics and rules of operation governing the components. Of course, many organizations cannot take this aggregate view of their operations because their own role is so relatively minute compared to the total system in which they operate.

Figure 3.1 shows an operating system as a "black box." Primary inputs

Figure 3.1 Operating System Viewed at the Highest Level of Abstraction

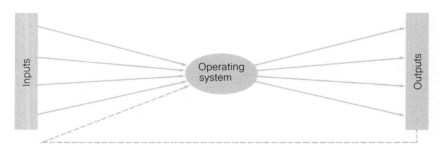

introduced into this box produce a set of outputs each differing from the inputs in physical state, location, point in time, and product mixture. In some systems, some or all of the output is recycled through the system, as shown by the dashed line in the figure. Our principal interest here is the specification and arrangements of those components that will efficiently yield desired outputs from the system.

The Total System

In Chapter 1, we stated that the total system is established by definition; that is, by defining the meaningful boundaries of the system in question. In most systems organized for profit, these boundaries will fall within those limits where direct decision making occurs, even though the environmental influence of other systems is noted. In economic, political, and social systems the scope of analysis can be much greater, and the criteria for defining the system might be an influence rather than a decision-making capability. In every instance the definition should be made in full realization of the relationship of the defined system to its environment. We can emphasize this point by considering the cross-relationships of some of our economic, political, and social problems relating to pollution. Figure 3.2 illustrates

Figure 3.2   A System Look at Pollution

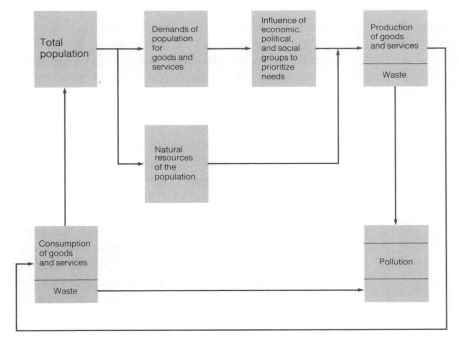

how pollution (waste) is a product of both production and consumption, but, even more basic, that the amount of pollution depends on many factors relating to all systems:

1. the total population and its rate of growth,
2. the demand of the population for goods and services,
3. the kind of goods and services which are produced as determined by priority,
4. the degree to which resource transformation can occur without waste,
5. the degree to which consumption can occur without waste.

When population is expanding, and the demand for goods and services is growing, waste creates little concern. Eventually, waste becomes excessive and is regarded as a negative factor in an evaluation of general living conditions.

Defining the total system as it pertains to pollution is very difficult, and defining the total system for a large corporation may be almost as illusive. Figure 3.3 shows a general model of the operation of the Weyerhaeuser Company, illustrating the material flow from the timber resource through the various processing stages to the products produced. The model represents the total system of material flow for the Weyerhaeuser Company and is the base upon which each subsystem can be defined and developed in relation to the whole.

Inputs to Operations

A system operates on the inputs it receives; primary inputs of materials, energy, or information. The operations on the inputs will include any of a number of possibilities—transforming, servicing, moving, holding, mixing, or aggregating. Secondary inputs, such as direct and indirect labor, capital goods, supplies, and other services also come into play. Behind both primary and secondary inputs, all of which are physical, lie the financial resources needed to support them.

Primary inputs may be unplanned or they may be regulated to fit costs, profits, or other objectives. Garbage is an instance of an unplanned input; all of it must be accepted by the garbage disposal system. The number of persons permitted to continue through the stages of a public education system represents a regulated type of input. We get some insight into the importance of the distinction between fixed and regulated inputs by considering the design of public transportation systems in urban areas. If we assume that the system has been designed to meet current and predicted needs, we can expect it to respond to anticipated growth. However, that same system can serve as an instrument of public policy by determining the direction of future growth. That is to say, future development is likely to occur adjacent to the site of the system. In this instance, the inputs to the system are determined by the system itself.

Some latitude is permissible in the selection of secondary inputs. One may substitute capital for labor, for example, or one type of capital equipment

Figure 3.3 Weyerhaeuser, A Materials Flow Company

Input and output figures are frequently affected by inventory changes, additives and waste, conversion and other factors. Output figures show either shipments or transfers. Items shown as net are net of sales and purchases.

ADT: Air dry ton
BDT: Bone dry ton
MBF: Thousand board feet
MSF: Thousand square feet
MCCF: 100,000 cubic feet

Internal flow

Outside purchases

Sales

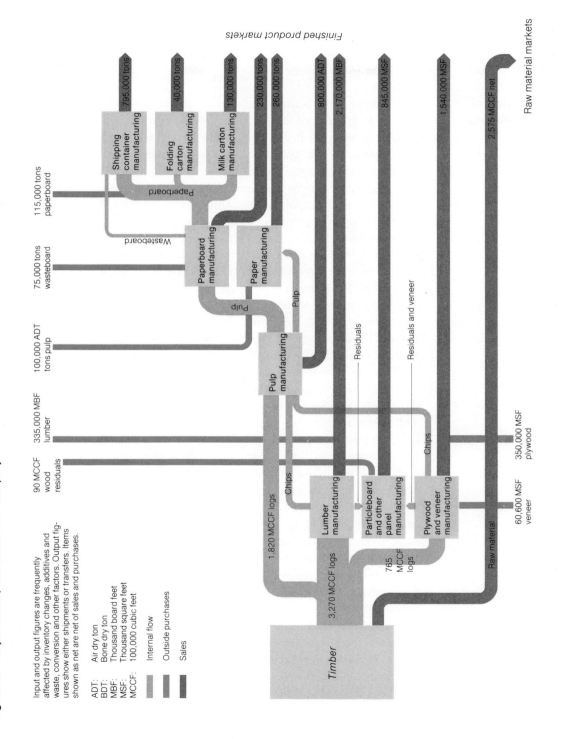

for another while maintaining the system's capabilities. A close relationship exists between inputs to system design and system operation. System design is established by capital expenditures for buildings, equipment, and machines, which may be substituted for direct energy inputs (labor) in the operation of the system.

Outputs of Operations

Depending on the nature of the operating system, the objective of the system may be to provide goods at a certain place in a given time, or to provide a product within specified quality limits for a given number of dollars. Since the operation of a system is rarely deterministic, the statement of the desired primary outputs should include a definition of the acceptable variation. Random elements in almost all operating systems combine to produce a distribution of outputs. A recognition and understanding of the inherent variability of system output is necessary to the proper interpretation of behavior which is observed. This point will be discussed in greater length in Chapter 9 which deals with statistical control models.

In some cases, available inputs determine what will be the outputs from the system. When this happens, the objective becomes one of selecting and producing outputs which maximize return or benefits within the resource constraints. Take, for example, an oil refinery serving an oil field with an input of crude oil having specific chemical characteristics. Output from the refinery would then be limited to certain petroleum products. In Chapter 4, we illustrate an analysis of this type of situation.

Another way to analyze the output of a system is in terms of the trade-offs which can be made between outputs that are obtained from the system, and factors such as cost, resources used, and method of operation. In this case, the study is directed toward determining the trade-off curve rather than maximizing output from a given input, or in minimizing those inputs necessary for a given output. For example, a fire protection system may be analyzed to determine the trade-off curve between cost and the average time to place equipment at a fire. When there are more fire stations and more equipment, cost is higher, but response time is lower. Conversely, with fewer stations and less equipment, cost is lower, but response time increases. Figure 3.4 illustrates the shape of the curve. From such a curve, we can assess the benefits derived from incremental investments in the fire protection system. If we could relate functionally average losses due to fire to average time taken for equipment to arrive, a further step might be to analyze the optimal level of fire protection where the marginal cost of protection is just equal to the marginal gain achieved from reduction in losses. However, functional relationships of this nature may be impossible to obtain, and in many cases the analysis would be directed simply at obtaining the trade-off curve.

Figure 3.4 Time-Cost Trade-off Curve for Typical Fire Protection System

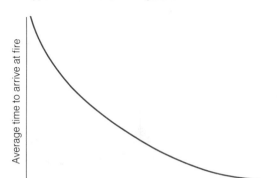

Secondary outputs of many operating systems are waste materials, depleted resources, and similar undesired by-products of operations. These secondary outputs from operations were once largely disregarded because of their lack of direct economic consequence. Wastes often were dumped onto the land, into the water, or into the air with little or no cost to the operating systems which produced them, but at considerable cost to the surrounding environment and the public at large. Increasingly, the point of view being adopted, primarily through regulatory legislation, is that those secondary outputs must be eliminated or made harmless—or that the operating systems which are responsible must bear the costs which have been inequitably borne by others before. Regulation of strip mining activities, dumping of oil from ships, and disposal of wastes in rivers and streams are illustrative of the increasing attention being given to the effects of secondary outputs from some operations, and any analysis of the operations involved must consider the consequences of these secondary outputs and their regulation.

Representation of Systems of Operations as Networks

Think of an operating system as a network of links and nodes, as in Figure 3.5. The inputs and outputs in this illustration are all primary. The secondary ones which tend to be numerous are omitted. Furthermore, the links, or straight lines, denote transportation, whereas the nodes, or junctions, represent the points at which transformation, some service, or storage occurs.

The network approach to an operating system may seem clearer when the inputs move physically through the links and nodes, but it applies equally well to service systems. Here the flow through the network is a movement of services rather than of physical inputs. In addition, the network concept proves useful in other contexts, as we shall see later on in this book.

Figure 3.5   Representation of a System of Operations as a Network of Links and Nodes

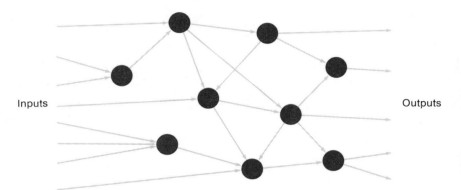

Figure 3.6 roughly depicts the network approach to a manufacturing process. This network contains a number of inputs, even more than those shown in the representation, but only a single primary output. The establishment of such a network requires several things. It calls for analyses of the number and locations of nodes, the operations to be performed at each node, the party responsible (prime manufacturer, subcontractor, or supplier) for the work at each junction, and the mode of transport between

Figure 3.6   Network Representation of a Manufacturing System

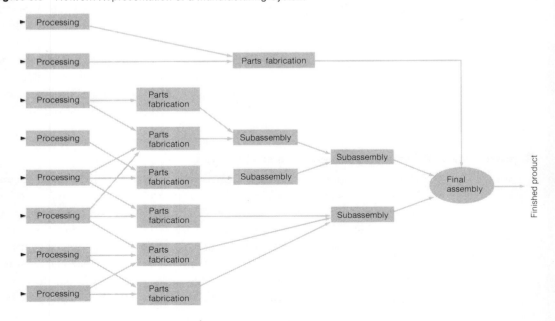

nodes. There is also a need to devise controls that will assure an effective flow through the network. This flow will support the desired rate of output, will minimize costs, and will not overtax the capabilities of the network.

A characteristic worth noting is that the network is not always tightly held together. Raw materials, parts, and subassemblies may be held in storage areas before and after moving from one node to another, and in some cases may be assembled into lots. The design of the control systems that regulate the flow through the network must recognize that movement need not be continuous and balanced at all times.

Unlike the rather loose network in Figure 3.6, the network in Figure 3.7

Figure 3.7 Petroleum Refining and Distribution System

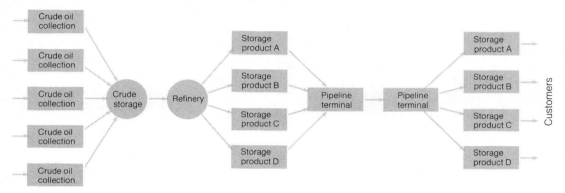

is more tightly coupled. This particular network covers the collecting, refining, and distributing of petroleum products. Because the network has this quality of tight physical coupling, balancing capacities of its elements and maintenance of a balanced flow through the network are critical.

Figure 3.8 diagrams a system of criminal justice. The flow in this system consists of persons accused and convicted of crimes. Two characteristics of this system are of special interest: (1) the amount of feedback of the output back into the system, and (2) the length of time it takes to process people through the system and return them to society.

Components of Networks

Although the specific characteristics of links and nodes in the operating system are peculiar to each system, we can make some general comments on the factors which are relevant in specifying the components of the system.

Transformation and Service Nodes. The principal factors of interest with regard to transformation and service nodes are capabilities, capacity, and cost characteristics of each node. Nodes may be specialized, performing only a single function, or they may have the ability to perform a variety of functions, perhaps on a number of different types of entities or transactions

Figure 3.8 Criminal Justice System

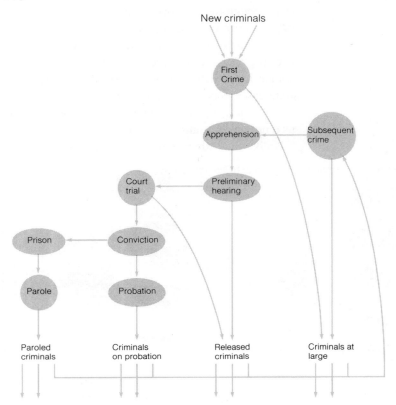

flowing through them. Specialized nodes are more likely to be suited to continuous processing operations while nodes with general purpose capabilities are more frequently associated with one-at-a-time, short-run, or batch-type operations. For example, the crude oil refinery node in Figure 3.7 is a special purpose processing facility designed for continuous processing of crude oil with limited capability for altering the mix of inputs and outputs. In contrast, the fabrication facilities in Figure 3.6 would probably have capabilities for producing various types of parts, and successive lots processed through them are likely to be quite different in nature.

The measurement of the capacity of a service or transformation node involves consideration of the basic operating rate in the node and the length of time that the facility operates. Some facilities, such as electric generating plants, are designed for continuous operation, but most are not utilized continuously. In determining the size or number of facilities to be incorporated in the system, comparisons must be made between the marginal costs of higher utilization rates and the costs of providing additional facilities to be operated at lower rates of utilization.

Break-Even Analysis. A common graphic model is the break-even chart which illustrates cost-volume-profit relationships. In such charts, as shown in Figure 3.9, costs are divided into two categories, fixed and variable. Sales revenue and variable costs are assumed to change in direct proportion to the volume of output. The assumptions (1) that there is a direct linear relationship between volume, revenue, and variable costs; and (2) that fixed costs remain constant break down when we consider the entire range of volume variations. However, for many situations, there are narrow "relevant ranges" of volume for which the assumptions do provide an adequate approximation. Note that the two variations of a break-even graph illustrated in Figure 3.9 reach identical conclusions.

Figure 3.9 Break-Even Graphs

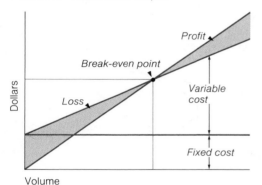
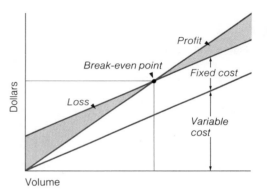

Multi-Facility Analysis. In determining the size or number of facilities to be incorporated in the system, comparisons must be made between the marginal costs of higher utilization rates and the costs of providing additional facilities to be operated at lower rates of utilization. Figures 3.10 and 3.11 illustrate this relationship.

A factor affecting capacity, particularly of general purpose facilities, is the amount of time lost in process change as different entities flow through the facilities. Where setup time is appreciable, capacity is severely reduced when a number of different entities are processed in small lot sizes. Operating policies, then, determine in part the capacity of a service or transformation node. In cases where the effect of a learning curve is significant, another determinant of capacity is the number of consecutive similar units that have been processed. The learning curve will be discussed in greater detail in Chapter 10.

We have already illustrated fixed and variable costs in Figure 3.9, and in Figure 3.10 in connection with the utilization of facilities. The same factors of fixed and variable costs are relevant in selecting the number of transformation or service nodes with similar capabilities to include in a system. Technological advances often offer opportunities for lower variable cost

Figure 3.10   Total Cost of Second Shift and Second Facility Operations

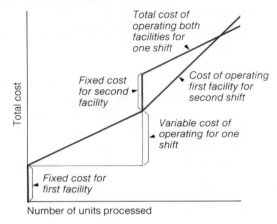

Figure 3.11   High Capacity-Single Facility Operations versus Low Capacity-Multiple Facility Operations

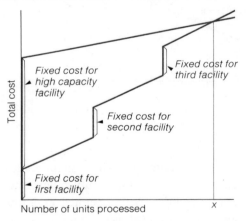

of operations but usually with higher fixed costs. Where volume is high enough in the system, choices may be made between providing a single facility with high capacity, high fixed cost, and low variable cost or a number of facilities with smaller capacity, low fixed cost, but higher variable cost. Figure 3.11 illustrates a typical situation. Below the volume X, multiple facilities are more economical, whereas above this volume, a single facility of higher capacity is less costly. The use of a single facility above the break-even volume, however, may also produce additional problems of scheduling the facility, geographic inconveniences, and exposure to risk in case of malfunction.

Storage Nodes. Within the operating system, storage nodes decouple or interrupt the flow in portions of the network, which permits a degree of temporary imbalance between preceding and succeeding activities in the network. The storage node acts as a buffer so that activities do not have to be precisely coordinated and tightly linked with one another. Management reduces the problems of coordinating flow through the network by using storage nodes; but a penalty is paid for the gain in organizational flexibility in terms of the costs for providing storage or waiting facilities, handling charges, and capital investment in inventories. The capacity of a storage node determines the amount of decoupling that can be obtained. In effect, organizational flexibility is purchased by providing storage nodes in the network. Management can increase flexibility by providing more costly storage nodes of higher capacity, but eventually a point is reached at which marginal savings obtained by decoupling the network are not sufficient to offset marginal costs of storage.

In addition to the organizational justification for storage nodes, such nodes also serve as points at which entities moving through the network can be aggregated, stored, disaggregated, and mixed together as necessary. For example, in a distribution system storage nodes may perform the function of bringing together shipments from different sources, regrouping them into mixed lots, and sending them out through the next link in the network. The airline terminal in the air transport system serves somewhat similar functions in that it provides a place where passengers arriving by auto and plane can be disaggregated and reaggregated into loads suitable for outgoing transportation links. The terminal also provides a place for storing passengers, the entities moving through the system, until such time as suitable transportation links are available.

Transportation Links. Transportation links may provide intermittent movement of entities in the system as in the case of passenger aircraft in an airline system, or flow may be continuous as in a pipeline. We can also characterize transportation links by their capacity for handling different types of entities.

Physical characteristics such as maximum load and speed of movement determine the maximum capacity of a transportation link. The degree to which maximum capacity is utilized through maximum loading and minimum delays determines actual capacity. Less than maximum utilization may result, for instance, when the design of the transportation link is not matched to the entities in the system. Cargo aircraft are often under-utilized when space in the cargo compartment is exhausted before maximum weight is reached.

The physical characteristics of transportation links are important to the overall network because they impose constraints on operations at preceding and succeeding nodes. Cost characteristics of transportation links must also be analyzed in terms of the impact on the total operation of the network. A link which offers the lowest transportation cost does not necessarily result in minimum cost for the system. Such things as the amount of intransit inventory required and the impact of the speed and responsiveness of the link on operations at preceding and succeeding nodes must be considered. In a spare parts supply system, for example, it may be more economical to maintain a single inventory of parts at a central location and air freight the parts to locations of demand rather than to maintain separate inventories at various geographical locations and ship parts to these dispersed inventories by a cheaper but slower mode of transportation. Airlines frequently find that, for many items, a single location or a few central locations for a spare parts inventory can provide nearly the same parts availability as multiple locations, and with a much smaller total inventory investment. However, in order to determine the lowest total systems costs and at the same time to maintain an effective system, the overall network must be analyzed.

Variations in Networks. The specific configurations of networks are a function of the systems being analyzed and the particular emphasis in the analysis. Different systems have different numbers and types of links and nodes. In addition, the same system may be modeled with different network configurations depending on the purposes of analysis and level of abstraction desired. Primarily, the network is a way of looking at systems of operations in an orderly way and forms the basis for meaningful analysis of alternative ways to organize and manage a total system.

Theoretical Analysis of Networks

Suppose that a network has certain fixed capacities in the links and we wish to determine the maximum capacity of the network—or maximum flow that can be obtained through the network. Figure 3.12 (A) shows a small network with capacities of the links indicated by the number above each link. We assume that nodes have infinite capacity and that, with the exception of the first and last nodes which are viewed as a source and a sink (destination), the flow into a node must equal the flow out. In addition, sources and destinations lie outside the boundaries of the system under study, and are given no further consideration in the model. A source might be a readily available supply of raw materials, and a sink might be customers who receive the system's output. The arrows in the figure indicate the direction of flow for the capacity which is given. Although flow is allowed in only one direction between any pair of nodes in Figure 3.12 (A), there is no reason why double links cannot exist, thereby permitting flow in either direction.

Flow Analysis

To find the maximum flow through the network, we start at the source and search for a path through the network from source to sink with unused

Figure 3.12 Determination of Maximum Capacity of Network

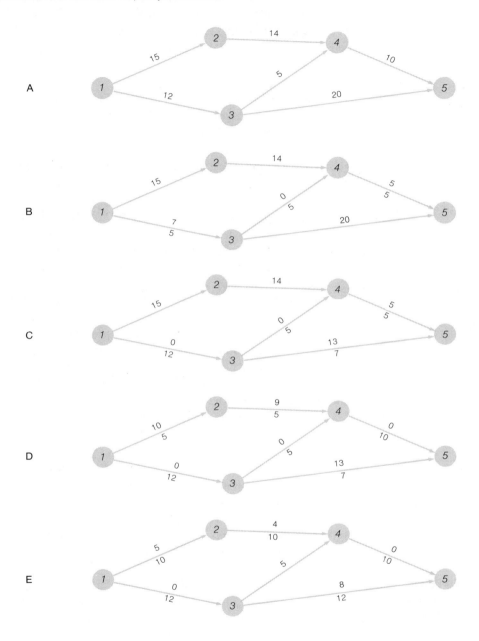

capacity on each link.[1] While there are several such paths in our network, we can choose any one arbitrarily (such as 1-3-4-5). We now find the link

[1] For a matrix approach to the same problem see G. Hadley, *Linear Programming* (Reading, Massachusetts: Addison-Wesley Publishing Co., Inc., 1962), pp. 344–351.

on the path with the smallest capacity, and establish a flow through the path equal to the minimum capacity. In Figure 3.12 (B), this flow is recorded beneath the links, and capacities above the links have been adjusted to reflect the net capacity still available. We repeat the process; this time we choose the path 1-3-5 with minimum unused capacity of 7 on link 1-3. Figure 3.12 (C) shows the network with capacities and flows adusted to reflect a flow of 7 through the path 1-3-5. In the next step, we find that path 1-2-4-5 has a minimum unused capacity of 5, and Figure 3.12 (D) reflects a flow of 5 added to 1-2-4-5.

It now appears that we can find no path with unused capacity from the source node to the sink node since all direct paths have at least one link with zero unused capacity. However, we can obtain an additional 5 units of flow by reducing the flow in link 3-4. Since link 3-4 has a forward flow of 5 units, we can reduce the flow in that link up to 5 units, and send an additional 5 units over the path 1-2-4-3-5. Note that we are not actually moving from node 4 to node 3, because the arrow goes in the opposite direction. But since we originally placed a flow of 5 units in link 3-4, a backflow of 5 units has the effect of reducing the forward flow to zero.

The result of these calculations appears in Figure 3.12(E), and at this point we can obtain no further increase in flow because we have evaluated all the paths. We determine the maximum possible flow through the network by examining the total flows out of the source node or into the sink node. This flow limits the capacity of the network. The total flow out of the source is the sum of flows in links 1-2 and 1-3, $10 + 12 = 22$, and the total flow into the sink node is the sum of flows in links 3-5 and 4-5, $12 + 10 = 22$. Therefore, the maximum possible flow in the network is 22. We can use this type of analysis to determine the capacities of transportation systems or distribution systems.

Networks with multiple inputs and outputs can be analyzed using the same technique by adding a single source node connected to each of the inputs by links with unlimited capacity, and by adding a single link node to each of the outputs. Capacity restrictions on nodes can be added to the network by replacing each node having a capacity limit with a pair of nodes connected by a single link with the desired capacity.

Optimum Shipping Patterns

A recurrent problem is to determine optimum shipping patterns between sources and destinations. Managers may have little difficulty in choosing shipping routes when they can supply each customer from the nearest plant or warehouse, but the problem usually is not that simple. Plants and warehouses have limited capacities, which may restrict the number of nearby customers who can be supplied from each. If Customer A is supplied from Plant 1, there may not be sufficient capacity to supply Customer B who also is closer to Plant 1 than to any other. Whenever we have a group of limited resources which must be used to supply competing demands, the problem is to find the optimum combination by matching resources and demands.

A manufacturer has two plants from which it must supply the requirements of three customers, as shown in Figure 3.13. Plant A has a capacity

Figure 3.13   Supplying Three Customers from Two Sources

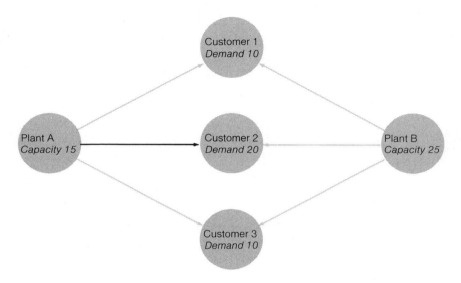

of 15 units, and Plant B has a capacity of 25 units. Customer 1 needs 10 units, customer 2 needs 20, and customer 3 needs 10. Figure 3.14 shows

Figure 3.14   Data for Transportation Problem

		Demands			Available at Sources
		1	2	3	
Supply	A	$4	$2	$1	15
	B	$1	$3	$5	25
Required at Destinations		10	20	10	40

the costs for shipping from each plant to each customer; for example, it costs $4 to ship one unit from Plant A to customer 1. The rim of the table also shows the amount available at each source and the amount demanded at each destination.

Note that requirements and availabilities are balanced—a total of 40 units is available and a total of 40 is required. If we had a situation in which supply and demand were not equal, we could create a dummy source by adding an extra row (a slack row) or an extra column (a slack column) to make a balanced table. A cost of zero would be assigned to each of the squares in the dummy row or column, because they would represent unused supply or unsatisfied demand.

In the present example, costs represent only shipping costs for each route. We can use the same formulation and the same method to analyze problems of where to produce and where to ship by adding production costs to the shipping cost in each square. The upper left hand square would then represent the cost to produce at Plant A and to ship to customer 1.

We apply the network flow concept by abitrarily assigning identical "prices" to each of the supplies. Suppose that we assign "prices" of $10 per unit to the supplies. Then the cheapest source for demand or customer 1 is supply B and the "price" for demand 1 is $10 + $1 = $11. Similarly, the lowest "price" for demand 2 is $10 + $2 = $12 from Source A, and the lowest "price" at demand 3 is $10 + $1 = $11 from source A. Figure 3.15(A) summarizes where the lowest cost routes are circled. We now construct a network flow problem, as shown in Figure 3.15(B), using only the lowest cost routes to connect supply and demand. The links between supply and demand are assumed to have infinite capacity. In addition, links with capacities equal to the amount of supply available connect all supplies to a single source node, and links having capacities equal to the amount demanded at each point connect all demands to a sink node. We then solve the network flow problem to find the maximum flow in the network; Figure 3.15(C) shows the results.

Since not all demand has been met, nor all of the supply utilized, the solution has not been found. The search for a solution proceeds by deleting any rows and columns, as shown in Figure 3.15(D), that have been fully utilized and determining the minimum reduction in supply "price" that will cause each of the remaining supply rows to be utilized. The only supply row that has not been deleted is row B, and the minimum reduction in "price" is $1. This will cause a flow to occur from supply B to demand 2. If more under-utilized supply rows existed in the problem, the minimum reduction in price would be computed for each such row and the minimum of the minimums determined. The price of the row with minimum price reduction, in this case, row B, is then adjusted,[2] and the entire procedure of setting demand prices, establishing the links, and solving the network flow problem is repeated. The second iteration is shown in Figure 3.16(A)-(C). We have found the minimum cost solution since all supplies and demands have been utilized. In larger problems more iterations are generally required, but the solution would proceed as we have shown in these two iterations.

---

[2] Only one row price is adjusted at each iteration.

Figure 3.15   First Iteration of Network Flow Solution to Transportation Problem

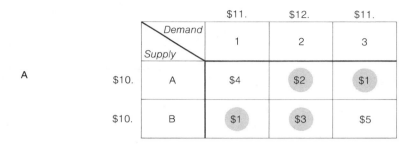

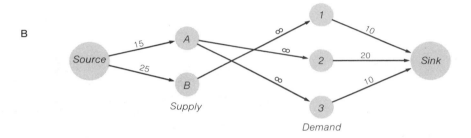

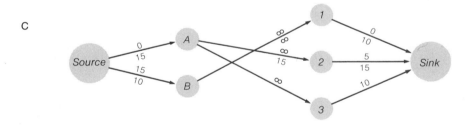

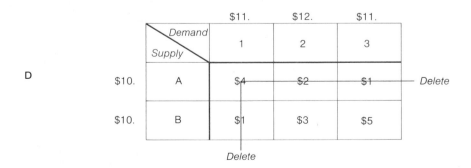

Figure 3.16 Second Iteration in Network Flow Solution

A.

	Demand / Supply	$10. 1	$12. 2	$11. 3
$10.	A	$4	$2	$1
$ 9.	B	$1	$3	$5

B.
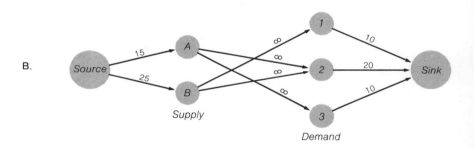

C.
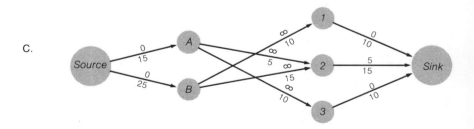

The optimum routing of shipments, as shown in Figure 3.17, is 5 units over route A-2, 10 units over A-3, 10 units over B-1, and 15 over B-2. Total cost of this solution is $(5 \times \$2) + (10 \times \$1) + (10 \times \$1) + (15 \times \$3) = \$75$. Only the costs shown in the original problem in Figure 3.14 are used in calculating total cost since the "prices" of supply and demand are introduced as a device for solving the problem by the network flow method. However, the "prices" do have an economic interpretation. We first subtract the minimum "price" in Figure 3.16(A), which is $9, from all "prices." The resulting "prices" shown in Figure 3.17 are marginal costs or shadow prices

Figure 3.17 Optimum Solution to Transportation Problem with Shadow Prices

		$1.	$3.	$2.	
Demand / *Supply*		1	2	3	*Available at Sources*
$ 1.	A	$4	$2	$1	15
			5	10	
$ 0.	B	$1	$3	$5	25
		10	15		
	Required at Destinations	10	20	10	40

of the constraints. For example, the shadow price for supply A is $1 since a unit added to the amount available from that source permits a shift of one unit from route B-2 to A-2 at a saving of $1. Similarly, the shadow price of demand 3, for example, is $2. If demand 3 is reduced by one unit, $1 is saved in shipping cost over the route A-3 and another $1 can be saved by shifting a unit from route B-2 to route A-2.

Transportation Method of Linear Programming

Linear programming is one of a group of analytic tools which has been developed in recent years for the solution to the problem of allocating scarce resources among competing demands. Mathematical programming is probably a better title to describe the whole area, because linear programming refers to one group of methods. Mathematical programming is not just an improved method for solving problems; it is an entirely new one which permits us to solve problems which were unsolvable before. One of the linear programming methods is called the distribution or transportation method which we can illustrate by applying it to the problem in the previous section. Another linear programming technique, the simplex method, will be discussed in the appendix to this chapter.

Recall that the manufacturer in the previous example had two plants and three customers. Figure 3.18 contains the relevant information for the prob-

Figure 3.18 Transportation Matrix for Two Plants and Three Customers

Supply \ Destination	1	2	3	4	Capacity
A	$4	$2	$1	$0	15
B	$1	$3	$5	$0	30
Requirements	10	20	10	5	45

lem. Plant A has a capacity of 15 units, Plant B, 30 units. Customer 1 requires 10 units, Customer 2 requires 20 units, and Customer 3 requires 10 units for a total of 40. Since a solution to the problem by the distribution method requires that the supply and demand be equal, we make them equal by creating an artificial or dummy customer, Customer 4, who will take up the slack. Any goods included in the final solution for this customer will represent excess capacity. No goods will be shipped to this customer, so we enter a cost of zero from each plant to Customer 4. From our previous example, the costs from Plants A and B to the other customers are put in the upper corner of the appropriate square.

The optimum solution to this problem appears in Figure 3.19. The

Figure 3.19 Optimum Solution to Transportation Problem

Supply \ Destination	1	2	3	4	Capacity
A	4	2 (5)	1 (10)	0	15
B	1 (10)	3 (15)	5	0 (5)	30
Requirements	10	20	10	5	45

amount sent from each plant to each customer is circled in the matrix. Five units are sent from Plant A to Customer 2; 10 units are sent from Plant A to Customer 3; and so on. The total cost for this solution is:

Route A-2:	$5 \times \$2 = \$10.$
Route A-3:	$10 \times \$1 = \$10.$
Route B-1:	$10 \times \$1 = \$10.$
Route B-2:	$15 \times \$3 = \$45.$
Route B-4:	$5 \times \$0 = 0.$
Total	$\$75.$

The solution is optimum because no lower cost combination of routes can be found. The appendix to this chapter explains the method of solution.

Summary

An aggregate, or overall view of systems enables us to understand the role of system components. A total system is defined by its boundaries. An operating system may be viewed as a black box which produces a set of outputs from its inputs. Primary inputs are materials, energy, or information. Secondary inputs are auxiliaries such as supplies and services. Primary outputs are the goods and services produced. Secondary outputs are the by-products of the operations.

Systems can be viewed as networks composed of links and nodes. Inputs into the system and resultant flows produce responses in the form of outputs. Systems of operations vary considerably in terms of the number and characteristics of links and nodes and the degree of coupling and feedback in the system. The design of such systems involves the selection of proper amounts of resources such as capital and labor to be used, determination of the structure, and flows through the system. Techniques like marginal analysis and network theory can be useful in understanding the design and operation of such systems. Another technique (linear programming) is useful in allocating scarce resources among competing demands to optimize some stated characteristic, for example, costs. The transportation method of linear programming is reviewed in this chapter, while the simplex method of this technique will be discussed in the appendix to this chapter.

Selected References

Daellenbach, Hans G., and Bell, Earl J. *User's Guide to Linear Programming.* Englewood Cliffs, N.J.: Prentice-Hall, Inc., 1970.

The authors present an extensive discussion of linear programming and its application.

Hare, Van Court, Jr. *Systems Analysis: A Diagnostic Approach.* New York: Harcourt, Brace, and World, Inc., 1967, Chapters 1–3.

The book provides a discussion of the characterization of systems and some methods of analysis.

Wagner, Harvey M. *Principles of Operations Research with Applications to*

Managerial Decisions. Englewood Cliffs, N.J.: Prentice-Hall, Inc., 1969, Chapters 6 and 7.

This text presents an extensive discussion of networks, their application to a variety of problems, and solution algorithms.

Questions

1 Give illustrations of the following:
   a. A system in which inputs are fixed and the obective is to maximize output.
   b. A system in which the output requirement is fixed and the objective is to minimize the cost of attaining that output.
   c. A system in which neither input nor output is fixed but we wish to know the response of the system to varying inputs.

2 What is meant by "feedback" in a system? Give an illustration.

3 Under what conditions will a secondary input to a system, such as capital, be substituted for labor? Give an illustration of a case in which this has actually happened.

4 Diagram some of the major inputs and outputs between the United States and the rest of the world.

5 Give illustrations of other emergency response systems that might be analyzed in terms of a trade-off curve such as the one in Figure 3.4.

6 Discuss the risks associated with the use of a single high capacity facility rather than several low capacity facilities as diagrammed in Figure 3.11.

Problems

1 Construct network diagrams for each of the following:
   a. The ordinance and law-making system of the state.
   b. The manufacturing and distribution system for a consumer product such as breakfast cereal.

2 The structure of a logistics system can be represented by the network shown below. Numbers above the links are the maximum capacities per period of the transportation equipment available for use over the links. What is the maximum amount of material that can be moved through this system per period and what routes should be used?

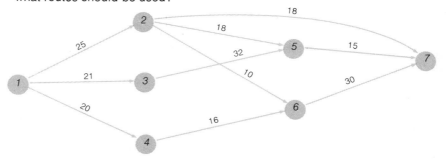

3 In the previous problem no capacity limits are given for the nodes in the system. Suppose that the capacity limits of the nodes are as follows.

Node	Units
1	80
2	23
3	25
4	15
5	20
6	20
7	70

What is the maximum capacity of the network in this case?

4 Determine the break-even points for an organization when the fixed cost is $20,000 for each 3,000 units of production, and when the demand is 5,000 units this year, the selling price is $30. per unit, and the variable cost is 70 per cent of the selling price. Draw the break-even graph.

5 Find the optimum pattern of shipments for the following transportation problem using the technique illustrated in the text of this chapter. (Interpret the data in the table below in the same way as in Figure 3.14.) What do the shadow prices represent?

		Demand			Available
		1	*2*	*3*	
	A	$2	$4	$2	15
Supply	B	$1	$3	$3	30
	C	$1	$4	$5	25
Required		10	40	20	

6 A low capacity processing facility has fixed costs of $2 million per year. It can produce up to 500,000 units per year using single shift operations at a variable cost of $10 per unit. Second shift operations can produce 400,000 additional units per year with no addition to fixed costs but with variable costs of $16 per unit due to inefficiencies and premium pay. A high capacity facility has fixed costs of $9 million per year, and it can produce up to 1,500,000 units per year using single shift operations at a variable cost of $7 per unit. Projected requirements are for processing 1,300,000 units per year. What are the costs of the alternative way of achieving this output? Discuss the intangible factors that might be considered for each alternative.

Appendix:
Mathematical
Programming

A useful tool for analyzing both large and small systems is mathematical programming. A programming problem is a particular kind of optimization which seeks to maximize or minimize a numerical function of a number of variables which are subject to certain constraints. Many optimization problems were first encountered in the physical sciences and engineering. The development of calculus led to the solution of many such problems. Later, calculus was found to be useful in analyzing various economic problems.

However, classical optimization techniques have proved to be of limited value in analyzing many of the problems of an economic nature which have developed and received a great deal of attention over the past few decades. As a class, these problems are referred to as programming problems and are widely found in government, military and industrial operations.

Broadly defined, programming problems deal with the classic economic problem: the optimal allocation of scarce resources among competing demands. These problems are concerned with situations in which a number of resources such as men, machines, and materials are combined to yield one or more products or services. Typically, there are restrictions on the availability of each resource as well as on the quantity of each product produced. Within these restrictions many feasible solutions will exist—that is, many ways of allocating the resources. A programming problem is one in which we seek, from among all permissible allocations of resources, the one allocation which minimizes or maximizes some numerical quality such as cost or profit.

The actual conversion of resources to outputs may be a simple operation such as mixing raw stock gasolines to form various motor fuels, or a complicated production process involving many types of machines and operations at various geographical locations. In some cases, conversion may be in the temporal and/or spatial dimension with no physical transformation taking place. For example, one might seek the best method of transporting goods from a set of origins to a set of destinations. Or, one might seek the best method of allocating production capacity existing at one set of points in time to demand at other points in time.

There are a variety of mathematical programming methods. Linear programming has been the most widely used. It applies to cases in which relationships are linear both in the constraints or restrictions and in the function to be optimized. Integer programming is a particular type of linear programming in which the solution variables must be integer values. Nonlinear programming obviously applies to cases where some of the relationships are nonlinear. Dynamic programming is a process for optimizing a sequence of decisions where a decision at one stage affects subsequent decisions. Parametric programming includes the consideration of risk or uncertainty in the values of the program variables.

While all of the above programming methods might be useful in analyzing operating systems, only linear programming will be considered in this book. It is the most useful and also the most comprehensible of the programming methods. The others are left for more advanced study. The use of linear programming in analyzing complex aggregate systems will be demonstrated in the next two chapters. We will introduce the solution techniques involved in linear programming in a relatively simple example.

Linear Programming

The general linear programming problem can be stated as follows: Given a set of m linear inequalities or equations in r variables, find non-negative (zero or positive) values of these variables which satisfy the constraints and maximize or minimize some objective function of the variables.

The above statement means there are m equations or inequalities which contain r unknowns of the form

$$a_{11}x_1 + a_{12}x_2 + \cdots + a_{1r}x_r \leq b_1$$
$$\vdots \qquad \vdots \qquad \qquad \vdots \qquad \vdots$$
$$a_{m1}x_1 + a_{m2}x_2 + \cdots + a_{mr}x_r \geq b_m$$

where the x_i's indicate the unknown quantities of the r variables and the a_{ij}'s and b's are coefficients which are a function of the system being described. Some of the a_{ij}'s may equal zero.

We seek non-negative values for the x_i's which maximize or minimize a linear function of the form

$$z = c_1x_1 + c_2x_2 + \cdots + c_rx_r$$

where the c_i's are value coefficients which are a function of the system being described.

Sample Problem

A wood working plant produces two kinds of products: doors and window frames. Sufficient market demand exists for the firm to sell everything it produces. Both products require processing on two machines, M_1 and M_2. The linear programming problem is to allocate the scarce resource of time on M_1 and M_2 among the two products in such a manner that total marginal profit is maximized.

The time requirements for the system are:

Machine	Hours to Produce 100 Units of Product		Total Machine Hours Available per Time Period
	Doors	Window Frames	
M_1	3	5	120
M_2	5	2	80

The marginal profit is $2 per door and $1 per window frame. Let X_1 be the number (times 100) of units of doors produced per time period and X_2 be the number (times 100) of window frames. Mathematically the problem is

$$\text{maximize } Z = 200X_1 + 100X_2$$

subject to the constraints

$$3X_1 + 5X_2 \leq 120 \quad (M_1 \text{ time})$$
$$5X_1 + 2X_2 \leq 80 \quad (M_2 \text{ time})$$
$$X_1, X_2 \geq 0$$

We can also state the problem graphically as in Figure 3A.1. Taking the first constraint, we see that if only X_1 is produced, sufficient capacity exists on M_1 to process 40 units. If $X_1 = 0$, then M_1 could process 24 units. M_1 could process 40 doors and 0 window frames or 0 doors and 24 window frames or any combination of doors and window frames found on the line connecting the above two points. Any point on the line would utilize all 120 available hours of M_1 time. Combinations falling below the line could also be produced and some M_1 time would remain unused. Since processing is required on both M_1 and M_2, the two constraints together determine the area of feasible production in the shaded area in Figure 3A.1. Therefore, although sufficient capacity exists on M_1 to produce 20 units of doors and 10 units of window frames, this point falls outside the M_2 constraints since 120 hours of M_2 time would be required and only 80 are available. The shaded portion in Figure 3A.1 defines the area of possible production.

Out of all the feasible combinations, we want to obtain the one point which produces the greatest profit per time period. The profit equation $Z = 200X_1 + 100X_2$ determines the relative profitability of the two products. Let us choose some arbitrary profit figure, say $5,000. The objective function becomes

$$5000 = 200X_1 + 100X_2 \quad \text{when } X_1 = 25, X_2 = 0$$
$$\text{or when } X_1 = 0, X_2 = 50.$$

Figure 3A.1   Linear Programming Sample Problem

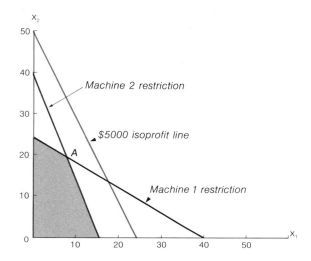

The line connecting those two points in Figure 3A.1 is the $5,000 isoprofit line. We cannot achieve a profit of this magnitude since the whole line lies beyond the range of feasible production. All other isoprofit lines will be parallel to the $5,000 isoprofit line. Therefore to find the maximum profit, we simply move a straight-edge parallel to the $5,000 profit line toward the area of feasible production until it touches it at some point. In our problem, this occurs at point A at which X_1 is approximately $8\frac{1}{2}$ and X_2 is approximately 19. Inserting those values in the objective equation we have total profit $= 200(8.5) + 100(19) = \$3600$, the maximum possible value.

Note that if we produce as much of product one as possible (since it is the most profitable product), we would produce 16 units for a total profit of only $3200 since there would be no remaining capacity on M_2 to produce product two. Although the optimal solution in this problem was to produce both products, it would not always be the case. For example, if the profit margins had been $100 for product one and $200 for product two, the optimal solution would have been $X_1 = 0$, $X_2 = 24$.

Such a graphical solution is easy to apply when there are only two products as in the previous example. It is also possible, although difficult, to use the graphical method when there are three products by drawing a third axis and expressing the constraints and the objective function as two-dimensional planes rather than one-dimensional lines. When there are more than three products, however, it is impossible to use the graphical method since additional dimensions cannot be represented graphically. Most linear programming problems, therefore, are solved algebraically rather than graphically, and the only limit to the number of products and processes is the ability of the analyst to cope with the required computations.

Simplex Algorithm

Algebraic methods for solving linear programming problems are composed of a series of repetitive steps which lead to an optimal solution. This process is called an algorithm. The most widely used and most general linear programming algorithm is the simplex method. It can be used to solve any linear programming problem which is solvable. Other algorithms such as the transportation method, which will be discussed later, are not as difficult to solve, but apply only to specific types of linear programming problems.

Detailed consideration of all the intricacies of the simplex method is beyond the scope of this book, but the basic steps employed in the process will be considered.

Initial Solution

Our example is restated as follows:

Maximize $P = \$200X_1 + \$100X_2$

Subject to the restrictions:

$$3X_1 + 5X_2 \leq 120 \quad \text{for machine 1}$$
$$5X_1 + 2X_2 \leq 80 \quad \text{for machine 2}$$
$$X_1, X_2 \geq 0$$

To use the simplex method, we must convert the restrictions which are now inequalities to equalities because it is much easier to manipulate equalities algebraically. We accomplish the conversion by introducing "slack variables" to the equations. These slack variables represent unused capacity in the restrictions. We will define IM_1 as the number of units (hours) of unused capacity on machine 1 and IM_2 as the units (hours) of unused capacity on machine 2. Now the machine restrictions are:

$$3X_1 + 5X_2 + IM_1 = 120$$
$$5X_1 + 2X_2 + IM_2 = 80$$

We can see that these machine restrictions are equivalent to the previous restrictions when $IM_1 \geq 0$ and $IM_2 \geq 0$.

The simplex algorithm starts with an obvious feasible solution in which all of the real production or allocation is equal to zero and the only allocations in the solution are idle capacity equal to the total unused capacity for each restriction. In our example, the starting solution is 120 units of IM_1 and 80 units of IM_2, each with zero profit contribution per unit. The initial solution is shown in matrix form in Table 3A.1

The next step in the simplex algorithm is to determine which real product makes the largest profit contribution per unit and to bring the maximum possible amount of that product into the solution. In our problem, we see from the profit equation that product 1 makes the greatest contribution at $200 per unit. To determine the amount to bring into solution, we examine the requirements for producing each unit of product 1 and the total amount

Table 3A.1 Starting Solution Matrix

Row \ Column		1	2	3	4	
	Solution	$0	$0	$200	$100	
	Variables	IM_1	IM_2	X_1	X_2	
A	$0 IM_1	1	0	3	5	= 120
B	$0 IM_2	0	1	5	2	= 80

of resources of each type available. In this case, machine 1 has enough capacity to produce 40 units of product 1 ($120 \div 3$), but machine 2 has only enough capacity to produce 16 units of product 1 ($80 \div 5$). Therefore, we are limited to bringing 16 units of product 1 into the solution since production on both machines is required to produce product 1.

These steps are shown in Table 3A.2 under the heading, "Starting Solu-

Table 3A.2 Simplex Solution to Sample Problem—Starting Solution and Initial Matrix

Row \ Column		1	2	3	4	
	Solution	0	0	200	100	
	Variables	IM_1	IM_2	X_1	X_2	
A	$0 IM_1	1	0	3	5	= 120/3 = 40
B	$0 IM_2	0	1	5	2	= 80/5 = 16
	Row evaluations:			$200 − 0	$100 − 0	
				$200	$100	

$$X_1 = 3IM_1 + 5IM_2$$
$$5IM_2 = 1X_1 - 3IM_1$$
$$IM_2 = 1/5X_1 - 3/5IM_1$$

$$X_2 = 5IM_1 + 2IM_2$$
$$= 5IM_1 + 2(1/5X_1 - 3/5IM_1)$$
$$= 19/5IM_1 + 2/5X_1$$

$$X_1 = 3IM_1 + 5IM_2$$
$$= 3IM_1 + 5(1/5X_1 - 3/5IM_1)$$
$$= X_1 + 0IM_1$$

$$IM_1 = 1IM_1 + 0IM_2$$
$$= 1IM_1 + 0(1/3X_1 - 3/5IM_1)$$
$$= 1IM_1 + 0X_1$$

tion and Initial Matrix." First the maximum amount of idle time is assigned to each capacity restriction and the coefficients for each equation are placed in the matrix. (Thus $IM_1 = 120$, $IM_2 = 80$, $X_1 = 0$, and $X_2 = 0$) Next, each alternative not in the starting solution (that is, X_1 and X_2 in columns 3 and 4) is evaluated to determine the product that will make the largest contribution to profit per unit by calculating the sum of the profit for each unit minus the cost of the resources used to produce it. (In a cost minimization problem rather than a profit maximization problem, selection would be of the largest negative value.) This leads to the selection of product 1 with a $200 per unit contribution. Then the rows are evaluated, using the coefficients in the column for the alternative that is being brought into the solution (column X_1) and the most restrictive row is determined (row B where $80/5 = 16$). Since all of the capacity represented by this row, the 80 hours of machine 2 time, will be used up when the maximum number of units of product 1 are brought in, IM_2 will be eliminated from the solution, and the new variable X_1, will be brought into the solution in its place. Each of the new X_1's will require 3 hours of processing on machine 1 for a total of $3 \times 16 = 48$ hours. Thus, since not all the capacity of machine 1 is utilized, IM_1 will remain a solution variable, but its value will be reduced from 120 to 72.

Revised Solution

Since a new variable is brought into the solution and an old variable eliminated, a new set of coefficients must be calculated, so that all the alternatives (columns) are expressed in terms of the new solution variables, X_1 and IM_1. This is done by solving first of all the column expressions that will be eliminated from the solution for the equivalent of the variables that will now be in the solution. In this problem $IM_2 = 1/5X_1 - 3/5IM_1$. This expression is then substituted into the other column relationships and the resulting expressions are simplified as shown at the bottom of Table 3A.2. For example, it is found that $X_2 = 19/5IM_1 + 2/5X_1$. This equation defines the relationship between X_2 and the variables currently in the solution IM_1 and X_1. Thus, in order to produce one unit of X_2 it would be necessary to reduce production of IM_1 by 19/5 units and reduce production of X_1 by 2/5 unit. We have now defined a new set of matrix coefficients which uses only the variables in the new solution, IM_1 and X_1. These coefficients are used in the new matrix in Table 3A.3 which calls for the production of $16X_1$ and $72IM_1$.

The columns of the new matrix are now evaluated. If the net contribution that would be made by bringing in one unit of the variable in each column is zero or negative, an optimum solution has been reached. No further changes can be made that would raise the total contribution to profit and overhead. However, if one or more of the columns yield a plus evaluation, then the column with the largest plus value is brought into the new solution.

In Table 3A.3, the second matrix is evaluated to find out if it would be profitable to make additional changes in the solution. There is now only one real product not in the solution, product X_2. Product X_2 cannot be made unless the amount of X_1 in the solution is reduced, since cutting back on the number of X_1's is the only way to get the machine 2 capacity required to make any X_2. If we produce one unit of X_2 we will require two hours of time on machine 2. Since each unit of X_1 is using five hours of capacity on machine 2, we can produce one unit of X_2 by reducing production of X_1

Table 3A.3   After First Iteration—Second Matrix

Column / Row		1	2	3	4	
	Solution Variables	$0 IM_1	$0 IM_2	$200 X_1	$100 X_2	
A	$0 IM_1	1	-3/5	0	19/5	$= 72\frac{19}{5} = 18\frac{18}{19}$
B	$200 X_1	0	1/5	1	2/5	$= 16\frac{2}{5} = 40$
	Row Evaluations:	0	0	200	100	
		-0	+0	-0	-0	
		-0	-40	-200	-80	
		0	-40	0	+20	

$$X_2 = 19/5IM_1 + 2/5X_1$$
$$19/5IM_1 = -2/5X_1 + 1X_2$$
$$IM_1 = -2/19X_1 + 5/19X_2$$

$$IM_2 = -3/5IM_1 + 1/5X_1$$
$$= -3/5(-2/19X_1 + 5/19X_2)$$
$$+ 1/5X_1$$
$$= 5/19X_1 - 3/19X_2$$

$$X_2 = 19/5IM_1 + 2/5X_1$$
$$X_2 = 19/5(-2/19X_1 + 5/19X_2)$$
$$+ 2/5X_1$$
$$= 1X_2 + 0X_1$$

$$X_1 = 0IM_1 + 1X_1$$
$$= 0(-2/19X_1 + 5/19X_2)$$
$$+ 1X_1$$
$$= 1X_1 + 0X_2$$

by 2/5 of a unit. This relationship is given by the coefficient 2/5 in row X_2 and column X_1 in the matrix in Table 3A.3.

Thus, it can be seen that the coefficients in the matrix describe the rate of tradeoff between variables. Now, if one unit of X_2 is added to the solution it will provide a $100 contribution to profit and overhead. However, it will be necessary to reduce X_1 by 2/5 of a unit, thus reducing the X_1 contribution to profit and overhead by $2/5 \times (\$200) = \$80$. Thus production of X_2 provides a net increase of profit of $20 for each unit added to the solution. It is also necessary to give up idle time on machine 1 in order to produce X_2. Each unit of X_2 requires five units of capacity on machine 1. However, producing one unit of X_2 reduces the production of X_1 by 2/5 unit and releases the $2/5(3) = 6/5$ unit of machine 1 time from the production of X_1. Thus each unit of X_2 requires $5 - 6/5 = 19/5$ unit of the unused machine 1 capacity.

Optimum Solution

The next step in the simplex method is to determine how far to go in giving up the production of X_1 in order to make X_2. This is determined in Table 3A.3 by dividing the available units of IM_1 (72) and X_1 (16) by the amounts of $IM_1(19/5)$ and $X_1(2/5)$ required to produce each unit of X_2. The available units of IM_1 will permit $(72 \div 19/5) = 18\frac{18}{19}$ units of X_2

to be produced. This is the bottleneck since the reduction of production of X_1 would allow $(16 \div 2/5) = 40$ units of X_2 to be produced (if sufficient time on machine 1 was available). Since IM_1 is the bottleneck, it will be eliminated from the solution as X_2 is brought in. Since it is necessary to reduce production of X_1 by 2/5 of a unit for every unit of X_2 produced, the total production of X_1 is reduced by $(2/5 \times 18\frac{18}{19}) = 7\frac{11}{19}$ units to $8\frac{8}{19}$ units. Next new coefficients are computed, yielding the matrix shown in Table 3A.4.

Table 3A.4 After Second Iteration—Third Matrix

Row \ Column		1	2	3	4	
	Solution Variables	0 IM_1	0 IM_2	200 X_1	100 X_2	
A	$100 X_2	5/19	−3/19	0	1	$= 18\frac{18}{19}$
B	$200 X_1	−2/19	5/19	1	0	$= 8\frac{8}{19}$

Row Evaluations:	0	0	200	100
	−26.32	+15.79	− 0	−100
	+21.05	−52.63	−200	0
	− 5.27	−36.84	0	0

Profit $= 8\frac{8}{19}$ ($200) $+ 18\frac{18}{19}$ ($100) $= \$3579$

Capacity Check:		*Needed for*		*Total*
		$8\frac{8}{19}X_1$	$18\frac{18}{19}X_2$	*Needed*
Machine 1 Capacity		$25\frac{5}{19}$	$94\frac{14}{19}$	120
Machine 2 Capacity		$42\frac{2}{19}$	$37\frac{17}{19}$	80
There is no unused capacity.				

Shadow Prices

At this point all of the capacity of each machine is fully utilized. All of the column evaluations now yield zero or negative values as shown in Table 3A.4, indicating that an optimum solution has been obtained. For example, in order to bring one unit of IM_2, idle time on machine 2, into the solution, it would be necessary to reduce production of X_1 by 5/19 reducing revenue by $200 (5/19) = \$52.63$. However, the resources thus released would allow 3/19 more units of X_2 to be produced providing additional revenue of $100 (3/19) = \$15.79$. The total cost of bringing one unit of IM_2 into solution is thus $\$52.63 - \$15.79 = \$36.84$. These numbers resulting from the column evaluations are called shadow prices. The shadow prices give the value of the resources, given the current solution. Thus if one additional unit of IM_2 was brought into the solution, the total profit would be reduced by $\$36.84$. Conversely, if one additional unit of machine 2 capacity was available total profit could be increased by $\$36.84$

The computations required in the simplex can become tedious even for problems of rather moderate complexity. Computer codes are readily available and normally large problems are solved on the computer. Linear programming problems ranging into several hundred variables and equations have been solved using a computer.

The Transportation Method

Another linear programming technique is the transportation method which is useful for solving allocation problems in which the requirements and resources are stated in terms of homogeneous units. We will use a problem similar to the one in Figure 3.18 to illustrate the method for solving these types of problems. Recall that in that problem we have two plants which are to supply three customers. Assume the same situation, except that the plants have a total capacity of 45 units. Since the plants have a capacity of 45 units and the three customers require only 40 units, we create a fourth dummy customer to absorb the difference.

In the transportation method we begin with an initial solution, evaluate the various alternatives to it and change the solution to incorporate more desirable alternatives. The process of evaluation and change is repeated until an optimum solution is found. This process is called an iterative procedure.

Initial Solution

We can begin with an initial solution in which assignments are made from sources to destinations in an arbitrary fashion without regard to costs, but one which is a feasible solution in that all the physical restraints of the problem are satisfied. The initial solution determined by the so-called northwest corner allocation is shown in Figure 3A.2.

Figure 3A.2 Transportation Matrix for Two Plants and Four Customers with Initial Northwest Corner Allocation

Destination / Supply	Customer 1	Customer 2	Customer 3	Customer 4	Capacity
Plant A	4 (10)	2 (5)	1	0	15
Plant B	1	3 (15)	5 (10)	0 (5)	30
Requirements	10	20	10	5	45

We begin the allocation in the upper left (northwest) corner, and assign 10 units from plant A to customer 1. Since plant A has a capacity of 15 units, we move across the first row and assign the remaining 5 units from plant A to customer 2. Next we move down the column to plant B and assign the other 15 units required by customer 2 from plant B. The balance of plant B's capacity of 15 units is allocated to customer 3 (10 units) and to customer 4 (5 units).

The total cost of this initial solution is

$$10(4) + 5(2) + 15(3) + 10(5) + 5(0) = \$145.$$

Evaluation of Alternatives

Next we examine each of the alternative routings—those that were not assigned in the initial solution—to determine if an improvement can be made. That is, we determine if any other solution will result in a lower total cost. Figure 3A.3 illustrates the evaluation of square B-1. If we add one unit to

Figure 3A.3 Evaluation of Square B–1

B–1: +1 − 4 + 2 − 3 = −4
A–3: +1 − 5 + 3 − 2 = −3
A–4: +0 − 0 + 3 − 2 = +1
Move to square B–1.

square B-1 we must subtract one unit from square A-1 in order to maintain a total of 10 units destined for customer 1. We continue around a closed path, alternatively adding and subtracting one unit, until we return to the square being evaluated. If we subtract one unit from A-1, we must then add one unit to A-2 and subtract one unit from B-2. The process is called the stepping-stone method because we include in the path only squares that have circled outlines—stones—in them. In tracing this closed path we are permitted to make only right angle turns at a square containing a "stone," moving diagonally is not permitted.

What is the change in cost of making this shift? This is determined by adding and subtracting the cost of each affected square. Thus, if we move one unit into square B-1 we would have net reduction of cost:

$$+1 - 4 + 2 - 3 = -4.$$

Before we shift any units into square B-1, we evaluate the other empty squares to determine the change in cost associated with each one.

We can trace a similar closed path for square A-3: A-3, B-3, B-2, A-2. The cost change for square A-4 is then −3 as shown in the figure. Similarly the cost change for square A-4 is +1. Note that the closed path for square A-4 is: A-4, B-4, B-2, A-2.

Revised Solution

Having evaluated each of the empty squares, we see that square B-1 yields the greatest reduction in cost, $4 per unit. For the revised solution we move as many units as possible into square B-1. Looking at the closed path for square B-1, we see that there are minus signs in squares A-1 and B-3. As we shift units around the closed path we must subtract units from each of these squares. Therefore, the most units we can shift into square B-1 is the smallest quantity in one of the squares with a minus sign, which in this case is 10 units. Adding 10 units to squares B-1 and A-2, and subtracting 10 units from squares A-1 and B-3 yields the revised solution shown in Figure 3A.4. The total cost for this solution is $15(2) + 10(1) + 5(3) + 10(5) + 5(0) = \$105$.

Figure 3A.4   Revised Solution

Supply \ Destination	Customer 1	Customer 2	Customer 3	Customer 4	Capacity
Plant A	4	2 (15)	1	0	15
Plant B	1 (10)	3 (5)	5 (10)	0 (5)	30
Requirements	10	20	10	5	45

A–1: +4 − 2 + 3 − 1 = +4
A–3: +1 − 5 + 3 − 2 = −3 ◄——————
A–4: +0 − 0 + 3 − 2 = +1

We next evaluate each of the empty squares in the revised solution to determine if a further reduction in cost is possible using the same procedure as before. The cost evaluation for the empty squares is shown in Figure 3A.4, where we see that a further cost reduction can be made by shifting units into square A-3.

Optimum Solution

We move the maximum possible number of units, 10, into square A-3 and we have the solution shown in Figure 3A.5. Now when we evaluate the empty squares we find that since no further cost reduction is possible, we have obtained an optimum solution. The total cost for the optimum solution is

$$5(2) + 10(1) + 10(1) + 15(3) + 5(0) = \$75.$$

Notice that we have made allocations to five of the eight possible routes. If we have a transportation matrix comprised of m rows and n columns, an optimum solution will in general never require more than $m + n - 1$ allocations.

Figure 3A.5 Optimum Solution to Transportation Problem

Destination / Supply	Customer 1	Customer 2	Customer 3	Customer 4	Capacity
Plant A	4	2 ⑤	1 ⑩	0	15
Plant B	1 ⑩	3 ⑮	5	0 ⑤	30
Requirements	10	20	10	5	45

A–1: +4 − 2 + 3 − 1 = +4
A–4: +0 − 0 + 3 − 2 = +1
B–3: +5 − 3 + 2 − 1 = +3

Degeneracy

Degeneracy in a transportation problem occurs when we have less than $m + n - 1$ allocations and cannot trace a closed path for all of the empty squares. Consider the problem in Figure 3A.6 which is like the previous

Figure 3A.6 Transportation Matrix with Initial Northwest Corner Solution

Destination / Supply	Customer 1	Customer 2	Customer 3	Customer 4	Capacity
Plant A	4 ⑩	2 ⑩	1	0	20
Plant B	1	3 ⑩	5 ⑩	0 ⑤	25
Requirements	10	20	10	5	45

A–3: +1 − 5 + 3 − 2 = −3
A–4: +0 − 0 + 3 − 2 = +1
B–1: +1 − 4 + 2 − 3 = −4 ◄———

problem except that Plant A has a capacity of 20 units and Plant B has a capacity of 25 units. The initial northwest corner solution and the evaluation of the empty squares are shown in the figure. Square B-1 has the greatest cost improvement, −4. Shifting 10 units into this square results in the revised solution of Figure 3A.7.

Figure 3A.7 Revised Solution Showing Degeneracy

Supply \ Destination	Customer 1	Customer 2	Customer 3	Customer 4	Capacity
Plant A	4	2 ⑳	1	0	20
Plant B	1 ⑩	3	5 ⑩	0 ⑤	25
Requirements	10	20	10	5	45

After the shift we see that there are only 4 allocations, and it now is not possible to trace closed paths for the empty squares. For example, we cannot evaluate B-2 because the occupied squares in the same row do not have entries in corresponding columns. Therefore, we have a case of degeneracy.

Degeneracy may be resolved by creating an artificial quantity, which we shall denote by the Greek letter ϵ (epsilon), and placing it in one of the squares in which an allocation disappeared, as in Figure 3A.8. It is an arti-

Figure 3A.8 Resolution of Degeneracy

Supply \ Destination	Customer 1	Customer 2	Customer 3	Customer 4	Capacity
Plant A	4 ⓔ	2 ⑳	1	0	20
Plant B	1 ⑩	3	5 ⑩	0 ⑤	25
Requirements	10	20	10	5	45

A–3: $+1 - 5 + 1 - 4 = -7$
A–4: $+0 - 0 + 1 - 4 = -3$
B–2: $+3 - 1 + 4 - 2 = +4$

ficial quantity because it represents a zero allocation, and does not affect the capacity restrictions or destination requirements. The ϵ allocation is then used to trace closed paths in the evaluation of empty squares in the usual manner. If the ϵ allocation happens to limit a shift in assignment to an empty square the ϵ is moved into the empty square, and the computation proceeds as before until an optimum solution is found.

Mathematical Formulation of Transportation Problems

Transportation problems may be formulated mathematically as other linear programming problems and solved by the simplex method. To use the simplex method, we express the requirements of the transportation problem as restraint equations:

1. the sum of the quantities shipped from each source is equal to the capacity of that source, and

2. the sum of the quantities received at each destination is equal to the requirements of that destination.

There will be a restraint equation for each source and destination. The objective function for the problem is the sum of the products of the quantities shipped from a source to a destination times the cost of shipping from the source to the destination.

Refer to the transportation problem in Figure 3A.2. We will let x represent the quantities shipped, and use subscripts to identify the source and destination for each shipment. As an example, X_{A1} will represent the quantity shipped from plant A to customer 1. The restraint equations representing the capacities of the two plants are:

$$X_{A1} + X_{A2} + X_{A3} + X_{A4} = 15$$
$$X_{B1} + X_{B2} + X_{B3} + X_{B4} = 30$$

The restraints representing the requirements of each customer are:

$$X_{A1} + X_{B1} = 10$$
$$X_{A2} + X_{B2} = 20$$
$$X_{A3} + X_{B3} = 10$$
$$X_{A4} + X_{B4} = 5$$

The objective function is:

$$4X_{A1} + 2X_{A2} + 1X_{A3} + 0X_{A4} + 1X_{B1} + 3X_{B2} + 5X_{B3} + 0X_{B4}$$
$$= \text{minimum}$$

These equations can then be solved by the simplex method to obtain an optimum solution to the problem.

Chapter 4
Aggregate
Evaluation of
Operating
Systems

Our discussion will now turn to some of the approaches to total system analysis. Although it is impossible to cover all forms of analysis, our illustrations are representative of the applications of modern techniques, relying heavily on mathematical model building. As in the preceding chapter, our interest is in the gross or aggregate analysis of operations. Details of the operating characteristics and decision rules system are treated in later chapters. Principal emphasis at this point is in the aggregate direction and rate of flow, number and location of components in the system, and gross operating characteristics of system components. Depending on the type of system, resource constraints, availability of data, and availability of solution techniques, analyses may be directed toward different objectives such as maximization of return, cost minimization, or determining the operating characteristics of the system. We will illustrate each of these forms of analysis.

Cost Minimization

In analyzing some operating systems the objective of achieving a specific level of performance may be stated in terms of minimizing the cost or value of inputs required to achieve desired output. Consider a military logistics system which must have a certain capability to deliver material to multiple destinations. At different times in the operation of such a system, various types of questions must be analyzed. For example, at one point in time, we may wish to examine alternate transportation forms. At another time, capacities of facilities may be the principal issue. At still another time, the design or redesign of the entire system may be possible. Since no one form of analysis is suitable for all situations, constraints on possible solutions and the appropriate form of any necessary models must be determined uniquely.

Figure 4.1 illustrates a small logistics system consisting of a single base supply point at node 1, two forward areas at nodes 3 and 4 with certain material requirements, and a proposed forward supply point at node 2. The system requires a delivery of either 20,000 units of material to node 3 or 40,000 units to node 4 within a specified time. Delivery can be accomplished either by direct movement by air from node 1 or by ground and water transportation from stocks maintained at a forward supply point at node 2. Between nodes 1 and 3, each aircraft can deliver 500 units within the specified time; between nodes 1 and 4, each aircraft can deliver 1200 units within the specified time. Fifty cargo aircraft are available which cost $1 million per year per aircraft to maintain in readiness. Yearly cost of operating the forward supply point together with maintaining adequate ground and water transportation capacity to meet delivery requirements to either node 3 or node 4 is $1000 per unit.

To permit a mathematical representation of the system, we denote the flow through each node in Figure 4.1 by x_i, and the flow through each link

Figure 4.1   Simplified Logistics System

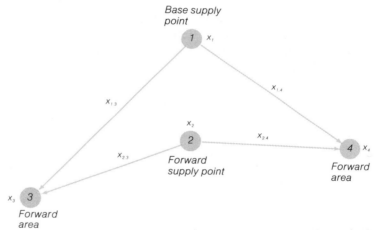

by $x_{i,j}$ where i and j are the beginning and ending nodes. Restrictions on the values of the x_i's and $x_{i,j}$'s are as follow:

Material availability:
$$x_1 \geq x_{1,3}$$
$$x_1 \geq x_{1,4}$$
$$x_2 \geq x_{2,3}$$
$$x_2 \geq x_{2,4}$$
$$x_3 \leq x_{1,3} + x_{2,3}$$
$$x_4 \leq x_{1,4} + x_{2,4}$$
Material requirements:
$$x_3 = 20{,}000$$
$$x_4 = 40{,}000$$

If we denote the number of aircraft utilized in the system by x_a, additional restrictions are:

$$x_a \leq 50$$
$$x_a \geq x_{1,3}/500$$
$$x_a \geq x_{1,4}/1200$$

The objective is to minimize total cost on a per year basis as given by

$$\text{Minimize } Z = 1000x_2 + 1,000,000x_a$$

Note that the restrictions are written to provide specified requirements at either node 3 or node 4, but not at both simultaneously. A different set of restrictions would be used if the objective were the ability to satisfy both requirements simultaneously.

The model of system operations as formulated above is a linear programming problem. The optimal solution is to maintain 28 aircraft and 33,600 units of material at node 1 and to establish a forward supply point at node 2 with 6,400 units of material. The total yearly cost of the optimal solution is $34,400,000. (Since the number of aircraft in the optimal solution must be an integer, the problem is technically an integer linear programming problem. In actuality, the optimal solution was found by solving the problem as a standard linear programming problem and then checking integral values of x_a close to the nonintegral value obtained in the solution.) Although our model is very elementary, we can use the same concepts to examine more complicated systems with multiple sources and destinations, alternate transportation modes, necessity for simultaneous delivery, and time phasing of deliveries.

Maximization of Return

Conversion operations for transforming raw materials into finished products are often most appropriately analyzed using an objective of maximizing return or profit. In the short run, a firm, such as a timber company or an oil company, may find that raw material supply and conversion capacity are available within upper bounds and that the firm must decide how best to utilize these resources. Typically, the firm can manufacture a range of products and can direct the flow of materials to alternate conversion facilities so that different end products are obtained. Under these circumstances the objective is to maximize return within the constraints imposed by raw material availability, conversion capacity, and size of markets.

Figure 4.2 shows a hypothetical system of conversion operations. In an actual case, we might have more raw material inputs and many more products. Raw material availability, capacity, size of markets, and technical characteristics of the conversion process all limit the flow through the system. We assume no limits on the capabilities of transportation links in the system, although we could include limits, if desired. The decision variables are the amounts of flow through each link and node in the system, and the objective is to determine these aggregate flows and maximize return while satisfying all restrictions.

**Basic
Model**

We denote the flow through each node in Figure 4.2 by x_i and the flow through each link by $x_{i,j}$ where i and j are the beginning and ending nodes. From Figure 4.2 we see that there are 36 such decision variables, 16 x_i's and 20$x_{i,j}$'s.[1]

Figure 4.2   System of Conversion Operations and Markets

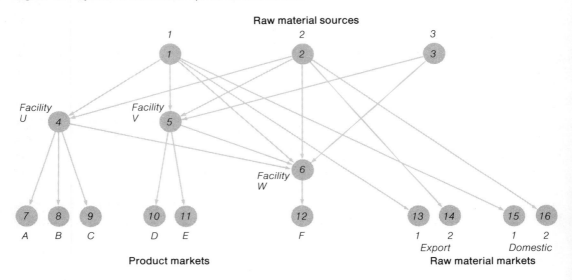

Restrictions on the operation of the system are:

Raw material:
 $x_1 \le$ supply of raw material 1
 $x_2 \le$ supply of raw material 2
 $x_3 \le$ supply of raw material 3
Capacity:
 $x_4 \le$ capacity of facility U
 $x_5 \le$ capacity of facility V
 $x_6 \le$ capacity of facility W
Product market:
 $x_7 \le$ market for product A
 $x_8 \le$ market for product B
 $x_9 \le$ market for product C

[1] The flows through nodes 7 through 16 are identical to the flows in the single links into these nodes. Therefore, we could eliminate either the links or the nodes to reduce the size of the model. However, we will include both the links and nodes in the model to show clearly that costs are incurred in the transportation links and revenues are obtained in the markets represented by the nodes.

$$x_{10} \leq \text{market for product } D$$
$$x_{11} \leq \text{market for product } E$$
$$x_{12} \leq \text{market for product } F$$

Raw material market:

$$x_{13} \leq \text{export market for raw material 1}$$
$$x_{14} \leq \text{export market for raw material 2}$$
$$x_{15} \leq \text{domestic market for raw material 1}$$
$$x_{16} \leq \text{domestic market for raw material 2}$$

Material flow:

$$x_1 = x_{1,4} + x_{1,5} + x_{1,6} + x_{1,13} + x_{1,15}$$
$$x_2 = x_{2,4} + x_{2,5} + x_{2,6} + x_{2,14} + x_{2,16}$$
$$x_3 = x_{3,5} + x_{3,6}$$
$$x_7 = x_{4,7}$$
$$x_8 = x_{4,8}$$
$$x_9 = x_{4,9}$$
$$x_{10} = x_{5,10}$$
$$x_{11} = x_{5,11}$$
$$x_{12} = x_{6,12}$$
$$x_{13} = x_{1,13}$$
$$x_{14} = x_{2,14}$$
$$x_{15} = x_{1,15}$$
$$x_{16} = x_{2,16}$$

Capacity utilization (where the $a_{i,j}$'s are the units of capacity j required for each unit of input of raw material from source i. For example, if a unit of raw material flowing in link $1-4$ requires .09 units of processing capacity at node 4, then $a_{1,4}$ is equal to .09. In the case of facility W, inputs are either raw materials or by-products from facilities U and V):

$$x_4 = a_{1,4}x_{1,4} + a_{2,4}x_{2,4}$$
$$x_5 = a_{1,5}x_{1,5} + a_{2,5}x_{2,5} + a_{3,5}x_{3,5}$$
$$x_6 = a_{1,6}x_{1,6} + a_{2,6}x_{2,6} + a_{3,6}x_{3,6} + a_{4,6}x_{4,6} + a_{5,6}x_{5,6}$$

Technological capability (where the $a_{i,j,k}$'s are the technological conversion capabilities of the facilities. These coefficients indicate the number of units of output to node k obtained by processing a unit of input from source i at facility j; the restrictions are equal to or less than restrictions to permit excess production of some products which cannot be utilized if that is part of the optimal solution):

$$x_{4,6} \leq a_{1,4,6}x_{1,4} + a_{2,4,6}x_{2,4}$$
$$x_{4,7} \leq a_{1,4,7}x_{1,4} + a_{2,4,7}x_{2,4}$$
$$x_{4,8} \leq a_{1,4,8}x_{1,4} + a_{2,4,8}x_{2,4}$$
$$x_{4,9} \leq a_{1,4,9}x_{1,4} + a_{2,4,9}x_{2,4}$$
$$x_{5,6} \leq a_{1,5,6}x_{1,5} + a_{2,5,6}x_{2,5} + a_{3,5,6}x_{3,5}$$
$$x_{5,10} \leq a_{1,5,10}x_{1,5} + a_{2,5,10}x_{2,5} + a_{3,5,10}x_{3,5}$$

$$x_{5,11} \leq a_{1,5,11}x_{1,5} + a_{2,5,11}x_{2,5} + a_{3,5,11}x_{3,5}$$
$$x_{6,12} \leq a_{1,6,12}x_{1,6} + a_{2,6,12}x_{2,6} + a_{3,6,12}x_{3,6} + a_{4,6,12}x_{4,6}$$
$$+ a_{5,6,12}x_{5,6}$$

Restrictions are all in the form of linear equalities or inequalities, and with the addition of an objective function the model becomes a standard linear programming problem. We represent costs contributed by each node and link by c_i and $c_{i,j}$ respectively and revenue from sales of raw materials and finished product by r_j. The objective is:

$$\begin{aligned}
\text{Maximize } Z = {} & r_7x_7 + r_8x_8 + r_9x_9 + r_{10}x_{10} + r_{11}x_{11} + r_{12}x_{12} \\
& + r_{13}x_{13} + r_{14}x_{14} + r_{15}x_{15} + r_{16}x_{16} - c_1x_1 - c_2x_2 \\
& - c_3x_3 - c_4x_4 - c_5x_5 - c_6x_6 - c_{1,4}x_{1,4} - c_{1,5}x_{1,5} \\
& - c_{1,6}x_{1,6} - c_{2,4}x_{2,4} - c_{2,5}x_{2,5} - c_{2,6}x_{2,6} - c_{3,5}x_{3,5} \\
& - c_{3,6}x_{3,6} - c_{4,6}x_{4,6} - c_{5,6}x_{5,6} - c_{1,13}x_{1,13} \\
& - c_{1,15}x_{1,15} - c_{2,14}x_{2,14} - c_{2,16}x_{2,16} - c_{4,7}x_{4,7} \\
& - c_{4,8}x_{4,8} - c_{4,9}x_{4,9} - c_{5,10}x_{5,10} - c_{5,11}x_{5,11} \\
& - c_{6,12}x_{6,12}
\end{aligned}$$

Figure 4.3 illustrates the structure of the model more clearly by giving the matrix of coefficients. The decision variables appear at the head of each column with the contribution of each decision variable to the objective function given above each variable. Numbers in brackets are hypothetical data to illustrate results obtained from a linear programming solution.

Table 4.1 Summary of Optimum Conversion System Operation

System Components	Capacity	Utilization	Cost or Revenue per Unit Flow	Total Cost	Total Revenue
Nodes:					
1	11000	11000	− 60.00	$ 660,000.00	
2	25000	25000	− 60.00	1,500,000.00	
3	3000	3000	− 30.00	90,000.00	
4	1500	1341	−1200.00	1,609,200.00	
5	1000	791	− 800.00	632,800.00	
6	1100	1100	− 600.00	660,000.00	
7	5000	5000	462.25		$2,311,250.00
8	4000	4000	430.25		1,721,000.00
9	10000	7317	371.50		2,718,265.50
10	9000	4434	234.75		1,040,881.50
11	7000	7000	203.75		1,426,250.00
12	22000	18700	99.75		1,865,325.00
13	3000	3000	113.75		341,250.00
14	10000	5197	90.75		471,627.75
15	2500	2500	111.50		278,750.00
16	3000	3000	137.50		412,500.00

Table 4.1 Continued

System Components	Capacity	Utilization	Cost or Revenue per Unit Flow		Total Cost	Total Revenue
Links:						
1–4			—	5.25		
1–5		5500	—	4.50	24,750.00	
1–6			—	3.75		
1–13		3000	—	8.75	26,250.00	
1–15		2500	—	6.50	16,250.00	
2–4		12195	—	6.50	79,267.50	
2–5		4608	—	5.00	23,040.00	
2–6			—	4.25		
2–14		5197	—	7.00	36,379.00	
2–16		3000	—	5.75	17,250.00	
3–5	No Capacity Restriction	3000	—	5.25	15,750.00	
3–6			—	3.00		
4–6		2200	—	1.50	3,300.00	
4–7		5000	—	12.25	61,250.00	
4–8		4000	—	15.00	60,000.00	
4–9		7317	—	11.50	84,145.50	
5–6			—	1.70		
5–10		4434	—	9.25	41,014.50	
5–11		7000	—	6.75	47,250.00	
6–12		18700	—	5.25	98,175.00	
					$5,786,071.50	$12,587,099.75

Optimum System Operation. Figure 4.4 shows optimum flows through the system obtained by a solution of the linear programming problem using data from Figure 4.3. Total cost and revenue from system operation are given in Table 4.1. Return, obtained by subtracting cost from revenue in Table 4.1, is about $6.8 million. This optimum solution utilizes all of the raw materials but does not fully utilize facilities U and V. Moreover, excess market potential exists for products C, D, and F, and raw material 1 in the export market.

In addition to the optimum pattern of operations shown in Figure 4.4, the linear programming solution can provide information useful in further analysis of the problem. For example, the shadow prices of the constraints binding supply, capacity, and the market are shown in Table 4.2. In the case of raw materials supply and facility capacity, these shadow prices show the increase in the objective function obtained by relaxing each constraint by one unit, thereby indicating the price that should be paid for an additional unit of each of the constraining resources. For example, Table 4.2 indicates that an additional unit of conversion capacity at facility W will increase net return by $1003.50, or an increase of one unit in supply of raw material 1 will increase net return by $31.87. Note that these shadow prices reflect the

Figure 4.3   Matrix Form of Model for Maximizing Return

	$(-60.)$ $-c_1$ x_1	$(-60.)$ $-c_2$ x_2	$(-30.)$ $-c_3$ x_3	$(-1200.)$ $-c_4$ x_4	$(-800.)$ $-c_5$ x_5	$(-600.)$ $-c_6$ x_6	(462.25) r_7 x_7	(430.25) r_8 x_8	(371.50) r_9 x_9	(234.75) r_{10} x_{10}
Raw material	1	1	1							
Capacity				1	1	1				
Product market							1	1	1	1
Raw material market										
Material flow	1	1	1				1	1	1	1
Capacity utilization				1	1	1				
Technological capability										

(203.75) r_{11} x_{11}	(99.75) r_{12} x_{12}	(113.75) r_{13} x_{13}	(90.75) r_{14} x_{14}	(111.50) r_{15} x_{15}	(137.75) r_{16} x_{16}	(−5.25) $-c_{1,4}$ $x_{1,4}$	(−4.50) $-c_{1,5}$ $x_{1,5}$
1	1						
		1	1	1	1		
						−1	−1
1	1	1	1	1	1		
						(−.09) $-a_{1,4}$	(−.05) $-a_{1,5}$
						(−.24) $-a_{1,4,6}$ (−.76) $-a_{1,4,7}$ (−.59) $-a_{1,4,8}$ (−.24) $-a_{1,4,9}$	(−.17) $-a_{1,5,6}$ (−.38) $-a_{1,5,10}$ (−.51) $-a_{1,5,11}$

Figure 4.3 Continued

	(-3.75) $-c_{1,6}$ $x_{1,6}$	(-8.75) $-c_{1,13}$ $x_{1,13}$	(-6.50) $-c_{1,15}$ $x_{1,15}$	(-6.50) $-c_{2,4}$ $x_{2,4}$	(-5.00) $-c_{2,5}$ $x_{2,5}$	(-4.25) $-c_{2,6}$ $x_{2,6}$	(-7.00) $-c_{2,14}$ $x_{2,14}$	(-5.75) $-c_{2,16}$ $x_{2,16}$	(-5.25) $-c_{3,5}$ $x_{3,5}$	(-3.00) $-c_{3,6}$ $x_{3,6}$
Raw material										
Capacity										
Product market										
Raw material market										
Material flow	-1	-1 -1	-1 -1	-1	-1	-1	-1 -1	-1 -1	-1	-1
Capacity utilization	$(-.60)$ $-a_{1,6}$			$(-.11)$ $-a_{2,4}$	$(-.06)$ $-a_{2,5}$	$(-.60)$ $-a_{2,6}$			$(-.08)$ $-a_{3,5}$	$(-.70)$ $-a_{3,6}$
Technological capability	(-7.2) $-a_{1,6,12}$			$(-.33)$ $-a_{2,4,6}$ $(-.41)$ $-a_{2,4,7}$ $(-.38)$ $-a_{2,4,8}$ $(-.60)$ $-a_{2,4,9}$	$(-.32)$ $-a_{2,5,6}$ $(-.32)$ $-a_{2,5,10}$ $(-.65)$ $-a_{2,5,11}$	(-7.0) $-a_{2,6,12}$			$(-.45)$ $-a_{3,5,6}$ $(-.29)$ $-a_{3,5,10}$ $(-.40)$ $-a_{3,5,11}$	(-6.3) $-a_{3,6,12}$

(-1.50) $-c_{4,6}$ $x_{4,6}$	(-12.25) $-c_{4,7}$ $x_{4,7}$	(-15.00) $-c_{4,8}$ $x_{4,8}$	(-11.50) $-c_{4,9}$ $x_{4,9}$	(-1.70) $-c_{5,6}$ $x_{5,6}$	(-9.25) $-c_{5,10}$ $x_{5,10}$	(-6.75) $-c_{5,11}$ $x_{5,11}$	(-5.25) $-c_{6,12}$ $x_{6,12}$	
								$\leqslant$ supply raw material 1 (11000)
								$\leqslant$ supply raw material 2 (25000)
								$\leqslant$ supply raw material 3 (3000)
								$\leqslant$ capacity facility U (1500)
								$\leqslant$ capacity facility V (1000)
								$\leqslant$ capacity facility W (1100)
								$\leqslant$ market product A (5000)
								$\leqslant$ market product B (4000)
								$\leqslant$ market product C (10000)
								$\leqslant$ market product D (9000)
								$\leqslant$ market product E (7000)
								$\leqslant$ market product F (22000)
								$\leqslant$ export market material 1 (3000)
								$\leqslant$ export market material 2 (10000)
								$\leqslant$ domestic market material 1 (2500)
								$\leqslant$ domestic market material 2 (3000)
								$= 0$
								$= 0$
								$= 0$
								$= 0$
	-1							$= 0$
		-1						$= 0$
			-1					$= 0$
								$= 0$
				-1				$= 0$
					-1			$= 0$
						-1		$= 0$
							-1	$= 0$
								$= 0$
								$= 0$
								$= 0$
$(-.50)$ $-a_{4,6}$				$(-.50)$ $-a_{5,6}$				$= 0$
1								$\leqslant 0$
	1							$\leqslant 0$
		1						$\leqslant 0$
			1					$\leqslant 0$
				1				$\leqslant 0$
					1			$\leqslant 0$
						1		$\leqslant 0$
(-8.5) $-a_{4,6,12}$				(-8.3) $-a_{5,6,12}$			1	$\leqslant 0$

Figure 4.4 Optimum Flow in Conversion System

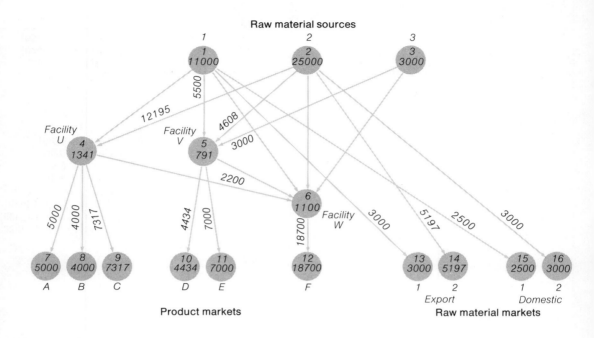

Table 4.2 Shadow Prices of Binding Constraints

Constraint	Shadow Price
Supply of raw material 1	$ 31.87
Supply of raw material 2	23.75
Supply of raw material 3	5.89
Capacity of facility *W*	1003.50
Market for product *A*	434.76
Market for product *B*	415.25
Market for product *E*	97.63
Export market for raw material 1	13.13
Domestic market for raw material 1	13.13
Domestic market for raw material 2	48.25

impact *on the entire system* of changes in any one of the binding constraints. This is particularly evident in the case of the shadow prices for the market constraints where these prices reflect not only the effects of an expansion in a market but also the indirect effects of diversion of materials from other uses.

The model also provides a methodology for analysis of possible alterations in the system. We can analyze the effects of the addition of a new facility by representing the characteristics of the facility and flows through the facility by additional equations and rerunning the model. Any changes in return which result can then be compared with the cost of the new facility. Use of the linear programming model to evaluate the new facility assures that interactions throughout the entire system are taken into account. Some other possibilities that can be explored in the same way are: purchase of additional supplies of raw materials from other sources; sales in different markets at different prices; effects of transportation restrictions; and effects of multiple shift operations.

System Response

Not all system operations are susceptible to optimization using monetary criteria. We may also direct analysis toward developing a model that is useful in understanding the behavior or operating characteristics of a system.

Consider the criminal justice system in Figure 4.5. (This is a more detailed flow diagram of the system shown in Figure 3.7. Figure 4.5, however, is still a superficial abstraction of the real world.) The diagram shows the general flow of criminals through the system with some individuals feeding back through the system. We may question the relevance of optimization to the analysis of this system. However, we can construct a simulation model of the system which will enhance our understanding of the behavior of the system and estimate probable effects of any changes made in it.

Simulation models may take either of two forms. They may be micro simulations which simulate on an individual basis or macro simulations which deal with the total numbers passing through the system. We prefer the macro version since the observation of hundreds of thousands of individuals would consume too much computer time.

Figure 4.6 depicts a simulation of the criminal justice system written in DYNAMO, one of the special computer languages conceived for such purposes. DYNAMO takes a model written in equation form and moves it ahead in a simulated period of time. The elements of the model are recomputed for each length of simulation desired, DT, and the results are printed and plotted to show the values of the items of interest throughout the entire run of the simulation. The first three cards following the RUN card in the model depicted in Figure 4.6 show the length of DT, total length of the run,

Figure 4.5 Criminal Justice System Model

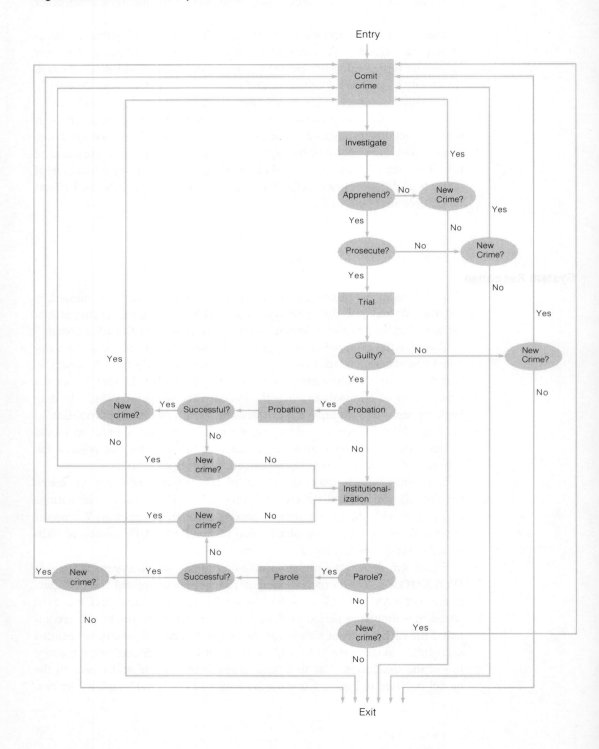

Figure 4.6   Criminal Justice System Model in DYNAMO

RUN		
SPEC	DT=.01/LENGTH=200/PRTPER=1/PLTPER=1	
PRINT	1)CRIME/2)INVST/3)TRIAL/4)PROBA/5)INSTI/6)PAROL/7)EXTOT	
PLOT	CRIME=C,INVST=I,TRIAL=T,PROBA=B,INSTI=J,PAROL=L,EXTOT=E	

CRIMINAL JUSTICE MODEL

8R	CRIME.KL=ENTRY.K+RPCR1.K+RPCR2.K	TOTAL CRIME
16A	RPCR1.K=(A2)(NOTAP.JK)+(A4)(NOTPR.JK)+(A6)(NOTGL.JK)+(A14)(NOPAR.J	
X1	K)	REPEAT CRIMES
16A	RPCR2.K=(A9)(SUCPR.JK)+(A10)(UNSPR.JK)+(A11)(UNSPA.JK)+(A15)(SUCPA	
X1	.JK)	REPEAT CRIMES
1L	INVST.K=INVST.J+(DT)(CRIME.JK−FININ.JK)	INVESTIGATIONS
20R	FININ.KL=INVST.K/INTIM	INVESTIGATIONS FINISHED
12R	APPRH.KL=(FININ.JK)(A1)	APPREHENSIONS
18R	NOTAP.KL=(FININ.JK)(1−A1)	NOT APPREHENDED
12R	PROSE.KL=(APPRH.JK)(A3)	PROSECUTIONS
18R	NOTPR.KL=(APPRH.JK)(1−A3)	NOT PROSECUTED
1L	TRIAL.K=TRIAL.J+(DT)(PROSE.JK−FINTR.JK)	TRIALS
20R	FINTR.KL=TRIAL.K/TRTIM	TRIALS COMPLETED
12R	GILTY.KL=(FINTR.JK)(A5)	GUILTY
18R	NOTGL.KL=(FINTR.JK)(1−A5)	NOT GUILTY
12R	PRBAT.KL=(GILTY.JK)(A7)	PROBATIONS
1L	PROBA.K=PROBA.J+(DT)(PRBAT.JK−ENDPR.JK)	ON PROBATION
20R	ENDPR.KL=PROBA.K/PRTIM	PROBATIONS COMPLETED
12R	SUCPR.KL=(ENDPR.JK)(A8)	SUCCESSFUL PROBATION
18R	UNSPR.KL=(ENDPR.JK)(1−A8)	UNSUCCESSFUL PROBATION
18R	INSPR.KL=(UNSPR.JK)(1−A10)	INST. AFTER PROBATION
18R	NOPRO.KL=(GILTY.JK)(1−A7)	NO PROBATION
52L	INSTI.K=INSTI.J+(DT)(NOPRO.JK+INSPR.JK+INSPA.JK−FINIS.JK)	INST.
20R	FINIS.KL=INSTI.K/ISTIM	COMPLETE INST.
12R	PROLE.KL=(FINIS.JK)(A12)	PAROLES
1L	PAROL.K=PAROL.J+(DT)(PROLE.JK−ENDPA.JK)	ON PAROLE
20R	ENDPA.KL=PAROL.K/PATIM	PAROLES COMPLETED
12R	SUCPA.KL=(ENDPA.JK)(A13)	SUCCESSFUL PAROLE
18R	UNSPA.KL=(ENDPA.JK)(1−A13)	UNSUCCESSFUL PAROLE
18R	INSPA.KL=(UNSPA.JK)(1−A11)	INST. AFTER PAROLE
18R	NOPAR.KL=(FINIS.JK)(1−A12)	NO PAROLE
18A	EXIT1.K=(NOPAR.JK)(1−A14)	EXIT FROM SYSTEM
18A	EXIT2.K=(NOTAP.JK)(1−A2)	EXIT FROM SYSTEM
18A	EXIT3.K=(NOTPR.JK)(1−A4)	EXIT FROM SYSTEM
18A	EXIT4.K=(NOTGL.JK)(1−A6)	EXIT FROM SYSTEM
18A	EXIT5.K=(SUCPA.JK)(1−A15)	EXIT FROM SYSTEM
18A	EXIT6.K=(SUCPR.JK)(1−A9)	EXIT FROM SYSTEM
10R	EXTOT.KL=EXIT1.K+EXIT2.K+EXIT3.K+EXIT4.K+EXIT5.K+EXIT6.K	EXIT

CONSTANTS

C	A1=.70
C	A2=.50
C	A3=.45
C	A4=.35
C	A5=.94
C	A6=.35
C	A7=.44
C	A8=.63
C	A9=.25

```
C          A10=.23
C          A11=.32
C          A12=.85
C          A13=.48
C          A14=.25
C          A15=.25
C          INTIM=.5
C          TRTIM=2
C          PRTIM=4
C          PATIM=5
C          ISTIM=4
              INITIAL VALUES
6N         INVST=0.
6N         TRIAL=0.
6N         PROBA=0.
6N         INSTI=0.
6N         PAROL=0.
6N         ENTRY=100000.
              STEP FUNCTIONS
45A        ENTRY.K=STEP(150000,100)
```

frequency of printing, PRTPER, frequency of plotting, PLTPER, variables to be printed, PRINT card, and variables to be plotted, PLOT card.

The 36 equations under the heading CRIMINAL JUSTICE MODEL form the main body of the model. Labels following each equation tend to make the model self-explanatory. Nevertheless, let us mention a few illustrations of the correspondence between the DYNAMO model and the system presented in Figure 4.5. The first equation, TOTAL CRIME, for example, defines crime rate, CRIME.KL, as the sum of new entries, ENTRY.K, into the system and the total number of repeat criminals reentering the system through the two feedback loops shown in Figure 4.5, namely, RPCR1.K and RCPR2.K. Total repeaters appear in the second and third equations. The fourth equation defines the current level of investigations, INVEST.K, as the previous level, INVEST.J, plus DT multiplied by the difference between new crimes under investigation, CRIME.JK, and investigations completed, FININ.JK. The fifth equation defines the rate of completion of investigations. This rate equals the number of cases under investigation divided by the average investigation time, INTIM, a device often used in DYNAMO to obtain delays in the system.

The sixth equation links apprehensions of crime, APPRH.KL, to finished investigations by the factor A1. This factor represents the fraction of apprehended criminals who are actually investigated, and its value appears in the model under the heading CONSTANTS. All told there are fifteen such factors which direct the flow through various parts of the system. Listed also under CONSTANTS are values for investigation time, trial time, probation time, parole time, and institutionalization time. These values determine the average delays in the specified parts of the total system.

The INITIAL VALUES section of the model stipulates that the system starts in an empty state with an entry rate of 100,000 new criminals per year. This rate increases to 150,000 per year at period 100 during the running of the simulation, as shown on the STEP card.

Results of over 200 periods, assumed to be years, appear in both tabulated and plotted forms in Figures 4.7 and 4.8. The first 100 periods serve

Figure 4.7   Tabulated Output from Criminal Justice Model

TIME	CRIME	INVST	TRIAL	PROBA	INSTT	PAROL	EXTOT
E+00	E+03	E+03	E+03	E+03	E+03	E+03	E+03
0.00	100.00	0.00	0.00	0.00	0.00	0.00	0.00
5.00	144.90	72.04	78.28	31.38	44.01	13.37	65.05
10.00	151.88	75.63	92.67	61.31	97.29	56.48	76.35
15.00	157.04	78.30	97.27	74.03	130.71	100.00	84.17
20.00	160.57	80.14	100.06	79.66	152.03	133.38	89.37
25.00	162.96	81.38	101.93	82.57	166.09	156.97	92.85
30.00	164.58	82.22	103.18	84.28	175.49	173.16	95.18
35.00	165.67	82.79	104.03	85.36	181.81	184.17	96.75
40.00	166.40	83.17	104.60	86.07	186.07	191.61	97.81
45.00	166.90	83.43	104.99	86.54	188.94	196.64	98.52
50.00	167.23	83.60	105.25	86.86	190.87	200.03	99.00
55.00	167.45	83.72	105.43	87.07	192.18	202.32	99.33
60.00	167.61	83.80	105.55	87.21	193.06	203.86	99.55
65.00	167.71	83.85	105.62	87.31	193.65	204.90	99.69
70.00	167.78	83.89	105.68	87.37	194.05	205.61	99.79
75.00	167.82	83.91	105.72	87.42	194.32	206.08	99.86
80.00	167.86	83.93	105.74	87.45	194.50	206.40	99.91
85.00	167.88	83.94	105.76	87.47	194.63	206.61	99.94
90.00	167.89	83.95	105.77	87.48	194.71	206.76	99.96
95.00	167.90	83.95	105.77	87.49	194.77	206.86	99.97
100.00	217.91	83.95	105.78	87.50	194.80	206.92	99.98
105.00	240.36	119.98	144.92	103.19	216.83	213.65	132.51
110.00	243.86	121.77	152.12	118.16	243.49	235.24	138.17
115.00	246.44	123.11	154.42	124.52	260.21	257.02	142.08
120.00	248.20	124.03	155.82	127.34	270.88	273.73	144 68
125.00	249.40	124.65	156.75	128.79	277.91	285.53	146.42
130.00	250.21	125.07	157.38	129.65	282.62	293.63	147.59
135.00	250.75	125.35	157.81	130.19	285.78	299.14	148.37
140.00	251.12	125.54	158.09	130.54	287.91	302.86	148.90
145.00	251.37	125.67	158.29	130.78	289.35	305.38	149.26
150.00	251.54	125.76	158.42	130.94	290.32	307.07	149.50
155.00	251.65	125.82	158.50	131.04	290.97	308.22	149.66
160.00	251.72	125.86	158.56	131.12	291.41	308.99	149.77
165.00	251.78	125.89	158.60	131.16	291.71	309.51	149.85
170.00	251.81	125.90	158.63	131.20	291.91	309.86	149.90
175.00	251.83	125.92	158.65	131.22	292.04	310.10	149.93
180.00	251.85	125.92	158.66	131.23	292.13	310.26	149.95
185.00	251.86	125.93	158.67	131.24	292.19	310.37	149.97
190.00	251.87	125.93	158.67	131.25	292.24	310.44	149.98
195.00	251.87	125.94	158.68	131.26	292.26	310.49	149.99
200.00	251.88	125.94	158.68	131.26	292.28	310.52	149.99

Figure 4.8 Plotted Output from Criminal Justice Model

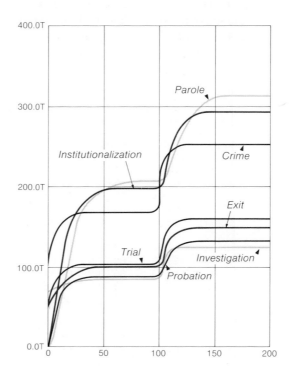

to stabilize the model and permit the system to fill up and reach a state of equilibrium. At period 100, the annual rate of new criminals entering the system mounts to 150,000 according to the STEP card, the behavior of the system thereafter reflecting the impact of this new rate. Delays and feedback gradually cause the system to reach a new equilibrium after a number of years. Essentially, the run enables us to observe what we may expect to happen when the crime rate rises. And this information proves useful for those concerned with the effect of growing crime rates on the various parts of the criminal justice system.

We can perform other experiments with the model, such as determining the effects of changing the fraction of convicted criminals placed on probation or the fraction paroled. The model offers a convenient way of explicitly stating the underlying mechanisms in the criminal justice system and observing the behavior of the system as elements of it are changed. In contrast to the models discussed in previous sections of this chapter, the simulation model focuses on the response of the system to changes rather than on optimization of an operating system.

System Cost Effectiveness

Operations which cannot be evaluated in terms of clear-cut monetary objectives may often be approached through cost-effectiveness calculations. Although cost-effectiveness analyses do not lead to optimizing solutions, they may provide an understanding of the operating characteristics of a system, which may be helpful in assessing alternative methods of operation. We will illustrate one type of cost-effectiveness study with an analysis of a statewide library system.

Public libraries typically are operated as local systems supported and controlled by city and county governments. Since libraries vary widely in size, local library resources are distributed unevenly when we consider the number of volumes immediately available to the user. To make additional resources available, inter-library loan arrangements have developed which permit some sharing of resources among libraries. Usually, however, inter-library loans are slow; they function through very loose organizational arrangements, and lack comprehensive catalogs of materials in all libraries.

One suggestion for improving the present situation is to develop formal library networks across wider geographic areas to provide rapid inter-library loans and more extensive sharing of materials. As an illustration of how we may evaluate such proposals at least in an overall fashion, let us examine two alternate systems proposed for a state. In one of these systems, local libraries would be organized into regional groupings to facilitate sharing of resources within the region. The largest library in the region would be the central point in the regional network. The other proposed system is a statewide network with all libraries linked to the largest library in the state.

Table 4.3 shows available statistical data regarding the number of volumes available in libraries within the system and the population served. The data has been tabulated by region and for the state as a whole. We assume that the regional groupings of libraries are not at issue in the analysis, being largely predetermined by natural geographic, economic, and political factors. Since there is no natural measure of effectiveness for the system, one must be constructed which is both credible and calculable from available data. We define the measure of system effectiveness as the number of persons served multiplied by the number of volumes immediately available to each person. For the present system of individual libraries, volumes immediately available are those in the local library; for the regional system volumes immediately available are those in the region; and for the statewide system, volumes immediately available are all volumes in the state. Admittedly the measure is crude and very broad, but it does provide a starting

Table 4.3 Library System Statistics

Region	Library	Population served (thousands)	Volumes (thousands)
1	1	68	175
	2	20	44
	3	192	308
2	1	6	16
	2	118	174
	3	156	285
	4	46	60
	5	232	372
3	1	26	36
	2	24	64
	3	16	24
	4	380	482
	5	40	38
4	1	42	74
	2	9	22
	3	112	246
5	1	687	1,335
	2	163	372
	3	60	87
	4	12	35
Statewide Totals	20	2,409	4,249

point for evaluating the alternate systems and can be refined later in the analysis.

For the present system the measure of effectiveness E_p is defined as:

$$E_p = \sum_j \sum_i p_{i,j} v_{i,j}$$

where i refers to the library, j refers to the region, $p_{i,j}$ is the population served by the ith library and the jth region, and $v_{i,j}$ is the number of volumes in the ith library in the jth region. For the network with regional grouping of libraries, system effectiveness E_r is

$$E_r = \sum_j \left(\sum_i p_{i,j} \sum_i v_{i,j} \right)$$

And, for a network with all libraries linked to the largest library, system effectiveness E_s is:

$$E_s = \sum_j \sum_i p_{i,j} \sum_j \sum_i v_{i,j}$$

Table 4.4 shows the calculation of each measure of effectiveness.

Table 4.4 Library System Effectiveness

Region	Library	p_{ij}	v_{ij}	$p_{ij}v_{ij}$	
1	1	68	175	11,900	
	2	20	44	880	
	3	192	308	59,136	
		$\sum_j p_{i,1} = 280$	$\sum_j v_{i,1} = 527$	71,916	$\sum_j p_{i,1} \sum_j v_{i,1} = 147,560$
2	1	6	16	96	
	2	118	174	20,532	
	3	156	285	44,460	
	4	46	60	2,760	
	5	232	372	86,304	
		$\sum_j p_{i,2} = 558$	$\sum_j v_{i,2} = 907$	154,152	$\sum_j p_{i,2} \sum_j v_{i,2} = 506,106$
3	1	26	36	936	
	2	24	64	1,536	
	3	16	24	384	
	4	380	482	183,160	
	5	40	38	1,520	
		$\sum_j p_{i,3} = 486$	$\sum_j v_{i,3} = 644$	187,536	$\sum_j p_{i,3} \sum_j v_{i,3} = 312,484$
4	1	42	74	3,108	
	2	9	22	198	
	3	112	246	27,552	
		$\sum_j p_{i,4} = 163$	$\sum_j v_{i,4} = 342$	30,858	$\sum_j p_{i,4} \sum_j v_{i,4} = 55,746$
5	1	687	1,335	917,145	
	2	163	372	60,636	
	3	60	87	5,220	
	4	12	35	420	
		$\sum_j p_{i,5} = 922$	$\sum_j v_{i,5} = 1,829$	983,421	$\sum_j p_{i,5} \sum_j v_{i,5} = 1,686,338$

$$\sum_i \sum_j p_{ij} = 2,409 \qquad \sum_i \sum_j v_{ij} = 4,249 \qquad E_p = \sum_i \sum_j p_{ij}v_{ij} \qquad E_r = \sum_i \left(\sum_j p_{ij} \sum_j v_{ij} \right)$$

$$E_s = \sum_i \sum_j p_{ij} \sum_i \sum_j v_{ij} = 10,235,841 \qquad\qquad = 1,427,883 \qquad\qquad = 2,708,734$$

The measures of effectiveness found in Table 4.4 may be criticized on several counts. The calculations assume that any book in a regional or state-wide network is immediately available to any patron in that region or state. This, of course, is not the case since even a very efficient network operation using rapid communication and data processing equipment would still result in some delay, although not as substantial as with the present inter-library loan procedures. Another major criticism is that the calculated measures of effectiveness are based on the implicit assumption that all books in the system are different, whereas a great deal of duplication both within and between libraries exists in the system. Finally, the measures do not take into account the quality of the books available; a factor of great significance in a library system.

These criticisms argue that the proposed systems are not as effective as the calculations would indicate; therefore, the calculated measures of effectiveness should be viewed as upper bounds on potential system effectiveness. Although accurate measures are desirable, even an upper bound may be helpful since alternatives which appear ineffective in this most favorable context will certainly not be viable when the measure is refined.

Let us now compare effectiveness with the costs of the alternative systems. Suppose that operation of the regional system will cost $50,000 per year, whereas the statewide system will cost $800,000 per year because of greater communications costs and the need for more sophisticated data processing procedures. We may calculate benefit-cost ratios as follows:

	Additional benefits	Additional costs	Benefit/Cost
Present vs. regional system	1,280,851	$ 50,000	8.5
Present vs. statewide system	8,807,958	800,000	11.0

The statewide system, although more expensive, has the higher benefit to cost ratio and appears to be the preferred alternative at this point in the analysis. Note, that further refinements of the measures of effectiveness would be required before making a final decision.

In contrast to the other approaches we have discussed, the analysis of library operations relies much less heavily on formal model building. Rather, data which are available are used to gain a better understanding of the effectiveness of proposed alternatives. The emphasis is less on formal mathematical structure and more on devising measures of effectiveness and ways of approaching a problem which lacks data and has an inadequate structure.

Summary

Analysis of aggregate system operations gives useful insights into the behavior of such systems. Details of operations are not considered when systems are analyzed in the aggregate, and only gross flows in the system and gross behavior of components are included in the analysis. The purpose of the analysis may be to achieve optimum system operations by maximizing return or minimizing cost, or it may be simply to understand the behavior of the system. Models which are helpful in analyzing total system operations range from those with elementary mathematical structures such as the library effectiveness model to more sophisticated models such as the linear programming structure used in the resource conversion model. The choice of the type of model to use depends upon the nature of the system, purpose of the analysis, and availability of computational techniques and data at reasonable cost.

Selected References

Daellenbach, Hans G. and Bell, Earl J. *User's Guide to Linear Programming.* Englewood Cliffs, N.J.: Prentice-Hall, Inc., 1970, Chapter 8.

The authors provide a detailed presentation of an application of linear programming to a large-scale corporate system.

Hamilton, H. R., Goldstone, S. E., et al. *Systems Simulation for Regional Analysis: An Application to River Basin Planning.* Cambridge: M.I.T. Press, 1969.

The book is an application of simulation to the analysis of a large river basin system.

Forrester, Jay W. *Urban Dynamics.* Cambridge: M.I.T. Press, 1969.

This book is a systems analysis of the problems of urban areas.

Quade, E. S. "Systems Analysis Techniques for Planning-Programming-Budgeting." Rand Publication P-3322 (March, 1966). Santa Monica, California: The RAND Corporation.

The author presents a philosophical discussion of the objectives and techniques of systems analysis.

Questions

1 How does the aggregate evaluation of systems differ from detailed analyses of the components and flows in the system?

2 Give an example of the application of the military logistics system illustrated in the text to a similar system in the private sector.

3 Discuss the different objectives which might be emphasized in systems analysis and give examples of situations in which each might be used.

4 In the text, several possibilities for further analysis using the model of the system of conversion operations are listed. Describe how the model would be modified to explore each of these possibilities.

5 Output from the criminal justice model shown in Figures 4.7 and 4.8 covers a period of 200 years. Of what usefulness is it to obtain output for such an extended period of time when it is almost certain that the actual system will not operate without substantial modification for that period of time?

6 Compare the criminal justice model in the text with Forrester's urban dynamics models. (See references for location of Forrester's models.)

7 How could the measure of effectiveness used in the library system analysis illustrated in the text be modified to take into account the criticisms mentioned in the chapter?

8 Select a large system in the private sector and discuss how you might go about modeling and analyzing the system. What would be the objective in the analysis?

9 Repeat question 8 for a system in the public sector.

Problems

1 The following problem relates to the logistics system model in the text of this chapter. A suggestion has been made to utilize floating warehouse ships in addition to the aircraft and forward supply point. Considering ship capacity, speed, and likely location of deployment, it is estimated that each ship can deliver 4,000 units to node 3 within the specified time or 4,500 units to node 4 within the specified time. Such ships can be deployed at an annual cost of $4.2 million per ship. Analyze this proposal.

2 A system of conversion operations consists of one raw material source, two processing facilities, and two products. Flows which may exist in the system are shown below. A unit of raw material costs $10 and 1200 units are available. Facility A has a capacity of 500 units, and it costs $20 to process a unit of raw material at A. Facility A yields ¼ of a unit of by-product and *either* ¾ unit of product 1 *or* ¾ unit of product 2 from each unit of raw material. Facility B can process 1000 units of raw material or by-product from A at a cost of $40 per unit. Output from B is one unit of product 2 for each unit of raw material or by-product. Up to 400 units of product 1 can be sold at $40 per unit, and up to 950 units of product 2 at $60 per unit. Prepare an analysis of the system.

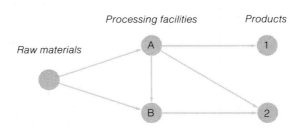

Processing facilities *Products*

Raw materials

A — 1

B — 2

3 Construct a simplified model of the criminal justice system by eliminating the possibility of probation and parole. Other than adjustments necessary for this change in structure, leave all constants and initial values the same. Analyze the behavior of this new system when the following changes are made.
a. Increase in the entry rate of new criminals to 150,000 per year.
b. Reduction in prosecution rate from .45 to .35 of those apprehended.
c. Reduction in verdicts of guilty from .94 to .75.

4 In the library system analysis in the text, the model does not consider the volume to title ratio. That is, libraries often have multiple volumes of the same title. Suppose that a study in another state shows the following average relationship between size of library and the volume of title ratio.

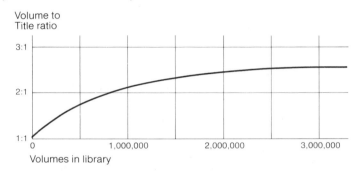

Construct a new measure of effectiveness for each of the three library system configurations. Comment on the adequacy of the new measure.

5 A city with a population of 500,000 is serviced by a single fire station located at the center of population. The city boundaries are in the shape of a square 10 miles on each side, and the population is evenly distributed across the area. Fire alarms are approximately proportional to the population in any area. A proposal has been made to disperse the fire equipment to multiple sites around the city to improve the time of response to alarms. Devise and compute a measure of response time for the present system and for systems with 2, 3, 4, and 5 sites.

Chapter 5
Facility
Location
and Layout
Analysis

Throughout the life of most organizations, decisions to establish, abandon, or relocate facilities occur infrequently. Most smaller organizations simply construct facilities at a location convenient to owners and operators and never seriously consider movement from that spot. Larger organizations find that the substantial investment in physical facilities and manpower at an established facility tends to restrict the decision to move, even though substantial operating diseconomies may develop. Despite its infrequency, the facility location and capacity decision is extremely important, for the level of many of the costs in the operating system is determined by the establishment of the physical facilities. Indeed, an inappropriate location or an uneconomical capacity level alone can relegate an organization to ultimate failure no matter how efficiently the organization may be managed.

In Chapter 4, we discussed the analysis of flows through operating systems which were represented as networks. We operated under the assumption that the network nodes, at which operations occurred, were fixed in the spatial dimension, and also that the number of nodes and the capacity of each had been established. In this chapter, that assumption will be relaxed.

Few existing systems preclude the opportunity to revise the spatial and capacity configuration. Even though there may be substantial costs for moving physical facilities and manpower, and other obstacles such as long-term leases and restrictive labor union contracts, some shifting of capacity can be accomplished if there are sufficient operating benefits which may result. At the other extreme, very few opportunities exist to establish a large-scale operating system network without some restrictions imposed by existing facilities. Large multiple facility operating systems typically are not established in one step. Rather, they tend to grow over time with additions of nodes or facilities one, or a few, at a time as economic opportunities and the resources of the organization warrant. Thus, the facility location and capacity problem must usually be analyzed in the face of numerous restrictions of varying degrees of rigidity imposed by existing established facilities.

Organizations operate in a dynamic environment. It is not sufficient to look at economic conditions today in selecting a facility site. Markets are continually changing with demand for some products and services increasing while demand for others may be diminishing. At the same time, the market may be shifting geographically. Similarly, the existing sources of inputs such as manpower, raw materials, and so forth, may become depleted and new sources may be required. The need to maintain flexibility and to react to such changes requires that a long-range view be taken in locating facilities.

Facility Location as an Economic Process

The establishment of an economic facility is an investment which is made because of the expectation that the facility will earn a profit in the future. As with most investments, the prime objective is to maximize the profit on the investment where the profit is equal to the revenue minus operating costs divided by the amount invested, or

$$\text{Annual Profit} = \frac{\text{Yearly Revenue} - \text{Yearly Operating Costs}}{\text{Investment}}.$$

Or, to treat the investment by the models to be developed in Chapter 8 on investment decisions, the future costs and revenue patterns may be properly discounted with the objective of maximizing the present value or the discounted rate of return.

The location of the facility may affect all three of the elements in the profit equation. Yearly revenue may be very sensitive to location. Firms dealing directly with consumers such as retailing institutions, banks, transportation firms, and laundries are often willing to invest in expensive property in order to achieve a prime location. The selling of their products and services depends heavily on close proximity to mass markets. For such firms, marketing conditions are the predominant factors in the location decision. Since operating costs are much less sensitive to location than revenues, these firms seek sites from which they can control a large market area. The geographic distribution of customers and competitors determines the choice. We will not consider these marketing-dominated location decisions here, since such problems are customarily treated in the marketing literature.

In most manufacturing firms and many wholesaling firms, revenues do not vary greatly with location. Manufacturing firms producing standardized products maintain inventories at their plants and at warehouses to provide quick delivery to nonadjacent areas. In firms which produce products to specific order, the transportation time usually is a small portion of the total production time. Thus, the effect of delivery time on sales is not usually significant except for widely separated sites. The cost of transporting goods to the market may prohibit a firm from covering the complete potential market area and, in this sense, revenue is dependent on location. But, in many cases, firms may need additional plants to provide complete coverage. Large firms, which do utilize several facilities to service their entire potential market, often follow a geographically uniform pricing policy throughout the market. Therefore, regardless of the location of any specific facility, total revenue remains the same.

Although revenue is relatively independent of location for manufacturing and wholesaling firms, the operating costs are strongly affected by facility location. The operating costs include the cost of acquiring the inputs to the transformation process, the cost of transforming these inputs into products, and the cost of distributing the products to the market. Factors such as the availability and costs of trained labor, power, and water will affect transformation cost. For labor-intensive products, the wage rates may be the most significant factor in the location decision. However, the costs of acquisition and distribution, that is, transportation costs, for most firms are the most important, at least in the early stages of the location decision process. The firm usually first determines the location that minimizes the cost of transportation. Once the firm has selected this area, it can make alterations to secure the necessary facilities for the conversion process. If a move from the intial area decreases conversion costs more than it increases transportation costs, it should be made. For high-value, low-weight items such as watches and jewelry, differences in the conversion cost would outweigh differences in transportation cost, whereas for heavy bulky material such as coal and lumber, only minimal movement from the raw material and market areas would be practical.

In some cases, the production process requires special environmental conditions. Some processes produce disagreeable odors or other irritants and pollutants which require either the installation of expensive cleansing equipment or location in an area where the pollutants do not create either short-term or long-run problems. Some firms use processes which require special temperature and humidity conditions. Such firms can either locate where such conditions exist naturally, or can attempt to create them through internal weather control. Still other processes require vast quantities of water or electricity, such as the production of aluminum which usually is located close to inexpensive supplies of electrical power. Some special process requirements can be placed within the framework of operating costs and others, such as vast requirements of electricity, must be placed in the category of transportation costs of raw materials.

The third element in the profit equation, investment, will also vary with location, since the costs of land and construction will both be affected. For example, cold climates require more substantial construction than temperate climates. In addition, land values may vary by several hundred per cent depending upon whether an urban or a rural location is chosen.

Determining the Minimum Transportation Cost Location

The initial step in the facility location process is to determine the location which minimizes the cost of transporting the inputs from a set of source nodes to the facility, and distributing the outputs from the facility to the next set of nodes in the system network. This same minimum transportation cost location problem also occurs in a number of other contexts. For example, in locating a machine or department within a factory, managers seek the location which minimizes the cost of moving men and material to and from it. Similarly, duplicating and other office equipment are often located to minimize the total walking distance of the employees who use the equipment. Public recreation areas, schools, and so forth, should presumably be located to minimize total user travel subject to land availability and other constraints.

We wish to minimize the sum of transportation costs,[1]

$$C = \sum_{i=1}^{n} T_i V_i D_i \tag{5.1}$$

where C is the total cost of transporting goods through distances D_i between the location point and the n known sources and destinations. V_i is the weight of the material going between facility i and the location point, and T_i is the transportation cost per unit weight per unit distance for the material going between facility i and the location point. Using a coordinate system described by X and Y axes, and with the location point described as (X,Y), the distance D_i between it and source or destination point i at (X_i,Y_i) is, by the Pythagorean Theorem,

$$D_i = \sqrt{(X - X_i)^2 + (Y - Y_i)^2}$$

Therefore,

$$C = \sum_{i=1}^{n} T_i V_i \sqrt{(X - X_i)^2 + (Y - Y_i)^2} \tag{5.2}$$

To minimize an expression such as equation 5.2, we normally take the first (partial) derivatives with respect to the variables X and Y, set the resulting expressions equal to zero and solve for X and Y.[2] Here, the partial derivative equations are:

$$\frac{\partial C}{\partial X} = \sum_{i=1}^{n} T_i V_i \frac{(X - X_i)}{\sqrt{(X - X_i)^2 + (Y - Y_i)^2}} = 0.$$

$$\frac{\partial C}{\partial Y} = \sum_{i=1}^{n} T_i V_i \frac{(Y - Y_i)}{\sqrt{(X - X_i)^2 + (Y - Y_i)^2}} = 0.$$

[1] This location analysis is adapted from Roger C. Vergin and Jack D. Rogers, "An Algorithm and Computational Procedure for Locating Economic Facilities," *Management Science* 13, no. 6 (February 1967): 240–254.

[2] For a review of differentiation see the appendix of this chapter.

Unfortunately, due to their complex form, the above equations cannot be solved simultaneously. Other methods are required to find the optimal (X, Y) location.

It has been proven mathematically that the cost equation 5.2 is convex, that is, it has a bowl-like shape. A little deductive analysis should confirm this fact. There is a best (minimum cost) area for locating the new facility. As the facility location deviates from that area, the cost increases, and the larger the deviation in any direction the greater the increase in cost. We may undertake an optimum seeking search process which systematically leads down the bowl-like cost surface to the minimum cost area. Even though we cannot solve the partial derivative equations directly, we can compute the numerical values of the partial derivatives for any particular set of X,Y coordinates. Then, if $\partial C/\partial X$, which is the slope of a line tangent to the cost curve in the X dimension at the particular X,Y value selected, turns out negative, one knows that the particular X value just evaluated lies to the left of the optimal value in the region where the cost curve is sloped downward, and that a larger value for X is required. If $\partial C/\partial X$ is positive, a smaller X is required. Figure 5.1 illustrates the cost curve in two dimensions. The same reasoning, of course, applies to the Y dimension.

Figure 5.1 Simplified Cost Curve

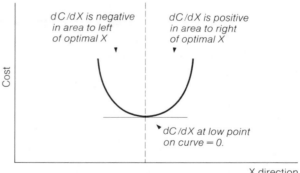

We find the minimum cost point, or the bottom of the bowl, by searching in each dimension, one at a time, and using the value of the partial derivative computed at each stage to select the next point to be evaluated. First X is varied until $\partial C/\partial X = 0$, then Y is varied until $\partial C/\partial Y = 0$. Since varying Y will alter the value of $\partial C/\partial X$ and varying X will alter the value of $\partial C/\partial Y$, the process of successively changing X and Y must be continued until $\partial C/\partial X$ and $\partial C/\partial Y$ reach zero simultaneously. If the cost surface were symmetrical, one search in each dimension would be sufficient to find the minimum cost point. However, since the source and destination points are normally not symetrically distributed in space, the bowl-shaped cost curve is somewhat misshaped. Therefore, taking successive slices of the cost curve and plotting the iso-cost slices might produce a series of curves such as shown in Figure 5.2, rather than concentric circles which exist in a perfectly symmetrical bowl-like cost surface. The iso-cost curves are developed by connecting on the graph all points with a given cost. With the irregular curves, several search iterations in each direction may be required, as shown in Figure 5.2, before the minimum cost point is found.

Figure 5.2   Search for Minimum or Maximum Point on a Surface C = f(X,Y)

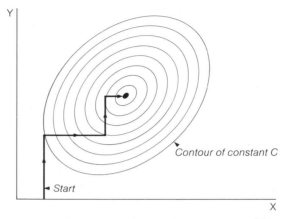

The mathematical computations become tedious in a large problem. However, the calculations are easily programmed for computer evaluation. For example, using in IBM 7094, a FORTRAN program produced the optimum (X,Y) location in 5 seconds of computation time for a problem with 100 existing facilities.

The computer printout in Table 5.1 gives an example of the search process. First, several simple initial estimations are computed and the one resulting in the lowest transportation cost is used as the starting point for the search process. The first partial derivative in the example is computed as follows:

$$\frac{\partial C}{\partial X} = \sum_{i=1}^{n} T_i V_i \frac{(X - X_i)}{\sqrt{(X - X_i)^2 + (Y - Y_i)^2}}$$

$$= 4 \cdot \frac{(7.300 - 4.)}{\sqrt{(7.300 - 4.)^2 + (6.733 - 4.)^2}}$$

$$+ 2 \cdot \frac{(7.300 - 6.)}{\sqrt{(7.300 - 6.)^2 + (6.733 - 7.)^2}}$$

$$+ 3 \cdot \frac{(7.300 - 14.)}{\sqrt{(7.300 - 14.)^2 + (6.733 - 10.)^2}}$$

$$+ 1 \cdot \frac{(7.300 - 5.)}{\sqrt{(7.300 - 5.)^2 + (6.733 - 20.)^2}}$$

$$= 2.514$$

Table 5.1 Optimal Location Sample Problem

PRESENT LOCATIONS		
X DIRECTION	Y DIRECTION	RATE X VOLUME
4	4	4
6	7	2
14	10	3
5	20	1

INITIAL ESTIMATORS OF MINIMUM COST LOCATION			
65.41	7.250	10.250	SIMPLE MEAN
57.53	7.500	8.000	WEIGHTED MEAN
55.62	7.300	6.733	SQUARED WEIGHTED MEAN
57.40	4.534	4.322	TENTH POWER WEIGHTED MEAN

COST	X LOCATION	Y LOCATION	X RATE OF CHANGE (PARTIAL DERIVATIVE) (WITH RESPECT TO X)	Y RATE OF CHANGE (PARTIAL DERIVATIVE) (WITH RESPECT TO Y)
55.62	7.300	6.733	2.514	
54.79	5.289	6.733	−2.954	
53.79	6.470	6.733	1.780	
53.60	5.758	6.733	−1.911	
53.34	6.141	6.733	.714	
53.31	5.998	6.733	−.359	
53.31	6.070	6.733	.226	
53.30	6.024	6.733	−.136	
53.30	6.024	6.733		−.911
53.15	6.024	6.916		−.715
53.12	6.024	6.987		.318
53.12	6.024	6.987	1.284	
53.11	5.992	6.987	−1.538	
53.11	6.012	6.987	.836	
53.10	6.001	6.987	−.340	
53.10	6.001	6.987		−.725
53.10	6.001	6.996		−.653
53.10	6.001	6.996	.022	

TRANSPORTATION COST	OPTIMAL LOCATION	
	X	Y
53.10	6.001	6.996

This positive value for $\partial C/\partial X$ indicates that a smaller value for X should be selected next. The final derivatives do not reach values of exactly zero. In order to conserve computer time, a stopping point was inserted in the computer program so that when no further shift would reduce cost by as much as .001, the search process would stop.

Traditional Evaluative Approach

Determination of the minimum transportation cost location is only the first step in the facility location decision process. Next, we must consider all the other factors (both objective and subjective) which pertain to the location decision. For most operating systems, labor would be the next major consideration. Not only is the cost of labor important, but the availability of an adequate labor pool from which the company can draw must be determined. In addition, the availability and costs of all the other locally acquired inputs such as water and power will affect the location decision.

Beyond this, firms are also interested in obtaining a somewhat broader picture of the communities they are considering. Firms obtain data on the local tax rates, amount of bonded indebtedness of the community, adequacy of local transportation, and so forth.[3] During this stage of the decision process, the firm will usually consider shifting from the minimum transportation cost location. In doing so, however, the extra transportation cost of such movement must be added in the evaluation for each community.

After a firm has selected a community, management selects a specific plant site. Typically, direct-cost calculations can be made for the alternative sites including the cost of the land itself, the cost of site preparation, connection to city utility and other services, and so forth. Moreover, factors such as the adequacy of public transportation, availability of additional land for future expansion, compatability with surrounding land use, and so on, will be evaluated.

In establishing an economic facility, the size or capacity of the facility must be determined as well as its location. A reasonable short term approach would be to establish sufficient capacity to meet immediate demand and then expand later if demand increases. This approach, however, may be inefficient. Because of economies of scale, a firm can probably obtain a more economical production process if a large plant is built immediately than if a series of expansions are added on to a small original facility. This process, however, entails the risk of excess capacity if the expected demand increase does not materialize.[4] Long-range forecasting and planning are required.

For most smaller and newly established firms, the capacity decision is made almost by default. These firms generally have only enough capital to establish a minimal size facility. Established organizations with existing facilities must consider the impact of the existing capacity when establishing the new facility. The new facility becomes an integral part of the larger system rather than an independent entity.

Economic theory casts some light on the choice of the proper capacity level. The principle of the economies of scale and the law of diminishing returns combine to help define the optimal size. It is an accepted techno-

---

[3] For a listing of factors to be evaluated in selecting the community along with suggested point weightings, see "Plant Site Selection Guide," *Factory Management and Maintenance,* May 1957, p. 180, and R. Reed, *Plant Layout,* 1961, pp. 361–366.

[4] For a discussion of size choice in an expanding market, see Robert M. Lawless and Paul R. Hass, "How to Determine the Right Size Plant," *Harvard Business Review* 40, no. 3 (May–June 1962): 97–112.

logical fact that many processes increase in efficiency as their size increases. Among the causes of such "economies of scale" are (1) the substitution of machine power for man power; (2) the use of standardized, interchangeable parts; (3) the breakdown of complex processes into simple repetitive operations; (4) and the specialization of function and division of labor. Initially, therefore, unit costs decrease as the scale of operations increases. Beyond a certain point, however, costs begin to increase. In particular, transportation costs begin to rise rapidly. As the number of units produced and sold increases, the firm must ship raw materials over longer distances and ship the finished products farther as the immediate market areas become satisfied. Thus, the unit cost curve is generally U-shaped. Beyond a certain capacity level, establishing additional facilities is more economical than increasing the size of the existing units.

Although economic theory regarding scale of operations is straight forward, applying it is not. Firms seldom have the necessary cost data to implement the theory. They are frequently changing product mix and operating costs are changed constantly. In addition, firms seldom can forecast and evaluate accurately the moves of competitors and their effect on demand.

Multi-Facility Location-Allocation-Size Problem

Firms with more than one facility find the location decision particularly complex. Not only must the firm evaluate all the factors encountered in the single facility case, but it must also consider the interactions of each new facility with existing facilities. The establishment of an additional facility will change the pattern of goods moving through the existing facilities. In addition, as soon as more than one facility is planned, optimal size must be considered along with optimal location.

Thus, three distinct types of decisions are required: decisions concerning the location of the new facilities; decisions concerning the proper allocation of products, markets, and raw materials to each facility; and decisions concerning the optimal size or capacity of each facility. We might attempt to solve each type of problem independently of the others. However, obtaining the optimal decision for each variable separately, or while holding the others constant, is not the same as obtaining an overall optimal decision. But, trying to determine the overall optimal decision considering all three areas presents a problem of substantial complexity, one well beyond the scope of the traditional mathematical and statistical models employed in solving organizational problems. We do not have precise algorithms available which produce well-defined solutions. Yet the problem remains and must be solved. Although obtaining the solution is probably still more of an art than a science, we can rely on more than subjective judgment and analyze the problem in a systematic manner. Methods exist for evaluating each portion of the problem separately and, by proper adjustment and use of the resulting solutions, a reasonable overall solution for the whole system may be obtained. In addition, some models have been developed which attempt to treat the entire multi-facility problem. First, we will consider methods for handling the separate parts, and then suggest some means of attempting to obtain overall solutions.

Multi-Facility Location Computational Procedure

The general methodology applied in the single facility case extends to the case of locating several facilities which have movements of goods between each other as well as movements between themselves and the existing facilities.

Where there are m existing facilities and n new facilities to be located, we wish to minimize:

$$C = \sum_{i=1}^{m} \sum_{j=m+1}^{m+n} T_{ij}V_{ij}\sqrt{(X_i - X_j)^2 + (Y_i - Y_j)^2}$$
$$+ \sum_{i=m+1}^{m+n} \sum_{j=1}^{m+n} T_{ij}V_{ij}\sqrt{(X_i - X_j)^2 + (Y_i - Y_j)^2} \qquad (5.3)$$

The first term is the cost of moving goods between the m existing facilities and each new facility, and the second term is the cost of movement among the n new facilities. Equation 5.3 has $2n$ unknowns. The partial derivatives with respect to these unknowns are more complex than those in the single facility case, thus defying straight-forward mathematical minimization.

The optimal location for the $(m + 1)$th facility, the first new facility, is dependent on its interactions with not only the existing m facilities, but also with the remaining $n - 1$ new facilities. The effect of the latter set of interactions on the location of the $(m + 1)$th facility depends on the locations of the other $n - 1$ new facilities. Therefore one cannot minimize equation 5.3 by sequentially locating each new facility independently of the other new facilities nor is it feasible to try to locate them all simultaneously.

The location problem can be solved by the following process: (1) each new facility is located at a *temporary* optimum point, that is, an optimum given the current (and in some cases temporary) location of the other $m + n - 1$ facilities; (2) after all the n new facilities are located in this manner, the process is repeated and the location for the $(m + 1)$th facility is adjusted to a new temporary optimum point which may be different than the previous temporary optimum since the locations of the other $n - 1$ new facilities may have similarly shifted since the previous location assignment for the $(m + 1)$th facility; (3) the readjustment process is continued until no further movements occur during a complete round of adjustment evaluations. At each step in the above process, a computer subroutine, such as we described in the single facility location model, can be used to find the temporary optimal locations for each facility.

The operation of the successive optimization computation process in an actual problem is perhaps best demonstrated by a very simple case with few interactions so that the logic of the process can be followed. Consider an example with four existing facilities and two new facilities to be located. (1) Facility 5, the first new facility, will be located on the basis of its relationships with the existing facilities 1 through 4. (2) Next, facility 6 will be located optimally with respect to the four existing facilities and with respect to the temporary location of facility 5. (3) Facility 5 will then be relocated based now on its interactions with 1 through 4 plus the interaction with the temporary location of 6. (4) Steps 2 and 3 will be repeated until the locations of both 5 and 6 remain constant, giving the final solution.

The problem data are (see Figure 5.3 for a plot of the data and the progress of the solution):

i	X_i	Y_i	$V_{i,5}T_{i,5}$	$V_{i,6}T_{i,6}$
1	10	10	10	0
2	20	10	0	10
3	10	20	10	0
4	20	20	0	10
5			0	10
6			10	0

Operation of the computation process:

	i	X_i	Y_i	Cost of Movement Between i and Others	Total Cost
Round 1	5	10.00	15.00	100.00	
	6	17.09	15.00	186.00	286.60
Round 2	5	12.85	15.00	157.50	
	6	17.09	15.00	158.10	273.20
Round 3	5	12.85	15.00	157.50	
	6	17.09	15.00	158.10	273.20

The true optimal set of locations, which can be found by trial and error and taking advantage of symmetry, is at (12.87, 15.00) and (17.13, 15.00) with a total cost of $273.20. Just as before, the reason that the computation procedure does not finally settle on precisely these points is that stopping points have been established in the computer program in order to reduce the computer running time so that the program will terminate when no further movement will reduce cost by as much as $.001. Note that the total cost is not simply the sum of the individual costs. Each facility is located on the basis of its interactions with the remaining facilities. Therefore, both of the in-

Figure 5.3 Example of Optimal Location for Multiple Facilities

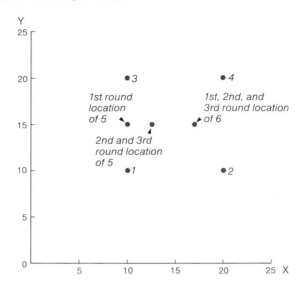

dividual cost figures for facilities 5 and 6 include the cost of movement between 5 and 6. The total cost includes that movement only once. Thus, for
rounds 2 and 3, total cost is equal to $157.50 + 158.10 - (17.09 - 12.85) \times 10 = \$273.20$.

The above process involves solving equation 5.3 by successively minimizing small portions of it and repeating the process until a stable state is
reached. In general, the result of a series of successive suboptimal decisions
may not be an overall optimal decision. Thus, the process of dividing a large
problem into a series of smaller problems does entail the risk that the solutions will not satisfy the larger problem. For example, the above location
process occasionally fails to produce optimal locations for situations in
which the interactions of two or more new facilities with each other are
large in comparison to their interactions with the existing facilities. When
interactions among new facilities are extensive, the optimal locations of
these new units generally are immediately adjacent to each other. Such
clusters of new facilities occasionally are improperly located by the multi-
facility location process, as we will see in the following example.

Existing facilities are at locations *A* and *B*. Two new facilities, *C* and *D*,
are to be located. Facility *C* has 1 load per day interaction with *A* and 5
loads per day with *D*. Facility *D* has 2 loads per day interaction with *B* and
the same 5 loads per day with facility *C*. If facility *C* is brought into solution
first, it will be placed at the location of existing facility *A*. Next, facility *D*
also would be located at *A* because of the attraction of facility *C*. The
optimal solution places both *C* and *D* at the location of *B*, but the computation procedure, which moves only one at a time, would never move either

new facility from location *A* because of their mutual attraction. This phenomenon is only a minor weakness since a close to optimal location for the cluster can be obtained if the computation process is run repeatedly, varying the order in which the new facilities are located. Note that in the above example bringing facility *D* into solution first would have produced the optimal solution.

The time required to reach a solution varies, of course, with the number of facilities and with the patterns of interactions among them. The number of readjustment cycles depends on the interaction patterns with anywhere from three to ten cycles required. The cost of the temporary solution after the second cycle is almost always within a small fraction of one per cent of the final solution cost and further location readjustments are of a very small magnitude. Average computation times on the IBM 7094 for various sized problems are listed below:

Number of Existing Facilities	Number of New Facilities	Computation Time in Minutes
5	5	.52
10	10	.81
15	15	1.46
40	15	2.52

Scale of Operations

The problem of determining the optimal capacity or size for multi-facility firms is one which has received very little attention in the management literature. When adding new facilities, many organizations regard the capacities of the existing facilities as fixed and concentrate only on determining the optimal size for the new facility, given the constraint of existing capacities. Determination of the optimal size for the new facility is then typically made on the basis of market studies on the potential volume of sales in the area assigned to the new facility. Few firms consider or attempt to evaluate the possibility of completely revising the existing plant capacities when considering the addition of new facilities.

One notable exception is a study undertaken for a New England manufacturing firm.[5] The company had acquired more than a dozen warehouses in the five states served from its manufacturing plant. Warehouses had been added in some areas and discontinued in others as changing conditions seemed to dictate. These decisions had been made on a "common sense" basis, and often had proved advantageous to warehouse operations in one area but at too great a cost in reduced operating efficiency in adjoining areas. The problem was complicated by the fact that two basic delivery methods were used. One type of distribution involved semi-trailer delivery from plant

[5] E. H. Bowman and J. B. Stewart, "A Model for Scale of Operations," *The Journal of Marketing* 20, no. 3 (January 1956): 242–247.

to warehouse, unloading and storage, and then individual deliveries to the market, whereas in the manufacturing plant area, individual or direct delivery to the market was the rule.

The problem was to determine how large a territory should be served by a warehouse to result in a minimum total cost for warehousing, trucking between plant and warehouses, and delivery from warehouse to customers. The "measure of efficiency" chosen, after examination of warehouse operations, was cost per dollar's worth of goods distributed. Since sales were fixed, minimizing cost for the entire distribution system would maximize profits.

The company obtained available data from its records. Examination of these data revealed that the cost of material handled in each warehouse district appeared to be primarily dependent upon two opposing factors: the volume of business passing through the warehouse and the area served by the warehouse. The greater the volume handled, the smaller would be the cost per dollar's worth of goods distributed. However, the greater the area served, the greater would be the cost per dollar's worth of goods distributed.

Finding this relationship was, of course, no surprise. The crucial job was to establish the precise relationship between these factors, that is, their relative importance and the rate at which their variation affected the overall economy of the system. To be satisfactory, the analysis would have to handle both factors simultaneously. With this done, the company could predict the cost of distributing goods as the area served by and the volume handled in each warehouse changed. More importantly, the systems could be arranged so that total cost would be minimized.

The analysts recognized that many other variables in this situation affect the measure of effectiveness. For instance, the price paid for gasoline in each warehouse area would affect the cost of operations in the area and undoubtedly varied throughout the New England states. The particular design of the warehouse (for example, whether the loading platform was at tailgate level of the trucks or on the ground) might also affect these costs. However, the analysts wished to keep the study fairly simple and so included only the two factors they considered most important.

Warehouse District Model. The analysts chose a mathematical model to study this problem because of the precision with which it could portray the relationships involved and with which it could reveal minimum-cost solutions. To build the mathematical model, the analysts had to understand the economics of the problem. Warehousing costs per dollar of goods handled tend to decrease with increasing volume: costs of supervision and other overhead are spread over more units, labor can usually be used with a lower proportion of idle time, and so forth. Since distance traveled is the main factor determining costs associated with area, this cost tends to vary approximately with the square root of the area. (Radius and diameter vary with the square root of a circle.) As concentric rings of equal area are added, rings rapidly become narrower, that is, additional distance traveled becomes smaller.

Therefore, the cost per dollar's worth of goods distributed (the warehouse efficiency) is equal to certain costs which vary inversely with the volume plus certain costs which vary directly with the square root of the area plus certain costs which are affected by neither of these variables. Placing this last factor first, these same variables put as a mathematical expression are

$$C = a + \frac{b}{V} + c\sqrt{A} \qquad (5.4)$$

where:

$C =$ cost (within the warehouse district) per dollar's worth of goods distributed—the measure of effectiveness.

$V =$ volume of goods handled by the warehouse per unit of time.

$A =$ area in square miles served by the warehouse.

$a =$ cost per dollar's worth of goods distributed independent of either the warehouse's volume handled or area served.

$b =$ "fixed" costs for the warehouse per unit of time, which divided by the volume will yield the appropriate cost per dollar's worth distributed.

$c =$ the cost of the distribution which varies with the square root of the area; that is, cost associated with miles covered within the warehouse district such as gasoline, truck repairs, driver hours, and so forth.

Before attempting to solve the model, the analysts examined the firm's cost records. The company had over a dozen warehouses, and the analysts determined, for each warehouse, the cost per dollar's worth of goods distributed (C), the volume of goods handled by the warehouse (V), and the area served by the warehouse (A). Then, by the statistical method of least-squares multiple regression, they used this warehousing experience to determine mathematically the values of the coefficients or parameters a, b, and c, which made the model the closest predictor of the actual cost for all present warehouses using the individual volume and area figures.

In order to confirm the accuracy of the model, a Cost (C) was computed for each warehouse using the determined values of a, b, and c from the multiple regression calculation and the warehouse's specific figures for V and A. By comparing these computed costs with the actual warehousing costs, the correlation coefficient was found to be .89, indicating a fairly high degree of correlation.

Developing a model such as this one is only the first step in predicting costs. The application of the model to minimize costs is the ultimate goal.

However, in this case, the analysts had to convert a part of the model mathematically in order to minimize costs. The object was to express cost as a function on only one unknown (area). A relationship was found between volume and area for each section of New England. This sales density (K), expressed in dollar volume per square mile of area, was

$$K = V/A.$$

Therefore, $V = KA$, and this expression is substituted for V in the original model, giving

$$C = a + b/KA + c\sqrt{A} \qquad (5.5)$$

Then the model is solved by differentiation which gives

$$\frac{dC}{dA} = \frac{-b}{KA^2} + \frac{c}{2\sqrt{A}} = 0$$

Therefore,

$$A = \left(\frac{2b}{cK}\right)^{2/3} = \left(\frac{2b}{c}\right)^{2/3} \left(\frac{1}{K}\right)^{2/3}. \qquad (5.6)$$

This expression for the area A indicates that area which would yield a minimum cost and which is a function of b and c (costs calculated from the empirical data) and K (the sales density of the area in question).

Equation 5.6 can now be used to establish the size and area served by warehouses. Consider two separate districts: the first with sales density, K_I, of \$1000 per square mile per year, and the second with sales density, K_{II}, of only \$1 per square mile per year. Then

$$A_I = \left(\frac{1}{1000}\right)^{2/3} \left(\frac{2b}{c}\right)^{2/3} = \left(\frac{1}{100}\right) \left(\frac{2b}{c}\right)^{2/3}$$

$$A_{II} = (1)^{2/3} \left(\frac{2b}{c}\right)^{2/3}$$

The area served by a single warehouse would be 100 times as large in district II as in district I. However, the warehouses in district I are 10 times as large as in district II since

$$V = KA$$

$$V_I = 1000 \left(\frac{1}{100}\right) \left(\frac{2b}{c}\right)^{2/3} = 10 \left(\frac{2b}{c}\right)^{2/3}$$

$$V_{II} = 1(1) \left(\frac{2b}{c}\right)^{2/3} = 1 \left(\frac{2b}{c}\right)^{2/3}$$

The explicit cost within the warehouse district is the minimized cost. The implicit cost such as interest on investment in inventory and equipment was analyzed and found to be insignificant for the purposes of this study. The costs also did not include the expense of loading semi-trailer trucks at the plant and transporting them to the branch warehouses, since as long as goods are handled from a branch warehouse, these costs will be incurred and will not be affected by volume handled or area served by each branch warehouse.

The company's actual branch warehouse areas ranged from about 95 to 150 per cent of the individually computed optimum areas. This disclosed that most of the branch warehouse areas were too large and that there were not enough warehouses in outlying districts.

The problem of how large an area to serve from the manufacturing plant was solved by a separate model, since, for the goods delivered directly from the plant, it was not necessary to ship them in semi-trailers and store them in warehouses before delivery. The company decided that the area to be serviced from the plant should be increased to about five times its original size.

Although the warehouse district model was developed for a specific application, the general procedure could be used for problems such as determining the best size for salesmen's territories, the best number of branch production facilities, or other issues which are fundamentally problems in the scale of operations.

Many firms do not have the extensive cost records which were available in this firm for such a large number of facilities. When the cost records are not available, the coefficients in the model might be determined from a management estimate or cost accounting type of approach. Through detailed cost

Figure 5.4   Distribution Network

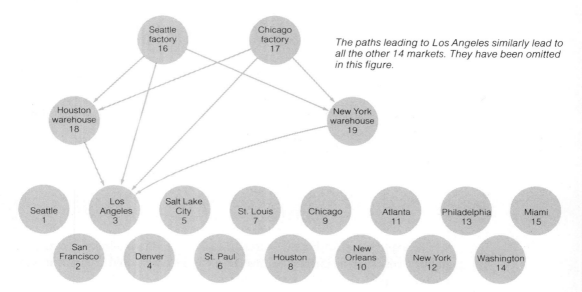

The paths leading to Los Angeles similarly lead to all the other 14 markets. They have been omitted in this figure.

estimations and projections, the cost of distribution per dollar's worth of goods could be determined for various combinations of area, size, volume, and other important variables.

Allocation

Another portion of the aggregate capacity-location problem is the division of territories to be served by each facility, or, the allocation of inputs and outputs to each node in the network. The following example illustrates the use and value of linear programming as an analytical tool for solving the allocation problem.

A firm operates factories located at Seattle and Chicago each with the capacity to produce 20,000,000 units of product per year. The firm operates a warehouse located at Houston with the capacity of handling 10,000,000 units per year and another at New York with 15,000,000 unit capacity. The product is sold in 15 different markets in the following quantities:

All markets must be satisfied. Shipments may be made to the markets either directly from the factories or from the warehouses at a cost of $.02 per unit per mile. Because of special handling and shipping methods for large quantities, goods can be shipped from factories to warehouses at a cost of $.01 per unit per mile. Figure 5.4 shows the distribution network. For example, each

	Market	Quantity (*in Thousands*)
1.	Seattle	733
2.	San Francisco	2241
3.	Los Angeles	4368
4.	Denver	564
5.	Salt Lake City	275
6.	St. Paul	1117
7.	St. Louis	1681
8.	Houston	807
9.	Chicago	5495
10.	New Orleans	685
11.	Atlanta	495
12.	New York	12912
13.	Philadelphia	3671
14.	Washington	1464
15.	Miami	495

factory could ship to any of two warehouses and fifteen markets. Each market could receive from any of two warehouses and two factories. In order to keep computations simple for this example, the map in Figure 5.5 will be used to compute distances between the network nodes.

The problem can be formulated as a linear program. Let

X_{1601} = the number of units in thousands shipped directly from node 16 to node 01, and so on. The restrictions on the system are

Factory Capacity

$$X_{1601} + X_{1602} + \cdots + X_{1615} + X_{1618} + X_{1619} \le 20{,}000$$
$$X_{1701} + X_{1702} + \cdots + X_{1715} + X_{1718} + X_{1719} \le 20{,}000$$

Warehouse Capacity

$$X_{1618} + X_{1718} \le 10{,}000$$
$$X_{1619} + X_{1719} \le 15{,}000$$

Market Requirements

$$X_{1601} + X_{1701} + X_{1801} + X_{1901} = 733$$
$$X_{1602} + X_{1702} + X_{1802} + X_{1902} = 2241$$
$$\vdots$$
$$X_{1615} + X_{1715} + X_{1815} + X_{1915} = 495$$

Figure 5.5 Markets for Distribution Problem (Quantities in Thousands of Units)

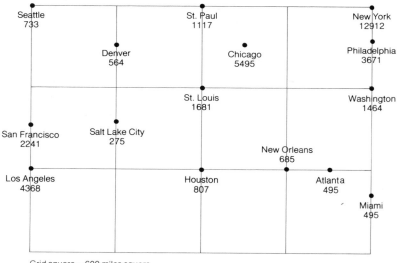

Grid square = 600 miles square

The problem is to pick the least expensive transportation links to satisfy the fifteen markets. We find the total cost by multiplying the number of units shipped on each link by the cost of shipping each unit on that link by summing the results. The link transportation costs are found by computing the distance from the simplified map in Figure 5.5 and multiplying by the transportation cost per mile. In order to keep computation simple in this example, we assume that movement is made only in direct North-South and East-West directions. Therefore, for example, the distance from Seattle to St. Louis is 1200 miles east plus 600 miles south. At a cost of $.02 per unit per mile, it costs $36.00 to ship one thousand units from the Seattle factory to St. Louis. In working through the actual problem, we would use the freight rates between cities.

The objective function is

$$
\begin{aligned}
\text{Minimize } Z = \quad & 0X_{1601} + 18X_{1602} + 24X_{1603} + 18X_{1604} \\
+ & 30X_{1605} + 24X_{1606} + 36X_{1607} + 48X_{1608} \\
+ & 36X_{1609} + 60X_{1610} + 66X_{1611} + 48X_{1612} \\
+ & 54X_{1613} + 60X_{1614} + 78X_{1615} + 24X_{1618} \\
+ & 24X_{1619} + 36X_{1701} + 42X_{1702} + 48X_{1703} \\
+ & 18X_{1704} + 30X_{1705} + 12X_{1706} + 12X_{1707} \\
+ & 24X_{1708} + 0X_{1709} + 24X_{1710} + 30X_{1711} \\
+ & 12X_{1718} + 12X_{1719} + 48X_{1801} + 30X_{1802} \\
+ & 24X_{1803} + 30X_{1804} + 18X_{1805} + 24X_{1806} \\
+ & 12X_{1807} + 0X_{1808} + 24X_{1809} + 12X_{1810} \\
+ & 18X_{1811} + 48X_{1812} + 42X_{1813} + 36X_{1814} \\
+ & 30X_{1815} + 48X_{1901} + 66X_{1902} + 72X_{1903} \\
+ & 42X_{1904} + 54X_{1905} + 24X_{1906} + 36X_{1907} \\
+ & 48X_{1908} + 24X_{1909} + 36X_{1910} + 30X_{1911} \\
+ & 0X_{1912} + 6X_{1913} + 12X_{1914} + 30X_{1915}
\end{aligned}
$$

Figure 5.6 shows the optimal distribution pattern determined by solving the above linear program. The total distribution cost is $620,934. There are alternative optimal solutions in this problem because some markets can be reached by more than one path at the same relative cost. In addition, we see that the Seattle factory has 2997 unused units of capacity, that the Houston warehouse has 7518, and the New York warehouse has 2088 units.

Combined Problem

Solutions obtained separately for each of the three segments of the general multi-facility location problem will not constitute an overall optimal plan. Rather, we must determine simultaneously the three variable factors. Unfortunately, the three-variable problem is so complex that the traditional mathematical and statistical approaches do not suffice. However, a number of heuristic approaches have been suggested for analyzing this multi-facility problem. Heuristic methods have been used to solve many problems in operating systems as well as in other types of human endeavors. Heuristic in the broadest sense simply refers to any rule-of-thumb or other simplification process that aids in problem solving. The term has been used to denote "any principle or device that contributes to the reduction in the average search to a solution."[6] Heuristic programs are problem-solving programs

[6] A. Newell, J. C. Shaw, and H. A. Simon, "The Processes of Creative Thinking," *The RAND Corporation Paper, P–1320,* August 1958.

Figure 5.6 Optimal Distribution Pattern

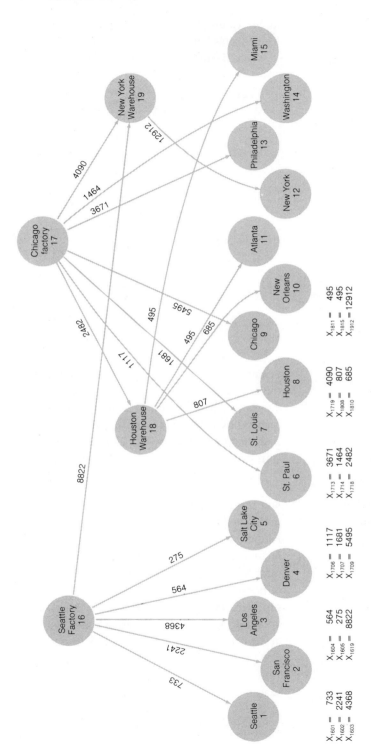

organized around such principles or devices. Some problem-solvers have attempted to distinguish between such programs and algorithms (such as linear programming) by suggesting that only the latter guarantee an optimal solution to the program.

If we examine the processes which have been called heuristic models (or heuristic programs) and have been used to solve production and other organizational problems, certain common characteristics emerge. Heuristic approaches recognize the trade-off between optimal solutions and the cost of problem solving. Heuristic techniques are used where an acceptable goal is to obtain a reasonable, rather than an optimal, solution. If, as a result of using heuristic techniques in solving such problems, the amount of computational effort is substantially reduced, the extra cost of the (reasonable) solution may be more than offset by the reduction in the cost of obtaining the solution compared to the cost necessary to obtain an optimal decision. Thus, the solution might still be termed optimal if one defined the objective criteria broadly enough. The heuristic approach attempts to find the solution that minimizes total costs including not only the normal objective cost criteria (such as the cost of the facilities, manufacturing, and transportation in the location problem currently under consideration), but also the cost of the problem solving or decision making itself.

Most of the problems for which heuristic programs have been developed are problems for which optimal solutions are at least theoretically possible. For example, heuristic models have been developed for solving the traveling salesman problem, the job-shop scheduling problem, the line-balancing problem, the plant layout problem, all of which will be covered in later sections of this book. For all of these cases, the absolute optimal solution could be obtained by complete enumeration of all alternatives. The combinatorial nature of such problems, however, renders this approach uneconomical and in many cases prohibits it because of the time which could be required to obtain solutions. Some of the techniques commonly employed in heuristic programs include:

1. Immediate elimination of all alternatives, which by some logical rule, are not very likely to be found in the optimal solution.
2. Consideration of only the major cost elements rather than all affected costs during preliminary stages of analysis.
3. Separation of complex problems into simpler components with provisions for modifying the results of the component solutions.

An obvious risk of using heuristics methods is the possibility that the best alternative may be eliminated accidentally.

The multi-facility location-allocation-size problem fits into the category of problems for which an optimal solution is theoretically possible. We can obtain an optimal solution by making cost computations of all possible combinations of sizes, locations, and allocations. Because of the enormous number of possible combinations, this would obviously be a task beyond the scope of the fastest computers for even small problems. Heuristic techniques are needed to bring the number of alternatives to a reasonable level.

One heuristic approach to the multi-facility problem is that of Kuehn and Hamburger, who developed a process of locating regional warehouses.[7] Regional warehouses perform a variety of functions in the distribution of a manufacturer's products including: (1) the reduction of transportation costs relative to direct shipment to customers by permitting bulk or quantity shipments from factory to warehouse; (2) the reduction of delivery costs by combining products manufactured at several factories into single shipments to individual customers, and (3) the improvement of customer relations by decreasing delivery time relative to direct factory shipment, thereby permitting customers to reduce their inventories. There are, however, substantial costs associated with the operation of a regional warehouse system. The basic problem to be solved by their heuristic program is, according to the authors, "to determine the geographical pattern of warehouse location which will be most profitable to the company by equating the marginal cost of warehouse operation with the transportation cost savings and incremental profits resulting from more rapid delivery."

The heuristic program for locating warehouses consists of two parts: (1) the main program, which locates warehouses one at a time until no additional warehouses can be added to the distribution network without increasing total costs, and (2) the bump-and-shift routine, entered after processing in the main program is complete, which attempts to modify solutions arrived at in the main program by evaluating the profit implications of dropping individual warehouses or of shifting them from one location to another. The three principle heuristics used in the main program are:

1. Most geographical locations are not promising sites for a regional warehouse; locations with promise will be at, or near, concentrations of demand.

The use of this heuristic to search and screen potential warehouse locations permits concentration on less than 1/100 of 1 per cent of the total area, thereby eliminating mountains, marshes, deserts, and other desolate areas from consideration. The program may, as a result, miss a good location. However, computer time is put to better use in screening and evaluating a finite number of concentrations of demand than in searching blindly for a possible profitable desolate location.

[7] A. A. Kuehn and M. J. Hamburger, "A Heuristic Program for Locating Warehouses," *Management Science* 9, no. 4 (July 1963): 643–666.

2. Near-optimum warehousing systems can be developed by locating warehouses one at a time, adding at each stage of the analysis that warehouse which produces the greatest cost savings for the entire system.

The use of this heuristic reduces the time and effort expended in evaluating patterns of warehouse sites. Thus, if there are M possible warehouse locations, the above heuristic would reduce the number of cost evaluations necessary from 2^m which would be required if all combinations were considered to approximately $N \cdot M$ where N is the size of an intermediate buffer which is discussed below.

3. Only a small subset of all possible warehouse locations need be evaluated in detail at each stage of the analysis to determine the next warehouse site to be added.

To insure adding the warehouse location that produces the greatest cost savings would require complete evaluation of each of the remaining potential warehouse sites. The time required by such an approach can, however, be reduced very substantially with the addition of only slight risk with a good, easily computed method of screening potential sites. The heuristic used for screening calls for N of the M potential warehouse locations to be evaluated in detail at each stage. The N potential warehouse sites chosen at each stage are those which, considering only local demand, would result in the greatest cost savings (or smallest increase in costs) if serviced by a local warehouse rather than by the system existing in the previous stage. In other words, it is assumed that at any stage, one can do reasonably well by locating the next warehouse in one of the N areas chosen on the basis of local demand and related warehousing and transportation costs.

In the detailed evaluation of each of the N locations placed in the buffer at each stage, the program either eliminates the site from further consideration, assigns a warehouse to that location, or returns the location to the list of potential warehouse sites for reconsideration at later stages in the program. Any site whose addition would not reduce total distribution costs is eliminated from further analysis in the main program. Of those sites which reduce total costs, that location which affords the greatest savings is assigned a warehouse; all others are returned to the list of potential warehouse sites. When the list of potential warehouse is depleted, all sites having been either eliminated or assigned a warehouse, the program enters the Bump-and-Shift Routine.

The Bump-and-Shift Routine is designed to modify solutions reached in the main program in two ways. It first eliminates (bumps) any warehouse which is no longer economical because some of the customers originally assigned to it are now serviced by warehouses located subsequently. Then, to insure the servicing of each of the territories established above from a single warehouse within each territory in the most economical manner, the program considers shifting each warehouse from its currently assigned location to the other potential sites within its territory.

We will illustrate the operation of the program with four sample problems. The problems represent four levels of fixed warehouse costs, $7,500, $12,500, $17,500, $25,000, for each warehouse in the system. Each of the sample problems considers only a single product. We assume that transportation costs and costs associated with shipping delays are proportional to the railroad distance between shipping points. For purposes of illustration, bulk shipping rates from the factory to warehouses are evaluated at $0.0125 per mile per unit, whereas the sum of the shipping and delay costs from warehouse to customer is $0.0250 per mile per unit. To simplify the four distribution problems further, we assume that the variable costs of operating the warehouses are linear with respect to the volume of goods processed. Consequently, these costs do not affect the optimal warehouse system and need not be considered in the sample problems. The size of the buffer (N) is equal to five in each of the problems.

The market structure in the sample problems consists of 50 concentrations of demand scattered throughout the United States. Twenty-four of these centers of demand are treated as potential warehouse sites. The metropolitan population of each of these areas is used to represent sales potential, a population of 1,000 representing one unit of demand (see Table 5.2).

The results obtained for each of the four cases are shown in Table 5.3. This table summarizes:

1. The warehouse locations selected by the main program, in the order of selection.
2. The modifications introduced into the main program solution by the Bump-and-Shift Routine.
3. Alterations to the heuristic warehouse network which will lower total distribution costs.
4. The total distribution costs at each stage of the heuristic solution and for the warehouse network which incorporates subsequent improvements.

In both of the cases in which an improvement upon the heuristic solution was discovered, the improvement consisted of replacing a warehouse in Houston with a warehouse in Dallas. This improvement was not found by the shift portion of the Bump-and-Shift Routine, since Dallas was not being serviced from the Houston warehouse. The shift routine as currently programmed considers as alternatives only those warehouse sites which are located within the territory served by the warehouse under examination. The rationale for limiting the alternatives considered in this fashion is (1)

Table 5.2 Sales Potential of Concentrations of Demand Used in Sample Populations (Population in Thousands)

Concentrations of Demand	Sales Potential	Concentrations of Demand	Sales Potential
Albuquerque, N. Mex.	146	Knoxville, Tenn.	337
Amarillo, Tex.	87	Los Angeles, Calif.*	4368
Atlanta, Ga.*	672	Louisville, Ky.	577
Baltimore, Md.	1337	Memphis, Tenn.	482
Billings, Mont.	31	Miami, Fla.*	495
Birmingham, Ala.	559	Mobile, Ala.	231
Boston, Mass.*	2370	Nashville, Tenn.	322
Buffalo, N.Y.*	1089	New Orleans, La.*	685
Butte, Mont.	33	New York, N.Y.*	12912
Cheyenne, Wyo.	32	Oklahoma City, Okla.	325
Chicago, Ill.*	5495	Omaha, Nebr.	366
Cincinnati, Ohio*	904	Philadelphia, Pa.*	3671
Cleveland, Ohio*	1466	Pittsburgh, Pa.*	2213
Columbia, S.C.	143	Portland, Oreg.	705
Dallas, Tex.*	615	Richmond, Va.	328
Denver, Colo.*	564	St. Louis, Mo.*	1681
Des Moines, Iowa	226	St. Paul, Minn.*	1117
Detroit, Mich.*	3016	Salt Lake City, Utah*	275
Duluth, Minn.	253	San Antonio, Tex.	500
El Paso, Tex.	195	San Francisco, Calif.*	2241
Fargo, N. Dak.	38	Seattle, Wash.*	733
Houston, Tex.*	807	Spokane, Wash.	222
Indianapolis, Ind.	551	Tucson, Ariz.	49
Jacksonville, Fla.	304	Washington, D.C.*	1464
Kansas City, Mo.*	814	Wichita, Kansas	222

*Potential warehouse sites.
Source: *The World Almanac, 1960* (New York: New York World-Telegram and the Sun, 1960).

it provides a convenient method of identifying most of the nearby unactivated warehouse sites, and (2) computation time would be minimized by not considering the realignment of regions at this point in the program.

Another heuristic approach is to try to combine the solutions obtained when treating the three location-allocation-size variables independently, making proper adjustments for the interactions of the variables. For example, the multi-facility location process and the linear programming algorithm might be used together in the following manner. First, establish a beginning set of plant and warehouse locations by inspection in order to provide a starting point for solving the allocation problem. Second, solve the allocation problem by use of the linear programming algorithm assuming the locations established above. Next, use the location computational procedure to determine the optimal set of locations assuming the allocations fixed by the linear programming solution. Since the new locations may change the

Table 5.3 Heuristic Solutions to Sample Problems Factory Location: Indianapolis

FIXED COSTS OF WAREHOUSES

$7,500		$12,500		$17,500		$25,000	
Warehouse Located at Each Stage	Cost of System at Each Stage	Warehouse Located at Each Stage	Cost of System at Each Stage	Warehouse Located at Each Stage	Cost of System at Each Stage	Warehouse Located at Each Stage	Cost of System at Each Stage
Main Program		*Main Program*		*Main Program*		*Main Program*	
No warehouses	$1,248,688	No warehouses	$1,248,688	No warehouses	$1,248,688	No warehouses	$1,248,688
Philadelphia	1,075,120	Philadelphia	1,080,120	Philadelphia	1,085,120	Philadelphia	1,092,620
Los Angeles	910,514	Los Angeles	920,514	Los Angeles	930,514	Los Angeles	945,514
Seattle	876,429	Seattle	891,429	Seattle	906,429	Seattle	928,929
San Francisco	861,967	San Francisco	881,967	San Francisco	901,967		
Houston	850,645	Houston	875,645	Houston	900,645	*Bump-Shift Routine*	
Chicago	839,853	Chicago	869,853	Chicago	899,853	No change	928,929
New York	830,424	New York	865,424			*Improvements not Found by the Heuristic Program*	
Detroit	824,721	Detroit	864,721	*Bump-Shift Routine*		None known	
Denver	819,073	Kansas City	860,484	Replace Houston with Dallas	896,864		
Pittsburgh	815,818	Atlanta	859,125	*Improvements not Found by the Heuristic Program*			
Washington, D.C.	813,321	Cleveland	858,764	None known			
Kansas City	809,827	*Bump-Shift Routine*					
Boston	808,203	Drop Detroit	857,725				
Atlanta	801,845	Replace Phila. with Wash.	856,257				
Bump-Shift Routine		*Improvements not Found by the Heuristic Program*					
Drop Denver	801,748	Replace Houston with Dallas	854,672				
Improvements not Found by the Heuristic Program							
Replace Houston with Dallas	800,163						

Source: A. A. Kuehn and M. J. Hamburger, "A Heuristic Program for Locating Warehouses," *Management Science* 9, no. 4 (July 1963): 649.

optimal allocations, new allocations are made by re-solving the allocation problem using the linear programming algorithm. The process of successively solving the location and the allocation problems continues until the point is reached at which neither locations nor allocations change.

The additional variable of warehouse size could also be added by solving the above location-allocation problem for 0, 1, 2, . . . warehouses and then adding the fixed costs for operating the warehouses to the transportation costs. Or, alternatively, general size recommendations could be obtained from the application of a scale of operations model and then placed into the location-allocation problem.

By using good judgment in the application of the above process, an overall solution to the multi-facility problem can be obtained which would intuitively appear to be reasonably close to the optimal solution.

As an example of this process, consider the two-factory, two-warehouse, fifteen-market problem illustrated earlier in this chapter. Based on the use of the locational model and the linear programming algorithm, the factories were relocated in New York and Los Angeles and with no warehouses used, distribution cost was only $515,070. With the addition of warehouses in Chicago and New Orleans, distribution cost was reduced to $363,072.

In existing systems, the above type of analysis is still useful. If sufficient operating economies can be achieved, some existing facilities could be closed, relocated, or changed in capacity, or, additional facilities could be established. The shadow prices, which the linear programming algorithm produces as a by-product, can be used to assist the analyst in determining logical facility configurations for detailed examination.

We have suggested a wide variety of approaches for handling either portions or all of the multi-facility location problem. The most reasonable approach when confronted with real problems of this type probably is to utilize all of the available models as aids in the decision process. The biggest task in locating facilities is still likely to be data-gathering. Large firms may spend thousands of dollars simply gathering information on labor, transportation, taxes, markets, land and so forth. The incremental cost of applying the models of this chapter to use data efficiently may be relatively small in comparison. And, since facilities location decisions involve sums reaching into the millions of dollars, the extra time and money spent in evaluating the alternatives through the use of the above models is money well-spent.

Layout Planning

Layout planning is another spatial arrangement problem. The term layout or, more commonly, plant layout, describes the arrangement of departments, machines, storage areas, and so forth, usually within the confines of some physical structure such as a factory, a warehouse, or an office. The layout planning problem determines a spatial configuration of activity areas which optimizes the location relationships between these areas. The complexity of the layout problem depends on the number of factors considered during the solution process. Some of these factors are the criteria to be used in evaluating layouts, restrictions on locations of certain activity areas, restrictions on the shape of the physical structure, restrictions on aisles, shipping docks, and proximity to utility services and the need for flexibility. To arrive at an optimal solution to a layout planning problem, some comprehensive means of structuring the criteria and restrictions must be found. Although multiple criteria generally exist, the minimization of travel or materials handling between activity areas normally dominates the layout decision, particularly when a product has any appreciable cost of moving. An office is an example of a case in which travel minimization might not be a dominant factor. Although minimizing the in-office movement of clerical workers is important, the grouping of compatible work activities may be an even greater consideration.

There are two basic types of arrangements of facilities, product layout and process layout, along with many variations and combinations of the two. They are employed in the flow production process and the job-shop production process respectively.

Product Layout

The product layout is used when the entire production process is devoted to a single product or activity. Examples of such processes are the typical automobile assembly line and the medical exams given on a mass basis to hundreds of army recruits or entering college freshmen. The arrangement of machines and work stations is in accordance with the sequence of operations for the given product or activity. The relative location problem is in large measure dictated by the process with the physical arrangement in the same order as the operations in process. Normally, the only layout problem is to fit the work centers into the available space with the given sequence.

Process Layouts

The second basic method of arranging activity areas is to group all work stations of a given type together. The location of a work center depends on the operation performed in the center, not on the sequence of operations on any particular product. Thus, all drill presses are grouped together in one area, all milling machines in another area, all painting equipment in a third area, and so forth.

The process layout is employed in a job-shop type organization where insufficient volume of any single product or activity exists to economically justify devoting a separate set of facilities to it. The facilities must be shared jointly by many different products, each with its own unique sequence of operations. Since different products have different sequences, no single facility arrangement will satisfy all products. A particular product or order is produced in a batch, and the batch is moved from one department to another following the sequence of operations for that particular product.

Consider minimization of the cost of travel as the prime objective in the layout of a job-shop type of system, which can be stated rather simply in the following formula:

$$\text{Minimize } C = \sum_{i=1}^{n} \sum_{j=1}^{n} T_{ij} V_{ij} D_{ij} \tag{5.7}$$

where

D_{ij} = distance from work center i to work center j,

V_{ij} = number of "loads" of material going from work center i to work center j in a basic time period,

T_{ij} = transportation cost per load per unit distance for material moved from work center i to work center j,

n = the total number of work centers,

C = total movement cost .

Examining equation 5.7, we see that the V_{ij}'s are fixed values. That is, the number of loads to be shipped between any two work centers does not depend on where the centers are located; it depends on the type and number of products to be produced. We can also consider the T_{ij}'s as fixed values. That is, the cost of moving a given load per unit distance does not depend on the total distance involved; it depends on the type of materials handling system used between the two points. Although it may be true occasionally that the type of materials handling system chosen for use between two departments depends on their distance apart, this would not often be the case. Therefore, only the D_{ij}'s vary with the spatial locations of the activity centers. Thus, the layout problem is to arrange the activity areas in a manner such that the areas with large $T_{ij} V_{ij}$ values are situated relatively close together so the corresponding D_{ij} values are small and total transportation cost is minimized.

Since most layout problems involve only a modest number of activity areas, it may seem reasonable to rotate the areas into the various possible configurations, measure the transportation cost for each, and select the layout with the lowest cost figure. However, the number of alternative configurations may be exceedingly large. Consider a problem with n activity areas of equal size and shape within a building. There are $n!$ different configurations that can be generated since the first area can be placed in any of n locations, the next area in any of $n - 1$ locations, and so on. A number of these configurations will have identical distances between activity areas since each layout would have another layout which is a mirror image, and both could be rotated about their length and width, giving different absolute locations but the same relative locations. Thus, the total number of different relative locations is $n!/8$. In the case of 16 areas of equal size located in a rectangular area, there are $20.923 \cdot 10^{12}$ absolutely different arrangements and $2.615 \cdot 10^{12}$ relatively different arrangements. The exhaustive search method of determining the optimal layout is beyond the capacity of even the largest computers for problems of even moderate size.

The layout problem often has been solved graphically. Activity areas are shifted around on a floor plan of the facility in an attempt to locate areas with heavy interaction relatively close to each other. This approach works reasonably well when the number of activity areas is small, but it is rather ineffective as the number of departments increases because of the difficulty of visualizing which changes will result in net improvements.

Computer Method of Layout Planning

A number of heuristic approaches to the layout problem have been developed recently. A computer program called CRAFT,[8] an acronym for Computerized Relative Allocation of Facilities Technique, is used which computes the cost of alternative configurations and progressively selects only layouts that reduce total transportation cost.

Figure 5.7 shows a vastly simplified flow diagram which describes the basic structure of the program.

Input Data. The program requires three types of input data: an initial layout configuration, a load matrix, and a material-handling cost matrix. Figure 5.8 represents an initial layout for a plant with twenty departments with physical dimensions of 200 feet by 300 feet. The initial solution may be completely arbitrary, any suggested layout felt to be good, or perhaps the existing layout. The initial solution is arranged so that each line is represented by one punched card. The card is punched with the sequence of letters representing the various departments; for example, line 1 would be punched AAAAAABBBLLLLLLL.

Figure 5.9 shows the load matrix, which is simply a tabulation of the number of loads which flow between all combinations of departments. The matrix is symmetrical on its main diagonal; for example, the flow from A to B is shown as 120.0, and this is also shown as the flow from B to A, though the reverse flow is unusual. This information could be summarized from records of past orders, or for very large plants, it would probably represent a random sample of orders.

Figure 5.10 shows the interdepartmental material-handling cost per unit load for each 100 feet moved. For this particular example, three methods of material handling were used: manual truck, fork-lift truck, and low-bed lift truck, with respective costs of $0.026, $0.015, and $0.012 per unit load per 100 feet. In some instances, figures other than these appear in Figure

---

[8] The CRAFT program is now available through the IBM SHARE library under number SDA 3391.

Figure 5.7 Flow Diagram for CRAFT Program

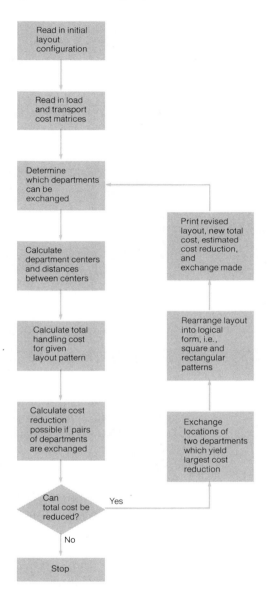

5.8, and these are weighted averages of the base figures and indicate that more than one method of material handling is in use between the departments concerned.

The Simulation. With the three items of basic data available, the program operates as follows (see the flow diagram of Figure 5.7):

Figure 5.8 Initial Relative Location Pattern, Iteration 0

	Location Pattern																						Iteration 0						
	1	2	3	4	5	6	7	8	9	10	11	12	13	14	15	16	17	18	19	20	21	22	23	24	25	26	27	28	29	30
1	A	A	A	A	A	A	B	B	B	B	L	L	L	L	L	L	L	S	S	S	S	S	S	S	S	W	W	W	W	W
2	A	A	A	A	A	A	B	B	B	B	L	L	L	L	L	L	L	S	S	S	S	S	S	S	S	W	W	W	W	W
3	A	A	A	A	A	B	B	B	B	B	L	L	L	L	L	L	L	S	S	S	S	S	S	S	S	W	W	W	W	W
4	A	A	A	A	A	B	B	B	B	B	L	L	L	L	L	L	L	S	S	S	S	S	S	S	S	W	W	W	W	W
5	A	A	A	A	A	B	B	B	B	B	L	L	L	L	L	L	L	S	S	S	S	S	S	S	S	W	W	W	W	W
6	C	C	C	C	C	C	D	D	D	D	L	L	L	L	L	L	L	S	S	S	S	S	S	S	S	W	W	W	W	W
7	C	C	C	C	C	C	D	D	D	D	L	L	L	L	L	L	L	G	G	G	S	S	S	S	S	W	W	W	W	W
8	C	C	C	C	C	D	D	D	D	D	L	L	L	L	L	L	L	G	G	G	S	S	S	S	S	W	W	W	W	W
9	C	C	C	C	C	D	D	D	D	D	L	L	L	L	L	L	L	G	G	G	S	S	S	S	S	W	W	W	W	W
10	C	C	C	C	C	C	D	D	D	D	N	N	N	N	N	N	H	H	H	T	T	T	T	T	T	T	T	T	T	T
11	E	E	E	E	E	E	F	F	F	N	N	N	N	N	N	H	H	H	T	T	T	T	T	T	T	T	T	T	T	T
12	E	E	E	E	E	E	F	F	F	N	N	N	N	N	N	H	H	H	T	T	T	T	T	T	T	T	T	T	T	T
13	E	E	E	E	E	E	F	F	F	P	P	P	P	P	P	P	J	J	J	T	T	T	T	T	T	T	T	T	T	T
14	K	K	K	K	K	K	F	F	F	P	P	P	P	P	P	P	J	J	J	T	T	T	T	T	T	T	T	T	T	T
15	K	K	K	K	K	K	F	F	F	P	P	P	P	P	P	P	J	J	J	U	U	U	U	U	U	T	T	T	T	V	V
16	K	K	K	K	K	K	F	F	F	P	P	P	P	P	P	P	R	R	R	U	U	U	U	U	U	U	V	V	V	V	V
17	K	K	K	K	K	K	M	M	M	M	M	M	M	R	R	R	R	R	R	U	U	U	U	U	U	U	V	V	V	V	V
18	M	M	M	M	M	M	M	M	M	M	M	M	M	R	R	R	R	R	R	U	U	U	U	U	U	U	V	V	V	V	V
19	M	M	M	M	M	M	M	M	M	M	M	M	M	R	R	R	R	R	R	U	U	U	U	U	U	U	V	V	V	V	V
20	M	M	M	M	M	M	M	M	M	M	M	M	M	R	R	R	R	R	R	U	U	U	U	U	U	U	V	V	V	V	V

Total cost $10,164.34   Estimated cost reduction 0   MOVEA   MOVEB

Scale: One Matrix Element Equals 100 Square Feet. Each Row and Column Equals 10 Feet.
Source: E. S. Buffa, *Operations Management* (New York: John Wiley and Sons, 1968), p. 402.

1. The program determines which of the departments can be exchanged. A limitation in the program specifies that the only candidates for exchange are departments of equal size, or departments adjacent to each other even though they may not be of equal size. Although this restriction may limit the direct exchanges that can be made, any pair of departments may eventually be exchanged through a sequence of exchanges.

2. The program calculates the physical centers of the various departments and then determines the distances between all combinations of departments.

3. Data is now available to calculate the total handling cost for a given layout pattern. This cost is computed from the input data on loads and unit transport costs between departments and the matrix of distances calculated in the second step. Of course, the first layout pattern for which total material-handling costs are calculated will be the initial pattern.

4. The program now evaluates what changes in total cost would occur if each department were exchanged in location with all other eligible departments. It does this by exchanging temporarily the two departments in question and recalculating total material-handling costs. This requires $(n^2 - n)/2 = 190$ evaluations for our example.

Figure 5.9 Interdepartmental Product Flow in Tens of Unit Loads per Annum

	A	B	C	D	E	F	G	H	J	K	L	M	N	P	R	S	T	U	V	W
A	0.	120.0	80.0	0.	0.	0.	0.	0.	0.	40.0	80.0	0.	0.	80.0	0.	0.	0.	0.	0.	0.
B	120.0	0.	80.0	1630.0	30.0	0.	930.0	0.	80.0	90.0	0.	0.	0.	0.	0.	0.	0.	0.	460.0	0.
C	80.0	80.0	0.	0.	0.	130.0	0.	0.	210.0	260.0	0.	0.	0.	870.0	0.	0.	0.	100.0	910.0	0.
D	0.	1630.0	0.	0.	60.0	380.0	500.0	0.	130.0	0.	0.	70.0	0.	0.	90.0	0.	0.	0.	1050.0	0.
E	0.	30.0	0.	60.0	0.	0.	150.0	90.0	0.	60.0	0.	30.0	0.	0.	0.	0.	0.	70.0	0.	0.
F	0.	0.	130.0	380.0	0.	0.	410.0	0.	0.	0.	0.	0.	0.	0.	0.	0.	0.	0.	0.	0.
G	0.	930.0	0.	500.0	150.0	410.0	0.	1600.0	0.	110.0	0.	0.	0.	0.	0.	0.	0.	110.0	0.	250.0
H	0.	0.	0.	0.	90.0	0.	1600.0	0.	0.	0.	0.	0.	0.	0.	0.	0.	0.	0.	500.0	2230.0
J	0.	80.0	210.0	130.0	0.	0.	0.	0.	0.	0.	0.	0.	500.0	0.	0.	0.	500.0	0.	0.	0.
K	40.0	90.0	260.0	0.	60.0	0.	110.0	0.	0.	0.	30.0	0.	0.	1240.0	160.0	0.	0.	0.	0.	0.
L	80.0	0.	0.	0.	0.	0.	0.	0.	0.	30.0	0.	800.0	150.0	200.0	80.0	1500.0	350.0	90.0	0.	0.
M	0.	0.	0.	70.0	30.0	0.	0.	0.	0.	0.	800.0	0.	0.	200.0	0.	0.	0.	0.	560.0	0.
N	0.	0.	0.	0.	0.	0.	0.	0.	500.0	0.	150.0	0.	0.	500.0	40.0	500.0	0.	0.	0.	0.
P	80.0	0.	870.0	0.	0.	0.	0.	0.	0.	1240.0	200.0	200.0	500.0	0.	40.0	500.0	0.	60.0	0.	0.
R	0.	0.	0.	90.0	0.	0.	0.	0.	0.	160.0	80.0	0.	40.0	40.0	0.	1000.0	350.0	0.	0.	0.
S	0.	0.	0.	0.	0.	0.	0.	0.	0.	0.	1500.0	0.	500.0	500.0	1000.0	0.	1000.0	0.	0.	0.
T	0.	0.	0.	0.	0.	0.	0.	0.	500.0	0.	350.0	0.	0.	0.	350.0	1000.0	0.	0.	0.	0.
U	0.	0.	100.0	0.	70.0	0.	110.0	0.	0.	0.	90.0	0.	0.	60.0	0.	0.	0.	0.	310.0	0.
V	0.	460.0	910.0	1050.0	0.	0.	0.	500.0	0.	0.	0.	560.0	0.	0.	0.	0.	0.	310.0	0.	0.
W	0.	0.	0.	0.	0.	0.	250.0	2230.0	0.	0.	0.	0.	0.	0.	0.	0.	0.	0.	0.	0.

Source: E. S. Buffa, *Operations Management* (New York: John Wiley and Sons, 1968), p. 403.

Figure 5.10 Interdepartmental Material Handling Cost Per Unit Load per 100 Feet Moved in Dollars

	A	B	C	D	E	F	G	H	J	K	L	M	N	P	R	S	T	U	V	W
A	0.	0.015	0.015	0.	0.	0.	0.	0.	0.	0.026	0.014	0.	0.	0.015	0.	0.	0.	0.	0.	0.
B	0.015	0.	0.012	0.015	0.026	0.	0.015	0.	0.015	0.015	0.	0.	0.	0.	0.	0.	0.	0.	0.015	0.
C	0.015	0.012	0.	0.	0.	0.017	0.	0.	0.015	0.015	0.	0.	0.	0.015	0.	0.	0.	0.015	0.015	0.
D	0.	0.015	0.	0.	0.018	0.015	0.015	0.	0.018	0.	0.	0.020	0.	0.	0.015	0.	0.	0.	0.015	0.
E	0.	0.026	0.	0.018	0.	0.	0.015	0.015	0.	0.026	0.	0.	0.	0.	0.	0.	0.	0.	0.015	0.
F	0.	0.	0.017	0.015	0.	0.	0.015	0.	0.	0.	0.	0.015	0.	0.	0.	0.	0.	0.015	0.	0.
G	0.	0.015	0.	0.015	0.015	0.015	0.	0.015	0.	0.017	0.	0.	0.	0.016	0.	0.	0.	0.015	0.	0.015
H	0.	0.	0.	0.	0.015	0.	0.015	0.	0.	0.	0.	0.	0.	0.	0.	0.	0.	0.015	0.	0.015
J	0.	0.015	0.015	0.015	0.015	0.015	0.015	0.	0.	0.	0.012	0.015	0.015	0.015	0.	0.	0.015	0.	0.	0.
K	0.026	0.015	0.015	0.018	0.026	0.	0.017	0.	0.	0.	0.	0.015	0.	0.015	0.012	0.015	0.	0.	0.015	0.
L	0.014	0.	0.	0.	0.	0.	0.	0.	0.	0.012	0.	0.015	0.	0.015	0.012	0.	0.	0.	0.015	0.
M	0.	0.	0.	0.020	0.	0.015	0.	0.015	0.	0.015	0.015	0.	0.	0.015	0.015	0.	0.015	0.	0.015	0.
N	0.	0.	0.	0.	0.	0.	0.016	0.	0.	0.	0.	0.	0.	0.016	0.026	0.012	0.	0.	0.	0.
P	0.015	0.	0.015	0.	0.	0.	0.	0.	0.015	0.015	0.015	0.	0.016	0.	0.015	0.	0.	0.015	0.	0.
R	0.	0.	0.	0.	0.015	0.	0.	0.	0.	0.012	0.012	0.015	0.026	0.015	0.	0.	0.	0.	0.	0.
S	0.	0.	0.	0.	0.	0.	0.	0.	0.015	0.	0.	0.	0.012	0.	0.	0.	0.012	0.	0.	0.
T	0.	0.	0.	0.015	0.	0.	0.	0.	0.	0.	0.	0.015	0.	0.015	0.015	0.012	0.	0.	0.	0.
U	0.	0.	0.	0.	0.	0.015	0.015	0.	0.015	0.	0.	0.	0.	0.	0.	0.	0.	0.	0.015	0.
V	0.	0.015	0.015	0.015	0.	0.	0.	0.015	0.	0.015	0.015	0.015	0.	0.015	0.	0.	0.015	0.015	0.	0.
W	0.	0.	0.	0.	0.	0.	0.015	0.015	0.	0.	0.	0.	0.	0.	0.	0.	0.	0.	0.	0.

Source: E. S. Buffa, *Operations Management* (New York: John Wiley and Sons, 1968), p. 404.

5. If any changes in location produce a reduction in material-handling cost, the program proceeds. If not, the program stops, for no further improvement can be made by the program.

6. If there are exchanges that produce cost reduction, the program selects the exchange of the two departments that yield the largest cost reduction and executes their exchange in the layout pattern.

7. Since some of the exchanges will be for departments of unequal size, program subroutines rearrange the layout into logical forms, that is, square or rectangular patterns.

8. The program now calls for the printing of the revised layout, the new total cost, the estimated cost reduction, and the record of the exchanges just made. Figure 5.11 shows the print-out for the first iteration of the problem. It shows that by exchanging the locations of departments A and V, a net improvement in material-handling cost of almost 12 per cent has been obtained.

Figure 5.11   First Improved Relative Location Pattern

```
                    Location Pattern                      Iteration 1
    1  2  3  4  5  6  7  8  9 10 11 12 13 14 15 16 17 18 19 20 21 22 23 24 25 26 27 28 29 30
 1  V  V  V  V  V  V  B  B  B  L  L  L  L  L  L  L  L     L  S  S  S  S  S  S  S  S  W  W  W  W  W
 2  V              V  B     B     L           L     S                          S  W              W
 3  V        V  B  B        B     L           L     S                          S  W              W
 4  V        V  B           B     L           L     S                          S  W              W
 5  V  V  V  V  V  B  B  B  B  L           L     S                          S  W              W
 6  C  C  C  C  C  C  D  D  D  L           L  L  S  S  S                    S  W              W
 7  C              C  D     D        L     L  G  G  G  S                    S  W              W
 8  C           C  D  D     D  L     L  G        G  S                       S  W              W
 9  C           C  D        D  L  L  L  L  L  L  G  G  G  S  S  S  S  S  S  S  W  W  W  W  W
10  C  C  C  C  C  D  D  D  D  N  N  N  N  N  N  H  H  H  T  T  T  T  T  T  T  T  T  T  T  T
11  E  E  E  E  E  E  F  F  F  N              N  H     H  T                                T
12  E              E  F     F     N  N  N  N  N  N  H  H  H  T                             T
13  E  E  E  E  E  E  F     F     F  P  P  P  P  P  P  P  J  J  J  T                       T
14  K  K  K  K  K  K  F     F     F  P              P  J     J  T  T  T  T  T  T        T  T  T
15  K              K  F     F     F  P  P  P     P  J  J  J  U  U  U  U  U  U  T  T  T  T  A  A
16  K              K  F  F  F  F  F  P  P  P  P  R  R  R  U           U  U  A  A  A  A  A
17  K  K  K  K  K  K  M  M  M  M  M  M  M  R  R  R  R  R  U           U  A              A
18  M  M  M  M  M  M  M              M  R              R  U           U  A              A
19  M                             M  R              R  U           U  A              A
20  M  M  M  M  M  M  M  M  M  M  M  M  M  R  R  R  R  R  R  U  U  U  U  U  U  U  U  A  A  A  A  A  A

Total cost  $8,979.26      Estimated cost reduction   $1,185.08      MOVEA A       MOVEB V
```

Source: E. S. Buffa, *Operations Management* (New York: John Wiley and Sons, 1968), p. 406.

9. The program now repeats the basic steps until no further cost reduction can be achieved, the last iteration representing the best possible solution. Figure 5.12 shows the seventh and final iteration for the sample problem. The final solution shows a 23 per cent reduction in material-handling cost compared to the initial layout configuration, and the entire solution required 0.62 minutes to execute

on an IBM 7094 computer. The final block diagram of Figure 5.10 would be used as a basis for the development of a more detailed layout.

Figure 5.12 Final Iteration of Location Problem—Suboptimum Relative Location Pattern

	Location Pattern																	*Iteration 7*												
	1	2	3	4	5	6	7	8	9	10	11	12	13	14	15	16	17	18	19	20	21	22	23	24	25	26	27	28	29	30
1	E	E	E	E	E	E	F	F	F	L	L	L	L	L	L	L	S	S	S	S	S	S	S	S	S	U	U	U	U	U
2	E				E	E	F		F	L							L	S							S	U				U
3	E	E	E	E	E	F	F		F	L							L	S							S	U				U
4	E	C	C	C	C	F			F	L							L	S							S	U				U
5	C	C			C	F	F	F	F	L							L	S							S	U				U
6	C						C	C	D	D	D	L				L	L	S	S	S					S	U				U
7	C						C	C	D		D	L				L	G	G	G	S					S	U				U
8	C	C	C	C	C	D			D	L						L	G			G	S				S	U	U	U	U	U
9	C	V	V	V	V	D			D	L	L	L	L	L	L	G	G	G	S	S	S	S	S	S	W	W	W	W	W	U
10	V	V							V	D	D	D	N	N	N	N	N	N	H	H	H	H	T	T	T	W	W	W	W	W
11	V								V	V	B	B	B	N					N	H		H			T		W	W		W
12	V								V	B			B	N	N	N	N	N	N	H	H	H	T			T	T	W		W
13	V	V	V	V	V	V	B			B	P	P	P	P	P	P	P	J	J	J	J	T				T	W			W
14	K	K	K	K	K	K	B			B	P							P	J			J	T			T	W	W		W W W
15	K						K	B			B	P							P	J	J	J	J	T		T	T	W W W W	A A	
16	K						K	B	B	B	P	P	P	P	P	P	P	R	R	R	R	T					T	T	A A A A A	
17	K	K	K	K	K	K	M	M	M	M	M	M	M	R	R	R	R			R	T					T		A		A
18	M	M	M	M	M	M	M							M	R					R	T					T		A		A
19	M															M	R					R	T				T		A		A
20	M	M	M	M	M	M	M	M	M	M	M	M	M	R	R	R	R	R	R	T	T	T	T	T	T	A	A	A	A	A

Total cost $7,862.09   *Estimated cost reduction* $213.54   *MOVEA E*   *MOVEB C*

Exchanging any two departments from their locations above here would increase the objective function, annual material handling expense.

Source: E. S. Buffa, *Operations Management* (New York: John Wiley and Sons, 1968), p. 407.

The most recent version of the computer program handles a maximum of forty departments and fixes the location of any number of the departments. The latter feature is often important, since sometimes not all departments can be changed in location. For example, the existing location of a railroad spur or road may determine the desirable location for receiving and shipping facilities. In such an instance, the best location of the other departments is determined, given the fixed location of the receiving and shipping departments. The present version of the program also considers candidates for exchange three at a time, rather than two at a time.

Summary

The level of many of the costs of operating systems is determined by the establishment of the physical facilities. The location of a facility affects the revenue, operating costs, and investment costs of the system.

Decisions to locate single-facility systems are not nearly as complex as those of locating facilities in multi-facility systems. In multi-facility systems, it is necessary to determine (1) how many facilities there should be and the size of each facility, (2) where each facility should be located, and (3) what portion of markets and distribution patterns should be allocated to each facility. Since all three problems are related, they must be treated within a single analytical framework.

Plant layout is a special kind of spatial problem in which facilities must be arranged within the confines of a building. In a product layout, the physical arrangement of facilities is in the same order as the sequence of work dictates. In a process layout, departments are arranged in a manner to minimize the cost of moving material between them.

Selected References

Armour, G., and Buffa, E. "A Heuristic Algorithm and Simulation Approach to the Relative Location of Facilities." *Management Science* 9 (January 1963).

Bowman, E. H., and Stewart, H. B. "A Model for Scale of Operations." *Journal of Marketing* 20 (January 1956): 242–247.

Drysdale, J. "Heuristic Warehouse Location." *Canadian Operational Research Society Journal,* March 1969.

Greenhut, M. *Plant Location in Theory and Practice.* Chapel Hill, N.C.: University of North Carolina Press, 1956.

Kuehn, A. A. and Hamburger, M. J. "A Heuristic Program for Locating Warehouses." *Management Science* 9 (July 1963): 643–668.

Magee, J. *Physical Distribution Systems.* New York: McGraw-Hill Book Co., 1967.

Mossman, F. H., and Morton, N. *Logistics of Distribution Systems.* Boston: Allyn and Bacon, 1967.

Nugent, C. E., Vollman, T. E., and Ruml, J. "A Experimental Comparison of Techniques for the Assignment of Facilities to Locations." *Operations Research* (1968): 150–173.

Vergin, R. C., and Rogers, J. D. "An Algorithm and Computational Procedure for Locating Economic Facilities." *Management Science* 13 (February 1967): 240–254.

Questions

1 How would the method of analysis vary for a marketing-dominated location decision as opposed to an operations-dominated location decision?

2 In the warehouse territory problem, why would the area served by the factory be much larger than the area served by each warehouse?

3 Linear programming was used to solve a problem for an organization with a single product. How could linear programming be used for an organization with several product lines? How could the acquisition of raw materials be incorporated into the problem?

4 What justification is there for using heuristic methods of problem solving rather than seeking optimal solutions?

5 What economic functions do warehouses perform?

6 What factors determine the selection of a product or process type of plant layout?

7 Explain how fewer computations are required in the CRAFT layout model than if complete enumeration of all alternative layouts were considered.

8 In the CRAFT model, how might the optimal solution be missed? What can be done to reduce the risk of missing the optimal solution?

9 Consider the problem of establishing a school system in a large city. Can the tools of analysis considered here be of use in this system?

10 In the Kuehn-Hamburger model, what are the specific risks that the optimal solution will not be found as a result of using the heuristic rules?

Problems

1 A new facility is to be located. It will have shipments between it and three existing facilities as follows:

Facility	Location X_i	Y_i	V_i	T_i
1	4	2	3	1
2	6	6	6	1
3	1	5	4	1

Make an intuitive estimate of the minimum transportation cost location for the new facility. Compute the direction in which the optimal location lies from your original estimate.

2 A persistent myth that can be found in many articles and books dealing with facility location is that the minimum transportation location is at the weighted average, also called the center of gravity, in each dimension. The weighted average is

$$\frac{\sum_{i=1}^{n} (V_i T_i) X_i}{\sum_{i=1}^{n} (V_i T_i)} \quad \text{in the } X \text{ direction and}$$

$$\frac{\sum_{i=1}^{n} (V_i T_i) Y_i}{\sum_{i=1}^{n} (V_i T_i)} \quad \text{in the } Y \text{ direction.}$$

Show that this is not the minimum cost location.

3 Consider a location problem in one dimension; an oil pipeline that moves oil only on a single east-west line for example. A single maintenance crew and spare part depot is to be located on the line from which repairmen will make periodic trips to pumping stations on the line. The line is 200 miles long with stations located and trips required as follows:

Location from origin in West	Average No. of Trips per Month
10	4
30	2
40	1
190	6

A simple, commonly used, arithmetic term describes the minimum transportation cost location for the one dimensional case. What is the term?

4 Using the warehouse size model from the chapter, determine how size and volume for two territories would compare when territory A has a sales density 8 times that of territory B.

5 In the 15-market allocation problem in the chapter, determine the optimal allocation pattern and distribution cost with:
a. 2 factories only, located at Los Angeles and New York with 20,000,000 unit capacity each;
b. 2 factories at Los Angeles and New York and 2 warehouses at Chicago with 15,000,000 and at New Orleans with 10,000,000 capacities.

6 For the 15-market allocation problem, where should the factory be located if only one factory and no warehouses were included in the system?

Appendix:
Review of
Differentiation

Calculus is often employed to find a maximum or a minimum value of a mathematical equation. Many of the economic relationships described by mathematical equations expressed in this book can be solved for a minimum cost or maximum profit value by following a few simple mathematical manipulations. These manipulations employ calculus by taking a derivative. The first derivative of an equation represents the slope of a line tangent to that equation. For example, suppose we have a u-shaped cost curve which is a function of a variable, X, such as below:

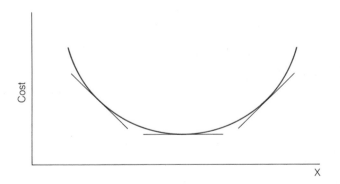

We can draw a series of lines tangent to the curve at various points on the curve. All will have either positive, zero, or negative slopes. Only at the bottom of the curve, the minimum point, will the line tangent to the curve have a zero slope. Thus, if we can find the point at which the slope of the line tangent to the curve is zero, then we also have the minimum (or maximum) point on the curve.

To find this point mathematically, we can take the first derivative, set it equal to 0, and solve for X. The derivative can be obtained by using the following rules:

Derivatives of Elementary Functions

a The derivative of a constant function is 0; for example, if $f(X) = 3$, then $f'(X) = 0$.

b The derivative of X^n is:

$$\frac{d(X^n)}{dX} = nX^{n-1}.$$

For example,

$$\frac{d(X^2)}{dX} = 2X^1.$$

Basic Rules of Computing Derivatives

a The derivative of a product of two functions is given by:

$$\frac{d(YZ)}{dX} = Z\frac{dY}{dX} + Y\frac{dZ}{dX}$$

where Y and Z are functions of X.
For example, if $Y = X$ and $Z = X^2$, then

$$\frac{dY}{dX} = 1X^0 = 1; \quad \frac{dZ}{dX} = 2X^1;$$

$$\frac{d(X \cdot X^2)}{dX} = X^2\frac{d(X)}{dX} + X\frac{d(X^2)}{dX} = X^2 + 2X^2 = 3X^2.$$

b The derivative of a quotient of two functions is given by:

$$\frac{d}{dX}\left(\frac{Y}{Z}\right) = \frac{Z\left(\frac{dY}{dX}\right) - Y\left(\frac{dZ}{dX}\right)}{Z^2}$$

For example, if $Y = X^3$ and $Z = X - 1$,

$$\frac{d}{dX}\left(\frac{Y}{Z}\right) = \frac{(X-1)3X^2 - X^3(1)}{(X-1)^2} = \frac{2X^3 - 3X^2}{(X-1)^2}.$$

c The derivative of a function such as $F(X) = [f(X)]^n$ is given by:

$$\frac{dF(X)}{dX} = n[f(X)]^{n-1}\frac{d[f(X)]}{dX}$$

For example, $F(X) = (3X - 2)^5$

$$\frac{dF(X)}{dX} = 5(3X - 2)^4 \cdot 3 = 15(3X - 2)^4.$$

Example 1:

$$C = aX + \frac{b}{X}$$

$$\frac{dC}{dX} = a - \frac{b}{X^2}.$$

Example 2:

$$C = (X - X_i)^2$$

$$\frac{dC}{dX} = 2(X - X_i) \cdot \frac{d(X - X_i)}{dX} = 2(X - X_i) \cdot 1 = 2(X - X_i).$$

Example 3:

$$C = \sqrt{(X - X_i)^2 + (Y - Y_i)^2}$$

$$C = [(X - X_i)^2 + (Y - Y_i)^2]^{1/2}$$

$$\frac{dC}{dX} = \tfrac{1}{2}[(X - X_i)^2 + (Y - Y_i)^2]^{-1/2} \cdot \frac{d[(X - X_i)^2 + (Y - Y_i)^2]}{dX}$$

$$= \tfrac{1}{2}[(X - X_i)^2 + (Y - Y_i)^2]^{-1/2} \cdot 2(X - X_i)$$

$$= \frac{(X - X_i)}{\sqrt{(X - X_i)^2 - (Y - Y_i)^2}}.$$

Partial Derivatives

Many problems with two variables can be solved with partial derivatives. The partial derivatives of f with respect to X, evaluated at the point X_0, Y_0, gives the slope of the tangent to the surface $Z = f(X, Y)$ in the direction parallel to the X-axis. The partial derivative with respect to Y gives the slope of the tangent in the direction parallel to the Y-axis. To solve for the optimal X and Y values, the partial derivatives are set equal to zero and the resulting equations are solved. The rules for differentiation for functions of one variable apply to obtain partial derivatives.

Chapter 6
The
Design
of Systems

What will a new subsystem contribute to the total system? How will it relate to other subsystems or nodes in the structure? Where should the facilities be located and arranged? The relationship of a subsystem to the larger system is not always easy to determine, but organizing its contribution to optimize the total system is crucial.

The principles that apply in macro-design also apply for subsystems, although detail becomes more important with each expansion of the subsystem hierarchy. The design of subsystems exercises man's ingenuity to the greatest degree, for assignments are more succinct and the results of creativity coincide more closely with individual contributions. Once the objectives of a system are determined, the design process starts. The first step is to outline the project, plan strategy, and schedule milestones for completing each significant phase of the program. Second, it is wise to determine those constraints which influence or limit design. Third, the proposed system is described in detail, using the most appropriate techniques of description. Fourth, the preliminary design is analyzed and reviewed. Finally, the accepted system is introduced, tested, and debugged.

Design and Creativity

Man has acquired most of what he knows and stores in his brain through learning. From the stimulus, response, and reinforcement sequence, he tests new experiences and patterns future behavior. This knowledge and understanding is called mental capacity or intelligence. Creativity, on the other hand, refers to the ability to create new knowledge from that which is known.

There are various degrees or kinds of creativity; the innovative work of a nuclear scientist would be in the "big leagues" compared to the achievements of war prisoners in engineering an escape from a high-security prison with few, if any, tools at their disposal. Interestingly, the process of creativity may be the same in either instance, however. It is suspected that most people possess unused and latent capacity to be creative.

The Process of Creativity

Although very little is known about the brain or how it works, we do know that man has the ability to recall information stored in his brain cells. In attempting to generate new ideas or solve problems, the process which occurs would include the recall of information pertinent to the situation. In Figure 6.1, for example, ten units of information have been recalled

Figure 6.1 The Process of Creativity

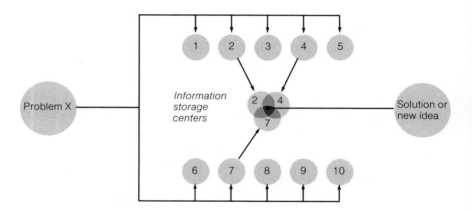

The search procedure may follow a testing of each storage area individually, then each combination of two, and so on until all possible combinations are considered.

relating to situation X. The next stage in the process concerns the orderly testing of this information in various combinations. Let us suppose that the use of information units 1, 3, and 7 provide the genesis of an idea which will solve the problem, and create something new.

Why are some people more creative than others? Is it because the creative person has greater capability, or is the difference attributable to a more effective use of potential? Probably it is a combination of both, a premise which may be more apparent to the reader after reviewing the model diagrammed in Figure 6.2.

We all possess a certain level of native intelligence which is measurable to some degree by (1) the amount of information accumulated from past learning experiences, (2) the ability to understand and organize this information, (3) the ability to recall information when needed, and (4) the capacity to visualize or create a mental picture of actual or hypothetical situations.

Some people are motivated to use their intelligence much more than others. This may be inspired because they are curious about everything they

Figure 6.2   A Model of Creativity

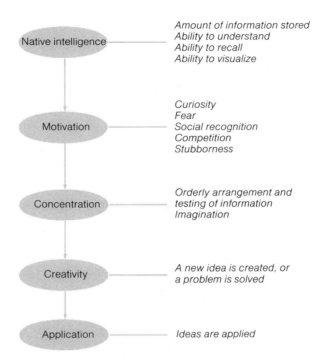

observe (for example, how do salmon find their way back to the stream in which they were spawned?). Some are motivated by fear (for example, of losing their job or being rejected). Most people are motivated because they wish to gain social recognition, or to achieve economic gain which they associate with social recognition. Many like to compete and will exert great effort in a competitive situation. Finally, some people are stubborn and enjoy tackling those problems which seem to defy solution.

When we are motivated, we tend to focus maximum attention—to concentrate. At this stage, the creative process is assisted if there is orderly arrangement and testing of known information. Rather than "going in circles," a logical procedure or method will enlarge the scope of the investigation and more often bring success. Imagination also is important, that is, the willingness of the researcher to branch out from the usual arrangement of information and try new and untried combinations.

The creative person can gain great personal satisfaction from his achievement, providing that he applies his ideas and others recognize his work as a genuine contribution. Following a creative act comes the period of presentation and verification, of review and testing. It is tragic when an ineffective presentation causes genius to go unrecognized, but such an occurrence is not uncommon.

Stimulating Creativity. Very few people use their basic creativity; many are lazy, overly modest, or afraid to fail. Unfortunately, their potential to be creative is seldom realized. An organization can stimulate latent creativity among its employees by encouraging everyone to try, and expecting occasional failure; by a program of rewards and recognition; and by increasing employee potential through education and special training.

Many techniques have been used to stimulate ideas. Three examples are brainstorming, the checklist, and value analysis.

1. Brainstorming: a group approach for problem solving where members are encouraged to drop all inhibitions and suggest ideas or build on the ideas of other members of the group. All suggestions are reviewed and evaluated later.

2. Checklist: a method of getting idea-clues by checking items on a prepared list against the problem. There are many variations of this technique, such as listing the characteristics of the problem.

3. Value analysis: a technique to test the value of any part or product, with the object of increasing the total value secured. Questions are asked concerning (a) what it is, (b) what it must do, (c) the costs, (d) possible substitutes, and (e) cost of substitutes.

The relevance of creativity to systems management and/or the systems approach is analogous to what a good wine can contribute to a dinner. The ordinary can become the exceptional by the generation of new ideas through the exercise of imagination and logic, by the addition of an extra ingredient.

The Crooked Tailpipe. In the early 1960's most automobile exhaust tailpipes were manufactured in the Detroit area. The tailpipes made for the replacement market were shipped from Detroit to garages and service stations throughout the country. A tailpipe carries the exhaust from the muffler to the rear of the car and is shaped to avoid touching any part of the body or frame. Therefore, a tailpipe may have several bends and a shape unique to the particular make and model of the car for which it was designed. As the number of makes and models of cars increased, it became more difficult to predict which particular pipes to stock. It also became more expensive to ship and inventory these pipes as their shape became more irregular.

An initial solution to this problem was to decentralize the manufacturing facility, which tended to reduce the amount of inventory that individual service units were required to store. Unfortunately, the cost of manufacturing increased as the volume per producing facility decreased, and so the trade off between the manufacturing subsystem and the distribution subsystem resulted in a negative improvement for the total system.

The ultimate solution was to manufacture a straight tailpipe at a centralized location and to ship this pipe to local service units. The local unit installed a small pipe bending machine that reacted to punched card instructions to bend the pipe exactly as it was programmed for each particular make and model. This was a creative solution which resulted in optimizing the total system, improving customer service, and reducing costs.

Systems Determination

An organization establishes broad plans primarily in the form of goals and objectives. Organizational goals are translated into more detailed and specific plans, which are translated again throughout the organization to even more detailed and specific plans.

The allied invasion of Europe during World War II presents a well-documented example of the hierarchical relationship of plans. First, the broad objective of the invasion was established, and this led to a series of secondary goals and objectives, such as requirements for weather conditions, goals for the numbers and types of military men needed, and determination of material needs. These secondary objectives were translated into more detailed plans which were then translated throughout the military hierarchy down to the most detailed plans at the lowest operating level. The entire planning process was extremely difficult because of the need for secrecy concerning the entire operation.

We can see the hierarchical relationship in planning for a more recent national effort, the National Aeronautics and Space Administration (NASA) program leading to man's exploration of the moon. In May 1961, President Kennedy set forth the broad national objectives: "I believe that this nation should commit itself to achieving the goal, before this decade is out, of landing a man on the moon and returning him safely to earth." With this broad objective as a guideline, the Office of Manned Space Flight was established within NASA, with prime responsibility for the Man-Lunar landing. Three major projects were established under the Manned Space Flight Program—Mercury, Gemini, and Apollo. They constituted a step-by-step approach in the program to develop a broad capacity for manned exploration of space. Given the broad goal, planning for each of these projects was initiated and integrated into the complete program. In July of 1969 man landed on the moon and the objective was accomplished.

Each subsystem's objectives serve those of the next higher system in the hierarchy. Therefore, the total mission, in view of such major subsystem relationships, must be subdivided into segments with distinct and measurable units of input and output, and at a scale where operations are economical. Determining the total combination and nature of subsystems necessary to complete the task, although not as glamorous and exciting as outlining total systems objectives, is the key to effective and efficient operations, or achievement of organization goals.

One of the most difficult tasks associated with system-subsystem determination pertains to the establishment of proper boundaries of operation. To the extent that goals are specific and distinct, the boundaries are easier to set. Still other factors such as environmental influence, the availability of man and machine resources, the time schedule for design and operation, cost of alternative design decisions, and the particular wishes or biases of the designers must be considered. In systems management, there is yet another decision criterion, the need to identify and measure all significant inputs and outputs in the proposed task division. No meaningful parameters of operation can be established when this criterion is not met.

Another premise related to systems management concerns the optimization of the total system. If a change in subsystem performance causes a negative result on the total system, even though it may improve the efficiency of the subsystem, it should not be enacted. The design of subsystems, thus, is limited by the output required for the next level in the system hierarchy.

Constraints on the Design Function

In order to place the design alternatives in their proper perspective, it is important to outline the various constraints which may be placed on the system design program. The constraints which affect the typical program are classified as environmental, macro, and process.

External forces are ever-present constraints on system design, particularly when we are concerned with the systems which must adjust or adapt to outside influence (open or flexible systems). The external environment affects the total system, which in turn places constraints on the design of many of the subsystems. For example, unions often influence management's planning concerning working conditions and compensation of employees. Government regulations may dictate the nature of the information-decision system, (such as the cost data reporting system required for all government suppliers, or the tax reporting system specified for most organizations. Each system is, in fact, a part of a higher level or super-system that may elect to dictate or influence design and operation decisions.

The macrosystem imposes constraints on each of its subsystems. General design and operating policy limit the parameters within which each subsystem must function. These policies may include the standards of social and ethical conduct subscribed to by top managers of the system; the amount of capital and/or resources available for each subsystem; the kind of input furnished by outside systems and other internal systems; and the nature of output described for each subsystem as its contribution to macro goals.

The production process itself may restrict design details, that is, the technology available to process the input, or the layout prescribed by the use of a particular process. For example, the transformation or decomposition of nitrogen pentoxide (N_2O_5) in a carbon tetrachloride ($C\ Cl_4$) solution requires a specific temperature in order to maintain a predictable reaction. The processing may require computer control, which, in turn, will specify certain space and air conditioning facilities.

The constraints which we have outlined do not represent a comprehensive listing. Rather, they illustrate the importance of considering and analyzing constraints early in the design process.

Characteristics of Effective Systems

Why are some systems effective and efficient while other systems are not? Is success attributable to the skill exercised in design, or to the caliber of management practiced during the operation stage? Successful systems are characterized by their simplicity, flexibility, reliability, economy, and acceptability. Simplicity, flexibility, and reliability tend to be a function of design, whereas economy and acceptability pertain to both design and operation. Numerous relationships exist among these characteristics, for example, simplicity will affect economy and possibly reliability. Moreover, management must reach a compromise between economy and reliability—a balance that optimizes either short- or long-run objectives.

Simplicity

An effective system does not need to be complex. On the contrary, simplicity in design is an extremely desirable quality. Consider the task of communicating information about the operation of a system and allocation of its inputs. The task is not difficult when components are few and relationships among them are straightforward. The problems of communication, however, multiply with each successive stage of complexity.

The proper method for maintaining simplicity is to use precise definition, that is, to outline the specific task for each subsystem. Total systems often become complex because of the sheer size and nature of operations, but effectiveness and efficiency can still be achieved if each subsystem maintains its simplicity.

Flexibility

Conditions change and managers should be prepared to adjust operations accordingly. There are two ways to adjust to a changing operating environment: design new systems, or modify operating systems. An existing system should not be modified to accommodate a change in objectives, but every system should be sufficiently flexible to integrate changes which may occur in environmental conditions and/or the basic nature of the inputs. For example, a company should not use the same system to build missiles as the one designed to build airplanes, or the same system to sell insurance as the one designed originally to sell magazines. However, it should be possible to modify an existing system to produce different sizes, varieties, or types of the same product or service.

The system must be well designed, but, to be practical, it cannot be entirely rigid. There will always be minor variations from the general plan and a system should be able to adapt to such changes without breaking down. The advantages associated with having a flexible system become more apparent when the difficulty of administering change is considered.

Reliability

System reliability is becoming an important factor in organizations. Reliability is the consistency with which operations are maintained, and may vary from zero output (a complete breakdown or work stoppage) to a constant or predictable output.[1] The typical system operates somewhere between these two limits. The characteristics of reliability can be designed into the system by a careful selection and arrangement of the operating components; the system is no more reliable than its weakest segment. Where the requirements for a particular component, such as an operator with unique skills, are critical, it may be worthwhile to maintain a standby operator. In all situations, provisions should be made for quick repair or replacement when failure occurs. One valid approach in the reliability-maintenance relationship is to use modular construction to permit repair by substitution of complete modules. Reliability is not as critical when prompt repair and recovery can be instituted.

Economy

An effective system may be neither economical nor efficient. For example, the postal service may keep on schedule with mail deliveries, but only by hiring a large number of additional workers. In this case, the efficiency of the postal system would be reduced. In another example, inventories may be controlled by using a comprehensive system of storekeeping. However, if the cost of the storekeeping were more than the potential saving from this degree of control, the system would not be economical or efficient. It is often dysfunctional and expensive to develop one segment of a system with much greater capacity than some other part. Building in great redundancy or providing for every contingency usually neutralizes the operating efficiency of the system. Where the objectives of the system include the achievement of a particular task at the lowest possible cost, there must be some trade off between effectiveness and efficiency. When the objective of a system is to perform a certain mission regardless of cost, there will be no trade off.

Acceptability

Any system, no matter how well designed, will not function properly unless it is accepted by the people who operate it. If they do not believe it will benefit them, are opposed to it, are pressured into using it, or think it is not a good system, it will not work properly. Two things can happen: the system will be modified gradually by the people who are using it, or the system will be used ineffectively and ultimately fail. Unplanned alterations of an elaborate system can easily destroy any advantages associated with the system.

[1] Reliability may be defined as the mathematical probability of system survival or non-failure for stated environmental conditions and time periods.

Many system designers encourage the people who will operate the system to assist in its creation, knowing that they then are more apt to accept the design.

Design Techniques

Once the objectives of a subsystem have been carefully defined in proper relationship to the total system, various techniques of analysis are employed in design. One of the most popular techniques is network analysis. Other useful techniques include space and layout analysis; work simplification; analysis of records, forms, and report requirements; methods and procedure analysis; organizational studies; and analysis of communications or information flow.

Network Analysis

Network analysis is a useful tool in systems design because it assists the analyst in recognizing and identifying the relationships which exist among the subsystems. First, each separate segment, or link, of the system is described with respect to other components of activities in the system. This description of each segment clearly defines the total system and the interrelationships among the parts. The network is illustrated by a flow chart or diagram. The flow of materials and/or information is measured in terms of volume, specifications, or time. The visual representation of the system achieves a comprehensive description and therefore outlines the task to be accomplished. This technique allows the manager to reappraise the existing system and identify examples of duplication and overlapping which may detract from the efficiency of the systems' operation. Further, it helps management to evaluate the subsystems and their interconnecting networks continuously, consistent with the overall objectives of the system.

Continuous re-evaluation of the system is necessary and feasible through network analysis. The purpose of a system changes; different outputs are specified, and different inputs are required. It is important that subsystems are adjusted to these changes and that the total system is revised accordingly. Network analysis fosters this type of approach by representing the entire system visually. It also allows an evaluation of the impact of various subsystem changes on other subsystems and/or the total system. A change in the type of output or a change in scheduling in a particular subsystem can affect operations in other areas. The effect can be determined in units of time, money, facilities, or other resources.

Network analysis is a valuable technique because it encourages introspection of an existing system, or provides the framework for visualizing the make-up of a proposed system. Predesign auditing may identify variations in performance which could occur. However, network analysis provides no guarantee of effective systems design. There is always the danger of assuming relationships among segments which do not exist, ignoring important relationships which should be considered, or weighing existing relationships improperly. Moreover, a system is dynamic, and every analysis needs to be followed up as the system continues to function, for the relationships among the segments will change with time.

An important element in several techniques of design is flow charting. The use of symbols and directional arrows allows the designer to create a graphic representation of the proposed system. Flow charting may become as elaborate as deemed necessary. Starting with simple skeletal charts that describe the flow of material or information, these general symbols may be exploded or expanded to include many variations, and the actual operations to be performed may be written or coded in various blocks. In this way, a comprehensive description is obtained of the entire transformation process for either material or information flow. The flow charts often include photographs or models of documents, material, or equipment in order to portray the proposed system for analysis and review. Some of the early examples of flow charting were task (method analysis) or procedure (office information flows) oriented. More recently, flow charting has been used to describe the total system with less emphasis on details.

During World War II, a group of war prisoners decided that they would try to escape from the prison camp. To make their escape, they had to get outside of the barbed wire compound undetected, and also travel more than fifty kilometers to get back to friendly territory. Moreover, it was rumoured that the prisoners would be transferred to another camp in about three months, therefore, time was an important factor. The prisoners decided to dig a tunnel. But first they decided to outline everything that had to be done, and to determine the time that each activity would take.

Many of the activities were dependent upon the successful completion of some other activity. For example, before anything else could be done, they had to organize a spy system to keep prisoners informed about the whereabouts of the guards. A summary of the activities and the time each was estimated to take are:

1–2. Organize alarm system—25 days.

2–3. Secure material to make tools—5 days.

2–6. Secure materials for reinforcing tunnel—5 days.

2–7. Engineer tunnel—7 days.

2–4. Secure materials for civilian clothing—5 days.

2–5. Secure camera—10 days.

3–6. Manufacture tools for digging—8 days.

4–9. Manufacture civilian clothing—20 days.

5–8. Take pictures of participants—2 days.

6–10. Dig tunnel—60 days.

7–9. Prepare area map for participants—6 days.

8–9. Forge passports for participants—7 days.

9–10. Rehearse escape procedure—4 days.

Figure 6.3, a network diagram, represents all the activities and the time

Figure 6.3 A Network of the Escape Plan

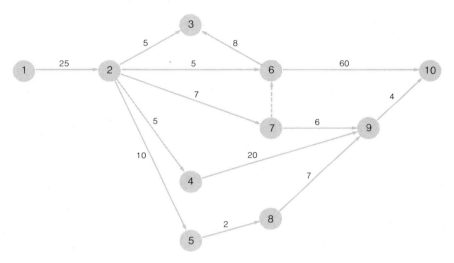

required to complete each. It would take 90 days, the longest time, to complete the sequence of activities 1–2–7–6–10 outlined in the escape plan. The prisoners would concentrate on these activities to shorten the required time.

One of the best known and widely used forms of network analysis is program evaluation and review technique (PERT). This technique will be described in some detail rather than critical path scheduling (CPS) or critical path method (CPM) only because it has been used so often by manufacturers in the aerospace industry, and because it is somewhat more involved than the others. In some of the recent applications of PERT, only one estimate of the predicted time is determined, which makes the difference between PERT and the other network techniques rather insignificant.

Program Evaluation and Review Technique (PERT). To overcome the inherent disadvantages of existing management planning and control techniques, the Special Project Office of the Navy, charged with the responsibility for system management of the Polaris design and production program, developed, in conjunction with the management consultant firm of Booz, Allen, and Hamilton and the Lockheed Aircraft Corporation, a new management planning and control tool. The tool was designed to determine and integrate all activity required to accomplish program objectives on time.

PERT is a technique of network analysis that presents a model of the activities which are necessary to complete a particular program. The representation of activities is made in terms of proper sequencing and with time estimates for each activity, allowing a range of estimates to accommodate the uncertainties associated with any forecast of achievement. The technique provides a representation for management concerning the manner in which subsystems should be structured to accomplish the stated objectives within specific deadlines. The PERT technique is based on the concept that in any program there are three significant variables: *time, resources* (personnel, facilities, funds), and *performance specifications.* Any one of these variables may vary within certain limits established for each program, while holding the other two constant. For example, holding time and performance constant, the requirements for resources may be determined. In its specific application to the Polaris program, the system held resources and performance specifications fixed while allowing the most critical element—time—to vary. However, time has a habit of becoming critical (reaching the maximum allowed by the customer), and when this occurs trades between resources and performance specifications are made.

Returning to our example, the sequencing of the activities for the escape is illustrated by the network in Figure 6.3 which shows the total task as a summation of each part, all in relation to each other. If the prisoners had prepared such a model, they would have been able to judge the feasibility of their plan in relation to the time constraint, and known where to concentrate any additional effort that might be needed. Each event is numbered for the purpose of identification. Thus Activity 1–2 (organizing the alarm system) is the activity which takes place between events numbered 1 and 2. Activity 8–9 (forging the passports) can start only after the pictures of the participants have been taken (Activity 5–8).

The length of the arrow (the activity) does not represent the time it takes to complete the activity or to get from one event to the next. However, it does represent the logical sequence of activities and events. The network also illustrates that activities which are not in the same path as other activities may be worked simultaneously. For example, the prisoners could be engaged in working Activities 2–3, 2–6, 2–7, 2–4, and 2–5 all at the same time. Event 9 indicates the completion of Events 7–9, 4–9, and 8–9, and the starting point of the final activity, that is, rehearsal of the escape procedure.

A Dummy Constraint is represented by a dashed arrow in the network and shows a relationship that does not require a time-consuming activity. The principal use of this symbol occurs when two separate activities both begin and end with the same event. The dummy constraint makes it possible to distinguish between such activities. In Figure 6.3, Activities 2–6 and 2–7 must both be completed before Activity 6–10 can start. It was necessary to secure materials to reinforce the tunnel and also to engineer the design before the actual construction could begin. In the chart a dummy event is added (7), and the relationship between Events 6 and 7 requires zero time. The difference, and also the relationship between the two activities can in this way be identified and computed.

Once the flow network has been outlined for the system, the next step is to obtain an estimate of the elapsed time required to accomplish each activity. In PERT this time forecast consists of three individual estimates: the "optimistic" estimate (a), the "pessimistic" estimate (b), and the "most likely" estimate (m).

The "optimistic" estimate assumes that everything will work out favorably, and if this occurs, the activity will require the least amount of time. The "pessimistic" estimate infers just the opposite, and every unfavorable contingency is considered in estimating the time the activity will take under such circumstances. The "most likely" estimate is the time that the experienced forecaster would predict in most instances. The difference in these time estimates provides a measure of the relative uncertainty involved in accomplishing the activity in question, as shown in Figure 6.4.[2] From

Figure 6.4 Estimating the Time Distribution

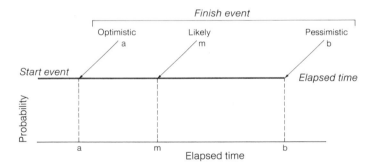

these estimates, the expected time (t_e) for each activity is computed by applying linear approximations to the data distribution developed for this purpose (Figure 6.5). The expected time is the average, or mean, time for the activity and may or may not be the most probable time (the estimator's most likely forecast). This discrepancy arises when the differences between the most likely estimate, the optimistic estimate, and the pessimistic estimate are not equal, thus tending to some degree to discredit the probability of the most likely estimate. The estimates (as well as the definitions of the events and activities) are outputs of the PERT planning technique, which

[2] Figures 6.4 to 6.7 are derived from *Production and Analysis Control Technique,* Special Project Office, Program Evaluation Branch, Department of the Navy, Washington, D.C., 8 February 1961.

Figure 6.5 Determining "Expected" Value and Variance of Time Intervals

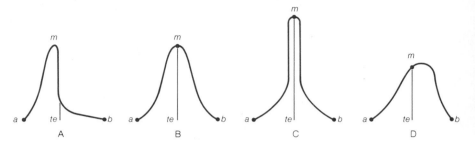

Problem: Given three estimates of elapsed time, find t_e, the expected value (mean) and σ_{te}^2 (variance) of distribution when distribution form varies as shown above

a—Optimistic estimate of interval
m—Most likely time of interval   } Obtained for each interval
b—Pessimistic estimate of interval

Solution: An estimating equation was developed which gives estimate of mean and variance for range of distributions to be encountered

$$t_e = \left[\frac{a + 4m + b}{6}\right]$$

Apply to each interval

$$\sigma_{te}^2 = \left(\frac{b - a}{6}\right)^2$$

have been based on a stipulated input of resources for the processing system. The estimate may change, however, if there is a change in resource allocation and/or a change in the task or product specifications.

The flow network, with its coded events, can be programmed for computer application. The computer solves the mathematical problems (calculation of each t_e) and, by adding the calculated expected times for each activity, computes the expected time for each event (E), as illustrated by Figure 6.6. Next, the computer identifies those events which determine the longest sequence to meet the end objective—the critical path. (The sum of t_e's on the critical path equals E_x.) Those events not on the critical path must therefore have some slack or spare time. Slack is computed by determining the latest time (E_L) that an event can take place without effecting the events on the critical path ($E_x - t_e$), and then subtracting that from an event (E) not on the critical path ($E_L - E = $ slack). Figure 6.7 illustrates this relationship graphically. Resources can be reallocated from the areas having slack to those areas on the critical path.

One of the most useful outputs of this system for management concerns the possibility of meeting critical schedule dates. These schedule dates, determined or stipulated by the customer, usually represent contractual commitments and will, at times, necessitate "trades" between resources and performance specifications as we described earlier.

Figure 6.6   Determination of Expected Time

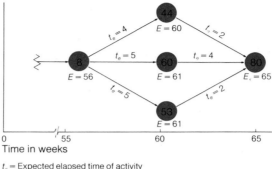

t_e = Expected elapsed time of activity
E = Expected absolute time of event

Note: "8" is the number of the first event illustrated just as 44 designates another event, and so forth. These numbers have no significance in the computation.

Figure 6.7   Determination of Slack

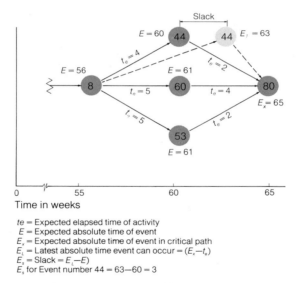

te = Expected elapsed time of activity
E = Expected absolute time of event
E_x = Expected absolute time of event in critical path
E_L = Latest absolute time event can occur = $(E_x - t_e)$
E_s = Slack = $E_L - E$)
E_s for Event number 44 = 63–60 = 3

PERT/Cost. PERT/Cost is a more recent development of the original PERT concept and includes the cost variable as well as time. When resources can be transferred from paths where there is slack to the critical path without adding cost, the decision is relatively simple. Unfortunately, additional costs usually are incurred by adding or redirecting resources to reduce time requirements.

The first step in this analysis is to determine costs. Presently there are four approaches to developing the cost estimates: (1) a single cost estimate of expected actual cost, (2) three cost estimates combined by a formula into expected cost, (3) optimum time-cost curves, and (4) three separate cost estimates.

The first method of estimating cost is to make the best estimate of actual costs by a summation of the elements of manpower, material, and other resources necessary to complete the task. Indirect costs then are apportioned to this activity to complete the total cost package.

The second method combines three cost estimates in a manner similar to the three time estimates made in PERT/Time. This adds the element of probability, and, assuming that three reasonable predictions can be made, improves the possibility of forecasting the expected cost.

The third approach is the optimum time-cost curve concept. The theory is that a relationship exists between time and costs for any activity, and that this relationship can be expressed as a continuous curve. The curve illustrates the relationship of time-cost tradeoffs that may be made. A variation of this method has been to use only two time-cost relationships, that is, for two conditions, normal or crash time. The analyst determines the cost to complete the task in the minimum possible time (crash) in comparison to the cost for normal time. Figure 6.8 illustrates this relationship.

Figure 6.8   Time-Cost Relationship

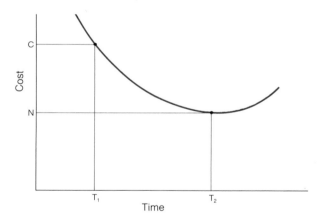

Under a crash program (T_1) the cost of the activity would be (C), whereas when the normal time (T_2) was taken the cost of the activity would be less (N). Management would have to decide whether or not the additional cost could be justified.

The fourth approach provides three possible time-cost-risk combinations from a range of alternatives. The three combinations are called the "most efficient," "direct date," and "shortest time" plans, and are rated respectively as low, medium, and high-risk alternatives for accomplishing the project. Managers can evaluate the effect of the three time, and risk factors for the particular project in question.

Human Factors in Systems Design

The systematic conception of the application of psychological principles to the invention, design, development, and use of complex man-machine systems is a growing field of study. Melton terms this field a theory of psychotechnology of man-machine systems and suggests that "it achieves integration of what has heretofore been variously called 'human engineering,' 'human factors engineering,' or 'engineering psychology' on the one hand and 'personnel psychology,' or 'personnel and training research' on the other hand. This union comes easily and naturally once the concept of *system* is examined and once the full implications of the concept of the human being as a *component* of a man-machine system are recognized.[3]

Research on integrating human factors directly into complex systems was stimulated by development of the weapon-system concept in the Air Force which brought together teams of scientists to deal with the problems of systems and their human and equipment components. This research has significance for many man-machine system developments.

Planning for human components of a system must be carefully integrated with planning for machine developments. The first stage is to determine the purposes or "missions" of the system and to develop an advanced operational design. From these, together with inputs about the current state of technological knowledge, are derived decisions about the major parts of the total system and the way in which they can be connected to fulfill the system's mission. This leads to the assignment of functions to men and machines. Gagné suggests the diagram shown in Figure 6.9 as a model to use in man-machines system development.

Psychotechnology has important implications. The basic assumption is that man should be considered as one of the major components of a total system rather than merely a user of the system once it is developed. It denies that systems development is purely an engineering problem—psychological and social factors must be considered. "Any reasonably complex system requires a true interaction between man and the other parts of the system, which may be machines, other men, or combinations of these. Some way must therefore be found for thinking about the functions of machines and the functions of men within a framework which makes possible the relations of these two kinds of functions to common goals—that is, to system goals."[4] In spite of the pioneering work pointed to by Gagné, there is a great deal to be done in the integration of man and equipment into large systems. Yet, the past efforts do point a new direction for psychologists and other behavioral scientists.

---

[3] Arthur W. Melton, in Robert M. Gagné (ed.), *Psychological Principles in System Development* (New York: Holt, Rinehart and Winston, Inc. ,1962), p. v.

[4] Robert M. Gagné, "Human Functions in Systems," ibid., p. 35.

Figure 6.9 Man-Machine System Development

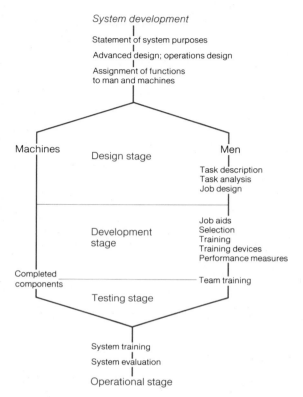

System development
|
Statement of system purposes
|
Advanced design; operations design
|
Assignment of functions
to man and machines

Machines   Men

Design stage

Task description
Task analysis
Job design

Development
stage

Job aids
Selection
Training
Training devices
Performance measures

Completed
components   Team training

Testing stage

System training
|
System evaluation
|
Operational stage

Source: Robert M. Gagné (ed.), *Psychological Principles in System Development* (New York: Holt, Rinehart and Winston, Inc., 1962), p. 4.

**New
Managerial
View**

The systems concept suggests a new role for management. In the traditional view, the manager operated in a highly structured, rigid system with well-defined goals, clear-cut relationships, tight controls, and hierarchical information flows. In the flexible or open systems view, the organization is not static but is continually changing to meet both external and internal disturbances. The manager's role is one of developing a viable organization, meeting change, and helping participants establish a dynamic equilibrium. "The one enduring objective is the effort to build and maintain a predictable, reciprocating system of relationships, the behavioral patterns of which stay within reasonable physical limits. But this is seeking a moving equilibrium, since the parameters of the system (the division of labor and the controls) are evolving and changing. Thus, the manager endeavors to introduce regularity in a world that will never allow him to achieve the ideal."[5]

[5] Leonard R. Sayles, *Managerial Behavior* (New York: McGraw-Hill Book Company, 1964), pp. 258–259.

The systems concept does not provide a prescription for making a manager's difficult and complex job easier. Rather, it helps him to understand and operate more effectively in the reality of complex systems. It suggests that operations cannot be neatly departmentalized but must be viewed as overlapping subsystems. Leadership patterns must be modified, particularly when dealing with professionals and highly trained specialists, and motivation must be directed toward active, willing participation rather than forceful subjugation.

Systems design involves the establishment of project and facilitating subsystems to accomplish certain tasks or programs. Under this approach, the network of human interdependence required to accomplish a given task is based on shared responsibility of the participating members of the subsystem. In contrast, the traditional organization is geared to functional performance and the integrating force is authority. Instead of gearing participant activities to rule obedience and closely structured behavior, the systems concept provides a basis for active participation in meeting task requirements. The manager is looked upon as a resource person who can help the group meet its goals as well as a source of authority and control. Thus, systems theory provides the structure by which the concepts of motivation, leadership, and participation can be applied effectively within the organization.

Design and Control

Control is not an end in itself, but rather a means to an end—a way to add flexibility and effectiveness to the operation of a system. The design of control in subsystems should be consistent with the objectives of the larger network, preventive rather than punitive, and no more elaborate than necessary to accomplish the desired purpose. A single definition can be used to describe all kinds of control, including machine-machine, and man-to-man systems; it is only the type and not the nature of control that changes.

Definition of Control

Control is *that function of the system which provides direction in conformance with plan; the maintenance of variations between operations and stated objectives within allowable limits.*

Control is maintained through a network of information in motion which is the vital flow of intelligence that establishes the basis for controlling a system. The "sensitivity" of a control system pertains to the degree of variation from the norm that occurs before an adjusting response is invoked. "Stability" concerns the ability of a system to maintain a predictable behavior pattern over time. "Rapidity of response" refers to the speed with which variations from stated objectives can be corrected.

Elements of Control

Every control system has four basic elements. They always occur in the same sequence and maintain a close relationship to each other. The elements are :

1. a controlled characteristic or condition;
2. a sensory device or method for measuring the characteristic or condition;
3. a unit which compares measured data with a standard or plan; and
4. a unit which activates a change in input.

Figure 6.10 illustrates the relationships among the four elements of control.

Figure 6.10   The Elements of Control

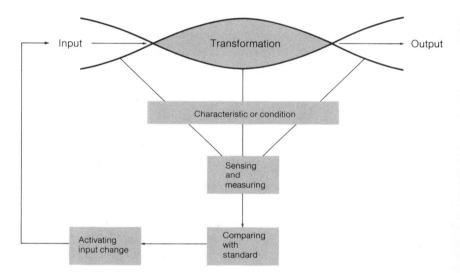

The first element, characteristic or condition, may simulate the system at any stage of the transformation process, or it may represent some segment of the input or output of the system, such as temperature, if the purpose of the system is to produce heat. It may also be a condition that, if it occurred, would be dysfunctional to the objectives of the system, such as shoplifting in a department store.

The sensor measures the characteristic(s) that is to be controlled. The thermometer is the sensor in a home heating system, whereas both clerks and detectives in a department store are the sensor to control theft.

The third element compares the measurement of operations and the established standard or plan. What is the difference, for example, between the temperature in the room and the desired setting? Or how do the costs compare with the estimates prepared in the budget? Some deviation from plan is usual and expected, but as significant deviations are recognized, information is released to adjust the operation of the system. Sometimes, it is possible to trace trends in performance and uncover problem areas before they become serious, which is indicative of effective control.

When there is a significant difference between performance and plan, the situation may be "out of control"—the system is ineffective, that is, the objectives are not being accomplished. If such a situation occurs, the objectives may have to be modified relative to the capability of the system, or the system may need to be redesigned. Suppose that a manufacturing plan schedules output of 1,000 units each month, but actual output is less than half of this figure. A goal of 1,000 units may not be possible even though employees work overtime. If the scheduled output is essential, the system must be redesigned to increase its output capacity. Positive feedback of this kind will cause systems to grow, a topic that will be discussed in more detail in Chapter 13.

The fourth element of control concerns the decisions that are made for changing input. The decision may be made automatically as variations exceed predetermined standards (for example, in a heating system), or it may be a decision made by a manager after a review of the information (for example, in a cost control system). The actual device or method used to release corrective inputs into operating systems occurs in many forms. The unit may be a hydraulic controller positioned by a solenoid or electric motor in response to an electronic error signal, or it may be an employee directed to rework defective parts.

Each control system encompasses the four elements: the controlled characteristic, a measurement, the comparison, and the effector of action—all interlinked by information flow.

Features of Control

Two features of control have significance for many systems. First, unlimited quantities of input may be controlled by a switch valve, or some other device. A small amount of energy can control jet airplanes, automatic steel mills, and hydroelectric power plants. The pilot turns a switch, and the landing gear of the airplane goes up or down; the steel-mill operator pushes a button, and a ribbon of white hot steel races through the plant; or a worker at a power station directs the flow of electrical energy throughout a regional network of substations. It takes but a small amount of control energy to release large amounts of input into the system (information, material, and energy), or to adjust transformation activity. It should be noted that the smaller the control energy expended, the more efficient the system will be.

Second, some of the control elements may be located far from the operating system. Measurement information may be transmitted to a distant point (the control unit) for comparison with a standard, and when deviations occur, the correcting input may be energized from a remote site. However, the input (activating unit), and usually the sensor,[6] will be lo-

---

[6] Remote measuring devices like radar are fundamental to some control systems.

cated in close proximity to the operating system. This means that planes can be flown by remote control: dangerous manufacturing processes can be operated from a safe distance; or a marketing system of a national organization can be directed from a centralized location.

Types of Control Systems

There are two kinds of control systems: open-loop and closed-loop. The difference between these two types of control concerns (1) whether or not all of the control elements are an integral part of the system being regulated, and (2) if allowable variations from a standard have been predetermined. In a closed-loop system, all elements are a part of the system and allowable variations have been predetermined.

A street-lighting system controlled by a timing device would be classified as an open-loop system. At a certain time each evening, the timing device closes the circuit and energy flows through the electric lines to light the lamps. It should be noted, however, that the timing device is an independent unit and is not measuring the operation of the lighting system. If on a dark, stormy day the lights should be needed, the timing device would not sense this variation and would not act on the need for energy input. In an open-loop system, the correct properties must either be built into the controller (for example, modify the time the lights are on as the days grow shorter or longer); or the sensing, comparison, and adjustment are made by action taken outside of the system. In the example given, one of the essential aspects of a closed-loop system, information flow, is missing.[7]

When control is exerted from within the system and as required to maintain the operation within prescribed limits, it is a closed-loop system. The home thermostat is the classic example of a control device in this category. When room temperature drops below the desired level, the control mechanism closes the circuit to start the furnace and the temperature rises. The furnace operating circuit is turned off as the temperature reaches the selected level.

The elements of control in an open-loop may not all be a part of the operating system, and may not be connected by predetermined information flow and standards. In contrast, the closed-loop control has all of the elements integrated into the operating system by the feedback of an information loop.

An essential part of a closed-loop system is feedback; that is, the output of the system is measured continually in terms of the control characteristic and the input or transformation plan is modified to reduce any divergence or error. Feedback control operates in a system expected to make errors, be-

---

[7] Some may argue that all control systems are closed-loop, otherwise there is no control; or that control occurs only when all elements needed to close the loop are present.

cause the system depends upon the error to bring about correction. The objective of such a system is to make the error as small as possible within practical limits.

Feedback control determines the extent of automation. For example, when a system is designed as an open-loop system, human intervention usually is required to keep the system "in control," whereas a closed-loop system is capable of keeping the system "on course" without human intervention. Feedback control, therefore, has added a new dimension to the capabilities of machines—the ability to simulate and replace the human nervous system.

In most situations, sensory inputs are relayed from many sources to a central location. Some of this feedback will be quantified, but in less-structured systems much will be subjective, involving both impressions and prejudices about the status of the system. Adjustments may be achieved through direct action or through informal pressure. For example, managers often rely on group interaction to motivate workers to increase output, reduce costs, and improve quality.

At one extreme, we have the black box (or the individual) that senses, compares, and corrects deviations at the site; while, at the other extreme, all control is centralized. This requires that feedback information from remote stations and corrective action be transmitted to the operation when action is warranted. Control may be decentralized effectively in human systems to the extent that the objectives of the remote elements of the system agree with those of the total organization, in other words, individuals have internalized the goals and objectives of the system.

Many of the patterns of information flow in organizations are found to have the nature of closed loops. The reason for such a condition is apparent when one recognizes that any system, if it is to achieve a predetermined goal, must have available to it at all times an indication of its performance or degree of attainment. In general, every goal-seeking system employs circuits, or feedback.

The principle of goal seeking as it relates to feedback and control has been used by Stafford Beer in his development of cybernetic control models. He has demonstrated the feasibility, using statistical feedback of current data, of generating predictive models which relate very closely with the real world.[8] Control models of this type are discussed in Chapter 9.

Problems of Control

Control is an important and necessary part of most biological, economic, behavioral, social, and mechanical systems. Nevertheless, the design and effective operation of control is not without problems.

[8] Stafford Beer, *Decision and Control* (New York: John Wiley and Sons, Inc., 1966), pp. 317–338.

A difficulty sometimes occurs in identifying the proper characteristic to control. Selecting the best characteristic often is a trade off between the one which most closely relates to the objectives of the system and the characteristic which can be identified and measured accurately. The effectiveness and efficiency of control, therefore, depends on the establishment of proper scales of measurement.

Subjective Measurement. The measure of system effectiveness, when the objectives are not described as quantitative output, is difficult to determine and subsequently perplexing to evaluate. Unfortunately, many of the characteristics pertaining to output do not lend themselves to quantitative measurement. This is true particularly when inputs of human energy result in unrelated units of output. The same situation applies to machines and/or other equipment associated with human involvement when output is not discrete. In evaluating man-machine or man-oriented systems, the difficulty of measuring the psychological and sociological factors becomes evident.

Human behavior interacting with other human behavior creates problems of measurement and evaluations that are difficult if not impossible to solve. Even when the units of measurement can be determined, and their magnitude gauged as a *unit of various stimuli,* the problem still remains to develop an agreeable *norm* against which individual variations can be evaluated. How do you measure and evaluate the effectiveness of a system in providing customer satisfaction? What unit of measurement can be used? How accurate will this measurement be? What standard of acceptable service does the customer have? These are questions which must be answered before an adequate system of measurement and evaluation can be designed.

Subjective readings may be transferred into numerical data, but there is always a danger that an incorrect rating and transfer may be made, and that the analyst may assume undue confidence in such data just because it has been quantified. Let us suppose, for example, that the decisions made by an executive are rated from one to ten, ten being the perfect decision. After determining the ranking for each decision, adding these, and dividing by the total number of decisions made, the average ranking would indicate the score of a particular executive in his decision-making role. On the basis of this score, judgments may be made about an executive's decision-making effectiveness which could be wrong.

Although some progress has been made in quantifying human behavior, most measures are still extremely subjective and lack the precise qualities of physical measurement.

Information Flows. A serious problem occurs when incorrect information is introduced into a feedback channel. This can occur in both computerized and human control systems, and may be caused by erroneous data collection, processing, or transmission, or through mistakes in judgment. Inadequate or improper feedback flows may cause a regeneration of output, leading to an oscillatory effect, for example, if a microphone in a public address system is placed too near the speakers. Errors in an algorithmic system are either mistakes in measurement or in quantifying input correctly, whereas most mistakes in a heuristic system are errors introduced through improper interpretation of the data.

Time or rapidity of response is a problem in the control of systems. The more rapid the response of the system to an error signal, the more likely it is that the system will overadjust. Yet, the need for prompt action is important because any delay in providing corrective input can be crucial. A system generating feedback inconsistent with current needs will maintain a continuous oscillation when disturbed if (1) the time delay in response to some frequency adds up to half a period of oscillation, and (2) the feedback effect is sufficiently large at this frequency to warrant adjustment. The most critical problem arises when the delay is exactly one-half a cycle, for then the corrective action is superimposed upon a deviation which, at the moment, is in the same direction as that of correction. This oscillatory behavior causes the system to overcorrect, then to correct too much in the other direction, and so on, until the oscillations become very pronounced (see Figure 6.11). One solution to this problem rests on *anticipation,* which involves measurement not only of the change, but of the rate of change as

Figure 6.11   Oscillation and Feedback

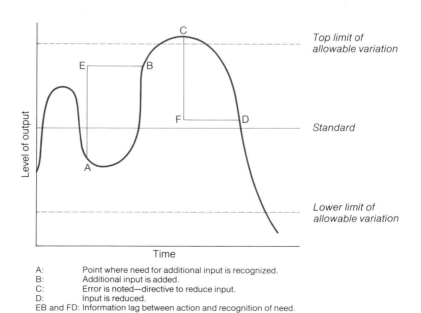

A: Point where need for additional input is recognized.
B: Additional input is added.
C: Error is noted—directive to reduce input.
D: Input is reduced.
EB and FD: Information lag between action and recognition of need.

well. The correction is directed as a factor of the type and the rate of the error. The difficulty also may be overcome by reducing the time lag between the measurement of the output and the correction of the input. Better still, a time lead can be introduced to compensate for the time lag, bringing about consistency between the need for correction and type and magnitude of the initiated correction. It usually is more effective for an organization to maintain continuous measurement of its performance, and to make small adjustments in operations constantly (high sensitivity). Information feedback, therefore, must be timely and correct to be effective, that is, the information must provide an accurate indication of the status of the activity.

Standards. Setting the right standards or control limits is a problem in many systems. Parents are confronted with this difficulty in outlining what is expected of their children, and managers face the same issue in establishing standards that are acceptable to workers. Some authorities suggest that workers should determine their own work standards on the assumption that the workers would be more apt to correct deficiencies in performance if they had taken part in planning acceptable levels of output.

Perhaps the most difficult problem in human systems is the unresponsiveness of individuals to indicated correction. This may take the form of opposition and subversion to control, or it may pertain to the lack of defined responsibility for taking action. Leadership and motivation, therefore, are significant factors in the control of human systems.

Standards should be as precise as possible and communicated to all persons concerned. Moreover, communication alone is not sufficient; understanding is necessary. Unfortunately, in many systems, standards tend to be vague; an allowable range or tolerance is difficult to determine in most systems involving human behavior. An element of discretion should be allowed managers of such systems in their determination of whether or not action is required.

In summary, most control problems relate to design and, therefore, the solution to such problems must start with design. Control subsystems, like operating systems, are subject to occasional breakdown. Some have attempted to solve this problem by designing simplicity into the system, adding redundant components, and building systems with capacity greater than necessary. Eventually, control systems may be designed which repair themselves.

Review and Evaluation of Systems

Most organisms tend to seek a state of homeostasis or a degree of stability. This trait is common among mankind because societies function within established norms. However, some men are continually looking for a "better way" and thereby changing the status quo.

The idea of progress is symbolized by the introduction of new processes, new ways to organize, as well as innovations of knowledge and product ideas. The rate at which such change occurs depends, in large part, on the difference between the countervailing forces of inertia and initiative. The same assertion applies to the management of systems for, unless there is a constant review of operations within the construct of sound analysis, any system, once designed, will tend to continue operating with a minimum of modification.

Few, if any, systems operate at optimum effectiveness or efficiency. Perhaps problems exist which relate to layout or arrangement; innovations in equipment may be added to improve operating efficiency; and sometimes more appropriate techniques of analysis can be applied to optimize resource inputs. The adjustment and improvement of operating systems, therefore, are necessary and continual processes.

Every system should be reviewed in relation to its objectives, and if the basic objectives change, the system as designed should be phased out of operation. When a project has been completed, a summary evaluation of performance provides useful information for designing better systems for future projects. The point should be emphasized, however, that change merely for the sake of change is foolish and wasteful and such a philosophy is not suggested in this text.

A discussion about the distinction between *control* and *evaluation* is appropriate at this time for, unfortunately, the two terms have been used interchangeably. We defined control as relating to the *operation* of systems, including those elements of measurement, comparison, and reallocation of resources necessary to maintain the system within prescribed operating limits. In contrast, evaluation is the analysis performed to determine how well the system has functioned, or if it has broken down, to determine why. The recommendations resulting from evaluation analysis most likely include changes in systems *design*. To illustrate the difference, we operate and *control* a machine (control pertaining to the regulation of material inputs, speed of operation, and so forth) relative to some predetermined standard; whereas we *evaluate* the performance of the machine to see how effective and efficient the design proved to be, or why it failed. In both instances a standard of comparison is necessary; control requires an operating plan or standard, whereas evaluation is conducted in comparison to the objectives of the system. Control decisions tend to adjust input, but evaluation decisions tend to adjust the kind or the arrangement of components in the system, or to change operating procedure.

A Program of Review and Evaluation

The program of review and evaluation may be organized in different ways but should always be logical and systematic. The approach selected will depend on the reason for the evaluation. Is the system being evaluated because it is not effective (accomplishing its objectives)? Is the system failing to achieve an expected standard of efficiency? Is the evaluation being conducted because of a breakdown or failure within operation? Or is it merely a periodic audit and review process?

Let us assume that the reason for the review is to determine if system objectives are being met. In this instance the review and evaluation may be organized in the following sequence:

1. Determine the objectives of the system, or the mission the system is designed to achieve.
2. Translate the objectives by describing in some detail those specifics which are to be accomplished.
3. Identify those key characteristics which bear a close relationship to goal achievement.
4. Choose the appropriate measuring techniques.
5. Gather and sort performance information.
6. Analyze the information that is collected.
7. Compare the analyzed information with the selected characteristics to determine the extent to which objectives have been achieved.
8. Proceed to the design phase if the need for redesign is indicated by the study.

We have stressed the need to declare clear-cut objectives for a system in many parts of this book. When the precise purposes for which the system exists are not understood, it is difficult, if not impossible, to establish criteria for evaluation or to select significant characteristics for analysis. Business institutions increasingly tend to highlight certain objectives which are not related directly to the profit motive, although decisions and actions still tend to be evaluated on the basis of the profit ethic (that is, the idea that the alternative which will maximize profits is selected). In contrast, public institutions may have objectives concerning specific kinds and levels of service to be performed in comparison to specific cost constraints, for example, police protection related to a budget (cost-benefit).

Within the general statement of objectives, the broad policies which are to be stressed in achieving the overall purposes of the system should be described. Such policies as the quality and reliability of the product, the level and nature of customer service, the kinds of social service performed in the community, and the stability and nature of the employment opportunity to be provided are examples of significant policies of business organizations.

Major goals for a distribution system may be to sell a specified family of products and, of course, to make a profit. Policies which are significant in achieving these goals could include the selection of a specific clientele to serve, or a liberal credit policy along with complete freedom to return merchandise. In this instance the credit and return policies become the strategy by which the organization plans to achieve its objectives.

Selection of Key Characteristics

Characteristics of operations are selected which provide specific evidence about the performance of the system. It is important to select characteristics that correlate closely with major policy achievement, but also to select those that can be isolated and measured in a practical way. There is an inherent danger that characteristics which lend themselves to measurement in algorithmic units may be selected, even when their association to systems performance is insignificant. For example, would the number of traffic citations made by a police department indicate whether or not the community was receiving adequate police protection at a reasonable cost?

Note that only in rare instances is it possible to plot the performance of a system by measuring a single characteristic, or even two or three. It usually is necessary to select many characteristics, all of which have relationships with each other and to total performance.

The nature and quality of service that a distribution system is providing can be measured, in part, by the characteristic of on-time deliveries. The number of orders which were available to the customer as scheduled would be a significant characteristic. This would not in itself be sufficient evidence to determine whether or not the system was fulfilling its objectives, however. The goods delivered may not meet specifications, may be of inferior quality, or may be made in a manner which increased cost unreasonably.

The same difficulties of measurement which pertain to control also apply to evaluation. In addition, some identical characteristics are measured in both the control of operations and the review and evaluation of systems design.

A system may be performing effectively but using an unreasonable amount of resources in the process. An evaluation of system efficiency would be appropriate whenever an inordinate amount of inputs are being allocated in order to accomplish the desired mission. Of course, how much input should be used, or what ratio should exist between input and output, is a difficult question to answer. The goal is to optimize this ratio or to achieve the maximum output with the minimum input.

In reviewing the efficiency of a system, an approach similar to that outlined for evaluating effectiveness may be followed. The standard of expected performance can be established by internal and/or external bench marks. For example, historical ratios serve as a guide to measure present performance, and industry figures provide some indication of the efficiency of the system's operation relative to competition.

When a system has failed or is in great difficulty, a different approach may be appropriate. Special diagnostic techniques are used to isolate the trouble area(s) and to identify the cause(s) of the difficulty.

Areas and Techniques of Analysis

In all programs of evaluation, the gathering of data for analysis and the choice of the proper measuring techniques are stages of the review procedures which go hand in hand. Knowledge of which techniques are to be used will influence the form in which the data are gathered, and the nature of the data will influence the kind of techniques that will serve the review and evaluation program best. The number of approaches, procedures, and analytical techniques are almost infinite.

Figure 6.12 and Table 6.1 summarize the areas in which the study may be organized, and the kind of analysis to be conducted. Figure 6.12 illustrates the areas of study within the context of the systems model. The clas-

Figure 6.12 Areas of Analysis

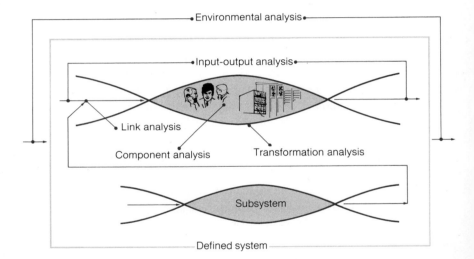

sification of review and evaluation by area is consistent with using an analytical approach for identifying problems that may occur in operations, or with a general review and evaluation of system performance. From a background of environmental analysis, the input-output relationships are studied. Link analysis, transformation analysis, and component analysis follow in this order when unidentified problems occur.

Table 6.1 illustrates the relationship between studies of effectiveness and efficiency. To survive, a system must perform effectively and, in the long run, it must also utilize resource inputs efficiently to optimize output. To be reliable or consistent, trouble must be identified quickly and corrections made before the general effectiveness and efficiency of a system are impaired.

To return again to the importance of clear-cut objectives, we can state categorically that knowing the exact mission to be accomplished will be the

Table 6.1 Types of Analysis

Kind of Analysis	Characteristics Analyzed	Illustrative Techniques of Analysis
EFFECTIVENESS	Service Provided	Customer Satisfaction Analysis
	Quality of Product	Performance Analysis
	Delivery Schedule of Product	Late Delivery Analysis
EFFICIENCY	Cost Relationships	Cost/Budget Analysis
	Volume Produced	Input-output Analysis
TROUBLE or BREAKDOWN	Diagnostic	Central Testing
		Stress Analysis
		Module Substitution

initial "giant step" toward actual achievement. The evaluation process will show whether or not objectives are transferred properly into detailed action decisions, and whether these decisions are carried out effectively and efficiently.

Because it is *difficult to identify characteristics which correlate directly with systems' objectives,* and because it is *not easy to measure such characteristics precisely,* it is this stage of analyzing and interpreting measurements which becomes crucial to sound evaluation. The quantitative techniques that have been described in other parts of this book are particularly useful in the analysis only if the proper measurements have been made.

Physical measurements may be either direct or indirect. They are direct when the actual scale of measurement is used; for example, the length of a building is determined by a tape which depicts the actual length. They are indirect, however, when an analog of the characteristic is measured; for example, the speedometer in the car indicates the speed the car is traveling. The two examples also illustrate whether the measurement is of *first or second order.* The length of the building can be measured in feet and/or inches which is a basic measurement (first order), whereas the state of an automobile can be measured in miles per hour which is a measurement derived as a ratio (second order).

It is important to establish physical measurements which contain general characteristics. When this is the case, the measurements can be applied to different systems and, thereby, the results of different systems can be compared and evaluated. Similarly, the measurement function in evolutionary systems will remain valid and comparable over time. Even though a system of measurement is designed to measure a specific system, the desirability of *establishing universal or standardized units* is quite apparent.

Within the quantifiable data, we can determine physical measures of output in terms of dollar cost related to units of output. Naturally, we would like to find a unit of measure which would be consistent over time. We can measure the number of automobiles produced by a specific manufacturer, but the automobile produced today is by no means the same car as the one produced in 1930. Consequently, when characteristics of the output are changing, some other means of measurement must be devised. Even the dollar, which is the most common unit of measuring, is not an error-free unit since its purchasing power changes over time. This kind of inconsistency can lead to a serious problem of comparability.

Aside from the selection of the proper characteristics and their accurate measurement, other significant factors relate to evaluation. We have, for example, alluded to the importance of using terminology which has meaning common to managers (comparability), but there is also the relationship between recording and storing the operational information which will be useful in evaluation. A transformation process, for example, may be changed over time, but if the change is not recorded there is no way to evaluate the significance of the change relative to output. A welder may change his equipment; a clerk may use a new procedure for checking inventory; or, a nurse may elect to skip certain procedures which appear to be a waste of time. If these changes were not recorded, there is little chance to measure their value, and problems that might be caused by the changes are difficult to identify.

It is easier to evaluate a structured system than an unstructured one. In a structured system where the transformation process is fixed and described in a precise manner, any changes become experimental in nature and the consequences of changing the design or of varying inputs can be recorded. In contrast, an unstructured system is difficult, or perhaps impossible, to evaluate in a meaningful way. Things happen, but nobody really knows just why or whether incidental changes have a positive or negative impact on total system performance.

There is great value in following a structured format in the evaluation process itself. The systems analysis model, for example, structures the evaluation in relation to objectives, imposed constraints, and the selection criteria used in the system's design. Based on this model, a thorough and consistent evaluation can be made and, when warranted, meaningful changes instituted. Nothing is left to chance; all factors are considered; and the framework of analysis is consistent.

Summary

People are able to solve design problems by developing and using new and better ideas. Most of us fail to develop our potential creativity. The creative process occurs when people are properly motivated and concentrate their abilities toward a particular project or problem. Orderly arrangement and testing of information, along with a good bit of imagination, can improve results.

The design of microsystems begins with the determination of the mission or objective to be accomplished by segments of the total system. Next, the constraints which may limit the design alternatives are carefully outlined. Alternative proposals are described, analyzed, and revised relative to the criteria listed for selection. Finally, the best alternative is selected, tested, and introduced.

Designers wish to create systems that are simple, flexible, reliable, economic, and acceptable to the people who will operate them. In other words, systems which are no more complex than necessary; which are able to adjust to changing environmental influences; which tend to perform consistently in a dependable and predictable manner; and which maximize output relative to input. These characteristics of good design apply to any man-to-man, man-to-machine, or machine-to-machine system.

After the objectives have been translated and the constraints have been outlined, the analysis begins. Every technique and tool that can improve the decision process should be used whenever practical. Network analysis and flow charting are very useful at the design stage for outlining the scope of the mission and describing the task in detail. One technique, PERT, has been used extensively during the design stage, although it also is used for cost and schedule control.

In designing a system, the planning for human components must be carefully integrated with planning for machine development. Some way must be found to relate the functions of machines and men to goals common to both, and also to the system. This suggests a new and challenging role for management.

Control is a necessary part of most systems. It includes the measurement of output and/or of inprocess operations, a comparison of this measurement with a standard, and corrective measures to adjust variations to acceptable norms when necessary. The energy needed to direct new inputs into the system is small relative to the inputs released. Control can be conducted from adjacent or remote locations, although the sensor and activating devices usually are near the operating system.

A control system may be open-loop or closed-loop. The difference between these two types of control concerns (1) whether the control element is an integral part of the system it regulates; and (2) if allowable variations from a standard have been predetermined. When both of these conditions are present, it is a closed-loop system.

Typical problems associated wtih the control function relate to the difficulty of identifying the proper characteristics to control. A characteristic must be used that is easy to measure and still represents objective achievement, and that can be measured accurately. In addition, the control needs a feedback of information without delay. Other problems include the difficulty of setting proper standards, and the administration of proper correction or adjustment.

Control and evaluation are derived from the same base, but they are different. Control maintains operations within acceptable variations from the standard or norm, but evaluation pertains to a review of systems performance as it relates to possible redesign. The evaluation may occur as a periodic review, or it may be instituted when the system goes "out of control" in terms of the objectives (effectiveness), costs (efficiency), or because some segment of the system has failed. The reason for the review and evaluation will establish the approach and technique(s) to be used. In every instance, a logical and systematic methodology should be followed.

The difficulty of making a sound evaluation is closely related to the problems of measurement. When units of measurement are made in quantitative form, the question arises about their proper classification and correlation with performance criteria. When measurement is subjective, these same problems exist and, in addition, there is the problem of quantification of the information if it is to be manipulated in a problem-solving technique.

Selected References

Anderson, Harold H., ed. *Creativity and Its Cultivation.* New York: Harper and Row, 1959.

This book presents an overview of the nature of creativity and the creative process as identified by creative individuals, research findings, and other sources.

Anthony, Robert N. *Planning and Control Systems—A Framework for Analysis.* Boston: Graduate School of Business Administration, Harvard University, 1965.

This book offers a conceptual framework for planning and control. It draws upon research in these areas, although it does not report on the research results. It has application beyond the business organization.

Beer, Stafford. *Decision and Control.* New York: John Wiley and Sons, Inc., 1966.

The author presents a combination of decision theory and control theory, and provides a theoretical framework for these fields of study.

Cleland, David I., and King, William R. *Systems, Organizations, Analysis, Management: A Book of Readings.* New York: McGraw-Hill Book Company, 1969, pp. 193–280.

The readings in this book include three articles on systems analysis and several on various social, military, and government applications.

Hare, Van Court, Jr. *Systems Analysis: A Diagnostic Approach.* New York: Harcourt, Brace & World, Inc., 1967.

The author stresses the fundamental theory of analysis rather than the more typical procedural application.

Kast, Fremont E., and Rosenzweig, James E. *Organization and Management—A Systems Approach.* New York: McGraw-Hill Book Company, 1970.

The book outlines the managerial role in the design and operation of systems.

Levin, Richard I., and Kirkpatrick, Charles A. *Planning and Control with PERT/CPM.* New York: McGraw-Hill Book Company, 1966.

The authors give a comprehensive description of the technique, including a bibliography of books, pamphlets, and articles on the subject.

Optner, Stanford L. *Systems Analysis,* 2nd ed. Englewood Cliffs, N.J.: Prentice Hall, 1968.

This book outlines the steps in systems redesign with particular reference to the introduction of computers. A number of case examples are included in the last half of the book.

Schellenberger, Robert E. *Managerial Analysis.* Homewood, Ill.: Richard D. Irwin, Inc., 1968.

The text describes and explains the process, tools, models, and evaluation of managerial analysis. Chapters 1, 2, 4, 5, and 19 have special application to the materials covered in this chapter.

Questions

1 How does intelligence contribute to the creative process?

2 What can an organization do to stimulate creativity among its workers?

3 How does the technique labeled "the checklist" relate to the model of creativity (Figure 6.2)?

4 List some of the constraints that may be considered by the designers of a system that is to care for elderly people under the medicare program.

5 In general terms, outline the subsystems that serve the automobile industry.

6 How does the efficiency of operating a system relate to the reliability of operations?

7 What are the chief advantages of the PERT/time technique? The limitations?

8 How would the application of PERT/cost affect the use of PERT/time?

9 Outline the steps you would follow in a program of system design.

10 Should the design of a system be a staff function? Why or why not?

11 Suggest an example of a closed-loop system in which the sensing and activating units are not in close physical proximity of each other.

12 Give examples in which the problems of control relate to the sensing element; to the activation.

13 A program may be reviewed following the eight-step sequence outlined in this chapter. Present an alternative procedure of review.

14 In what sequence should the various areas of analysis be performed, assuming that a general evaluation is in order?

Exercises

1

```
.   .   .

.   .   .

.   .   .
```

With four straight lines (all connected) cover all nine dots.

2

```
+   +   +   +   +

+   +   +   +   +

+   +   +   +   +

+   +   +   +   +

+   +   +   +   +
```

Connect 12 crosses to form the outline of a large cross, leaving 5 crosses untouched on the inside, and 8 on the outside.

3

How many squares are in this chart?

4 There are twelve travel bags; all appear identical except that each bag has a distinct number, one through twelve. One bag is very different, however. It contains a bomb. If it is lighter than the rest, it contains the type of bomb that can be deactivated by placing the bag in water. If the bag is heavier, the type of bomb would explode if it contacted water. Using only a balance scale, devise a system for identifying the bag with the bomb in three weighings of the scale, and be sure to determine if the bag is heavier or lighter than the rest.

5 A mayor organized a research team to solve the traffic problems facing a certain city. Proposals had been made to add another freeway system, a rapid transit system, and an extensive system of bus transportation. Assuming that you are a member of the research team, determine:
a. the objectives of the system you propose;
b. the constraints that may be present including natural and man-made, political and economic;

c. the information needed to describe and analyze alternative system proposals;

d. the tools which would be appropriate for use in the various stages of description and analysis.

Use the "systems analysis model" outlined in Chapter 1 in preparing your answer.

6 A nationwide system may be needed to provide an educational opportunity for minority races to prepare some members for employment in government, public institutions, and business organizations on an equal basis with others. Illustrate your general plan and strategy in designing such a system.

7 Diagram and find the critical path for the following project:

Task	Time (days)	Sequence*
a–b	4.2	a
a–c	6.7	a
b–d	3.4	b
c–e	4.0	c
d–f	5.0	d
d–g	7.2	d
d–h	6.4	d
e–h	5.6	e
e–i	3.6	e
f–j	5.8	f
g–j	7.0	g
h–k	1.2	h
i–k	4.7	i
j–l	3.4	j
k–l	2.8	k

*Milestone task must follow.

You have 22 days to complete the project. What alternatives would you investigate?

8 A community recently learned that their local hospital is bankrupt. As an outside consultant, outline a program of review which will provide sufficient information so that a revised system can be planned to replace the one that has failed.

Chapter 7
Information Systems and Computers

A revolutionary development of data processing components and techniques has occurred during the past decade; although the fundamentals governing information requirements, generation, storage, and use have changed very little.

The glamor and mystique of the computer, its tremendous potential to collect, store, process, and display information, have prompted many to concentrate on systems technology without sufficient regard for the basic concept of information flow. If we remember that mechanical data processing was thought to be very progressive in the 1940's, and recognize that in some applications it continues to be the most efficient approach, then the computer as today's "star" component in the information system can be placed in proper perspective. Even though it is a very advanced tool, it is conceivable that it may be replaced someday by another breakthrough in information technology.

On the information-handling continuum, we observe that the kind of components and the manner of processing used in the larger and more complex information systems have become increasingly sophisticated (see Figure 7.1). The key is to select the appropriate tool and the methods of

Figure 7.1 Development of Information Tools and Methodology

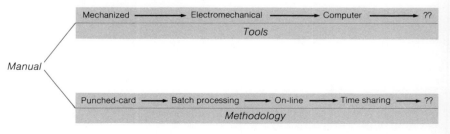

processing needed to meet the specific information requirements of each system.

The Role of Information Systems

In the broadest sense, information has been defined as that which is communicated, or as a patterned relationship among those events which add to knowledge or intelligence and can be evaluated in terms of their relevance for decision making.

Facts, numbers, and data are processed to provide meaningful information. For example, miscellaneous accounting data furnish information when arrayed in balance sheets and income statements. Ratio analysis and graphic displays of the pertinent relationships, however, will portray even more meaningful information. A close tie exists between information and communication. The latter is defined as the process of transferring information from a source to a receiver. The effectiveness of the transfer depends on the quality of transmission and the capability and receptiveness of the receiver. What constitutes meaningful information depends upon both the problem at hand and the decision maker's ability to use it; for example, certain facts and characteristics concerning an individual's health are more significant to someone trained in medicine.

Information can be conveyed in many ways, both formally and informally. Periodic reports in some standard format provide formal feedback for an operating system. The "grapevine" is an illustration of how informal impersonal relationships become channels of communication as well. Information exists in various forms, such as electronic impulses, written or spoken words, informal or formal reports, and each may provide the basic input for decision making.

Organizations are complex networks of systems with many decision points, ranging from individual decision makers at the lower operating levels to policy-making groups at the top. The information system supplies the premises for decisions at various levels in the organization; that is, each decision point may be considered a subsystem with inputs of data and information, transformation or analysis, and output or decisions.

A manager decides issues based on the information received in conjunction with previously developed strategies, procedures, or rules. Depending upon the level in the organization and/or the type of decision (programmed or unprogrammed), the decision maker may have several alternatives. If the matter is fairly commonplace and routine, he can handle it quickly, particularly if there are rules or procedures governing the situation. If the question is more complex, more of an unprogrammed nature, the decision maker may require additional inputs and may need to consult with subordinates, superiors, or peers. In every instance, the flow of proper information to decision points throughout an organization is vital.

Figure 7.2 represents a simplified system, a skeleton model of an organization, showing the basic flows of information necessary to accomplish system objectives. Internal capabilities are affected by environmental information and influence the process of setting goals and objectives. Premises with regard to governmental regulations, political conditions, the competitive situation, customer needs and desires, and other factors evolve over a period of time and form a frame of reference for planning. Plans for repetitive and nonrepetitive activities are transmitted to the operating system as standards which can be compared with operating results.

Figure 7.2   Information Flows in an Organization

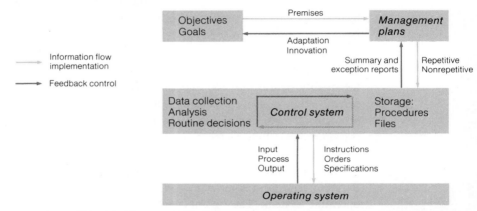

Source: Richard A. Johnson, et al., *The Theory and Management of Systems*, 2nd ed. (New York, McGraw-Hill Book Company, Inc., 1967), p. 106.

Information flow is an integral part of the control system. The operating system is monitored providing feedback on characteristics such as quality, quantity, and cost. Feedback from the various phases of the operating system is collected and analyzed. Decisions are made automatically within the control system if routine adjustment criteria are preprogrammed in the set of procedures or instructions. In addition, there is a flow of information from the operating system that may suggest changes to the program. Thus, procedures are changed and files updated simultaneously with the decision making pertaining to operations.

Summary and exception reports are generated by the control system and become a part of higher-level control in terms of adaptation or innovation of goals and objectives. Subsequent planning activity reflects such feedback and the entire process is repeated. This basic or simplified model of information flow can be applied to any organization; it shows the essential flow regardless of the sophistication of the techniques and equipment used.

We use the term information-decision system to emphasize that information should be generated relative to the decisions that will be made throughout the organization. Thus, an information-decision system should be designed as a communication process relating new inputs to the stored information and to the decisional requirements. Decisions at a given stage in the organization represent output from one subsystem which will be used for subsequent decision making at the same level, by a segment of that subsystem, or by the larger system. The number of patients and their status in the intensive care ward of a hospital, for example, would be information vital to that subsystem for scheduling nursing hours; it would be useful to the kitchen in planning the correct type and number of meals, and to the total hospital system as feedback information for its planning and/or budgeting decisions.

Blind adherence to organizational patterns for the flow of information will often hamper the development of an optimal system. The development of an information-decision system is particularly difficult when organizational adjustments have occurred and there is a mixture of a functional organization with product programs. Key decision points should be identified first, and then the best means devised to communicate meaningful information to these points.

The Functions of Information Systems

Common to all information systems are seven functions which occur in varying degrees of significance and/or intensity: (1) determination of information need, (2) data collection, (3) data or information reduction, (4) data or information storage, (5) data processing or information generation, (6) data or information transmission, and (7) information use. Figure 7.3

Figure 7.3 The Functions of an Information System

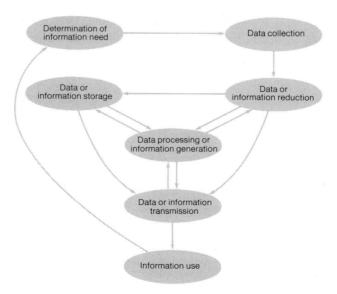

illustrates these functions in relation to their flow. Note that the sequencing of these functions may vary, or that some functions may be performed more than once, for example, data and information storage.

Determination of Informational Need

The first step in defining the informational need of a system is to determine the objectives of that system, such as what kind of information will be needed, when, and in what form. One approach is to analyze and define the information currently in use, but this approach has definite limitations, particularly if the current information system is not effective. It is much better to start by asking such questions as what information is needed, how will it be used, when is the information needed, and in what form should it be provided? This approach starts by examining the output requirements of the system and should be made in consideration of the long-range needs of the organization, which often change as the total system evolves within its environment. An organization must consider the environment in which a system will be operating, for the organization should expect to grow, change its operating objectives from time to time, and anticipate changes in competition and in the outside agencies influencing it.

One way to classify information by requirements is to organize it with respect to the level of management where it will be used. What information is required to determine which new systems are needed? What information is necessary for the design and allocation of resources to the new systems? What information is needed to operate the systems effectively and efficiently, including the control of operations within plan? What information is essential for the evaluation of the operating performance of the system?

We categorize the need for information under the four stages of Systems Management: Systems Planning, Design and Creation, Operation and Control, Review and Evaluation. Table 7.1 gives examples of specific activities

Table 7.1 Examples of Activities in the Four Stages of Systems Management

Systems Planning	Design and Creation	Operation and Control	Review and Evaluation
Choosing company objectives	Assignment of personnel	Planning activities and inputs	Measuring and appraising the performance of the system.
Setting personnel policies	Retraining of personnel		
Setting marketing policies	Designing new systems	Control of schedules, inventory, costs, and quality	General audit
New systems decisions	Capital expenditure decisions for redesign		Management appraisal
Decisions relative to existing systems			
Formulating budgets	Redesign of existing systems, e.g., different arrangement		

occurring under these four areas. The table shows how different the need for information is at the various levels. The kind of information needed for establishing objectives, for example, is very different from that needed for scheduling operations. An information system should be designed to collect the right information for the appropriate user.

Data Collection

The data used to plan and operate an organization is collected to provide the raw material for the function of data processing. In the modern organization the number of relevant facts for decision making at various levels is staggering. The number of daily activities is so high that only the most pertinent facts can be reported in the normal course of operations. The information system must be designed to garner pertinent facts and screen unwanted or unusable data.

Data collection involves the elements of sensing and recording. The discussion on control is applicable here for data must be sensed in some way and then collected and fed back for storage. The process of sensing can be carried out either by man or by machine.

The collection of data and generation of information are expensive, particularly if the decisions which follow do not result in an optimum operation. Substantial savings can be made by reducing the volume of data collected (by astute determination or by sampling), and by processing only that data into information that is meaningful.

One method of reducing the data collection requirement is to collect only that data which tends to suggest a change in operations. This would follow the exception principle of management, that is, all new data which indicates that previous strategy and decisions were proper would be filtered and not stored. A changing trend in operations would cause the data to be recorded and new information generated for decision making. Following this approach, control data would be recorded only when a trend might indicate a change in input allocation. Why, for example, maintain a daily schedule for a worker if his output is satisfactory?

Data or Information Reduction

There are two ways that data or information can be reduced: (1) data or information transformation—changing the physical form in which the data or information exists; and (2) data or information compression—reducing the physical volume or amount of the data or information.

Although original data may not have to be transformed to be transmitted or transported, other advantages may exist which would result from a change in its form. For example, a change in form may reduce the storage space requirement, or allow data and/or information to be processed, transmitted, or used.

One of the major concerns in the transformation process is the possibility of losing or misinterpreting the original data. When this possibility exists, the probability of the occurrence of this loss and the significance of the loss if it were to occur must be determined. When the probability or the consequences of a loss are small, it would not pay to install extensive safeguards. On the other hand, when the probability is great or the consequences are serious, it may be necessary to maintain the source documents even after the transformation (reduction) is made.

Obviously, the decision about what information is to be transformed relates to the information's use and, therefore, the decision concerning use must be made before the decision about transformation. Data transformation will not always take place at the source for, in some instances, transformation occurs at a later stage (see Figure 7.3). Minimizing the number of times data is transformed in the system is generally advisable. Once data or information has been transformed into machine language, for example, the systems analyst would prefer to keep the data or information in that form for subsequent processing by the computer.

Because of the amount of data that is involved in most information systems, its reduction by compression is almost essential. One method of compressing data is to reduce its physical size. Microfilm allows reductions in the size of material to the extent of about 250 to 1, and the technology continues to improve.

A second type of compression is accomplished through sampling. In the area of statistical sampling, a random selection of the population can be an approximate miniature of the total. The degree to which the sample represents all of the data depends on the size and design of the sample.

In some instances a change in the form of the data or information will also result in a substantial compression. A mathematical equation, for example, results in a basic change in the form of the data, but also permits the condensation of reams of data into one model. To the extent that models do not represent the real world, the possibility exists that some error will be included. The potential for errors from reducing data must be weighed against the benefits to be gained.

Data and Information Storage

When data and information are stored, the retention of documents and other data or information with their original quality and accessibility is important, so that the correct data or information can be recovered promptly and in the desired form. The fundamental operations of information data storage include indexing, storage, and retrieval. If the storage function is to be effective and efficient, each of these three operations must be considered carefully during the design stage of the system.

When an event is recorded and stored, it must be described in some way which will permit its retrieval within a desired time period. Just as we classify and inventory raw material or parts in a specific area or bin, we want to inventory the data that has been collected in a manner that aids easy identification of its classification.

Data should be classified according to a common attribute or characteristic, but the generation of information from this data should be in terms of the decision requirements of the organization. Classifying the raw data according to unique characteristics provides more flexibility for the system and, even if decision requirements change, the basic data are still valid and can be processed differently to meet the change. For example, data may be classified according to the incremental cost of material input and transformation, and decision information can be generated periodically by totalling these costs in various ways to test alternative courses of action.

Once data and information have been inventoried or stored, it is necessary to index their locations so that data can be retrieved when needed. If data and information are not properly indexed and are not available for decision making, the costs of their collection and/or generation has been wasted. Probably the most common form of indexing is the use of alphabetical subject headings or titles arranged in the same terminology as that used in the system. Another form is to study the information and summarize its contents with respect to its possible use for decision making, that is, the stage or level of decision making for which it applies.

Coding is another form of indexing whereby certain words or symbols are used to file and later recover data or information. Coding makes it possible to use the computer in the search process. The computer can make a complete search very rapidly and print out the results of that search in a form which would give detailed information on content and also the specific location.

The actual form in which data and information are stored varies greatly. Storage may be temporary or more permanent, and vary from the conventional library with hard copy documents and index cards to the storage of information in electronic coding. A magnetic tape will store approximately twenty million characters of data or information and can be attached quickly to the computer for retrieval.

The form in which data and information are stored is a function of volume, accessibility, and cost. They must be stored in the form in which they are recorded, or converted (coded) into another form which lends itself to storage and information generation. Similarly, data in a form which is compatible with the processing equipment will be more available and accessible for information generation and, consequently, more valuable to the decision maker. On the other hand, this type of storage may be more expensive; therefore, a trade off exists between these characteristics. The sheer magnitude of the data to be stored sometimes requires a reduction in the physical volume of the storage area by converting or coding data into a different language. This condensation does not destroy the validity of the original input, but merely converts it into another form.

Just as we try to maintain an up-to-date inventory of raw materials and goods and occasionally purge the out-of-date inventory, we must sometimes filter out insignificant and worthless data which has been collected. We will limit the problems of storage and/or retrieval to the extent that the data can be compressed or reduced in volume. Obviously, it is not always possible to determine how useful or relevant data may be after it has been supplemented by more current data, or after it has been generated into information for decision making. One approach is to use a purge system that will discard data and information automatically after a specified time has elapsed since the activity. Another approach is to classify data by age and regulate its accessibility for information generation accordingly. In other words, the more current the data the more accessible (in terms of time) it would be made to the decision maker, while older data would be transferred to less accessible storage areas.

Data Processing or Information Generation

The process of transforming data and information into material for decision making is outlined in Figure 7.4. The information on how the processing will take place (the object program), and the source data are reduced into

Figure 7.4   The Processing of Data into Information

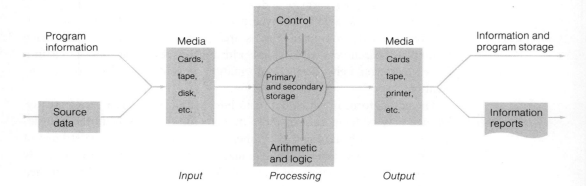

machine language (machine cards or tape) for computer processing. The program information is stored in the primary storage area (within the computer), while the source data is stored in both the primary and secondary (outside of the computer, such as on a tape or disc) storage area. The computer processes the data in relation to the programmed instructions and the resulting output is again reduced to some media such as a tape or punched card. Basic data or information are stored for subsequent processing, along with the program instructions. The important segment of the output, or that part which has been generated as a result of the instructions, becomes the information which will be presented in a variety of forms, including management reports for decision making.

This representation of a data-processing system is appropriate regardless of how elaborate the equipment might be at the input, processing, or output stages. This process can also represent a manual operation. For example, the same model may be used to describe a manual operation of computing the payroll and determining the periodic labor cost. A predetermined sequence of operations (the program) is followed and the source data (including such items as individual pay rates and hours worked) are converted into some media (e.g. a work sheet) which is easier to interpret and more convenient for the processor. The processing includes multiplying the rate by the hours for each individual, subtracting the various deductions, computing the size of the individual check, and adding the totals to the various expense accounts. From this work sheet the information can be reduced to other forms including the individual paychecks, payroll expense, and withholding reports. The basic information about the workers' pay grade, and so forth, and the sequence of operations necessary to complete the payroll procedure, would be stored for the next cycle.

The processing of data never ends, for the data base is continually updated by transactions (any event which tends to modify or change the data base) which occur in the operation of the organization. At periodic times the data are sorted, combined, and analyzed to present meaningful information for decision making. A part of this processing function will often include the computation of data to present relationships which have more meaning for analysis.

Transmission of Data and Information

The points at which information is generated and at which it is needed are often widely separated. Some method must be used to facilitate the accumulation, processing, and distribution of required information to decision points. Often this task is accomplished by a physical transfer. Modern communication equipment, however, can transmit coded data from its point of origin, to a processing area and subsequently to wherever the results are required. Long-range transmission over hundreds of miles is possible but costly. Short-range data transmission is practical and operational today.

Telephone wires are used to transmit data between the sender and the receiver. In such cases, adequate checking must be employed to ensure the data transmitted and data received are identical. Whenever an error is discovered by the control program built into such a receiver, it signals the sender to that effect. The sender will then back-up and retransmit what, in all probability, will be the correct data.

It may be necessary to change the form or coding of data in order to process it more efficiently; and it also may be necessary to change the form again in order to transmit the information from one geographic point to another. In other words, it often is advisable to encode the information for effective and efficient transmission and then decode the information at the other end for use as an information base for decision making.

The electronic transmission of information makes it possible to establish centralized decision-making centers. Lacking such communication, geographically separated subsystems would be more apt to institute their own information-decision systems, particularly for operations.

The Use of Information

The utilization of information depends on the quality of the information (its accuracy and pertinence), its form, and its timeliness. The degree of quality reverts back to the determination of informational needs. If the use is carefully planned ahead and the information system is well-designed, the user will receive accurate information. The form in which the information is presented is also a function of system planning so that human perception of this information will be relatively easy. A periodic display of the most current information will be made through periodic reports, reports triggered by some on-line operational problem, or special reports for evaluation and/or planning analysis.

The timeliness with which data and information are made available is very important to the user. The significance of current information varies with the nature of the decision to be made. For example, scientists studying the change in the depth of oceans may find that annual or semi-annual reports are sufficient, while an air traffic controller will need information as it changes by the second.

When a system has been designed to provide information for the user, its distribution is predetermined. When information is generated without this kind of planning, the question arises about who should receive various information outputs. A filtering process can be initiated to sort the information output, but usually there is a tendency to provide more information than required, rather than risk the possibility of omitting a potential user.

The Role of the Computer

The electronic computer was developed during World War II primarily to provide a faster means of computation in scientific problems. Earlier calculators had been used to supplant human effort and improve effectiveness and efficiency. However, their speed of computation was limited by the movement of mechanical parts, thus imposing a relatively low upper limit on the ultimate speeds of calculations. The significant principle of electronic computers is that the flow of electrons, acting as signals in the circuitry of the equipment, is susceptible to direction and control. Numbers and alphabetic characters are symbolized by electronic pulses or other manifestations, and the controlled movement, or flow, of these symbolic signals provides the basis for the data-processing tool. A computer, then, is "a machine that manipulates symbols in accordance with given rules in a predetermined and self-directed manner. Speaking more technically, an automatic computer is a high-speed, automatic, electronic digital data-processing machine."[1]

An important adjective is "high-speed," since speed of computation is one of the primary goals. The speeds obtained today by electronic computers are already fantastic and will increase. Increasing the computational speed, plus providing larger and larger storage capacity or memory, makes the electronic computer an even more versatile tool for use in a data-processing system.

The word "digital" is used in contrast to the term "analog" which describes an important group of machines that create a *physical* analogy or model as a way to solve the problem being studied. The digital computer, on the other hand, is based on the manipulation of *symbols* and counting (the binary number system).

The term "automatic" refers to the self-controlling characteristic of electronic computers, because they have internally stored programs (lists of instructions) that determine the sequence of operation in a processing of computational routine. These instructions are predetermined in the sense that human effort is required to plan and set forth in detail all the steps involved in any processing job. Once the program is designed, it acts as the control element in the data-processing system. During processing, the program itself can be modified, again according to predetermined rules, and hence, provide directions according to the situation represented by input data. This modification quality parallels the feedback-control concept of production automation and has led to the description of electronic data processing as office automation. The concept of internally stored, self-adjusting programs for controlling operations sets the electronic computer completely apart from its predecessors (electromechanical equipment). In this sense, the electronic computer is not just another stage in the evolution of mechanized equipment.

A computer provides a new dimension for data processing and allows much more sophisticated and imaginative systems of information flow to be developed. It can do work (fitted to its talents) faster and more economically than any other equipment. It is more accurate than people, or than other machines in use. It can easily perform operations previously considered impractical, if not impossible, in the area of research and analysis, but, most important, the electronic computer offers a rare opportunity to expand the scope of current mechanized information flow.

Because the computer is such a versatile tool and represents such an advance over its forerunners, it provides analysts with an opportunity for redesigning systems of information flow. Yet, it is in this area that progress

[1] Ned Chapin, *An Introduction to Automatic Computers* (Princeton, N.J.: D. Van Nostrand Co., Inc., 1957), p. 4.

has been extremely slow. Some reasons for the lack of progress include: (1) too much emphasis has been placed on immediate cost savings; (2) existing systems of procedures have been transferred to electronic data processing, resulting in the faster processing of the same old system of information flow; (3) the emphasis on immediate results in substantial cost savings has led to the predominance of a piecemeal approach with little regard for the overall picture. Integrated data processing is often considered a "cloud 9" concept, with little or no practical application; and (4) management has not been convinced of the merits of electronic computers in all instances. Management's attitude has, of course, contributed to the emphasis on immediate cost savings and the piecemeal approach.

In general, the problem in most data-processing installations has been a preoccupation with operational difficulties at the expense of time which could be devoted to long-range planning. This is not a unique problem; administrators in other functional areas also are susceptible to this tendency. For example, one manager in charge of a planning staff stated that his job had been created eighteen months before to deal with four functions: long-range planning, program planning, systems, and controls. He spent none of his effort on long-range planning. Of his time spent on systems, very little attention was given to the overall system of information flow, and, again, none of his effort had been spent on the long-range aspects of the system. This approach is typical and indicates why the full potential of electronic computers has not been attained. A complete reevaluation of a company's system of information flow must be undertaken in order to provide a proper reference point for every application put on the computer. If each application is related to the overall plan (or the information flow model), the ultimate result will be a completely integrated data-processing system.

Hardware and Software

Some computer programmers assert that the most trouble-free electronic data-processing installations seem to develop from operations that originally were manual, rather than mechanical. This assertion is reasonable because a computer performs the various steps of a program in essentially the same way as a person does. Each record or item is processed completely as a unit (in a file-maintenance approach) rather than bit by bit, as in the case of punched-card systems. The similarity to the manual approach allows a great deal of imagination in the design of systems incorporating electronic data processing. High-speed computers encourage analysts to rethink the entire flow of paperwork and reporting, thereby utilizing an expensive piece of equipment. At the same time, more detailed (step-by-step) procedures must be provided for the computer than for people; the machine will consider only those possibilities preprogrammed before making a decision.

The task of developing the minutely detailed program of procedural steps is arduous, time-consuming, and often frustrating. The earliest programs were written directly in a language the machine could use to perform the arithmetic and logic operations. Each instruction had to be coded and stored in a specific location in the computer's memory. Each step included a reference to a location where the next instruction could be found. Keeping track of used and unused space allotted to the program was a tedious task. Simplifying this programming chore has been the focal point of much research and development over the past decade. This aspect of data processing is called software and its development has paralleled to a degree that of the hardware or machinery.

Software includes all the programming systems used to facilitate effective and efficient utilization of computer hardware. Software research and development has been an extremely important part of the electronic data processing age, for advancement in programming systems can augment systems-design capabilities even more than additional sophistication of equipment. An early improvement in software involved the use of intermediate symbolic codes which the programmer could use to develop a set of instructions. These instructions were processed by an assembly program which prepared a set of machine language steps for actual data-processing operations.

The development of subroutines also made programming easier. Sets of instructions for typical calculations were developed in modular form and inserted into a larger system of programmed steps where needed. Libraries of subroutines have been accumulated by users over the years. Most computers have special instructions which incorporate subroutines automatically and programming can be accomplished by using simple reference statements.

Another phase of software development came with the compilers or translators, which are similar to assembly programs but usually much more complex. The language used by the programmer has been made as simple as possible, thus requiring a more complex compiler or translator program to develop the machine-language instructions (object program).

Figure 7.5 illustrates the procedural flow followed to develop machine-language instruction. The process is: (1) a programmer develops the general written instructions, (2) an operator processes the instructions into

Figure 7.5 Developing Machine-Language Instructions

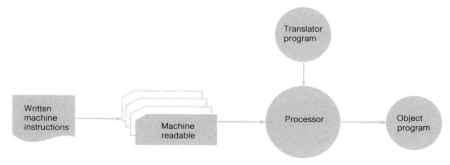

machine readable information, and (3) the computer prepares the objective program by interpreting the general instructions as outlined by the translator program.

The development of programming languages has progressed rapidly over the last decade. FORTRAN IV (Formula Translator), COBOL (Common Business-Oriented Language), ALGOL (Algorithmic Oriented Language), and BASIC (Beginners All-purpose Symbolic Instruction Code) are examples of widely used languages. There have been numerous suggestions for standardization in order that program packages may be used on a variety of computers. Some progress has been made in this area but much remains to be done.

NPL (New Programming Language for IBM equipment, later PL-1) was designed to meet the need for a language that could be used for both business and scientific applications. The absence of arbitrary restrictions allows a programmer to devote most of his effort to problem description and to express with freedom the procedure for its solution. The objective was to develop a language which would enable programmers to write more diverse application programs than heretofore possible.

A number of special-purpose languages have been developed for specific classes of problems, for example, investigation into artificial intelligence, linguistics, human behavior simulation, and a variety of problem-solving techniques requiring manipulation of non-numeric or symbolic data. List processing capability is the central theme for IPL-V (Information Processing Language), LISP and SLIP.

For another particular application, simulation, IBM developed GPSS (General Purpose Systems Simulator). SIMSCRIPT, a similar development by the Rand Corporation, is a pretranslator for FORTRAN IV. CSL (Control and Simulation Language), SIMPAC, and DYNAMO are other examples. SIMTRAN (Simulation Translator) is a language designed by the Boeing Company for internal use in the analysis of logical systems. Although an attempt was made to attain computer independence by writing interpretation and execution routines in FORTRAN IV, SIMTRAN provides several logical and arithmetical operations that are not present in other simulation languages.

Undoubtedly, many companies have developed their own programming language or have modified standard packages to fit their particular needs; but special purpose computer hardware is less common. There is a broad base of common programming systems—subroutines, assemblers, and compilers—as well as many tailor-made, intracompany innovations which represent individualized software packages. Moreover, there is still considerable freedom for innovation in designing data-processing systems; the creativity demonstrated by systems designers and programmers is still crucial.

Research and development in software has been focused upon alleviating the tedious, time-consuming, and often frustrating task of preparing machine-language or object programs. Sophisticated software allows the programmer more time to spend on systems design which facilitates his efforts in implementing data-processing systems efficiently.

Computer hardware includes the machines (mechanical and/or electronic) used in information systems, as well as all of the supporting equipment associated with input, storage, output, and transmission. The development of hardware is moving fast and changes occur constantly. A summary description of such equipment is outdated, therefore, before it can be published. System designers find it meaningful to report their specific needs to hardware manufacturers, who then relate their needs to the current hardware capabilities.

Integrated Data Processing

An integrated or total information system often is outlined as the goal of designers of information systems. Integrated data processing (IDP) suggests a close coupling of the components of the information system so that there will be a minimum of human intervention between each input and output stage, plus a common information base so that the flow among various subsystems of the organization can take place without difficulty.

One of the problems in many installations concerns the task of converting visable source material to machine-sensible language prior to processing. Normally, the justification for electronic data-processing equipment is the elimination of clerical-work stations and electrical accounting machines. More often than not, however, installations of supporting EAM (electrical accounting machines) equipment have increased with the addition of EDPM (electronic data-processing machines) equipment. The job of creating and checking the cards and/or tape for input into the computer has resulted in this increasing pressure on supporting equipment. Often, human intervention occurs between the initial source document and input into the computer. If so, the chance to make errors is obvious. Since impure input will compound errors (garbage in—garbage out), it is highly desirable to strive for error-free input. Integrated data processing appears to be a worthwhile development, particularly if it can reduce errors.

IDP coincides with the approach that original source material, both visible and machine sensible, are prepared simultaneously. A wide variety of machines have been developed which provide, for example, both a hard copy and a perforated tape. Or, more commonly, a punched card is developed initially and used to produce subsequent documents of information with a minimum of human intervention, thus cutting time, effort, and errors. At present the perforated tape is used most often as a common-language element of an integrated, data-processing system, and it can be produced by cash registers, typewriters, bookkeeping machines, desk calculators, teletype centers, and others. The tape can be used to actuate many pieces of equipment, including punch-card machines and computers.

In order to eliminate the handling of cards and paper tapes between initial recording and input to the computer system, some type of direct data-transmission system must be utilized. The data transmission among various subsystems of the organization provides the key for the broader aspect of integrated data processing. Many current and potential users of such devices are evident, such as multiplant companies with central data processing, companies with widespread sales offices, and companies with scattered, in-plant recording stations.

Many kinds of input data for computer processing originate outside of the system and, therefore, cannot be obtained through source-data by-product devices. The logical answer, rather than the laborious, costly, and sometimes inaccurate card-punch process, is to develop machines that "talk" to the computer without human intervention. The banking industry standardized the encoding of checks early in the 1960's, and other organizations are now adopting various scanning devices or readers to integrate their data processing.[2] Eventually, man will be able to communicate directly with the computer by speaking.

The advantages of integrated data processing or integrated information flow are probably more significant from an organizational point of view than from the efficiencies gained within the subsystem. In order to create a common information base for the entire organization, it is necessary to outline the proper role of each subsystem relative to the objectives of the total system. The advantages of such rethinking should be obvious to the reader.

Real-time Data Processing. Most data processing applications are examples of batch processing; that is, facts or data are collected manually or electronically over a period of time and then merged with a master file in a processing run. Such processing may take place bi-weekly, weekly, daily, or even at shorter intervals. However, batch processing implies that the system is not completely up-to-date at any given moment. Real-time processing, on the other hand, involves updating the master file or description of the current situation with every transaction, regardless of their frequency.[3] For example, a wholesaler may keep his inventory entirely in the magnetic

---

[2] Carl Heyel, *Computers, Office Machines, and the New Information Technology* (New York: Business Equipment Manufacturers Association, 1969), pp. 126–133.

[3] Even in a real-time system, some momentary delay in updating may occur subject to the capabilities of input and processing devices. A unique characteristic of real-time systems, however, is that they are always on-line, or available.

storage of a file computer; as orders are received and processed, the inventory status is updated immediately. Thus, a perpetual inventory record is maintained which is current in terms of transactions at any given point in time. Information on stockouts is obtained as an exception printout whenever this condition occurs, and a purchase order is printed the minute the re-order point is reached. Contrast this with a system in which transactions are collected for a week and then processed, and where serious gaps could be present in the information necessary for managerial decision making.

Real-time as a systems concept was popularized in the military application of the SAGE (Semi-automatic Ground Environment) system. SAGE is a continental air command warning system designed to maintain a complete, up-to-date picture of the air and ground situation in the continental United States and other parts of North America. It was designed to control modern air-defense weapons rapidly and accurately and to present appropriate filtered pictures of the air and weapon situations to those Air Force personnel who would conduct the air battle. The SAGE system includes numerous radar installations and a widespread interconnected network of air-defense direction centers which receive information from numerous sources and process the information rapidly on electronic data-processing equipment. Elaborate means are available for displaying pertinent information to the human decision makers stationed at the control centers. Signals directing interceptor aircraft and other weapons in the air-defense system can be issued if and when the situation calls for such action.

Airline reservation systems are examples of real-time information systems in everyday living. The problem involves matching customer demand with an inventory of seat schedules for future flights. The airlines wish to process inquiries about availability of space in a matter of seconds in order to make the system practical from a customer's point of view. The system accepts inquiries from numerous points: city ticket offices, airport ticket counters, airport check-in positions, airport standby control, and by telephone. A request initiates a sequence of processing steps which checks the availability of seats, reports status, and updates the inventory if a sale is made. The real-time reservation system for an airline is actually a small part of the total information system of the company. However, it does perform an exceedingly crucial function and hence deserves the attention that has been devoted to it. In addition, the reservation system for a given company often must be interrelated with those of other airlines as a passenger may need to transfer to complete his journey. Such a supersystem of multiple company coordination, or integration among systems, performs the ultimate benefit to the traveler.

Some companies have developed central "control rooms" which are designed to furnish information about company operations on a real-time basis. A console provides a means for management to interrogate the system with questions such as (1) the amount of overtime by project for the current month and for the year-to-date, (2) the schedule status of project XYZ, and (3) the turnover rate among research personnel. Most of these systems are not real-time in the same sense as the two other examples because the data are collected and processed periodically. Charts and graphs are developed from the data processed in the latest batch and become the current information stored in the system. On the other hand, it is conceivable that data could be collected on a real-time basis and illustrations developed and displayed by the system as each inquiry is directed to it. The charts and graphs would be produced whenever a real-time inquiry was ordered.

A combination of real-time with the central "control room" is used by several cities for freeway surveillance and control. Detectors are installed in the pavement at selected locations along the freeway lanes, along the entrance ramps, at the frontage road approaches to entrance ramps, and at the exit ramps. Detectors are used either to sense the presence of vehicles or to count the number of vehicles, or both. More specifically, detectors provide data for determining the speed of a vehicle and the gap size between vehicles; indicate the presence of a vehicle at the traffic signal; indicate the presence of a vehicle stopped in the ramp-freeway merge area; indicate a vehicle stopped in the frontage road approach to an entrance ramp; and provide the computer with data for determining whether a ramp driver's travel time after a traffic signal turns green exceeds a predetermined value.

A computer which is used in an on-line capacity actually divides information received from the detectors into three major categories: volume, occupancy, and speed. Occupancy and speed are functions of the length of time that a vehicle occupies a major area of pavement. Once the data has been gathered, processing amounts to a scanning or consulting of basic data stored in the computer to make the best possible decision as to how the actual traffic lights should be controlled. In effect, the computer functions as a kind of policeman with the capability of seeing not only one intersection at a given time, but of seeing all intersections at the same time. It can then resort to two basic kinds of decision processes. The first is to bring into play any one of many patterns of action stored in the computer. These patterns are generated beforehand by an off-line analysis and simulation. Second, it is possible to allow a traffic engineer to make second by second decisions at a particular intersection, and still, if he desires, coordinate that intersection with adjacent ones. In other words a traffic engineer could extract the control of one intersection from the total system and provide manual control while the computer system controls all of the other stations in relation to the one under manual control.

The traffic control signals are advanced from one phase to another by an electronic pulse transmitted directly to them from the computer. Because of its speed, the computer is able to examine the activity of each controller once every second to determine when it needs advancing. Automatically, the computer then sets up the proper commands, and sends simultaneous advance pulses to the controller that it selects. The computer also checks to make sure the controller has actually changed the light and has responded properly to the computer's command.

As an additional output of this on-line system, traffic engineers can obtain printed statistical information on traffic activity at the end of each day. In addition, since all information is stored and immediately retrievable within the computer, anytime that an engineer wants an answer to a specific question, he can obtain it by interrogating the system and getting an immediate printed answer. This would in no way interrupt the regular function of traffic control. At the end of the control period for each day, information such as the volume, stops, delay, average delay per vehicle, and probability of stops can be printed out for each detector. In addition, other information would be available for a more detailed analysis of operations.

Figure 7.6 illustrates this system, showing the input and output of the system. In August 1967, an IBM 1800 Data Acquisition and Control System was installed in Houston for use in investigating gap acceptance and

Figure 7.6   The 1800 Traffic Control System

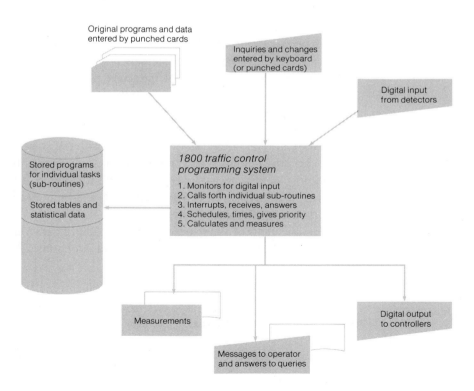

traffic interaction in the freeway merging process. Studies utilizing the 1800 as a ramp and freeway system controller were conducted over the next several months. As a result of this development work, an operational control system evolved which has been utilized as a primary control on the Gulf Freeway since January 1969. Such a system now controls 8 major entrance ramps along a six and a half mile northbound stretch of the Gulf Freeway approaching Houston. Sensing devices, located at intervals along the right-hand freeway lane, detect gaps in traffic during peak hours and relay information to the computer. When a gap of acceptable size is detected, the computer turns an entrance ramp traffic light green so that a motorist reacting in an average manner will reach the freeway at the right time to merge into the gap. Figure 7.7 illustrates how new vehicles are accepted on the freeway with respect to sufficient spacing.

Time Sharing. Computer information systems are sometimes organized on a time sharing basis. This permits concurrent utilization of the same system by two or more users tied directly to the same informational base. (Subsystems which may or may not be part of the same larger system.) Each of the subsystems has the ability to inquire and to add or alter information in the central storage.

The original meaning of time sharing pertained to the kind of circuitry which permitted more than one instruction or operation to be executed simultaneously by the computer. This allowed a greater utilization of the internal processing capability while inputting or outputting occurred. The second generation computers, such as the Honeywell H-800, permitted the loading of several programs at the same time, programs with large quantities of input and output. In such multiprogramming, an executive program is used to direct the utilization of input, processing, and output capability in terms of established priorities.[4]

The next level of time sharing occurred with the tying of remote locations into a central system. The computer in these systems was of the third generation of equipment, with program-interrupt features. It is this level of time sharing that incorporates characteristics of real-time processing (e.g., airline reservation system).

The meaning of time sharing relates to the utilization of central equipment by different users and with different programs. There are five basic characteristics:

1. On-line. The computer has the capability for remote entry of data and the receipt of responses from remote stations, on a continuous or intermittent basis.

---

[4] Heyel, *Computers, Office Machines, and the New Information Technology,* pp. 158–163.

Figure 7.7 Illustration of Gap Acceptance Strategy

Detection of acceptable gap

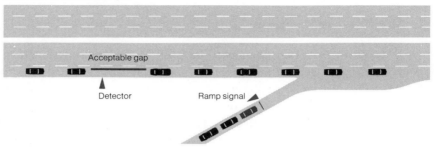

Projection of acceptable gap

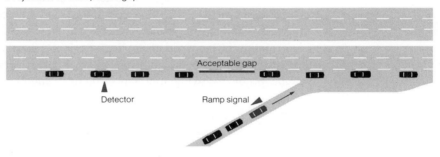

Vehicle merge

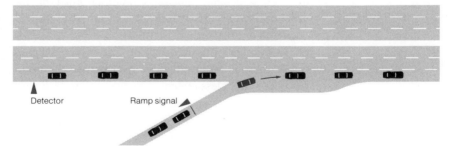

2. Real-time. The computer must be capable of serving all users on a real-time basis. This implies that the inputs to the computer are accepted at once and the results of the memory access or central processor computation are quickly available, that is, within the normally accepted limits for a given job.

3. Concurrent access. Two or more users must be able to interact with the computer from different remote locations at the same time.

4. *Autonomy.* The computer system must enable each subscribing subsystem to use the time-sharing computer as if it were dedicated exclusively for its own use.

5. *Functional latitude.* There is a significant acceptable range of jobs which can be performed.

Two arguments are used to justify the installation and operation of a general-purpose, time-sharing system. The first is a "performance requirements or objectives" argument: the need for accomplishment is so important that this type of facility is justified. Certain military applications would fall into this category. The second argument is the more usual and is basically a cost-benefit analysis rationale; the advantages, the disadvantages, and the cost of time sharing would be considered.

The major advantage of time sharing is the immediate availability of information for decision making.[5] Obviously, there are certain kinds of control operations in which having continuous and immediate knowledge of changes is extremely important, whereas a decrease in the response time of information in many other applications is not nearly as significant. Another real advantage is the ability to use or interact with the computer as a dynamic problem-solving tool (for example, simulation). Information is available on a current basis and the time required for problem solving or planning can be reduced substantially.

The principal disadvantage of time-sharing systems is the high cost, particularly because of the installation cost. A time-sharing system requires a larger central processing unit, memory, and auxiliary memory storage. In addition, the cost of high-speed auxiliary storage, terminals, communication controllers, and communication facilities must be included. Then, too, a comprehensive executive program is required as individual programs are developed and maintained.

As the number of users on an on-line service increases, and decreases the unit cost, there is the problem of overloading the time-sharing facilities and making the system less effective for the various units.

There are several special problems which may influence the decision to install and use time-sharing facilities. One of these involves the security and privacy of the user's data. Even though there are various mechanical devices as well as control built into the software systems, the danger always exists that data will be improperly used or distorted in the central system. There may also be problems or breakdowns, transmission difficulties, and, as mentioned previously, overloading.

---

[5] The assumption is made that the subsystem could not support its own computerized information system.

The Economics of Information

Information has value to the extent that it improves decision making. The value of an increment of new information could be determined if the marginal improvement resulting from the decision-making process which followed were known. New information which changes the model representing the real world is important if, in fact, the change is significant enough to cause a change in the subsequent decision. For example, new information about how students learn could bring about changes in the design of systems of education; or additional information concerning increasing inventory cost could cause a change in the allocation of resource inputs in an operating system. Similarly, control and evaluation information may cause a change in operations and/or systems design.

It has often been stated that much data and some information is generated for no real purpose and, thereby, should be eliminated. There seems to be a tendency to generate large quantities of information on the assumption that a direct correlation exists between the volume of information and the quality of decision making. This is a valid assumption only if there is a flow of the right information, properly presented, to the right parties, and at the right time. Perhaps it is this lack of knowledge about what information, by whom, and when it should be generated, that causes the difficulty. The tendency is to compensate for these uncertainties by furnishing quantities of information to administrators at all levels and at all times, and never to analyze whether these people are using the information which has been generated. It may be advisable to advocate a free inquiry system whereby decentralized decision centers receive information only to the extent that they request it from the central data processing center, and do not receive voluminous, periodic reports.

Ultimately, each user of information for decision making should develop a pay-off matrix to determine the cost of information relative to its utility for decision making. The cost of complete information can be weighed against the expected pay-off from good decisions as opposed to the consequences and probability of less desirable action. To construct such a model, we must know the incremental cost of information and the incremental gain from improving the quality of the decision. The difficulty of creating such a model which would represent reality should be obvious to the reader. Information for decision making is dynamic; any consideration of this process as a static model is indeed theoretical and of little value in practice.

The limitations in outlining any theoretical model to evaluate the economics of information should not cause the reader to discount this approach entirely, for a theoretical discussion is of considerable use. When the cost of information is formalized, particularly in making structured decisions, an estimate can be made of the value of improved information against the cost of acquiring this information. An understanding of the cost and value of improved information will be of significant value to managers and systems designers in providing the most appropriate information to the decision makers relative to the cost of acquiring this information.

Cost of Information

In many organizations the cost of information is summarized by the cost of operating the data processing department. Although this obviously is the real and determinable cost, it does not include the total cost of data collection, storage, processing, transmission, and use. For example, a decision maker often overlooks the time spent scanning meaningless reports or trying to extract information which may or may not pertain to his problem. Similarly, the costs of storing out-dated information are not always considered. Whenever the costs of information are to be determined, the information flow through all of the functions must be included to make it a meaningful analysis.

There is a tendency to assume that the costs of information are fixed; in the short run, this may be true. In other words, once the information equipment has been purchased or leased, the costs of this equipment will continue (within specified rental periods, if the equipment is leased) regardless of volume. The approach, therefore is to assume that additional information can be generated at a small incremental cost inasmuch as the computer may be idle otherwise. This philosophy sometimes results in a generation of information of marginal value and loads the system to the point where costs can increase quite rapidly. Loading the system also reduces its ability to respond to special information needs and requirements.

Costs are related directly to the response time required to identify, analyze, and present stored data into processed information. On one end of the spectrum, we have the real-time operation where the response time is instantaneous, or, at least, very short. At the other extreme, we have the periodic sequential processing where information is generated during specified intervals. Real-time information systems usually are more expensive because of the higher cost of storing data and information on-line and because of the higher transmission costs in connecting the remote input and output stations electronically. Figure 7.8 shows a theoretical example of the costs. The figure shows that as the response time in an on-line operation is increased, costs decrease only to the extent that additional storage and/or transmission circuits are released. A definite decrease in cost is achieved by using the sequential system of processing, and cost continues to decline as the time interval or response time is increased.

In the on-line information system, the output can be very selective as determined by the system design. Obviously this, too, adds to the initial cost. In contrast, the output from the sequential system can be rather general and produced rather inexpensively. It becomes necessary to determine the information needs of the decision maker and to decide whether selective informa-

Figure 7.8 Relation of Cost to Response Time

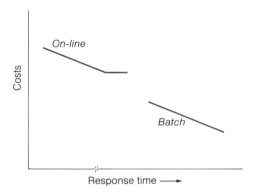

tion provided within a minimum response time will result in savings of users' time and the making of better decision.

The accuracy and reliability requirements of a system also will affect costs. To the extent that the ultimate in accuracy and reliability are achieved, increasing costs can be anticipated. Increases in these costs, in a given system, will be moderate to a point, beyond which the cost will increase at a much more rapid rate. The most feasible approach is to specify the accuracy and the reliability characteristics of a system within practical limits and then add control checks that will identify any serious errors which may occur.

In summary, it is the decision maker who must determine the value of information. He must analyze the sensitivity of the decision relative to the importance of additional and more current information as activities change the data base. He must weigh the importance of time and the importance of receiving only that information which pertains directly to the decision at hand. Superfluous and unnecessary information may be screened at his level or by the central information system, and to the extent that the cost of the two approaches are balanced, the optimum total system will be achieved.

Scale of Information Systems

A question arises about the optimum scale or size of information systems, particularly as it pertains to the use of large computers in centralized operations. A larger computer can produce information at a faster rate and in larger volume. In addition, it can do things that smaller computers cannot do. There is some evidence that, for computer equipment, average cost decreases as size increases. This position was maintained by Herbert R. Grosch in the late 1940's and became known as Grosch's law:[7]

[7] William F. Sharpe, *The Economics of Computers* (New York: Columbia University Press, 1969), pp. 315–316.

$$C = K\sqrt{E} \quad \text{or} \quad E = \left(\frac{1}{K^2}\right) C^2$$

where C = the cost of a computer system,
$\qquad E$ = the effectiveness (performance, speed, throughput) of the system, and
$\qquad K$ = some constant.

Concerning average cost (C/E), the law asserts:

$$\frac{C}{E} = \frac{K^2}{C} \quad \text{or} \quad \frac{C}{E} = \frac{K}{\sqrt{E}}$$

where K is some constant.

The relationships demonstrating the law are shown in Figure 7.9 (A)

Figure 7.9 Cost Per Unit of Effectiveness versus (A) Cost and (B) Effectiveness of System

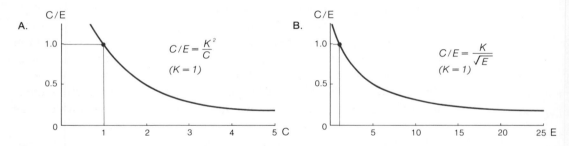

Source: William F. Sharpe, *The Economics of Computers* (New York: Columbia Press, 1969), p. 316.

and (B) with cost and effectiveness normalized so that $C = 1$ when $E = 1$. The question arises whether the cost of the system represents value to the user or cost of manufacture. "We conclude that price measures value relatively well and cost of manufacture rather poorly. . . It has been suggested that Grosch's law holds only because manufacturers use it to set prices."[8]

We may conclude that users should select computer systems which are compatible with their information requirements; requirements based on organizational, economic, and practical considerations. Assuming that computer power (in millions of operations per second) increases faster than cost, then there are advantages in using a large centralized computer providing that such gains are not offset by the increased costs of data transmission. The main reason for subscribing to a time sharing system is to gain access to a large computer with its economies of scale.[9]

[8] Ibid., p. 349.
[9] ". . . , an increase in computing costs by a factor of 2 may generate an increase in computing power by a factor of 2^3, or 8." John Dearden, et al., *Managing Computer-Based Information Systems* (Homewood, Ill.: Richard D. Irwin, Inc., 1971), p. 72.

Pricing in Time Sharing

The pricing structure of commercial time-sharing systems is by no means uniform, although charges may be determined by five categories of conditions. The first charge is the fixed installation fee, designed to cover the administrative expenses incurred in initiating the service to the user as well as the technical expense of installing the terminal. Next, there is a fixed minimum charge per time period, usually by the month. The third kind of charge is based on the usage of specific components of the time-sharing system. For example, such charges may include the central processing time used, the elapse time of terminal connect time, the on-line bulk storage of programs and/or data belonging to the user, the kind and type of communication facility which is incorporated into the system, and the rental of any facility (terminals) which are leased by the user. The fourth pricing condition pertains to the kind of priority which the user receives for his jobs. Instantaneous service, instead of waiting for the less active periods of the day, demands a premium charge. Even after the decision has been made whether to use instantaneous or delayed service, there is a price differential based on use during peak or less active hours of the day. The final major charge is made for performing various systems support services such as setting up special programs for the user. This classification of charges is made on a nonregular negotiated basis and it is not as significant to the user as the recurring charges. It is the costs associated with time sharing which determine the pricing structure, a point worthy of note.

Value and Cost

The design considerations of a management information system must include an appraisal of the possible value of such a system to the organization, as well as the cost associated with the design and operation stages. An organization must determine for each segment of the total system the benefits to be realized and estimate those costs associated with the different possible approaches being considered.

Improved management capability can result from a constantly evolving information system based on integrating the smaller systems developed from a unified data base. The success of an evolving system is more likely if an overall systems development pattern is pre-established. Some of the potential benefits include:

1. An improved understanding of the business, including internal effects of outside factors and their interaction.
2. Reduced response time in reacting to changing external conditions.
3. More objective analysis of business alternatives.
4. Reduced costs of operations when resources are organized properly.
5. An integrated data base offers accurate, uniform data for all users, eliminating duplication and minimizing hardware requirements.

Figure 7.10 Information System Development Activity Plan

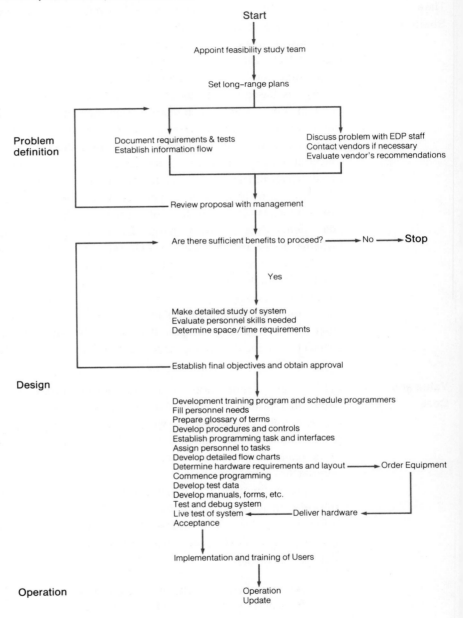

Source: R. E. Breen, et al., *Management Information Systems, A Subcommittee Report on Definitions* (Schenectady, N.Y.: General Electric, 1969), p. 21.

This list indicates the nature of benefits to be realized from an improved management information system. A study of the particular system is necessary to establish an approximate order of the dollar values to be gained for each segment of the organization. When the value of each management information system has been determined, the designer is in a position to work out preliminary system design from which cost estimates can be made. Included in the various alternatives will be systems with different reliability, time, and availability attributes. These can have different value-cost relationships for the individual user.

In general, it is advisable to develop management information systems in an evolutionary way which compliments the operational needs of the business, with particular emphasis on those functions that offer financial benefits to it. As these improvements bring about significant financial returns, marginal gains then can be achieved by improvements in those areas of lesser importance. The major fixed costs associated with the management information system will already have been justified, and the additional gains can be achieved with the expenditure of only incremental costs. Figure 7.10 illustrates an information system development activity plan. Although this methodology may be varied according to the particular assignment, Figure 7.10 does point out its relationship with three stages or levels of systems management, namely, problem definition, design, and operation.

Summary

Information is defined as that patterned relationship among events which adds to knowledge and can be evaluated in terms of its relevance for decision making. In some organizations decisions may be preprogrammed at the lower levels subject to anticipated inputs, while in other organizations and/ or at higher management levels, information is generated to make unprogrammed decisions. Information may be collected to plan new systems, to operate and control systems, or to analyze and review their performance. The idea, however, is to gather and process data into information only if it is helpful for making decisions.

The functions of the information system are (1) to determine the information need, (2) data collection, (3) data or information reduction, (4) data or information storage, (5) data processing or information generation, (6) data or information transmission, and (7) information use.

"The electronic computer is a machine that manipulates symbols in accordance to a predetermined and self-directed manner." Because the computer is so versatile, accurate, and extremely efficient, it has added new and dramatic design possibilities for information systems. Using such equipment only to replace electromechanical equipment, however, does not utilize its real potential.

Software includes all of the programming systems that facilitate the utilization of computer hardware. Software is the procedural instructions to the computer telling it what to do, and also the control of what is done. First, subroutines were developed so that programming was easier and less time consuming. These subroutines were called and used by the computer as designated in the general program. Next, compilers or translators were developed so that the programmers could use very simple language in programming. Many special language programs have been created.

Integrated data processing suggests a close coupling of all of the components in the information system so that human intervention at juncture points is not necessary. The greatest gain from IDP is the elimination of those errors which creep into the system when data is duplicated or converted into another form by human action. The essential requirement of such a system is the use of a common language, with machine inputs generated or created from the original input.

Real-time data processing means an on-line, or constantly available, operation involving the continuous updating of the master information file whenever transactions occur. Airline reservations systems are an example of this kind of an operation.

The time-sharing concept originally meant the carrying out of more than one instruction by the computer at one time. Next, several programs were processed simultaneously, and then remote stations were added when the interrupt feature was added to computer capability. Now when we talk of time sharing we mean on-line, real-time, concurrent access, autonomy of subscribers, and functional latitude capability.

The value of a unit of information is equal to the incremental improvement it makes in decision making. If we could measure this, we would know how much and what kind of information to provide. Because we do not know the cost of what is needed, we tend to over-supply. This is particularly true if we consider the cost of the information system fixed and believe that we might as well operate it at full capacity. This raises the question of the size of information systems. Although there is a general belief that efficiency improves with size, it is more rational to select equipment that is capable of handling specific information requirements.

Selected Readings

Dearden, John, McFarlan, F. Warren, and Zani, William M. *Managing Computer-Based Information Systems.* Homewood, Ill.: Richard D. Irwin, Inc., 1971.

The authors present a discussion of the construction and management of computer-based information systems with cases and illustrations. A basic knowledge of computers is assumed.

Hertz, David B. *New Power for Management.* New York: McGraw-Hill Book Company, 1969.

The book provides a summary of the information requirements of the various functional areas of a business. The applicability of the computer in such systems is reviewed.

LeBreton, Preston P. *Administrative Intelligence-Information Systems.* Boston: Houghton-Mifflin Company, 1969.

A book outlining the information-intelligence concept in management. It includes a discussion on the nature and role of information and the assessment of needs. It also has a section on the planning of such systems.

Sanders, Donald H. *Computers and Management.* New York: McGraw-Hill Book Company, 1970.

The role of the computer as a component of information systems is outlined in detail. Subject coverage includes planning, staffing, and control of computers.

Sharpe, William F. *The Economics of Computers.* New York: Columbia University Press, 1969.

The book presents a theoretical discussion of the economics of information systems, and particularly that of computers.

Questions

1 Outline the kinds of information needed to make rational decisions in:
   a. buying a home,
   b. operating a bowling alley,
   c. creating the "Peace Corps."

2 Does planning information differ from control information? How?

3 What is the difference between data and information? Give examples of each.

4 Is it advisable to classify data by the function it is to perform or by some characteristic unique to the data? Why? Contrast this with the classification of information.

5 How can the volume of data collected and stored be maintained within reasonable quantities?

6 What impact does electronic transmission have on information systems design?

7 Discuss the significance of computers relative to the design of information systems.

8 A phase of software development relates to compilers and translators. What is gained by this approach?

9 Outline the prerequisite of an integrated data processing system. How does this differ from real-time data processing?

10 What kinds of organization would be apt to use time-sharing installations? Why?

11 Discuss the relationship between system cost and response time. What cost factors are significant and how will they vary as response time increases?

Problems

1   Design a model of a real-time information system for one of the following:
    a. a department store,
    b. a football team,
    c. police department,
    d. cost control system in a factory.

2   Estimate the cost of any information system with which you are familiar. Include as many of the costs as you can, such as costs of equipment, systems design, and operation and control.

Chapter 8
Facilities Investment Decisions

Facilities investment decisions are perhaps the most crucial aspect of designing and operating systems. These decisions are part of the basic asset management problem of an enterprise, which is to utilize effectively the human, physical, monetary, and informational resources of the system. Present decisions to commit resources determine the future of an enterprise. Investment decisions are crucial to long-range success because they typically commit the organization for years to come, and, for most enterprises, physical facilities determine the capacity and operating characteristics of the system. The airlines' decision to convert from propeller-driven planes to jet aircraft is a notable example. Airlines which were slow to make the decision to convert were at a competitive disadvantage for several years.

When should old facilities be replaced? Which piece of equipment should be selected to perform a particular operation? Should equipment be leased or purchased? Should a particular service be performed within the organization or contracted to an outside service organization? Should the company have one big plant or several smaller ones? Should the plant utilize expensive highly automated equipment with low labor cost, or less expensive manually operated equipment with higher labor costs? Should an item be manufactured or purchased? Should the firm embark on a new research and development program? Should a new distribution system be introduced? These are some of the types of decisions with which management must continually deal. Our primary focus will be on two types of facilities decisions: (1) selection problems, comparing alternative methods of carrying out proposed projects; and (2) replacement problems, the retirement and replacement of existing facilities with new facilities.

Sources of Facilities Decisions

Decisions to invest in new facilities may arise from several sources. First, an organization may need to expand the capacity of its system. A growing firm needs more facilities to meet demands for higher levels of output. We discussed this kind of decision in Chapter 2. Second, an organization may need additional technical capabilities in the form of new manufacturing processes, computer information systems, research facilities, distribution systems, educational facilities, hospital patient-care facilities, and the like. Third, a firm may need to replace inefficient or obsolete equipment. As equipment gets older, it becomes more costly to maintain; and it may become obsolete because new equipment exists which can do the job more efficiently.

Strategic Importance of Facilities Investment Decisions

The strategic importance of facilities investment decisions is indicated by their magnitude. Facilities decisions typically involve very large expenditures. For example, in the United States, industry spent over $65 billion for new plant and equipment in 1968, nearly 8 per cent of the gross national product. An executive considering the expenditure of tens or hundreds of thousands or millions of dollars needs the best information he can obtain in order to make effective decisions.

It may take a long time for faulty decisions in this area to be recognized. In the current era of rapid technological change, many physical facilities become obsolete long before they are worn out. The failure to replace obsolete equipment may have no discernible effect for several years until a firm finds itself in an uncompetitive position. There are numerous examples of companies that continue to operate obsolete equipment, not recognizing that with each passing month or year, their operating costs relative to those of competitors are getting higher and higher until they reach a point at which the companies are no longer able to compete in the market. By contrast, an ineffective marketing program or a poorly designed product may be apparent much sooner than a faulty equipment decision.

Decisions Reflect Choice Among Alternatives

Managerial decisions are made on the basis of intuitive judgments or on the basis of careful analysis of the expected effect from carefully delineated alternatives. Facilities investment decisions are often incorrect, because managers fail to identify carefully alternatives and the relevant differences among them. Such difficulties often arise because of the complexities introduced by common elements among the alternatives. The equipment, machines, and buildings which are the subject of facilities investment decisions are usually parts of a complex system, and the interactions among system components may make it difficult to differentiate clearly the effects of alternatives.

Decisions are made in terms of future events and are based upon predictions of the future. Investment decisions refer to commitments of resources with the hope of realizing future benefits. Because decision makers cannot know the future with certainty, investment decisions involve the assessment of risk. What has happened in the past is irrelevant to such decisions except as it affects the future or aids in predicting the future. Whatever has already happened cannot be affected by future choices. This implies that past expenditures should not be included in the analyses of facilities, nor should apportionments of those expenditures be included.

A decision to invest resources generally depends upon a favorable answer to the question, "Will the investment earn enough in the form of benefits to recover the initial investment plus a return on the investment in keeping with the risk involved and the return available from alternative investments?" Finding such a basis is complicated by the fact that we are often faced with choosing among various options for which there is no readily apparent measure of superiority. An asset may have a high original cost which is offset by such factors as operating advantages in the form of lower operating costs; durability, reflected in lower maintenance costs; or increased technical capability, reflected in higher precision or reliability of the service provided.

Like other management decisions, facilities involve elements that cannot be measured or reduced to identifiable costs. Facilities decisions are based partly upon technical and engineering factors related to the physical capability of the equipment, partly upon economic factors such as costs and revenues, and partly upon human factors related to the impact on the facility on the organization. Environmental factors are becoming increasingly important, some of which are difficult to measure and evaluate. It is desirable insofar as possible to reduce the alternatives to numerical data that can be compared on an economic basis, and to identify the irreducibles, those factors which cannot be reduced to numerical data, so that they may be weighed in the final decision. Elements which are common to alternatives and which will not be affected by the choice of one or the other alternative need not be considered in the analysis.

Systems Concept

Since individual facilities are components of larger systems, the decision maker must consider the systems of which they are a part. However, the systems are often too complex to analyze as a unit. It is desirable to consider the entire system, but there are many instances in which the interrelationships among the system components are so complex that we could not identify all the possible alternatives and compare them in a reasonable time. In such cases, we may examine the entire system and then divide it into several parts in order to analyze the alternatives in each part. While analyzing each part, we can consider its impact on the whole system.

The example of a large drug distributor who was planning to change the materials handling system in one of its distribution centers illustrates a systems approach to facilities analyses and some of the difficulties that may be encountered.[1] The distribution center, one of eight company centers, served an area with a population of 10 million people and carried about 30,000 items in stock. Most orders were for small lots of about 10 to 50 different items. The company faced the decision of what combination of manual, mechanical, and automatic materials handling systems to use for filling customer orders.

The company, to satisfy customer wants, needed to have the ability to make prompt and complete shipments accompanied by a final invoice. Invoices were prepared with several copies which served as shipping lists, delivery receipts, accounts receivable billing records, and inventory control records. Although the problem dealt primarily with the materials handling system, the company found that the information system was so closely related to the material handling system that the two systems had to be considered together.

The distributor identified three major systems which had to be integrated: materials handling, customer order and invoice processing, and packing for shipment. For each subsystem, several alternatives were available. Thus, the complete warehouse system contained one of the alternatives from each of the five subsystems. A total of 300 possible combinations would meet the restraints imposed on the system. Examination of each of the 300 possible combinations was not practical or necessary because many of the combinations were incompatible. For example, to choose an underfloor tow chain for incoming materials and a belt conveyor system for order picking would be incompatible because of the duplicate investments in equipment and their interference with one another. Similarly, to choose a fully automatic materials handling system and manual order processing and inventory control systems would be incompatible because information for the materials handling system would have to be machine processed.

In the analysis of this problem, combinations of materials handling alternatives and information processing alternatives were compared, and combinations were chosen so that the two subsystems would be compatible. This substantially simplified the system analysis and permitted the examination of alternatives for the subsystems. Had an attempt been made to examine only complete systems, it is quite possible that some important alternatives would have been overlooked. Conversely, had an analysis been made of only individual alternatives, it is likely that the requirements of the complete materials handling-information processing system would not have

---

[1] This case is described in more detail in Eugene L. Grant and W. Grant Ireson, *Principles of Engineering Economy*, 5th ed. (New York: The Ronald Press Company, 1970), pp. 237–241.

been met. This case is typical of many facilities problems in which several subsystems are so interrelated that they must be considered simultaneously in order to design the best complete system.

The Role of Operating Managers

A company's important investment decisions are almost always approved by the board of directors or by the chief operating executive. In large organizations, top-level executives cannot be familiar with the technical and economic details of all the proposals presented to them, and they must rely upon evaluations made at lower levels in the organization. This requires close coordination among operating, design, and financial sectors of the enterprise, and between those initiating capital investment requests and those approving them.

Operating managers have an important role in capital investment decisions, because they must operate within the constraints imposed by the physical facilities of the system, and they initiate many of the proposals for altering those facilities. Lower-level operating managers carry the responsibility for carefully evaluating existing facilities and proposing changes, and they are required to weigh the alternatives on the basis of economically measurable criteria and evaluation of the irreducibles. They must be aware of the information needed at the top levels of the enterprise in order to furnish proper justification for their proposals. These information requirements make it increasingly necessary that, insofar as possible, economic justifications for various proposals be made on some comparable basis, such as those presented in this chapter.

Classification of Costs

The economic analysis for facilities decisions requires data on expected cost differences between future alternatives and consideration of the time value of money. Accounting data are important sources of information in making estimates for facilities decisions, but they cannot be used without careful evaluation because accounting data represent a record of past expenditures and receipts. Accounting data do not consider alternatives nor the time value of money, yet they do involve allocations of joint costs between divisions, departments, or products, and involve allocation of past expenditures to future time periods.

It is important to understand the distinction between average costs, incremental costs, and sunk costs if we expect to utilize cost data effectively. Average costs are often determined from accounting data and involve the allocation of joint costs, as in the allocation of overhead items to departments or product lines. For example, the salary of a department head or supervisor may be apportioned to various activities under his jurisdiction.

These indirect or overhead items may be allocated on some basis such as direct labor hours. If the overhead rate is determined to be $5.00 per dollar of direct labor cost, each task is charged $5.00 for each dollar of direct labor incurred In examining a prospective reduction in direct labor cost, the reduction will not necessarily result in a comparable reduction in overhead. The reduction in overhead may be zero, small, or large depending upon the particular alternative chosen. In comparing two alternatives, the only way to judge this effect is to analyze the expected effect on the various items which comprise the overhead expense.

Incremental cost refers to differences in costs among alternative actions. This is the cost with which we are concerned in making economic analyses for facilities decisions. Incremental costs are often difficult to define and to identify, but it is necessary to make as careful an estimate as possible when alternatives are being evaluated on the basis of cost differences. Consider the case of a manufacturer deciding whether to continue to make a particular part or to discontinue its production and to purchase the part from an outside supplier. The costs relevant to this decision are those which would actually be reduced or eliminated by discontinuing production and those which would actually be incurred by purchasing from an outside supplier. The extent to which costs will be reduced depends partly upon the use that is to be made of existing equipment and the space it occupies. Certain costs may be readily identified, such as the raw materials involved, direct labor cost, power to run the machines, and the costs of supervising the operation. Others which are included in the total cost of producing the item may not be reduced, such as costs of administration and the cost of maintaining that part of the building in which the work is done. The important factor for the analysis is to determine which costs would actually be reduced or eliminated by making the change.

Since we are considering differences in future effects of alternatives, past costs should be considered as sunk costs which are irrelevant except as they affect the future. Although this concept seems simple enough, it may be difficult to apply in specific situations. Treatment of past expenditures will be explored more fully when we consider the question of placing a value on existing items of equipment in a replacement study, but a familiar example will serve to illustrate the point. Suppose that you purchase a new automobile for $3,000, accept delivery and drive it home. Suppose further that the dealer might be induced to repurchase the car for his cost of approximately $2,500 and that this is your only option for disposing of it. Now the question is what is the value of the automobile? If your neighbor asks the value of the car, you might tell him $3,000, but if you suddenly find yourself in need of funds and are forced to sell the car, it is clear that the car is only worth $2,500. Before you bought the car, your decision was whether or not to spend $3,000 for it, and up to the point at which you actually made the purchase the relevant cost was $3,000. However, after you bought the car, the purchase price became irrelevant to any future decisions. When you own the automobile, the relevant value is the amount you could realize by selling it.

In the methods of analysis which follow, our attention will be directed to the use of cash flows as opposed to expense items. Since we are concerned with the actual money differences between alternative courses of action, this will remind us that we are concerned with expected future cash receipts and disbursements.

The Life Span of Assets

We may define the life of capital equipment in at least three ways: physical life, economic life, and tax life. The economic life span of equipment may differ considerably from its physical life, and the life span for income tax purposes may differ from both of these. Obsolescence and increasing maintenance charges may reduce the economic life of equipment to a mere fraction of its physical life. For equipment analysis purposes, it is the economic life of an asset that should be considered as the length of the investment period. The analysis will have to take into account, however, the length of time allowed for depreciation of the asset for tax purposes, because depreciation affects after-tax cash flow and therefore the investment decision.

We may approach the selection of asset life in several ways. A firm may use the guidelines published by the United States Internal Revenue Service as the basis for both depreciating assets and for economic analysis of investment proposals. Or a firm may make a separate forecast of what it considers a reasonable life, taking into account the state of the art in the industry and the rate of technological advance. Another approach is to calculate an optimum life which minimizes cost or maximizes present worth or rate of return on an asset.

Time Value of Money

Since facilities problems involve decisions which have long-run affects, money flows are adjusted for time value in order to make direct comparisons between alternatives. Money has time value, because people are willing to pay for its use. Banks pay interest for the use of money in savings accounts, borrowers pay lenders for the use of their money, and capital investments are expected to yield enough to return the initial investment plus interest on the money committed over the life of the investment. Because of interest, a dollar in hand now is worth more than the prospect of a dollar to be received at some future date.

Compound
Interest
and the
Concept of
Equivalence

Fundamental to the analysis of long-term capital investment decisions is a clear understanding of the concept of equivalence as related to the time value of money and compound interest. The time value of money arises in this way. If you have $1,000 today and invest it at a rate of 10 per cent, one year from now you will have $1,000 plus $100 interest for a total of $1,100. For an interest rate of 10 per cent, $1,100 due one year from now is said to be equivalent to $1,000 in hand today. If the investment were for two years and interest earned at the end of one year were left to accumulate at the same 10 per cent, interest is compounded and the amount due at the end of two years would be $1,210.

We will use the following symbols to explain the calculations in more general terms:

P = a present sum of money
R = a uniform series of end-of-period payments over t periods
S = a sum of money at the end of t periods from the present time
i = interest rate per period (expressed as a decimal)
t = the number of time periods
T = terminal time period

Using this notation, the preceding example may be expressed in terms of the basic formula for compound interest:

$$S = P(1 + i)^t, \tag{8.1}$$

where $(1 + i)^t$ is the single payment compound amount factor $(CAF'_{t,i})$ for t years at i rate of interest. Using the formula, the value of our $1,000 investment at the end of five years would be:

$$S = P(1 + 0.10)^5 = \$1,000(1.611) = \$1,611.$$

If we are given the value of a future sum of money, we may wish to convert it into the equivalent present value, or to find its present worth. To accomplish this, we take the reciprocal of the single payment compound amount factor which is called the single payment present worth factor $(PWF'_{t,i})$.

$$P = S(PWF'_{t,i}) = S\frac{1}{(1 + i)^t} \tag{8.2}$$

The interest tables in the appendix of tables at the end of the book show single payment present worth factors, series present worth factors, and capital recovery factors for interest rates between 1 and 50 per cent. Table values represent values for one dollar in each case; to convert to any other amount, simply multiply the appropriate table value by that amount. For instance, we may ask, "How much would have to be invested now at 5 per cent interest in order to accumulate $5,000 at the end of three years?" Or,

"What is the present value of $5,000 due at the end of three years at an interest rate of 6 per cent?" Using the value from the table, we find that:

$$P = S(PWF'_{3,\ 0.06}) = \$5,000(0.840) = \$4,200.$$

If we had a uniform series of payments or receipts due at the end of each of t periods, we could find the present worth of this series by adding the present worth of each of the individual payments, or we could add together each of the single payment present worth factors and multiply this sum by the amount of the uniform payment.

The expression for this summation is

$$
\begin{aligned}
P &= \sum_{t=1}^{T} \frac{R}{(1+i)^t} \\
&= R\frac{1}{1+i} + R\frac{1}{(1+i)^2} + \cdots + R\frac{1}{(1+i)^T} \\
&= R\left(\frac{1}{1+i} + \frac{1}{(1+i)^2} + \cdots + \frac{1}{(1+i)^T}\right).
\end{aligned}
\tag{8.3}
$$

The summation of this geometric series is

$$P = R\frac{(1+i)^t - 1}{i(1+i)^t}.\tag{8.4}$$

The expression

$$\frac{(1+i)^t - 1}{i(1+i)^t}$$

is called the series present worth factor $PWF_{T,i}$. The present value of $200 per year for 10 years at an interest rate of 6 per cent is

$$P = R(PWF_{10,\ 0.06}) = \$200(7.360) = \$1,472.$$

If we deposited $1,472 today at 6 per cent we could withdraw $200 at the end of each of ten years and leave nothing in the account.

The present worth of an infinite uniform series is the annual amount divided by the interest rate:

$$P = \frac{R}{i}.\tag{8.5}$$

At an interest rate of 10 per cent the present worth of $300 per year forever is $300/0.10 = $3,000. This is often referred to as a capitalized cost.

The reciprocal of the series present worth factor is called the capital recovery factor $(CRF_{t,i})$ which is used to determine the uniform end of period payments which are equivalent to a present sum.

$$R = P(CRF_{t,i}) = P\frac{i(1+i)^t}{(1+i)^t - 1}.\tag{8.6}$$

If we take a lender's point of view, it gives the uniform end of period payments necessary to repay a debt. If we assume only one annual payment, the amount required to repay a $15,000 mortgage over 20 years at 6 per cent is:

$$R = P(CRF_{20,\ 0.06}) = \$15,000(0.08718) = \$1,317.70.$$

Over the twenty-year life of the loan, a total of $20(\$1,317.70) = \$26,354$ would have been paid representing the loan principle and interest. In a facilities investment analysis, the capital recovery factor is used to convert the amount of the original investment into an equivalent uniform annual cost figure.

These examples assume that cash flows occur at the end of each period. In many situations, cash flows do not occur at the end of a period, but rather throughout a period. With continuous cash flows we might use continuous compounding of interest as discussed in the next section. For most situations, periodic compounding of interest and an end-of-period convention are used, because they are easier and their use will usually not introduce a significant error.

Continuous Compounding of Interest[2]

If the interest in equation 8.1 were compounded more often than once per year, we find the compound amount by dividing the annual nominal interest rate and multiplying the number of periods by the number of times per year interest is compounded.

$$S = P\left(1 + \frac{i}{m}\right)^{mt} \tag{8.7}$$

where

$$m = \text{number of compounding periods per year.}$$

If we let

$$k = \frac{m}{i}$$

then

$$m = ik$$

and

$$S = P\left(1 + \frac{1}{k}\right)^{ikt}$$
$$= P\left[\left(1 + \frac{1}{k}\right)^{k}\right]^{it}. \tag{8.8}$$

---

[2] This section may be omitted without loss of continuity.

As the number of compounding periods increases without bounds, k approaches infinity, $k \rightarrow \infty$.

From calculus, we know the limit of this expansion is

$$\lim_{k \to \infty} \left(1 + \frac{1}{k} \right)^k = e$$

and

$$e = 2.71828. \ldots$$

Therefore, for continuous compounding of interest e^{it} is the single payment compound factor, and from equation 8.1

$$S = Pe^{it}. \tag{8.9}$$

Single payment present worth is

$$P = Se^{-it} \tag{8.10}$$

and present worth of a series is

$$P = \int_0^T R(t) e^{-it} \, dt \tag{8.11}$$

where

$$R(t) = \text{annual rate of cash flow.}$$

Selection

In the selection phase of capital equipment facilities analysis, we choose from among alternative proposals one which will accomplish an operation. As part of the decision analysis, we are interested in determining whether we will recover the proposed investment plus a return commensurate with the risks involved, usually by means of a discounted cash flow analysis. Four basic discounted cash flow methods by which alternatives may be compared are:

1. present worth of cost comparison,
2. equivalent uniform annual cost comparison,
3. present worth of savings or income from incremental investment, and
4. rate of return on savings or income from incremental investment.

The first three methods require that a minimum attractive rate of return be specified, and alternatives are then compared on the basis of this rate. The fourth computes the expected return on the additional investment required for higher cost alternatives. As we shall see, each of these approaches will give comparable results in the sense that each will give the same relative ranking to alternatives.[3]

A number of quite complex mathematical models have been developed to analyze many of the special problems which arise in facilities selection and replacement decisions and project analyses. A thorough understanding of these four methods of analysis is essential to an understanding of more complex and sophisticated models, because these methods represent the basis for more sophisticated analytic models.

Cash Flow

Comparison of facilities alternatives begins with a determination of prospective cash flow representing expected receipts and disbursements. The concept of cash flows is central to the analysis. In some situations, such as selection of individual pieces or groups of equipment, there may be little or no impact on revenues, and we are concerned primarily with expected costs or disbursements except for receipts generated by salvage value. In this regard, the decisions are typical of many of those encountered at the design level of the system. The alternatives under consideration often will not affect expected revenues. In other situations, such as building a new facility or expanding existing facilities, expected revenues will be affected and would be included in the cash flows. In either case, the basic methods of comparison are the same.

When the expected cash flows for each alternative have been enumerated, it may be possible to determine directly which alternative is the more attractive. If one alternative has a lower initial investment and lower operating costs over the study period than the other alternative, it is obviously more attractive from the standpoint of those economic factors. But unfortunately the comparison is usually not this simple. Difficulties arise because cash flows often are not directly comparable, such as in the situation in which one alternative involves a higher initial investment but has some advantage over another in terms of lower operating costs, higher salvage value, or a longer expected life. Then we are back to our original question of whether these advantages will offset the higher initial investment.

Consider the following example. A part of a firm's operation involves a service which can be performed manually or can be done by certain equipment. Two equipment modules have been proposed, giving three alternatives for evaluation. Under the manual operation, called Plan A, annual operating costs are estimated at $36,000, which includes direct labor expense and those items of indirect cost which are related to this operation. Plan B, which requires an initial investment of $44,000, has expected annual operating costs of $24,400. The firm anticipates that this equipment module

---

[3] One exception to this statement will be noted in the section on rate of return.

will have a useful life of ten years, which coincides with the expected requirement for the length of the service, and that it will have just enough scrap
value at the end of the ten-year period to cover the cost of its removal. Thus,
we assume that the module has no terminal salvage value. Plan C, which
requires an initial investment of $70,000, is expected to reduce operating
cost to $20,900 per year, to have the same ten-year life, and to have a net
terminal salvage value of $9,500. Table 8.1 gives a tabulation of expected

Table 8.1 Table of Cash Flows for Three Alternatives

Year	Plan A	Plan B	Plan C
0		−$44,000	−$70,000
1	−$36,000	−$24,400	−$20,900
2	−$36,000	−$24,400	−$20,900
3	−$36,000	−$24,400	−$20,900
4	−$36,000	−$24,400	−$20,900
5	−$36,000	−$24,400	−$20,900
6	−$36,000	−$24,400	−$20,900
7	−$36,000	−$24,400	−$20,900
8	−$36,000	−$24,400	−$20,900
9	−$36,000	−$24,400	−$20,900
10	−$36,000	−$24,400	−$20,900
			+$ 9,500
TOTALS	−$360,000	−$288,000	−$269,500

cash flows over the ten-year study period. In the table, cash outflows are
shown as negative amounts, and cash inflows are shown as positive amounts.
A cursory examination of the table may suggest that Plan C should be
chosen because it has a projected lower total cash flow. Cash flows, however,
are not directly comparable because of variations in their timing. The timing
of cash flows for Plan C is portrayed in Figure 8.1.

In this example, we assume uniform annual operating costs over the
ten-year period. Such factors as rising labor costs, increased maintenance
costs, and reduced operating efficiency of equipment as it ages may create
situations in which a uniform cash flow assumption is not appropriate. The
analyst should be careful to include such changing cost patterns in the analysis whenever necessary.

**Present
Worth of
Cost**

Present worth and uniform annual cost comparisons are based upon a specified rate of interest, or discount rate, which is often referred to as a minimum
attractive rate of return, and represents the minimum return the firm expects
for investments with commensurate risks. This usually places the rate at a
level higher than bank borrowing rates, and should reflect the cost of capital
to the enterprise, because every investment decision competes with all other

Figure 8.1 Cash Flows for Plan C

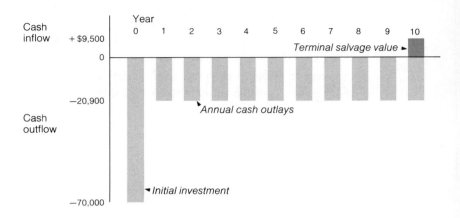

investment decisions in the organization. We assume that the firm has determined a minimum attractive rate of return of 22 per cent before income
taxes and a rate of 12 per cent after income taxes of 48 per cent for this
class of investment.

For the models which follow, we will use this notation:

$$PW = \text{present worth}$$
$$c_t = \text{operating cost for year } t$$
$$c = \text{uniform operating cost}$$
$$i = \text{interest rate}$$
$$I = \text{initial investment in the facility}$$
$$S_T = \text{terminal salvage value}$$
$$t = \text{year}$$
$$T = \text{terminal year of the study}$$

We determine present worth of cost for each alternative by converting all
cash flows to equivalent present worths at the specified interest rate. If the
cash flows are not uniform, the cash flow for each time period must be multiplied by the single payment present worth factor for that period, and
summed. This process is summarized in the following expression:

$$PWC = I - S_T(PWF'_{T,i}) + \sum_{t=1}^{T} c_t(PWF'_{t,i}). \tag{8.12}$$

Note that the present worth of the terminal salvage value is subtracted because it is a cash inflow. If the cash flows are uniform, we may shorten the
computation considerably by using the series present worth factor:

$$PWC = I - S_T(PWF'_{T,i}) + c(PWF_{T,i}). \tag{8.13}$$

Applying this expression to the data for Plan C, we obtain

$$PWC_C = I - S_{10}(PWF'_{10,\ 0.22}) + c(PWF_{10,\ 0.22})$$
$$= \$70,000 - \$9,500(0.1369) + \$20,900(3.932)$$
$$= \$150,700.$$

Similarly, for Plans A and B, we obtain

$$PWC_A = c(PWF_{10,\ 0.22}) = \$36,000(3.932)$$
$$= \$141,200, \text{ and}$$
$$PWC_B = I + c(PWF_{10,\ 0.22}) = \$44,000 + \$24,400(3.932)$$
$$= \$139,700.$$

Based upon the present worth of cost, Plan B is the most economical plan. Even though Plan C requires a lower total cash outlay over the ten-year period, the timing of the disbursements and receipts makes it less attractive than either of the other two plans at this interest rate.

Equivalent Uniform Annual Cost

A comparison of annual costs requires the conversion of cash flows into an equivalent uniform annual series. This procedure may be thought of as the inverse of finding present worths. For present worth calculations, all cash flows are converted into equivalent sums at zero date, whereas for uniform annual cost calculations cash flows are spread out over the life of the study period by converting them into an equivalent uniform annual series. We calculate uniform annual cost (UAC) by using the procedure represented by the following expression:

$$UAC = (I - S_T)CRF_{T,i} + iS_T + c \qquad (8.14)$$

Uniform annual cost is initial investment minus terminal salvage value times the capital recovery factor, plus interest on terminal salvage value, plus uniform operating costs.

For the three plans under consideration, equation 8.14 gives the following results:

$$UAC_A = c$$
$$= \$36,000$$
$$UAC_B = (I)CRF_{10,\ 0.22} + c = \$44,000(0.2549) + \$24,400$$
$$= \$35,600$$
$$UAC_C = (I - S_T)CRF_{10,\ 0.22} + 0.22S_{10} + c$$
$$= (\$70,000 - 9,500)0.2549 + 0.22(\$9,500) + \$20,900$$
$$= \$38,400.$$

Plan B is still the preferred plan. Where there is a terminal salvage value, as in Plan C, total capital recovery is made up of two components, the uniform annual costs on the initial investment less the terminal salvage value, and the interest on the terminal salvage value. A loan repayment analogy may be helpful in understanding the rationale for this. If we borrow $70,000 and expect to repay $60,500 of this plus interest in equal annual payments, and to repay $9,500 in one lump sum at the end of the ten-year period, our total yearly payment would consist of two parts: the uniform annual payment necessary to repay the $60,500 plus interest, and the annual interest on the end-of-period lump sum payment. In this illustration, the annual payments would be $60,500 times the capital recovery factor for 22 per cent for 10 years, or $15,400 per year, and the annual interest would be $2,100.

Another way in which to find uniform annual cost is to subtract the present worth of terminal salvage value from the initial cost and multiply this difference by the capital recovery factor.

$$UAC = [I - S_T(PWF'_{T,i})](CRF_{T,i}) + c. \qquad (8.15)$$

In the case of Plan C, this would yield

$$\begin{aligned} UAC_C &= [\$70,000 - \$9,500(0.1369)](0.2549) + \$20,900 \\ &= \$38,400 \end{aligned}$$

which is the same as the result obtained before.

If the cash flows are different from year to year, the general procedure is to convert cash flows into their present worths and multiply the sum of these present worths by the appropriate capital recovery factor. Applying this concept gives

$$UAC = \left[I - S_T(PWF'_{T,i}) + \sum_{t=1}^{T} c_t(PWF'_{t,i}) \right](CRF_{T,i}). \qquad (8.16)$$

Equation 8.16 is a general form which can be used with any series of cash flows. Equations 8.14 and 8.16 yield the same results which we illustrate by converting the previously computed present worth of cost for Plan C to uniform annual cost:

$$UAC_C = (PWC_C)(CRF_{10,\ 0.22}) = \$150,700(0.2549) = \$38,400.$$

This is the same result achieved by computing equivalent uniform annual cost directly from cash flows. Conversely, present worths may be computed by multiplying equivalent uniform annual costs by the appropriate series present worth factor.

Since both present worth and uniform annual cost methods yield equivalent results (by this, we mean that the particular option favored by one method will also be favored by the other method in a like ratio), the choice of which method to use depends on the preference of the analyst or the manager making the decision. Present worth methods seem to be favored in the capital budgeting literature, while many authors of the literature on engineering economy seem to prefer uniform annual cost methods. In the case of irregular series of cash flows, present worth methods are easier to use, because the cash flows must first be converted into present worths before uniform annual costs may be computed. On the other hand, uniform annual cost is easier to use when comparing assets with different life spans, and some feel that they are easier to understand.

Comparison on the Basis of Savings on Income

So far, we have compared alternatives on the basis of costs. To evaluate income-producing investments, we compare expected cash outflows with expected cash inflows over the life of the project. We wish to determine whether the income or savings produced is sufficient to return the initial investment plus an adequate rate of interest on that investment. The same criterion may be applied to projects which promise cost savings, as well as to income-generating projects. Leaving aside questions of measurement and apportionment, the basic accounting expression for net profit is:

$$\text{Net Profit} = \text{Revenue} - \text{Expense}.$$

If, as in the case of many investment decisions, the proposed investment will not materially add to the revenue of the enterprise, but promises to reduce cost for some portion of the operation, it will have the same effect on net profit as will an increase in revenue. Thus, for purposes of analysis, savings resulting from cost reduction may be treated in the same manner as net income from income-generating projects. This is illustrated in Table 8.2

Table 8.2 Table of Cash Flows Comparing Plans A and B

Year	Cash Flows Plan A	Cash Flows Plan B	Difference in Cash Flows Plan B–Plan A
0		−$ 44,000	−$44,000
1–10	−$ 36,000 per year	−$ 24,400 per year	+11,600 per year
TOTALS	−$360,000	−$288,000	+$72,000

which compares the differences in cash flows between Plans A and B. Figure 8.2 compares the timing of the savings from Plan B to that from Plan A. When tabulating cash flows, it is convenient to show cash inflows or receipts as positive values, and cash outflows or disbursements as negative values. This makes it possible to directly compare cash flows for the alternatives under consideration. In our example, Plan B requires an incremental investment of $44,000 over Plan A and has incremental annual savings of $11,600.

To find the savings for Plan C, we determine the difference in cash flows between Plans C and B, as in Table 8.3.

Table 8.3 Table of Cash Flows Comparing Plans B and C

Year	Cash Flows Plan B	Cash Flows Plan C	Difference in Cash Flows Plan C—Plan B
0	−$ 44,000	−$ 70,000	−$26,000
1–10	−$ 24,400 per year	−$ 20,900 per year	+$ 3,500 per year
10		+$ 9,500	+$ 9,500
TOTALS	−$288,000	−$269,500	+$18,500

Figure 8.2 Difference in Cash Flows Between Plan B and Plan A

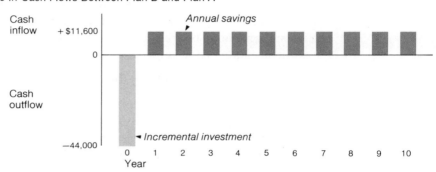

Why do we compare Plans C and B rather than Plans C and A? The answer is that we are dealing with mutually exclusive alternatives, and we expect each increment of investment to justify itself. If we can accomplish the same task with the investment of $44,000 required by Plan B as with the investment of $70,000 required by Plan C, we expect that extra $26,000 of investment to earn more than the preceding increment in order to be considered. Remember, we have assumed that no benefits may be derived from Plan C other than those revealed in the economic analysis, and that the two plans are otherwise equal. If Plan B were not available to us, then it would be appropriate to compare Plan C with Plan A, but since Plan B is available to do the same task for a lesser investment, no meaningful comparison can be made between Plans A and C for this decision.

In general, when dealing with multiple alternatives, they should be ranked in order of increasing initial investments and the savings, if any, resulting from the larger investment compared with the required incremental investment.

Inclusion of Income Taxes

In any economy in which income taxes are levied at high rates, the impact of such taxes should be taken into account in facilities selection and replacement decisions. We may do this directly by computing the impact of income taxes on cash flows and including them in the analysis, or, indirectly, by establishing a before-tax minimum attractive rate of return which is proportionately higher than the required after-tax return. The former approach is preferable because it enables the analyst to explore directly the impact of income taxes on the decisions to be made. Obviously we cannot explore the details of any tax laws or regulations in the space available; therefore, we will restrict our discussion to a consideration of a few of the general principles involved, based primarily on practice in the United States.

The basic procedure required to incorporate taxes into the analysis is to calculate the extra income taxes which are likely to be incurred and to subtract these from the before-tax cash flows. To find the amount of extra income tax, we compute extra taxable income and apply the appropriate income tax rate. In facilities studies, taxable income will usually be the before-tax savings or income less an allowance for depreciation.

Depreciation

Although the term depreciation has several meanings in common usage, we shall use it in the accounting concept of amortizing the cost of capital assets over their expected lives of service. Since depreciation used in this context is not a process of valuation of assets, book values have no necessary relationship to asset market values. In facilities replacement studies, distinctions between book value and market value are important because they are used differently in the analysis.

In the United States, three methods for computing depreciation are in common use: straight-line, sum-of-years digits, and double-declining balance methods. Under the straight-line method, the annual depreciation allowance is the original cost of the asset minus its projected terminal salvage value divided by the estimated life of the asset. Since Plan B has no terminal salvage value, annual depreciation is $44,000/10$ years $= \$4,400$ per year. For Plan C, it would be $(\$70,000 - 9,500)/10$ years $= \$6,050$ per year.

Under the sum-of-years digits method, the amount of depreciation allowed each year changes and is determined from a fraction, the numerator of which is the number of years of life remaining in the asset from the year being calculated, and the denominator of which is the sum of the years digits for the life of the asset. In the example being considered here, we have assumed a life of 10 years. For this life, the denominator of the depreciation fraction is the sum of the numbers one through ten. The sum of a series of integers may be determined from the following formula:

$$1 + 2 + 3 + \cdots + n = \frac{n(n + 1)}{2}. \tag{8.17}$$

Thus, the denominator of the depreciation fraction for an asset with a ten-year life span is $10(11)/2 = 55$. Depreciation to be charged in the first year is $10/55$ of the original cost minus the estimated terminal salvage value. Charge for the second year is $9/55$ of the original cost minus estimated terminal salvage value, and the fraction decreases by $1/55$ each year through the tenth year. The depreciation charge for Plan C for the first year would be (10/55) ($70,000 − 9,500) = $11,000. In the second year, it would be (9/55) ($70,000 − 9,500) = $9,900, and so on. The depreciation would decline by $1,100 each year. For Plans B and C, this method writes off approximately 73 per cent of the depreciable cost of the asset in the first half of its life. In general, the sum-of-years digits method would write off 70 to 75 per cent of the depreciable cost during the first half of an asset's life, depending upon the length of life used.

Under the double-declining balance method, a depreciation rate is applied to the remaining book value, the rate being 200 per cent/estimated life. For a ten-year life, the rate would be 200 per cent/10 years = 20 per cent per year. For Plan B, the depreciation allowed for the first year would be 0.20 ($44,000) = $8,800. At the end of the first year, the remaining book value is $44,000 − $8,800 = $35,200, and the depreciation charged for the second year would be 0.20($35,200) = $7,040. The terminal salvage value of the asset is disregarded since there will be a small book value remaining at the end of the depreciation period. For Plan B, the remaining book value at the end of the tenth year is approximately $4,700. In general, this method writes off about two-thirds of the initial cost of the asset in the first half of its life. Table 8.4 shows a comparison of annual depreciation for

Table 8.4 Annual Depreciation for Plans B and C

	PLAN B			PLAN C		
Year	Straight-Line	Sum-of-Years Digits	Double-Declining Balance	Straight-Line	Sum-of-Years Digits	Double-Declining Balance
1	$4,400	$8,000	$8,800	$6,050	$11,000	$14,000
2	4,400	7,200	7,040	6,050	9,900	11,200
3	4,400	6,400	5,632	6,050	8,800	8,960
4	4,400	5,600	4,506	6,050	7,700	7,168
5	4,400	4,800	3,604	6,050	6,600	5,734
6	4,400	4,000	2,884	6,050	5,500	4,587
7	4,400	3,200	2,307	6,050	4,400	3,670
8	4,400	2,400	1,845	6,050	3,300	2,936
9	4,400	1,600	1,476	6,050	2,200	2,349
10	4,400	800	1,181	6,050	1,100	1,879

Plans B and C, and Figure 8.3 shows the end-of-year book values for Plan B for each of the depreciation methods. These figures illustrate the differences in the rate of write-off under each depreciation method.

After-Tax Cash Flows

If we assume an income tax rate of 48 per cent and straight-line depreciation, the calculation of after-tax cash flow for Plan B is as follows:

Figure 8.3 Plan B—End-of-Year Book Values for Three Depreciation Methods

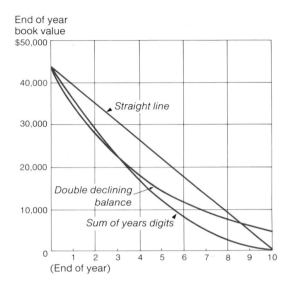

After-Tax Cash Flow for Plan B—Straight-Line Depreciation		
Before-Tax Annual Savings		$11,600
Less extra income tax		
Before Tax Savings	$11,600	
Less Extra Depreciation	− 4,400	
Change in Taxable Income	$ 7,200	
Extra Income Tax = 0.48 ($7,200)		−3,456
After-Tax Cash Flow		$ 8,144

The extra depreciation is $4,400 which, when subtracted from before-tax savings, results in a change in taxable income of $7,200. The extra income tax is then 48 per cent of this, or $3,456. This calculation can be reduced to a single expression:

$$f(a)_t = f(b)_t - r[f(b)_t - d_t] \qquad (8.18)$$

where:

$$f(a)_t = \text{after-tax cash flow year } t$$
$$f(b)_t = \text{before-tax cash flow year } t$$
$$r = \text{income tax rate}$$
$$d_t = \text{extra depreciation year } t.$$

Tables 8.5 and 8.6 show the calculations of after-tax cash flows for Plans B and C with sum-of-years digits depreciation. In the case of an investment that has a terminal salvage value, such as Plan C, it is ordinarily convenient to show the recovery of salvage value as a separate entry in the terminal year in the cash flow tabulation in order to distinguish it from the taxable income arising from savings for that year. Since salvage value represents the recovery of invested capital, and is not taxable income, there would be no impact

Table 8.5 After-Tax Cash Flow, Comparing Plans B and A
Sum-of-Years Digits Depreciation (Income Tax Rate 48 Per Cent)

Year	Difference in Before-Tax Cash Flow Plan B–A	Extra Depreciation	Change in Taxable Income	Cash Flow For Extra Income Tax	Difference in After-Tax Cash Flow Plan B–A
0	−$44,000				−$44,000
1	11,600	−$ 8,000	$ 3,600	−$ 1,728	9,872
2	11,600	− 7,200	4,400	− 2,112	9,488
3	11,600	− 6,400	5,200	− 2,496	9,104
4	11,600	− 5,600	6,000	− 2,880	8,720
5	11,600	− 4,800	6,800	− 3,264	8,336
6	11,600	− 4,000	7,600	− 3,648	7,952
7	11,600	− 3,200	8,400	− 4,032	7,568
8	11,600	− 2,400	9,200	− 4,416	7,184
9	11,600	− 1,600	10,000	− 4,800	6,800
10	11,600	− 800	10,800	− 5,184	6,416
TOTALS	$72,000	−$44,000	$72,000	−$34,560	$37,440

Table 8.6 After-Tax Cash Flows, Comparing Plans C and B
Sum-of-Years Digit Depreciation (Income Tax Rate 48 Per Cent)

Year	Difference in Before-Tax Cash Flow Plan C–B	Extra Depreciation	Change in Taxable Income	Cash Flow For Extra Income Tax	Difference in After-Tax Cash Flow Plan C–B
0	−$26,000				−$26,000
1	3,500	−$ 3,000	$ 500	−$ 240	3,260
2	3,500	− 2,700	800	− 348	3,116
3	3,500	− 2,400	1,100	− 528	2,972
4	3,500	− 2,100	1,400	− 672	2,828
5	3,500	− 1,800	1,700	− 816	2,648
6	3,500	− 1,500	2,000	− 960	2,540
7	3,500	− 1,200	2,300	− 1,104	2,396
8	3,500	− 900	2,600	− 1,248	2,252
9	3,500	− 600	2,900	− 1,392	2,108
10	3,500	− 300	3,200	− 1,536	1,964
	9,500				9,500
TOTALS	$18,500	−$16,500	$18,500	−$8,800	$ 9,620

on income tax from such recovery unless the amount realized were different from the ending book value. In such a case, it would be treated as a gain or loss which affects that year's taxes according to the applicable regulation.

Present Worth of Savings or Income

When cash flows resulting from expected savings or income for a project have been calculated, present worths may be calculated by following a procedure similar to that for determining present worth of cost. If we let s_t equal savings or revenue for year t, substitute s_t for c_t in equations 8.12 and 8.13, and change signs to reflect the direction of cash flow, we obtain these expressions for present worth of savings:

$$PWS = -I + S_T(PWF'_{T,i}) + \sum_{t=1}^{T} s_t(PWF'_{t,i}) \qquad (8.19)$$

$$PWS = -I + S_T(PWF'_{T,i}) + s(PWF_{T,i}). \qquad (8.20)$$

With an after-tax discount rate of 12 per cent and using the after-tax cash flows for savings resulting from Plan B in Table 8.5, and for Plan C in Table 8.6, we find $PWS_B = \$4,001$ and $PWS_C = -\$7,438$. This analysis reveals that even though there is a net positive cash flow of $9,620 resulting from Plan C, it is insufficient to yield the minimum attractive rate of return, because of the timing of the positive cash flows. This result is consistent with those of the before-tax present worth of cost and equivalent uniform annual cost analyses.

Rate of Return on Incremental Investment

Present worth and uniform annual cost criteria assume a specified minimum attractive rate of return. Often it is desirable to compute the expected return on the investment required for a particular facility project. Several methods have been described in the operations management, accounting, and finance literature which yield answers called rate of return, but many of these do not take into account the time value of money and compounding of interest. The discounted cash flow method (DCF) described here is the correct method for determining internal rate of return, because it involves a discounting process which takes into account the time value of money. Other methods which do not consider the time value of money should be referred to by some phrase to distinguish them from correct procedures, such as "approximate rate of return," or "so-called rate of return."

The basic procedure for calculating the true rate of return by the discounted cash flow method is to find the rate of interest at which the present worth of the net cash flows resulting from the investment over its expected life is zero. Or, stated in another way, the procedure is to find the rate of interest at which the present worth of the net cash receipts (either income or savings) expected from the investment is equal to the initial investment.

Finding this interest rate usually involves a trial and error process of computing net present worths of the stream of cash flows at interest rates above and below the rate of return, and interpolating them. Present worth of after-tax savings from Plan B at interest rates of 14 per cent and 16 per cent are calculated in Table 8.7. At 14 per cent, the present worth is

Table 8.7 Present Worth of After-Tax Savings for Plan B
Sum-of-Years Digits Depreciation

Year	After-Tax Cash Flow	*i = 14 per cent* Single Payment Present Worth Factor	Present Worth	*i = 16 per cent* Single Payment Present Worth Factor	Present Worth
0	−$44,000	1.0000	−$44,000	1.0000	−$44,000
1	9,872	.8772	8,660	.8621	8,510
2	9,488	.7695	7,301	.7432	7,051
3	9,104	.6750	6,145	.6407	5,832
4	8,702	.5921	5,163	.5523	4,816
5	8,336	.5194	4,329	.4761	3,969
6	7,952	.4556	3,623	.4104	3,264
7	7,568	.3996	3,024	.3578	2,678
8	7,184	.3506	2,518	.3050	2,191
9	6,800	.3075	2,091	.2630	1,788
10	6,416	.2697	1,731	.2267	1,454
TOTALS	$37,440		$ 585		−$ 2,446

$585, which indicates that the rate of return is higher than 14 per cent. The −$2,446 presents worth at 16 per cent indicates that it is less than 16 per cent. Linear interpolation between these values yields an interest rate of return of 14.4 per cent:

$$i = 14\% + \frac{585}{585 - (-2,446)} (2\%) = 14\% + 0.4\% = 14.4\%.$$

A similar calculation for Plan C yields an interest rate of return of 5.3 per cent, which is considerably below the minimum attractive return of 12 per cent established as the criterion in this case. This computation confirms our earlier observation that Plan C is a less economical choice than Plan B.

If the cash flow is a regular series, the series present worth factor can be computed directly from equation 8.20. We are trying to find the interest rate at which

$$0 = -I + s(PWF_{T,i})$$
$$I = s(PWF_{T,i})$$
$$PWF_{T,i} = \frac{I}{s} \tag{8.21}$$

Recall that for straight-line depreciation, the annual after-tax cash flow for Plan B is $8,144. Substituting this figure into equation 8.21, we have

$$PWF_{10, \imath} = \frac{\$44,000}{\$8,144} = 5.403.$$

Examination of the table for series present worth factors reveals that 5.403 lies between the factors for 12 and 14 per cent.

$$PWF_{10, \; 0.12} = 5.650$$
$$PWF_{10, \; 0.14} = 5.216$$

By linear interpolation, we find that the interest rate is 13.1 per cent.

The rate of return may also be computed from present worth of cost or equivalent uniform annual cost for each alternative. This is based upon the observation that the rate of return is the interest rate at which the present worth of costs or the uniform annual costs for the two alternatives are equal.

The DFC rate of return method may yield ambiguous results in some situations. If there are one or more reversals in the direction of cash flows over the life of the project, calculation of rate of return by the trial-and-error method outlined here may yield two or more interest rates for which the present worth is zero. This type of situation may arise in the mineral and petroleum industries. For example, an oil company may have a well that, after recovery of the primary oil reserve, will require an additional sub-stantial investment in order to recover the remaining secondary oil reserve. The additional investment would inject a large negative cash flow into the calculation. This may result in present worths which follow the pattern in Figure 8.4.

Figure 8.4 Present Worth of an Investment Involving a Reversal in Cash Flows

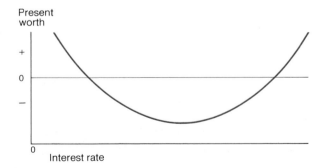

In such a situation, use of the present worth criterion at the firm's mini-mum attractive rate of return will avoid the ambiguity. This phenomenon does not negate the value of rate of return calculations because such cases do not arise in normal facilities studies.

Table 8.8 is a summary of the results of the analysis of Plans A, B, and

Table 8.8   Results of Analysis of Plans A, B, and C

	Plan A	Plan B	Plan C
Initial Cost	0	$ 44,000	$ 70,000
Terminal Salvage Value	0	0	9,500
Annual Operating Cost	$ 36,000	24,400	20,900
Present Worth of Cost Before Taxes at 22%	141,200	139,700	150,700
Equivalent Uniform Annual Cost			
Before Taxes at 22%	36,000	35,600	38,400
Incremental Investment		44,000	26,000
Annual Savings Before Taxes		11,600	3,500
Present Worth of Savings After Taxes at 12%			
Straight-line Depreciation		2,000	−8,200
Sum-of-Years Digits Depreciation		4,000	−7,400
Double-Declining Balance Depreciation		3,600	−6,200
Rate of Return after Taxes			
Straight-Line Depreciation		13.1%	5.0%
Sum-of-Years Digits Depreciation		14.4%	5.3%
Double-Declining Balance Depreciation		14.1%	5.9%

C. We note that each of the criteria gives a consistent result in that Plan B is indicated as the preferred alternative in each case.

Payback Period

The crude payback period is the length of time required to recover the amount of an investment without consideration of interest, or for net cash flow to equal zero. The crude payback period is a useful supplemental criterion because it illustrates the cash flow requirements for a proposal. Earlier, we found the after-tax cash flow for Plan B using straight-line depreciation to be $8,144 per year. Using this cash flow, the payback period would be

$$\text{Crude Payback Period} = \frac{\$44,000}{\$8,144/\text{year}} = 5.4 \text{ years.}$$

A crude payback period is shown graphically in Figure 8.5 which is a graph of the cumulative cash flow for Plan B using sum-of-years digits depreciation. Cash flows were calculated in Table 8.5. From the graph we see that the payback period occurs at the point where cumulative cash flow becomes positive, or at approximately 4.8 years.

The crude payback period is not an appropriate criterion to use by itself to rank investment proposals, because it ignores the impact of cash flows after the payback period. It is essentially cash flows after the payback period which determine rate of return from an investment. Because the payback period ignores subsequent cash flows, it may reject proposals with very attractive returns and consequently tend to favor retention of uneconomical

Figure 8.5   Cumulative After-Tax Cash Flow Comparing Plans B and A
(Sum-of-Years Digits Depreciation, Income Tax Rate 48 Per Cent)

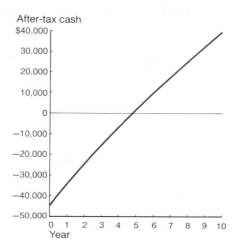

defenders. The only case in which it would be appropriate to use payback period as a sole criterion would be one in which investment funds were so restricted that no investments could be made unless they could be recovered in a very short time.

Replacement

Equipment in an operating system is continually in a defensive position with regard to its survival because it competes with challengers that are potentially more attractive due to increased capability or superior operating performance. Prospective challengers may provide superior performance because existing equipment is inadequate to meet the demands placed upon it, because challengers have been developed which can perform the same functions at lower cost, because existing equipment deteriorates and is increasingly expensive to operate, or because of some combination of these factors. Two aspects of the problem are the time to replace equipment, and choosing the best available alternative. Our discussion to this point has focused on the latter of these, and we now turn to consideration of when to replace existing equipment.

In general, it is time to replace the defender when buying the challenger becomes more attractive than retaining the defender. The decision is what to do now with regard to retaining, replacing, or retiring a defender, but our forecast of future occurrences may affect the present decision. This implies that we look not only at the challenger which has appeared but at prospective future challengers.

**Study
Horizon**

In any event, we must establish a time horizon for the study which will encompass the economic lives of challenger and defender. A number of ways for determining the study period have been proposed. These range from assuming physical lives or tax lives for the comparison to calculations of optimal economic life spans. An optimal replacement policy is one which maximizes the value or minimizes the cost of providing a service over the entire length of time that the service is required.

Because of the difficulties of forecasting the appearance and operating characteristics of challengers very far into the future, a more reasonable approach is to gear the study horizon to the length over which it is possible to forecast disturbances to the system. These disturbances may take any one of several forms. The defender may deteriorate which would be reflected in increased cost of operation and in increased maintenance costs. At the point at which it becomes more expensive to extend the service life of the defender than the average cost of owning and operating a new challenger, it becomes economic to replace the defender with the challenger, even if there have been no technological changes to generate new challengers. Another form of disturbance is technological change which results in the appearance of a new challenger which is better suited to perform the task. Disturbances may also arise in the form of a change in the level of demand for the service provided by the equipment which would make it unsuitable for providing that service. And, of course, a disturbance occurs when there is a termination of the need for the service.

**Uniform
Annual
Cost of
Challenger**

To illustrate some of the differences between handling replacement problems and selection problems, assume that we invested in Plan B based upon our previous analysis, that 4 years have now passed, and that a new module of equipment, which we will refer to as Plan D, has come onto the market. We will assume a study period of 6 years. The challenger (Plan D) would cost $40,000 installed and is estimated to have a salvage value at the end of 6 years of $4,000. Annual operating expenses would be somewhat less than for the defender, $17,100 per year for the first year, and would increase $2,000 per year for each of the 6 years of the study period.

The defender (Plan B) had an original cost of $40,000 and its book value is $26,400 based upon straight-line depreciation. The defender may be sold for a net amount of $16,400. Current operating expenses are $24,400 per year, but we now estimate that these will increase by $2,000 per year for each of the remaining 6 years. We will make a before-tax comparison of uniform annual costs for the defender and challenger at the same 22 per cent interest rate used previously.

We determine the uniform annual cost for the challenger in the same way as in the previous example.

$$UAC_D = (I - S_T)(CRF_{T,i}) + iS_T + \left[\sum_{t=1}^{T} c_t(PWF'_{t,i}) \right](CRF_{T,i})$$

$$= (\$40,000 - 4,000)(0.31576) + 0.22(\$4,000)$$
$$+ [\$17,100(0.81967) + \$19,100(0.67186) + \$21,100(0.55071)$$
$$+ \$23,100(0.45140) + \$25,100(0.37000)$$
$$+ \$27,100(0.30328)](0.31576)$$
$$= \$33,200.$$

Capital Recovery of Owned Assets

The determination of capital recovery for assets already owned is different than for assets yet to be purchased. We have noted previously that equipment selection and replacement analyses are based upon comparing the consequences of alternative future courses of action, and that costs incurred in the past are irrelevant. In a before-tax analysis, the original purchase price of equipment already owned or its book value are irrelevant. The relevant value is the amount that can be realized from disposing of the asset. In the present case, the alternatives are to retain the defender or to dispose of it. If we dispose of the defender, we will realize a net positive cash flow of $16,400; if we keep it, we will forego this amount. Consequently, the relevant value for assets already owned is the amount that could be realized from their disposal. Applying this to the defender, we obtain

$$UAC_B = (I)(CRF_{T,i}) + \left[\sum_{t=1}^{T} c_t(PWF'_{t,i}) \right](CRF_{T,i})$$

$$= \$16,400(0.31576) + \left(\sum_{t=1}^{6} c_t PWF'_{t,0.22} \right)(0.31576)$$

$$= \$33,400.$$

On the basis of this analysis, we should replace the defender with the challenger.

Tax Impact

The current book value of the defender becomes relevant in an after-tax analysis because of the impact on income taxes of gains or losses incurred in the disposal of assets. In the present example, we will assume that the firm is using single-item asset accounting for this equipment, that it has no offsetting gains or losses, and that any loss on the sale of the asset may be fully deducted from income for tax purposes. Under this set of assumptions, disposal of the defender will result not only in receiving the $16,400 market value, but the loss on the sale will result in a reduction in income taxes. If the asset is sold for this amount, there will be a loss on the sale of

$$\$26,400 - \$16,400 = \$10,000.$$

At a tax rate of 48 per cent, this will result in a tax savings of $4,800. Under these conditions, the after-tax value of the defender is

$$\$16,400 + \$4,800 = \$21,200.$$

Using an after-tax minimum attractive rate of return of 12 per cent, we obtain an annual cost of

$$UAC_B = \$21,200(0.24323) + \left[\sum_{t=1}^{6} c_t(PWF'_{t,0.12})\right](0.24323)$$
$$= \$33,900.$$

To determine the annual cost of the challenger, we add the extra income tax attributable to its lower operating cost offset slightly by the higher depreciation allowance for the challenger.

$$\text{Extra Income Tax} = 0.48[(\$24,400 + 4,400) - (\$17,100 + 6,000)]$$
$$= \$2,700.$$

Since operating costs for both challenger and defender are expected to increase at the rate of $2,000 per year, the difference between them will remain constant and the extra income tax will be approximately $2,700 for each of the 6 years. Adding this to the cost of the challenger, we obtain a uniform annual cost of

$$UAC_D = (\$40,000 - 4,000)(0.24323) + 0.12(\$4,000)$$
$$+ \left[\sum_{t=1}^{6} c_t(PWF'_{t,0.12})\right](0.2432)$$
$$= \$33,400.$$

Thus, on the basis of this analysis, we should replace the defender with the challenger.

Optimum Life

In the preceding replacement example, we assumed a study period of 6 years and compared the equivalent uniform annual costs of defender and challenger on this basis. Because capital recovery costs decline and annual operating costs increase as an asset is retained for longer periods, there will be a point at which the total equivalent uniform annual cost is at a minimum. If we assume a schedule of salvage values for the defender, as shown in Table 8.9, we may compute uniform annual costs for alternative life spans and determine that length of life for which these costs are minimum. In Table 8.9, we note that the annual cost of maintaining the defender is at a minimum in 4 years, and that the differences between years are very small.

In Table 8.10, we show the cost of extending the life of the defender for

Table 8.9 Equivalent Annual Costs for Alternative Lives for Plan B (22 Per Cent Interest)

Year	Ending Salvage A	Uniform Annual Capital Recovery B	Operating Expenses C	Uniform Annual Operating Expenses D	Total Equivalent Uniform Annual Cost B + D
0	$16,400				
1	10,000	$10,008	$24,400	$24,400	$34,408
2	5,000	8,743	26,400	25,301	34,404
3	2,500	7,356	28,400	26,137	33,493
4	1,000	6,396	30,400	26,908	33,304
5	0	5,727	32,400	27,618	33,345
6	0	5,179	34,400	28,267	33,446
7	0	4,802	36,400	28,859	33,661
8	0	4,531	38,400	29,396	33,927
9	0	4,331	40,400	29,882	34,213
10	0	4,180	42,400	30,319	34,499

Table 8.10 Cost to Extend Asset Life for 1 Year for Plan B (22 Per Cent Interest)

Year	Year-End Value	Decline During Year	Interest on Beginning Value	Capital Recovery Cost	Operating Cost	Total Cost
0	$16,400					
1	10,000	$6,400	$3,608	$10,008	$24,400	$34,408
2	5,000	5,000	2,200	7,200	26,400	33,600
3	2,500	2,500	1,100	3,600	28,400	32,000
4	1,000	1,500	550	2,050	30,400	32,450
5	0	1,000	220	1,220	32,400	33,620
6	0	0	0	0	34,400	34,400
7	0	0	0	0	36,400	36,400
8	0	0	0	0	38,400	38,400
9	0	0	0	0	40,400	40,400
10	0	0	0	0	42,400	42,400

one more year for each of these lives. To find capital recovery cost for one year, the capital recovery portion of equation 8.14 may be simplified somewhat. Setting $T = 1$, we have

$$
\begin{aligned}
CR &= (I - S_1)CRF_{1,i} + iS_1 \\
&= (I - S_1)\frac{i(1 + i)}{(1 + i) - 1} + iS_1 \\
&= (I - S_1)(1 + i) + iS_1 \\
&= (I - S_1) + iI
\end{aligned}
\tag{8.22}
$$

Since I represents the value at the beginning of the year and S_1 the value at the beginning of the following year, capital recovery cost for one year is the decline in salvage value during that year plus interest on the beginning value. If we add to that capital recovery cost the operating expense for that year, we obtain the cost of extending the life of the asset for one year.

The relationship between total equivalent uniform annual costs for alternative lives and the cost of extending asset life for one year is shown graphically in Figure 8.6. Examination of this figure and of Tables 8.9

Figure 8.6 Equivalent Annual Cost for Alternative Lives for Plan B (22 Per Cent Interest)

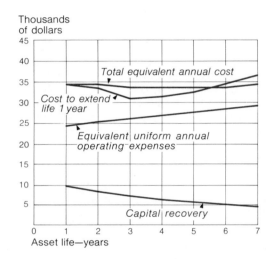

and 8.10 indicates that the minimum equivalent uniform annual cost is reached at the time at which the cost of extending asset life for one year is just equal to the uniform annual cost.

The minimum uniform annual cost calculated in this way is an optimum economic life only in a very narrow sense. The primary assumption underlying this concept of economic life is that the asset will be replaced with an identical new unit, that is, that future challengers will have the same initial cost, the same expected salvage values for each year, and the same expected operating expenses for each year. This approach also assumes that the minimum attractive rate of return remains the same, and that the need for the service rendered by this equipment continues indefinitely. In other words, it is assumed that there will be an infinite chain of replacements with identical units. Under these conditions, an asset should be replaced when the marginal cost of operating it for an additional year exceeds the equivalent uniform cost at that date.

The flatness of the uniform annual cost curve indicates that if there were no changes in technology or prices, the timing of replacements need not be very precise. However, in a dynamic economy, managers must be continually alert to the appearance of challengers and to appropriate timing of replacements.

The uniform annual cost may be converted to the present worth of the infinite series of renewals by dividing the uniform annual series by the interest rate as shown in equation 8.5. In this case, replacements would be indicated in the year in which the present worth is at a minimum.

It is apparent that these assumptions are in general quite unrealistic in these times of rapid advances in technology, changing price levels, and fluctuating interest rates. While there may be a few types of equipment that somewhat fit these assumptions, they constitute a very small portion of the replacement problems faced by management. The issue in replacement decisions is not the age of the defender, but rather to retain the defender no matter how old it is or to replace it with the most suitable available challenger. This approach is also useful in selecting a remaining life that is most suitable for the defender.

For these reasons, we have suggested that the analyst select a time period for the equipment study in keeping with the ability to forecast future disturbances to the system—disturbances in the form of anticipated technological advances and changes in requirements for the service being provided. Although it may not be possible to forecast precisely the costs and operating characteristics of future challengers or changes in service requirements, they may be sufficiently well-known to be included in the analysis on an approximate or qualitative basis. The availability of modern computers makes it feasible to perform sensitivity analyses by examining the impact in the replacement decision of several different forecasts. Such analyses will reveal whether the present decision is sensitive to a range of errors in forecasts about future challengers or service requirements.

Even with these shortcomings, this type of minimum-cost analysis is useful because it illustrates some of the fundamental and theoretical aspects of replacement analysis. A thorough understanding of this type of approach is essential to an understanding of more sophisticated models appearing in the literature.

Post-Audit of Capital Investment Decisions

We have noted previously the difficulties in isolating and measuring cash flows associated with individual modules of equipment, and difficulties of accurately forecasting these cash flows over the long time periods associated with investment decisions. As discussed in Chapter 6, a control system requires feedback of information about the results achieved by the system. Post-audits of capital investment decisions can serve this function in facilities selection and replacement. Because of measurement and forecasting difficulties, it is difficult in the absence of a post-audit to determine the accuracy of analyses upon which investment decisions are being made.

An audit of an investment involves basically three steps: (1) measurement of actual performance of the investment, (2) comparison of the actual performance to forecast performance, and (3) a report on variances with appropriate explanation regarding deviations from the forecast. It is apparent that auditing investment decisions is not fundamentally different from other auditing procedures, but it is an important part of facilities selection and replacement analyses.

Such post-audits cannot change the original investment decision, but a systematic program of evaluation can help to improve the quality of future analyses, and they can serve as a basis for evaluating the performance of analysts. In addition, a post-audit program may offer positive incentives to operating departments to improve the quality of their analyses, because they know their work is to be audited.

Risk Analysis

A fundamental limitation of the approaches suggested so far for evaluating facilities decisions is that they fail to take into account the uncertainties inherent in forecasts of the input factors—costs, savings, investments, and so forth—upon which the analysis depends. Companies often find that investments fail to turn out as expected, due to such uncertainties. Suppose that a firm establishes a minimum rate of return criterion of 10 per cent after taxes, and that all facilities investment projects approved must meet or exceed that rate. Post-audits may well reveal that only a relatively small proportion of approved projects actually achieve that return. Why? Largely because the evaluations are based upon single-valued forecasts of cost and savings input factors. Such single-valued forecasts represent "best guess" or most likely estimates of the factors that do not incorporate information of the expected range of variability. In addition, most likely value is equal to expected value only when a frequency or probability distribution is symmetrical, a circumstance that often may not occur.

In Chapter 2, we saw that a decision tree approach is one way to incorporate uncertainties and to evaluate risk in project evaluation. Another method which may be even more useful for the types of project evaluation under consideration is computer simulation using a Monte Carlo approach. Using simulation techniques, we can determine expected values and probability profiles for each of the criteria being used to evaluate a proposal.

To illustrate how simulation can be used in the evaluation of investment proposals, consider the case of a company contemplating an investment of $300,000 in facilities. These facilities have an anticipated life of 5 years, and the firm will evaluate the proposal by the present worth criterion with a minimum attractive rate of return of 10 per cent after taxes. The best estimate of most likely net cash inflow is $80,000 per year after taxes. From this, we calculate the net present worth of the net cash inflow as

$$PW = PWF_{5,0.10}(\$80,000) = 3.79(\$80,000) = \$303,200.$$

On the basis of this criterion, the project would be accepted. However, a closer examination reveals that the $80,000 per year cash flow estimate is not certain; that there is a 40 per cent likelihood that cash flow in a year will differ from the most likely estimate by more than $20,000, and a 20 per cent chance that it will differ by more than $40,000. After further analysis and questioning of the experts who prepared the cost and revenue estimates, a probability distribution of the range of cash flows was developed, as depicted in Table 8.11.

Table 8.11 Probability Distribution of Annual Cash Flows

Annual Net Cash Inflow	Probability of Occurrence	Cumulative Probability	Corresponding 2-Digit Random Numbers
−$20,000	.05	.05	00–04
0	.05	.10	05–09
20,000	.05	.15	10–14
40,000	.10	.25	15–24
60,000	.15	.40	25–39
80,000	.25	.65	40–64
100,000	.20	.85	65–84
120,000	.10	.95	85–94
140,000	.05	1.00	95–99

Once a probability distribution has been established for each input factor, we can use the Monte Carlo model sampling process to simulate the range of probable outcomes for the proposed investment in terms of the investment criteria which will be used to evaluate the proposal. In the Monte Carlo process, we repeatedly sample from the distributions of the input factors and build up frequency distributions or probability profiles of the various criteria. We illustrate this process in Table 8.12, in which we have

Table 8.12 Simulation of Cash Flows for One Trial

Year	Random Number	Net Cash Flow	Present Worth Factor i = 10 Per Cent	Present Worth
1	42	$ 80,000	.909	$ 73,000
2	66	100,000	.826	83,000
3	22	40,000	.751	30,000
4	60	80,000	.683	54,000
5	56	80,000	.621	50,000
TOTALS		$380,000		$290,000

made one trial. The first random number drawn is 42. Referring to Table 8.11, we see that this corresponds to a cash flow of $80,000. The second

Figure 8.7 Investment Risk Analysis Simulation

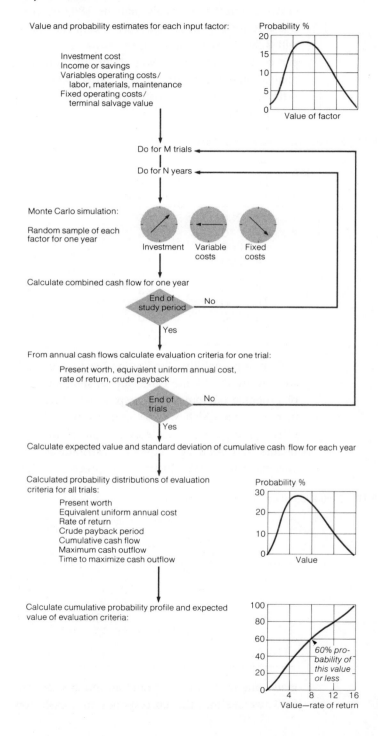

random number, 66, corresponds to a cash flow of $100,000. A sample is drawn for each year, the cash flows are recorded, and the present worth is $290,000. The sampling process is repeated for many trials, and the trial results are combined into frequency distributions.

The flow diagram in Figure 8.7 portrays the entire process. For a typical investment analysis, we will have several probability distributions, each representing an input factor. The interactions of several probability distributions are difficult, if not impossible, to evaluate by means other than computer simulation techniques. A computer can make many trials and develop the desired probability distributions very rapidly. The culmination of the process is the development of cumulative probability profiles for each of the desired evaluation criteria. A cumulative probability profile is, as the name implies, a cumulative probability distribution which shows the probability of achieving a particular value or less. The graph shows that there is a 60 per cent probability of an 8 per cent or less return on the hypothetical investment represented. These profiles are useful because they indicate the range of variability which may be expected from the investment. Profiles such as these give management a great deal more information upon which to base decisions than from single-value analysis. For example, consider the two alternatives represented in Figure 8.8 which we will assume require

Figure 8.8   Cumulative Probability Profiles

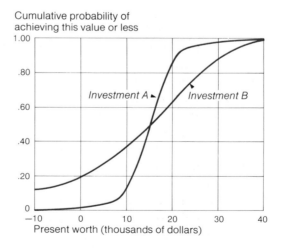

the same initial investment and have the same life spans. Although both investments, A and B, have a median (.50 probability) present worth of $15,000, investment B has substantially more variability than investment A. There is a .20 probability that alternative B will yield a zero or less present worth, while alternative A is not likely to vary significantly from a present worth of between $10,000 and $20,000. Clearly, then, single-value analyses of present worth or rate of return do not necessarily provide the best basis for management decisions.

Summary

Facilities investment decisions, a part of the basic asset management problem of an enterprise, are perhaps the most crucial aspect of designing and operating systems. Facilities investment decisions commit the organization for several years. Careful identification of alternatives and of the relevant differences between them are essential for effective investment decisions. In the analysis of facilities investment proposals, the analyst generally attempts to answer the question of whether the investment will be recovered plus a suitable return. Effective utilization of cost data in the analysis requires a distinction among average, incremental, and sunk costs.

The two major aspects of facilities investment decisions are selection from among alternative proposals, and replacement of existing equipment. In the selection phase, four discounted cash flow methods are used for comparison of alternatives: (1) present worth of cost, (2) equivalent uniform annual cost, (3) present worth of savings or income, and (4) rate of return on savings or income. Each method will give comparable results except when there are one or more reversals in the direction of cash flows over the life of the project. Payback period may also be useful as a supplementary criterion.

In analysis of replacement problems, an appropriate time horizon for the study is the time period over which it is possible to forecast disturbances to the system. Present worth, equivalent uniform annual cost, and rate of return methods may be used to determine when to replace a defender with a challenger. The relevant investment cost for assets already owned is the amount that can be realized, including tax adjustments, from disposal of the asset. Optimum economic life in a narrow sense may be determined as the point in time at which the cost to extend the life of an asset for one more year is just equal to the uniform annual cost up to that time. This assumes that there will be an infinite chain of replacements with identical units, an assumption that may not be realistic in a dynamic economy.

Monte Carlo simulation methods are one means by which uncertainties in forecasts may be taken into account in an analysis. Simulation permits the development of cumulative probability profiles for the evaluation criteria.

Selected References

Bierman, Harold, Jr., and Smidt, Seymour. *The Capital Budgeting Decision.* New York: Macmillan Company, 1961.

The authors present the case for favoring the present value method of analyzing capital investment.

Grant, Eugene L., and Ireson, W. Grant. *Principles of Engineering Economy.* 5th ed. New York: The Ronald Press Company, 1970.

The authors present a very thorough and clear coverage of basic fundamentals of investment and equipment replacement decisions. They include many examples.

Hertz, David B. "Risk Analysis in Capital Investment." *Harvard Business Review* 42 (January–February 1964): 95–106.

A more detailed presentation of the use of a Monte Carlo simulation model in evaluating investment proposals is given in this article.

Terborgh, George Willard. *Business Investment Management.* Washington, D.C.: Machinery and Allied Products Institute, 1967.

Questions

1 Why are facilities investment decisions of such crucial importance to the design and operation of systems?

2 Distinguish between selection and replacement in facilities investment decisions.

3 What is meant by a systems approach in facilities decisions?

4 Distinguish among average costs, incremental costs, and sunk costs.

5 Why should facilities investment analyses consider only cash flows and not all expense items?

6 Explain how make-versus-buy and lease-versus-purchase decisions may be analyzed using the approaches presented in this chapter.

7 Of what value is a post-audit of capital investment decisions?

8 What information may be obtained from a simulation approach to project analysis that is not available from single-valued analyses?

Problems

1 What is the present value of $6,500 due at the end of 4 years if the interest rate is 6 per cent?

2 What is the present value of $350 received at the end of each year for the next 5 years if the interest rate is 8 per cent?

3 Mr. Green has a son aged 5 years. He estimates it will cost $8,000 to send his son through 4 years at the university. How much will he have to deposit in his savings account at the end of each year to accumulate this amount by the time his son reaches age 18 if the interest is 6 per cent?

4 A machine which costs $18,000 will yield an estimated $4,000 per year savings over its expected life of 10 years. It will have no salvage value at the end of 10 years. What is the before-tax present value of these savings if the minimum attractive rate of return is 15 per cent?

5 Compute the before-tax rate of return on the investment required for the machine in problem 4.

6 A piece of equipment has an installed cost of $32,000, estimated annual operating cost of $4,500 over its expected life of 7 years, and an estimated terminal salvage value of $3,000. Compute the equivalent uniform annual cost of this equipment at 12 per cent.

7 Mr. Brown is considering the purchase of an automobile for $4,000. He can borrow $3,000 on the car for 24 months at 1 per cent per month interest. Compute his uniform monthly payments and the total amount he will have to pay.

8 A proposal has been made to install mechanical material handling equipment to replace the current manual system. The equipment has an installed cost of $10,000 and zero salvage value at the end of its expected life of 8 years. Cost savings are estimated at $2,400 the first year, but will decline according to the following schedule because of increased maintenance costs.

Year	Savings	Year	Savings
1	$2400	5	$2000
2	$2400	6	$1800
3	$2400	7	$1500
4	$2200	8	$1300

Compute the before-tax rate of return on the investment required for this equipment.

9 The Bilbo Company has decided to obtain a Datacomp V computer, and is considering whether to lease or purchase it. The 5-year lease under consideration costs $87,000 per year, payable at the beginning of each year. The purchase price is $414,000, the maintenance contract costs $13,200 per year, payable at the beginning of each year, and the computer has an estimated market value at the end of 5 years of $145,000.
   a. Prepare a tabulation of before-tax annual cash flows for each plan and for the difference between the purchase and lease plans.
   b. Compare the present worth of the purchase and lease plans using a before-tax minimum attractive rate of return of 12 per cent.
   c. Compare the before-tax equivalent uniform annual costs of the two plans at 12 per cent.
   d. Find the interest rate that makes the before-tax present worths of the two plans equal.

10 In problem 9, assume an effective income tax rate of 50 per cent. Rental and maintenance paid at the beginning of each year will be deductible from income taxes paid at the end of the year. If the computer is purchased, straight-line depreciation will be used assuming a 10-year life and 10 per cent terminal salvage value.

a. Prepare a tabulation showing the annual difference in after-tax cash flows between the purchase and lease plans for 5 years. Assume that the computer will be sold at the end of 5 years at the estimated market value, and that any loss on the sale will be deducted from income tax.

b. Compute the after-tax present worth of the difference between the purchase and lease plans at 6 per cent.

c. Find the interest rate that makes the after-tax present worths of the two plans equal.

d. What other factors should be considered before the lease-buy decision is made?

11 Oron Wood Products Company is considering the installation of an automatic machine to replace two machines that now provide the same total capacity. This company uses straight-line item depreciation for accounting and tax purposes. Economic data on the defenders (old machines) are estimated as follows:

Initial cost (both machines)	$ 9,000	
Life (economic and tax)		15 years
Salvage value (end of 15 years)	$ 0	
Present age		5 years
Present market value (both machines)	$ 400	
Annual operating expenses (both)	$24,000	

Estimates for the challenger (new machine) are as follows:

Installed cost	$22,000	
L fe (economic and tax)		10 years
Salvage value (end of 10 years)	$ 2,000	
Operating expenses per year	$18,000	

Assume that the firm is profitable and that the income tax rate is 50 per cent. Assume that any "loss" on disposal of the defender will be fully deductible from income in the year of retirement; consider the tax saving resulting from the sale as an addition to the net salvage value of the defender.

a. What is the value of the present investment in the defenders?

b. Compute the after-tax annual savings attributable to the challenger.

c. What is the after-tax crude payback period?

d. What is the after-tax rate of return on the net investment needed to acquire the challenger?

Chapter 9
Statistical
Control
Models

The control process measures and regulates system behavior to accomplish the objectives of the organization. Control attempts to insure the quality and quantity of system output according to predetermined plans and standards of performance through a negative feedback mechanism. A central part of system design is the design of effective control systems compatible with the goals and operating requirements of the organization (Chapter 6). Although an effective control system should accommodate the capabilities and response pattern of the system under control, attempts are often made to operate control systems which do not reflect the variations inherent in the system behavior.

All our information is about the past. Although we cannot be certain about the future, managerial planning is concerned with predicting this uncertain future. Prediction and forecasting inevitably involve the projection of information about the past. The sophistication and quality of predictions will vary greatly, depending upon a number of factors such as the ability of the predictor, the adequacy of his information and the stability of the system with which he is dealing. Hence, the manager must continuously evaluate information about the quality and stability of the system.

Statistical analysis of data, including probability theory, can be used to aid in this evaluation, and thus help refine control methods. Although mathematics cannot replace managerial judgment in planning and decision making, reveal imaginative alternative courses of action, nor identify the objectives of the manager and his organization, it can aid in the prediction of future conditions and the consequences of decisions. Many of the mathematical models applicable to managerial control involve complex applications using probability theory and statistical inference; however, the rudiments of these ideas are not difficult, and a working knowledge of them can be of great aid to the manager in dealing with technical specialists. In the 1920's, Walter A. Shewhart of the Bell Telephone Laboratories, applied sampling theory to the problem of quality control of manufactured products.[1] In the course of his research he invented the statistical control chart which used sampling theory as a basis for monitoring a process to determine whether it is meeting expectations. We will examine some fundamental aspects of Shewhart control models, which are useful for monitoring systems to detect changes over time. These statistical models are based upon the same concepts as statistical estimation and hypothesis testing.

Variation and Stability

No system is totally unstable or chaotic, but neither does any system appear to be perfectly stable. Stability is a relative matter, because all systems exhibit some degree of variation in performance. Fortunately, in many systems the variations are of such a minor nature that they can be tolerated. It is the manager's problem to distinguish those tolerable minor fluctuations from major changes in the system which require correction. In order to make this distinction, he must know the inherent capability of the system, and decide what variation is acceptable. Having done this, he may establish decision rules and procedures which will insure that changes beyond a certain degree are brought to his attention, so that he can decide what is to be done.

Variation in system behavior may be introduced at any point in the operation of the system, as illustrated in Figure 9.1. Inputs may vary either

Figure 9.1   Sources of Variation in a System

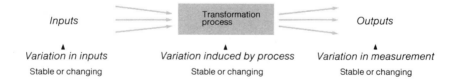

Inputs ➔ Transformation process ➔ *Outputs*

▲   ▲   ▲
Variation in inputs   *Variation induced by process*   *Variation in measurement*
Stable or changing   Stable or changing   Stable or changing

as to quality characteristics or timing of arrival. Because input items are not exactly alike, the transformation process is designed to accommodate normal variation in inputs. The transformation process itself induces variation, because it does not operate repeatedly in exactly the same way. Besides variations in output resulting from variations in inputs and in the process, additional observed variation is introduced by imprecision and errors in measuring quality characteristics of the output.

If we recognize that variation in system performance is inevitable, the statistical techniques of the Shewhart control model may be employed to estimate the amount of residual variability in system behavior. We can

[1] Walter A. Shewhart, *Economic Control of Manufactured Product* (New York: D. Van Nostrand Co., Inc., 1931).

predict the pattern of expected system behavior resulting from a relatively stable underlying set of causal factors. In this case, behavior, in the form of dispersion of system outputs around the average level of output, is due to a *stable system of chance causes*. As long as the underlying causal factors remain unchanged, the average level and dispersion of output will continue as expected, and in such a relatively stable system we may predict that future behavior will follow this pattern. In systems which are constantly changing, the problem confronting the manager is whether the change is significant enough to warrant correction.

Now, if there is a disturbance to the system and underlying causal factors have changed, the change will be reflected in a new or abnormal pattern of behavior, which will take the form of a shift in average level of output or a change in the distribution of output around the average. The system is then no longer operating from the previous stable system of chance causes and the shift in behavior is due to *assignable causes of variation*. If the change is undesirable, remedial action may be taken to correct it. If the change is desirable, that is, it results in improved performance, action may be taken to incorporate the change into normal operation of the system.

Detecting Change and Making Decisions

The Shewhart control model applies to monitoring the output of a process in order to maintain stability of system outputs. We regard the process as a black box, because we are concerned with the output flows and not with internal operating characteristics of the process. The system may be a single process, such as the processing of customers at one service facility, the preparation of invoices by one clerk, parts assembly at one work station, package filling by one machine, or machining of components by one machine tool. Or the system may be defined at a higher level of aggregation to include the output of a group of processes, such as an entire work center, department, division, enterprise, project, or community. The measured outputs of the system may include costs, volumes, performance times, quality of service, quality of products, labor turnover, absenteeism, and utilization of facilities.

Maintaining Stability

From the manager's viewpoint, the problem of maintaining stability has three aspects: monitoring, decision making, and taking corrective action. Monitoring involves inspecting the output and measuring pertinent characteristics. An inspector samples output and compares it with some performance standard. If the sample deviates from normal performance by some amount determined by the Shewhart control model, he records that the system appears to have changed. If the sample does not deviate from normal performance, he records that the system has not changed.

If there is an apparent change in the system, a decision must be made about what action is to be taken. This is an application of the exception principle. Stability is maintained by detecting and correcting disturbances which cause changes in the system.

Systems in Control

A system is *in control* when the observed variation in process output is within the normal pattern of variation. Thus, bringing a process under control does not eliminate all variation, but eliminates assignable causes of variation and restores the process to its normal pattern of variation. The Shewhart control model indicates when to leave the process alone because it appears to be functioning normally, and when to take remedial action to correct the process.

The model also discloses whether a given process is capable of meeting the requirements placed upon it. If the process cannot produce the required output, then appropriate action may be taken by revising the system, putting in a new system, or relaxing the requirements. These two aspects of the model—indicating when to leave the system alone and determining whether the system is capable of meeting performance standards—often, in themselves, result in significant reductions in operating costs.

Using Sampling Information

Since it is rarely possible or economically feasible to examine all the information about a system, a manager may rely upon sample data for control purposes. By drawing a sample from a population and examining the characteristics of the sample, the costs of inspection, monitoring, and auditing can be reduced greatly in comparison with the costs of examination of the entire population. If the sample is a random sample, in which each item in the population has an equal chance of being selected, then inferences based upon probability theory can be made about the population from which the sample was drawn.

There are three primary interrelated types of information sought from the use of statistical sampling. One is for estimating unknown values of certain characteristics of members of a large population, another is for testing hypotheses about certain characteristics of the members of a population, and the third is for monitoring changes in a process over time.

Risks in Using Sampling Information

The use of sampling information is not without risk, however. We attempt to amass evidence upon which to make an informed judgment. Since, by using sampling information, we are inferring certain characteristics of a population without examining the entire population, we can be lead to a wrong conclusion.

We stand in a position analogous to that of a jury in a court of law. The defendant before us is either guilty or innocent, and it is our task to weigh the evidence to determine his guilt or innocence. Figure 9.2 is a contingency table illustrating the situation. There are two possible states for the defendant and two decisions. The legal system of the United States

Figure 9.2 Contingency Table of Error Types in Legal System (Hypothesis of Innocence)

True state of defendant	Decision	
	Acquit	Convict
Innocent	Correct	Type I error
Guilty	Type II error	Correct

presumes that a defendant is innocent until he is proven guilty. In such circumstances the null hypothesis, H_0, may be, "the defendant is innocent." If he is in fact innocent and we acquit him, we accept the hypothesis correctly. If he is guilty and we convict him, we reject the hypothesis of innocence correctly. If he is in fact innocent and we convict him, we have rejected the hypothesis when it was true and we have made a *Type I error*. If he is guilty and we accept the hypothesis of innocence, we acquit him and have made a *Type II error*. In a sampling scheme the probabilities of making each type of error usually are not the same. Therefore, we must decide which type of error is worse and reduce the probability of making that type of error to an acceptable level. The contingency table in Figure 9.3 shows the types of error expressed in terms of acceptance or rejection

Figure 9.3 Contingency Table of Error Types in Decision Making

True state of system	Decision	
	Accept hypothesis	Reject hypothesis
Hypothesis is true	Correct	Type I error
Hypothesis is false	Type II error	Correct

of hypotheses. In most sampling schemes it is easier to reduce the risk of making a Type I error. For this reason, we stated the hypothesis in Figure 9.2 in the form of the defendant's innocence. In a control system the null hypothesis, H_0, may be: the stability of the process has not changed. If the sample result falls within predetermined control limits, then the hypothesis is accepted.

The question of importance to management is what this rule will lead to under different circumstances. In other words, the manager should know what are the two types of errors that may be made, the probabilities of making each type of error, and their expected cost.

System Requirements

The criteria for selecting a control system are based upon the desire to minimize the expected costs of running the system under control. Since these costs may be difficult or impossible to determine in many situations, we may make some general observations about the requisites for the use of the Shewhart model and sampling techniques for management control.

Perhaps the most important factor is that of defining and measuring system performance. We must be able to identify and measure the output of the particular system by some objective means. Measurement scales may be nominal, ordinal, interval, or ratio, as illustrated in Table 2.1 of Chapter 2. Measurements may be expressed as numerical values (money, time, quantity, size, weight, percentages, and so forth) or as dichotomies (right-wrong, good-bad, correct-incorrect, acceptable-defective, on time-late, and so forth). Definition and measurement of quality characteristics of physical products are often difficult; definition and measurement of quantities and quality characteristics of organizational units are not only often very difficult, but they may appear to be impossible. A great deal of imagination and experimentation may be required to identify appropriate objective control variables in nonproduct situations.

Some systems are inherently so stable that they do not require constant monitoring; others are so unstable that a monitoring system to indicate instability would be redundant. In some, the consequences of instability are so minor that continuous monitoring would be too expensive; some systems are so critical that they require constant, total inspection and re-inspection to assure as perfect an output as possible. Even in these situations, however, a sampling monitoring control scheme may be a good check on inspection and control systems themselves.

A large group of management systems exists to which the Shewhart control model may be effectively applied to provide management with prompt feedback of system changes. These are systems whose outputs are measurable, significant, and generally, but not always, stable.

Statistical Measures of Process Output

Before we consider the problems of constructing and interpreting statistical control charts and of making decisions based upon inferences from information obtained from samples, we will review some important measures of distributions of data and fundamental concepts of sampling. Measured variation in process output gives rise to frequency distributions and probability distributions. These distributions may be used to describe in an orderly fashion some of the characteristics of the set of process outputs.

Normal Probability Distribution

The normal probability distribution is important in statistics, because many natural phenomena can be approximately described by it, and because it has a unique place in the field of sampling. The normal distribution also describes the outputs of many production processes. It received the name "normal" from work done in the late eighteenth century, when it was derived as the limiting form of the binomial expansion, and when it was observed that this distribution seemed to describe errors in measurement. It was thought by some that this distribution represented a natural universal law of chance. In the field of sampling, the importance of the normal distribution is derived from the fact that means of samples drawn from a population tend to be normally distributed, even if the original distribution is not.

A normal distribution is one which follows the formula and takes on the shape of the distribution shown in Figure 9.4. Note that the distribution is completely described by its average or arithmetic mean, μ, and its standard deviation, σ.[2]

Recall that the standard deviation, σ, is the square root of the variance σ^2, which is the average of the squared deviations from the arithmetic mean:

$$\sigma^2 = \frac{\sum_{i=1}^{N} (x_i - \mu)^2}{N}. \tag{9.1}$$

To compute the variance, we square the deviations from the mean of each item in a population and take their average. For computational purposes, it is often easier to compute the variance from the following expression:

$$\sigma^2 = \frac{\sum_{i=1}^{N} (x_i)^2 - \mu^2}{N}. \tag{9.2}$$

In this form, we take the sum of the squares of each value, divide by the number of items in the population, and subtract from this result the square of the arithmetic mean.

If we measure the area under the curve lying between the mean and one standard deviation above and below, $\mu \pm 1\sigma$, we find that 68.3 per cent of the total area is included. Similarly, 95.4 per cent of the total area lies between the mean and 2 standard deviations above and below, $\mu \pm 2\sigma$, and 99.7 per cent lies between the mean and 3 standard deviations above and below, $\mu \pm 3\sigma$. The larger the standard deviation, the more widespread is the normal distribution, but the proportion of the area under the curve in these intervals remains constant. Table D in the Appendix at the end of the

---

[2] The Greek μ is read "mu" and refers to population means. The Greek σ is read "sigma" and refers to population standard deviations.

Figure 9.4   Density Function of Normal Distribution Showing Areas Included under the Curve

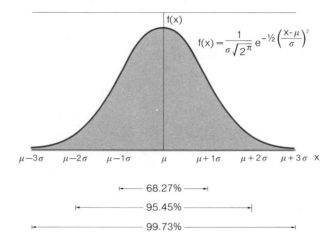

book gives cumulative proportions of the area under the normal curve between $-\infty$ and $+\infty$ in multiples of σ on either side of μ.

**Process
Capability**

We can use the above information to determine the capability of a process. Suppose we have a process producing an item whose length has a specified tolerance of $1.000'' \pm 0.004''$. Suppose further that we have determined that the items being produced have a mean length of $1.000''$, the standard deviation of the population is estimated to be $0.002''$, and the outputs are approximately normally distributed. The proportion of process output expected to fall within the tolerance limits may be determined by converting them to multiples of σ and finding the area included. The upper tolerance limit is $+2\sigma$ from the mean and the lower tolerance limit is -2σ from the mean. The area under the normal curve included in these limits is 95.45 per cent, which is the proportion of items falling within the tolerance limits as shown in Figure 9.5.

We may use this information to forecast the future behavior of the process. As long as the process remains stable, we expect about 4.55 per cent of the items produced to be outside the tolerance dimension. Any shift in the process average will greatly increase out-of-tolerance items. If a 4.55 per cent defective level is unacceptable, it may be necessary to produce this item by some other process which is capable of closer tolerances.

If we have an empirical distribution whose form is unknown, we can utilize Tchebycheff's inequality to make somewhat less satisfactory forecasts. Tchebycheff's inequality states that less than $1/k^2$ of the items in any distribution can fall outside the interval $\mu \pm k\sigma$, where k is not less than 1, and at least $1 - 1/k^2$ of the items will fall within. If $k = 3$, less than $1/3^2 = 1/9 = 0.111$ of any group of numbers may fall outside the interval $\mu \pm 3\sigma$,

Figure 9.5 Proportion of Items Within Tolerance Limits

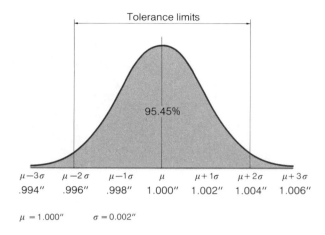

and at least 0.889 of the numbers must fall within that interval. We can compare the areas of the normal distribution and the limits of Tchebycheff's inequality.

Limits	NORMAL DISTRIBUTION The indicated percentages will fall outside the limits.	TCHEBYCHEFF Less than the indicated percentages will fall outside the limits.
$\mu \pm 2\sigma$	4.55	25.0
$\mu \pm 3\sigma$	0.27	11.1
$\mu \pm 4\sigma$	0.006	6.3

Obviously, if we can use the normal distribution, we can make much better decisions.

We can also use this information to monitor process output. Given a normal distribution and good estimates of the mean and standard deviation, we can set up a time based chart, as in Figure 9.6, on which we have indicated the process mean and 3σ intervals. We would expect that 99.7 per cent of the items produced would fall within these limits. If we plot measurements sequentially and observe several points outside the 3σ limits, we may conclude that the process has changed in some manner—the mean has shifted, or the distribution is no longer normal, or the dispersion of outputs has changed. Although these data indicate the inherent capability of the process, they are not sufficient as a basis for managerial control. Since the data are not based upon samples, they do not permit us to test the hypothesis that the process is in control, and they are relatively insensitive to shifts in the mean output.

Figure 9.6   Time-Based Chart of Process Output

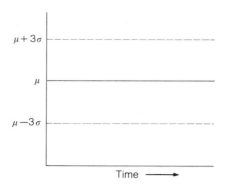

Statistical Inference

The Shewhart control model is based upon and closely related to the concepts involved in estimating arithmetic means of populations from information obtained from random samples, and in testing hypotheses about those means. Before proceeding to the construction of control charts, we will review the procedure for estimating the value of the arithmetic mean of a population from data obtained from random samples.

We first draw a random sample of size n, and compute the arithmetic mean of the sample $\bar{x}$.[3] We can use the information from this sample to make inferences about the entire population. If we repeat this process and draw many samples of size n and compute the mean of each sample, we would have a distribution of numbers. From the distribution, we can build up a frequency distribution of the sample means $\bar{x}$, called a *sampling distribution*. This term is used to distinguish between the distribution of sample mean values and the parent distribution from which the samples were drawn. Like any distribution of numbers, the sampling distribution will have its own arithmetic mean and standard deviation. We will use the symbol $\bar{\bar{x}}$, meaning grand average or average of averages, to refer to the arithmetic mean of the sampling distribution, and $\sigma_{\bar{x}}$, called the standard error of the mean, to refer to the standard deviation of the sampling distribution.

Relationship of Sampling Distribution to Population

The value of random sampling becomes apparent when we examine the relationship of sampling distributions to the distribution of the parent population. Suppose we have a set of 10,000 invoices whose amounts are normally distributed with a mean of $20 and a standard deviation of $5. From our previous discussion of the normal distribution, we know that the proportion of invoices which will fall in various intervals may be determined from a table of areas under the normal curve as follows:

[3] $\bar{x}$ is read "x-bar" and refers to sample means.

$$68.27\%: \mu \pm \sigma \ = \$15 - \$25$$
$$95.45\%: \mu \pm 2\sigma = \$10 - \$30$$
$$99.73\%: \mu \pm 3\sigma = \$\ 5 - \$35$$

This distribution is illustrated in Figure 9.7 which shows the relationship

Figure 9.7 Relationship Between Population Distribution and Sampling Distributions

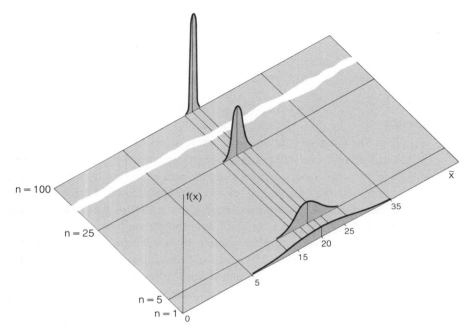

between the distributions of the original population (a distribution of samples of size $n = 1$) and the sampling distributions for samples of size 5, 25, and 100 drawn from that population. Three very important aspects of this relationship can be observed here. First, the arithmetic mean of each of the sampling distribution, $\bar{\bar{x}}$, is equal to the mean of the population, μ, that is $\bar{\bar{x}} = \mu$.

Second, the distribution of sample means is a normal distribution, as was the original population distribution. If the original population were not normally distributed, we would find that, as the sample size was increased, the sampling distribution would approach a normal distribution. This would be true regardless of the shape of the original population distribution. This phenomenon, which can be mathematically proved, results from the *central limit theorem*. The central limit theorem states that the distribution of sample means approaches normality as the size the sample is increased, provided the population has a finite mean and variance.

The convergence of distributions of sample means toward the form of a normal distribution is such a powerful tendency that for many distributions the means of samples of size 4 or 5 already approximate a normal distribution. One of Shewhart's experiments illustrates this tendency. Figure 9.8

Figure 9.8 Distributions of Sample Means for Samples of Size 4
From Rectangular and Right Triangular Universes

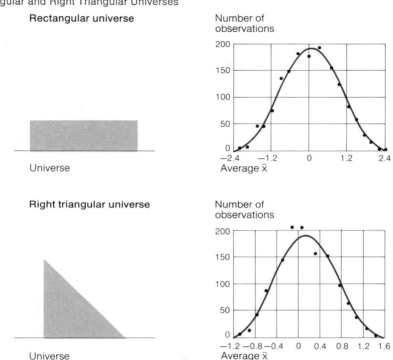

shows the results of his experiments. Shewhart drew 1,000 samples of size 4 from a rectangular universe and a right triangular universe and compared the distributions of sample means with normal distributions. In Figure 9.8, it is apparent that the distribution of sample means, shown as points, very closely approximates a normal distribution. These facts permit us to use relatively small samples in the construction and use of control charts.

Third, the standard deviation of the sampling distribution, called the standard error of the mean, is related to the population standard deviation, as follows:

$$\sigma_{\bar{x}} = \frac{\sigma}{\sqrt{n}}. \tag{9.3}$$

The standard error of the mean $\sigma_{\bar{x}}$, is the standard deviation of the population σ, divided by the square root of the sample size n. These three relationships are the essence of sampling theory, and show why it is possible to rely upon data from samples.

Confidence Interval

The proportion of sample means lying within given intervals around the population mean, can be determined because we know that the sampling distribution is normal and that we can compute the value of the standard error of the mean, $\sigma_{\bar{x}}$. In Figure 9.7, if we examine the distribution of the means of samples of size 5, drawn from the population of invoices, we find that the mean of the distribution is equal to $20, but that the probability intervals have become considerably smaller. The standard error of the mean of this new distribution is

$$\sigma_{\bar{x}} = \frac{\sigma}{\sqrt{n}} = \frac{\$5}{\sqrt{5}} = \frac{\$5}{2.24} = \$2.24.$$

For this sampling distribution, the proportion of sample means lying within various intervals is

$$68.27\%: \mu \pm \sigma_{\bar{x}} = \$17.76 - \$22.24$$
$$95.45\%: \mu \pm 2\sigma_{\bar{x}} = \$15.56 - \$24.48$$
$$99.73\%: \mu \pm 3\sigma_{\bar{x}} = \$13.38 - \$26.72.$$

These values give us the probability that one sample mean lies within any given interval of $\sigma_{\bar{x}}$ around the population mean. Thus, for a sample of 5 invoices, there is a probability of .9545 that the sample mean will lie in the interval from $15.56 to $24.48. For samples of size 25, the sampling distribution has a standard error of $5/ \sqrt{25} = \$5/5 = \$1.00$. For this sampling distribution, 99.73 per cent of the sample means lie in the interval $20 \pm $3, or between $17 and $23. If we increase the sample size to 100, the intervals contract further, since the standard error reduces to $0.50. The 99.73 per cent interval is from $18.50 to $21.50.

Now, if we have one sample mean, $\bar{x}$, we can state, with a corresponding probability of being correct, that the population mean, μ, lies within any given interval of the standard error of the mean around the mean of our sample. This interval is called the *confidence interval*. Note that we did not say that there was a certain probability that the population mean lies within a given interval of the sample mean. The population mean is either in this interval or it is not. The probability is 1.00 if the population mean is in the interval, and 0.00 if it is not. We made the statement that we believe the population mean to be in this interval, and supported it with a statement about how confident we were that our statement was correct. The probability or degree of confidence associated with a particular confidence interval is called a confidence level.

Probability used in this sense refers to frequency of occurrence. When we draw a sample, compute its mean, calculate a $\pm 3\sigma_{\bar{x}}$, or 99.73 per cent confidence interval, and use this information to make inferences about the population mean, we are basing this confidence on the notion that if we were to repeat the experiment many times, about 99.73 per cent of the time our statement would be correct, and our statement would be wrong about three in one thousand times.

For example, suppose we drew three different samples of size $n = 25$, as shown in Figure 9.9. In this example, the population mean, μ, which we

Figure 9.9   Sampling Distribution and Confidence Intervals for Three Samples

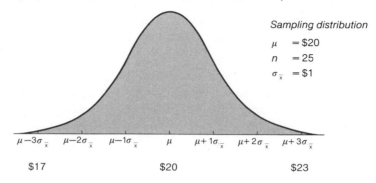

Sampling distribution
$\mu = \$20$
$n = 25$
$\sigma_{\bar{x}} = \$1$

$\mu - 3\sigma_{\bar{x}}$ $\mu - 2\sigma_{\bar{x}}$ $\mu - 1\sigma_{\bar{x}}$ μ $\mu + 1\sigma_{\bar{x}}$ $\mu + 2\sigma_{\bar{x}}$ $\mu + 3\sigma_{\bar{x}}$

$\$17$ $\$20$ $\$23$

Sample a: $\bar{x} = \$19.25$

Confidence interval

$\bar{x} - 3\sigma_{\bar{x}}$ $\bar{x}$ $\bar{x} + 3\sigma_{\bar{x}}$

$\$16.25$ $\$19.25$ $\$22.25$

Sample b: $\bar{x} = \$21.63$

Confidence interval

$\bar{x} - 3\sigma_{\bar{x}}$ $\bar{x}$ $\bar{x} + 3\sigma_{\bar{x}}$

$\$18.63$ $\$21.63$ $\$24.63$

Sample c: $\bar{x} = \$23.35$

Confidence interval

$\bar{x} - 3\sigma_{\bar{x}}$ $\bar{x}$ $\bar{x} + 3\sigma_{\bar{x}}$

$\$20.35$ $\$23.35$ $\$26.35$

are trying to estimate is $20 and the standard error of the mean, $\sigma_{\bar{x}}$, is $1. At a 99.73 per cent level of confidence, the $\pm 3\sigma_{\bar{x}}$ confidence interval is $\pm\$3. The mean of sample (a) is $19.25 and the confidence interval is from $16.25 to $22.25. Our contention is that the population mean, μ, lies within the interval $16.25 to $22.25, and we are 99.73 per cent certain that this contention is correct. From the figure, we see that we are right in this instance, because the true population mean does lie within this interval.

Similarly the mean of sample (b) is $21.63 and confidence interval is from $18.63 to $24.63. Again, our contention that the population mean lies within this interval is correct. Now, consider sample (c). The mean of this sample is $23.35 and the corresponding confidence interval is from $20.35 to $26.35, which we claim contains the population mean. We are still 99.73 per cent certain that we are correct, but this time we are wrong. Such samples do occur with a frequency of about three in one thousand times. This is an illustration of a Type I error.

Reducing the Risk of Error

Suppose we feel that we cannot run the risk outlined above. Several alternatives are open to us. We could take a complete count of the population and then determine the population mean precisely except for errors of measurement, but this may be too costly. Or, we could set a larger confidence interval. A $\pm 4\sigma_{\bar{x}}$ confidence interval would correspond to a probability of 99.994 per cent. Our confidence interval for sample (c) would then have been from $19.35 to $27.35 [$\bar{x} \pm 4$ ($1)] and would include the population mean. We have gained confidence but lost precision. Note that for a given sample size, the precision of the estimate and the level of confidence are inversely related. A 68 per cent level of confidence corresponds to a confidence interval of $\bar{x} \pm 1\sigma_{\bar{x}}$, while a 99.7 per cent level of confidence corresponds to a confidence interval of $\bar{x} \pm 3\sigma_{\bar{x}}$.

To increase the precision of an estimate at a given level of confidence, we must increase the size of sample. An increase in the sample size by a factor of 4 would reduce the confidence interval by one-half, as illustrated earlier in Figure 9.7, because the standard error of the mean varies inversely with the square root of the sample size. Whether it is desirable to increase precision by increasing sample size depends upon the added cost of inspection. The manager would have to weigh the added cost against the value of the more precise estimate.

We can use equation 9.3 and our understanding of confidence intervals to determine the sample size required for a particular estimate. Ignoring cost for now, the required sample size depends upon three factors: (1) variation in the population, (2) precision desired, and (3) permissible risk.

The expression for the confidence interval is $\mu \pm k\sigma_{\bar{x}}$, where k is the factor associated with the level of confidence. If we let A be the desired precision of the estimate, or the permissible error range, $\bar{x} - \mu$, then

$$A = k\sigma_{\bar{x}} = k \frac{\sigma}{\sqrt{n}}.$$

Solving for n, we get

$$n = \frac{k^2\sigma^2}{A^2}. \tag{9.4}$$

Suppose we wish to determine the size sample required to estimate the mean value of the invoices in the previous example within a precision of $\pm\$.50$ at a confidence level of .95. From the table of areas under the normal curve, we find $k = 1.96$ for a confidence level of .95. Substituting into equation 9.4, we find that

$$n = \frac{(1.96)^2(5)^2}{(.50)^2}$$
$$= 384.$$

A sample of 384 would be required for this estimate. Note that n does not depend upon the proportion of the sample size to the size of the population. If the population is large and the sample small relative to it, the population size does not enter the calculations. If these conditions are not met, a correction factor is applied. Many statistics texts illustrate the use of this correction factor.

Using Estimated Values

So far in our discussion, for purposes of explanation and comparison, we have assumed that we know the mean and standard deviation, μ and σ, for the population from which samples were drawn. This is seldom, if ever, the situation. Most populations encountered by managers are unknown empirical distributions for which μ and σ must be estimated. Predictions are based upon samples drawn from these populations. Since the means of samples are closely clustered around the mean of their parent population, we may use the mean of a sample $\bar{x}$ as an estimate of μ, the mean of the population.

The variance in a single sample, σ_s^2, tends to underestimate the variance of a population σ^2, because the average of the distribution of variances of samples is only $(n - 1)/n$ times the variance of individual values in the population. If we multiply a sample variance, σ_s^2, by $n/(n - 1)$, we correct for the downward bias and obtain an unbiased estimate of the variance of the population:[4]

$$s^2 = \sigma_s^2 \frac{n}{n - 1} = \frac{\sum_{i=1}^{n} (x_i - \bar{x})^2}{n - 1} \tag{9.5}$$

where s^2 refers to an estimate of the variance of a population. For large-size samples, the correction factor $n/(n - 1)$ is often ignored, because the resulting error is small. For a sample of size $n = 25$, the correction factor would

---

[4] However, s is not an unbiased estimate of σ. To correct for bias, s is multiplied by the factor c_2. Values of c_2 for various values of n are given in Table F in the Appendix.

be $25/(25 - 1) = 1.042$, and its omission would cause an error of approximately 4 per cent.[5]

We substitute the value of s^2 into equation 9.3 to obtain an estimate of the standard error of the mean,

$$s_{\bar{x}} = \sqrt{\frac{s^2}{n}} = \frac{s}{\sqrt{n}} \cdot \tag{9.6}$$

The estimated standard error of the mean may be used in setting confidence intervals from sample data.[6]

For example, suppose that we had drawn a sample of 25 invoices and computed the mean of the sample to be $\bar{x}_s = \$19.00$ and the variance of the sample to be $\sigma_s{}^2 = \$4.80$. To find the estimated variance of the population s^2 we would use equation 9.5:

$$s^2 = \sigma_s{}^2 \frac{n}{n - 1} = 4.80 \left(\frac{25}{24}\right) = 4.80(1.04) = 4.99.$$

Then, to estimate the standard error of the mean $s_{\bar{x}}$ we would use equation 9.6:

$$s_{\bar{x}} = \frac{s}{\sqrt{n}} = \frac{4.99}{\sqrt{25}} = \frac{4.99}{5} = .998.$$

Following this, we could proceed to find the confidence intervals as before.

Control Charts

A statistical control chart is a time-based graphic display of the performance of some characteristic of an operating system or subsystem, which shows whether a system has remained stable or has undergone some significant change. Control charts based upon sampling theory outlined in preceding sections are used to monitor a process. When properly applied and maintained, control charts are useful detective devices. They will not indicate the cause of changes in the system, but they will indicate the probable nature of the shifts; and if the samples are taken periodically and the information

---

[5] For a finite population, a correction factor should be applied,

$$s^2 = \frac{\sum\limits_{i=1}^{n} (x_i - \bar{x})^2}{n - 1} \left(\frac{N - 1}{N}\right)$$

where N is the size of the population. The populations usually encountered in statistical control problems are of such size that the correction factor can be ignored.

[6] When estimating both μ and σ for sample data from small samples in which $n < 30$, Student's t distribution is used for probability statements rather than the normal distribution.

plotted, they will indicate the time at which the difficulty appeared. This is of material benefit to the manager, since he can investigate whether there were any changes in the system which might contribute to the shift, such as a new batch of raw material or a change in operators.

Two classes of charts are used, one for monitoring variables and the other for monitoring attributes. When measurements of a quality characteristic are recorded, such as dimensions, temperature, weight, and tensile strength, quality is expressed as a variable. When information is recorded only about whether an item conforms or fails to conform to a specified requirement, quality is expressed as an attribute. For example, a piece of glass is either broken or not; a column of numbers is either totaled correctly or not. Charts for monitoring variables are used with measurements, such as weights or dimensions, and are called $\overline{X}$ and R charts. An $\overline{X}$ chart is used to monitor the means of samples drawn from a population. It would be used in conjunction with an R chart (range chart) which is used to monitor the variation within samples drawn from a population. Control charts used to monitor attributes are called p charts or c charts. For control of output that can be counted, such as the number of errors or defective items, p charts are used to monitor the fraction or proportion of defective output or errors, and c charts are used to monitor the number of defects or errors.

The basic procedure for developing control charts may be summarized in the following steps:

1. Determine the purpose of the chart, the variable to be measured, the measurement to be used, and the size and frequency of the subgroups (samples).

2. Measure the appropriate variable, calculate the center line and trial control limits, plot the chart, and draw preliminary conclusions.

3. Revise the control limits if necessary, and continue plotting the chart.

Average and Range Control Charts

To illustrate the construction and application of $\overline{X}$ and R charts, let us consider a control problem. A frozen food processing company has an automatic package filling machine which is supposed to be set for an average package weight of 18.0 ounces. For this illustration we will assume the population of package weights is approximately normally distributed as shown in Table 9.1 with $\mu = 18.0$ ounces and $\sigma = 0.4$ ounces. Of course, the manager would not know this information but we will use the data to demonstrate the operation of a control chart for variables. Since average package weight is the characteristic that will be measured, $\overline{X}$ and R charts would be used to monitor the centering and dispersion of the process. We will assume that the manager decided to use the traditional $3\sigma_{\overline{x}}$ control limits, and samples of size 4.

Table 9.1 Cumulative Distribution of Package Weights

Package Weight (ounces)	Cumulative Probability of Occurrence
16.8	.002
16.9	.004
17.0	.009
17.1	.017
17.2	.030
17.3	.052
17.4	.084
17.5	.130
17.6	.190
17.7	.265
17.8	.354
17.9	.450
18.0	.550
18.1	.646
18.2	.734
18.3	.810
18.4	.870
18.5	.916
18.6	.948
18.7	.970
18.8	.983
18.9	.991
19.0	.996
19.1	.998
19.2	1.000

Table 9.2 shows the results from drawing 25 samples of 4 packages from the population distribution in Table 9.1 and computing the mean weight $\bar{x}$ and the range R for each sample. The samples were selected using the Monte Carlo procedure outlined in Chapter 2. The 25 sample means have a grand average, $\bar{\bar{x}}$, of 18.06 ounces, which is remarkably close to μ, and an average range, $\bar{R}$, of 0.876. The 25 sample means are plotted on the $\bar{X}$ chart in Figure 9.10.

To analyze historical data, we set the center line of an $\bar{X}$ chart at $\bar{\bar{x}}$, the average of the sample means. For control purposes, the center line may be derived either from historical data or from some target central line, specified by management, at which the process is supposed to be centered. In this example, the central line may be set at 18.0 ounces, the population mean μ, and control limits set at:

$$\mu \pm 3\sigma_{\bar{x}} = 18.0 \pm 3\left(\frac{0.4}{\sqrt{4}}\right) = 18.0 \pm .6.$$

Table 9.2 Package Weights of 25 Samples of 4 Items

Sample Number	Weight of Individual Packages				$\bar{x}$	R
1	17.5	17.9	17.5	18.9	17.95	1.4
2	17.5	18.2	17.6	18.4	17.925	0.9
3	18.1	18.3	18.9	17.5	18.20	1.4
4	18.4	18.5	19.0	18.2	18.525	0.8
5	18.3	18.2	18.2	17.5	18.05	0.8
6	18.5	18.3	17.9	17.5	18.05	1.0
7	18.1	18.1	17.6	18.6	18.10	1.0
8	17.9	17.7	17.3	17.0	17.475	0.9
9	17.9	18.1	18.0	17.8	17.95	0.3
10	18.2	17.7	18.0	18.7	18.15	1.0
11	18.8	17.8	18.3	18.3	18.30	1.0
12	17.6	18.3	18.0	17.5	17.85	0.8
13	18.0	18.2	18.8	18.9	18.475	0.9
14	17.7	17.7	17.4	18.2	17.75	0.8
15	18.1	18.2	18.2	18.7	18.30	0.6
16	17.7	17.3	18.0	18.4	17.85	1.1
17	18.6	18.4	17.7	18.0	18.175	0.9
18	17.6	18.6	19.0	17.9	18.275	1.4
19	17.3	18.0	17.4	18.7	17.85	1.4
20	18.3	18.1	18.4	17.7	18.125	0.6
21	18.6	18.0	18.1	17.4	18.025	1.2
22	18.1	18.3	17.8	18.2	18.10	0.5
23	18.1	18.1	18.4	18.4	18.25	0.3
24	18.0	18.0	17.8	17.8	17.90	0.2
25	18.3	18.1	17.7	17.6	17.92	0.7

$$\bar{\bar{x}} = 18.06 \qquad \bar{R} = 0.876$$

Figure 9.10 $\bar{X}$ Control Chart

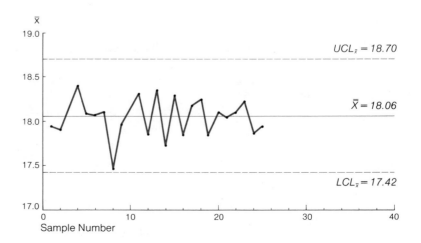

or, at 18.6 and 17.4. But we will illustrate the construction of the chart from the sample data, which yields a central line at $\bar{\bar{x}} = 18.06$ ounces.

Upper and lower control limits are derived from equation 9.7:

$$UCL_{\bar{x}} = \bar{\bar{x}} + ks_{\bar{x}}$$
$$LCL_{\bar{x}} = \bar{\bar{x}} - ks_{\bar{x}} \tag{9.7}$$

where k is the multiple of $s_{\bar{x}}$ which corresponds to the desired confidence level. Since calculation of the standard deviation for each sample is time consuming, and may be difficult for those expected to maintain the control chart, we make use of the following relationship between the average range and standard deviation:

$$d_2 = \frac{\bar{R}}{\sigma} \tag{9.8}$$

We can compute the estimated standard deviation from:

$$s = \frac{\bar{R}}{d_2} \tag{9.9}$$

Values of the factor d_2 for various sample sizes are given in Appendix Table G.

Calculation of upper and lower control limits for an average chart with $3s_{\bar{x}}$ control limits can be considerably shortened by using the following relationship:

$$UCL_{\bar{x}} = \bar{\bar{x}} + A_2\bar{R}$$
$$LCL_{\bar{x}} = \bar{\bar{x}} - A_2\bar{R}. \tag{9.10}$$

Values of A_2 for various sample sizes are given in Appendix Table G.[7] For the samples drawn, which had $n = 4$, shown in Table 9.2, we find that $A_2 = 0.729$, and the control limits are:

$$UCL_{\bar{x}} = 18.06 + (0.729)(0.876) = 18.70$$
$$LCL_{\bar{x}} = 18.06 - (0.729)(0.876) = 17.42$$

which are the limits indicated in Figure 9.10.

---

[7] The factor A_2 is derived in the following way: For $3s_{\bar{x}}$ control limits, $k = 3$, and from equations 9.7 and 9.8

$$UCL_{\bar{x}} = \bar{\bar{x}} + 3s_{\bar{x}} = \bar{\bar{x}} = 3 + \frac{s}{\sqrt{n}}.$$

Substituting for s

$$UCL_{\bar{x}} = \bar{\bar{x}} + 3\frac{\bar{R}/d_2}{\sqrt{n}} = \bar{\bar{x}} + \frac{3}{d_2\sqrt{n}}\bar{R}.$$

If we let

$$A_2 = \frac{3}{d_2\sqrt{n}},$$

then

$$UCL_{\bar{x}} = \bar{\bar{x}} + A_2\bar{R}.$$

The control chart for ranges, the R chart, shown in Figure 9.11, is used to monitor the dispersion of process output and is based upon the distribution of ranges. Its construction follows the same procedure as the $\overline{X}$ chart.

Figure 9.11 R Control Chart

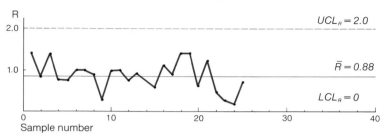

The central line is the average range, $\overline{R}$, of the samples, 0.88 in this example. Control limits are determined from the estimated standard error of the range s_R:

$$UCL_R = \overline{R} + ks_R$$
$$LCL_R = \overline{R} - ks_R. \qquad (9.11)$$

Although the distribution of ranges is not normal, the probability of a sample range falling outside $3s_R$ control limits is so small that points falling outside are a strong indication of the presence of assignable causes of variation.[8] The following expression may be used to calculate upper and lower $3s_R$ control limits for a range chart:[9]

$$UCL_R = D_4 R$$
$$LCL_R = D_3 R. \qquad (9.12)$$

Values for the factors D_4 and D_3 are given in Appendix Table G. For $n = 4$, $D_4 = 2.282$ and $D_3 = 0$. Using these values

---

[8] For a discussion of the distribution of ranges, see Acheson J. Duncan, *Quality Control and Industrial Statistics,* 3rd ed. (Homewood, Ill.: Richard D. Irwin, Inc., 1965), Chapter 6.

[9] The factors D_4 and D_3 are derived in the following manner:

$$UCL_R = \overline{R} + 3s_R$$
$$LCL_R = \overline{R} - 3s_R$$

If we let,

$$D_4 = 1 + \frac{3s_R}{\overline{R}}$$

and

$$D_3 = 1 - \frac{3s_R}{\overline{R}}$$

we obtain by substitution

$$UCL_R = D_4\overline{R}$$
$$LCL_R = D_3\overline{R}$$

$$UCL_R = (2.282)(0.876) = 2.0$$
$$LCL_R = 0$$

which are the control limits in Figure 9.11.

Control charts may be computed on the basis of standard deviation, but the range is more often used because it is easier to calculate and understand, and the range and standard deviation are likely to fluctuate together for small samples. Factors for computing control limits for standard deviation charts are included in Appendix Table D.

The charts illustrated in Figures 9.10 and 9.11 indicate that the process is in control, which we expect since the samples are from an unchanging population. At this point, the manager should ask whether the performance of the system is acceptable, even though it is in statistical control. If, for example, the manager desired an average package weight of 17.0 ounces, the charts indicate that at present the process is clearly not producing packages of that average weight. The manager would take action to correct the process if this were the case.

If the process average were to shift from the present value of 18.0 ounces, or if the dispersion in the process were to increase, sample means or ranges would fall outside the control limits. The appearance of sample means outside control limits would serve as an indication of the presence of a shift, and would call for management attention. A single value outside the control limits might be due to chance (we expect that about three in one thousand $\bar{x}$ values will fall outside the $3\sigma_{\bar{x}}$ control limits). But for more than one sample mean in a sequence to fall outside the limits would be extremely unlikely. Consequently, if one mean falls outside, the manager might take a second sample before shutting down the process to look for an assignable cause for the variation.

It is not necessary to wait for means or ranges to fall outside the limits before taking action. A long run of means (7 or more) on one side of the center line or a discernible trend in means in one direction are indications that the mean has shifted and would signal management attention.

Control Chart for Fraction Defective

Many control situations exist in which the quality of the output from a process cannot be measured conveniently, but can be observed as attributes. There are other situations in which it may be desirable to convert measurements into attributes. In these cases, we use a dichotomous classification, such as good-defective. Two types of charts are often used for these instaces: a p chart for the fraction of defective output (fraction defective), and a c chart for the number of defects per unit. Fraction defective is the ratio of the number of defective articles to the total number of articles inspected. Fraction defective charts are particularly useful in nonproduct applications, such as observing clerical errors, absenteeism rates, and usage rates of equipment.

Fraction defective charts are not as sensitive to changes as are variable charts, and larger sample sizes are required. Often fraction defective charts are based upon 100 per cent inspection. The sample size should be large enough so that each sample is likely to contain some defective items in order to detect fluctuations in quality levels. If 10 per cent of the items are defective, a sample size of 10 is required to include an average of one defect per sample. If only 1 per cent are defective, the sample size must be at least 100. Consequently, the better the quality of the process, the larger must be the sample.

A p chart is useful for monitoring clerical operations in which an invoice or form is classified as good if it contains no errors and defective if it contains one or more errors. Table 9.3 shows the result of drawing a daily sample of

Table 9.3 Results of Checking Invoices for 30 Days

Day	Invoices Inspected n	Number of Defectives np	Fraction Defective p
1	30	8	.267
2	30	7	.233
3	30	7	.233
4	30	6	.200
5	30	11	.367
6	30	12	.400
7	30	7	.233
8	30	8	.267
9	30	4	.133
10	30	9	.300
11	30	7	.233
12	30	7	.233
13	30	4	.133
14	30	6	.200
15	30	5	.167
16	30	5	.167
17	30	6	.200
18	30	11	.367
19	30	7	.233
20	30	8	.267
21	30	10	.333
22	30	9	.300
23	30	11	.367
24	30	6	.200
25	30	7	.233
26	30	8	.267
27	30	11	.367
28	30	4	.133
29	30	8	.267
30	30	6	.200
Totals:	900	225	

30 invoices and checking them for accuracy. We find the average fraction defective by treating the data as a single sample:

$$\bar{p} = \frac{225}{900} = 0.250.$$

To set up a control chart for fraction defective, p, we first establish preliminary control limits based upon the estimated standard error of the proportion s_p from the binomial probability distribution:

$$s_p = \sqrt{\frac{\bar{p}(1 - \bar{p})}{n}} \qquad (9.13)$$

where

$$\bar{p} = \text{average proportion defective}$$
$$n = \text{sample size.}$$

The binomial distribution applies to situations involving infinite populations where the probability of occurrence is constant from sample to sample. As long as the universe fraction defective remains unchanged, the relative frequency of the sample fraction defectives may be expected to follow the binomial distribution. The populations encountered in management control problems are usually large enough so that the binomial distribution serves as a good approximation of the distribution of proportions. Control limits may be set at $\pm 3s_p$ from the following expression:

$$UCL_p = \bar{p} + 3s_p$$
$$LCL_p = \bar{p} - 3s_p. \qquad (9.14)$$

Applying these expressions to the observed data in Table 9.3, we have

$$s_p = \sqrt{\frac{(0.25)(0.75)}{30}} = \sqrt{\frac{0.1875}{30}} = \sqrt{0.00625} = 0.0791$$

and

$$UCL_p = 0.25 + 3(0.791) = 0.487$$
$$LCL_p = 0.25 - 3(0.791) = 0.013$$

These preliminary limits have been plotted on the p chart in Figure 9.12, along with the 30 observations. We note that the process appears to be in control. Had points fallen outside the control limits, we would investigate to determine the cause of out-of-control points. If some unusual circumstances existed for those days which were out of control, we would eliminate those days' observations and recompute the control limits. When the process appears to be in control, the chart may be used for continued monitoring.

Periodically it is necessary to recompute control limits, because the average universe fraction defective may change. For example, the institution of

Figure 9.12 Control Chart for Fraction Defective

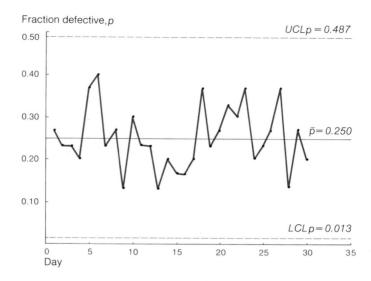

control charts for process monitoring often results in improved performance, requiring new control limits.

For charts based upon observation of the entire output of a process for some time period, the subgroup size may vary. In this case, the sample is the output from the entire period. Then it is necessary to use variable control limits for each subgroup, because s_p depends upon the number of items observed.

A p chart may be used to judge whether a process is meeting some desired quality level established by the manager by setting $\bar{p}$ at the desired objective. When setting up a p chart based upon a standard fraction defective rather than upon historical data, the manager needs evidence that the standard is actually attainable, or the chart may show an apparent lack of control. To be effective there must be evidence that the standard is attainable. Without such evidence the purpose of the chart may be defeated, because of antagonism toward an apparently unattainable standard of performance.

Control Charts for Number of Defects Per Unit

In many systems it is more appropriate to deal with the number of defects per unit rather than with the proportion of defective units. A defective unit is one that does not conform to some standard of quality, because of one or more defects. In product quality applications defects per unit may refer to the number of poor electrical connections in a TV set or the number of surface blemishes in a painted surface of a given area. In nonproduct applications, the term might apply to the number of errors made in filling out a complex form, the number of accidents along a stretch of highway, the number of crimes committed in a given area, or the number of arrivals at a service facility within a given time.

These situations have a common factor: that there are a large number of opportunities for occurrence of errors or defects, and that the probability of a particular defect occurring is small. In such situations the c chart, which applies to the number of defects in samples of constant size, may be used to monitor the process and detect changes. Control limits for the c chart are based upon the Poisson probability distribution.

The Poisson distribution is a close approximation of the binomial distribution when the probability of occurrence p is small and the sample size n is large. The applicability of the Poisson distribution to defects per unit situations may be explained if we translate defects per unit into a proportion. If in filling out a complex form there are 200 possibilities for error, the number of errors may be expressed as the proportion of errors to the total possible number of errors (fraction defective p). If the proportion of errors p is small, say less than 0.10, and the sample size (the number of possible occurrences) is large, then the distribution of the sample fraction defective is approximated by the Poisson distribution. If we take p to be the proportion of occurrence (of defects) in a population and n to be the size of sample (the opportunity for occurrence), np is the average number of defects per sample. The probability of c occurrences in a sample is:

$$P(c) = \frac{(np)e^{-np}}{c!} \tag{9.15}$$

which is the formula for the Poisson distribution. The variance of the Poisson distribution is equal to the mean, $\sigma^2 = np$, and the standard deviation is the square root of the mean, $\sigma = \sqrt{np}$. If we use the average number of occurrences $\bar{c}$ as an estimate of the population mean np, then we may establish 3-sigma control limits for a c chart as follows:

$$UCL_c = \bar{c} + 3\sqrt{\bar{c}}$$
$$LCL_c = \bar{c} - 3\sqrt{\bar{c}}. \tag{9.16}$$

Development and operation of a c chart follows the same procedure as that for $\bar{X}$, R, and p charts. However, the Poisson distribution is not symmetrical as is the normal distribution used as a basis for $\bar{X}$ charts; consequently, probabilities of points falling outside the upper and lower 3-sigma control limits are not equal. Equal probability limits may be established on c charts by use of equation 9.15, or by referring to a table or graph of the Poisson distribution (see Appendix Table F).

To illustrate the use of the c chart to monitor changes in a process, consider a multi-channel service facility set up to accommodate arrivals, such as toll booths on a toll bridge. We determine the desired capacity of the system by using queuing theory models, as discussed in Chapter 12, and a *c* chart to indicate when the system has changed. Data for 25 hours of operation of the system are shown in Table 9.4. The estimated average number of arrivals per hour is:

$$\bar{c} = \frac{229}{25} = 9.2.$$

Table 9.4   Number of Arrivals per Hour at Service Facility

Hour	Number of Arrivals c	Hour	Number of Arrivals c
		13	4
1	9	14	11
2	11	15	4
3	3	16	9
4	11	17	11
5	8	18	10
6	12	19	4
7	8	20	17
8	12	21	10
9	8	22	9
10	9	23	4
11	17	24	4
12	10	25	14
		Total	229

Applying equation (9.16) the control limits are:

$$UCL_c = 9.2 + 3\sqrt{9.2} = 9.2 + 3(3.03) = 9.2 + 9.1 = 18.3$$
$$LCL_c = 9.2 - 3\sqrt{9.2} = 9.2 - 3(3.03) = 9.2 - 9.1 = 0.1.$$

These are drawn on the *c* chart in Figure 9.13 which shows the system to be in control. When used for continual monitoring, values falling outside the control limits signal the need to alter the system capacity, because of an apparent change in the average arrival rate. Closer control limits (say 2-sigma) could be established for a more sensitive warning signal, but, at the expense of increasing the risk of Type II error, or making a change in capacity when there is no change in the mean arrival rate.

A *c* chart requires a constant sample size, that is a constant opportunity for occurrences. In those situations in which there is a varying sample size, it is necessary to weigh the number of defects by the sample size and use variable control limits.

Economic Design of Control Charts

One of management's goals is to design control systems which will minimize the expected costs of running the system under control. There are several

Figure 9.13 Control Chart for Number of Arrivals per Hour

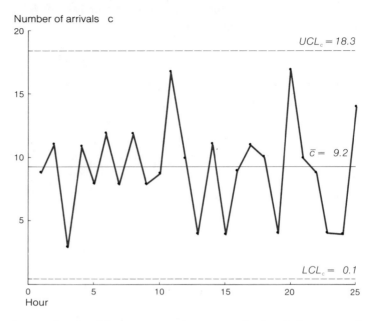

types of costs involved in any control system, whether it is a control system based upon the Shewhart control model which uses statistical sampling techniques, or a more traditional control system. Figure 9.14, using the

Figure 9.14 Contingency Table of Economic Factors in Control System

True State of System	Decision	
	Accept Hypothesis	Reject Hypothesis
Unchanged: Stable system of chance causes operating	No additional cost	Cost of looking for nonexistent trouble C_{12}
Changed: Assignable cause of change present	Cost of failing to detect change C_{21}	Cost of locating trouble C_{22}

C_{11} = Cost of inspection

hypothesis that the system is unchanged, shows the types of costs involved in a control system. We may classify the costs:

1. The costs of monitoring the process and making investigations, C_{11}. These costs would apply regardless of what the manager's decision is about the state of the system.

2. The costs of looking for nonexistent trouble if the decision is to reject the hypothesis that the system has not changed when, in fact,
the hypothesis is true, C_{12}.

3. The costs of failing to detect a change in the system if the system,
in fact, has changed, C_{21}.

4. The costs of finding the cause of trouble and correcting it if the
system has changed and the hypothesis is correctly rejected, C_{22}.

The manager attempts to minimize the total of the expected value of these
costs through his decisions about the characteristics of the control system
to be used, and his decisions about what action to take when confronted
with the results of inspecting the system. If all the costs and probabilities
were known with certainty, the decision might be reduced to a statistical
decison-theory problem. Since they are not, the manager, must utilize his
judgment and knowledge about the way in which the system operates.

**Operating
Characteristics
Curve**
Fundamental to the concept of a minimum cost control plan is the concept
of operating characteristics functions. Operating characteristics curves show,
for various states of the system, the probability of discriminating between
the alternative hypotheses established for testing. For variables control
charts ($\overline{X}$ charts), an operating characteristics curve indicates the probability of a sample mean value $\overline{x}$ falling within the control limits when the process
average has shifted, and consequently shows the probability of failing to
detect a change in the system (a Type II error).

For an $\overline{X}$ chart with $\pm\ 3s_{\overline{x}}$ control limits, the probability of a Type I
error, a false indication that the system is out of control, is the proportion
of the area under a normal curve outside the 3-sigma limits, or 0.0027, an
unlikely event. The probability of making a Type II error depends upon
the magnitude and the shift of the process mean.

Consider the package filling process in Table 9.1, in which the desired
process mean $\mu\ =\ 18.0$ ounces and 3 $\sigma_{\overline{x}}$ control limits are 18.6 and 17.4
for a sample size of $n = 4$. Figure 9.15 shows the sampling distribution of $\overline{x}$
for five possible states of the system with different means, but constant dispersion. State 1 is the desired state of the system in which $\mu_1 = 18.0$. In
State 2, the mean of the process has shifted to $\mu_2 = 17.8$, which is one
standard error away from the desired state. If there were a shift to this new
mean, there would be a new sampling distribution centered on μ_2 as shown.
The lower control limit of the chart now falls at $\mu_2 - 2\sigma_{\overline{x}}$ and from Appendix Table D, 98 per cent of the new sampling distribution is still within
the control limits. Thus $\beta = 98$ per cent, the probability of making a
Type II error, failure to detect the shift. This may also be referred to as P_a,
the probability of accepting the hypothesis of no change in the system. Similarly the probability of failing to detect a shift in the process mean to 17.6

Figure 9.15 Determination of Type I and II Error for an $\overline{X}$ Chart. (Shift in process mean, Constant variance, $\sigma = 0.4$, $n = 4$, $\sigma_{\bar{x}} = 0.2$)

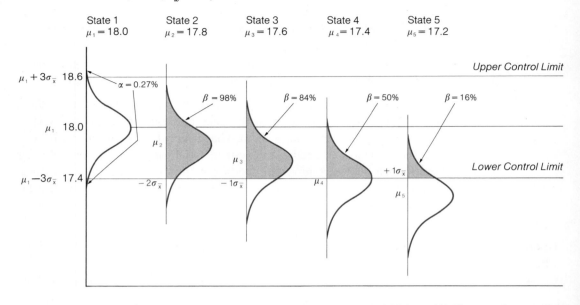

$(\mu_1 - 2\sigma_{\bar{x}})$ is 84 per cent. When the probabilities of failing to detect each of the possible shifts in process mean from 18.0 to 16.8 (0 to $-6\sigma_{\bar{x}}$) are plotted, as in Figure 9.16, we have an operating characteristics curve for this sampling plan.

Figure 9.16 Operating Characteristic Curve for an $\overline{X}$ Chart (Shift in Process Mean, Variance Constant)

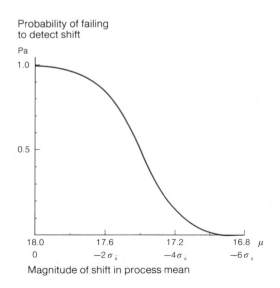

If the population dispersion is also variable, the probability of failing to detect the shift depends upon both the mean and standard deviation, and the operating characteristics function would be a surface rather than a curve. Operating characteristics functions for fraction defective, p charts, and number of defects per unit, c charts, may be derived in a similar manner. For p charts the probabilities are from the binomial distribution, and may be closely approximated from the Poisson distributions for $p \leq 0.10$ and from the normal distribution for $p \geq 0.10$. For c charts, the Poisson distribution is used to compute probabilities.

Optimal Control Plans

The management problem in the economic design of control charts is to determine a combination of sample size, frequency of sampling, and control limits which will minimize the total expected cost of running the system. Finding such combinations is a difficult problem in cost accounting and statistical theory, but we can outline some general aspects of the problem. From Figure 9.14, we see that the expected total cost, $E(TC)$, of running a control system is:

$$E(TC) = C_{11} + E(C_{12}) + E(C_{21}) + E(C_{22}). \qquad (9.17)$$

The cost of inspection and maintaining the control chart C_{11} is a function of the cost of inspection, the size of sample, and the frequency of sampling. If the cost to take a sample and inspect an item is high, and frequent large samples are taken, costs would be high. The expected cost of looking for nonexistent trouble $E(C_{12})$ is a rather complicated function which depends upon the average cost of looking for trouble that is not there, the frequency of sampling, the probability that the system remains in control, and the probability that a sample mean falls outside the control limits when the system has not changed. This latter probability depends upon where the control limits are set. We would expect more false alarms with 2-sigma control limits than with 3-sigma limits. The expected cost of failing to detect change $E(C_{21})$ is an even more complicated function which depends upon the loss incurred from an undetected defect, the rate of output of the system, and the probability that the system is out of control while undetected. The final term, the expected cost of locating trouble $E(C_{22})$ is a function of the average cost of locating trouble, and the probability that the process is out of control and detected.

To determine a minimum expected total cost, we could develop the equations for each of the expected cost factors in equation 9.17, and use calculus techniques to solve for a minimum in terms of sample size, frequency of sampling, and control limits. This has been done for one set of assumptions, and one algorithm for an exact solution to the model has been developed.[10] The procedures are quite complex and beyond the scope of our discussion, but we will examine some of the conclusions which have come out of these studies.

The optimum sample size appears to be determined primarily by the degree of shift in process mean which we desire to detect, as indicated below:

Degree of Shift	Optimum Sample Size
$\mu + 2\sigma$	2 to 6
$\mu + 1\sigma$	8 to 20
$\mu + 0.5\sigma$ or less	40 or more

The loss incurred from an undetected out of control process primarily affects the interval between samples. For large values of loss, more frequent samples should be taken than for small values.

The costs of looking for nonexistent trouble, C_{12}, and of locating trouble when it does occur, C_{22}, mainly affect the optimum control limits and somewhat affect sample size. Charts with 2.5 $\sigma_{\bar{x}}$ control limits are appropriate for small values of C_{12} and C_{22}, and 3.5 to 4 $\sigma_{\bar{x}}$ control limits for large values.

The variable cost of inspection, the cost to take a sample and inspect an item affects sample size, control limits, and frequency of sampling. Large inspection costs call for small samples, narrow control limits, and less frequent samples. The fixed cost of taking a sample affects mainly the sampling interval and has some effect on sample size.

The problem of control plan design is even more complex than we suggest here. As we pointed out in the discussion of operating characteristics functions, the degree of shift in process mean is not a single stable multiple of σ. Nor is it subject to only one assignable cause, but is itself a distribution and one which may vary over time. Various cost factors are probably themselves complex variables subject to the kind and extent of change in the process. Different troubles require different costs to locate and correct the trouble. The costs of defects may depend upon the amount of change in the system and the type of defect.

Even though we have no simple solution to this complex problem, the type of analysis suggested here does serve to define more precisely the problem and to increase the manager's understanding of the problem. It also

---

[10] Acheson J. Duncan, "The Economic Design of $\overline{X}$ Charts Used to Maintain Current Control of a Process," *Journal of the American Statistical Association* 51, no. 274 (June 1956): 228–242, and A. L. Goel, S. C. Jain, and S. M. Wu, "An Algorithm for the Determination of $\overline{X}$ Charts Based on Duncan's Model," *Journal of the American Statistical Association* 63, no. 321 (March 1958): 304–320.

indicates some of those aspects of the problem requiring managerial judgment. The analysis also suggests the potential value of a simulation approach in which different parameters are inserted into the simulation model, and their impact upon the cost of running the system are explored.

Acceptance Sampling

Another use for sampling in control of operating systems is acceptance sampling, in which a random sample is drawn from a population, and if the number of defective items is not more than a predetermined number, the population is judged acceptable. If the number of defective items is greater than the acceptance number, the population is either rejected or set aside for rectification—a complete inspection is made and defective items removed.

Acceptance sampling is widely used in purchasing to protect a buyer from an inferior quality of merchandise. If a supplier is submitting lots of products within acceptable limits, the buyer accepts the lots on the basis of the sample, and thus greatly reduces the cost of inspection, an important factor when large volumes of items are to be processed. If a supplier is submitting materials which have too large a percentage of defectives, they are either returned or subjected to 100 per cent inspection. Acceptance sampling is also used in internal auditing and control where samples of work (say invoices) are taken and the lot passed or rejected, based upon the number of errors observed in the sample.

Acceptance sampling is useful when inspection costs are high, and the cost from defective items getting through is not high, when the inspection procedure destroys the item inspected, or when 100 per cent inspection may not produce as adequate a control as sampling. It is well known that 100 per cent inspection is not a guarantee of perfect detection of defective items; inspectors may be careless or become fatigued.

The design of acceptance sampling plans has been worked out and published for various types of situations and varying degrees of protection. These published tables are built upon the sampling theory outlined in our discussion of control charts, and eliminate the need for computing the parameters of the plan. Consequently, we will not discuss the technical details of acceptance sampling plans, but will restrict our discussion to some of the characteristics of single sampling plans.

A single sampling plan is one in which a lot is accepted or rejected on the basis of a single sample. The plan is characterized by the size of the sample n, acceptance number c, and size of lot N. The power of a sampling plan to discriminate is revealed by its operating characteristics curve, which relates the quality of the lot to the probability of accepting it, as discussed earlier (see Figure 9.16).

Figure 9.17 shows the operating characteristics curve for the sampling plan $n = 100$, $c = 2$ for large lot sizes ($N \geq 1,000$). The curve shows, for example, that if the fraction defective $p = 0.008$, the probability of acceptance $P_a = 0.95$. If, as shown, the acceptable quality level AQL is $p = 0.011$, then there is a $1.00 - 0.90 = 0.10$ probability of rejecting lots of this quality or better (Type I error). This risk is known as *producer's risk α*. The *consumer's risk β* is the probability of accepting lots of, or worse than, a stated quality level called the lot tolerance fraction defective LTPD. This is the probability of a Type II error. In this example the probability of accepting lots with a fraction defective $p = 0.053$ or greater is 0.10.

Figure 9.17 Operating Characteristic Curve

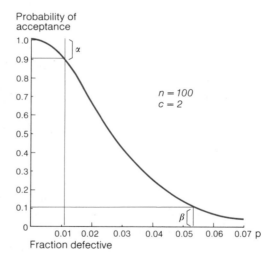

For large lot sizes the binomial probability distribution is used to compute an OC curve, but when the fraction defectives are small, the Poisson distribution may be used as a close approximation to the binomial, as we did here. The probability of acceptance may be read from the summation terms for the Poisson distribution, given in Appendix Table F. Consider a sample of 100, with p of 0.02, and $np = 2.0$. An np of 2.0 and a c of 2 correspond to P_a of $677/1000 = 0.677$. This process is repeated by varying p to obtain the points of the OC curve.

Another important measure of an acceptance sampling plan is an average outgoing quality AOQ curve, as shown in Figure 9.18, which illustrates AOQ for different levels of incoming quality p. The maximum value of the curve is the average outgoing quality limit, $AOQL$, and indicates that over the long run the outgoing quality will not be worse than this. For an incoming quality of $p = 0.01$, the probability of acceptance of a lot is 0.92.

Figure 9.18 Average Outgoing Quality Curve

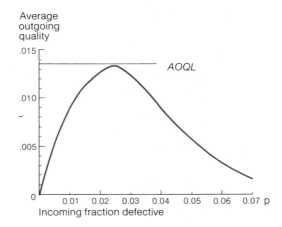

Over the long run, 92 per cent of the lots will be passed, containing an average of 1 per cent defectives. Assuming that rejected lots will be subjected to 100 per cent inspection and that all defectives will be replaced with good articles, 8 per cent of the lots will have no defectives. The AOQ will be $(P_a)(p) = (0.92)(0.01) = 0.0092$. For finite lots of size N, a correction factor is applied to account for the proportion of accepted lots which are inspected and screened for defectives:

$$AOQ = (P_a)(p)\left(\frac{N - n}{N}\right).$$

(9.18)

The specification of $AOQL$ is particularly appropriate to nonproduct applications, such as checking clerical work, where it is desirable to distinguish between the work of capable and incapable individuals.

Acceptance sampling of process inputs to distinguish between good and bad lots of incoming materials or work is not a substitute for control at the source. Carefully maintained control charts to monitor process output at the source can be used to eliminate duplication of inspection systems at a subsequent stage in the system. As management control devices, control charts are superior to acceptance sampling plans because they record data over time and reveal trends and changes in the process.

Managerial Implications of Variance Controls

Although the Shewhart control model and many of its underlying statistical techniques were developed for and have been applied primarily to product quality control problems in manufacturing operations, they have broad implications for management control in any operating system. Let us examine some of these implications and their impact on the behavior of the organization being controlled. In this broader context, we may use the term *variance controls* to include the variance control charts and techniques associated with statistical quality control.[11]

Critics of traditional management control systems argue that inattention to behavioral consequences results in control designs which frequently do not achieve improved performance, but may actually hinder the accomplishment of organizational objectives. The approach found in the Shewhart control model may offer a starting point for constructing a behaviorally sound and technically effective approach to control system design.

In traditional control systems, actual performance is measured against pre-established goals such as standards, budgets, quotas, and so forth.

Proper application of variance controls avoids one of the principal shortcomings of these traditional control systems, absolute, inflexible performance standards which do not explicitly take into account the likelihood of normal variation. Variance controls do not focus attention on absolute levels of performance but on variation in the total pattern of performance from period to period.

Using either approach, actual performance may not reach the desired level and management may well wish to raise the average level of performance. The difference is that variance controls provide a means for analyzing and evaluating performance on the basis of what is and what is likely, rather than exclusively on the basis of what ought to be.

It is argued that although management may gather information on discrepancies and attempt to restore conformance to standards, it is the individuals in the organization who actually exercise control as they accept or reject standards, do or do not exercise care in performing their duties, or accept or resist efforts to change their behavior. Management's task is then to act and design control systems in such a way that they utilize rather than antagonize the energy and creativity of organizational members.

Variance controls require an objective definition of levels of performance in terms of what the system is normally capable of accomplishing under a given set of conditions. Normal performance is ordinarily derived by measuring actual performance over a period of time. Although standards based upon past performance may reward previously poor performance or penalize good performance, they are an indication of actual capabilities of the system and provide a basis for realistic short-range planning and long-range efforts for improvement of performance. Variance controls have the potential for

---

[11] Much of the material in this section is adapted from Raymond E. Miles and Roger C. Vergin, "Behavioral Properties of Variance Controls," *California Management Review* 8, no. 3 (Spring 1966).

creating a positive, problem-solving, rather than punitive, atmosphere for the exercise of necessary corrective action, because management may generally refrain from acting on the basis of only minor variations in performance, and because there is a presumption of some unusual circumstance, or assignable cause, contributing to abnormal performance outside the limits of normal variation.

Variance control charts are potentially both simple to apply and easy to understand and can be maintained within the organizational unit or at the individual work place. The supervisor or employee may maintain his own control chart, posting performance data and periodically recomputing performance averages and control limits. This provides them with direct means to monitor such factors as quantity, quality, cost, savings and equipment utilization. The control chart, as a visible analog of actual performance, may provide an incentive for good performance, and maintaining the chart further involves the individual in the control process.

In the area of budgeting, concern has been voiced on possible negative effects of unilaterally imposed rigid budget figures. Structuring budgets based on performance data within the format of normal variation provided by variance control theory may overcome some of these problems. Where past performance data are insufficient to meet the requirements of variance controls, managers can estimate cost figures for budgets and include their own subjective probabilities of variation. These probabilities can then be incorporated into control limits which may be used to guide investigation of abnormal variation.

Recent work in the area of job enlargement, the process of adding to the scope and variety of tasks performed by an individual in an effort to improve performance and increase job satisfaction, indicates that when quality inspection and certification are added to an employee's responsibility productivity may be improved. Where the individual is responsible for performing his own quality adjustments, variance control charts may provide him with objectives, obtainable standards and efficient, understandable decision rules to guide his performance.

There are, of course, innumerable problems in defining and measuring performance in nonproduction situations and in implementing variance controls. Many of the potential benefits of variance controls may be lost if the people using them do not understand completely how they work and what they are intended to accomplish.

Major benefits from the use of variance control techniques may accrue from management's explicit recognition of normal variation in process performance and in the resulting removal of close and intensive supervision when it is unlikely to produce beneficial results. Management's full and dedicated acceptance of the underlying philosophy of variance controls may prove equally if not more beneficial than the control techniques themselves.

Summary

Statistical analysis and probability theory are the basis for managerial variance control, which, when properly used, overcome many of the objections to traditional management control systems. All systems are subject to variability, but none is totally unstable. The Shewhart control model is considered as a technique for distinguishing between tolerable minor fluctuations and major changes in a system which require attention. A system in control is said to be operating under a stable system of chance causes. A system out of control is one which has changed because of some assignable cause of variation. Sampling information is the basis for variance controls, but the use of sample information is subject to risk. Type I error is the rejection of a true hypothesis. Type II error is acceptance of a false hypothesis. Systems in which the Shewhart control model may be effectively used are those whose outputs are measurable, significant, and generally stable.

Sampling theory and the normal probability distribution are the basis for statistical control models. Sample information is used to estimate the mean, variance, and standard error of sampling distributions from which inferences about populations can be made. $\overline{X}$ and R charts are used to monitor variables. Fraction defective is monitored with p charts, and number of defects is monitored with c charts. Optimal control systems should be based upon the economic factors associated with running a statistical control model. Acceptance sampling is used to distinguish between good and bad lots of incoming materials or work. Control charts are generally superior to acceptance sampling for management control because they record dynamic changes in the system being controlled.

Selected References

Duncan, Acheson J. "The Economic Design of $\overline{X}$ Charts Used to Maintain Control of a Process." *Journal of the American Statistical Association* (June 1956): 228–242.

Duncan, Acheson J. *Quality Control and Industrial Statistics.* 3rd ed. Homewood, Illinois: Richard D. Irwin, Inc., 1965.

This text is very comprehensive. It contains all you are likely to want to know about the subject. The author includes an extensive discussion of experimental statistics.

Grant, Eugene L. *Statistical Quality Control.* 3rd ed. New York: McGraw-Hill Book Company, 1964.

A readable standard work on statistical control models. It is very thorough, and includes many examples.

Miles, Raymond E., and Vergin, Roger C. "Behavioral Properties of Variance Controls." *California Management Review* 8 (Spring 1966).

The authors compare some of the implications of variance controls (statistical control models) with traditional management control systems.

Shewhart, W. A. *Economic Control of Manufactured Product.* New York: D. Van Nostrand Co., Inc., 1931.

The pioneering work on statistical quality control.

Questions

1 What effect do uncertainties and variation in a system have on management planning and control?

2 Select an operating system with which you are familiar and identify the major sources of variation in system behavior.

3 What is meant by the phrase "a stable system of chance causes"? Give an example.

4 When is a system in control, as the term is used in the Shewhart control model? When is a system out of control? Give examples of each condition.

5 Under what kinds of conditions is the Shewhart control model applicable?

6 What are the major differences between variance control systems and traditional management control systems?

7 What information do variance control systems provide that is not likely to be found in traditional management control systems?

8 What benefits may be expected from variance control systems?

9 Under what conditions would p or c charts be used instead of $\bar{X}$ and R charts?

10 Should 3σ limits always be used for statistical control charts? Why or why not?

11 Describe a potential application of statistical control charts in a management control system. What charts would be required? What measures of system performance would be used? How would the charts be maintained?

12 For the example described in the previous question, identify the four types of expected costs which would apply to the control system. Specifically, what particular costs would make up each category? How would these expected costs vary with changes in the inspection procedure, that is, the size of samples, the frequency of samples, and the tightness of control limits?

Problems

1 Control charts for $\bar{X}$, and R are maintained on a particular dimension of a part produced by an operator. The sample size is 6. After 30 samples were inspected and the values of $\bar{X}$ and R computed for each sample, $\Sigma\bar{X} = 91.20''$ and $\Sigma R = 31.60''$. Compute the values of the 3σ limits for the $\bar{X}$ and R charts. Assume that the process is in statistical control.

2 Control charts for $\bar{X}$ and R are maintained on the weight of packages of dry cake mix filled by an automatic filling machine. The sample size is 5. After

25 samples and the values of $\bar{X}$ and R are computed for each sample, $\Sigma\bar{X} = 355.0$ ounces and $\Sigma R = 15.0$ ounces. Compute the values of the 3-sigma control limits for the $\bar{X}$ and R charts. Assume that the process is in statistical control.

3 Using the Monte Carlo procedure with the cumulative distribution of package weights in Table 9.1 and a table of random numbers, draw 20 samples of size $n = 6$. Compute the values of $\bar{X}$ and R for each sample, and the central line and values of the 3-sigma control limits for $\bar{X}$ and R control charts. Prepare the charts and plot the values of the 20 sample on them.

4 a. Using the data and $\bar{X}$ and R charts prepared in problem 3, draw an additional 10 samples of size 6. However, before computing the values of $\bar{X}$ and R for each sample, add 0.2 ounces to the value of each package weight. This will simulate a shift in process mean of $+0.2$ ounces. Plot the result on the charts. Did the charts signal the shift in process mean?

b. Repeat the procedure in problem 4(a). Draw an additional 10 samples of size 6, but this time add 0.4 ounces to the value of each package weight. Compare the results with those of problem 4(a).

c. Repeat the procedure in problem 4(a). Draw an additional 10 samples of size 6, but this time add 0.8 ounces to the value of each package weight. Compare the results with your previous results.

d. Discuss the implications of the results of this simulation with respect to sample size and degree of shift in process mean.

5 Daily output of an item is 300 units. Each day's output is given 100 per cent inspection. For the first 25 days' output a total of 165 units were defective. Determine the 3-sigma trial control limits for a p chart showing fraction defective. Estimate the process average fraction defective, assuming that all the points fall within the control limits.

6 The manager of the Thompson Company is interested in the possibility of applying statistical control charts, variance controls, to company clerical operations. The operation selected for study was the preparation of invoices. It was decided to investigate application of control charts for fraction defective, p charts.

An invoice is classified as good if it contains no errors, and defective if it contains one or more errors. A daily random sample of 50 invoices was checked for accuracy for 30 days, with the results shown in the table below. On the basis of this sample information, the manager planned to establish a trial control chart and evaluate its value as a management control tool.

Compute the 3-sigma control limits for a p chart for fraction defective based upon the data in the table. Set up a p chart with these limits and plot the 30 observations.

Does the process appear to be in control? How might these charts be used for management control purposes?

Day	Number of Invoices Inspected n	Number of Defectives np	Fraction Defective p
1	50	6	.12
2	50	4	.08
3	50	2	.04
4	50	5	.10
5	50	3	.06
6	50	6	.12
7	50	5	.10
8	50	5	.10
9	50	4	.08
10	50	9	.18
11	50	6	.12
12	50	6	.12
13	50	2	.04
14	50	6	.12
15	50	6	.12
16	50	5	.10
17	50	4	.08
18	50	8	.16
19	50	6	.12
20	50	3	.09
21	50	4	.08
22	50	3	.09
23	50	6	.12
24	50	6	.12
25	50	7	.14
26	50	1	.02
27	50	5	.10
28	50	5	.10
29	50	5	.10
30	50	7	.14
Totals:	1500	150	

7 A control chart for per cent defective (100 p) is maintained for an item subject to 100 per cent inspection. At the end of the first month the average fraction defective was computed and a standard value of fraction defective established to apply to the coming month. For the month of October the standard fraction defective was established at 0.043. Compute individual 3σ control limits based upon the standard fraction defective for the first four days in October from the following data. Plot the results on a per cent defective chart and indicate whether the per cent defective fell within the control limits for each day.

Day	Number Inspected	Number of Defectives
1	225	7
2	81	5
3	324	29
4	169	7

8 Administrators of the State Highway Patrol are interested in the possibility of applying statistical control charts to monitor highway accidents. It was suggested that the charts might be useful in determining when and where to assign extra patrol cars as accident patterns varied. The administrators decided to set up a trial c chart for defects for a particular section of heavily travelled freeway, and to record the number of accidents per week. An accident occurrence is classified as a defect. The following table gives the results for the previous 6 months.

Week	Number of Accidents	Week	Number of Accidents	Week	Number of Accidents
1	2	10	2	19	3
2	5	11	7	20	1
3	3	12	6	21	15
4	10	13	5	22	7
5	2	14	9	23	2
6	6	15	8	24	8
7	5	16	13	25	4
8	8	17	2	26	6
9	8	18	1		
				Total	148

Determine $\bar{c}$ and trial control limits, and plot a control chart for defects. Does the system appear to be in control? Recompute $\bar{c}$ and the control limits after eliminating any out-of-control points. How might these charts be used in this situation?

9 A single sampling plan uses a sample size of 120 and an acceptance number of 2. The lot size is large. Use the table of summation terms for the Poisson distribution in Appendix Table F to determine the approximate probabilities of acceptance for lots 0.5 per cent, 1 per cent, 2 per cent, 3 per cent and 5 per cent defective.

10 You are a dealer in a product. Recently the quality of the product furnished by your supplier has been rather poor, and your customers have been returning defective items with increasing frequency. Although you would like to inspect each item to insure that they are all of good quality, you feel this task is too large and tedious to be a good solution. Your friend, who is studying operations management, suggests that you take a sample of 10 from each lot of 1,000 and reject any lots which have 3 or more defectives in the sample. If 30 per cent of the items you receive are defective, how much would this sampling plan improve the quality of items you are selling (what would be the average outgoing quality)?

11 A single sampling plan uses a sample size of 50 and an acceptance number of 1. The lot size is large. Use the table of summation terms for the Poisson distribution in Appendix Table F to compute and draw the operating characteristics curve and average outgoing quality curve for this plan. Identify the producers' and consumers' risk on the *OC* curve.

12 The following is suggested as a class demonstration. Mark 500 chips as follows:

Mark	Frequency	Mark	Frequency	Mark	Frequency
3	1	22	14	40	12
4	1	23	16	41	11
5	1	24	17	42	10
6	1	25	18	43	9
7	1	26	18	44	7
8	2	27	19	45	6
9	2	28	20	46	6
10	3	29	20	47	5
11	3	30	20	48	4
12	4	31	20	49	3
13	5	32	20	50	3
14	6	33	19	51	2
15	6	34	18	52	2
16	7	35	18	53	1
17	9	36	17	54	1
18	10	37	14	55	1
19	11	38	14	56	1
20	12	39	13	57	1
21	13				

a. Place the chips in a container and mix thoroughly. Draw 4 chips, record the numbers, and compute $\bar{X}$ and R for the sample. Replace the chips and mix thoroughly. Draw another sample of 4 chips. Repeat the process until 20 samples have been drawn. Compute control limits for $\bar{X}$ and R charts and plot the results from the 20 samples on the charts.

b. Use the charts prepared in part (a). Draw an additional 20 samples of 4 chips. However, before computing the values of $\bar{X}$ and R for each sample, add 10 to the value on each chip. Compute the values of $\bar{X}$ and R for each sample and plot on the charts. Did the charts signal the shift in process mean?

c. Repeat the procedure in part (b). Draw an additional 20 samples of 4 chips, but this time add 20 to the value on each chip. Plot on the $\bar{X}$ and R charts. Compare the results with your previous results.

Chapter 10
Inventory
Systems

Organizations provide goods or services for other organizations or individuals. Those which provide services lack the flexibility in the temporal and spatial dimensions possessed by the organizations which produce goods. A group of medical doctors cannot treat disease and injury until a patient brings the unique input of himself to the organization for treatment. The doctors must be located and keep hours convenient to some segment of the population in order to receive this unique input. The organizations which produce the medications and equipment used in treating the patient can, however, produce them at any convenient time and location. The use of inventories creates this flexibility.

Inventories are located at a variety of points in the operating system. All goods are produced from materials which originally existed in their natural state as animal, vegetable, and mineral matter. Some organizations convert the natural matter into raw materials such as lumber, iron and steel, hides, and so forth. Other organizations begin the conversion of raw materials into industrial and consumer goods. In producing complex products, such as computers or jet airplanes, hundreds of different organizations may be involved in converting and assembling the product and some individual components may pass through several organizational entities. After the physical transformation is completed, other organizations transport and transfer ownership of the products, often through several stages, until the product reaches the hands of the ultimate consumer.

Inventories provide the basic function of "decoupling" the operations involved in converting inputs into outputs. They allow both time and spatial separation between production and consumption of products and between the many nodes or operations within the operating system. We would find it difficult even to imagine human existence without inventories. Indeed, the most primitive societies find it necessary to accumulate stocks of food to supply part of their needs through winter seasons and dry spells.

Economic development provides increased output and efficiency through specialization. In the caveman's society, each man produced all of his own goods—food, clothing, and a few simple utensils. In modern industrialized societies, each individual produces only a minute fraction of the goods he consumes. Such a society cannot operate without large stocks of inventories. The high degree of specialization necessitates geographic and temporal separations. Inventories provide the buffer which allows these separations to exist. The tremendous advance in the standard of living during the last century in the advanced economies is due as much to changes in production methods, such as specialization and division of labor, as it is to technological invention. The time span required for producing an object such as an automobile from the conversion of raw material to final delivery would undoubtedly run into years. Yet, a person can purchase a new automobile in a matter of minutes because of the existence of inventories. Inventories also provide separations which allow economical levels of operations. Instead of requiring production of a single unit each time one is consumed, products can be produced in batches, thus achieving economies in handling and transporting the goods and setting up production processes.

Since inventories tie up assets, firms must keep them at a reasonable level. Additional direct charges accumulate because of storage space requirements, insurance and taxes, and so on. Firms, therefore, cannot afford to keep unrestricted inventories at every point in the production process despite the benefits they bring. Even with closely controlled inventories, manufacturing firms often find that as much as 25 to 50 per cent of their total assets are invested in inventories. Moreover, wholesalers and retailers occasionally find as much as 75 to 80 per cent of their assets in inventories.

All types of business and other organizations maintain some inventories. Manufacturing firms, whose primary task is the physical conversion of goods, maintain large stocks of raw materials, semi-finished and finished goods. Marketing firms, such as wholesalers and retailers, accumulate finished goods, maintain them at locations, and provide them at times convenient to their customers. Financial institutions, transportation firms, governmental organizations and other institutions that deal primarily in providing services rather than products still require stocks of office and operating supplies, cash, and so forth.

The institutions providing service cannot, unfortunately, accumulate inventories of the services that they provide. Their inability to accumulate inventories prevents the service industries from making the rapid strides in increasing efficiency and output that have occurred in the production of physical products. Banks must maintain sufficient facilities and people to handle peak hour loads even if they remain idle the remainder of the day. The railroads and the airlines must move their trains and planes on schedule even if only one-fourth of the seats are occupied. Contrast this to the factory in which lawn mowers can be produced all year long, although almost all of them are sold in a period of four or five months each year. The service industries continue to require a larger and larger portion of the total work force partially because they cannot automate operations and accumulate inventories of services.

Inventory Costs

The benefits obtained from the proper use of inventories are not obtained without penalty. There is a rather substantial cost of carrying inventories. A firm should consider the cost of capital which could be earning a return if invested elsewhere. In making this estimate, a firm takes into account the liquidity and risk involved. Money tied up in inventory is quite liquid—it may be converted into cash in a fairly short time, if the need arises. The cost of borrowing new capital is apt to be misleading for estimating the cost of capital invested in inventory unless the firm is actually willing and able to change its borrowing in response to changes in the inventory level. Most firms have more investment opportunities, which will earn returns in excess of the borrowing interest rate, than they can obtain funds to finance. Hence, a firm should charge inventories with an opportunity cost equivalent to the expected return on other investments with comparable risk and liquidity; a rate usually in excess of the borrowing rate.

Inventory is also subject to spoilage, obsolescence, and deterioration. Many firms carry fire insurance on inventories. Even when none is carried, the inventory carrying cost rate should reflect the existing risk of fire loss. Warehouses and storage areas must be built and maintained for the inventories. Space charges may include depreciation of racks, fixtures, and other handling and storing devices. Generally, these costs are apportioned uniformly among the various stored products on the basis of some percentage of the product's dollar value. Although a more accurate allocation of these costs may be on the basis of storage space required, such information is usually not readily available within the firm's normal data processing system. Generally, a cost-based allocation is sufficiently accurate for inventory decision-making purposes since some degree of correlation often exists between size and value within a firm.

When all the elements of cost are added together, the total annual carrying cost is often within the range of 20 to 25 per cent of the inventory's value. The inventory carrying cost curve is normally treated as a linear cost function. Thus, a firm with a 25 per cent carrying cost maintaining an average inventory of $1,000,000 would have an annual inventory cost of $250,000.

The benefits obtained from carrying inventory accrue at a decreasing rate. That is, a firm obtains large economies from adding the first units of inventory, but as the firm adds more inventory the cost reductions become smaller. Although a firm may obtain $500,000 in annual benefits per year from the first $1,000,000 of inventory held, the second $1,000,000 may produce only $100,000 worth of savings in other areas. Thus, relatively small inventories produce a large rate of return with the return becoming smaller as the size of the inventory is increased. The main decision problem in inventory control is to determine at what point the cost of carrying inventory outweighs the benefits which the inventory produces.

Determining Inventory Levels for Individual Products

Most products and materials are sold or consumed individually or a few units at a time. However, in order to decrease the amount of ordering, shipping, and handling, the products are purchased or produced in larger quantities. Determination of the optimal quantity to produce or purchase often is accomplished through the use of the economic production (or order) quantity formula.

The Economic Production Quantity

The economic production quantity (EPQ) formula applies to situations described by a number of restrictive, and sometimes unrealistic assumptions. The formula will be derived first and then examined in terms of its implicit restrictions. We will solve a specific problem as we derive the general formula. We have a product which starts at an inventory level of zero at time t_0, as shown in Figure 10.1. The product is produced for a length of time, $t_1 - t_0$, during which inventory builds to its maximum level at t_1. After production stops, inventory is sold until it is depleted at t_2 when another production run begins.

We define the following terms:

d = annual rate of demand for the product = 6400
p = annual rate of production = 9600
S = cost of setting up or preparing for a production run = \$100
C = cost per unit of producing the product = \$40
i = cost of carrying inventory per year = 20 per cent
Q_p = production quantity
$Q_p{}^*$ = economic production quantity
TC = total cost of policy
TC^* = minimum total cost policy when $Q_p = Q_p{}^*$

We have two opposing sets of costs: carrying cost which increases linearly as Q_p increases, and the set up cost which is inversely proportional to Q_p.

Annual set up cost = $\dfrac{d}{Q_p} S$, where d/Q_p is the number of set ups per year and S is the cost per set up.

Figure 10.1   Inventory Level for an Internally Produced Product

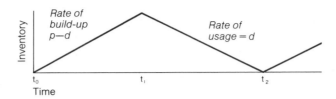

For our particular problem, annual set up cost is equal to $6400(100)/Q_p$ which gives us the curve in Figure 10.2. In determining the carrying cost, note that a triangular pattern exists with inventory going from zero to a maximum and back to zero. Thus, from geometry we know that the average inventory is equal to maximum inventory divided by 2. Since production is

Figure 10.2   Costs Associated with Inventory for a Single Product

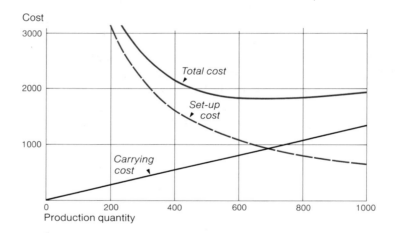

at the rate p and sales is at the rate of d, inventory increases at the rate of $(p - d)$ during production and is depleted at the rate d during nonproduction times. Thus the maximum inventory is $(p - d)(t_1 - t_0)$. Note that $Q_p = (t_1 - t_0)p$, or the quantity produced, is equal to the length of the production run times the production rate. Substituting, we find that:

$$\text{Maximum Inventory} = (p - d)\frac{Q_p}{p} = (1 - d/p)Q_p$$

$$\text{Average Inventory} = (1 - d/p)\frac{Q_p}{2}$$

$$\text{Annual Carrying Cost} = (1 - d/p)\frac{Q_p}{2}iC.$$

For our example, annual carrying cost is equal to $(1 - 6400/9600)$ $(Q_p/2)(.2)40 = (4/3)Q_p$.

The total annual cost is

$$TC = \frac{dS}{Q_p} + \frac{iCQ_p(1 - d/p)}{2}. \tag{10.1}$$

We find the minimum point on the total cost curve by taking the first derivative of the total cost formula with respect to Q_p and setting it equal to zero. This indicates the bottom of the cost curve, or the point at which a line tangent to the curve has a slope equal to zero.

$$\frac{d(TC)}{dQ_p} = \frac{dS}{Q_p{}^2} + \frac{iC(1 - d/p)}{2} = 0 \tag{10.2}$$

Solving, we get

$$Q_p{}^* = \sqrt{\frac{2dS}{(1 - d/p)iC}}. \tag{10.3}$$

Substituting $Q_p{}^*$ into equation 10.1,

$$TC^* = \sqrt{2dS(1 - d/p)iC}. \tag{10.4}$$

For our problem

$$Q_p{}^* = \sqrt{\frac{2(6400)100}{(1 - 6400/9600)(.20)(40)}} = 693 \text{ units}$$

$$TC^* = \sqrt{2(6400)100(1 - 6400/9600)(.20)(40)} = \$1848.$$

The number of production runs per year is:

$$N = \frac{d}{Q_p{}^*} = \frac{6400}{693} = 9.24.$$

The length of each run is:

$$t_1 - t_0 = \frac{Q_p{}^*}{p} = \frac{693}{9600} = .072 \text{ year.}$$

The maximum inventory level is:

$$(1 - d/p)Q_p{}^* = \left(1 - \frac{6400}{9600}\right)693 = 231 \text{ units.}$$

Economic Order Quantity

A more widely used formula is the economic order quantity (*EOQ*) for products which are ordered from an external supplier and for which a cost of placing an order, rather than a set-up cost, exists. The *EOQ* formula is a special case of the *EPQ* formula. When the product is ordered, all Q units are received at the same time. Thus "production" is instantaneous and the term $(1 - d/p)$ approaches 1 giving:

$$TC = \frac{dS}{Q} + \frac{Q}{2}iC \tag{10.5}$$

$$Q^* = \sqrt{\frac{2dS}{iC}} \tag{10.6}$$

and

$$TC^* = \sqrt{2dSiC} \tag{10.7}$$

If a product similar to the one in our previous example was purchased from a supplier at a cost of \$40/unit, and with S now being the fixed cost of preparing the order, receiving the goods, paying the bill, and so forth, the optimal order quantity would be:

$$Q^* = \sqrt{\frac{2(6400)100}{(.20)(40)}} = 400 \text{ units,}$$

and

$$TC^* = \sqrt{2(6400)(100)(.20)(40)} = \$3,200.$$

Sensitivity Analysis

One of the difficulties in applying mathematical models in decision making is to make accurate estimates of the costs used in the models. Extreme precision often is impossible to obtain because of measurement problems and the necessity to assign values to intangible items such as investment opportunities, lost sales, goodwill, and so on. We will examine the effect of errors in the estimation of parameters in the application of the EOQ formula.

Assume that we have errors in our estimates of d, S, i, and C. Let the estimates be K_1d, K_2S, K_3i, and K_4c. Now the apparent economic order quantity is:

$$Q = \sqrt{\frac{2K_1dK_2S}{K_3iK_4C}} \tag{10.8}$$

which yields a total cost of

$$TC = \frac{dS}{\sqrt{\dfrac{2K_1dK_2S}{K_3iK_4C}}} + \frac{iC}{2}\sqrt{\frac{2K_1dK_2S}{K_3iK_4C}}$$

Note that the true values remain d, S, i, and C. Though we presumably do not know what these values are, we must use the true values in order to determine the effect of the estimation errors. Simplifying,

$$TC = \sqrt{\frac{dSiC}{2}\left(\frac{K_3K_4}{K_1K_2}\right)} + \sqrt{\frac{dSiC}{2}\left(\frac{K_1K_2}{K_3K_4}\right)}$$

$$= \frac{1}{2}TC^*\left[\frac{(K_3K_4)^{1/2}}{(K_1K_2)^{1/2}} + \frac{(K_1K_2)^{1/2}}{(K_3K_4)^{1/2}}\right]$$

$$= \frac{1}{2}TC^*\left[\frac{K_1K_2 + K_3K_4}{(K_1K_2K_3K_4)^{1/2}}\right] \tag{10.9}$$

which reduces to TC^* if all K's equal one.

The percentage of extra inventory cost resulting from errors in parameter estimation is:

$$\frac{TC - TC^*}{TC^*}(100) = \left[\frac{K_1K_2 + K_3K_4}{2(K_1K_2K_3K_4)^{1/2}} - 1\right]100 \qquad (10.10)$$

To examine the effect of errors of estimation, we set all K's $= 2$, which means that all estimates were 100 per cent in excess of actual values.

$$\frac{TC - TC^*}{TC^*}(100) = \left[\frac{2\cdot 2 + 2\cdot 2}{2(2\cdot 2\cdot 2\cdot 2)^{1/2}} - 1\right]100 = 0$$

Despite the large estimation errors, $TC = TC^*$. Upon reflection, this is obviously correct since the errors will cancel out and the correct EOQ will be used.

To investigate the effect of errors in estimating just one parameter, set $3\ K$'s $= 1$. The formula reduces to:

$$\frac{TC - TC^*}{TC^*}(100) = \left[\frac{K_i + 1}{2\sqrt{K_i}} - 1\right]100$$

for the remaining K. Figure 10.3 shows the extra cost resulting from different values of K.

Figure 10.3 Effect of an Error in Estimating One Parameter in the EOQ Formula (Per Cent of Extra Cost)

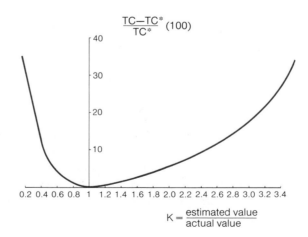

Total cost is more sensitive to underestimation of parameter values than to overestimation, but within a rather large range the total cost is relatively insensitive to errors in either direction. Although some combinations of errors, such as overestimating S and underestimating i, combine to accentuate each other, still other combinations will cancel out each other. Normally, it would therefore be a mistake to undertake an elaborate and expensive cost study if reasonably accurate estimations can be made by simpler and less expensive means.

Validity of EOQ Model

The *EOQ* model assumes that:

1. p is known and constant;
2. d is known and constant;
3. lead time, the interval between the time the order is placed and the time it is received, is known and constant;
4. carrying cost is linear throughout the entire inventory range and varies with average inventory;
5. price of the product does not depend on the quantity purchased; and
6. ordering of the product is independent of ordering other products.

Many of the above requirements are violated in most real-life situations. This does not mean that the *EOQ* approach lacks usefulness. Rather, the *EOQ* approach represents the first step in solving the inventory problem and it can be expanded to accommodate violations of the above assumptions which occur in practice. For example, p, the production rate, is subject to variation due to breakdowns and other events, d, the demand rate, is rarely known with certainty and is often subject to extreme fluctuations, and the lead time may also vary widely. Still, the *EOQ* may be used along with a buffer of safety stock which protects against the above uncertainties. If the firm has a limited amount of capital the carrying cost may not be linear, but it may increase as the level of inventory increases. In such a case, the *EOQ* formula may be slightly modified with the appropriate mathematical manipulations made to take into account the proper shape of the carrying cost curve. Similarly, a revised *EOQ* approach may be used when the price of the product varies with the quantity ordered.

When assumption six is violated, however, it is often desirable to abandon the *EOQ* approach and use a different type of inventory system. For example, when several products are ordered from the same supplier, substantial economies may result from combining orders for the several products which indicates an inventory system different from the *EOQ* system. Also, when more than one product is produced with the same set of facilities, conflicts may occur when more than one product requires the use of the equipment at a given time. Thus, a schedule must be developed which takes into account the available facility time as an additional variable. First, we will examine how the *EOQ* approach can be made more comprehensive and then we will consider methods of managing inventories for multiple-product systems.

Quantity
Discounts

The unit price paid for a product often decreases as the quantity purchased increases. If the cost of the product had been included in the previous analysis, the total cost equation for an ordered product would have been

$$TC = \frac{dS}{Q} + \frac{iCQ}{2} + dC$$

where C is the cost per unit, and dC is the annual cost of the product. Taking the first derivative of TC with respect to Q, the term dC would drop out of the resulting expression since we assumed that the price was independent of the order quantity.

Quantity discounts are given for a variety of reasons. There is a strong economic justification for them. The supplying firm can spread its fixed costs of handling each order among more units. In some cases, these fixed costs may be quite large. If the order is for a product which requires a special production run, then fixed costs may reach hundreds or thousands of dollars. Thus, an economically logical pricing policy which is used by some firms is that the cost of an order is $F + VQ$ where

F = supplier's fixed cost including normal markup for overhead and profit
V = variable cost of producing each unit including normal markup
Q = quantity ordered

The cost per unit is therefore, $(F + VG)/Q$. With such a pricing policy, the total cost is

$$TC = \frac{dS}{Q} + i\left(\frac{F + VQ}{Q}\right)\frac{Q}{2} + \frac{d}{Q}(F + VQ) \qquad (10.11)$$

where the last term is the annual cost of the product itself. Then,

$$TC = \frac{iF}{2} + iV\frac{Q}{2} + \frac{dS}{Q} + \frac{dF}{Q} + dV$$

$$= \frac{iF}{2} + iV\frac{Q}{2} + \frac{d}{Q}(S + F) + dV$$

$$\frac{d(TC)}{dQ} = \frac{iV}{2} - \frac{d}{Q^2}(S + F).$$

When

$$\frac{iV}{2} - \frac{d}{Q^2}(S + F) = 0,$$

$$Q^* = \sqrt{\frac{2d(S + F)}{iV}}. \qquad (10.12)$$

Consider our earlier example with $d = 6400$ per year, $i = 20$ per cent per year, $S = \$100$ per order. Let $F = \$300$ and $V = \$40$. Then

$$Q^* = \sqrt{\frac{2(6400)(100 + 300)}{.20(40)}} = 800.$$

This gives an *EOQ* twice as large as in the previous case.

The fixed cost of the supplier which is passed on to the purchaser has the same effect as the purchaser's own fixed costs. For purposes of determining the *EOQ*, they should both be lumped together.

Unfortunately from a decision making standpoint, most firms employ a pricing policy which is much more difficult to handle mathematically. The more common policy is to use a series of discrete points at which price is lowered. Such a pricing policy for a product with the same demand and costs that we used earlier might be: $40 per unit in lots of less than 500 units; $39.90 per unit in lots of 500 to 999; and $39.80 per unit in lots of 1,000 or more. Because of the discontinuities in this product cost expression, the problem cannot be solved by differential calculus. The total cost expression can, however, easily be evaluated for any particular value of Q. If we can determine which values of Q are good candidates for the minimum TC, we can evaluate those Q's and pick the one with the lowest TC. Fortunately, Q has only a few values which need examining. Recall that in our example the value which minimized the sum of the ordering cost and the carrying cost, but not the cost of the product, was $Q = 400$. The further we move from the point $Q = 400$, the greater will be the sum of the ordering and carrying costs. Thus, $Q = 400$ is obviously the only candidate for the minimum total cost value within the range of $O < Q < 500$ for which $C = \$40$ per unit; $Q = 500$ is the only candidate within the $39.90 price range of $500 \leq Q < 1000$; and $Q = 1000$ is the only candidate within the $39.80 price range of $Q \geq 1000$. These three points are evaluated in Table 10.1 and illustrated in Figure 10.4.

We find that $Q^* = 500$. The firm is justified in going to the first price

Figure 10.4 Costs for Quantity Discount Problem

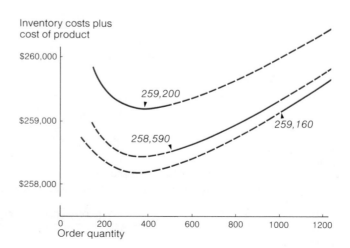

break, but the extra carrying cost of going to the second price break more than outweighs the savings in ordering and in the cost of the product itself.

Table 10.1   Total Inventory Associated Costs with Varying Lot Sizes

		Lot Size	
	400	500	1000
Product Cost (dC)	256,000	255,360	254,720
Ordering Cost $\left(\dfrac{dS}{Q}\right)$	1,600	1,280	640
Carrying Cost (QiC/2)	1,600	1,950	3,800
Total Cost	259,200	258,590	259,160

Determining Reorder Points

Organizations stock goods and materials in the expectation that they will be either used within the organization or sold. The amounts stocked and the times at which the goods and materials are ordered depend on forecasts of usage. In many cases the forecasts are quite informal, being nothing more than an intuitive extrapolation of past demand into the future. In other cases, very elaborate models, combining sophisticated statistical techniques with economic analyses of the conditions affecting usage, are employed. But, no matter what method is used, all forecasts have one thing in common —they are invariably inaccurate.

No matter how precisely measurements are taken or how many significant digits are carried in computations, numerous factors affecting usage remain that simply are unpredictable. Formal forecasting techniques typically separate complicated demand patterns into a series of components such as long term trends, seasonal patterns, and so forth. Some amount of unexplained variation, commonly known as random deviations, or noise, always remains after these efforts.

Because of the existence of random deviations in demand patterns, we cannot expect a smooth withdrawal of units from inventory which results in an arrival at the zero inventory position at precisely the time that the next order arrives. Instead, the inventory withdrawals may look more like the graph shown in Figure 10.5.

In addition to the uncertainty in the usage pattern, variation also exists in the lead time, the difference between the time an order is placed and the time it is received from the supplier. In order to allow for these uncertainties, a buffer layer of safety stock is added to the inventory picture.

The decision about how much safety stock to use and when to place an order depends on the expected pattern of demand during the lead time. The decision must take into account both the variation in demand per day and the variation in days per lead time, and the relative costs of carrying

Figure 10.5 Inventory Withdrawal Pattern

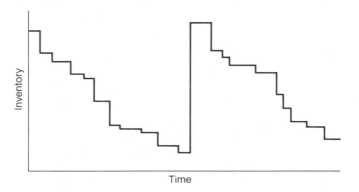

extra inventory versus the cost of running out of stock. Safety stock will be carried as long as the value of protection against stockouts, which the safety stock provides, is greater than the cost of carrying it in inventory. There are, however, diminishing returns to the investment in safety stock so that in most cases occasional stockouts should be allowed, as shown in Figure 10.6.

Figure 10.6 Cost of Stockouts and Carrying Safety Stock

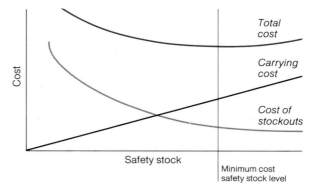

The cost of a stockout often is difficult to estimate with a high degree of accuracy. If a firm is out of material that it requires for producing a product, sometimes a reasonably accurate estimate can be made of the cost of obtaining the material on a rush basis and the cost of downtime (time when production is shut-down) of the production process which results from the stockout. When a stockout occurs for a product which is sold to a customer, however, the measurement problem is more difficult. In some instances the customer may simply return at a later time to purchase the product in which case the cost is zero. In other instances, he may purchase the product elsewhere, thus depriving the firm of the marginal profit which would have been earned on the sale. In more extreme cases, the customer may take all of his future business to another supplier because of the stockout.

As a result of the cost estimation difficulties, many firms attempt to avoid the problem of estimating the stockout cost by arbitrarily establishing some limit on stockouts, such as allowing stockouts to occur in 10 per cent of the lead times. Although such a policy can be instituted without making an explicit estimate of stockout cost, any policy implies something about the value of the stockout cost. Therefore, although management may not be aware of it, the establishment of such an arbitrary stockout policy imputes a precise value to the cost of a stockout. We will illustrate this imputed cost later in this section.

An alternative approach to determining the amount of safety stock and the reorder point is to estimate the stockout cost and then determine the reorder point which minimizes the sum of the stockout and carrying cost.

We define:

K = cost of stocking out of one unit

iC = cost of carrying one unit in inventory for one year

N = number of orders placed per year = d/Q
  where d = demand per year, Q = order quantity

P_j = probability that demand is equal to or greater than j
  units during the leadtime

R = reorder point, unknown

We will use a marginal cost approach to determine the reorder point inventory level. If we have a very low reorder point quantity l such that $P_l = 1.0$, we will always sell all of the goods before the next order arrives, and we will usually stockout since P_{l+1} will be large. We should therefore use a larger reorder point because the extra units would usually be sold during the lead-time and therefore would not accumulate carrying cost, but would prevent stockouts. Suppose, at the other extreme, we used a high reorder point m such that $P_m = O$, then we will never sell all the units during the lead time. Obviously, such a reorder point is too high since the last unit of inventory never prevents a stockout, but continually accumulates storage charges. At some point between l and m the expected value of the stockouts prevented by a single unit, the jth unit, is equal to the expected carrying cost of that j^{th} unit. This defines the optimal reorder point. Reorder points below j allow too many stockouts; reorder points above j have excess carrying costs.

We are looking for the jth unit at which we just break even on carrying that unit within our reorder point quantity, or the unit for which

Expected Cost of Stocking = Expected Cost of Not Stocking   (10.13)

If we stock the jth unit, the chance of selling it is P_j. If we sell it, there is no carrying cost. In the $(1 - P_j)$ proportion of the times in which we do not sell the jth unit, we must carry it in stock for one more inventory cycle or $1/N$ years. We will not have to hold the unit in stock for the entire year. For each ordering interval, it provides protection against a stockout and the appropriate carrying cost time period is $1/N$ year. Thus, the expected cost of stocking is $(1 - P_j)iC/N$. If the jth unit is not stocked (if our reorder point is $j - 1$), there will a penalty cost of K when the unit is demanded, but not on hand, or P_j of the time. There will be no cost if the unit is not demanded. Thus equation 10.13 becomes:

$$(1 - P_j)iC/N = P_jK. \tag{10.14}$$

Solving for P_j^*, the minimum cost value for P_j, gives

$$P_j^* = \frac{iC/N}{K + iC/N}. \tag{10.15}$$

Referring to the probability distribution of demand per lead time, we can determine the optimal reorder point, R^*, which corresponds to P_j^*.

The safety stock is the amount by which the reorder point exceeds the average sales during the lead time.

Consider the following example:

$$N = 3 \text{ orders per year}$$
$$iC = \$4 \text{ per unit per year}$$
$$K = \$3 \text{ per unit}$$

Demand per Lead Time

Units Demanded	Relative Frequency
10	.05
11	.10
12	.10
13	.15
14	.20
15	.15
16	.10
17	.10
18	.05
	1.00

Converting the relative frequency figures to a cumulative probability distribution, we obtain the graph in Figure 10.7 by adding together the relative frequencies of $j, j + 1, j + 2, \ldots$ for each j to obtain P_j. From equation 10.15, we find

$$P_j^* = \frac{4/3}{3 + 4/3} = .30.$$

Figure 10.7   Distribution of Lead Time Demand

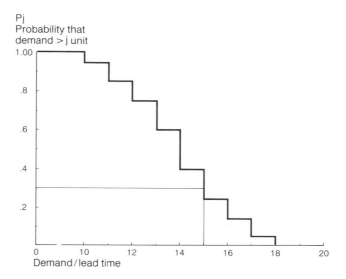

From Figure 10.7 we see that $R^* = 15$. Note that $P_{15} = .40$ and $P_{16} = .25$. Although $P_j^* = .30$ is closer to P_{16} than P_{15}, the optimal reorder point is 15 since there must be at least .30 chance of selling the unit to justify its inclusion within the reorder point quantity. The results can be checked by plugging the appropriate figures back into equation 10.13 and 10.14,

$$\text{Expected Cost of Stocking} = \text{Expected Cost of Not Stocking}$$

$$(1 - P_j)iC/N = P_jK.$$

For unit 15:

$$(1 - .40)4/3 < .40(3)$$
$$.80 < 1.20$$

Therefore, 15 units should be stocked.
For unit 16:

$$(1 - .25)4/3 > .25(3)$$
$$1.00 > .75$$

Therefore, 16 units should not be stocked.

The optimal policy is one which allows stockouts to occur during 25 per cent of the lead times.

Suppose that the inventory control manager had arbitrarily established a policy to allow stockouts in 5 per cent of the lead times without ever estimating the stockout cost. From Figure 10.7, $R = 17$ since demand is greater than 17 in 5 per cent of the lead times. The 17th unit will be sold .15 of the time and carried over for another inventory cycle .85 of the time. The expected carrying cost for unit 17 is $(1 - P_{17})iC/N = ((.85)4/3) = \$1.13$. Since unit 17 will be sold .15 of the time, it prevents a stockout .15 of the time. At the optimal point, from Equation 10.14, $(1 - P_j)iC/N = P_jK$. At $R = 17$ we can solve equation 10.14 for K', where K' is the value of K which would satisfy equation 10.14 and make $R = 17$ the optimal reorder point.

Solving, we find

$$(1 - .15)4/3 = .15K'$$
$$K' = \$7.53.$$

In setting $R = 17$, the firm is acting as if the cost of a stockout is \$7.53. Although the decision maker may think he is avoiding the problem of estimating K, any action he takes imputes some value for K.

Relationship Between EOQ and Reorder Point

The procedure covered in the previous sections provides for calculating the economic order quantity and the reorder point independently. Actually, the two values are related. For example, as the value of the order quantity Q increases, the number of orders per year decreases. There are fewer opportunities for stockouts and a given expected number of stockouts per year can be obtained with a smaller safety stock.

The mathematical calculations for obtaining the order quantity and the reorder point simultaneously are somewhat involved. The cost reduction obtained from this more precise simultaneous computation is typically quite small and for most situations the interaction can be conveniently ignored.[1]

Inventory Control Systems

The system illustrated in the previous section of determining an economic order quantity and a reorder point is often called the fixed quantity inventory system, or the two-bin system. This system minimizes the direct inventory associated costs for individual independent products. When the cost of administering the system is also considered, other inventory systems, which yield higher direct inventory costs, sometimes produce lower overall costs.

In instances when the product can be physically segregated into two containers, the costs of administering the fixed quantity system are minimal. When an order is received, an amount equal to the reorder point quantity is placed in the second bin and all of the rest of the order is placed in the first bin. When the first bin is emptied, there is an automatic signal to place an order and the stock in the second bin is used during the lead time interval. In most cases, however, the goods cannot be conveniently separated into two bins and the fixed quantity system then has the major disadvantage of

[1] For an illustration of the computations required, see H. Bierman, C. Bonini, and W. Hausman, *Quantitative Analysis for Business Decisions*, 3rd ed. (Homewood, Ill.: Richard D. Irwin, Inc., 1969), pp. 175–177.

requiring perpetual auditing of the inventory on hand to assure that an order is placed when the reorder point level is reached. In some instances the cost of this record keeping may be more than the cost of ordering and carrying the goods; and for very low valued items, such as nuts and bolts, pencils, and so forth, it may be more than the cost of the product itself. Thus, other inventory systems which require only an occasional tallying of inventory may be less costly for some products.

Most organizations manage inventories of hundreds or thousands of different materials and products. It is often possible to achieve economies by combining orders for several products into a single order. If a firm purchases twenty different products from the same supplier, the cost of ordering all twenty at one time is only a small fraction of the cost of twenty separate orders. Thus, inventory systems which allow a combination of orders may be more efficient than the fixed quantity system in which each product reaches its reorder point independently of the others.

The most commonly used inventory system is the base stock, or the s,S inventory system which is shown in Figure 10.8. This system sets two inven-

Figure 10.8   s,S Inventory System

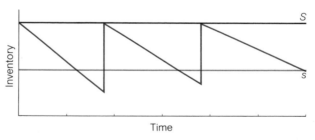

tory levels: S represents the maximum inventory amount which is reached when an order arrives; s represents the reorder inventory quantity. Inventory is reviewed periodically instead of perpetually. If the inventory is above the s level at review time, nothing is done; if it is below s, an order is placed. Reviewing all items at fixed periods of time allows a firm to combine orders, and thereby distributes the ordering cost among several products. The quantity ordered is an amount sufficient to bring inventory to the S level. The order quantity will vary by a small amount from order to order since the order is not placed as soon as s is reached, but at the first review period after that time. The amount ordered will be an economic shipping quantity. This amount will be much smaller than the economic order quantity of the fixed quantity system since the ordering cost per product ordered will be much smaller.

A disadvantage of the base stock system is that a somewhat larger safety stock is required. Under the fixed quantity system, safety stock provided protection against the random deviations in the demand pattern over the lead time interval. In the base stock system, the inventory position is evaluated only at the review time. Thus, if demand should suddenly spurt upward immediately after review, the increase would not be detected until the following review time. At that time, an order would be placed which would arrive a lead time later. Safety stock in the base stock system must provide protection against uncertainty over a review cycle plus a lead time. When the random deviations are independent of each other in time, demand per period follows the Poisson distribution and the standard deviation of forecast error is proportional to the square root of the length of the time span. Thus, if a safety stock of 10 units were used for a product with a one-week lead time under the fixed quantity system, the safety stock required to provide equal protection under a base stock system with a three week review time would be 10[Lead time + Review Cycle Time]$^{\frac{1}{2}}$ = 10[1 + 3]$^{\frac{1}{2}}$ = 20 units. In general, the safety stock for the base stock system would be larger than under the fixed cycle system by a factor of:

$$\frac{[RT + LT]^{1/2}}{LT^{1/2}} = \left[1 + \frac{RT}{LT}\right]^{1/2} \qquad (10.16)$$

where

$$RT = \text{review time}$$
$$LT = \text{lead time.}$$

ABC Inventory Value Classification

With thousands of items in inventory, it is often not possible or even desirable to exercise close control over all the items. One method frequently used to determine the degree of control desired is the A B C classification system.

In almost every organization, no matter what its function, a small number of items constitute a large proportion of the total investment in inventory, and a very large number of low valued items constitute only a small proportion of the total inventory value. Figure 10.9 shows a typical A B C classification. Although the precise figures may vary from firm to firm, it is not uncommon to find 10 per cent of the items accounting for as much as 75 per cent of the inventory value at the A end of the scale, and 75 per cent of the items falling in the C category, accounting for only 10 per cent of the inventory value. The remaining 15 per cent B items constitute 15 per cent of the dollar value of inventory in this example.

The A items deserve close controls. The inventory manager may want to study economic conditions in developing demand forecasts. Because each item represents a significant amount of money, the fixed quantity inventory system is often used, since it provides the closest control. The extra cost of individual orders may be more than offset by the lower safety stock requirements of the fixed quantity system. Demand forecasts for B items may be

Figure 10.9 A B C Inventory Classification System

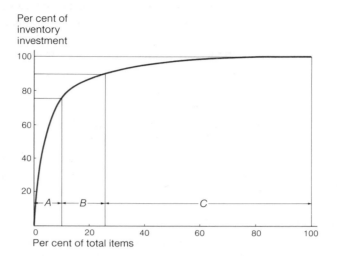

developed by statistically extrapolating past demand history, which would be less accurate, but also less expensive. Ordering may often be done under the base stock, or s,S inventory system. This allows the firm to combine orders for several items. Since the value of B items is less than of A items, it is rarely economical to treat each item independently.

A very loose policy may be applied to C items. In some cases the policy may be to review inventory levels quarterly and order a six months supply for all items with less than six months inventory on hand at the review time. In other firms, the policy may be to always take advantage of price breaks.

In a manufacturing firm, a relatively large safety stock of C items would be carried since the carrying cost is small, but the problem and cost of running out of nuts and bolts may be about as serious as the problem of running out of major components.

The absolute level of inventory investment, as well as the relative level, affects the amount of control given to inventories. Firms with small inventory investments may be justified in very informal (and non-mathematical) controls, while firms with millions of dollars of inventories may well want to develop elaborate forecasting models, to estimate accurately all inventory costs, and employ rather sophisticated mathematical inventory models.

Recently, many firms have computerized much of the inventory management function. Such systems automatically compute and periodically revise order quantities and review points, forecast demand, and keep summary data on demand patterns, stockouts, and so forth. Such information is useful not only in managing inventories, but also for scheduling production, evaluating the result of special sales promotions, determining sales trends, evaluating profitability of products, and so on. Most computer manufacturers supply inventory management programs as part of their software package. Usually, these ready-made programs can be used with only slight modifications to adapt them to an organization's particular operating conditions. The availability and low cost of such programs is making it profitable for even relatively small organizations to employ elaborate inventory management systems.

Computer programmed simulation models for inventory management are also available through computer manufacturers and other sources. These models allow testing of various forecasting methods and inventory decision rules. Simulation also provides a means of evaluating the effect of inventory management practices on other areas in the organization such as production scheduling.

The Single Period Inventory Problem

Some goods have such a high degree of obsolescence that if not sold within a short time period they will have no value, and in fact may incur expense in disposal. Newspapers and Christmas trees are common examples. Other products such as fashionable women's dresses have a rather short selling season and must be sold at a loss if they remain in inventory after the regular season. Organizations handling such goods have the problem of determining how many units to stock. If they stock fewer units than are demanded, they will lose a potential profit since there is insufficient time to replenish stocks. If they stock more units than are demanded, some must be disposed of at a loss.

Various service organizations face a similar problem. Airlines and hotels are faced with "no-shows" who make reservations but fail to keep them. Such organizations must decide how many extra reservations to accept. Too few will mean empty facilities while too many will require turning away customers with reservations. Either course has a penalty cost.

Manufacturing firms face similar problems in determining "reject allowances" when special products requiring special "set ups" of facilities are produced. If some of the completed goods will be rejected by subsequent inspections, some extra number should be produced, again with the obvious penalty costs for shortages and excesses.

The basic rule in all of the above problems is to add inventory as long as the expected reduction in penalty cost for a shortage is greater than the expected cost of stocking the unit.

We define

$$P = \text{probability of selling an additional unit}$$
$$MP = \text{marginal profit from selling a unit}$$
$$\text{(or from occupying a space)}$$

ML = marginal loss from disposing of unused unit
(or from turning away a customer with a reservation).

As we add an additional unit to our order quantity, the expected incremental profit is $P(MP)$. The probability of not selling it is $(1 - P)$ and the expected loss is $(1 - P)\ ML$. As long as the expected incremental profit is greater than the expected incremental loss we will add to the order quantity. Net profits will be maximized when

$$P\ (MP) = (1 - P)ML \tag{10.17}$$

for the last unit in the order.

Solving for P, we get

$$P = \frac{ML}{ML + MP}. \tag{10.18}$$

The probability of selling a unit must be at least $ML/(ML + MP)$ in order to justify the stocking of the unit.

Suppose that a merchant wishes to stock Christmas trees for sale during the holiday season. Assume that he knows the probability distribution of demand to be:

Demand	Probability of Demand Equal to the Given Number
6	.05
7	.15
8	.20
9	.40
10	.10
11	.10
	1.00

The merchant pays $2.00 for each tree and receives $6.00 for each tree sold. He must dispose of each tree not sold by December 25 at a cost of $.50 per tree. The ordering cost is fixed for all courses of action.

Solving:

$$MP = \$6.00 - \$2.00 = \$4.00$$
$$ML = \$2.00 + \$.50 = \$2.50$$
$$P = \frac{\$2.50}{\$2.50 + \$4.00} = .385.$$

From the demand distribution, P for unit $6 = 1.00$, since demand will always be at least 6 units, P for unit $7 = .95$, P for unit $8 = .80$, P for unit $9 = .60$, P for unit $10 = .20$. Thus, the best course of action is to order 9 trees.

Cost of Uncertainty

The analysis could be carried further to determine the cost of uncertainty in forecasting demand. If it were possible to predict demand precisely, how much could profit be increased?

First, we can determine expected profit under existing uncertainty. The policy is always to order 9 units. We will sell 6 units .05 of the time, earning $4.00 on each of the 6 units sold, but losing $2.50 on each of the extra 3. The expected profit would be $31.77, as shown below.

Profit Calculation

Sold	Probability	Profit	Probability × Profit
6	.05	$6(4) - 3(2.50) = 16.50$	.82
7	.15	$7(4) - 2(2.50) = 23.00$	3.45
8	.20	$8(4) - 1(2.50) = 29.50$	5.90
9	.60	$9(4) \qquad = 36.00$	21.60
			31.77

If perfect forecasts were possible, the merchant would order 6 units when demand was going to be 6, and so forth, so that the expected profit would be $34.60, as shown below. In this particular problem the gain from perfect forecasting would be a relatively small 8.9%, $[(34.60 - 31.77)/(31.77)] \times 100$.

Profit with Perfect Forecasts

Sold	Probability	Profit	Probability × Profit
6	.05	24	1.20
7	.15	28	4.20
8	.20	32	6.40
9	.40	36	14.40
10	.10	40	4.00
11	.10	44	4.40
			34.60

Managing Inventories

In managing inventories as well as in other endeavors, "a little learning can prove a dangerous thing." There have been numerous instances of managers arming themselves with economic order quantity formulas, but having little basic understanding of inventory management they create complete chaos out of systems which previously had been operating fairly smoothly. The experienced manager recognizes that he cannot take a few formulas out of context and expect that they will always fit smoothly into existing operations. Management of inventories requires a systems viewpoint, and should not be treated as a series of independent decisions on individual stock items.

The proper objective of the inventory system is to facilitate the overall operations of the organization. A series of decisions which appear optimal at a low organizational level (determining economic order quantities and reorder points for individual products) may be far from optimal when viewed in a broader context (that of the entire inventory system). But managers must consider events beyond the immediate realm of the inventory system in order to manage inventories efficiently and effectively. The inventory system is, after all, only a part of the overall operating system of the organization and it exists not for its own sake, but to facilitate the accomplishment of the goals of the organization. Thus, an inventory system in a manufacturing firm may minimize the direct inventory associated costs but result in production orders which would require large weekly changes in employment levels and excessive overtime and idle time of men and equipment. A more efficient inventory system may have somewhat higher direct inventory costs, but it may permit far less costly operations in the remainder of the organization. In Chapter 13, we will examine the relationship of the inventory system to the total operating system.

Does this mean that the discussion of inventories in this chapter, which was limited to the inventory system, is of no value when viewed in the broader framework of the entire organization? Certainly not. The design of the entire operating system is an extremely complicated task with no hard and fast rules to assure us of arriving at the best design. Indeed, the task is so complex that it is perhaps impossible for the human mind to properly conceptualize and analyze all of the nuances and interactions of the components of the organization. But, the rules developed when analyzing individual subsystems can be utilized to assist in designing the broader system. The effective administrater tempers and modifies the precise scientific methodology employed in the creation of mathematical models and decision systems and blends it with his own intuition and experience to arrive at an effective design.

Summary

Inventories decouple the operations involved in converting inputs into outputs. They allow separation in both the time and spatial dimensions between the many stages in the production process. This separation enables each stage in the production system to operate somewhat independently of the other stages and, therefore, at more economical levels than if the whole system were rigidly connected.

The law of diminishing returns applies to the use of inventories; that is, the first units of inventory added at each stage provide the greatest benefit with each successive unit providing successively smaller benefits. Since there are substantial costs for carrying inventories, it is essential that inventories are not maintained in excessive quantities. They should be used only to the extent that the benefits which they provide exceed the cost of carrying them.

Selected References

Brown, Robert G. *Statistical Forecasting for Inventory Control.* New York: McGraw-Hill Book Company, 1959.

Buchin, Joseph, and Koenigsberg, Ernest. *Scientific Inventory Management.* Englewood Cliffs, N.J.. Prentice-Hall, Inc., 1963.

Hadley, G. and Whitin, T. M. *Analysis of Inventory Systems.* Englewood Cliffs, N.J.: Prentice-Hall, Inc., 1963.

Hanssmann, Fred. *Operations Research in Production and Inventory Control.* New York: John Wiley & Sons, Inc., 1962.

Starr, Martin K., and Miller, David W. *Inventory Control: Theory and Practice.* Englewood Cliffs, N.J.: Prentice-Hall, Inc., 1962.

Wagner, Harvey M. *Statistical Management of Inventory Systems.* New York: John Wiley & Sons, Inc., 1962.

Questions

1   What is the decoupling function of inventories?

2   What are the components of inventory carrying cost?

3   How valid is the economic order quantity formula?

4   What is the relationship or interaction between the order quantity and the safety stock?

5   What is the cost of a stockout?

6   What are the advantages of the two-bin inventory system?

7   What is an s, S inventory policy?

8   How does the inventory ordering decision for products such as newspapers differ from ordering decisions for most products handled by a typical whole-saler or retailer?

9   How much accuracy in estimating cost parameters and forecasting demand is necessary in order to manage inventories effectively?

10   Why may the type of inventory control methods employed by a large firm vary considerably from the type employed by a small firm, even though the two firms are otherwise similar?

Problems

1   A firm purchases a component from an external supplier for use in its manufacturing process. A total of 10,000 units are used per year. It costs $10 in fixed charges for sending purchase orders, receiving goods, and paying bills, for each order. The firm uses a figure of 5 per cent of the cost of the goods as the annual charge for carrying inventory. The basic price for the component is $1/unit. If it is ordered in quantities of 125 or more, the unit price is reduced to $.95. The firm has been purchasing the goods in lots of 125 in order to take advantage of the price break. Determine the optimal lot

size. Compute also the extra cost per year of operating under the policy of ordering 125 as compared to the optimal policy.

2   For a purchased product,

$$d = 40,000$$
$$iC = \$.08$$
$$S = \$200.$$

What effect would an error of .02 (that is you estimate $iC = .10$ when it actually equals .08) have on yearly inventory costs?

3   Alpha Distributors purchases a product which it resells with the following demand distributions:

Demand/Week	Probability
12	.10
13	.15
14	.15
15	.20
16	.20
17	.10
18	.05
19	.05

The purchase price is $30/unit. The firm has an ordering cost of $20. In addition, it must pay a fixed cost of $500/order to reimburse the supplier, Beta Manufacturing, for its set-up costs for the production of the product for a total fixed cost of $520/order. The cost of carrying inventory is $3/unit/year. The cost of a stockout is $10/unit short. Order lead time is constant at one week. Calculate:

a. economic order quantity,
b. reorder point,
c. safety stock,
d. average stockout cost per year, and
e. the proportion of demand satisfied from inventory on hand throughout the year.

4   Beta Manufacturing, the supplier firm in the above problem, is considering the purchase of a new machine to produce the product. If Alpha Distributors will pay Beta the additional set-up cost for each order, it will sell Alpha the product for $29/unit. Because the new machine has more automatic feaures which require expensive adjustments, the set-up cost will be $2,060. Should Alpha take advantage of the offer? Calculate the costs to Alpha with both the old and the new machines.

5   A product with an annual usage rate of 10 per year has an economic order quantity of 5. The cost of carrying one unit of inventory for one year is $4.00, and each unit demanded when the firm is out of stock costs $3.00, since the customer takes his order elsewhere and the firm loses the potential profit on the sale. The distribution of demand during the lead time is as follows:

Units Demanded	Probability
1	.25
2	.50
3	.25

What is the optimal safety stock level? What is the reorder point?

6 You have a product which has average weekly sales of 600 units. By looking at past demand records, you find that the demand pattern has followed the distributions below:

Demand above	Per Cent of the time
400 units/week	100
450	90
500	79
550	64
600	50
650	22
700	8
750	3
800	0

There is a fixed cost for ordering of $72 for every order placed. Lead time is constant at one week. Inventory carrying charge is $1.80 per year. The stock-out policy has been set to allow 2 stockouts per year. Determine the order quantity and the safety stock which will minimize the variable costs.

7 A firm is operating a fixed quantity (Q) inventory system. One product has the following characteristics:

$$C = \$10$$
$$i = .20$$
$$S = \$12$$
$$d = 1200$$

Standard deviation of demand per week = 10 units
Demand per week is normally distributed.
Lead time is one week.

The firm has established a policy of allowing stockouts to occur in 5 per cent of the lead times.

a. Determine the safety stock required with this policy.
b. Determine the imputed stockout cost per unit (K) with this policy.
c. Estimate the percentage of orders handled from stock on hand with this policy.

8 An assembly plant of an automobile company orders various parts from fabrication plants of the same company. On part #4329, next year's requirement is estimated at 20,000 units. The plant uses an annual inventory carrying charge of 20 per cent on the average value of inventory. Part #4329 is valued at $20 per unit and all orders are delivered in one batch. The cost of processing an order is estimated at $100. The plant operates 250 days a year.

a. Compute the optimal ordering quantity.

b. How many orders should be placed per year with the production department?

c. If the average lead time is 10 working days; disbursements are continuous and uniform; and safety stock level is set at 500 units, what is the reorder point?

9 In problem 8, suppose the assembly plant produced part #4329 itself, employing intermittent processing.

a. If the production rate is 160 units per day and the rate of disbursement averages 80 units per day, what should be the order or production quantity?

b. How many orders should be placed per year with the production department?

c. If the production rate is cut to 100 units per day, what is the optimal quantity?

10 The probability distribution of demand for a product which is purchased and sold daily has been estimated as:

Demand	Probability
10	.05
11	.15
12	.30
13	.35
14	.10
15	.05
16	.00
	1.00

Each unit costs $30 and sells for $50. If not sold, the unit is completely worthless. The cost of ordering and carrying inventory is insignificant. How many units should be ordered? What is the expected profit? What is the value of a perfect forecast of demand?

Chapter 11
Scheduling of Operations— Physical Conversion

Organizations operate most efficiently with a smooth, even flow of goods and services passing through them. Unfortunately, the availability of inputs seldom matches the output requirements in either the temporal or spatial dimensions.

Organizations therefore face the task of scheduling—of planning physical, spatial, and temporal transformations. Scheduling is the task of specifying when and where certain events are to take place. In the physical conversion of goods, scheduling specifies which individuals and facilities are to be assigned to particular tasks and when these tasks are to be performed. Resources for service operations, such as maintenance and repair, transporting, and serving customers, are similarly allocated on a time basis.

The scheduling problems faced by service-producing organizations and the tools available to solve them are quite dissimilar to the problems of goods-producing organizations. Consequently, we will treat scheduling within the two types of organizations separately with goods-producing organizations considered in this chapter and service-producing organizations reviewed in Chapter 12.

The Scheduling Time Horizon

The scheduling process consists of the development of a series of plans or schedules with successively shorter time horizons. Firms forecast and plan conversion to some extent when they determine the proper capacity for and design factory buildings, warehouses, railroad systems, and so forth. Further scheduling is necessary in the selection of equipment and processes to assure that the processes selected are the most economical for the anticipated level of operations. After facilities are acquired, scheduling at a more detailed level is necessary to plan the best level of operations and employment throughout the year. Finally, monthly, weekly, and even daily schedules are developed to describe in detail the precise activities of individuals and facilities.

Previous sections of the book have dealt with the long-term forecasting and planning involved in the facilities design decisions. In this chapter, we assume that we are looking for the best *operating* schedules within the constraints of existing facilities.

A manufacturing firm producing goods requires two types of operating schedules. The manufacturer needs schedules of the aggregate or total level of production for the intermediate time span of up to 12 months in order to plan for the hiring of people, acquisition of raw materials, and creation of inventories. Short-term schedules of perhaps less than a month's duration are then developed within the confines of the aggregate schedule. The short-term schedules assign individuals and facilities to specific products and orders based upon up-to-date information about orders and inventory levels. Such short-term scheduling typically is labeled production control.

Planning the Aggregate Production Level

The necessity for planning aggregate production, employment, and inventory levels arises because of uneven time patterns of either inputs or outputs. If inputs were available at a uniform price throughout the year and if sales requirements were evenly spread, the optimal schedule would be to produce at the average demand level with no seasonal inventory buildup and no necessity for hiring and layoff, or for overtime to adjust employment to the production schedule. Unfortunately, most firms contend with some seasonality in the demand for their products. In industries producing products such as boats, toys, lawn mowers, farm equipment, and antifreeze, as much as 80 to 90 per cent of annual sales may occur in substantially less than half the calendar year. Even necessary items such as food and clothing, which have a more stable consumption pattern, often exhibit an appreciable degree of seasonality.

Some organizations also face the constraint of an uneven rate of raw materials input. For example, fruit and vegetable canneries receive all their input of each basic product within an interval of a few weeks out of each year. Firms with seasonal inputs usually have a limited number of production alternatives available. Canneries, for example, must produce all their canned peas within a few weeks because of the spoilage rate of the raw material. Such schedules give rise to high cost because the firm must maintain expensive equipment which it uses for only a small part of each year.

The alternatives open to the firm with a seasonal demand pattern are more numerous because of the capacity to transport products over time through the use of inventory. At one extreme, the firm can meet each change in demand with a change in the production rate, accomplishing this by hiring and laying off employees and by the use of overtime and idle time. At the other extreme, the firm can maintain an even production and employment pattern and accommodate the seasonal sales pattern by building up inventories during the slack sales periods and reducing them during the peak times. Other alternatives consist of all combinations of the two extremes, using some inventories and having some variation in the production and employment rates.

**Costs of
Seasonality**

Specific penalty costs are associated with all of the alternatives for smoothing production. Level production schedules result in large stocks of seasonal inventories with their related storage and carrying charges. Overtime operations usually require a 50 per cent wage payment premium and result in increased inefficiency when large increments are scheduled. Idle time may be even more costly. Changing the employment level may be relatively simple in some firms where a low skill level is required, but extremely expensive in firms where several months of training may be necessary in order to bring employees to an acceptable productive level. In addition, a schedule which utilizes a varying production rate will require more capacity than a stable pattern.

It is no simple matter to arrive at accurate cost estimates for hiring, carrying inventory, and so forth, since many of the cost components may be real but intangible economic costs, and others may be allocated jointly among a variety of accounts. The estimation problem is complicated because the costs do not remain constant and may vary considerably over a short period of time. Three critical factors are suggested as determinants of the total incremental costs of changing production and employment levels:[1]

1. The production output rate and inventory and employment levels of the period about to end, that is, the point of departure.

2. The magnitude of the change in the production rate, the employment level and inventory level.

3. The length of the period of the production schedule.

The current operating level represents some point in the total production cost curve of the firm. This cost curve is not a straight-line function; the marginal costs vary throughout the curve. For example, if a firm has been operating at 75 per cent of normal single-shift capacity, a 10 per cent increase in the production rate can be accomplished by hiring more workers. If the firm had been operating at 100 per cent of normal capacity, however, an increase of the same magnitude might require a second-shift operation, and increased supervision in addition to hiring more workers. Similarly, a reduction in the production rate from the 100 per cent level could be accomplished by a small reduction in the work week, or by laying off per-

[1] See R. E. McGarrah, *Production and Logistics Management* (New York: John Wiley & Sons, Inc., 1963), pp. 110–113.

sonnel with the lowest seniority and least skill. If the production rate were down to 50 per cent of normal capacity, however, further reductions in employment might necessitate laying off highly skilled employees whom the firm may not be able to rehire at some later time.

The effect of the magnitude of the change is fairly obvious. It costs more to hire and train ten employees than to hire and train one. In fact, it may well cost more than 10 times as much. Normally, a few people with the required skills probably are available in the local labor market. However, large increases in the employment level will require more intensive recruiting, covering a wider geographic area and the hiring of some people without the desired skills. Thus, the cost per employee hired will increase as more are hired. The same relationship will hold with respect to reductions in the employment level. There is usually some attrition plus those recently hired who can be layed off at little cost to the firm. Larger layoffs may require some restructuring of the organization and direct penalty costs because of union restrictions and state unemployment compensation laws.

The length of the production schedule affects the choice of alternative methods of adjustment. Some of the costs occur only once while others are imposed over several successive production periods. Consider the alternative of producing a unit during regular time some number of time periods before it will be sold, or of producing it during overtime in the same period that it will be sold. The premium overtime charge occurs just once, whereas an inventory carrying charge for the product produced ahead of time will accumulate for each period it is held in storage. It may be less expensive to carry a unit in inventory for a few periods than to produce it during overtime, but the best decision will change if it is necessary to carry the inventory for many time periods.

Planning Horizon

Firms typically follow a practice of planning the aggregate production rate for monthly increments for a year into the future. The schedule is based on forecasts of sales. As a result of the deviations between actual and forecast sales, firms must revise the original schedule frequently, perhaps as often as once a month.

Thus, the planned production rate for a specific month may be changed as many as twelve times in the year prior to that month. Despite the frequent schedule changes, the development of schedules for a year into the future is not a wasted effort. Consider what would happen if a one-month time span were used. Figure 11.1 shows the seasonal pattern of demand for a firm's products. Starting in January, the schedule which minimizes the total cost for the next one-month period is one in which the production rate matches the demand rate. The same is true for February and the subsequent months. Following this practice, there would never be any buildup of inventory in anticipation of the later peak demand periods. As a result, the schedules in September, October, etc., would be very costly to meet since production would have to match the high demand rates for those months.

Figure 11.1   Seasonal Demand Pattern

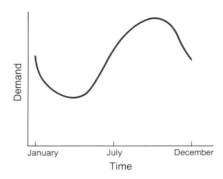

The proper objective is to minimize cost over the entire year. A firm must develop a schedule for the next month which is consistent with a minimum cost *yearly* plan. This is not the schedule which minimizes cost for the next month. That schedule would be a suboptimal schedule; it optimizes at a lower level—the one-month period. The optimal schedule will have higher costs through the early part of the year because of the buildup of seasonal inventory so that the production rate and the costs in the later part of the year can be kept at a reasonable level. Even though this schedule must be changed frequently, the revisions are usually minor and are made in order to react to deviations in the actual demand from the forecast level to bring the overall yearly plan back into adjustment. The revisions do not invalidate the original schedule, they merely adjust it more precisely.

Linear Decision Rules for Aggregate Scheduling

Firms have used a variety of approaches to determine aggregate production schedules including graphical methods, trial-and-error simulation analysis, and linear programming. A linear decision rule model developed by a research group at the Carnegie-Mellon University helps not only to develop the original schedule but also to modify and adjust it in the light of unforeseen developments.

The linear decision rule model minimizes the total cost of meeting demand over the yearly horizon. It begins with the development of a total cost formula consisting of the variable costs associated with the aggregate schedule. We define the following terms:

P_t = scheduled production rate in period t
W_t = work force level in period t
I_t = net inventory at end of period t

S_t = sales forecast for period t

A_t = actual sales in period t

C_i = cost coefficients and system parameters for particular organizations

Figure 11.2 illustrates the cost curves of a typical firm for inventory, overtime, and hiring and laying off employees. The total payroll cost per month, Figure 11.2 (A), is simply the size of the work force, W_t, times the average cost per worker including wages and fringe benefits, C_1.

Figure 11.2 Cost Behavior as a Function of Planning Variables

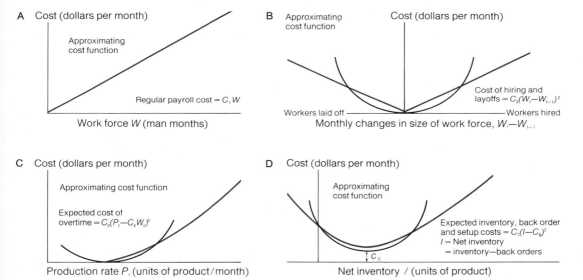

A Cost (dollars per month)

Approximating cost function

Regular payroll cost = $C_1 W$

Work force W (man months)

B Approximating cost function

Cost (dollars per month)

Cost of hiring and layoffs = $C_2(W_t - W_{t-1})^2$

Workers laid off ———— Workers hired

Monthly changes in size of work force, $W_t - W_{t-1}$

C Cost (dollars per month)

Approximating cost function

Expected cost of overtime = $C_3(P_t - C_4 W_t)^2$

Production rate P_t (units of product/month)

D Cost (dollars per month)

Approximating cost function

Expected inventory, back order and setup costs = $C_7(I - C_8)^2$

I = Net inventory = inventory—back orders

C_8

Net inventory I (units of product)

Source: C. C. Holt, F. Modigliani, and H. A. Simon, "A Linear Decision Rule for Production and Employment Scheduling," *Management Science* 2, no. 1 (October 1955).

We find the cost of changing the employment level, Figure 11.2 (B), by computing the size of the change, $W_t - W_{t-1}$, and squaring it (to include the effect that larger changes are more costly per unit than small changes), and multiplying by C_2, a cost coefficient. An organization determines this cost coefficient by estimating the cost of employment changes of varying magnitudes, plotting the values on a graph, and fitting a curve to the points. Trial and error will determine the particular value of C_2 which describes the curve that best fits the points. By its symmetrical nature, the curve in Figure 11.2 (B) indicates that hiring and laying off are equally costly. If one is more costly than the other, the asymmetry can be handled by the inclusion of another term in the mathematical expression.

The overtime cost expression consists of a series of curves, one for each possible employment level. Only one curve is shown in Fig. 11.2 (C). Each employment level, W_t, has an ideal production rate equal to $C_4 W_t$ where C_4

is the average number of units produced per worker per time period. A lower production rate results in an inefficient use of manpower, and a higher rate requires overtime with its increased costs. In overtime cost expression, $C_3 (P_t - C_4 W_t)^2$, the cost term C_3 is determined in the same manner as the term C_2.

Comparison of the actual inventory level I_t to C_8, the ideal inventory level, determines the inventory cost expression. The ideal inventory level consists of the raw materials, safety stock, inventory in process, and the like required to handle the normal daily transactions. If I_t is greater than C_8, the firm will have excessive inventory carrying costs. If I_t is lower than C_8, extra costs will occur because of stockouts, abnormally short production runs, and other delays. The inventory cost expression is $C_7(I_t - C_8)^2$. The C_7 cost term is determined in the same manner as C_2 and C_3. Note that the terms C_5 and C_6 appear to be missing in the sequence of numbers used. The original linear decision rule model developed by the Carnegie research group included the terms C_5 and C_6 along with C_9, C_{11}, and C_{12} cost terms. The researchers who developed the model used these terms to make the model conform more closely to the actual cost patterns in the firm for which the model was developed. But the terms have been omitted here since they are not essential to the operation and understanding of the model.

The total cost for a period is:

$$
\begin{aligned}
TC_t = \ & C_1 W_t && \text{Payroll cost} \\
& + C_2(W_t - W_{t-1})^2 && \text{Hiring and layoff cost} \\
& + C_3(P_t - C_4 W_t)^2 && \text{Overtime and idle time cost} \\
& + C_7(I_t - C_8)^2 && \text{Inventory cost} && (11.1)
\end{aligned}
$$

Solving the above equation results in a schedule that minimizes costs over the next period. A series of such schedules, each minimizing cost over the next period, is not the same as minimizing total cost over a longer period. Equation 11.1 produces a schedule which would never build up seasonal inventory since there is no advantage in doing so *for the current time period*. A schedule that might be more costly in the next period but that will lead to lower costs later is preferable. Thus, a firm must minimize total cost over a longer time horizon:

$$
TC_T = \sum_{t=1}^{T} TC_t \tag{11.2}
$$

where T is the appropriate time, usually 12 months. Equation 11.2 is subject to the constraint

$$
I_t = I_{t-1} + P_t - A_t.
$$

To obtain the scheduling rules that minimize total cost, we differentiate the equation with respect to each decision variable, $P_1, P_2, \ldots P_{12}, W_1, W_2,$

... W_{12}, and then solve the resulting expressions. We then have a pair of linear decision rules that specify the production and employment levels. Since the mathematical derivation is rather long and complex, we will not cover it here.

For the firm in which the model was originally developed, the following cost terms were specified:

$$C_1 = 340$$
$$C_2 = 64.3$$
$$C_3 = .20$$
$$C_4 = 5.67$$
$$C_7 = .0825$$
$$C_8 = 320.$$

The linear decision rules were:

$$P_t = \begin{Bmatrix} +.464S_t \\ +.236S_{t+1} \\ +.112S_{t+2} \\ +.047S_{t+3} \\ +.014S_{t+4} \\ -.001S_{t+5} \\ -.007S_{t+6} \\ -.008S_{t+7} \\ -.008S_{t+8} \\ -.007S_{t+9} \\ -.005S_{t+10} \\ -.004S_{t+11} \end{Bmatrix} + 1.006W_{t-1} + [153. - .464I_{t-1}]$$

$$W_t = .742W_{t-1} + [2.00 - .010I_{t-1}] + \begin{Bmatrix} +.0101S_t \\ +.0088S_{t+1} \\ +.0071S_{t+2} \\ +.0055S_{t+3} \\ +.0042S_{t+4} \\ +.0031S_{t+5} \\ +.0022S_{t+6} \\ +.0016S_{t+7} \\ +.0011S_{t+8} \\ +.0008S_{t+9} \\ +.0005S_{t+10} \\ +.0004S_{t+11} \end{Bmatrix}$$

where

P_t = number of units to be produced during the coming month t

W_t = number of persons to be employed during the coming month t

W_{t-1} = number of employees at the beginning of the month (end of previous month)

I_{t-1} = number of units of inventory minus number of units on backorder at the beginning of the month

S_t = sales forecast for month t (S_{t+1} is the forecast for the next month, and so on).

The two decision rules are applied at the beginning of each month. The computations are simple and require only a few minutes to perform. The rules support the kind of behavior that we would intuitively expect. Both the production rate and the employment rate depend upon future sales, with the immediate future weighted more heavily than the distant future, upon the current employment level, and upon the current inventory position. The terms $[153. - .464I_{t-1}]$ represent the inventory influence on the production rate. If the net inventory level is large, the sum of the two terms in the brackets will be negative thus pushing production downward. If the net inventory level is small, the sum of the two terms is positive and exerts an upward pressure on production in order to bring inventory back toward the desired level.

Tables 11.1 and 11.2 show the application of the scheduling equations to a firm. The firm has had a stable demand of 500 units per month which suddenly increases to 1000 units. Table 11.1 illustrates the optimal schedule when the change was not foreseen. Table 11.2 shows the optimal reaction when the increase is perfectly forecast. The linear decision rules minimize the total cost of reacting to changes in the demand patterns. Obviously, we can develop a more effective schedule when we can anticipate the changes. Thus, by determining the optimal schedule with a perfect forecast and with various degrees of error in the forecast and comparing the costs of such schedules, we can obtain a precise measure of the value of accurate forecasts for future sales. This information may then be used to decide whether it is worthwhile to develop more elaborate and expensive forecasting techniques in an effort to improve the accuracy of forecasts.

The automatic control feature of the linear decision rules operates through the inventory term. If, for example, sales during period t are 100 units less than forecast, then I_t will be 100 units more than anticipated. During the next period, the term $(153. - .464I_{t-1})$ will total 46.4 units less than the value if sales had been as forecast, thus reducing production for that period by 46.4 units to bring inventory toward the desired level. The adjustment would continue through the following periods until inventory is finally at the desired level.

Several published reports indicate that organizations gain significant savings by using the linear decision rules. In the paint factory in which the original research was performed, the application of the rules over a three-

Table 11.1   Costs of Fluctuations in Production, Work Force, and Inventory Levels
(Permanent Change in Demand Level—Not Forecast)

		Determination of Production, Work Force, And Inventory Levels from Decision Rules		
Period	Forecast Sales	Actual Sales	Production	Employment	Inventory
1	500.	500.	496.44	84.57	316.44
2	500.	500.	495.66	84.49	312.11
3	500.	500.	495.09	84.72	307.20
4	500.	500.	494.10	85.34	301.30
5	500.	1000.	493.46	86.41	−205.24
6	500.	1000.	725.57	93.07	−479.67
7	500.	1000.	856.10	101.85	−623.57
8	500.	1000.	926.70	111.36	−696.87
9	500.	1000.	977.27	121.25	−719.61
10	500.	1000.	1020.75	131.56	−698.85
11	500.	1000.	1076.99	142.56	−621.87
12	500.	1000.	1168.82	154.35	−453.05

		Variable Cost by Time Period		
Period	Payroll	Hiring and Layoff	Overtime	Inventory	Total
1	28753.77	11.89	1711.11	1.04	30477.81
2	28725.35	0.45	1692.50	5.14	30423.44
3	28804.02	3.44	1586.41	13.53	30407.39
4	29015.08	24.78	1338.80	28.86	30407.51
5	29378.75	73.56	987.08	22759.93	53199.32
6	31642.82	2851.23	18828.68	52756.49	106079.19
7	34629.82	4962.76	30734.75	73452.06	143779.38
8	37862.44	5812.51	33593.55	85307.69	162576.13
9	41224.27	6286.42	32760.98	89164.81	169436.44
10	44731.04	6840.18	30396.05	85640.81	167608.06
11	48469.50	7773.91	29521.82	73187.19	158952.38
12	52477.68	8936.07	33720.99	49302.89	144437.56

	Total Variable Cost			
Payroll	Hiring and Layoff	Overtime	Inventory	Total
435714.31	43577.20	216872.50	531620.38	1227784.00

year period using a simple moving average forecast would have resulted in a 7.84 per cent reduction in costs (Table 11.3). Actually the costs in Table 11.3 are not all variable. Even if there were no seasonality or random deviations in demand, there would still be a regular payroll cost somewhere in the range of 600 plus. Thus the reduction in true variable costs is much greater than 7.84 per cent.

Despite its apparent value, the linear decision rule scheduling process has not yet enjoyed wide application. This is partially because of the effort required to obtain accurate cost data to fit into the cost expression. Although

Table 11.2   Costs of Fluctuations in Production, Work Force, and Inventory Levels
(Permanent Change in Demand Level—Perfect Forecast)

		Determination of Production, Work Force, And Inventory Levels from Decision Rules			
Period	Forecast Sales	Actual Sales	Production	Employment	Inventory
1	500.	500.	478.94	91.52	298.94
2	500.	500.	518.27	99.32	317.21
3	500.	500.	573.13	108.47	390.34
4	500.	500.	664.90	118.93	555.24
5	1000.	1000.	827.90	130.10	383.13
6	1000.	1000.	918.97	140.10	302.11
7	1000.	1000.	966.62	148.33	268.73
8	1000.	1000.	990.38	154.78	259.11
9	1000.	1000.	1001.32	159.65	260.43
10	1000.	1000.	1005.61	163.26	266.04
11	1000.	1000.	1006.63	165.88	272.67
12	1000.	1000.	1006.19	167.75	278.86

		Variable Cost by Time Period			
Period	Payroll	Hiring and Layoff	Overtime	Inventory	Total
1	31116.76	2733.33	0.0	36.58	33886.67
2	33768.20	3910.33	0.0	0.64	37679.16
3	36880.44	5387.67	0.0	408.16	42676.28
4	40437.09	7036.16	640.48	4565.15	52678.88
5	44232.48	8012.45	7460.71	328.81	60034.45
6	47633.81	6435.02	10788.81	26.42	64884.06
7	50433.09	4358.59	10963.52	216.90	65972.06
8	52623.64	2669.08	9760.87	305.88	65359.47
9	54281.73	1529.21	8252.15	292.75	64355.84
10	55507.54	835.79	6889.90	240.22	63473.44
11	56398.02	441.06	5802.26	184.81	62826.14
12	57036.21	226.54	4983.46	139.67	62835.87

	Total Variable Cost			
Payroll	Hiring and Layoff	Overtime	Inventory	Total
560348.69	43575.22	65542.13	6745.98	676212.13

this may seem like a reasonable excuse not to use the linear decision rule model and other systematic scheduling processes, it is not a valid reason. Any kind of scheduling process, even an intuitive shuffling around of rates and times is presumably based on at least an informal estimate of relative costs. If no consideration at all is given to costs, the resulting schedules are likely to be far from optimal, no matter how they are obtained. Although the results obtained with the linear decision rule model will improve as the cost estimates become more accurate, it is not essential to have completely accurate cost estimates in order to use the model. The model may be used even when substantial errors in cost estimation exist. The results are still likely to be better than if no consideration is given to the cost of adjusting for seasonality.

Table 11.3 Cost Comparison of Company and Decision Rule Performance

Costs for 3-year period	Company Performance	Decision Rule, Moving Average Forecast
Regular Payroll	643.1	588.3
Overtime	42.0	48.6
Inventory	139.8	152.6
Backorders	166.9	126.0
Hiring and Layoffs	8.2	6.1
Total Cost	1000.0	921.6

Source: C. C. Holt, et al., *Planning Production, Inventories, and Work Force* (Englewood Cliffs, N.J.: Prentice-Hall Inc., 1960), p. 24. The costs were scaled so that the total cost company performance equals 1000.0.

Scheduling of Conversion Operations

After long-range planning decisions have been made to establish the capacity of the operating system and intermediate term plans have established the aggregate level of employment, production, and inventories, an organization then must establish schedules for the conversion of individual units and products which fit into the broader plans and constitute an efficient use of its facilities. Short-term operating schedules, with time horizons varying from a few weeks to a few months, form the final step in this scheduling process. This short-term scheduling process is often encompassed within the term "production control" in the firm. At this stage, the firm must look at each individual node and link in the production network and determine the rates and times at which raw materials, components, and subassemblies flow through the network as well as the appropriate levels of inventories and manpower assigned to each product and process.

The operating system at this level of decision making is often extremely complex. For example, in Chapter 4, Figure 4.5 shows a network representation of a manufacturing system. When one considers that several dozen or even several hundred different products may be produced by such a system with each product possessing a unique set of inputs and operations and a unique path through the network, the enormity of the scheduling task becomes apparent. It is not surprising that even in well run organizations, stockouts of products occur and slack time will exist at one node while long lines of products are waiting at another node.

Fortunately, not all production operating systems are as complex as the one in Figure 4.5. However, even a production system consisting of a single node may present considerable scheduling difficulties when several different products must pass through the system.

In the vast majority of production operating systems, it is uneconomical to try to develop the best or optimal schedule because of the systems' complexity. Even if a firm could determine the best schedule for the next month, the firm probably could not follow the schedule very closely since new inputs are constantly entering the system and even a minor malfunction at one node may produce a substantial chain reaction throughout the entire network of the system. Thus, the development of a reasonable schedule—one that will work fairly well most of the time—is a satisfactory objective.

The criteria or measures of effectiveness that may be used to evaluate the scheduling process include the level of finished goods and work-in-process inventory, the percentage of facility utilization, the percentage of orders shipped on time, the average production time per order, the percentage of stockouts or inventory shortages, and the percentage of time spent in setting up or changing over facilities to produce a different product. None of the above can be used as the sole measure of the production control process; all of them must be kept at a reasonable level. A firm can easily develop a schedule that would excel in meeting any one of the above indicators if the others were ignored. For example, a firm can gain a very low inventory level by limiting the number of orders in process, but that gain would be at the cost of poor facility utilization.

Types of Physical Conversion Systems

A number of different classification schemes have been used to describe physical conversion systems. However, the number of different variables describing a system is so large that no classification scheme is very successful in fitting such a diverse assemblage of systems into a few precise categories. There are, however, a few distinctions between systems which should be made. First, systems produce products either to specific order or for stock. If a substantial majority of the customers desiring a product are content with a product of a standard or customary set of specifications of size, color, capacity, and the like, it is usually economical to produce the product in relatively large quantities for stock, that is, before specific orders arrive. Examples of such products are canned peas, electric toasters, bedroom sets, and bicycles. If, on the other hand, each customer has a unique set of product specifications, the manufacturer must wait until the order arrives before production can take place. Examples of this type of product are generators for hydroelectric plants, expensive men's suits, architectural drawings, and false teeth.

The production processes used and the scheduling problems encountered differ considerably between the two classifications. When production is to specific order, the production process must be of a general-purpose rather than a specialized type. Since each order is different from the others, the process must have sufficient flexibility to accommodate the differences. This flexibility requires workmen of a relatively high skill level with the capability of determining their own work methods, setting up equipment, and in some cases even designing some part of the product. The technological needs of production by specific order requires machines and other physical facilities. But the producer uses relatively fewer and less specialized pieces of equipment since the physical equipment does not possess the flexibility of humans to make changes from one order to the next.

When production is for stock, the conversion process can begin and even be completed well in advance of the time the customer decides he wants the product. The process can be automated since it is more repetitive. The human skills requirements are not as great. The workers can be trained to follow closely specified methods and need not deviate substantially from them.

Scheduling is more difficult when production is to order. With production for stock, a manufacturer can use forecasts of demand to establish production goals. Based on these forecasts, he can determine the requirements for raw materials and purchased components. Since the output is standardized, fewer different kinds of materials are needed. Manpower and facilities may be utilized at a more constant rate; since flexibility exists in the time dimension, conversion need not be tied to specific orders. Movement between nodes in the conversion network may be scheduled in advance. Movement is easier because the products tend to follow a more consistent path through the network and the adjoining nodes in the process can be located next to each other.

Another important classification dimension depends upon sales volume. If the expected sales volume of a product is sufficiently large, production can be accomplished most economically on a continuous basis. A firm may establish a separate set of facilities devoted exclusively to a single product. Substantial economies accrue to large-volume continuous production. Highly automated physical facilities can be designed, built, and used for the conversion process. Although such equipment may reduce the cost per unit of production, the capital cost is warranted only when a sufficiently large volume of sales exists. In addition, no time is lost in starting, stopping and changing over from one product to another. Movement between nodes in the process is minimal and can be handled automatically.

If sales volume is small, production is accomplished on an intermittent or a jobbing basis because the use of expensive, highly automated facilities is uneconomical. Even less expensive general-purpose facilities must be shared by several products when the volume of each is at a level which utilizes only a small portion of the available equipment time. In a job shop production process, a given department may produce a product for a week and build up sufficient inventory to last for several weeks or months. During the next week, the department produces another product and so on.

Again, the scheduling problems encountered vary considerably between a continuous and an intermittent or jobbing process. In a continuous process, much of the scheduling is built into the design of the process itself. In a continuous process, such as a bottling plant or an automobile assembly line, it is essential that the work load at each node or each work station be equal. The slowest station limits the speed of the process. Since each station is closely linked to the whole process, a slowdown at one station will delay the entire process. This balancing of the work load takes place at the time the process is designed and after that little scheduling is necessary. We will examine the line balancing problem in more detail later in this chapter.

In a discontinuous process, all the problems of coordinating the conversion of several products in the same facilities exist and the scheduling task is formidable for even a relatively simple system.

At this point the reader can appreciate the difficulty of trying to fit individual organizations into exact categories. Some products are produced to order and others for stock, or part of a product may be produced on a for-stock basis with other stages in the process taking place only after a specific order has been received. Similarly, a given organization may produce some products continuously, others discontinuously, and others partially with both types of processes. Also, some products may be produced continuously by one organization and discontinuously by another depending on the individual organization's sales volume. Thus, our method of classifying conversion systems represents, at best, simply a way of looking at the factors determining how conversion should take place and the kinds of scheduling problems encountered in each kind of process. This will be useful in examining the production control problems and the scheduling techniques used to handle them.

We have insufficient time and space to try to consider scheduling of every type of conversion process. We can, however, examine a few of the more interesting cases. We will consider first the line balancing problem of the continuous production process. Secondly, we will look at a single-node system with discontinuous production for stock. Next, we will consider how we can attempt to schedule conversion on a complex multi-node system with discontinuous production both for stock and to specific order (the job shop scheduling problem). Finally, we will look at some of the problems of estimating the processing times used in the scheduling process.

The Line-Balancing Problem

In a continuous production system with a separate set of facilities devoted to a single product, the primary scheduling problem is to obtain the desired level of output with the minimum input of labor and other resources. For example, an automobile assembly line may be set up with a pace of operation to produce a finished automobile every 60 seconds. The scheduling task is to assign the work in a manner which minimizes the number of work stations and workers required to perform all the assembly operations within the 60 second time period. Work assignment scheduling is not done for each individual unit, but the schedule is built into the structure of the conversion process, and the assignment of individual tasks to specific work stations remains the same until the structure of the entire process is changed.

The first step in balancing the line is to define the job and the work tasks constituting it. We define work tasks as the smallest meaningful segments of work which can be assigned to an individual work station. Any further subdivision will result in substantial additional work. In defining the tasks, we also specify their sequence requirements. Each task has some time relationship with all other tasks. It either must precede or follow, or it is independent of the performance of every other task. For example, Figure 11.3 shows a network drawing of a conversion process.

Figure 11.3 Work Tasks in Conversion Process

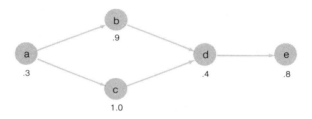

The network suggests, for example, that task b cannot be started until a is completed; b must be done before d can be started, and b can occur either before or after c. The figures below the nodes give the average task performance time in minutes.

Consider now the assignment of the tasks to work stations. The total time available at each station depends on the required output of the process which in turn depends on the expected sales or usage rate of the output. In the example above, suppose that a unit must be produced every 1.0 minutes. A quick examination of Figure 11.3 reveals that no two tasks could be combined within a single station. Tasks a and d, if combined, would fall within the 1.0 minute time limit. They cannot be assigned to the same station, however, since tasks b and c must be performed between a and d. Thus, the job would require five separate work stations. This results in a rather low labor utilization level. The total amount of actual work accomplished is equal to the sum of the task times, or 3.4 minutes in this case. However, five workers are occupied for 1.0 minutes each for a total labor time of 5.0 minutes or a labor utilization rate of $3.4/5.0 = .68$.

In practice, it might be difficult to achieve even this level of output. The time figures given for each task represent the average performance time. Considerable variation in the time requirement for each task may exist from unit to unit. There may be some variation in the specific work involved in a given task from one unit to the next. For example, on an automobile assembly line, each automobile is somewhat different than the next in terms of body, transmission, and engine configuration as well as in the number and kinds of special accessories. The average time for installing a transmission may well vary with the kind of transmission.

In cases where the product specifications and the work assignments remain exactly the same from unit to unit, variations in time requirements still exist. Some inherent and unavoidable variation exists in the time in which the work is completed owing to a variety of causes such as parts being slightly out of proper shape, wear in tools, accidental dropping of parts, or simply because the workers change their pace.

When the production process is rigidly paced as it is when the product moves along a conveyer line, the effect of this variation is substantial since the rigid pace ties all the work stations together. Suppose that on two successive units the worker on task b requires 1.1 and .7 minutes respectively, while the worker on task e requires .5 and 1.1 minutes during the same two cycles. Even though each was working at his average pace, the line could move only after all workers completed their work on a given cycle. In this case, the line could move only after 1.1 minutes on each cycle. The longer the line, the more serious is the time variation problem.

It becomes very difficult to achieve high labor utilization on a continuous process system because of the limited divisability of work tasks and variation in the processing times. Fortunately, there are ways of reducing the effect of these obstacles. Back-up operators are sometimes used. Their job is to step into the line at points where the individual operator is falling behind. Also, inventory can be used to partially decouple the work station. A bank of goods in process between stations can absorb many of the variations in time from unit to unit instead of having the repercussions felt immediately throughout the entire line.

Despite the problem of balancing the line, the continuous process has economic advantages, such as reduced materials handling, smaller facility and tool investment, and lower skill requirements, that can be achieved when sales volume is sufficiently large. Since such systems exist, they must be designed and scheduled. Much work has been done to develop models that produce optimally balanced lines. We will consider first a method useful in handling problems of moderate size and then consider a model for handling very large problems.

Rules for Balancing Assembly Lines

The first method for balancing an assembly line uses two fairly simple rules to assign tasks to stations:

1. construct all possible combinations of tasks at each succeeding stage;

2. eliminate combinations when:
   a. all tasks in one set are contained in another; or
   b. when one differing task exists in a combination set but requires less time than the task in another set and does not permit the inclusion of any different subsequent task combinations at succeeding stages.

The line balancing problem is a combinatorial problem, that is, one of seeking the right combination among many possible combinations of assignment of work tasks. Rule number 1 forms all possible combinations. Its use alone would be sufficient and would assure that the best solution was obtained. However, the number of different combinations is exceedingly large for even moderately sized problems, and rule 2 helps to reduce the number of alternatives under consideration by eliminating those alternatives for which others equally good or better exist.

We will solve the problem in Figure 11.4 to illustrate the use of the rules. Cycle time is 10 minutes. The sum of the task times is 46 minutes. Thus, at least five work stations will be required. The reader can verify the usefulness of the systematic rules at this point by attempting to balance the line by inspection. The optimal five station solution is not easy to see.

At stage 1, the list of alternative combinations becomes:

$$(a \ b \ c)$$
$$(a \ b \ h)$$

Neither can be eliminated by rule 2.

Stage 2:

$$(a \ b \ c) \ fh$$
$$(a \ b \ c) \ gh$$
$$(a \ b \ c) \ ih$$
$$(a \ b \ h) \ cf$$
$$(a \ b \ h) \ cg$$
$$(a \ b \ h) \ ci$$

The last 3 combination sets contain the same work tasks as the first 3 sets and can be eliminated by rule 2(a). We apply rule 2(b) to a comparison of the first and second sets with the differing tasks f and g. The first set can be eliminated since f requires less time than g. In comparing the second and third sets, neither can be eliminated since differing tasks i and g have different succeeding tasks which might be included in subsequent stations.

Stage 3:

$$(abc, ih) \ fj$$
$$(abc, ih) \ g$$
$$(abc, gh) \ i$$
$$(abc, gh) \ fd$$

Applying rule 2(a) eliminates the third set.

Stage 4:

(abc, ih, fj) gd
(abc, ih, g) fj
(abc, ih, g) fd
(abc, gh, fd) i
(abc, gh, fd) e

Applying rule 2(a) eliminates the fourth set.

Figure 11.4 Precedence Diagram for Line Balancing Problems

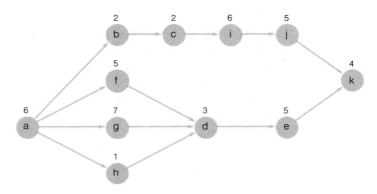

Stage 5: The only remaining tasks after the first set (abc, ih, fj, gd) are e and k which are now assigned to station five. The other three sets will all result in six station lines. Table 11.4 gives the optimum solution.

Table 11.4 Optimum Balance for Sample Problem

Station	Tasks	Time
1	abc	10
2	ih	7
3	fj	10
4	gd	10
5	ek	9

Computer Method for Balancing Lines

The number of possible combinations increases rapidly with problem size. Although the previous set of balancing rules will always produce the best solution, the rules become too unwieldy for lines with a large number of tasks. For large complex products, several hundred separate work tasks must be performed. An interesting and useful approach for balancing large lines is through the use of COMSOAL,[2] which is an acronym for Computer

[2] A. L. Arcus, "COMSOAL: A Computer Method of Sequencing Operations for Assembly Lines," E. S. Buffa (ed.), *Readings in Production and Operations Management* (New York: John Wiley & Sons, 1966), pp. 336–360.

Method of Sequencing Assembly Lines. This process uses a high-speed digital computer to generate a random sample consisting of a large number of solutions. Even though the probability is very small that any one of the solutions is optimal, there is a reasonably good chance that at least one of the solutions generated will be optimal if a large enough sample is taken. As we will see, the probability of obtaining an optimal solution can be calculated precisely. We will illustrate the process through the solution of a simple problem, the one shown in Figure 11.5.

Figure 11.5   COMSOAL Line Balancing Example

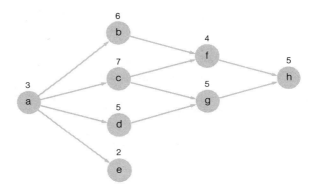

This problem with eight tasks has 112 different feasible ways of combining the tasks. One or more of the combinations requires the minimum number of stations; one or more, the minimum number plus one; and so on. Table 11.5 shows the distribution of sequence combinations for our problem.

Table 11.5   Distribution of Feasible Sequence Combinations for COMSOAL Example

Stations Required	Number of Sequences
4	25
5	84
6	3
Total	112

Suppose that a process generates random feasible sequences and that r is the proportion of the universe of feasible sequences which require the minimum number of stations. The probability that the first sequence generated will be optimal is r and the probability that it is not is $(1 - r)$. If n sequences are generated, the probability that all are non-optimal is $(1 - r)^n$, and Pn, the probability is $1 - (1 - r)^n$ that at least one sequence drawn is optimal. *Pn* approaches 1, absolute certainty, as *n* increases even when *r* is very small. Table 11.6 gives a few selected computations for *Pn*.

Table 11.6 Pn, the Probability that at Least One Sequence is Optimal

		n, the number of sequences randomly generated		
		100	*500*	*1,000*
r, the proportion of optimal sequences in the universe	*.001*	.095208	.393621	.632305
	.01	.633968	.993430	.999957
	.1	.999973	1.000000	1.000000

We must know the value of *r* in order to compute *Pn*. Unfortunately, *r* rarely can be determined with precision. In our example, $r = 25/112 = .223$. In this case, we enumerated all possible sequence combinations, a task that is obviously impossible for large-scale problems. Although no short cut exists to determine *r*, a reasonably good solution would normally suffice in a practical problem. We can hypothesize that an economic sample will, in most cases, contain at least one optimal sequence; and that in the comparatively few cases that possess a very small *r*, at least one sequence in the economic sample will require only one station in excess of the optimal number.

The problem of rapidly and economically generating sequences still remains. COMSOAL uses a process which involves progressive selection of tasks from among those which have no unassigned preceding tasks. The COMSOAL approach for our problem is:

Step 1: Form an availability list which includes all tasks which now have no preceding unassigned tasks. (At the first step, only a is in the list.)

AVAILABILITY LIST
a

Step 2: Form a fit list which includes those tasks from the availability list which require times equal to or less than the time left available in the station to which work is now being assigned. (Since 10 minutes are available and a requires only 3, it satisfies the requirement.)

FIT LIST
a

Step 3: In the simplest form of COMSOAL, a random selection is made from the fit list and the task is assigned to the work station to which work is now being assigned. (In this case, a is assigned to the first station.)

Steps 1, 2, and 3 are repeated until all tasks have been assigned. The result is a sample of size 1. Additional solutions are generated by repeating the generation process until the desired number of solutions have been generated. The randomness of the selection process in step 3 assures that a different solution will result in each successive run.

Following our example a bit further, we have:

AVAILABILITY LIST

b

c

d

e

FIT LIST

b

c

d

e

Suppose that d is the randomly selected task. Now (a) and (d) have been assigned to station 1 and continuing:

AVAILABILITY LIST

b

c

e

FIT LIST

e

and so on, repeating steps 1, 2 and 3.

The COMSOAL generating process we have described was improved by biasing the selection of tasks from the fit list instead of selecting them at random. A total of nine different biasing rules were tested which tended to favor the selection of fewer station combinations, thus tending to increase *r,* the probability of generating an optimal sequence. Among the more effective biasing procedures were:

RULE 1. Weight tasks that fit in proportion to task time. The effect of this rule is to give large tasks a greater chance of assignment early at each station and in the entire sequence. This leaves the shorter tasks to the end. The time space is filled efficiently by loading the longer time spans first and leaving the smaller time spans to fill the reduced time spaces.

RULE 2. Weight tasks that fit in proportion to the number of immediately following tasks. This rule increases the chances of selection of tasks which will lead to an expansion of the availability list.

The computer time requirements of COMSOAL can be estimated from Arcus' examples. He found that a 45-task problem generated optimal 8-station assignments in an average of 32 seconds of time on an IBM 7090. He states that Chrysler Corporation implemented an earlier version of

COMSOAL and that for a 1000 task job, a 203 station sequence resulting in 1.48 per cent idle time was computed in about 2 minutes of 7090 time.

Having found a computing procedure that produced optimal or near-optimal solutions for basic line-balance problems, Arcus proceeded to provide for a series of other more realistic constraints on the program. In essence, these constraints affect the fit list which must satisfy the new constraints in addition to those stated earlier. These additional constraints will not be described in detail, but the following list should serve to describe their general nature:

1. Tasks larger than the cycle time.
2. Tasks that require two men.
3. Tasks fixed in location.
4. Space for parts.
5. Time to obtain a tool.
6. Time for the worker to change position.
7. Time to change the position of a unit.
8. Grouping tasks by criteria.
9. Wages related to tasks.
10. Worker movement between units being assembled.
11. Mixed production on the same line.
12. Stochastic task performance times.

Scheduling of Multiple Products through a Single Facility

There are a large number of production processes which intermittently produce several different kinds of products for stock on the same set of physical facilities. For example, oil refineries or chemical processing plants may produce one product or a set of products for two weeks during which inventories of these products are built up. At the end of two weeks, processing facilities are used to produce other products and sales demand for the first set of products is met by the inventory which was previously accumulated. It may be several months before the first set of products is produced again. Similarly, an assembly line in an appliance factory may assemble dishwashers one week, clothes dryers the next, stoves the following week, and so on. The lack of sufficient sales volume of any single product to justify its own separate process necessitates the sharing of facilities.

Despite the very common occurrence of this type of production process, no one has yet devised a method for determining the optimal production schedule. To illustrate the scheduling complexities which are introduced by facility sharing, we will attempt to develop a schedule for a very simplified situation, one in which two products share a process.

There are two products A and B with the following characteristics:

	d	p	S	C	i
A	10,000	25,000	$6,000	$10	.20
B	10,000	25,000	$3,000	$20	.20

where
d = annual rate of demand
p = annual rate of production
S = cost of setting up or preparing for a production run
C = cost per unit of producing the product
i = cost of carrying inventory per year

The production process can operate 250 days per year. In Chapter 10, we derived a formula to determine the optimal production quantity, Q_p^* for each production run, that is, the quantity that minimizes the sum of the setup and carrying costs. Equation 10.3 stated that

$$Q_p^* = \sqrt{\frac{2dS}{(1 - d/p)iC}}. \tag{11.3}$$

Applying equation 11.3, we get

$$Q_{P_A}^* = 10,000 \text{ units}$$
$$Q_{P_B}^* = 5,000 \text{ units}$$

The results suggest that product A should be produced once per year $(d_A/Q_{P_A}^* = 10,000/10,000)$ with a production run of 10,000 units which would require .4 $(Q_{P_A}^*/p = 10,000/25,000)$ of a year or 100 production days. Product B should be produced twice a year with runs of 5,000 units each time, each run requiring .2 of a year or 50 production days.

The only remaining problem is to try to fit the production runs for both products into the time schedule of the single facility that must produce both. Either A or B could be produced at the start of the year. We will arbitrarily schedule B first. Product B will be produced for 50 days. During that period 5,000 units will be produced and .2 of the year's demand or 2,000 units will be sold leaving an inventory accumulation of 3,000 units on hand at the end of day 50. This inventory is 3,000/10,000 = .3 of a year's supply and should last until the end of day 125. Thus, the second production run for product B must begin on day 126. Figure 11.6 illustrates this inventory level for product B.

The production process is now available for producing product A from day 51 through day 125, and from day 176 through day 250. Despite the fact that 150 days are available, no single segment is long enough for the 100 days of production that product A requires. We can try scheduling A at the start of the year or try maneuvering the schedule around in other ways, but there is no conceivable schedule which will allow both A and B to be produced at the quantities $Q_{p_A}^*$ and $Q_{p_B}^*$ with each production run beginning at the time inventory for the respective product has just been depleted.

Figure 11.6   Inventory Level for Product B

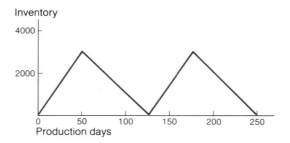

$Q_{p_A}^*$ and $Q_{p_B}^*$ minimizes the sum of the ordering and setup costs only when they are combined into a feasible schedule on the same process. Since a feasible schedule cannot be arranged using those quantities, some type of workable compromise schedule must be developed. We see, from Figure 11.6, that if product A were produced in 50-day runs of 5,000 units each, the run could be fitted into the periods between the runs of product B. This compromise, however, would increase the sum of the setup plus carrying costs for product A. Figure 11.7 illustrates the costs for products A and B as they vary with the quantity produced. With $Q_{p_A}^* = 10,000$ and $Q_{p_B}^* = 5,000$, the total annual carrying and setup costs for each product are $12,000 for a total of $24,000 for both products. Changing the production quantity of A to 5,000 units increases the total annual carrying and setup costs for product A to $15,000, or a total of $27,000 for both products.

Another feasible schedule would result if each product were produced once per year in quantities of 10,000 units. A could be produced from day 1 through day 100, and product B from day 101 through day 200. Such a schedule leaves the total annual carrying and setup costs for product A at $12,000, but increases the cost for product B to $15,000, for a total of $27,000 for both products.

Actually, any schedule that calls for the same number of production runs for all products produced on the same facility will be a feasible schedule, no matter how many products share the facility or how many runs of all the products are made per year provided, of course, that the facility has sufficient production capacity. Such a schedule would work even if demand for the several products required that the process operate every day of the year. This is in sharp contrast to the first schedule that we tried in the above example where the process operated at only .80 of full capacity, but still could not produce at $Q_{p_A}^*$ and $Q_{p_B}^*$ because of time overlaps. A schedule

Figure 11.7 Carrying and Setup Costs for Products A and B

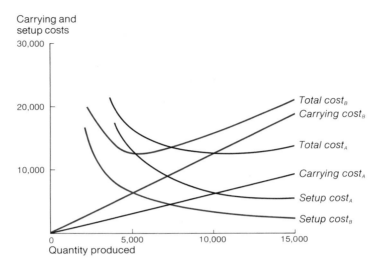

for producing each product the same number of times per year will be feasible, and it will not have time overlaps on the facility because each run of each product is offset from the previous run of that product by the same time span. Thus, if the number of runs per year is three, then the second run of product A will begin exactly one-third of a year after the first run began, and so on for products B, C, and all the rest although the quantities produced of each product and the time required to produce each product varies considerably from one product to the next.

The production of all products which are made by the same facility the same number of times per year may not necessarily be the optimal schedule. It is, however, a workable schedule and may be as close as possible to the optimal schedule in a practical case. If a producer were to operate such a schedule, he would attempt to determine the best value for the number of times of production per year. For our two-product example, let us redraw Figure 11.7 in a slightly different form, this time illustrating how cost varies with N, the number of production runs per year. Since N is a function of Q_p ($N = d/Q_p$), the curves have a similar shape. The horizontal variable, N, has been scaled so that the curves for A and B from Figure 11.8 exactly fit Figure 11.7. (This is possible only because $d_A = d_B$.) Adding the two curves together produces curve TC which has a minimum point about halfway between $N = 1$ and $N = 2$ at an approximate total annual carrying plus setup cost of $25,500.

Economic Production Cycle

We can usually analyze and determine the value of N mathematically. The total cost equation to be minimized is very similar to equation 11.3, which was developed for a single product. The basic differences are that we must

Figure 11.8 Carrying and Setup Costs for Products A and B

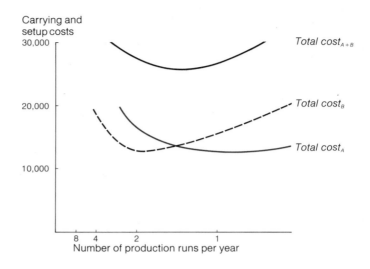

now state costs in terms of N rather than in terms of Q_p and we must sum the costs for all products together. Thus,

$$TC_{All} = \Sigma \text{ Setup Costs} + \Sigma \text{ Carrying Costs}$$

$$= N \sum_{i=1}^{m} S_i + \frac{1}{2N} \sum_{i=1}^{m} i_i C_i d_i (1 - d_i/p_i). \qquad (11.4)$$

where m is the number of products produced on the facility and the other terms are as previously defined.

Taking the first derivative, setting it equal to zero, and solving for N gives

$$N^* = \sqrt{\frac{\sum_{i=1}^{m} i_i C_i d_i (1 - d_i/p_i)}{2 \sum_{i=1}^{m} Si}}. \qquad (11.5)$$

For the example,

$$N^* = 1.414.$$

Substituting $N = 1.414$ in equation 11.4 gives $TC^* = \$25,452$.

The resulting value of N^* does not necessarily give the best schedule. It merely gives the best value of N, given that we wish to produce all products the same number of times per year. It is conceivable that a lower cost schedule exists. However, since no method exists for finding the optimal schedule, the above process of calculating N^* for the group of products may be used to set the basic schedule. Next we may calculate N_i^* for each product as if it were an independent product without the facility-sharing constraint. ($N_i^* = d_i/Q_{p_i}^*$ where $Q_{p_i}^*$ is obtained from equation 11.3). Then, for products in which N_i^* is significantly different from N^*, some manipulation of the schedule can be made by trial and error in order to try to fit the product into the basic N^* schedule either more or less frequently as dictated by N_i^*. The degree to which this trial and error manipulation is successful depends upon the utilization of the facility. If a great deal of slack time exists, it may be reasonably successful; but if the facility must operate at close to 100 per cent of capacity, no changes from the N^* schedule may be possible. In any case, the efficiency of any trial and error schedule may be determined by adding up the carrying and setup costs for all the products.

Variation in the Rate of Demand

In an actual system, the operation of a schedule such as we have determined may be difficult for any extended time period. The above schedule assumes a rather constant rate of demand. Although we have discussed a situation in which products are for stock, the predicted level of sales and the rate of depletion of inventories are developed from sales forecasts. These forecasts are inevitably in error as the rate of demand changes over time due to causes that are not entirely predictable. Even a small increase in the rate of demand for a single product can have an enormous effect on the production schedule. Suppose, for example, that a production system is scheduled to produce four different products three times a year, with the length of each production run being one month or 20 working days. Product A is produced in January. At the end of January, sufficient inventory of product A has been built up to last 60 more working days until A again is scheduled for production starting in May. However, at the beginning of February the sales rate for product A increases by ten per cent. Therefore, inventory of product A is depleted in approximately 54 working days. If the cost of being without a stock of product A is sufficiently large, a new production run of A will have to be started immediately. This will cut into the schedule of product D, which is normally produced for 20 days in April, after only 14 days of production. As a result, the inventory buildup of product D is insufficient to last the normal 60 working days until D is next scheduled for production. Since only .70 (14 days/20 days) of the normal production run occurred, the accumulated inventory will last only about .70 x 80 = 56 days from the start of the run. Thus, D would be in a stockout condition 16 days after the beginning of the production run of product B. At this point, the firm may cut short the run of B and switch to product D. In 4 more days, product C has run out. The implication of this adjustment and the snowballing effect of the first small increase in demand is obvious. A firm may easily find itself in a position of continually reacting to the latest crises and rapidly shifting production from one product to another as a result of an initially small change in the normal demand pattern. As a result, setup costs are excessive and stockouts still continue to occur at a high rate.

To some extent, the effect of disturbances to the original schedule can be dampened by the use of a buffer or safety stock. Most small disturbances can be absorbed by buffer inventory which can then be brought back to normal levels as time permits. Let us examine the relationship between safety stock and the length of the production run and how variation in the rate of demand effects the production schedule.

Figure 11.9 shows how the carrying and setup costs vary for a single product. The sum of the two costs is a minimum at point A. The level of safety stock required to provide a specific level of protection against stock-outs varies with the quantity produced. If N is large and the length of each production cycle is short, a relatively small amount of safety stock is required since variations in the demand rate would not have had sufficient time to cause large inventory deficits or surpluses. As N becomes smaller and Q_p for each product becomes larger, the time span between successive uses of a product correspondingly increases. Since the effect of variations in the rates of demand increases over time, the safety stock must similarly increase in order to provide the same level of production.

If demand conforms to the Poisson distribution, as it does for many products, the standard deviation of demand is proportional to the square root of the time span. Thus, a four-month production cycle would require $\sqrt{4}$ or 2 times as much safety stock as a one-month cycle for every product. As shown in Figure 11.9, the safety stock is increasing with increasing Q_p. The minimum cost value for Q_p is shifted to the left, to Point B, as the safety stock cost is added to the carrying and setup costs. Thus, if a manufacturer

Figure 11.9 Effect of Safety Stock on Economic Production Quantity

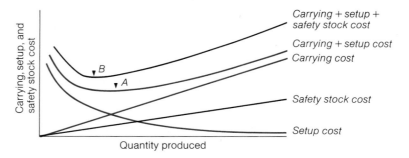

were attempting to use equation 11.5 as the basis for scheduling production, the resulting N^* value should be adjusted upward and the production runs shortened to account for the safety stock carrying cost which equation 11.5 ignores. The amount of the adjustment will depend upon the amount of variation in the demand rates and the relative cost of carrying safety stock as opposed to the costs of setup and carrying the cycle stock.

In practice, it remains exceedingly difficult to stick to any schedule in the multi-product single-facility production system. Despite safety stocks, stockouts still occur. In addition, breakdowns occasionally delay production. As stockouts occur, pressure is exerted from various points in the organization to begin producing the out-of-stock items. When the preplanned schedule is interrupted, the problems are not avoided. They are only temporarily delayed and, in fact, increased, as we have seen. Once the scheduler succumbs to the temptation to ignore the schedule and react to an immediate crisis, the number of stockouts and the size of the crises invariably increase. The scheduler must accept the fact that he cannot avoid all stockouts, and when they do occur he must resist the temptation to immediately revise the schedule. The out-of-stock items should be produced only when their insertion will not cause an even greater imbalance.

Job Shop Scheduling

Certainly the most difficult type of scheduling for a production process is the job shop. The job shop is characterized by a broad product mix with production in batches representing individual jobs either to specific order or for stock. Typically, each job is produced intermittently on several different facilities with transportation of the semi-finished goods between operations. Each job may follow a unique path through the network, and the facilities may require extensive alterations between jobs. The common example of a job shop is the metal working shop which contains a diversity of equipment and produces a wide variety of products and components. A wood working shop which produces cabinets, doors, window frames, and the like is also a job shop.

The job shop scheduling task is to plan operations on literally hundreds of jobs in dozens of work centers in order to meet the multiple scheduling objectives described earlier in this chapter. The complexity of the scheduling task is readily apparent. Historically, most job shops have operated almost without schedules. That is, most have been operated with little attempt at planning the timing of individual jobs.

The major attempt at "scheduling" has been through the use of various visual aids which plot the progress of jobs and the level of facility utilization. These visual devices may be in the form of control boards using pegs and strings, card control systems, graphs, or computer printouts. No matter what the form, they are all basically derived from the Gantt chart, a device developed in the early 1900's by Henry L. Gantt, a pioneer in the scientific management movement of that era.

Figure 11.10 shows two variations of the Gantt Chart. In the top section the projected four-week schedule is shown for various parts listed in the first column. The horizontal lines indicate the planned or projected time for which the job will be scheduled in the numerically indicated department.

Figure 11.10 Gantt Charts

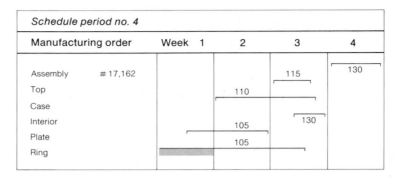

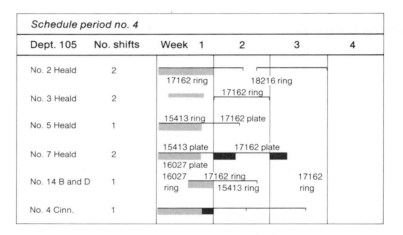

Source: Gordon B. Carson (ed.), *Production Handbook*, 2nd ed. (New York: Ronald Press, 1958), p. 321.

The lower part of the chart shows the scheduled load on each of a number of machines listed in the first column and represents graphic machine loading. In both the part schedule and machine loading schedule, the progress of jobs is updated by the heavier black lines.

The Gantt chart, or its variations, are not typically used to plan the progress of each individual job. They provide a visual description of the current plant status. This information is used for broader aggregate scheduling decisions and also for "exception" scheduling, that is, for establishing priorities for those jobs which the charts reveal to be lagging behind the normal rate of progress. At the aggregate level, the charts disclose where bottlenecks are likely to appear, where extra capacity exists, the level of work backlogs in each department, and so forth. This information can then be used to schedule overtime and to shift workers as well as some processing from department to department. It also is used to estimate production lead times so that the due dates promised by the sales force will have some reasonable expectation of being met.

The optimal sequencing of individual jobs is usually of academic interest only. What might appear to be an optimal sequence for some time period into the future is often obsolete after a single day of operations. The delay in the completion of a single job in a single department because of a machine malfunction or an erroneous time estimate-is enough to throw off the entire schedule because of the complex interrelationships that exist between jobs and the availability of capacity. In addition, the continual entrance of new orders into the system also requires frequent schedule revision.

Consequently, sequencing is usually established on real-time, using some basic framework or decision criteria to establish which job is to be processed next at a given facility. Real-time sequencing means that the choice of the processing sequence is not planned ahead of time but rather the decision is made at the same time that it can be executed. The real-time decision is typically based on some local decision rule. That is, the choice of the next job to be processed on a given facility is based on the situation at that single (local) facility and not based on what the status is at any of the other facilities.

For purposes of analysis, the job shop may be visualized as a network of waiting lines. Jobs arrive and join a waiting line at a work station or service facility. As the facility completes a job, the job is moved on via the materials handling system to another waiting line at another facility. As one job leaves a facility, another job is selected for processing from the waiting line in front of that facility based on some local decision rule.

Considerable research has been performed on the effectiveness of various types of sequencing rules through computer simulations using both artificial and real job time dates. We will look briefly at the results of this research.

An investigation by Nanot[3] tested ten different decision rules on six different job shop configurations with over two million simulated orders passing through the system. The rules tested were:

Rule	1	(FCFS)	—first come, first served.
Rule	2	(SOT)	—shortest operation time.
Rule	3	(SS)	—static slack; due date minus time of arrival at work center.
Rule	4	(SS/PT)	—static slack / remaining processing time.
Rule	5	(SS/RO)	—static slack / remaining number of operations.
Rule	6	(FISFS)	—first in system, first served.
Rule	7	(LCFS)	—last come, first served.

[3] Y. R. Nanot, "An Experimental Investigation and Comparative Evaluation of Priority Disciplines in Job Shop-Like Queueing Networks" (Ph.D. diss., UCLA, 1963).

Rule 8 (DS) —dynamic slack; time remaining to due date minus remaining processing time.

Rule 9 (DS/PT) —dynamic slack / remaining expected processing time.

Rule 10 (DS/RO) —dynamic slack / remaining number of operations.

Table 11.7 shows the resulting mean times for job completion and variation in job completion times for one of the six job shop configurations. This particular job shop consisted of four work centers operating under a moderate work load. The pattern of results was similar for the other five configurations.

Table 11.7 Job Completion Mean Time and Standard Deviation of Completion Times

Rule		Mean	Standard Deviation
(1)	FCFS	1.67	1.96
(2)	SOT	.99	1.87
(3)	SS	1.71	2.10
(4)	SS/PT	2.53	3.96
(5)	SS/RO	1.99	2.92
(6)	FISFS	1.69	1.55
(7)	LCFS	1.68	3.52
(8)	DS	1.86	1.62
(9)	DS/PT	2.54	5.43
(10)	DS/RO	1.78	3.66

Source: Y. R. Nanot, "An Experimental Investigation and Comparative Evaluation of Priority Disciplines in Job Shop–Like Queueing Networks" (Ph.D. diss. UCLA, 1963).

In both the Nanot study and other research investigations, the shortest operating time (SOT) rule consistently has the fastest flow-through of jobs, as shown by the smallest mean job completion time in Table 11.7. This result is not surprising. By selecting the job which can be processed the fastest, jobs are most quickly moved from work centers with waiting lines to idle work centers. Also, the smaller, shorter jobs are readily moved through the plant to completion. Long, bottleneck jobs are not allowed to tie up long lines of shorter jobs. The SOT rule is also effective in minimizing inventory in process and machine idle time.

There is, however, a problem in using the SOT rule: a few jobs which require lengthy processing at a work station may be kept in line for an excessive period of time as shorter jobs which continue to enter the waiting line are given priority. Thus, while the SOT rule is effective in getting most jobs completed by their due dates, excessive delays or lateness in a few jobs may make it too costly. Table 11.7 reveals that both the first-in system, first-served (FISFS) rule and the dynamic-slack (or DS) rule have smaller standard deviations in the job completion time distributions. This suggests that both the FISFS and the DS rules are more effective in avoiding the long delays in individual jobs which are occasionally caused by the SOT rule. The employment of either of these rules, however, will substantially increase the mean job completion time.

An ideal rule would have both a small mean completion time (such as the SOT rule produces) and a small variation in the completion time distribution (such as the FISFS or DS rules produce). A compromise rule which may work better than any of these ten rules is to use the SOT rule most of the time to gain the advantage of a fast flow time for most jobs and to alternate it with some other rule to periodically pick up those individual jobs which have waited for an excessive period of time.

A simulation run by Conway and Maxwell[4] truncated the SOT rule after waits of various lengths. A simple SOT rule produced a mean job completion time of 218.2 time periods with a standard deviation of 354.2 periods. The mean waiting time per waiting line was approximately 40 periods. Thus, a truncation number such as 100 periods means that a job which has been in line 2.5 times (100/40) as long as the mean waiting time will be given priority, or selected on a FCFS rule basis. Table 11.8 shows the results of various truncation levels.

Table 11.8   Performance of Truncated SOT Rule (TS,C; C = Truncation Number)

Rule	Mean Job Completion Time	Standard Deviation of Completion Time	Facility Idle Time, Per Cent
TS, 0 (FCFS)	244.5	174.5	16.69
TS, 100	236.1	190.5	13.36
TS, 300	229.3	226.7	11.98
TS, 1000	220.4	275.7	7.60
TS, ∞ (SOT)	218.2	354.2	6.79

Source: R. W. Conway and W. L. Maxwell, "Network Scheduling by the Shortest Operation Discipline," *Operations Research* 10, no. 1 (1962): 51–73.

As the SOT rule is subject to truncation, the mean completion time increases but the standard deviation of the completion time distribution decreases. Truncation also increases facility idle time.

The experimental results suggest that a rational selection of a priority rule for job sequencing is worthwhile for a manufacturing firm. All of the studies indicate a clear dominance of the SOT rule over other rules that were tested. It had the best performance in several of the measures of effectiveness and was also very effective when combined with other measures. Implementation of the SOT rule is simple and does not require an

---

[4] R. W. Conway and W. L. Maxwell, "Network Scheduling by the Shortest Operation Discipline," *Operations Research* 10, no. 1 (1962): 51–73.

elaborate data processing system. The rule can easily be modified or combined with other rules to diminish the effect of its few relative disadvantages.

More complex rules based on due dates, customer classifications, order value, and the like can certainly be devised and may even be more effective in meeting the objectives of the job shop. However, in most cases the priority computations and the order selection will be made by the machine operator who may lack the initiative to undertake a complex mathematical computation for each of several wating jobs before making a selection for processing.

In the normal manufacturing shop, contingencies develop and specific orders take on critical importance because of various reasons such as the importance of the customer, the critical need for the order, and an idle facility waiting for something to process. Some expediting process is necessary to remove the critical orders from their normal sequence and assure their rapid progress through the production process. This may be done by red-tagging an order or by having some individual act as an expediter and personally push the critical orders through the shop. Although some expediting is necessary in the best run shops, a large amount of it is an indication of a basically inefficient sequencing process. It is expensive not only from the standpoint of the resources devoted directly to the expediting function but also from the standpoint of the indirect, but very real costs, of disrupted schedules.

Improvement Curves

A forecast estimate of the time required to perform each element of work is a basic necessity for scheduling any type of system. These estimates are obtained in a variety of ways. In some cases, a foreman or a scheduler simply uses his judgment and past experience to estimate processing time. In other cases, historical records are kept of processing time. When a new job is to be scheduled, the records are examined and a time estimate is obtained by comparing it to similar jobs processed in the past. In still other cases, time studies are made for new jobs. Time study involves timing a worker's performance while he performs the job a few times. The person making the time study rates the worker or compares his performance to what he considers a normal performance for the people who will eventually be doing the work, and then establishes time estimates.

No matter what process is used, rather large errors in time estimates are inevitably found when the work is finally performed. This, of course, compounds the scheduling problem. The errors are due to a variety of causes. In some cases, improvements in processing are introduced, thereby reducing processing time. In other cases, unforeseen technological difficulties, delays in materials, employee problems, and the like cause time overruns. In still other cases, time estimating errors occur because many schedulers fail to recognize the magnitude of improvement derived from repetition of the task.

Most people know that improvement in the amount of time required to perform a task or group of tasks occurs with repetition. A worker can perform a task better the second time, and each succeeding time he performs it. However, many people are not aware that the pattern of improvement can be predicted because of its regularity. Nor are they aware that such patterns can apply not only to individual performance, but also to performance of groups and organizations.

This improvement from repetition generally results in a reduction of man-hour requirements for the accomplishment of tasks and consequently an improvement in operating and production costs. From empirical evidence, the pattern of this improvement has been quantified in the improvement curve,[5] which is described by the following relationship: each time the output quantity doubles, the unit man-hours are reduced at a constant rate.[6]

We may illustrate this relationship with an example in which 1,000 man-hours are required to manufacture the first unit of a product. If we assume that the constant rate of improvement is 80 per cent, then we forecast that the second unit requires only 80 per cent as many man-hours as the first, 1,000 x 80 per cent, or 800 man-hours. The fourth unit requires only 80 per cent as many as the second, and so on.

Unit		Man-hours
1st		1,000
2nd	1,000 × 80%	800
4th	800 × 80%	640
8th	640 × 80%	512
16th	512 × 80%	410

We may also express the relationship mathematically.

$$Y_x = K(X)^n \qquad (11.6)$$

and

$$T_x = \sum_{i=1}^{x} (Y_i), \qquad (11.7)$$

or

$$T_x = K\left[\frac{(X + 1/2)^{n+1} - (1/2)^{n+1}}{n + 1}\right] \qquad (11.8)$$

[5] Improvement curves are also called learning curves, industrial progress curves, cost curves and experience curves.

[6] Another relationship used in some situations is that the *cumulative average* man-hours are reduced at a constant rate each time the output quantity doubles. Our discussion will utilize the *unit* man-hours relationship.

where:

Y_x = the man-hours required for the single unit X

T_x = the cumulative total man-hours required from the first unit through unit X

X = the number of the unit for which the man-hours are being determined

K = the man-hours for the first unit

$n = \log r/\log 2$

r = improvement ratio (80 per cent, etc.), expressed as a decimal (.80, etc.).

We can readily calculate equation 11.6 for a specific value of X, but equation 11.7 is tedious by manual calculations since it involves calculating every unit value from 1 to X. Formula 11.8 is a close approximation of 11.7 that is satisfactory for many practical estimates.

If we plot this relationship on an arithmetic chart, with linear coordinates, as in Figure 11.11, we observe that it is a curve which shows a rapid initial

Figure 11.11 80 Per Cent Improvement Curve on Arithmetic Scales

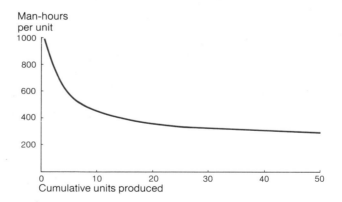

decline that later tapers off. The relationship, however, is of a hyperbolic nature, that plots on a log-log chart as a straight declining line, as in Figure 11.12. The units of the scales on a log-log chart are proportioned in logarithmic ratios. Such a straight-line relationship is easier to draw and use for estimation purposes.

Tables have been developed which give the factor for each unit and for various improvement ratios. They allow greater precision than we can obtain from reading a graph and eliminate the need for cumbersome calculations required by the formula. Table 11.9 shows factors for unit man-hours, and Table 11.10 shows the factors for cumulative total man-hours.

Using Tables 11.9 and 11.10, we determine the man-hours for each unit, the cumulative total man-hours, and the cumulative average unit man-hours for the previous example.

Figure 11.12 80 Per Cent Improvement Curve on Logarithmic Scales

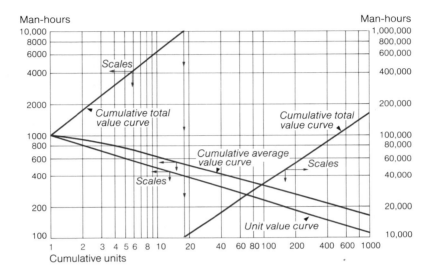

Unit (1)	Unit man-hours (2)	Cumulative total man-hours (3)	Cumulative average unit man-hours (col. 3 ÷ col. 1) (4)
1	1,000	1,000	1,000
2	800	1,800	900
3	702	2,502	834
4	640	3,142	785
5	596	3,738	748
8	512	5,346	668
10	477	6,315	632
100	227	32,650	327
1,000	108	158,700	159

The cumulative total and cumulative average curves are also plotted in Figure 11.12. When the unit and cumulative average curves are plotted on the same scale, they approach a parallel condition.[7] Note the graphical device used to extend the cumulative total value curve beyond about 19 units by shifting the vertical scale by two fields.

[7] The cumulative average curve is asymptotic to a line parallel to the unit curve.

Table 11.9 Improvement Curves: Table of Unit Values

Unit	Improvement ratios							
	60%	65%	70%	75%	80%	85%	90%	95%
1	1.0000	1.0000	1.0000	1.0000	1.0000	1.0000	1.0000	1.0000
2	.6000	.6500	.7000	.7500	.8000	.8500	.9000	.9500
3	.4450	.5052	.5682	.6338	.7021	.7729	.8462	.9219
4	.3600	.4225	.4900	.5625	.6400	.7225	.8100	.9025
5	.3054	.3678	.4368	.5127	.5956	.6857	.7830	.8877
6	.2670	.3284	.3977	.4754	.5617	.6570	.7616	.8758
7	.2383	.2984	.3674	.4459	.5345	.6337	.7439	.8659
8	.2160	.2746	.3430	.4219	.5120	.6141	.7290	.8574
9	.1980	.2552	.3228	.4017	.4930	.5974	.7161	.8499
10	.1832	.2391	.3058	.3846	.4765	.5828	.7047	.8433
12	.1602	.2135	.2784	.3565	.4493	.5584	.6854	.8320
14	.1430	.1940	.2572	.3344	.4276	.5386	.6696	.8226
16	.1296	.1785	.2401	.3164	.4096	.5220	.6561	.8145
18	.1188	.1659	.2260	.3013	.3944	.5078	.6445	.8074
20	.1099	.1554	.2141	.2884	.3812	.4954	.6342	.8012
22	.1025	.1465	.2038	.2772	.3697	.4844	.6251	.7955
24	.0961	.1387	.1949	.2674	.3595	.4747	.6169	.7904
25	.0933	.1353	.1908	.2629	.3548	.4701	.6131	.7880
30	.0815	.1208	.1737	.2437	.3346	.4505	.5963	.7775
35	.0728	.1097	.1605	.2286	.3184	.4345	.5825	.7687
40	.0660	.1010	.1498	.2163	.3050	.4211	.5708	.7611
45	.0605	.0939	.1410	.2060	.2936	.4096	.5607	.7545
50	.0560	.0879	.1336	.1972	.2838	.3996	.5518	.7486
60	.0489	.0785	.1216	.1828	.2676	.3829	.5367	.7386
70	.0437	.0713	.1123	.1715	.2547	.3693	.5243	.7302
80	.0396	.0657	.1049	.1622	.2440	.3579	.5137	.7231
90	.0363	.0610	.0987	.1545	.2349	.3482	.5046	.7168
100	.0336	.0572	.0935	.1479	.2271	.3397	.4966	.7112
120	.0294	.0510	.0851	.1371	.2141	.3255	.4830	.7017
140	.0262	.0464	.0786	.1287	.2038	.3139	.4718	.6937
160	.0237	.0427	.0734	.1217	.1952	.3042	.4623	.6869
180	.0218	.0397	.0691	.1159	.1879	.2959	.4541	.6809
200	.0201	.0371	.0655	.1109	.1816	.2887	.4469	.6757
250	.0171	.0323	.0584	.1011	.1691	.2740	.4320	.6646
300	.0149	.0289	.0531	.0937	.1594	.2625	.4202	.6557
350	.0133	.0262	.0491	.0879	.1517	.2532	.4105	.6482
400	.0121	.0241	.0458	.0832	.1453	.2454	.4022	.6419
450	.0111	.0224	.0431	.0792	.1399	.2387	.3951	.6363
500	.0103	.0210	.0408	.0758	.1352	.2329	.3888	.6314
600	.0090	.0188	.0372	.0703	.1275	.2232	.3782	.6229
700	.0080	.0171	.0344	.0659	.1214	.2152	.3694	.6158
800	.0073	.0157	.0321	.0624	.1163	.2086	.3620	.6098
900	.0067	.0146	.0302	.0594	.1119	.2029	.3556	.6045
1,000	.0062	.0137	.0286	.0569	.1082	.1980	.3499	.5998
1,200	.0054	.0122	.0260	.0527	.1020	.1897	.3404	.5918
1,400	.0048	.0111	.0240	.0495	.0971	.1830	.3325	.5850
1,600	.0044	.0102	.0225	.0468	.0930	.1773	.3258	.5793
1,800	.0040	.0095	.0211	.0446	.0895	.1725	.3200	.5743
2,000	.0037	.0089	.0200	.0427	.0866	.1683	.3149	.5698
2,500	.0031	.0077	.0178	.0389	.0806	.1597	.3044	.5605
3,000	.0027	.0069	.0162	.0360	.0760	.1530	.2961	.5530

Source: Albert N. Schrieber, Richard A. Johnson, Robert C. Meier, William T. Newell, Henry C. Fischer, *Cases in Manufacturing Management* (New York: McGraw-Hill Book Company, 1965), p. 464.

Table 11.10   Improvement Curves: Table of Cumulative Values

Units	60%	65%	70%	Improvement ratios 75%	80%	85%	90%	95%
1	1.000	1.000	1.000	1.000	1.000	1.000	1.000	1.000
2	1.600	1.650	1.700	1.750	1.800	1.850	1.900	1.950
3	2.045	2.155	2.268	2.384	2.502	2.623	2.746	2.872
4	2.405	2.578	2.758	2.946	3.142	3.345	3.556	3.774
5	2.710	2.946	3.195	3.459	3.738	4.031	4.339	4.662
6	2.977	3.274	3.593	3.934	4.299	4.688	5.101	5.538
7	3.216	3.572	3.960	4.380	4.834	5.322	5.845	6.404
8	3.432	3.847	4.303	4.802	5.346	5.936	6.574	7.261
9	3.630	4.102	4.626	5.204	5.839	6.533	7.290	8.111
10	3.813	4.341	4.931	5.589	6.315	7.116	7.994	8.955
12	4.144	4.780	5.501	6.315	7.227	8.244	9.374	10.62
14	4.438	5.177	6.026	6.994	8.092	9.331	10.72	12.27
16	4.704	5.541	6.514	7.635	8.920	10.38	12.04	13.91
18	4.946	5.879	6.972	8.245	9.716	11.41	13.33	15.52
20	5.171	6.195	7.407	8.828	10.48	12.40	14.61	17.13
22	5.379	6.492	7.819	9.388	11.23	13.38	15.86	18.72
24	5.574	6.773	8.213	9.928	11.95	14.33	17.10	20.31
25	5.668	6.909	8.404	10.19	12.31	14.80	17.71	21.10
30	6.097	7.540	9.305	11.45	14.02	17.09	20.73	25.00
35	6.478	8.109	10.13	12.72	15.64	19.29	23.67	28.86
40	6.821	8.631	10.90	13.72	17.19	21.43	26.54	32.68
45	7.134	9.114	11.62	14.77	18.68	23.50	29.37	36.47
50	7.422	9.565	12.31	15.78	20.12	25.51	32.14	40.22
60	7.941	10.39	13.57	17.67	22.87	29.41	37.57	47.65
70	8.401	11.13	14.74	19.43	25.47	33.17	42.87	54.99
80	8.814	11.82	15.82	21.09	27.96	36.80	48.05	62.25
90	9.191	12.45	16.83	22.67	30.35	40.32	53.14	69.45
100	9.539	13.03	17.79	24.18	32.65	43.75	58.14	76.59
120	10.16	14.11	19.57	27.02	37.05	50.39	67.93	90.71
140	10.72	15.08	21.20	29.67	41.22	56.78	77.46	104.7
160	11.21	15.97	22.72	32.17	45.20	62.95	86.80	118.5
180	11.67	16.79	24.14	34.54	49.03	68.95	95.96	132.1
200	12.09	17.55	25.48	36.80	52.72	74.79	105.0	145.7
250	13.01	19.28	28.56	42.08	61.47	88.83	126.9	179.2
300	13.81	20.81	31.34	46.94	69.66	102.2	148.2	212.2
350	14.51	22.18	33.89	51.48	77.43	115.1	169.0	244.8
400	15.14	23.44	36.26	55.75	84.85	127.6	189.3	277.0
450	15.72	24.60	38.48	59.80	91.97	139.7	209.2	309.0
500	16.26	25.68	40.58	63.68	98.85	151.5	228.8	340.6
600	17.21	27.67	44.47	70.97	112.0	174.2	267.1	403.3
700	18.06	29.45	48.04	77.77	124.4	196.1	304.5	465.3
800	18.82	31.09	51.36	84.18	136.3	217.3	341.0	526.5
900	19.51	32.60	54.46	90.26	147.7	237.9	376.9	587.2
1,000	20.15	34.01	57.40	96.07	158.7	257.9	412.2	647.4
1,200	21.30	36.59	62.85	107.0	179.7	296.6	481.2	766.6
1,400	22.32	38.92	67.85	117.2	199.6	333.9	548.4	884.2
1,600	23.23	41.04	72.49	126.8	218.6	369.9	614.2	1001.
1,800	24.06	43.00	76.85	135.9	236.8	404.9	678.8	1116.
2,000	24.83	44.84	80.96	144.7	254.4	438.9	742.3	1230.
2,500	26.53	48.97	90.39	165.0	296.1	520.8	897.0	1513.
3,000	27.99	52.62	98.90	183.7	335.2	598.9	1047.	1791.

Source: Albert N. Schrieber, Richard A. Johnson, Robert C. Meier, William T. Newell, Henry C. Fischer, *Cases in Manufacturing Management* (New York: McGraw-Hill Book Company, 1965), p. 465.

Factors Determining Improvement Ratios

The improvement curve phenomenon was first observed in airframe manufacturing in the 1930's, when it was found that the number of man-hours required to build an airplane declined at a regular rate. The original formulation of the improvement curve concept is generally attributed to T.P. Wright.[8]

In practice, the improvement ratio may vary from about 60 per cent, representing very great improvement, to 100 per cent representing no improvement at all. Generally, as the difficulty of the work decreases, the expected improvement also decreases and the improvement ratio that is used becomes greater. On the other hand, as the difficulty increases, we have a greater opportunity for improvement; therefore, the improvement ratio that is used will be a lower percentage. The proportion of the labor content in an operation also affects the improvement ratio: lower percentages occur in operations with higher labor content. Moreover, operations having similar proportions of labor-paced to machine-paced work tend to have similar improvement ratios.

Some other factors which have an important effect on determining the rate of improvement are:

1. Familiarization with the job by both workers and supervisors.
2. Length of service on the job of workers and supervisors.
3. Improvement in organization and procedures which improve the flow of work and availability of materials.
4. Design and engineering changes in the product.
5. Improvement in tooling used to produce the product.
6. Expectation of improvement by workers and management.

This list of factors is by no means comprehensive nor are the factors readily quantifiable. Much research remains to be done to define the contributing factors and the extent of their contribution.

For example, an airframe assembly, in which the proportion of labor-paced work is around three-fourths, often has an 80 per cent improvement ratio. As the proportion of labor-paced work declines to one-half and one-fourth, the improvement ratio may increase to 85 per cent and 90 per cent respectively. On the basis of several studies on improvement ratios, made since the end of World War II it appears that average rates of improvement are similar for similar types of manufacturing work. To determine the rate of improvement appropriate for forecasting in a specific situation, a scheduler should use the past experience of the individual firm. These rates can be estimated by statistical regression analysis techniques.

[8] T. P. Wright, "Factors Affecting the Cost of Airplanes", *Journal of Aeronautical Sciences,* February 1936, pp. 122–128.

Estimating the Cost of a Production Lot

On a new job, estimation of the man-hours required for the first unit is necessary. This information generally is derived from experience on work that is similar to the new situation. A second estimate is required to establish the improvement ratio. With these two factors, prediction of the man-hours required for an individual unit or for any cumulative group of units is possible by the use of Tables 11.9 and 11.10, respectively. For example, if it is assumed that the first unit will require 600 man-hours and the improvement ratio is 85 per cent, then in a production lot of 30 units, the 30th unit will require 270 man-hours (600 × .4505 from Table 11.9) and the cumulative man-hours required for the entire lot of 30 units will be 10,254 man-hours (600 × 17.09 from Table 11.10).

A very common problem in the use of improvement curves is the estimation of the cost of a follow-on lot of production when the costs of the previous lots are known. The generalized method of solving this problem is: the cost of a follow-on lot is determined by subtracting the cumulative costs of all previous lots from the cumulative cost of the previous and proposed lots combined. The cost of follow-on lots is based on a consideration of the total costs from the very first unit produced through the units under consideration. We illustrate the application of the generalized rule for determining succeeding lot cost in the following example.

Assume that the first production lot of 40 units of an item actually required a total of 12,900 man-hours and the first unit required 750 man-hours. The ratio of the total man-hours to the man-hours for the first unit is 12,900 ÷ 750 = 17.20. From Table 11.10, we find for 40 units a cumulative improvement factor of 17.19 for an 80 per cent improvement ratio. Based on this experience, we wish to calculate the man-hours for a second follow-on production lot of 160 units. The cumulative number of units will be 200 (40 on the first and 160 on the second lot). If we assume that the follow-on lot will also follow an 80 per cent improvement curve, then the cumulative total required for both lots will be 39,540 man-hours (equal to 750 × 52.72 from Table 11.10). The follow-on lot will then require 26,640 man-hours (39,540–12,900).

The average man-hours of the first lot was 12,900 ÷ 40 = 322.5, and the average man-hours on the second lot will be 26,640 ÷ 160 = 166.5. We calculate the average direct labor cost for each lot by multiplying the average man-hours by the labor rate per hour. By linear interpolation between the values for number 40 and 45 from Table 11.9, we determine the expected time required for the first unit of the follow-on lot, unit number 41:

$$750 \times [.3050 - \tfrac{1}{5}(.3050 - .2936)] = 750 \times .3027 = 227 \text{ man-hours}$$

Unit number 200 should require $750 \times .1816 = 136$ man-hours. These values are plotted in Figure 11.13.

Figure 11.13   Improvement Curve of Unit Man-Hours (80 Per Cent Improvement Ratio)

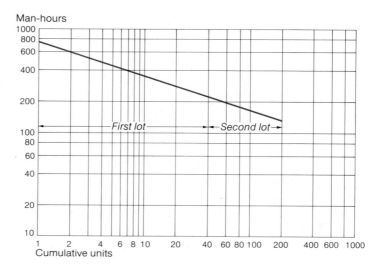

The information from this type of analysis is useful as a basis for pricing and negotiation in procurement of nonstandard special products. In such situations, in which only a single source of supply often exists, there may be no comparative prices and little opportunity for competitive bidding. Costs of follow-on contracts can be estimated from improvement curve calculations, and provide important information for buyer and seller alike.

Schedule Forecasts and Project Feasibility Analysis

Another important application of improvement curves is in manpower planning and scheduling. If the improvement rate concept is applicable in a particular situation, then for a constant output rate the size of the required workforce should decline. Conversely, for a constant workforce size, the output rate should increase.

Suppose that an airplane manufacturer is considering the development and introduction of a new type of commercial jet aircraft. Preliminary design work has been completed at a cost of $45 million and has demonstrated the technical feasibility of the new plane. The firm estimates that to complete the design and engineering, and to tool up to produce the plane will require 4 more quarters (12 months) and will cost $25 million per quarter.

As part of the project feasibility and financial analysis, a schedule of direct labor man-hours and work force size is needed. In a real situation, a monthly schedule would be more precise, but a quarterly schedule will serve to illustrate the procedure.

Figure 11.14 Manpower Schedule for Airplane Project (80 Per Cent Improvement Ratio)

Line	Item	1	2	3	4	5	6	7	8	9	10	11	12	13	14	15	16
										Quarter							
1.	Delivery Rate						5	15	20	20	20	20	20	20	20	20	20
2.	Cumulative Deliveries						5	20	40	60	80	100	120	140	160	180	200
3.	Improvement Curve Cumulative Factor						3.74	10.48	17.19	22.87	27.96	32.65	37.05	41.22	45.20	49.03	52.72
4.	Cumulative Direct Labor Man-Hours (millions)						3.74	10.48	17.19	22.87	27.96	32.65	37.05	41.22	45.20	49.03	52.72
5.	Total Man-Hours for Units Delivered During Quarter (millions)						3.74	6.74	6.71	5.68	5.09	4.69	4.40	4.17	3.98	3.83	3.69
	Man-Hours Incurred During Quarter (millions)																
6.	Delivery 2 Quarters Later				1.25	2.25	2.24	1.89	1.70	1.56	1.47	1.39	1.33	1.28	1.23		
7.	Delivery Following Quarter					1.25	2.25	2.24	1.89	1.70	1.56	1.47	1.39	1.33	1.28	1.23	
8.	Delivery Current Quarter						1.24	2.24	2.23	1.90	1.69	1.57	1.46	1.39	1.32	1.27	1.23
9.	Total Man-Hours Incurred (millions)				1.25	3.50	5.73	6.37	5.82	5.16	4.72	4.43	4.18	4.00	3.83	2.50	1.23
10.	Direct Labor Manpower Requirements (men) (500 hours/man/quarter)				2,500	7,500	11,460	12,740	11,640	10,320	9,440	8,860	8,360	8,000	7,660	5,000	2,460

Fabrication on the first plane may begin during the following fourth quarter. Each plane will require 3 quarters for fabrication and assembly. Direct labor man-hours will be divided evenly among the 3 quarters. Deliveries could begin in the sixth quarter. The delivery rate is expected to be 5 planes in quarter 6, 15 in quarter 7, and 20 per quarter thereafter. The manufacturer expects to sell 200 planes at a price of $6.0 million each. The company estimates that the first plane will require 1.0 million man-hours, and expects that direct labor hours will follow an 80 per cent improvement curve.

With this information, we prepared the manpower schedule shown in Figure 11.14. The schedule gives the delivery schedule, man-hours requirements, and manpower requirements for the 200-plane project. The general procedure for calculation of the schedule is to determine cumulative total man-hours for deliveries up to each quarter, and then to break these totals down into man-hours required during each quarter. We have illustrated this procedure in the schedule.

Cumulative direct labor man-hours, line 4, are found by multiplying the 1.0 million estimated man-hours for the first unit by the cumulative improvement curve factor from Table 11.10. Total man-hours for units delivered during the quarter, line 5, are computed by subtracting the cumulative hours for the prior quarter from the cumulative hours for the quarter. The 20 units produced by the end of quarter 7 would require 10.48 million man-hours, and the 5 units produced in quarter 6 require 3.74 million man-hours. The 15 units produced during quarter 7 would take $10.48 - 3.74 = 6.74$ million man-hours. This work is divided into 2.25 in quarter 5, 2.25 in quarter 6, and 2.24 in quarter 7, and entered in lines 6, 7, and 8.

From the total direct labor man-hours incurred in each quarter, line 9, we found the work force size, line 10 (assume 500 working hours per man

Figure 11.15 Airplane Project Manpower Schedule

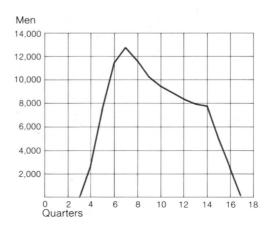

per quarter), which is plotted in Figure 11.15. We see that the work force size rises rapidly as the project gets under way, reaches a peak in quarter 7, and then gradually declines as the group gains experience.

Computation of a before-tax cash flow schedule uses these data and other cost data. Figure 11.16 illustrates a cumulative cash flow break-even graph for this project. For the financial analysis, we have assumed the following additional costs: average direct-labor costs of $4.00 per hour plus 50 per cent variable overhead, purchased materials costs of $1.3 million per plane plus 20 per cent variable overhead, and fixed administrative and marketing overhead costs of $15.0 million per quarter. Details of the cash flow projection are left as an exercise at the end of the chapter.

Figure 11.16 Airplane Project Cumulative Cash Flow

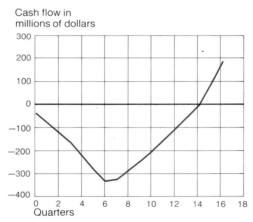

In Figure 11.16 we see that, although there is a net positive cash flow of $184 million for the entire project, the cumulative cash flow is negative until quarter 15. The maximum cumulative cash outflow is $330 million, and occurs in quarter 6. If the company goes ahead with the project, it must have this amount of money available.

The analysis of the project feasibility could be carried further to compute expected rate of return and to include a probability forecast of sales volume. These are suggested in the problems at the end of the chapter.

Other Uses

From the examples in this section, we see that improvement curve concepts have a wide range of potential applications. Although improvement curves originated in the aircraft industry, they have been found applicable in many other industries, such as shipbuilding and electronics.

An important use of improvement curve concepts is in management planning and control. Cost estimation, forecasting, scheduling, and project analysis based upon the improvement curve can be important inputs in performance evaluation of systems and system components. Improvement curve analysis can make a significant contribution by providing more objective information for management decision making.

The improvement curve, however, is not a universal panacea, nor is its application without difficulties. It is a statistical device designed to measure average improvement in a system. As such, it is subject to the limitations of the use of statistical averages and of attempts to predict human activity.

A vital prerequisite for the use of these concepts is to identify and accumulate the relevant cost information. Existing, sound cost-accounting systems can provide the necessary information when pertinent costs have been defined. Costs must be related to activities and production lots, which requires that standard cost data be kept continually current.

There is an apparent mathematical sophistication to the functions that describe improvement phenomena which may not be justified. This apparent sophistication can lead to blind acceptance or rejection. The validity of the analysis depends upon the factors used in it.

An improvement curve will not create improvement. System improvement depends upon a number of complex factors in the environment, such as the expectations of the people in the system and their willingness to continually seek improved performance. But when used with an understanding of its potential and limitations, the improvement curve can serve as an effective management tool in internal planning and control.

Summary

Scheduling specifies when and where conversion operations are to take place. Firms with seasonal demand for their products must determine aggregate operating schedules which specify the overall or total production, employment, and inventory levels for a future period of time. Some of the alternative methods of reacting to the seasonal demand pattern include changing production levels by hiring and laying off employees, changing production levels by the use of overtime, building up inventories during slack demand periods, subcontracting a portion of the demand, and adding secondary product lines which have counter-seasonal demand patterns.

After the aggregate schedule has been established, it is necessary to schedule the production of individual products within the constraints established by the aggregate schedule. The type of scheduling process employed depends upon the characteristics of the production process, particularly whether production is to fill a particular order or is made for inventory, and whether the process is continuous or intermittent.

A basic necessity for scheduling any type of conversion is a forecast estimate of the time required to perform each element of work. When improvement in processing can be expected, the total time is reduced. An estimate of the impact of such gains in efficiency can be predicted by using improvement curves.

Selected References

Buffa, E. S. *Production-Inventory Systems: Planning and Control.* Homewood, Ill.: Richard D. Irwin, Inc., 1968.

Conway, R. W., and Shultz, A. "The Manufacturing Progress Function." *Journal of Industrial Engineering,* January–February 1959.

This article provides a thorough background for evaluation of the improvement curve concept. The implications of the use of the improvement curve are based upon a study of the experiences of four companies.

Greene, J. H. *Production Control: Systems and Decisions.* Homewood, Ill.: Richard D. Irwin, Inc., 1965.

Hirschmann, Winfred B. "Profit From the Learning Curve." *Harvard Business Review,* January–February 1964, pp. 105–119.

The author discusses the improvement curve as a primary planning tool of management. He includes examples of its application to a variety of situations.

Holt, C. C., Modigliani, F., Muth, J., and Simon, H. *Planning Production, Inventories, and Work Force.* Englewood Cliffs, N.J.: Prentice-Hall, Inc., 1960.

Magee, J. F., and Boodman, D. M. *Production Planning and Inventory Control.* New York: McGraw-Hill Book Company, 1967.

Muth, J. F., and Thompson, G. L. *Industrial Scheduling.* Englewood Cliffs, N.J.: Prentice-Hall, Inc., 1963.

Young, Samuel, L. "Misapplications of the Learning Curve Concept." *Journal of Industrial Engineering,* August 1966, pp. 410–415.

The author presents an analysis of budgetary and other management directed influences which, in his opinion, may obscure the significance of the improvement curve.

Questions

1 What is the proper time horizon for production scheduling?
2 What are the alternative methods of accommodating seasonal demand and what are the costs of each alternative?
3 What is the effect of the "point of departure" in the aggregate production schedule?
4 How does the automatic control feature of the linear decision rule model work?
5 What are the economic factors that determine whether a product is produced on a continuous or an intermittent basis?
6 Why is it difficult to achieve close to 100 per cent utilization of labor input in an assembly line?
7 What is the most effective job shop scheduling decision rule?
8 Why is it difficult to follow an established schedule in a job shop?
9 What is the improvement curve concept, and how was it developed?
10 Under what states can the improvement curve concept be used effectively?
11 What factors account for the reduction represented by the improvement curve?

12 What degree of precision can be expected from improvement curve estimates?

13 Your company, the buyer, and a subcontractor, the vendor, have agreed on an 80 per cent improvement ratio, and on the proper number of direct labor hours for the first unit of an improved product. Up to the present time, 100 units of the earlier version have been produced. To whose advantage is it to treat this improved version as a completely new model and call the first unit number one on the improvement curve? To whose advantage is it to treat it as a continuation of a previous model, and call the first unit number 101 on the improvement curve?

14 What potential dangers can you foresee in applying the improvement curve concept? How can they be minimized?

Problems

1 The following linear decision rules have been derived for a firm:

$$P_t = \begin{matrix}(.5S_t) \\ (+.2S_{t+1}) \\ (+.1S_{t+2})\end{matrix} + .9W_{t-1} + 150. - .5I_{t-1}$$

$$W_t = \begin{matrix}(.020S_t) \\ (+.012S_{t+1}) \\ (+.008S_{t+2})\end{matrix} + .7W_{t-1} + 3.0 - .01I_{t-1}$$

One worker during regular time produces 7.5 units per month. Beginning inventory is 250 units. Beginning employment is 40.

a. Forecast sales are 300 units per month for every month throughout the year. Actual sales turn out as follows:

J	F	M	A	M	J	J	A	S	O	N	D
300	300	300	300	300	300	600	600	600	600	600	600

Calculate and plot graphically the production, employment and inventory levels for the year.

b. Suppose that the forecast had been perfect; that is, increase to the level of 600 units had been anticipated. Calculate and plot graphically the production, employment, and inventory rules for this situation.

2 An assembly line is to be set up (balanced). The operations required, their times required in minutes, and the ordering constraints (for example a before b and c; b before d and e; and so forth) are shown below:

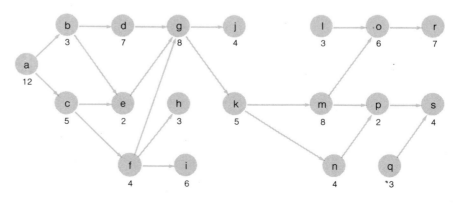

Each of these operations will be performed one at a time on the assembly line. The operations cannot be split between work stations on the line: that is, they must be contained wholly within one work station. One work station may, of course, do more than one operation if time permits.

a. If four assemblies are required per hour, what is the minimum number of work stations required? Obtain an optimal balance.

b. What is the efficiency of the schedule obtained in part (a)?

3 An assembly line has tasks as listed below:

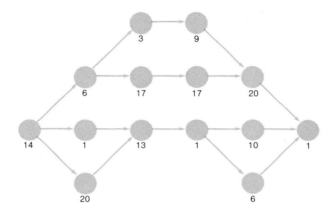

a. Three completed assemblies are required per hour. Balance the line.

b. What is the labor efficiency?

4 For a firm producing five different products on the same facilities:

Product	Annual Demand	Production per Shift	Inventory Carrying Cost	Setup Cost
1	5,000	100	1.00	40
2	10,000	75	.90	25
3	7,000	50	.30	30
4	15,000	80	.75	27
5	4,000	40	1.05	80

The firm has capacity to operate 3 shifts per day for 250 days per year. Determine:

a. The number of times each product is to be produced per year and the total costs when all products are produced on the same facilities.

b. The number of times each product is to be produced per year and the total carrying and setup costs if each product had a separate set of productive facilities with the same production rate as indicated above.

5 A firm produces five different products with the following characteristics on a single facility:

Product	Annual Demand	Production per Day	Inventory Carrying Cost	Setup Cost
1	80,000	1,600	.020	16.
2	110,000	2,200	.030	22.
3	40,000	1,600	.016	36.
4	180,000	2,400	.044	20.
5	70,000	2,000	.010	15.

The firm operates 250 days per year. Solve for (a) and (b) as in problem 4.

6 A company is preparing a cost estimate for 50 units of a special machined part. The company estimates that the first unit should require 230 man-hours, and that an 85 per cent improvement ratio is applicable. Compute the expected total man-hours for 50 units, average man-hours for the 50 units, and man-hours for the 50th unit. Plot the unit man-hour curve on a sheet of log-log paper.

7 Production of an initial order for 60 units of a new type of hydraulic system required a total of 2,474 man-hours and had followed a 75 per cent improvement ratio. An estimate is being prepared for a follow-on contract of 190 units.
a. Estimate the total and average man-hours for the follow-on contract.
b. Estimate the man-hours required for the first and last units of the follow-on contract.
c. Plot the unit values on a sheet of log-log paper.

8 The first unit of a production run of an item required 400 man-hours, and the first 50 units required a total of 4,924 man-hours. How many hours should the next 50 units require if the same rate of improvement applies? How many hours should the 100th unit require?

9 These questions relate to the airplane scheduling project described in the text:
a. Compute the annual before-tax cash flows and cumulative annual cash flows for the project.
b. Based upon the cash flows computed in part (a), determine the discounted cash flow rate of return for the project at the projected sales volume of 200 planes.
c. Assume that, instead of a single sales volume estimate of 200 units, the following forecast has been prepared showing a range of possible sales and estimates of the likelihood of achieving each:

Units	Probability of selling that quantity
160	.10
180	.20
200	.40
220	.20
240	.10

Discuss the implications of this additional information about the decision whether to proceed with the project. Prepare an analysis to support your conclusions.

10 Electronic Associate Company was preparing a bid on a contract to produce 180 electronic control units. Payment would be made as units were delivered in the month following delivery. The company purchasing agent estimated that purchased components and materials would cost $500 per control unit, and that one month would be required to order and receive materials. Payment for materials would be made in the month following receipt. The production manager estimated that the first control unit would require 1145 man-hours, and that work on the project would follow a 75 per cent improvement ratio. Preparation and tooling up before production could begin on the first unit would require one month and would cost $10,000. Direct labor and variable overhead would be $8.00 per direct labor hour. Fixed overhead would be $5,000 per month commencing with the beginning of actual production. A profit of 10 per cent on the selling price was desired. The production manager planned to assign 30 operators to the project. For planning purposes the company assumed that 165 working hours per operator were available each month.

a. Compute the bid price for the contract.

b. Prepare a production schedule for the project.

c. Prepare a cash-flow schedule for the project.

Chapter 12
Scheduling of Service and Transportation Systems

In goods-producing systems, the use of inventories dampens the effects of irregularities in the time patterns of inputs and outputs. Service systems, however, usually depend upon a unique input provided by the beneficiary of the service, and conversion or production cannot take place until that unique input is available. Inventories of services cannot be accumulated.

Because of the inherent time dependence of production in service systems, they typically cannot achieve the same level of efficiency in utilizing the time capacity of people and facilities as goods-producing systems can achieve. Some service systems approach full utilization of their resources by scheduling the arrival of the unique inputs provided by the "customer." Systems which provide medical (a doctor's office) and legal (lawyer's office) services and some transportation systems (scheduled trains, buses, and the like) fall into this category. The apparent internal efficiencies of these systems are substantially reduced when the time spent waiting by the "customer" before being served is considered. In other service systems, such as highways, hospitals, and supermarkets, very little control over the arrival of the "customer" exists and it may be necessary to provide sufficient capacity to serve peak loads even though peak load conditions exist only a very small proportion of the time and most of the facility remains idle most of the time. In this chapter, we will examine service systems in which little or no control over arrivals can be exercised and also transportation systems with fixed-schedule movement patterns.

Service Systems with Non-Controllable Inputs

The vast majority of service-producing systems exercise little control over the time of arrivals to the system. Although individual arrivals may follow specific time-behavior patterns, the overall pattern of arrivals for many service systems is completely random. Arrival patterns give rise to queuing or waiting line systems when they occur with some type of time distribution. Service or transformation is performed, again, over some kind of a time pattern, and the individuals leave the queuing system. Because of the uneven patterns of arrivals and service times, waiting lines are formed from time to time.

Queuing or waiting line analysis is a branch of probability theory. The original work was begun in 1905 by A. K. Erlang, a Danish telephone engineer. He viewed telephone service as a waiting line process with the telephone call arrivals being serviced on the telephone lines and exchanges. He investigated the effect of fluctuating service demand on the utilization of equipment. In the past twenty years queuing analysis has been applied to other kinds of problems, and today a wide variety of seemingly diverse processes are analyzed within the waiting line format.

Waiting lines are encountered frequently in normal daily existence. One joins a waiting line for service at a department store or a supermarket check-out counter, at a traffic stoplight, or at a bank. In other cases, the arrivals are things rather than people. For example, applications for entrance arrive at the admissions office of a university, orders for production arrive at a factory, and jobs arrive at a computer center for processing. In some cases, the service center goes to the waiting line. When someone calls a repairman to fix a home appliance, the repair order call joins the repairman's waiting line of jobs where it remains until the service center or the repairman reaches that point on the waiting line. The above are just a few examples. A very wide variety of situations fits the general waiting line model.

The methods used to describe and analyze waiting line systems depend upon the structure of the particular system. Some of the basic characteristics which vary from system to system include:

1. The number of servicing units. Variation exists in the number of channels and in the number of phases within a single channel—a single-phase system is mathematically the simplest. When the arrival has the option of going to any one of two or more servers, the system is multi-channel. When the arrival must be serviced by two or more servers in sequence, the system is multi-phase.

2. The size of the population from which arrivals come, whether it is finite or infinite. In a (small) finite population, the size of the waiting line materially affects the rate of arrival and makes mathematical analysis difficult.

3. The queue discipline, that is, whether arrivals will join the line if it is long, whether they will leave, whether some arrivals have priority over others, and so forth.

4. The distribution of time of arrivals. Arrival patterns may vary from constant time intervals to a completely random pattern.

5. The distribution of times required to perform the service.

Analysis of Waiting Lines

We can analyze queuing situations by at least three different methods. First, we may experiment physically with the queuing system and observe the results. For example, if an administrator is trying to determine the optimal number of ambulances to have at a hospital, it is a simple matter to try each of the various alternative numbers for a month, record the average time to respond to an emergency call and the costs of maintaining the ambulance service centers, and then make a decision about the best alternative. Such a method of decision making is obviously costly, but it is still by far the most common approach used in analyzing waiting line situations. To test this point, question your local supermarket manager or restaurateur about how he determines his employment level throughout the week.

Simulation is a second method of analyzing queuing problems. This technique requires the gathering of information on arrival and service patterns, costs, customer behavior, and the like. The analysis is conducted by manipulating a model of the real system, using a computer or a pencil and paper and employing the Monte Carlo sampling method. Simulation can result in a substantial improvement in predictability over experimentation with the real system and is being used with increasing frequency, particularly where the structure of the problem is complex.

Finally, queuing problems may be amenable to direct mathematical solution through the use of probability theory. Simulation and mathematical analysis of waiting lines will be considered in this chapter.

Random Arrival and Service Time Patterns

A variety of arrival patterns occur in practice. If arrivals are generated by a completely automatic machine, there may be a constant interval between arrivals such as curve (a) in Figure 12.1. If a human operator working on a machine generated the arrivals, there is likely to be some variation in the time interval between arrivals, and a distribution such as curve (b) may result. When arrivals are drawn from a large pool of potential arrivals, each operating independently of all the others, a random pattern, such as (c), will exist.

Figure 12.1 Arrival Distributions

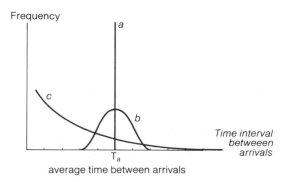

average time between arrivals

The random pattern of arrivals results in a relatively simple probability distribution. Since the random pattern frequently occurs in waiting line systems, we will examine it closely. Randomness does not mean that things happen at any time. The condition defining a random pattern of arrivals is that the probability of an arrival in the next time period is independent of the time the last arrival occurred. When arrivals are random, the number of arrivals in a time period is a random variable which follows the Poisson distribution, one of the most commonly encountered distributions in probability theory. The probability of exactly x arrivals per time period is

$$P(x) = \frac{\lambda e^{-\lambda}}{x!} .$$
(12.1)

where λ (lambda) is the average arrival rate and e is 2.718, the base of the natural logarithm. If $\lambda = 10$ arrivals per hour, the probability of any specific number of arrivals per hour as obtained from equation 12.1, or from Appendix Table F, is given in Table 12.1.

Corresponding to the Poisson arrival *rate* for random arrivals is a distribution of *times between arrivals*. It can be shown that this forms a negative exponential distribution such as curve (c) in Figure 12.1. The probability that no arrival occurs during the next t time units is

$$F_0(t) = e^{-\lambda t}$$
(12.2)

Thus, if $\lambda = 10$ arrivals per hour, the probability of having no arrival in the next three minutes is

$$F_0(\tfrac{1}{20}) = e^{-10(1/20)} = .606$$

The probability of at least one arrival during the next three minutes, regardless of when the last arrival occurred, is $1 - .606 = .394$.

Empirical research has shown that a wide variety of queuing situations have random arrival patterns including arrivals of customers at banks, barber shops, supermarkets and other stores, mechanics at tool cribs, failed machines at repair stations, telephone calls at an exchange, fire alarms at a fire department, or practically any situation where a large population of potential arrivals exists with each operating independently of the rest. Stating that the above situations have random arrivals does not imply that the rate is the same at all times. In many of the above cases, there are distinct changes in λ throughout the day or week. The supermarket for example has a much larger λ Friday afternoon than Tuesday morning, but within each of these periods the arrival pattern is still random.

The negative exponential distribution is sometimes described as the only probability distribution "without memory." That is, it does not help at all to know when the last event occurred in order to predict when the next event

Table 12.1 Probability of n Arrivals per Hour when $\lambda = 10/\text{hour}$

n	Probability of n Arrivals
0	.000
1	.000
2	.003
3	.007
4	.019
5	.038
6	.063
7	.090
8	.113
9	.125
10	.125
11	.114
12	.095
13	.072
14	.053
15	.034
16	.022
17	.013
18	.007
19	.004
20	.001
21	.001
22	.001
	1.000

will occur. This characteristic makes the distribution particularly attractive for use in queuing theory, since it substantially simplifies the mathematical description of the behavior of the waiting line.

The reader, in his first exposure to the negative exponential distribution often expresses surprise that the curve has the shape shown in curve (c) of Figure 12.1 rather than a horizontal straight line shape since the probability of an arrival in the next time period is independent of when the last arrival occurred. A simple example will demonstrate that the frequency of short time intervals between arrivals will be greater than the frequency of long intervals. The probability of an arrival during the next period is a constant (time independent). Say the probability of an arrival during the next minute is .1. The proportion of time intervals of one minute duration will then be .1. In only .9 of the time intervals will the system go beyond one minute without an arrival. The probability of an arrival during the next (second) minute remains .1, but since only .9 of the intervals get to the second minute the relative frequency of two minute intervals between arrivals is $(.1)(.9) = .09$. Continuing this example the relative frequency of three minute intervals will be $(.1)(.81) = .081$, and so on, giving the shape shown in curve (c) of Figure 12.1.

Random service rates also follow the Poisson distribution with a mean rate of μ (mu) services per unit time. Service times are exponentially distributed with average time of $1/\mu$. Random service time means that the probability of completing the service in the next time period is independent of when service began. Empirical research reveals fewer instances of exponentially distributed service times than exponentially distributed arrival times. There are, however, numerous cases in which variation is only slightly less than exponential for which the assumption of complete randomness will suffice. A distribution shown to be exponential is the length of local telephone calls. Thus, if we were attempting to estimate the average length of local telephone calls, we could measure the length of a sample of calls from start to completion, or we could begin measuring calls five minutes after they had begun until completion, or we could even begin measuring them at any random point in time until completion and always come up with the same average length. The implications of the last statement should be examined closely.

Derivation of Queuing Formulas

Consider the mathematically simplest waiting line case. Arrival and service times are random. The arriving population is infinite. All arrivals will join a queue and be served by a single service station on a first-come, first-served basis. We will now develop formulas describing the characteristics of the waiting line system such as

$$P_n = \text{probability of n units in the system}$$
$$L = \text{average number of units in the system}$$
$$L_q = \text{average number of units in the waiting line}$$
$$W = \text{average time that units spend in the system}$$
$$W_q = \text{average time that units spend in the waiting line}$$

where

$$\lambda = \text{average arrival rate}$$
$$\mu = \text{average service rate}$$
$$\rho = \lambda/\mu, \text{utilization parameter, rho}$$
$$\mu > \lambda$$

The probability of an arrival occurring in a very short interval of time Δt is $\lambda \Delta t$. The probability that a unit under service will be completed during time interval Δt is $\mu \Delta t$. With Δt very small we can ignore the possibility of two or more arrivals and/or services occurring during Δt since $(\Delta t)^2$ is sufficiently close to zero. Thus, only three things can occur during Δt, a net addition to the system of one by an arrival with probability $\lambda \Delta t$, a net reduction of one in the system by a service completion with probability $\mu \Delta t$, or a maintenance of the same number in the system by no arrivals or service completions with probability $1 - (\lambda \Delta t + \mu \Delta t)$. (Remember that the above is true only for random arrivals and service times.) The transition from one state to another during the time interval Δt is shown in Figure 12.2. Note the special situation for state 0 which arises because the state of having -1 in the system does not exist.

Figure 12.2 Rate of Transition in the Number of Units in the System

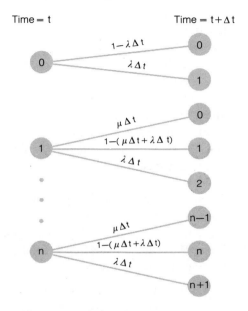

Probability of being in each ending state at time $t + \Delta t$, given each starting state at time t.

The state n can be reached at time $t + \Delta t$ by three paths: being in state $n - 1$ at time t and having an arrival (with probability $\lambda \Delta t$); being in state n at time t and having neither an arrival nor service completion [with probability $1 - (\lambda \Delta t + \mu \Delta t)$]; or by being in state $n + 1$ at time t and having a service completion (with probability $\mu \Delta t$). Since the three paths constitute all possible ways of arriving at state n, the probability of n in the system at time $t + \Delta t$ is

$$P_n = \lambda \Delta t P_{n-1} + [1 - (\lambda \Delta t + \mu \Delta t)]P_n + \mu \Delta t P_{n+1}. \tag{12.3}$$

Dividing by Δt and simplifying, we get:

$$0 = \lambda P_{n-1} - (\lambda + \mu)P_n + \mu P_{n+1} \tag{12.4}$$

where $n > 0$.

For the special case where $n = 0$, we have

$$P_0 = [1 - \lambda \Delta t]P_0 + \mu \Delta t P_1. \tag{12.5}$$

Dividing by Δt, produces

$$0 = -\lambda P_0 + \mu P_1. \tag{12.6}$$

Equations 12.4 and 12.6 are called difference equations and can be solved by successive substitution as follows:

$$P_1 = \lambda/\mu P_0$$
$$P_2 = (\lambda/\mu)^2 P_0$$
$$\vdots$$
$$P_n = (\lambda/\mu)^n P_0 \quad \text{for all } n \tag{12.7}$$

Thus, the values for all of the states are a function of state 0, that is, for no units in the system. A bit of deductive analysis will give us the value of P_0. If there are λ arrivals per hour and the system has the capacity for μ services per hour, the system will be busy λ/μ proportion of the time, or idle $1 - \lambda/\mu$. Thus,

$$P_0 = 1 - \lambda/\mu$$

and substituting into equation 12.7

$$P_n = (\lambda/\mu)^n (1 - \lambda/\mu). \tag{12.8}$$

Average Length of Lines and Waiting Times

Other characteristics of waiting lines may be required to analyze waiting line systems. The average number of units in the system, including the one being served, is

$$L = \sum_{n=0}^{\infty} n P_n$$

Substituing for P_n from equation 12.8 yields

$$L = \sum_{n=0}^{\infty} n(\lambda/\mu)^n (1 - \lambda/\mu)$$
$$= (1 - \lambda/\mu) \sum_{n=0}^{\infty} n(\lambda/\mu)^n.$$

The term $\sum_{n=0}^{\infty} n(\lambda/\mu)^n$ is an infinite geometric series with a sum of

$$\frac{(\lambda/\mu)}{(1 - \lambda/\mu)^2} .$$

Therefore

$$L = \frac{(1 - \lambda/\mu)(\lambda/\mu)}{(1 - \lambda/\mu)^2}$$

which reduces to

$$L = \frac{\lambda}{\mu - \lambda} . \tag{12.9}$$

We determine L_q, the mean number in the waiting line, by subtracting from L the average number being served. This is not 1 as it may first appear since the system is completely empty part of the time. With a capacity to serve μ per unit time and λ arrivals per unit time the service station is busy λ/μ proportion of the time, or the average number being served is λ/μ. Thus,

$$L_q = L - \lambda/\mu = \frac{\lambda^2}{\mu(\mu - \lambda)}. \tag{12.10}$$

We determine W, the average time in the system including the time being served, by dividing the average number in the system by the number that arrive each time period. This yields the average time each arrival spends in the system. Thus,

$$W = \frac{L}{\lambda} = \frac{1}{\mu - \lambda}. \tag{12.11}$$

The time spent in the system is spent either waiting or being served. W_q, the average waiting time, can be determined by subtracting the average service time from the average time in the system. Thus,

$$W_q = W - \frac{1}{\mu} = \frac{\lambda}{\mu(\mu - \lambda)}. \tag{12.12}$$

Queuing Problem

A new hospital is being designed in a downtown metropolitan area. The design team is trying to determine the amount of emergency ambulance equipment required in order to provide a reasonably fast response to emergency calls. The cost of waiting cannot be valued monetarily. The design team has established a policy to keep waiting to a bare minimum. An ambulance should be sent immediately to the vast majority of emergency calls. Because of the random nature of calls for service, the design team recognized that occasionally some calls would have to wait but the amount of waiting should never be more than a few minutes. Based on data from hospitals serving similar areas, the team estimated that the calls for emergency ambulance service would occur at random with an average of one per hour with about half due to accidents and the other half due to various illnesses. The time required to make the round trip and unload the ambulance was estimated as randomly distributed and at an average of one-half hour.

$$\lambda = 1 \quad \mu = 2$$
$$W_q = \frac{\lambda}{\mu(\mu - \lambda)} = \frac{1}{2} \text{ hour}$$
$$P_0 = \frac{\lambda}{\mu} = \frac{1}{2}$$

Although a single ambulance would be busy only half of the time, the average wait, W_q, before it could be sent to respond to an emergency call would be one-half hour, a time which was obviously too long.

Multiple Channel Queues

When more than one channel (ambulance) is available for service, the formulas derived for the single server case no longer apply. With the utilization parameter $\rho = \lambda/M\mu$, where M is the number of parallel channels, the queuing formulas are

$$P_0 = \frac{1}{\left[\sum_{n=0}^{M-1} \frac{(M\rho)^n}{n!}\right] + \left[\frac{(M\rho)^M}{M!(1 - \rho)}\right]} \qquad (12.13)$$

$$P_n = \frac{(M\rho)^n}{n!} \cdot P_0 \qquad \text{for } 0 < n < M \qquad (12.14)$$

$$P_n = \frac{M^M \rho^n}{M!} \cdot P_0 \qquad \text{for } n \geq M \qquad (12.15)$$

$$L_q = \frac{(M\rho)^{M+1}}{(M - 1)!(M - M\rho)^2} \cdot P_0 \qquad (12.16)$$

$$L = L_q + \frac{\lambda}{\mu} \qquad (12.17)$$

$$W_q = \frac{L_q}{\lambda} \qquad (12.18)$$

$$W = \frac{L}{\lambda}. \qquad (12.19)$$

Although the computations may become somewhat complicated in practice, Figures 12.3 and 12.4 have been developed which can be used by computing only ρ. Thus, it is not necessary to use formulas 12.14 through 12.19 although they do provide somewhat greater accuracy than reading values from Figures 12.3 and 12.4.

In our example, with 2 ambulances the utilization factor is

$$\rho = \lambda/M\mu = 1/2(2) = 1/4.$$

Reading from Figure 12.4, the average number in the waiting line is

$$L_q = .033$$

From equation 12.18, the average wait is

$$W_q = .033 \text{ hour} = 2.0 \text{ minutes}$$

Also, from equations 12.13, 12.14, and 12.15, we can find the probabilities of various numbers of units in the system:

$$P_0 = .600$$
$$P_1 = .300$$
$$P_2 = .075$$
$$P_3 = .019$$
$$P_4 = .005$$
$$P_5 = .001$$
$$\overline{}$$
$$1.000$$

With 2 ambulances in the system at least one would be busy .975 $(P_0 + P_1 + P_2)$ of the time. Thus .025 of the calls could not be serviced immediately. Although the average wait for all service calls is only 2 minutes, the average wait for the .025 which actually waited would be $2/.025 = 80$ minutes.

With 3 ambulances in service, $\rho = 1/3(2) = .167$ and from Figure 12.4:

$$L_q = .003$$
$$W_q = .003 \text{ hour} = 11 \text{ seconds}$$

With the system operating characteristics now determined, the choice between two or three ambulances could be made after a cost-benefit analysis.

Figure 12.3 Behavior of Multi-Channel Queuing Systems (Mean Number in System)

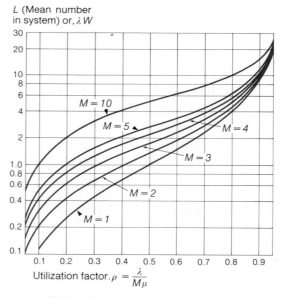

L (Mean number in system) or λW for different values of M, versus the utilization factor ρ. $L = \lambda W$.

Another alternative to the two-ambulance system is to equip one ambulance to specialize in accident calls and the other to specialize in emergency

Figure 12.4 Behavior of Multi-Channel Queuing Systems (Mean Number in Queue)

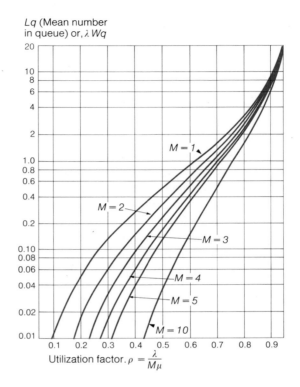

L_q (Mean number in queue) or λW_q for different values of M, versus the utilization factor ρ. $L_q = \lambda W_q$.

illness calls. Because of the specialized equipment used, the design team estimated that the average service time could be reduced from 30 minutes to 25 minutes. There would now be two separate single channel queuing systems each with

$$\lambda = .5 \text{ per hour} \quad \mu = \frac{60}{25} = 2.4 \text{ per hour}$$

$$W_q = \frac{\lambda}{\mu(\mu - \lambda)} = \frac{.5}{2.4(2.4 - .5)} = .110 \quad \text{hour} = 5.5 \text{ minutes}$$

Although the average service time was reduced from 30 to 25 minutes, the average waiting time increased from 2.0 to 5.5 minutes for the two separate queuing systems. This is not as surprising as it might at first appear. The increase occurs because there are times when the accident ambulance has calls waiting and the illness ambulance is idle and vice-versa. This does not occur when both ambulances are part of the same queuing system and each can handle either type of call.

Simulation Analysis of Waiting Lines

The structure of operating systems with unscheduled arrivals is often quite complex along one or more of the dimensions of waiting line systems mentioned earlier. In many cases the mathematical expressions describing the system behavior cannot be reduced to a solvable form.

We may use the process of simulation to analyze such service systems. Simulation provides a method of analyzing alternative system configurations and operating rules without touching the real physical system. A simulation model of the system is manipulated rather than the system itself.

Simulation has been used to analyze a wide variety of organizational systems. Within a physical production context, the operation of processes under various scheduling rules has been simulated. For example, operations of maintenance departments and inventory control systems have been studied. Within transportation organizations, simulation has been applied to determine scheduling and routing patterns and to select the proper number and kinds of vehicles. In a broader transportation context, traffic control systems, highway systems, and public transportation systems are often studied through simulation models. Even ecological systems within fields such as forestry and fisheries are being managed more effectively because of analysis by simulation.

Simulation is used for complex systems where mathematical analysis is too costly or complex. Examples are systems in which the arrival or service distribution did not comply with one of the simple standard forms for which analytical solutions have been developed, systems with a sequence of service operations required, or systems with some selection rule for determining service priority such as value or expected time for service. The development of simulation models for such systems is often quite simple although mathematical analysis may be extremely complex. The simulation model takes the random inputs to the system, moves them through the system according to the specified rules of operation, and sends them out of the system while periodically recording the important operating conditions being evaluated. Simulation models are extremely flexible and can be adapted readily to changing environmental and operating conditions.

Monte Carlo Sampling

The process of sampling from some random probability distribution is known as the Monte Carlo method, a name presumably adopted because the method is somewhat similar to the use of certain gambling devices. We will use the Monte Carlo method in the following example.

The Canadian government operates a tourist information service on a large highway a few hundred feet from the United States border. A study of the pattern of arrivals at the station during a certain portion of the day produced the distribution of times between arrivals shown in Figure 12.5. Since a clustering of cars often occurred at the customs station just before the information station, the arrival times were not random.

Figure 12.5 Time Between Arrivals Distribution to Nearest One Minute Interval

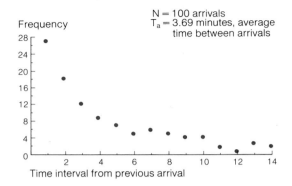

Figure 12.6 shows the distribution of times required for service that was revealed in a time study of the service to tourists. Analysis of the two distributions shows that the average time between arrivals is 3.69 minutes and the average time required for service is 6.00 minutes.

Arrivals at the station will occur according to the pattern of Figure 12.5 and will be serviced according to the pattern of Figure 12.6. Each individual arrival time and service time is a random variable from these patterns. In

Figure 12.6 Service Time Distribution

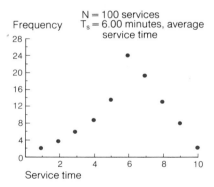

order to simulate the system, we must establish a process of taking random draws from these known distributions—the Monte Carlo process. In the Monte Carlo process all of the possible events, that is, times, are assigned to the outcomes of some random process in the same proportion as they occur in the distributions. The random process may be the spinning of a roulette wheel, drawing of numbered cards from a box, or some similar device. In practice a table of random numbers such as the one found in Appendix Table E is often used. As each random number is drawn, the corresponding point on the distribution is selected and that value is used in the simulation.

In our problem, Table 12.2 shows the assignment of random numbers. There are 100 two digit random numbers, each having a probability of .01 of being the next number drawn in a random process. In the arrival distribution, the probability that the next arrival occurs zero minutes from the last one is .04. Hence four random numbers (01, 02, 03, 04) are assigned to that event. An arrival one minute from the previous arrival has a probability of .27 and 27 random numbers (05–31) assigned, and so on.

Table 12.2 Assignment of Random Numbers to Specific Arrival and Service Times

ARRIVAL DISTRIBUTION			SERVICE DISTRIBUTION		
Time Interval from Previous Arrival	Probability	Random Numbers Assigned	Service Time	Probability	Random Numbers Assigned
0	.04	01–04	1	.02	01–02
1	.27	05–31	2	.04	03–06
2	.18	32–49	3	.06	07–12
3	.12	50–61	4	.09	13–21
4	.09	62–70	5	.14	22–35
5	.07	71–77	6	.24	36–59
6	.04	78–81	7	.18	60–77
7	.05	82–86	8	.13	78–90
8	.04	87–90	9	.08	91–98
9	.03	91–93	10	.02	99–00
10	.03	94–96		1.00	
11	.01	97			
12	.00	—			
13	.02	98–99			
14	.01	00			
	1.00				

Once the arrival and service times have been generated by the Monte Carlo process, the actual running of the simulation is a rather straight forward process of moving arrivals into the system, determining when they are serviced and recording the characteristics of the system that are of concern, such as the waiting time of the arrivals, the idle time of the servers, and the length of the waiting line.

In the case of the tourist information bureau, the government wants to maintain a sufficiently large staff so that the tourists can normally be served without lengthy waiting periods. At least two people will be required to man the station because arrivals occur at an average of every 3.59 minutes, and an average of 6.00 minutes are required for service. This service system is simulated for thirty arrivals in Table 12.3.

The simulation run of Table 12.3 is a test of one alternative level of capacity. An examination of the results shows that the average time between arrivals for the 30 arrival sample was 4.40 minutes. Since the average time between arrivals is known to be 3.59 minutes, a significant amount of error exists in the simulation. The error results because the sample size is too small. The precision of the measurements produced by simulation increases as the sample size increases. Although we cannot develop quite the same kinds of rules concerning simulation that we can develop to state the accuracy of statistical sampling for hypothesis testing or parameter estimation, we can take a few common sense measurements to test the accuracy of the simulation. The sample should be large enough so that the average arrival and service times in the sample comply with the known distributions, and the measurements of average waiting time and idle time should stabilize with only minor shifts in these values as the simulation continues. Usually a sample size of at least 200 is needed to satisfy these requirements.

Simulation may appear to be an expensive means of gathering information and evaluating alternatives, particularly considering the large number of samples required. However, after a little practice one quickly becomes adept at running the simulation and a run of size 200 can be carried out within an hour for a relatively simple system. Most complex systems are analyzed using a computer. Special simulation computer languages such as SIMSCRIPT, DYNAMO, and GPSS have been developed to ease the task of programming. For most systems, several years of operations can be simulated in less than a minute of computer time.

Simulation of Large Systems

The advantage of using simulation to analyze service systems is that it provides a means of testing alternative designs and operating rules for complex as well as simple systems. In the tourist information bureau example, the analyst could evaluate the difference caused by the addition of a third person to wait on arrivals. If a certain portion of the arrivals declined to wait for service when the waiting line reached a specified length, this factor could readily be added to the original simulation model and its importance measured. If the highway leading to the station is being improved and the flow of traffic is expected to increase by some proportion, the effect of the increased arrival rate can be determined in advance. For many complex service systems, simulation is the only tool available for analyzing behavior.

As an example of a more complex system, a flow chart of a service system for maintaining and repairing equipment is shown in Figure 12.7. Forty seconds of computer time were required to simulate 5,000 hours of operation for a system consisting of 5 machines.

Scheduling of Transportation Systems

Movement of goods and people constitutes a major portion of the activities of an advanced economy. Studies have shown that more than 50 per cent of the eventual production cost of goods is accumulated in movement and

Table 12.3 Information Booth Simulation

Arrival Number	Random Number	Arrival Interval	Arrival Time	Random Number	Service Duration	Server #1 Starting Time	Server #1 Completion Time	Server #1 Idle Time	Server #2 Starting Time	Server #2 Completion Time	Server #2 Idle Time	Waiting Time of Arrival	Number Waiting at Arrival Time
1	65	4	04	42	6	04	10	4				0	0
2	73	5	09	28	5				09	14	9	0	0
3	22	1	10	43	6	10	16	0				0	0
4	17	1	11	61	7				14	21	0	3	1
5	38	2	13	70	7	16	23	0				3	2
6	36	2	15	12	3				21	24	0	6	2
7	20	1	16	39	6	23	29	0				7	2
8	29	1	17	65	7				24	31	0	7	3
9	99	13	30	35	5	30	35	1				0	0
10	96	10	40	51	6				40	46	9	0	0
11	00	14	54	40	6	54	60	19				0	0
12	91	9	63	48	6				63	69	17	0	0
13	64	4	67	78	8	67	75	7				0	0
14	03	0	67	61	7				69	76	0	2	1
15	46	2	69	61	7	75	82	0				6	1
16	81	6	75	62	7				76	83	0	1	1
17	77	5	80	32	5	82	87	0				2	1
18	41	2	82	11	3				83	86	0	1	1
19	37	2	84	96	9				86	95	0	2	1
20	67	4	88	04	2	88	90	1				0	0
21	23	1	89	51	6	90	96	0				1	1
22	62	4	93	23	5				95	100	0	2	1
23	48	2	95	69	7	96	103	0				1	1
24	04	0	95	48	6				100	106	0	5	2
25	00	14	109	38	6	109	115	6				0	0
26	78	6	115	73	7				115	122	9	0	0
27	64	4	119	70	7	119	126	4				0	0
28	48	2	121	30	5				122	127	0	1	1
29	83	7	128	32	5	128	133	2				0	0
30	67	4	132	23	5				132	137	5	0	0
Totals		132			177			44			49	50	

Average Time Between Arrivals = 132/30 = 4.40 min.
Average Service Time = 177/30 = 5.90 min.

Figure 12.7 Simulation Model for Determining Operating Characteristics of Multi-Machine Maintenance System Under Alternative Maintenance and Repair Scheduling Rules

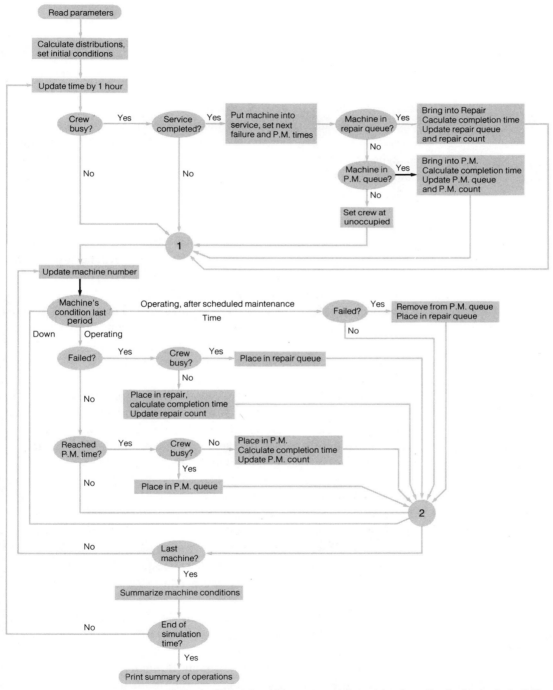

Source: R. C. Vergin, "Scheduling Maintenance and Determining Crew Size for Stochastically Failing Equipment," *Management Science* 13, no. 2 (October 1966): 59.

handling. This includes both the movement of materials and semi-finished goods from department to department within a single organization and the movement from one organization to another through the manufacturing-distributing chain. In addition, the cost of moving people is substantial, including the movement of people from their residences to their places of employment and the movement of people in the course of their work. Indeed, most computer time is spent in moving information from one internal location to another.

Many organizations are devoted completely to the movement of goods and people. The railroads, trucking and bus lines, airlines, and pipelines are obvious examples. Governmental agencies involved in designing and operating highway systems, airports, navigable waterways and port facilities, and public transportation systems are also concerned primarily with transporting goods and people. In other organizations in which transportation is not the primary concern, such as factories, schools, and construction, it is still of vital interest.

The transformation performed by the transportation firms is in the spatial dimension. Goods are moved to locations where they have increased value. People are moved to locations to which they desire to go. This transformation is also accomplished in a temporal dimension. The systems operate on time schedules and the movement itself requires time. The scheduling problem faced by an organization is to have its services comply as closely as possible in the spatial and temporal dimensions to the desires of its customers and to provide these services at a reasonable cost.

Goods and people are normally accumulated into "loads" and then transported together from one node to another in a transportation network. For example, a freight train leaves Kansas City bound for San Francisco every day at 3:00 p.m. All goods arriving at the freight station for shipment are accumulated until it is time for the train to leave. But this type of movement pattern does not follow the pattern of demand for transportation service in either the temporal or spatial dimensions. Each user desires service that will begin at his doorstep at precisely the time he is ready for it and terminate at the desired destination without any intermediate stops. Such a system would require a continuous flow of transportation capacity between every pair of nodes and is quite obviously impossible. At the other extreme, a transportation organization that provided infrequent service between inconvenient nodes would not receive much patronage no matter how economically the service was provided.

An economic relationship exists between the service provided and the usage the system will receive and also between service provided and the cost of providing it. This relationship is expressed graphically in Figure 12.8.

The horizontal scale is defined as simply the amount of transportation service provided by the organization, including both the number of nodes

Figure 12.8 Economics of Transportation Service

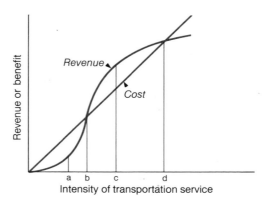

serviced and the frequency with which they are served. The units on the scale are merely dollars worth (including both the operating cost and the capitalized fixed cost) of transportation service, thus producing the straight line cost-service relationship. The revenue or value produced is not proportional to the cost of providing service. Some reasonable minimum amount of service is necessary for the system to be profitable. In Figure 12.8, the marginal cost of each new unit of transportation service is less than the marginal benefit until point (a) is reached. From (a) to (c), the slope of the revenue line is greater than the slope of the cost line, and the marginal revenue is greater than the marginal cost. The organization becomes profitable at point (b) with maximum profit at point (c). Beyond (c), the marginal revenue is less than marginal cost. Unprofitable service is now being added as excess nodes are served and too frequent trips occur. The familiar economic principle of diminishing returns applies to transportation organizations as well as to other types of systems.

Nodes that cannot be served economically by one transportation organization can be served profitably by either a less costly or a more costly system. For example, although construction of a limited access highway on a straight line between your place of residence and place of work may not be feasible, some secondary system of roads will allow you to make the trip. Or, although the city bus may not stop at your door, you can hire a taxi to do so. Paying a still larger amount, you can buy an automobile and hire a chauffeur so that not only are the spatial movements accomplished, but they are done without any waiting, completely satisfying the temporal dimension of transportation.

In designing the facilities and determining the operating schedule for a transportation organization, the designer should start with an analysis of the market—what are existing and future transportation needs and how well are they being met by existing organizations? From that point, the entire facility and schedule problem should be treated within a single analytical framework. Unfortunately, this usually proves excessively difficult because of the complexity of the system. Analysis of the overall problem one piece at a time is usually necessary and then the use of intuition and experience to blend the solutions to the pieces together to obtain a cohesive system.

We will consider analytical methods for some of the pieces of the problem in the remainder of this chapter. In many instances, part of the solution to the overall problem is specified and only one part remains. For example, a firm may have an existing fleet of vehicles and the problem is to maximize their usage. Or, the routing and frequency of trips may be specified by governmental agencies and the problem is to operate with the minimum number of vehicles.

Fixed Schedule Fleet Size Problem

Passenger service on railroads, buses, airlines, as well as some freight service, is provided on a fixed schedule. One need only consult a timetable to predict the movements within each system. If we follow the format established earlier in the book and describe a transportation system as a series of terminals or nodes and links connecting nodes, then a fixed schedule system would require the specification of arrival and departure times for each node and the link to be taken by the departing vehicles. This is a rather complex task and we will examine here some of the more manageable portions of this problem.

A ferry system runs between the mainland and two island terminals, as shown in the network in Figure 12.9. The indicated times include allowance

Figure 12.9   Ferry System Routing

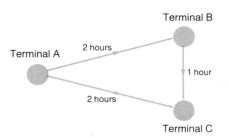

for unloading, traveling, and loading. Table 12.4 gives a fixed schedule for the system. The problem is to determine the minimum number of vessels required to service this schedule.[1] Although this simple case could undoubtedly be solved by inspection, larger, more complex problems of the same type may require more systematic analysis.

---

[1] The analysis of this problem is adapted from T. E. Bartlett, *An Algorithm for the Minimum Units Required to Maintain a Fixed Schedule* (La Fayette, Ind.: Management Sciences Research Group, Purdue University, 1956).

Table 12.4   Fixed Schedule for Ferry System

| TERMINAL A | | TERMINAL B | | TERMINAL C | |
Arrival	Departure	Arrival	Departure	Arrival	Departure
8	5	7	6	7	6
13	7	9	9	10	11
17	13	15	13	14	15
2	17	19	18	19	24

Note: Twenty-four hour day. For example, Terminal A has first arrival at 2 A.M. and first departure at 5 A.M.

The scarce resource whose consumption is being minimized can be stated as vessels or as vessel-hours. Determining the minimum number of vessel-hours required allows immediate conversion into the required fleet size. At any instant of time a vessel is either running or idle,

$$\begin{pmatrix} \text{Total vessel-hours} \\ \text{required} \end{pmatrix} = \begin{pmatrix} \text{Vessel-hours} \\ \text{running} \end{pmatrix} + \begin{pmatrix} \text{Vessel-hours} \\ \text{idle} \end{pmatrix}$$

Since the running time is irreducible, the only opportunity is to reduce idle time to a minimum by assignment of incoming ferries to outgoing trips.

The idle time for the entire system is simply the sum of the idle times at the individual terminals. As long as the given schedule is met, a change in idle time at terminal A will not affect idle time at terminal B. The system can thus be "cut up" and studied from the viewpoint of the individual terminals. Consider first the situation at terminal C. The simplest pattern is to assign incoming ferries to departures in the same order in which they arrive. Since none arrives before the scheduled six o'clock departure, that trip must be assigned to the last one arriving from the previous day.

Plan I	Arrival	Departure	Idle Time
	19	6	11
	7	11	4
	10	15	5
	14	24	10
Vessels held over = 1		Total Idle Time =	30

Several other plans are:

Plan II	Arrival	Departure	Idle Time
	14	6	16
	10	11	1
	7	15	8
	19	24	5
Vessels held over = 1		Total Idle Time =	30

Plan III	Arrival	Departure	Idle Time
	10	6	20
	19	11	16
	7	15	8
	14	24	10
Vessels held over = 2		Total Idle Time = 54	

Plan IV	Arrival	Departure	Idle Time
	7	6	23
	14	11	21
	19	15	20
	10	24	14
Vessels held over = 3		Total Idle Time = 78	

We see that idle time depends only upon the number of vehicles held over from one day to the next. As long as this number is held constant, any match of arrivals to departures will yield the same idle time. We show this relationship mathematically as follows:

$$a_{ij} = \text{time of } i^{th} \text{ arrival at terminal } j$$
$$d_{ij} = \text{time of } i^{th} \text{ departure from terminal } j$$
$$I_j = \text{vessel-hours of idle time at terminal } j$$
$$T = \text{length of scheduling period}$$

For plan I;

$$I_c = (d_{1c} - a_{4c} + T) + (d_{2c} - a_{1c}) + (d_{3c} - a_{2c}) + (d_{4c} - a_{3c})$$
$$= \sum_i d_{ic} - \sum_i a_{ic} + T.$$

In general, for K vessels held over,

$$I_j = \sum_i d_{ij} - \sum_i a_{ij} + KT.$$

This equation states that the total idle vessel-hours at the terminal can be found by adding up the departure times, subtracting the sum of the arrival times, and adding the product of the number of held-over vessels times the length of the scheduling period.

Clearly, the idle time depends upon K. The necessity of holding vessels over arises only when, at some time during the day, the number which has arrived is less than the number scheduled to depart up to that time. The difference must be made up of vessels held over from the previous day. The reader should verify that the minimum value of K at terminal A is one, and that at terminal B it is also one. The total idle vessel-hours for the system are

$$I = \sum_j \left\{ \sum_i d_{ij} - \sum_i a_{ij} + K_j T \right\} \quad (12.20)$$

where K_j refers to vessels held over at terminal j.

The running time can now be computed. If the ith departure from terminal j becomes the Kth arrival at terminal m, and the entire trip takes place within one scheduling interval, the running time is

$$a_{Km} - d_{ij},$$

or simply, arrival time minus departure time. The subscripts merely tie a particular arrival to a particular departing vessel.

If the running time begins in one period and arrives in the next, the running time is

$$a_{Km} - d_{ij} + T,$$

or, again, arrival time minus departure time, taking into consideration that the arrival is occurring in the next scheduling period (day). Adding the running times for the entire system gives

$$R = \sum_j \left\{ \sum_i a_{ij} - \sum_i d_{ij} \right\} + MT \quad (12.21)$$

where M is the number of trips which start in one period and are completed in the next. It is also the number of vessels which are in motion at the end of a scheduling period, although a trip extends over several scheduling periods (days).

The total fleet time is the sum of the idle and running times:

$$I + R = \sum_j K_j T + MT$$

since the arrival and departure time terms simply cancel out.

Dividing the fleet time by the length of the scheduling period gives the fleet size:

$$\frac{I + R}{T} = \sum_j K_j + M. \quad (12.22)$$

Verbally, the rule which has been formulated for finding the minimum fleet size to operate a fixed schedule is:

1. Find the maximum by which departures exceed arrivals during a scheduling period at each terminal. Add for all terminals.
2. Find the number of vessels in motion at the end of a scheduling period. The sum of these two numbers is the minimum fleet size.

Applying this rule to the network example will show that the minimum fleet size is four ferries. In addition, rather minor changes in the fixed schedule may reduce the required fleet size.

Fixed Schedule Departure Time Problem

Demand for transportation does not occur in a lump sum. Material or people arrive at a terminal singly or in small quantities desiring transportation to other terminals in the system. The transportation organization accumulates these arrivals and moves them together. It is a reasonable objective to have the scheduled departure times comply as closely as possible to the pattern of arrivals.

We will consider the specifications of departure times by studying a very simple system.[2] A fixed schedule will be designed for a single vehicle serving a two-node, single-link network. We will make a number of simplifying assumptions.

Assume that one departure will be made from each terminal during the scheduling period of length T. Assume also that the amount of material accumulating at a terminal never exceeds the capacity of the vehicle. We make these assumptions in order to keep the mathematical analysis simple. The methodology considered here can be expanded to relax these assumptions and to analyze more complex networks.

Our objective will be to minimize the amount of waiting time for departure of the arrivals. If we multiply the number of units that wait times the length of time they wait, we have the number of unit-periods of waiting.

We define:

$\bar{x}_{it}$ = average number of arrivals at terminal i during time period t

d_i = departure time from terminal i

$W(d_A, d_B)$ = average total unit-periods of waiting for a schedule with departures at d_A and d_B.

S = travel time between the two terminals; it is required that $2S \leq T$ in order that a round trip can be completed during the basic scheduling period, T.

To minimize waiting time, we must find values for two unknowns, d_A and d_B. The problem can be simplified even more if we specify a fixed layover period at one terminal. Let us state that the vehicle will arrive at terminal B and stay at B for a fixed length of time, Z, before leaving for terminal A. There is now just one unknown, d_A, the departure time from terminal A, since the departure time from terminal B will occur $S + Z$ hours after d_A,

$$d_B = d_A + S + Z.$$

The vehicle leaves terminal A, proceeds to terminal B for an interval of time, S, waits for Z time units, and departs for A. For any time period before

[2] This analysis is adapted from William T. Morris, *Analysis for Materials Handling Management* (Homewood, Ill.: Richard D. Irwin, Inc., 1962), pp. 33–40.

departure, or $t \leq d_A$, the material arriving at terminal A will wait $d_A - t$ time units before departing. Material arriving at terminal B during time period $t + S + Z$ will have the same length of time to wait before departure. (For example, if $S = 3$, $Z = 2$, $d_A = 6$, then $d_B = 6 + 3 + 2 = 11$ and material arriving at terminal A during time period $2(t = 2)$ would wait $d_A - t = 6 - 2 = 4$ periods. Similarly, material arriving at terminal B at $t + S + Z = 2 + 3 + 2 = 7$ would wait $d_A - t = 4$ periods.) The same approach suggests that material arriving at terminal A after departure for values of $t > d_A$ will have to wait through the end of the current scheduling period until departure the next scheduling period, or for time $T - t + d_A$. Material arriving at terminal B during period $t + S + Z$ will have the same wait, $T - t + d_A$, before departure.

We define:

$$X_t = \bar{x}_{A,t} + \bar{x}_{B,t+S+Z}$$

The first term is the average number of arrivals at terminal A during period t, and the second is the average number of arrivals at terminal B during the period $S + Z$ time units later, all of which will wait the same number of hours, either $d_A - t$ or $T - t + d_A$. Now, the function to be minimized is

$$W(d_A) = \sum_{t=1}^{d_A} X_t(d_A - t) + \sum_{t=d_A+1}^{T} X_t(T - t + d_A) \qquad (12.23)$$

where the first term gives the total amount of waiting for the units which arrive before departure time, each of which waits $d_A - t$ hours, and the second term gives the total amount of waiting for the units which arrive after departure time, each of which waits $T - t + d_A$ hours, at each respective terminal.

We now desire a value for d_A which will minimize the equation. Since we have assumed that time is a discrete variable, we do not have a continuous function with a first derivative. Instead, we must use the following conditions which characterize the points at which this function reaches its (local) minima. If D_A is a value of d_A for which the function reaches a local minimum, it must be true that

$$W(D_A + 1) - W(D_A) \geq 0$$

and

$$W(D_1 - 1) - W(D_1) \geq 0.$$

These two statements simply say that if D_A yields a minimum waiting time, the departure from terminal A in either the period before or the period after will have more waiting time. Taking the first of these conditions, we have:

$$W(D_A + 1) - W(D_A)$$

$$= \sum_{t=1}^{D_A+1} X_t(D_A + 1 - t)$$

$$+ \sum_{t=D_A+2}^{T} X_t(T = t + D_A + 1) - \sum_{t=1}^{D_A} X_t(D_A - 1)$$

$$- \sum_{t=D_A+1}^{T} X_t(T - t + D_A)$$

This reduces to

$$X_{D_A+1} \leq \frac{\sum_{t=1}^{T} X_t}{T} \tag{12.24a}$$

The second condition yields by a similar process the result:

$$X_{D_A} \geq \frac{\sum_{t=1}^{T} X_t}{T} \tag{12.24b}$$

This pair of inequalities, then, specifies the conditions which must be met by the minimizing values of d_A. The term on the right-hand side of these expressions is simply the average amount of material becoming available for shipment in the system per period. The inequalities require that we find a departure time such that the average amount of material becoming available at each terminal in the periods of departure is greater than or equal to the overall average amount (equation 12.24b), and that the average amount becoming available in the periods just after the departure is less than or equal to the overall average amount (equation 12.24a). Our intuition about the problem confirms this suggestion to some extent.

Consider a plant which divides the day into six four-hour planning periods, and the plant manager wishes to set up a fixed schedule for a single round-trip movement from the terminal point in the plant's production process (terminal A) to its warehouse (terminal B). At the warehouse, incoming material is picked up for delivery to the plant. Measuring time in four-hour intervals, suppose

$$T = 6$$
$$S = 2$$
$$Z = 1$$

then,

$$X_t = \bar{x}_{A,t} + \bar{x}_{B,t+3}.$$

The basic data on demand and the resulting values of X_t are given in Table 12.5.

Table 12.5 Average Number of Units Arriving at Points A and B During Each Hour

t	$\bar{x}_{A,t}$	$\bar{x}_{B,t}$	X_t
1	25 units	12 units	60 units
2	34	21	50
3	18	12	42
4	26	35	38
5	38	16	59
6	21	24	33
Totals	162	120	282

Thus, for example, if departure from A is scheduled at the end of hour 1, then departure from B will occur at the end of hour 4, and X_1 is equal to the 25 units that arrive at terminal A during hour 1 plus the 35 units that arrive at terminal B during hour 4, all of which would wait 0 hours.

The overall average amount of material becoming available per period is

$$\frac{\sum_{t=1}^{T} X_t}{T} = \frac{282}{6} = 47.$$

We then wish to find a value of $t = D_A$ such that

$$X_{D_A+1} \leq 47$$
$$X_{D_A} \geq 47.$$

An examination of the right-hand column of Table 12.5 indicates that there are two departure times which satisfy these conditions, $D_A = 2$ and $D_A = 5$. The problem thus exhibits two local minima, and we must compute the actual unit-periods of waiting for each in order to obtain the absolute minimum. By plugging both $D_A = 2$ and $D_A = 5$ into equation 12.23, we get

$$W(D_A = 2) = 665 \text{ unit-periods}$$
$$W(D_A = 5) = 677 \text{ unit-periods.}$$

Thus, the best departure time from terminal 1 is at time $t = 2$, and this will result in a departure time from terminal 2 at $t = 5$.

Management may also be interested in the effect of changing the layover time at terminal 2. Again, changing the values for Z in equation 12.23 produces the following:

Z	D_A	$W(D_A)$
0	2	641 unit-periods
1	2	665
2	2	641

In this simple problem, a layover at terminal B of 0 or 2 hours would be preferable to the originally chosen value of 1 hour.

**Optimal
Routing
Problem**

A frequently encountered problem is to determine the shortest route through a network in which each node is linked to every other node and each node must be passed through once and only once with a return to the starting node at the end. This is commonly known as the traveling salesman problem. The problem occurs when a salesman has to travel to each of n cities in his territory once during a time period and then return to his starting base. The problem also occurs frequently in scheduling various transportation organizations. Repairmen making house calls and other delivery men face this problem. Within a factory, materials handling systems are sometimes designed to operate on a fixed path passing through each department once. Even in scheduling the sequence of orders passing through a facility, the traveling salesman situation is encountered. Consider, for example, the ordering of jobs going through a computer system. The time required to set up or make ready the computer system for each job is dependent on which job precedes it. The objective here is to minimize the total set-up time for all jobs as each is passed through the system once.

Although the problem statement is simple, the solution is difficult. With n nodes, there are $(n - 1)!$ different tours through the network so that complete enumeration is possible for only rather small problems. Several attempts have been made to solve the problem with varying degrees of success. The method illustrated here is called a branch and bound technique.[3]

The basic method is to break up the set of all possible tours into smaller and smaller subsets and to calculate for each subset a lower bound on the cost or length of the best tour in the subset. The subsets of tours are represented as nodes of a network and the process of partitioning as a branching of the network.

The costs of the traveling salesman problem form a matrix. Let $C(i,j)$ be the cost of going from city i to city j. We will solve the six-city problem shown in Figure 12.10.

The branching process begins with a node which contains all possible tours. At the first branch the tours are subdivided into those in the (i,j) node and those in the $(\overline{i,j})$ as shown in Figure 12.11. The (i,j) node contains all the tours which include the city pair i to j in them, and the $(\overline{i,j})$ node represents all tours that do not. At the (i,j) node there is another branching. The node containing $(\overline{k,l})$ represents all tours that include (i,j) but not (k,l), whereas (k,l) represents all tours that include both (i,j)

[3] J. D. C. Little, et al., "An Algorithm for the Traveling Salesman Problem," *Operations Research* 11, no. 6 (November–December 1963).

Figure 12.10   Cost Matrix for a Six-City Problem

	To					
	1	2	3	4	5	6
1	∞	27	43	16	30	26
2	7	∞	16	1	30	25
3	20	13	∞	35	5	0
4	21	16	25	∞	18	18
5	12	46	27	48	∞	5
6	23	5	5	9	5	∞

From (rows 1–6)

A typical tour might be $t = [(1,3)(3,2)(2,5)(5,6)(6,4)(4,1)]$, which has the cost (length) $= 43 + 13 + 30 + 5 + 9 + 21 = 121$.

and (k,l). In general, by tracing from a node, X, back to the start, we can pick up which city pairs are committed to appear in the tours of X and which are forbidden from appearing. If the branching process is carried far enough, some node will eventually represent a single tour. Notice that at any stage the terminal nodes of all branches represent all possible tours.

Figure 12.11   Branching of Tours in Subdivisions

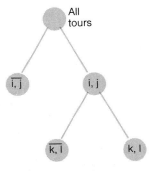

A useful concept in constructing lower bounds is that of reduction. If a constant, h, is subtracted from every element in a row of the cost matrix, the cost of any tour under the new matrix is h less than under the old matrix, because every tour must contain one and only one element from that row. The relative cost of all tours is unchanged, however, and so any tour that is optimal under the old will be optimal under the new matrix. The same possibility exists for reduction by columns. In our six-city problem, the process of subtracting the smallest number in each row from all numbers in the row and then proceeding by columns gives the matrix in Figure 12.12. The total reduction is 48; therefore, the cost of each of the tours is at least 48.

Figure 12.12 Cost Matrix After Reducing Rows and Columns

	1	2	3	4	5	6
1	∞	11	27	0 ⑩	14	10
2	1	∞	15	0 ①	29	24
3	15	13	∞	35	5	0 ⑤
4	0 ①	0 ⓪	9	∞	2	2
5	2	41	22	43	∞	②
6	13	0 ⓪	⑨	4	0 ②	∞

Circled numbers are values of $a(i,j)$.

Having reduced the matrix, we can begin the branching process. The goal in branching is to split each branch into one subset which is likely to include the best tour of that branch and another subset which is quite unlikely to include it. Possible low cost tours to consider are those involving an (i,j) for which $c(i,j) = 0$, that is, one with a zero relative cost between a city pair.

Now, consider all tours that do not contain (i,j). Since city i must connect to some city (other than city j), these tours must incur at least the cost of the smallest number in row i, excluding $c(i,j)$. Since city j must be reached from some city (other than city i), the tours must incur at least the cost of the smallest number in column j, excluding $c(i,j)$. Call the sum of these two costs $a(i,j)$. We shall choose as our branching city pair the one with the largest $a(i,j)$ from among those with $c(i,j) = 0$.

For the example, the $a(i,j)$ values are written in small circles placed in the cells of the zeroes of Figure 12.12. The largest is a $(1,4) = 10 + 0 = 10$ and so $(1,4)$ will be the first city pair used for branching. For the node $(\overline{1,4})$ the lower bound is now $48 + 10 = 58$ and the node is so labeled in Figure 12.13.

We can reduce the matrix further. Since the city pair $(1,4)$ is now committed to the tours, row 1 and column 4 are no longer needed and are deleted as shown in Figure 12.13. We can now set $c(4,1) = \infty$ since we cannot go from city 1 to city 4 and then immediately back to city 1. Looking for

Figure 12.13 (A) Matrix After Deletion of Row 1 and Column 4 (B) First Branching

	1	2	3	4	5	6
1	∞	11	27	0	14	10
2	0 +	∞	14 ~~15~~	0	28 ~~29~~	23 ~~24~~
3	15	13	∞	35	5	0
4	∞	0	9	∞	2	2
5	2	41	22	43	∞	0
6	13	0	0	4	0	∞

A

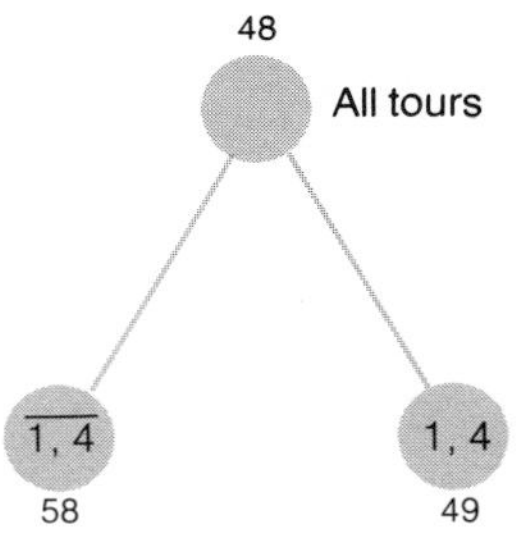

B

further reductions, we find that row 2 can be reduced by 1. This gives a lower cost bound for (1,4) of 48 + 1 = 49, as shown.

The same branch and bound technique is continued step-by-step until a complete tour is established with one entry from every row and column. The next node selected for branching is the one with the smallest lower bound. This leads to the fewest branches in the network. For our example, we would next select city pair (2,1). We could now delete row 2 and column 1 from the matrix. All of the tours on this node now include movement from city 2 to city 1 to city 4 as part of the route. Thus we can now also delete city pair (4,2) from the matrix, because movement from city 4 to city 2 would return us to a city which was previously visited without going to all the other required cities. We continue branching until we have the tour on the right hand branch of Figure 12.14. That tour would be from 1 to 4 to 3 to 5 to 6 to 2 and back again to 1.

Now we go back to examine those paths with lower bounds less than 63 to see if a better solution exists. Node $(\overline{1,4})$ has a lower bound of 58. After the next branching, both nodes have lower bounds at least as large as 63 and the problem is finished.

Of the $(n - 1)!$, or 120 different tours, we have selected the best one and have shown that all others are more costly. The larger the problem the more obvious the advantage of this method of systematically eliminating the nonoptimal tours. Computational times grow exponentially as the size of the problem increases. Problems of 10 cities can be solved by hand in approximately one hour. Experience with computer solution shows that a twenty-city problem takes a few seconds, a thirty-city problem requires about one minute, and a forty-city problem more than 8 minutes.

Figure 12.14 Final Network

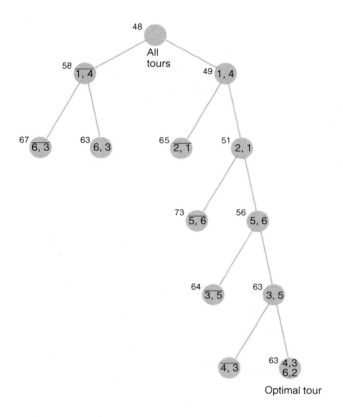

Optimal tour

**Expanding
the Analysis**

For reasons of mathematical simplicity, we have deliberately worked with highly simplified and fragmented versions of the system design and scheduling problem. The next series of steps involves refinement and enrichment, moving toward a more realistic analysis of the particular problem faced by the analyst. We might attempt to expand consideration to more terminals, to allow any number of departures per scheduling period, or to several different kinds of vehicles. Each attempt to make the analytical framework more general and more inclusive will make analysis more difficult.

Because of the difficulty of building large-scale models for transportation system and solving them mathematically, simulation also has been employed extensively in transportation scheduling problems. For example, airlines are faced with service to dozens of terminals, with several different types of airplanes of varying speed and capacity, with a multitude of rates, and with service demand that varies with the time of day, the day of the week, and month by month with different patterns between different terminals. The system schedulers find that simulation is the only available tool that can handle all of these variables at the same time.

The use of simulation does not preclude the use of the analytical models. Simulation only evaluates the schedules established by the analyst; it does not formulate the schedules. The analyst can use the analytical models to assist him in formulating the schedules that will be evaluated.

Summary

Some systems are designed to perform services rather than produce physical products. Transformation cannot usually take place in service systems until some unique input is provided by the beneficiary of the service. Some service systems, such as transportation systems, are able to maintain a high level of utilization of their facilities by requiring the customers to modify their service demands to fit the established transformation schedules. Scheduling problems faced by such systems include selection of the proper kind and quantity of transporting equipment and the determination of the times and the routes of movement. Other service systems, such as retailing organizations and fire-fighting organizations, can exercise little or no control over the arrival of the customer. The primary scheduling problem faced in these systems is to select the proper level of capacity to provide efficient service. The methodology of waiting line analysis is useful for such decisions.

Selected References

Cox, D.R., and Smith, W.L. *Queues.* London: Methuen and Company, 1961.

Morse, P.M. *Queues, Inventories and Maintenance.* New York: John Wiley and Sons, 1958.

Panico, J.A. *Queuing Theory.* Englewood Cliffs, N.J.: Prentice-Hall, Inc., 1969.

Saaty, T.L. *Elements of Queuing Theory.* New York: McGraw-Hill Book Company, 1961.

Questions

1 How does the level of operating efficiency of a service-producing system compare to that of a goods-producing system?

2 What are "random" arrivals?

3 What are the advantages of simulation for analyzing waiting line systems over direct mathematical analysis?

4 Why is the difference between L, the average number of units in the system, and L_q, the average number of units waiting, not equal to one?

5 Compare the efficiency of a single large (fast) service station with several small (slow) service stations from a waiting line point of view.

6 How is the problem of determining the minimum fleet size related to the problem of determining the schedule departure times?

7 How efficient would the rule, "pick the closest city," be in the traveling salesman problem?

Problems

1 A process has a random arrival rate with $\lambda = 4$ arrivals per hour.
   a. What is the probability that exactly 4 arrivals will occur in a given hour?
   b. What is the probability of more than 5 arrivals during a given hour?
   c. What is the probability of no arrivals during a 15-minute span immediately following an arrival?
   d. What is the probability of no arrivals during the next 15-minute span, given that 15 minutes have passed since the last arrival?

2 A small bank employs only one teller. Arrivals occur at the rate of 10 per hour, and are Poisson-distributed. How fast must the teller work in order to assure that the average customer will not have more than 5 minutes in line before being served? The length of service is exponentially distributed.

3 Cars arriving at a toll booth at a bridge are Poisson-distributed with an average of 20 seconds between arrivals. Toll collection time is distributed exponentially with an average of 6 seconds.
   a. What is the probability that an arrival will have to wait?
   b. The bridge authority will install a second toll booth when average waiting time reaches at least 20 seconds. By how much must the arrival rate be increased in order to justify a second toll booth?

4 A port has docking facilities for unloading and loading ships with capacity to handle two ships at a time. Ships arrive randomly at the rate of 5 per week, and the unloading rate is 2 ships per man-week. The time to unload and load a ship is inversely proportional to the number of workers on it. Unloading times are exponentially distributed. Currently, the entire crew of longshoremen works on the same ship until it is completed. Each man on the crew is paid $200 per week. The cost of an idle ship is estimated at $1000 per week.
   a. What is the optimal crew size and the average weekly cost?
   b. What change would occur in average weekly cost if the men were split into two crews?
   c. What advantages and disadvantages are there to such a split?

5 In the single-channel waiting-line system, with random arrivals and exponential service times, suppose that there were a limit to the waiting line of 2 spaces. Thus, if arrivals occur when there are two waiting, they cannot be accepted into the system, and will simply be sent to an external system. Derive the formula describing the average number of arrivals in the system in terms of λ and μ.

6 Consider the tourist information booth in the chapter. Use simulation to answer the following questions. Each question is independent of the others.
   a. If half the arrivals declined to wait when two or more arrivals were waiting, what proportion of the arrivals would not be served?
   b. What would average waiting time be with three servers.
   c. What would average waiting time be if the arrival rate doubled and three (or four) servers were used?

7 Check the answers produced by the waiting line formulas for the ambulance problem by simulating the waiting line operations.

8 Consider the following three-terminal transportation network.

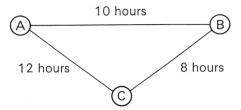

The schedule of departures is:

From A to B	3:00 AM
A to C	1:00 PM
A to B	11:00 PM
B to A	8:00 AM
B to C	4:00 PM
B to A	12:00 AM (midnight)
C to B	12:00 PM (noon)
C to A	12:00 AM (midnight)

a. Find the minimum number of vehicles required.
b. Cut travel time in half. Find minimum number of vehicles required.
c. Determine the percentage utilization of vehicles.

9 For the departure time problem in the chapter, determine departure time when the holdover time, 2, is two hours; also for $z = 0$ hours.

10 The following table gives the average number of parcels arriving at each of two cities for shipment to the other.

Hour	Arrivals at City A	Arrivals at City B
1	14	42
2	18	18
3	17	19
4	23	40
5	22	16
6	18	14
7	19	23
8	27	25

Travel time between the two cities is one hour.
a. Determine the best time for departures if one round trip is to be made per day between the cities.
b. How much would waiting time be reduced if four round trips were made per day with the same vehicle?

11 Using the mileage chart on page 442, solve the traveling salesman routing problem for any six (or seven, or eight, etc.) cities.

	Boston	Chicago	Cleveland	Denver	Detroit	Los Angeles	Miami	Minneapolis	New York	Philadelphia	San Francisco	Seattle
Boston		994	631	1997	699	3042	1542	1377	216	304	3162	3024
Chicago			341	1013	272	2092	1374	412	841	760	2187	2055
Cleveland				1366	167	2411	1310	746	507	426	2531	2393
Denver					1318	1157	2074	846	1866	1785	1264	1357
Detroit						2363	1381	698	667	586	2483	2345
Los Angeles							2733	1942	2797	2716	405	1170
Miami								1705	1336	1239	3072	3403
Minneapolis									1246	1165	1993	1637
New York										92	3031	2883
Philadelphia											2950	2812
San Francisco												845
Seattle												

Chapter 13
System
Dynamics

We may make two observations about the dynamics of system behavior. First, behavior of an organization is a result of the combined effect of individual decisions made throughout the organization. What appears to be, by itself, a wise decision may, when taken together with other decisions, have an adverse effect on the total organization. It is important to consider not only the initial impact of particular decisions, but also their effect in combination with others throughout the system.

Second, decisions must be evaluated on the basis of their impact on the organization over time. When we evaluate these time-based effects of decisions, it becomes apparent that time lags in the system have an important and indeed often overriding impact on outcome. Thus, we must consider not only actions occasioned by a decision, but also reactions of other components of the system and continuing interactions. The decision maker who must operate within this framework is concerned with dynamic system behavior, and not just with the projected outcome of some static analytical model.

Our knowledge of the effects of time lags has been quite limited until recently, even though the problem has long been recognized and a good deal of attention has been given to it. Recent literature on inventory theory has dealt with the effects of time lags. Queuing theory considers time lags and their effects on waiting time and idle time in a service system. Several economists have dealt with dynamic economic systems in the context of such things as trade-cycle models and the interindustry analysis suggested by input-output models.

Several interrelated developments have made it possible to evolve a methodology for analyzing the dynamics of socioeconomic system behavior. These developments include information feedback control theory or servomechanism theory which is the basis of cybernetics, simulation techniques which permit study of system dynamics, large digital computers which permit simulation of large-scale complex systems, and clearer understanding of managerial decision-making processes.

One important approach to analysis of system behavior is industrial dynamics developed at Massachusetts Institute of Technology by Jay W. Forrester. Industrial dynamics is a methodology for studying the role of decision makers in an interactive dynamic environment. It focuses on feedback structure and behavior in complex social systems. Forrester has defined industrial dynamics as:

> Industrial dynamics is the study of the information feedback characteristics of industrial activity to show how organizational structure, amplification (in policies), and time delays (in decisions and actions) interact to influence the success of the enterprise. It treats the interactions between the flows of information, money, orders, materials, personnel, and capital equipment in a company, an industry, or a national economy.
>
> Industrial dynamics provides a single framework for integrating the functional areas of management—marketing, production, accounting, research and development, and capital investment. It is a quantitative and experimental approach for relating organizational structure and corporate policy to industrial growth and stability.[1]

Feedback Systems

Feedback is the basis for self-regulating control systems. Such systems have a closed loop structure in which information about past activities of the system is fed back to a control center to regulate future activities. If feedback is negative, we have a homeostatic goal-seeking system. Deviations from the goal call up an opposing reaction to correct the deviation. If feedback is positive we have a growth system in which deviation is amplified.

A nuclear chain reaction is an example of positive feedback. Increases in animal populations are another. Two mature members of a species produce more than two offspring, who, when they mature, can produce more offspring. Unless the cycle is interrupted or retarded by limitations in food supply or predators, the population would grow at an exponential rate. The growth of cities, companies, and products are still other examples.

Feedback loop structures are found in biological and many mechanical systems, but our concern here is with feedback in social systems which involve interactions of individuals and groups. These groups range from small work groups to departments, business enterprises, governmental enterprises, and even national economies. When we view such groups from a systems perspective, we see that they are comprised of complex interactive information feedback networks.

Because all managerial decisions are made in the context of information feedback systems, decision makers must understand the structure and dynamic behavior of those systems. Engineers have generally studied be-

---

[1] J. W. Forrester, *Industrial Dynamics* (Cambridge, Mass.: The M.I.T. Press, 1961), p. 13. Copyright © 1961 by the Massachusetts Institute of Technology.

havioral characteristics of feedback systems by using complex formal mathematics. The mathematics are not only quite difficult, but are not adequate to the study of very complex systems. We will examine some of the fundamental concepts of system behavior through a simulation approach, and we will illustrate applications of information feedback concepts to many different types of socioeconomic systems.

Structural Characteristics of Feedback Systems

There are two fundamental components of feedback system structure: states and activities. The states of a system exist at points in time and change as a result of activities during some time period. Information about the state of the system is fed back and used to regulate future activities. In industrial dynamics models states and activities are called levels and rates.

Levels are the condition of the system and are accumulations of system resources. These resources include amounts of information, inventories, people, money, orders, and capital equipment. In information flows, levels represent information about past activities or events, such as the average sales rate for last month. Information levels may also exist as accumulations of ideas such as levels of confidence or satisfaction.

Rates are the activities or flows of the system, such as transmission of information, receipt and shipment of goods, arrival and departure of people, receipt and payment of money, and acquisition and disposal of capital equipment. Decision functions determine current rates based upon information about the state of the system.

Social systems are complex because they are comprised of multiple nonlinear feedback loops which are interconnected and interact with one another. Within a system we may find both positive and negative feedback loops, many of which will be of high order. The order of a feedback loop refers to the number of levels or accumulations present within the loop. We can study the dynamic behavior of social systems made up of multiple nonlinear feedback loops through simulation.

Some of the most important characteristics of system structure are the time lags or delays that exist in every activity. Time lags represent delays in flows through a system, such as in movement of goods, people, or information. In models which we shall examine, time lags are introduced by accumulations or reservoirs.

Information-Feedback Decision System

In Chapter 2 we discussed decision making as part of a complex feedback process and portrayed the feedback structure of the decision process in Figure 2.2. The decision-making process is composed of goal-seeking activities which attempt to bring the state of a system into conformity with a desired state. We will examine that decision process more closely in the context of a feedback loop structure.

The basic structure of an information feedback decision system, portrayed in the form of a flow diagram in Figure 13.1, is comprised of three primary functions in the feedback loop: the decision function which regulates activity, the action stream or flow which alters the system state, and information about the state of the system which is fed back to the decision function. The decision function is a goal-seeking process which attempts to correct differences between the perceived system state and the desired state. In the flow diagram, system levels are represented by rectangles, rates by valve symbols, information flows by dashed lines, and material flows by solid lines.

Figure 13.1   Basic Information-Feedback Decision System

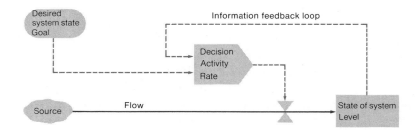

Decisions are based upon information about the state of a system, and not directly on its true state. The decision process may be complicated by discrepancies between the actual and perceived states of the system. These differences arise from distortions in information channels which comprise the information feedback loop; distortions which may take the form of random errors (noise), bias, and delays. The states of systems perceived by the decision maker will more or less represent actual states depending upon the quality of information transmitted through information channels.

Elementary Inventory System

We may illustrate the feedback decision process by an elementary inventory replenishment decision, as in Figure 13.2. The system is a first-order feedback system, because there is only one system level variable. In this system the purchase rate decision, PRCHR, controls the flow of goods from supplier into inventory, INVTY, and goods shipped rate, GSHPR, controls the flow out of inventory. No time delay exists between ordering and receiving goods, nor in the flow of information from inventory to the purchasing decision.

The purchase rate decision is based upon a goal of maintaining inventory at a desired level, DSINV, which in this illustration is assumed to be a constant value. Feedback is negative, since the purchase rate must be

Figure 13.2   Inventory Replenishment Decision System
(First-order Negative Feedback System)

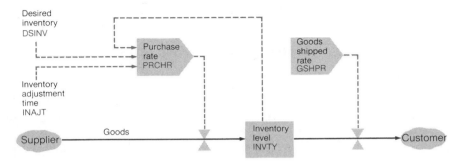

increased if inventory falls below the desired quantity, and must be negative if inventory rises above that quantity. A negative purchase rate would represent goods returned to the supplier.

Before proceeding to develop the equation model for this system, we must explain the subscript notation used to represent time. In keeping with notation used in industrial dynamics literature, we will designate the present instant of time by the letter K, the immediately preceding time by J, and the immediately succeeding time by L, as indicated in Figure 13.3. Current inventory level in this system is indicated by INVT.K. DT is the length of the time interval separating points in time in the model. The time interval preceding the present instant in time is designated JK, and the following interval KL. If, for example, DT is one week, PRCHR.JK would indicate the rate of flow of orders occurring during the preceding week, and PRCHR.KL the purchase rate of the following week. Constants, parameters which do not change over time, do not require a time subscript notation.

Figure 13.3   Time Notation Used in Industrial Dynamics Models

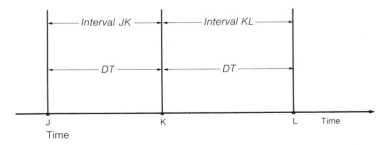

In the inventory replenishment system of Figure 13.2 the amount of goods currently in inventory depends upon the amount on hand last week plus the difference between the amounts purchased and shipped during

the preceding week. Since the purchase decision and shipment rate represent rates of flow (units per week), and we wish to determine the amount of goods on hand (units), we must accumulate the rates of flow over the time interval DT (weeks). This summation is accomplished by multiplying the difference between purchase rate and shipment rate by DT as follows:

$$INVT.K = INVT.J + (DT)(PRCHR.JK - GSHPR.JK) \qquad (13.1)$$

This summation is analogous to the process of integration in calculus. In calculus notation, the integration would be expressed as:

$$INVTY_t = INVTY_{t=0} + \int_0^t (PRCHR - GSHPR)\, dt \qquad (13.2)$$

where $INVTY_{t=0}$ is the beginning inventory. Industrial dynamics models use the difference equation structure of equation 13.1, because it is compatible with solution on digital computers.

To achieve the desired goal, the purchase rate depends upon the difference between desired and actual inventory and may be expressed as

$$PRCHR.KL = DSINV - INVTY.K$$

However this expression is not dimensionally correct, because the term on the left is measured in "units per week" and the term on the right is measured in "units." Consequently another term must be introduced on the right side of the equation. We may express the relationship between changes in inventory and order rate in many ways, but for now we will assume that this relationship is a linear function. For a linear relationship, the additional term in the expression would take the form 1/INAJT, where INAJT is inventory adjustment time in weeks. The purchase order rate would then be expressed as

$$PRCHR.KL = \frac{1}{INAJT} (DSINV - INVTY.K) \qquad (13.3)$$

Inventory replenishment is to be made at the rate of 1/INAJT per week of the difference between the desired and actual inventory. INAJT has no time notation because it is a constant.

To examine the dynamic behavior of this elementary information feedback system, we can simulate its operation and observe how it would correct inventory differences. We must always specify initial values for system levels to provide a level of departure. Assume that desired inventory, DSINV, and initial inventory value, INVTY, are each 1,000 units, inventory adjustment time, INAJT, is 4 weeks, and the model solution time interval, DT, is 1 week. Further assume that for this illustration no goods are being shipped from inventory, except in the third week when 500 units are shipped. Thus we will apply a pulse of 500 units in the third week to test response of the feedback system.

Using a pulse input for demand, rather than a more realistic demand schedule which might include seasonal and random fluctuations, permits us to analyze the inventory correction process without the added complication of fluctuating demand. The use of a standard test input signal, such as a pulse, permits the analyst to compare the dynamic response of alternative systems. In addition, system response to a standard test input usually correlates with its response to actual inputs. Other standard inputs employed in testing system response include a step input and a ramp input, which will be illustrated in subsequent models. After a model has been analyzed and adjusted to respond as desired to these test inputs, it is often run with more complex inputs.

Calculations to simulate the system of Figure 13.2 for 20 weeks are shown in Table 13.1. The entries for week 0 represent the initial state of the system in which inventory level contains 1,000 units and both shipping and purchasing rates are zero. This state prevails until the third week when the shipping rate GSHPR.KL, rises to 500 units/week for one week. Purchasing rate is still zero because it is based upon the inventory level at the beginning of the week.

We compute the new value of inventory for week 4 from equation 13.1:

$$INVTY.K = 1,000 + (1)(0-500)$$
$$= 500 \text{ units}$$

The purchase rate can now be calculated from equation 13.3:

$$PRCHR.KL = \tfrac{1}{4}(1,000 - 500)$$
$$= 125 \text{ units/week}$$

This purchase rate applies to the interval between the end of week 3 and week 4. These goods are received into inventory by week 5 and bring the level up to 625 units. Now the inventory difference is $1,000 - 625 = 375$ units and the purchase rate is $(1/4)(375) = 93.75$ units/week. Following this same procedure, we can calculate the values for subsequent periods and fill in the rest of the table. Figure 13.4 portrays graphically the results of the simulation. Purchase rate and the increase in inventory decline in an exponential fashion as inventory approaches the desired level. By the eighth week inventory has reached 842 units and by the twentieth week 995 units. Thus we see that the introduction of an inventory adjustment time lag slows the ability of a system to correct differences between desired and actual system states.

Representation of Delays

Another form of a negative feedback system with response similar to the previous one is found in the regulation of an outflow rate from a storage level. Consider the order filling process in Figure 13.5, in which the shipping rate is a function of the level of unfilled orders and average length of

Table 13.1 Calculation of First-Order Information Feedback System Response

TIME	INVTY	INVDF	GSHPR	PRCHR
E+00	E+00	E+00	E+00	E+00
.000	1000.0	.00	.00	.00
1.000	1000.0	.00	.00	.00
2.000	1000.0	.00	.00	.00
3.000	1000.0	.00	500.00	.00
4.000	500.0	500.00	.00	125.00
5.000	625.0	375.00	.00	93.75
6.000	718.8	281.25	.00	70.31
7.000	789.1	210.94	.00	52.73
8.000	841.8	158.20	.00	39.55
9.000	881.3	118.65	.00	29.66
10.000	911.0	88.99	.00	22.25
11.000	933.3	66.74	.00	16.69
12.000	949.9	50.06	.00	12.51
13.000	962.5	37.54	.00	9.39
14.000	971.8	28.16	.00	7.04
15.000	978.9	21.12	.00	5.28
16.000	984.2	15.84	.00	3.96
17.000	988.1	11.88	.00	2.97
18.000	991.1	8.91	.00	2.23
19.000	993.3	6.68	.00	1.67
20.000	995.0	5.01	.00	1.25

Figure 13.4 First-Order Information Feedback System Response

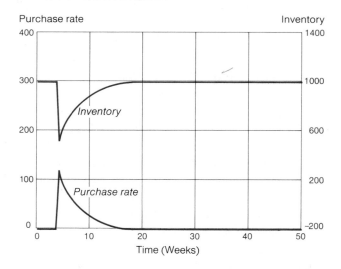

shipping delay time. A delay is created in the flow of orders because of the lag in response of shipping rate to changes in purchase rate. This system is a first-order exponential delay, comprised of a level and an outflow rate dependent upon the level and delay period. As in equation 13.1, the level of unfilled orders, UNFOR, accumulates the difference between purchase rate, PRCHR, and supplier shipping rate, SSHPR:

$$\text{UNFOR.K} = \text{UNFOR.J} + (\text{DT})(\text{PRCHR.JK} - \text{SSHPR.JK}) \quad (13.4)$$

The outflow rate SSHPR, of this type of delay is the amount in the level, UNFOR, divided by the average shipping delay time, SHPDL:

$$\text{SSHPR.KL} = \frac{\text{UNFOR.K}}{\text{SHPDL}} \quad (13.5)$$

In this equation the average time of the delay, SHPDL, may be either a constant or variable parameter. If it were a variable parameter, it would contain a time subscript notation, as SHPDL.K. This loop is a negative feedback loop because an increase in purchase rate adds to the amount of unfilled orders and increases the shipping rate, which in turn decreases the amount of unfilled orders. Its response follows the same pattern as shown in Figure 13.4.

Figure 13.5   First-Order Exponential Delay

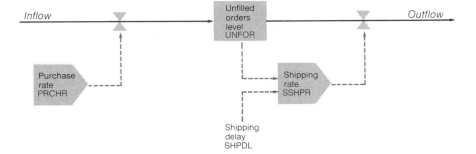

This type of delay for shipping rate can be justified on the basis that we are modeling at an aggregate inventory level which represents many different items, and that the delay represents an average shipping delay. If there is a sudden increase in unfilled orders, some of the increment would be shipped immediately, but it would take time before the system could adjust fully to the higher level of activity. The delay itself is an aggregation of different types of time lags, such as clerical, order filling, and transit delays.

We can choose not only appropriate average delay times, but we may introduce other types of delays into system flows to represent different types of system reactions. The transient response of a model may be regulated by choosing other kinds of time lags, such as a discrete time lag, or by cascading first-order exponential delays. In a discrete delay the entire input is held back until the end of the delay period when it is released. Discrete delays apply to delays of individual events. For example, a discrete delay would be used to represent the length of time required to process a single order. First-order exponential delays may be cascaded by chaining them together and dividing the total delay time among the parts, as shown in Figure 13.6, which demonstrates how a third-order exponential delay is formed.

Figure 13.6 Third-Order Exponential Delay Formed by Cascading Three First-Order Delays

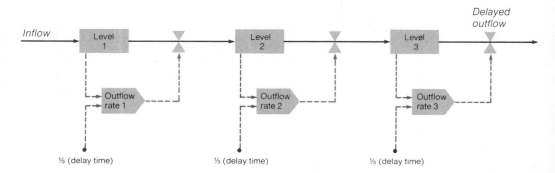

Closely related to the concept of delays in physical flows are time lags in transmission of information. Information time lags may take the form of discrete delays of individual messages, or smoothing of information time series. The impact on a system of transient fluctuations in a time series is delayed and the sensitivity of the system to high frequency fluctuations is altered by smoothing. Because of this, there is in selecting information smoothing a trade off between a desire to reduce the impact of random noise and a desire to reduce the time required to recognize significant changes in information.

Two techniques commonly used for smoothing time series are arithmetic moving averages and exponential moving averages or exponential smoothing. Where an arithmetic moving average gives equal weight to data from each time period included in the average, exponential smoothing gives greater weight to more recent data. In models of decision processes, exponential smoothing may often more appropriately represent human behavior than an arithmetic moving average.

An exponential moving average is usually expressed in the following form:

$$\bar{x}_t = \alpha x_t + (1 - \alpha)\bar{x}_{t-1} \qquad 0 < \alpha < 1 \tag{13.6}$$

where

$\bar{x}_t =$ moving average for period t

$x_t =$ data for period t

$\bar{x}_{t-1}$ = moving average for period $t - 1$

α = weight given to current data (between 0 and 1)

The value of the moving average for period t is α times the data for the most recent period plus $1 - \alpha$ times the value of the moving average from the preceding time period. Equation 13.6 may be rewritten in the form of a difference equation:

$$\bar{x}_t = \bar{x}_{t-1} + \alpha(x_t - \bar{x}_{t-1})$$ (13.7)

The value of the moving average for period t is the value of the average for the preceding period plus α times the difference between the data for period t and the previous value of the average.

In industrial dynamics models it is convenient to think of α in terms of a time interval of T periods, in which case α would be replaced by $1/T$. We may generalize the equation for first-order exponential smoothing to apply to any solution interval, DT, and express it in industrial dynamics notation as:

$$\text{AVG.K} = \text{AVG.J} + \frac{\text{DT}}{\text{T}} (\text{DATA.JK} - \text{AVG.J})$$ (13.8)

The average for period K equals the average for the preceding period J plus a fraction of the difference between the values of the rate of flow over the time interval JK and the average for the preceding period. In computing the moving average choice of larger values for T would give less weight to data flow and more to the old average, and would thereby delay the response of the moving average to variations in data flows. Exponential smoothing equations can also be cascaded for higher order delays. An important computational advantage of using exponential smoothing in computer programs is that only one value—the old average—need be stored in computer memory.

Differences in output rates of first-, second-, and third-order exponential delays and a discreet delay in response to step and pulse input signals are portrayed in Figures 13.7 and 13.8. The first-order exponential delay responds to the step input with a small increase in output at once and rises to approximately 63 per cent of the input rate by the time of the delay period. Second-order and higher order delays introduce a lag before any output appears. This may be seen in Figure 13.8 where output rate increases slowly, reaches a maximum, and then declines. A discrete delay is actually a cascading of an infinite number of exponential delays. For a discrete delay, there is no output until the end of the delay period, at which time output rises to reflect the input signal.

The choice of delay function depends upon the phenomena being represented in the model. A first-order delay would be used to represent an activity in which there is an immediate response followed by a gradual

Figure 13.7 Response of First, Second and Third Order Exponential Delay and Discrete Delay to a Unit Step Input

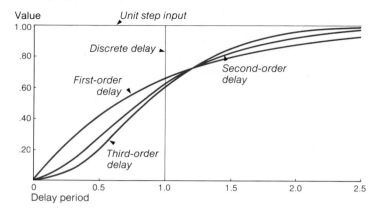

Figure 13.8 Response of First, Second and Third Order Exponential Delay and Discrete Delay to a Pulse Input

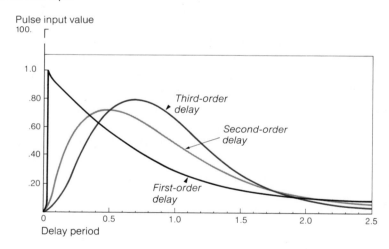

tapering off, such as response to an advertisement. A third-order delay might be used to represent an activity in which there is a time lag before anything happens followed by a rise to a peak and a gradual decline, such as a transportation system in which there is a time lag before any goods arrive at their destinations.

Second-Order Feedback System

If we expand the information feedback decision system of Figure 13.2 to include another system state variable, or level, in the feedback loop we have a second-order system which has a different type of dynamic response. We will expand the system to include part of the supplier sector and a time delay between purchasing and receiving goods, as depicted in Figure 13.9. Instead of goods flowing into inventory as an immediate result of the purchase decision, the purchase decision regulates the rate of flow of orders into the supplier's file of unfilled orders. The flow of goods sent from the supplier and received into inventory is regulated by a supplier's shipping rate function. As explained earlier, the shipping rate decision is a function of the number of units on order and the average shipping delay. Inclusion in the feedback loop of this second level and rate function introduces a time delay in the purchasing-receiving flow, and alters the system response.

Figure 13.9 Inventory Replenishment Decision System with Supplier Sector
(Second Order Negative Feedback System)

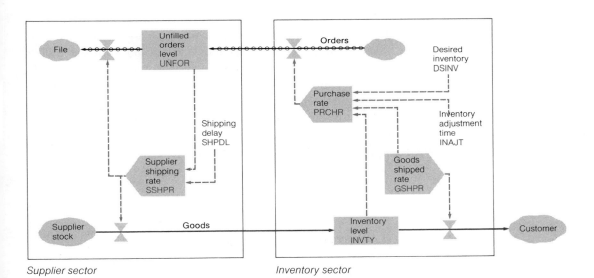

Supplier sector   *Inventory sector*

Model Equations   Three of the four equations required to model the expanded system were introduced above in equations 13.1, 13.4, and 13.5, but equation 13.1 for inventory level, INVTY, must be altered to provide for goods flowing into inventory as a result of the supplier's shipping rate, SSHPR:

$$\text{INVTY.K} = \text{INVTY.J} + (\text{DT})(\text{SSHPR.JK} - \text{GSHPR.JK}) \quad (13.9)$$

Repeating equations 13.4 and 13.5

$$\text{UNFOR.K} = \text{UNFOR.J} + (\text{DT})(\text{PRCHR.JK} - \text{SSHPR.JK}) \quad (13.4)$$

$$\text{SSHPR.KL} = \frac{\text{UNFOR.K}}{\text{SHPDL}} \quad (13.5)$$

$$SSHPR = \text{supplier shipping rate (units/week)}$$
$$UNFOR = \text{unfilled orders (units)}$$
$$SHPDL = \text{shipping delay (weeks).}$$

For a test of system response we will use a step input applied to the goods shipped rate, GSHPR, in the third week. The goods shipped rate will be 100 units per week for two weeks and in the third week will be stepped up to 200 units per week, where it will remain for the rest of the simulation. A step input represents an increase in demand and permits us to analyze system response to such an increase.

A decision function different from the previous model is required for the purchase rate decision, because of the addition of a continuous flow of goods out of inventory. There are of course many ways in which this decision might be modeled, since there are many ways in which buyers actually make such decisions, some of which are based upon the sophisticated analyses presented in Chapter 10. For the sake of simplicity, we will use here a realistic, but somewhat naive, decision rule consistent with the goal of maintaining inventory at its desired level, and consistent with information available in the system. Two things are considered: the replacement of goods shipped in the preceding time period and correction of differences between desired and actual inventory levels. This can be accomplished by adding to the inventory correction decision, developed in equation 13.3, the goods shipped rate from the prior time interval:

$$PRCHR.KL = GSHPR.JK + \frac{1}{INAJT} (DSINV - INVTY.K) \quad (13.10)$$

$$PRCHR = \text{purchase rate (units/week)}$$
$$GSHPR = \text{goods shipped rate (units/week)}$$
$$INAJT = \text{inventory adjustment time (weeks)}$$
$$DSINV = \text{desired inventory (units)}$$
$$INVTY = \text{inventory (units).}$$

System Behavior

We will simulate this system with the following parameter values:

$$INAJT = 4 \text{ weeks}$$
$$SHPDL = 8 \text{ weeks}$$
$$DSINV = 1,000 \text{ units}$$

The simulation will begin with the system in an equilibrium state, that is, with the three rates, GSHPR, PRCHR, and SSHPR, each at 100 units per week, and initial inventory, INVTY, of 1,000 units.

Table 13.2 Calculation of Second-Order Information Feedback System Response

TIME	INVTY	INVDF	UNFOR	SSHPR	GSHPR	PRCHR
E+00	E+00	E+00	E+00	E+00	E+00	E+00
.000	1000.0	.00	800.0	100.00	100.00	100.00
1.000	1000.0	.00	800.0	100.00	100.00	100.00
2.000	1000.0	.00	800.0	100.00	100.00	100.00
3.000	1000.0	.00	800.0	100.00	200.00	100.00
4.000	900.0	100.00	800.0	100.00	200.00	225.00
5.000	800.0	200.00	925.0	115.63	200.00	250.00
6.000	715.6	284.38	1059.4	132.42	200.00	271.09
7.000	648.0	351.95	1198.0	149.76	200.00	287.99
8.000	597.8	402.20	1336.3	167.03	200.00	300.55
9.000	564.8	435.16	1469.8	183.72	200.00	308.79
10.000	548.6	451.44	1594.9	199.36	200.00	312.86
11.000	547.9	452.08	1708.4	213.55	200.00	313.02
12.000	561.5	438.54	1807.8	225.98	200.00	309.63
13.000	587.4	412.56	1891.5	236.44	200.00	303.14
14.000	623.9	376.12	1958.2	244.77	200.00	294.03
15.000	668.7	331.35	2007.4	250.93	200.00	282.84
16.000	719.6	280.41	2039.4	254.92	200.00	270.10
17.000	774.5	225.49	2054.5	256.82	200.00	256.37
18.000	831.3	168.68	2054.1	256.76	200.00	242.17
19.000	888.1	111.92	2039.5	254.94	200.00	227.98
20.000	943.0	56.98	2012.5	251.57	200.00	214.24
21.000	994.6	5.41	1975.2	246.90	200.00	201.35
22.000	1041.5	− 41.49	1929.7	241.21	200.00	189.63
23.000	1082.7	− 82.70	1878.1	234.76	200.00	179.32
24.000	1117.5	−117.46	1822.7	227.83	200.00	170.63
25.000	1145.3	−145.29	1765.5	220.68	200.00	163.68
26.000	1166.0	−165.98	1708.4	213.56	200.00	158.51
27.000	1179.5	−179.53	1653.4	206.67	200.00	155.12
28.000	1186.2	−186.21	1601.8	200.23	200.00	153.45
29.000	1186.4	−186.44	1555.1	194.38	200.00	153.39
30.000	1180.8	−180.82	1514.1	189.26	200.00	154.80
31.000	1170.1	−170.08	1479.6	184.95	200.00	157.48
32.000	1155.0	−155.03	1452.1	181.52	200.00	161.24
33.000	1136.5	−136.55	1431.9	178.98	200.00	165.86
34.000	1115.5	−115.53	1418.7	177.34	200.00	171.12
35.000	1092.9	− 92.87	1412.5	176.56	200.00	176.78
36.000	1069.4	− 69.44	1412.7	176.59	200.00	182.64
37.000	1046.0	− 46.03	1418.8	177.35	200.00	188.49
38.000	1023.4	− 23.37	1429.9	178.74	200.00	194.16
39.000	1002.1	− 2.12	1445.3	180.67	200.00	199.47
40.000	982.8	17.22	1464.1	183.02	200.00	204.30
41.000	965.8	34.20	1485.4	185.68	200.00	208.55
42.000	951.5	48.52	1508.3	188.54	200.00	212.13
43.000	940.0	59.98	1531.9	191.49	200.00	215.00
44.000	931.5	68.49	1555.4	194.43	200.00	217.12

Table 13.2 Continued

TIME	INVTY	INVDF	UNFOR	SSHPR	GSHPR	PRCHR
45.000	925.9	74.07	1578.1	197.26	200.00	218.52
46.000	923.2	76.81	1599.4	199.92	200.00	219.20
47.000	923.1	76.89	1618.6	202.33	200.00	219.22
48.000	925.4	74.56	1635.5	204.44	200.00	218.64
49.000	929.9	70.12	1649.7	206.22	200.00	217.53
50.000	936.1	63.90	1661.0	207.63	200.00	215.97

An initial value must also be specified for the unfilled order level, UNFOR. For an initial equilibrium condition, the required amount of unfilled orders can be calculated by rearranging equation 13.5 like this:

$$UNFOR = (SSHPR)(SHPDL)$$

The initial value of unfilled orders is equal to the initial shipping rate multiplied by the shipping delay. Substituting the other initial values specified so far, we obtain an initial value of

$$UNFOR = (100 \text{ units/week})(8 \text{ weeks}) = 800 \text{ units}$$

Initial values for week 0 have been entered in Table 13.2. None of the values change for the first two weeks because the system is in equilibrium, but in the third week GSHPR is increased to 200 units per week. This causes 200 units to flow out of inventory during the week while only 100 units flow in. The amount of inventory in week four is computed from equation 13.9:

$$INVTY.K = 1,000 \text{ units} + (1 \text{ week})(100 \text{ units/week} - 200 \text{ units/week})$$
$$= 900 \text{ units}.$$

Unfilled orders remain at 800 units, as purchase and shipping rates for the preceding weeks did not change. Since there is now a difference of $1,000 - 900 = 100$ units between desired and actual inventory, the purchase rate is increased to

$$PRCHR.KL = 200 \text{ units/week} + (\tfrac{1}{4})(1,000 - 900)$$
$$= 225 \text{ units/week}.$$

Calculations for the simulation run of 50 weeks are shown in the table, and results are plotted in Figure 13.10. We see that, following a 100 per cent increase in goods shipped rate, GSHPR, in the third week, inventory begins to fall and continues to drop to about 45 per cent of its initial level in week 10. Then, instead of gradually recovering to its desired level, inventory continues to climb to a peak of 1186 units (about 19 per cent above the desired level) in week 29. Following that, it drops slightly below the desired level, and even by the end of the simulation run of 50 weeks has not returned to a new equilibrium condition.

Figure 13.10 Second-Order Information Feedback System Response

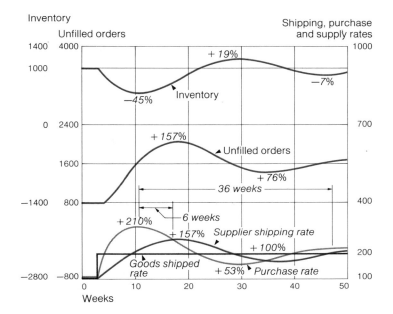

Thus, the system over-corrects differences between desired and actual inventories. Oscillation in the system is caused by addition of the unfilled orders level and the shipping delay in the supply sector, a delay which retards the response of inventory. Purchase rate rises to a peak of 210 per cent above the initial value, but then must be cut back below the new equilibrium rate of 200 units per week, because of the over-correction.

Compare the timing of the supplier shipping rate and the purchase rate. Purchase rate reaches a peak in week 11, and is then reduced. But because of delay in the system, supplier shipping rate continues to rise until week 17.

We also note that a time relationship exists between outflow rate, GSHPR, inflow rate, SSHPR, and inventory peaks and valleys. Inventory maximums and minimums occur when inflow and outflow rates are equal.

Altering the two delay constants, inventory adjustment time and shipping delay will change the system oscillations, but oscillation will not be completely eliminated as long as the second delay remains in the system. Experiments to show this are suggested in the exercises at the end of the chapter.

In this section we have explored some aspects of the feedback loop as a basic component of system structure and the dynamic behavior of negative feedback systems containing time lags. A system with a single negative feedback loop exhibits goal-seeking behavior which gradually approaches the goal. Feedback systems containing more than one state variable, or level, can exhibit oscillation. In later sections, we will apply these concepts to several types of systems, and we will also examine the dynamics of growth systems which contain positive feedback loops.

Multi-Stage Production-Distribution System

The concepts developed in the preceding sections may be applied to a multi-stage production-distribution system to illustrate its dynamic behavior. Inventories serve to provide time and place utility and to decouple stages of a system in order to damp out transient disturbances, but the system structure and interactions between sectors may create instability in the form of amplification and oscillation. Dynamics of an inventory system can be understood only within the context of the distribution system of which it is a part. To see how the concepts of industrial dynamics can be applied to such a system, we will examine the following distribution system.

System Description

The system represented here is of a company that produces goods, such as small electric appliances, that are sold to distributors, and in turn to retail dealers who sell them to customers. The company maintains a finished goods inventory. Orders from distributors are received by the company, and shipments are made to distributors from the finished goods inventory. The company production organization determines its production schedules from a sales forecast based upon orders received from distributors.

It has been observed that, based upon historical data, production rates in the factory seem to fluctuate much more widely than retail sales and warehouse deliveries. It also appears that production peaks and valleys often do not correspond to the rise and fall of retail sales or warehouse deliveries. Sometimes production is at a low level when retail sales are rising, and at other times production continues high while sales are declining.

Analysis of the problem begins with an examination of the company production-distribution system, the overall structure of which is pictured in Figure 13.11. One major flow represented there is the flow of materials from raw materials sources through the company production process, to distributors' inventories, to retailers' inventories, and finally to retail customers. Another flow is the flow of purchase orders in the opposite direction. In addition, there is a complex interconnection of information flows.

The system contains three major negative feedback loops. The first loop contains the retailers' inventories, their purchase decision, and the distributors' shipping function. The second loop contains the distributors' inventories, their purchase decision, and the company's shipping function. The third loop contains the company inventory and its production decision. The goal of each loop is to adjust inventory levels and purchase or production rates to correspond to customer demand. We will develop a model of this

Figure 13.11   Multi-Stage Production-Distribution System

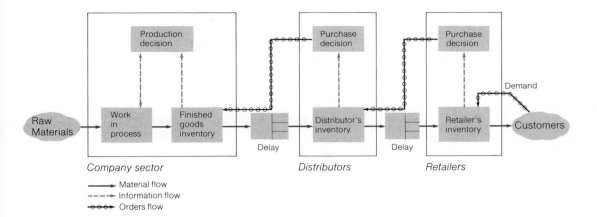

system and use it to analyze behavior of the system. As in the case of the elementary system in Figure 13.9, we will observe that the structure and time lags in the system cause amplification and instability.

**Retailers'
Operation
Feedback
Loop**

Two aspects of retailers' operations are of direct interest: receiving merchandise and shipping it in response to customer orders, and purchase decisions to replenish inventories. Figure 13.12 shows a detailed flow diagram of the feedback loop containing retail purchase rate. Note that it is similar to the second-order feedback loop of Figure 13.9, but that it has a more complex decision function. Before examining components of this system, trace around the major feedback loop.

Beginning in the lower right-hand corner of the diagram, we see that information about current inventory level flows into the purchase rate decision. Retailers' purchase rate generates a flow of purchase orders into distributors' unfilled order file. After an order filling delay, goods are shipped from distributors' inventories, and after a transit delay goods are received into retail inventories. This is a negative feedback loop because a decrease in inventory relative to its desired level causes an increase in purchase rate, unfilled order level, and distributor shipping rate. After some delay the inventory level then rises back toward its desired level.

Around this feedback loop is an alternating rate and level structure. As before, levels are represented by rectangles or boxes, and rates by valve symbols. Variables represented by circles are auxiliary variables which are structurally part of rate equations. They are used to break down complex rate or decision functions into subfunctions to show the individual factors comprising decision variables. The mnemonic names used in the model are included in the flow diagram and numbers in the symbols refer to equation numbers in the computer model listed at the end of the chapter.

Figure 13.12   Flow Diagram of Retailers' Inventory Replenishment Feedback Loop

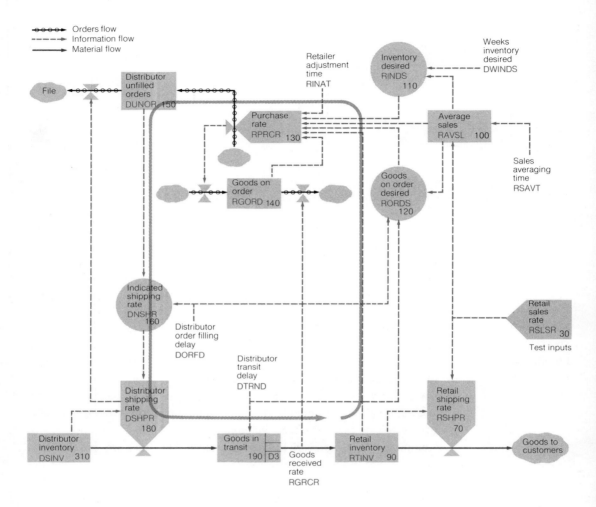

Retail Sales Rate. The exogenous input to the retail inventory feedback loop is retailers' sales rate, RSLSR. We will use a standard step test input to test response of the system. Because goods are delivered directly from inventory, the shipping rate, RSHPR, reflects the sales rate, RSLSR. Note, however, the information flow from retailers' inventory, RTINV, to shipping rate. This is included to place an upper limit on shipments; no goods can be shipped unless there is sufficient stock on hand.

Purchase Rate Decision. The retailers' purchase rate decision is based upon a set of goals designed to maintain a flow of goods into inventory which is consistent with a forecast rate of sales and to adjust the level of inventory to correspond to changes in business activity. Although the purchase rate decision may appear on the flow diagram to be rather complicated, it is actually based upon only four factors, the principles of which have already been discussed in previous sections:

1. a sales forecast based upon a projection of average demand,

2. an inventory adjustment to correct differences between desired and actual inventory levels,

3. an adjustment in the amount of goods on order to correspond to delays between placing orders and receiving goods, and

4. an adjustment time factor which represents the rapidity with which retailers adjust to changes in the rate of business activity.

Other more sophisticated decision rules could be used, but this one will serve to demonstrate characteristic system behavior.

The sales forecasting method used here is exponential smoothing which is obtained from a first-order exponentially smoothed moving average like the one described earlier in equation 13.8. In the model, this forecast is referred to as retail average sales, RAVSL. There are two inputs into the exponential smoothing function, the current sales rate, RSLSR, and a sales averaging time constant, RSAVT. In this system, a sales averaging time constant of four weeks is used.

Although few dealers may be likely to use any formal methods such as exponential smoothing for sales forecasts, in this situation it appears that the aggregate of their behavior may reasonably be represented by such a function. Since exponential smoothing gives greater weight to more recent data and progressively less weight to older information, it seems to be a good representation of intuitive smoothing of irregularities in information flows. Average sales rate (the sales forecast) is the primary component of the purchase rate decision; the other three factors pertain to adjustments of inventory and adjustments for orders placed but not yet delivered.

Desired inventory, RINDS, is a function of the anticipated rate of business activity. Retailers try to maintain an inventory equivalent to several weeks of sales. In this model the weeks' inventory desired, RWIND, is 8, which means that retailers attempt to keep on hand about a two-month supply of goods. An eight-week inventory is equivalent to an annual inventory turnover of $52/8 = 6.5$. Desired inventory, RINDS, is computed by multiplying average sales, RAVSL, by weeks inventory desired, RWIND. Desired inventory is then compared with actual retail inventory, RTINV, to determine the correction in purchase rate necessary to adjust inventory levels to bring them into conformity with desired levels.

In addition to average sales and inventory adjustment, the purchase rate decision contains an adjustment to account for orders placed but not yet received. This adjustment is accomplished by determining a desired amount to have on order, retail goods on order desired, RORDS, and comparing this with the amount of goods on order, RGORD. To maintain a flow of goods through the system the buyer would like to have enough goods on order to correspond to average sales over the lead time. Lead time is distributors' order-filling delay, DORFD, plus transit delay, DTRND. Goods on order desired, RORDS, is the average sales rate, RAVSL, times the sum of order-filling delay, DORFD, and transit delay, DTRND. This is compared with goods on order, RGORD, to determine the necessary adjustment in purchase rate.

In the discussion of equation 13.3, we pointed out that it is necessary to provide an adjustment time constant to specify how fast corrections in inventory and goods on order should be made. In the multi-stage model this reaction time constant is provided by RINAT, which has a value of four weeks.

The four factors described above when combined together form the purchase rate equation in the model.

$$RPRCR.KL = RAVSL.K + \frac{1}{RINAT}$$
$$\times (RINDS.K + RORDS.K - RTINV.K$$
$$- RGORD.K). \qquad (13.11)$$

Distributor Shipping Rate. Continuing around the feedback loop, orders generated by the purchase rate decision flow into the distributors' unfilled order file, DUNOR. The distributors' shipping rate, DSHPR, is a function of the level of unfilled orders and inventory on hand. Since orders are filled after an order-filling delay, DORFD, the indicated shipping rate, DNSHR, is the amount of unfilled orders divided by order-filling delay or DUNOR.K/DORFD. Note that the rationale for this formulation is the same as for the shipping rate in equation 13.5. The actual shipping rate, DSHPR, is equal to the indicated shipping rate as long as sufficient inventory is on hand. As in the case of retailers' shipping rate, inventory on hand puts an upper limit on shipping rate.

After goods are shipped from the distributors' inventory, it takes an average of about one week for them to reach the retailers. Some arrive earlier and a few take two weeks or more, but over half arrive in one week or less. This time lag is represented in this continuous-flow model by a third-order exponential delay with an average transit delay, DTRDN, of one week.

The output of the transit delay is the retailers' goods received rate, RGRCR, which is the rate of flow of goods into retail inventory. This completes the major feedback loop representing the replenishment of retail inventories.

Distributor Inventory Feedback Loop

Figure 13.13 shows the feedback loop containing distributors' inventory replenishment, which is similar in structure to the retail inventory loop. The distributors' purchase rate decision, DPRCR, is structurally identical to the retail purchase rate decision, RPRCR. The equations comprising this decision are identical to those in the retail inventory loop, but the numerical values of the time constants are different. Distributors attempt to keep a twelve-week supply of inventory on hand, their reaction time is eight weeks, and they use a sales averaging time constant of eight weeks.

Distributors' average sales, DAVSL, are taken from the flow of incoming orders, RPRCR. The distributors' purchase rate decision, DPRCR, causes orders to flow into the factory unfilled order file, FUNOR. Order filling at the factory is subject to an order-filling delay, FORFD, of two weeks. Goods shipped from the factory are subject to a three-week transit delay, FTRND, which reflects the presumed greater average distance between factory and distributors.

This distributor inventory loop is coupled to the retail inventory loop by the flow of incoming orders and shipment of materials. It is a negative feedback loop, because an increase in the incoming order rate causes a decrease in inventory and an increase in purchase rate. The increased purchase rate causes an increase in factory unfilled orders and an increase in the factory shipping rate, which results in an increase in distributors' inventory.

Company Production Decision Feedback Loop

The two major aspects of the company's operations which are of immediate interest to us in analysis of the multi-stage system are the flow of materials through the production process into finished goods inventory, and the flow of information upon which the production rate decision is based. These flows are the primary components of the feedback loop pictured in Figure 13.14. Although this feedback loop may appear more complex than those for the retail and distributor sectors, it has several features in common with them.

Beginning in the lower right-hand corner of the diagram, we see that information about the level of finished goods inventory, FGINV, flows into the production rate decision desired production, DEPRN. Desired production determines production started rate, PNSTR. Production started rate generates work in process, WPINV, and after a delay which represents production time, production finished rate, PNFNR, flows into finished goods inventory. This is a negative feedback loop because a decrease in finished goods inventory relative to desired inventory causes an increase in production rate to move the level of finished goods inventory back toward its desired level.

Production Rate Decision. The structure of the production rate decision follows the usual concept of attempting to bring the level of the system into

Figure 13.13 Flow Diagram of Distributors' Inventory Replenishment Feedback Loop

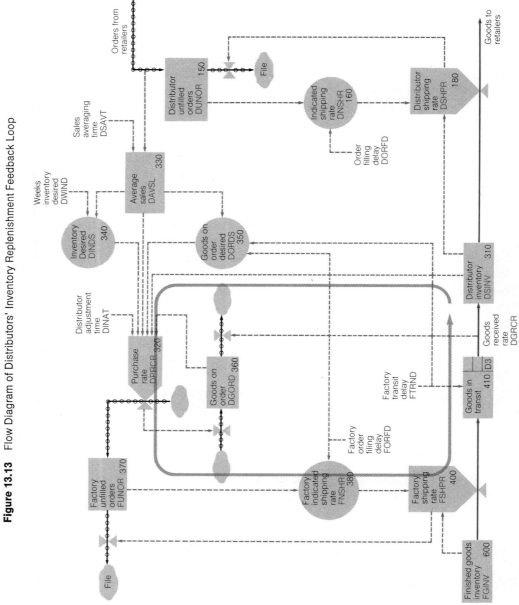

accord with some desired state. In Figure 13.14, the basic production rate decision is shown as desired production, DEPRN. The decision is based upon several components: sales forecast, finished goods inventory, backlog of unfilled orders, and work in process.

The sales forecast, called factory average sales, FAVSL, is an exponentially smoothed moving average of company sales. It is taken from the flow of incoming orders from distributors, and uses a sales averaging time constant, FSAVT, of eight weeks.

Note that the auxillary variables representing desired finished goods inventory, work in process, and unfilled orders are all functions of average sales and thus are related to anticipated business activity. The company desires to maintain a finished goods inventory equivalent to four weeks of sales. Desired work in process, WIPDS, is included in the production rate decision to account for average production time of six weeks. Unfilled orders desired, FUNDS, is average sales times an order-filling delay of two weeks.

A change in production rate cannot be made immediately. Time is required to hire workers, obtain raw materials, and adjust to a new higher production rate. Similarly, time is required to reduce production rates. In this system small changes can be made rapidly, but larger changes take longer. In general, the plant can be expected to operate at about 60 to 65 per cent of a planned new level within four weeks. This adjustment rate is represented here by a production adjustment time, PNAJT, of four weeks. Speeding up or slowing down this adjustment process would require several changes in purchasing, scheduling, hiring, and training procedures. Desired production is computed from the following equation which incorporates these variables:

$$DEPRN.K = FAVSL.K + \frac{1}{PNAJT}$$
$$\times (FINDS.K + WIPDS.K + FUNOR.K$$
$$- FGINV.K - WPINV.K - WIPDS.K).$$

(13.12)

Production Rate. The actual production started, PNSTR, is desired production as computed from equation 13.12, but it is restrained by production capacity, PNCAP, of 1,000 units per week. A third order delay is used to represent the time lag between the time production is started and finished. The length of the delay is the production time, PRNTM, six weeks, and work in process is the amount of production started but not finished. The production finished rate, PNFNR, is the input into finished goods inventory, FGINV.

The company inventory-production decision feedback loop is coupled to the distributor inventory loop through the inflow of orders and outflow of

Figure 13.14 Flow Diagram of Company Inventory-Production Decision Feedback Loop

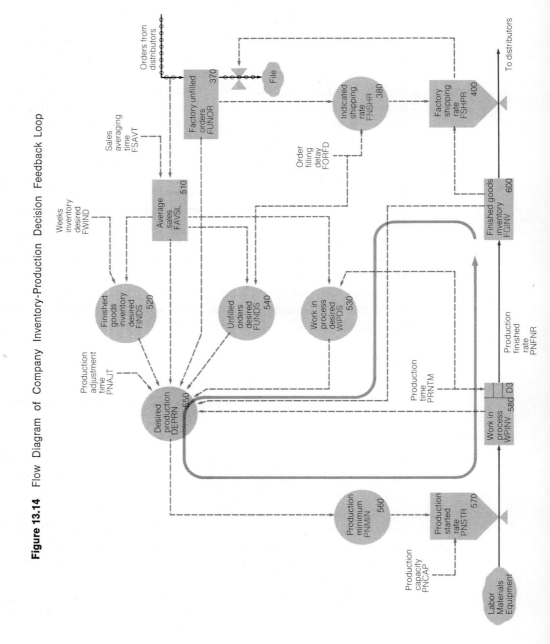

goods. This completes the description of the structure of the model, a complete listing of which may be found at the end of the chapter. We will now examine some aspects of the dynamic behavior of this model.

Dynamic System Behavior

A summary of the input parameter values used in the simulation of this system is provided in Table 13.3. Negative feedback loops are goal-seeking, but system adjustment to goals is not necessarily a smooth one. The multistage distribution system, which is a series of higher order negative feedback loops coupled together, exhibits a fluctuating behavior, as shown in Figure 13.15. The graph shows the plotted output from a simulation of 52 weeks

Table 13.3   Input Parameter Values Used for the Simulation Run of

	Retail Inventory Replenishment Feedback Loop	
STPHT	Retail Sales Step Height (Retail Sales Rate from week 3 on)	550 units/week
RSAVT	Retail Sales Averaging Time	4 weeks
RINAT	Retailers' Adjustment Time	4 weeks
RWIND	Retail Number of Weeks Inventory Desired	8 weeks
DORFD	Distributor Order Filling Delay	1 week
DTRND	Distributor Transit Delay	1 week
	Distributor Inventory Replenishment Feedback Loop	
DSAVT	Distributor Sales Averaging Time	8 weeks
DINAT	Distributor Adjustment Time	8 weeks
DWIND	Distributor Number of Weeks Inventory Desired	12 weeks
FORFD	Factory Order Filling Delay	2 weeks
FTRND	Factory Transit Delay	3 weeks
	Company Inventory-Production Decision Feedback Loop	
FSAVT	Factory Sales Averaging Time	8 weeks
FWIND	Factory Number of Weeks Inventory Desired	4 weeks
PNAJT	Production Adjustment Time	4 weeks
PRNTM	Production Time	6 weeks
PNCAP	Production Capacity	1,000 units/week

operation of the system, illustrating transient response to a sudden unexpected ten per cent increase in retail sales in the third week. The simulation began with the system in an equilibrium state. The rates (retail sales, retail purchase, distributor purchase, and factory production) were all initially at 500 units per week, and inventories initially were each equal to their desired levels: retail inventory = 4,000 units; distributory inventory = 6,000 units; and finished goods inventory = 2,000 units.

The system behaves with the type of lagged amplified response which we associate with coupled higher order feedback loops. After the ten per cent increase in retail sales, retail purchase rate increases by twenty per cent in

Figure 13.15   Response of Multi-Stage Distribution System to a 10 Per Cent Increase in Demand

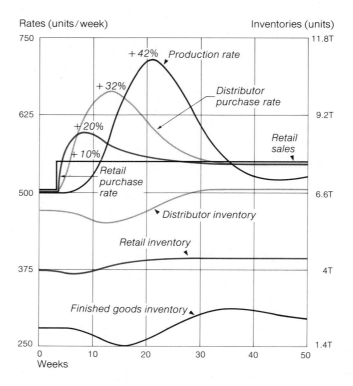

the eighth week (a five-week time lag). The sudden increase in retail sales causes a drop in the level of retail inventory, while desired inventory is increasing. Consequently the purchase rate rises not only to accommodate the new higher rate of business activity, but also to replenish the depleted inventory and build it up to a new level of 4,400 units.

In the distributor sector the increase in business activity, represented by the incoming retail purchase rate, is 20 per cent. This causes distributor inventory to drop by 7 per cent and the distributor purchase rate to rise 32 per cent by the thirteenth week (a ten-week time lag). The increased distributor purchase rate causes a 28 per cent decline in finished goods inventory at the company, and results in a 42 per cent increase in production rate by the twenty-first week (an eighteen-week time lag). Observe that the production rate then drops from a peak of 713 units per week in the twenty-first week to 522 units per week in the forty-fourth week, which is about 5 per cent below the new equilibrium level of 550 units per week. We see that it takes about five months for the step increase in retail sales to be reflected in the peak production rate, and that the system has not returned to an equilibrium state nearly a year later.

Seasonal Fluctuations. How would this system behave in response to rising and falling retail sales of the type we associate with seasonal fluctuations? Figure 13.16 depicts the response of the system to an unexpected rise and fall in retail sales of ten per cent occurring over a period of twelve months. This would correspond to a seasonal fluctuation with a peak occurring in the thirteenth week of the year, and valley in the thirty-ninth week of the year. Retail purchase rate leads the sales rate by two weeks and fluctuates from a high of +20 per cent to a low of −20 per cent of the

Figure 13.16   Response of Multi-Stage Distribution System to an Unexpected ± 10 Per Cent Seasonal Fluctuation

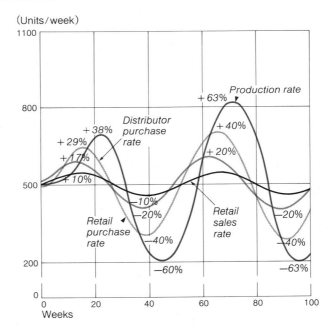

average. In distributor purchase rate and production rate, we see a more pronounced amplification than in the previous illustration. Distributor purchase rate coincides with retail sales rate, and after the first peak of 29 per cent, fluctuates between +40 per cent and −40 per cent. Production rate lags retail sales by about six weeks, and after the first peak of +38 per cent, fluctuates between +63 per cent and −63 per cent.

Amplification and Reaction Times. The extreme amplification observed in this system is a result of several factors. One is the necessity of filling and emptying the pipeline of inventories existing in the chain comprised of the three sectors of the distribution system. Another is the fact that each sector responds only to the incoming flow of orders. No prompt information is available at either the distributor or company sector about recent changes in retail sales rate. Another factor is the decision rules used which are designed to expand and contract inventory levels with changes in business activity.

Because we are dealing with a system comprised of coupled negative feedback loops of second order and higher, it is not possible to eliminate completely all overshoot and amplification. We observed this in the system portrayed in Figure 13.10. But it is possible to substantially alter the amplification by merely changing reaction time in each of the sectors. Figure 13.17 shows a comparison of five runs of the model with changed reaction times. Production rates for each of the runs are plotted in the graph. For this series of runs the two inventory adjustment times, retail inventory adjustment time and distributor inventory adjustment time, and production adjustment time were set equal to each other, and a series of runs were made using values of 1 week, 2 weeks, 4 weeks, 10 weeks, and 20 weeks. Recall from our description of the model that reaction time is used in a fraction which determines the amount of inventory and pipeline imbalance corrected in the following week.

Figure 13.17 Response of Production Rate in Multi-Stage Distribution System to Changes in Reaction Times of Inventory Adjustment (RINAT = DINAT = PNAJT)

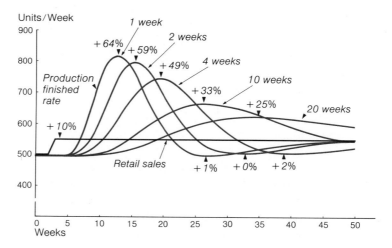

Observe in Figure 13.17 that increasing the reaction times has two effects: the amplitude of the overshoot is reduced and the time lag between the step increase in retail sales and peak production rate is increased. However, even in a system with a relatively slow reaction time of 20 weeks, there is still a 25 per cent increase in production as a result of the 10 per cent increase in retail sales.

Management Implications. What are the implications of these findings for the company management? One is that because of the decision policies which attempt to maintain inventories at levels which correspond to the rate of business activity, short reaction times imply that inventory is not serving as a buffer to absorb fluctuations, but actually is a cause of increased amplification and oscillation in the system. In order to utilize inventory as a buffer, a manager must be willing to allow it to fluctuate, and exercise some restraint in the rapidity with which he attempts to correct differences between desired and actual inventory levels.

In this model we may also observe the effect of an information system which does not provide information about what is happening in other sectors of the system. If an information flow directly from the retail sector to the company were included, it could be used to reduce fluctuations at the company. If the company is dealing with independent distributors and retailers, as is the case in many industries, it may not be feasible to get retailers to report the desired information. In these situations the company may turn to other information sources to learn more rapidly about the current rate of customer demand. A company operating in an industry in which there is a well-defined seasonal fluctuation would include this information in its scheduling decisions, as discussed in Chapter 11.

Elimination of the distributor sector would reduce amplification and oscillation at the company, but there would be costs associated with such a move. Some firms have done just that. Whether such a move would be desirable depends upon many factors, such as type of product and cost of transportation. To determine the effects of such a change, the model may be restructured to represent the proposed system, and simulation experiments performed.

This model has been structured and analyzed in the context of a distribution system in which each sector represents separate enterprises. Many of the conclusions we have reached may be applied equally well to distribution systems within an enterprise. Industrial companies, merchandising firms, transportation companies, and military and other governmental organizations may have internal inventory-distribution systems not unlike the one we have discussed here. For example, a multi-store merchandising firm may have a central purchasing office and distribution centers which store and transmit goods to retail stores. The analysis we have made on this system may also be applied to those types of systems. This model may be adapted if the system were similar, or a new model could be built which would incorporate the structure of the system under study.

The Dynamics of Growth Systems

Growth systems contain positive feedback loops, in contrast to the systems we have examined so far which have contained only coupled negative feedback loops. As we indicated earlier, a negative feedback loop is goal-seeking; deviations from the goal are corrected by opposing actions designed to bring the state of the system into conformity with some desired state. Positive feedback, on the other hand, is reinforcing; action which increases a state of a system results in more action which further increases the system state.

When we compare companies that grow rapidly and profitably with those that grow slowly and those that fail, we often observe that the difference between them is good management. But what is it that good management has done right and that poor management has done wrong? Why do some companies grow at annual rate of from 30 to 50 per cent, while others falter and either barely survive or fail? To understand this process better, we must take a systems approach and examine the interactions between a company and its environment. As a basis for our discussion we will take a detailed look at some aspects of the interaction between a company and its market.

Figure 13.18 shows some of the information and action flows which interconnect a firm and its market. As pictured here, the market is influ-

Figure 13.18 Flows Between Firm and Market

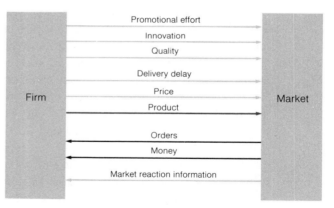

Source: Adapted from Jay W. Forrester, "Common Foundations Underlying Engineering and Management," *IEEE-Spectrum*, September 1964, p. 70.

enced by promotional effort, product or service innovation, quality, delivery delay, and price. Promotional effort, product or service innovation, and quality form part of the positive feedback loops in the system. Relative to competitors, increases in these factors tend to increase the flow of orders. On the contrary, an increase in delivery delay, here defined as the length of time a customer has to wait for delivery of goods or services, tends to decrease the flow of orders. The market usually responds in an inverse way to price—an increase in price reduces demand. The company responds not only to the flow of orders and money from the market, but also to information about the reaction of the market to variations in price, quality, innovation, and delivery delay. The system portrayed here is a closed system, but, of course, many other exogenous factors exist which affect behavior of a firm and the market. From the complex nature of the system of interactions we can readily see that a firm cannot give attention only to single factors if it is to understand the process of growth.

Corporate Growth Model

As a vehicle for exploring some aspects of growth dynamics, we will examine the structure and behavior of an elementary corporate system which incorporates several of these variables.[2] Figure 13.19 depicts the structure of the system we will consider. In order to keep the model of the system simple, we will examine only promotional effort and capacity expansion as positive influences on the market. Although we will omit such factors as product innovation and quality, remember that the fundamental concepts underlying them are similar to the ones we will consider. The specific nature and time lags of other interactions are different, but they have the same type of positive effect on growth as the factors we are considering.

In Figure 13.19, there are two major positive feedback loops and two major negative feedback loops in the system. In the promotional positive feedback loop, the firm's promotional efforts are represented by one aggregate variable, called promotional effort. Promotional effort includes all those things which a firm does to promote and sell its product, such as advertising, selling, and management attention given to marketing. This is a positive feedback loop because an increase in promotional effort leads to an increase in sales rate, order backlog, and production rate. An increased production rate yields higher revenues, which increases the promotion budget and results in a further increase in promotional effort.

The other positive feedback loop involves the expansion of production capacity. Tracing around the loop, an increase in sales causes an increase in backlog and ultimately an increase in production rate up to the limit of plant capacity. As the backlog increases relative to plant capacity, there will be pressures to expand. These pressures ultimately result in expansion of production capacity which permits an increase in the production rate. This generates an increase in the promotion budget and promotional effort, and leads to further increases in the sales rate.

The delivery delay loop is a negative feedback loop. Tracing around it, we see that an increase in sales rate increases order backlog and ultimately production rate up to the limit of plant capacity. Plant capacity and the

[2] The model discussed here is based partly upon one developed in Jay W. Forrester, "Market Growth as Influenced by Capital Investment," *Industrial Management Review,* Winter 1968, pp. 83–105.

Figure 13.19 Feedback Loop Structure of Long-Term Growth Model

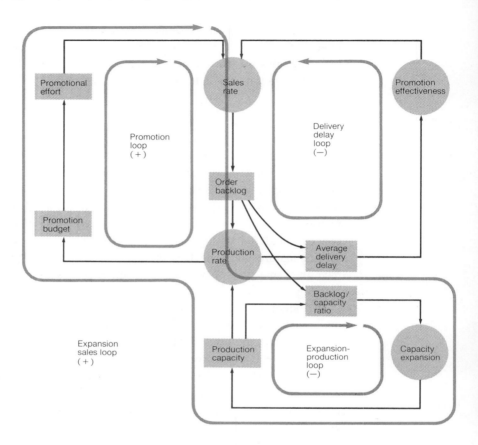

time lag required to change the production rate cause an increase in delivery delay. In the system we are considering, an increase in delivery delay lowers the effectiveness of the firm's promotional efforts, and tends to reduce sales. The other negative loop shown involves capacity expansion. At capacity an increase in backlog increases pressures to expand. As capacity is expanded the production rate increases and lowers backlog.

Promotional Effort Positive Loop

Figure 13.20 illustrates the detailed structure of the positive feedback loop which incorporates promotional effort. Within the symbol for each model variable is included the variable name, the mnemonic symbol used to represent it in the computer program, and the equation number.[3] Tracing

---

[3] A listing of the DYNAMO computer program for the complete model is at the end of the chapter for those who would like to examine the equation structure more closely or to experiment with it.

around the loop beginning with sales rate, we see that it causes orders to flow into order backlog. Order backlog is a level, or system state variable, and is represented by the same type of level equation which we have previously encountered. The backlog level is depleted by production rate, which is determined in another sector of the model. Production rate is averaged by first-order exponential smoothing, and this average is used as the basis for the promotion budget. The indicated promotion budget is a function of deliveries, or average production, and in this model is simply the amount allocated to promotion for each unit produced multiplied by the quantity produced. Actual promotional effort is indicated promotion budget delayed by promotion adjustment time. In an equilibrium condition promotional effort is equal to the indicated promotion budget, but the first-order delay used here serves to take into account the fact that it does take time before indicated budget changes can be realized. It requires time to hire salesmen, develop new advertising campaigns, and to adjust managerial effort.

Figure 13.20   Growth Model: Positive Feedback Loop for Promotional Effort

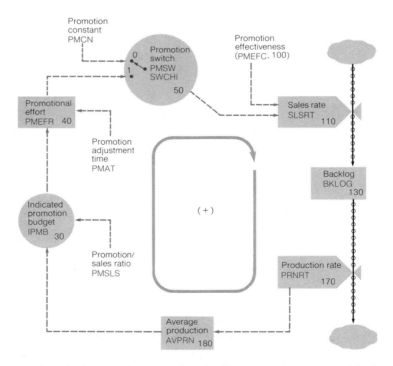

Promotion budget and promotional effort equations are critical components of the model. The particular formulation used here represents a situation in which the company bases its promotional effort on the level of

business activity. Many companies do this. Promotion budgets are often increased when business activity is rising, and are reduced when it is falling. One of the uses to which we can put this model is to explore whether this is a desirable policy.

Promotional effort multiplied by promotion effectiveness determines sales rate. The promotion switch shown at the top of the diagram is included to permit the simulation model to be rerun with the loop deactivated, and a constant amount of promotional effort substituted for the variable promotion budget.

Figure 13.21 illustrates the exponential growth of this positive feedback loop. The graph shows the results of a computer simulation run in which

Figure 13.21   Growth Model: Unlimited Exponential Growth of Positive Feedback Loop

other feedback loops of the model have been deactivated. Sales and production rates are initially at 1000 units per month, order backlog is 2000 units, and promotional effort is $5000 per month. In this model, promotional effectiveness is expressed as the average number of units of sales generated by each dollar of promotional effort. For this run promotional effectiveness is 0.2, that is, for each dollar spent on promotional effort an average of 0.2 units of product will be sold. Multiplying the $5000 promotional effort by the promotional effectiveness factor of 0.2 yields an initial sales rate of 1000 units per month. The initial production rate of 1000 units per month multiplied by the promotion to sales ratio factor of $12 per unit per month yields an indicated promotion budget of $12,000 per month. Delays around the loop are found in the time to adjust production (3 months), time to average production (1 month), and time to adjust promotional efforts (24 months). Increasing any of these delays would result in a slower growth rate, and conversely decreasing any of them would result in a faster growth rate. The exponential growth seen here is characteristic of unrestrained positive feedback systems. In subsequent simulation runs, we will examine what happens when positive and negative loops are coupled together.

Negative Market Loop

The negative feedback loop incorporating the effect of delivery delay on the effectiveness of promotional efforts is portrayed in detail in Figure 13.22. Delivery delay is a function of the ratio of order backlog to average production rate, and represents the length of time required to fill an order in the backlog. For example, if there is an order backlog of 2000 units and the

Figure 13.22 Growth Model: Negative Market Feedback Loop

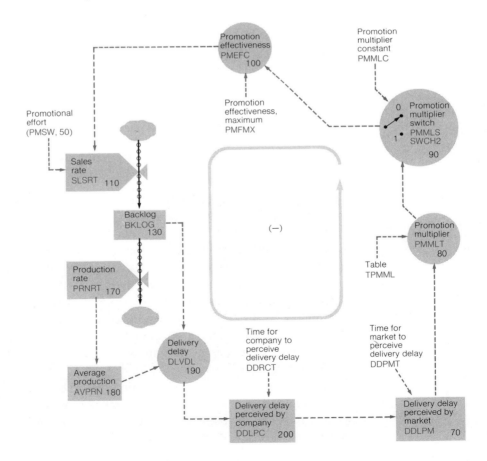

current production rate is 1000 units per month, then the factory will require two months at that rate to fill all the orders in the backlog. Observe that delivery delay feeds into a variable called "delivery delay perceived by company." This variable is included to account for the fact that decision makers in the company are unlikely to be aware of instantaneous changes in delivery delay. Instead, some time period will pass before changes come to their attention. Delay in this information flow is represented in the model by a first-order exponential delay. Additional time may elapse before changes in delivery delay are perceived by the market, as represented by the variable "delivery delay perceived by the market." Information about this variable determines the effectiveness of the company's promotional efforts.

The relationship between the market's perception of delivery delay and effectiveness of the company's promotional efforts is represented by a table function, as shown in Figure 13.23. In this table the independent variable

Figure 13.23   Table for Promotion Multiplier

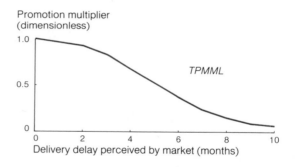

is delivery delay perceived by the market, and the dependent variable is a factor called promotion multiplier. This factor is a fraction between 0 and 1 by which the maximum value of promotion effectivenss is multiplied to determine effectiveness of the company's promotional efforts. As we explained earlier, the maximum value of promotion effectiveness is 0.2; for each dollar of promotional effort an average of 0.2 units of product will be sold. If delivery delay perceived by the market is 2 months, the promotion multiplier is 0.92, and promotion effectiveness is 0.184. As delivery delay rises, the effectiveness of promotional effort declines. We include a switch in the loop to permit substitution of a promotion multiplier constant for the table function.

An advantage of using a table relationship such as this one for promotion multiplier is that we may express a relationship between two variables without resorting to complex mathematical formulas. Although determination of the precise values for each point on the curve may be difficult, we can probably determine a general shape for the curve and a range of values that it should take. Such approximate values may be inserted into the model, and simulation runs made to perform sensitivity analysis. In this case sensitivity analysis would involve trying different curves to observe their effect on model behavior. If a model is found to be very sensitive to a particular variable, then additional resources can be devoted to an attempt to determine more precise values for that relationship. On the other hand, if the model is not found to be very sensitive to a particular variable, an approximation may serve.

Negative Production Feedback Loop

The production sector of the model is included in the negative feedback loop depicted in Figure 13.24. Order backlog and production capacity are compared in a backlog-capacity ratio. This ratio is used in the table of Figure 13.25 to relate size of the backlog to fraction of production capacity utilized. In the table we see that the entire production capacity is not utilized unless there is at least a two-month backlog-capacity ratio. Below

Figure 13.24 Growth Model: Negative Production Feedback Loop

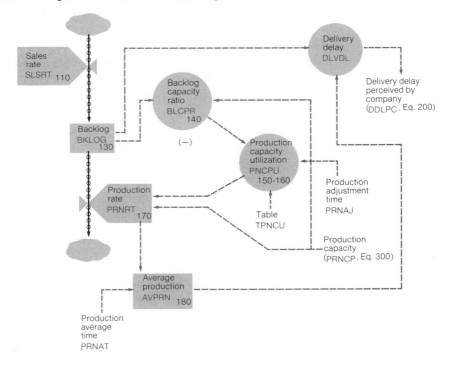

a two-month ratio, the fraction utilized drops off in proportion to the size of the backlog. Use of a table function relating backlog to capacity permits variation of the absolute size of backlog with variations in capacity. Pro-

Figure 13.25 Table for Production Capacity Utilization as a Function of Backlog

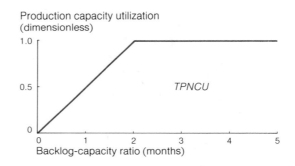

duction capacity utilization is multiplied by production capacity to obtain production started rate. The production rate is the output of a third-order delay which represents the length of time for the production cycle and the time required to make adjustments in production rate. Production rate is averaged and compared with backlog to determine the current value of delivery delay. Delivery delay is used in the market loop of Figure 13.22, and the backlog-capacity ratio is used in the capacity expansion sector. Tracing around the production and market loops we note that delays occur in production rate adjustment (3 months), production averaging (1 month), delivery delay perceived by the company (4 months), and delivery delay perceived by the market (10 months).

Figure 13.26 shows the results of a simulation run of the model in which promotional effort and production capacity are held constant. The run began with an initial disequilibrium state with backlog at 2000 units, production capacity 3000 units per month, and production rate at 1000 units per month. A constant promotional effort of $27,000 per month and delivery delay of 2 months result in an initial sales rate of 4970 units per month. With this sales rate, production rate rises rapidly to the level of capacity, but backlog continues to increase resulting in an increase in delivery delay. Note that although order backlog reaches a peak in the eleventh month, delivery delay as perceived by the market does not reach a peak until the twenty-second month. Sales rate is falling in the interval between the intial month and the twenty-second month because of reduced promotion effectiveness which accompanies increased delivery delay. As the sales rate falls below production rate, order backlog is reduced. Fluctuations around the equilibrium level continue over the simulation run of 100 months with reduced amplitude.

The situation depicted here is based upon an assumption that a firm's ability to deliver goods promptly affects its efforts to promote and sell its products. In this model the variable promotion effectiveness is meant to

Figure 13.26 Growth Model: Fluctuation in Negative Production and Market Feedback
Loops

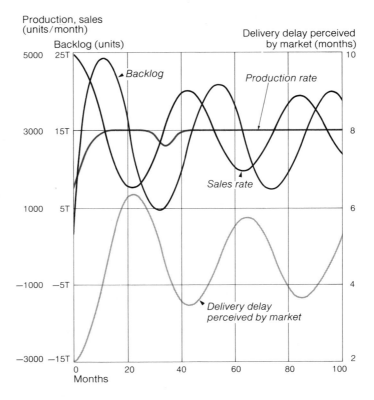

represent an average effect resulting from a complex set of factors, which
might include not only customers' reluctance to place orders when delivery
delay is long, but also the added amount of time required for the firm's
salesmen and management to devote to tracing, expediting, and explaining
late orders. If we were modeling a specific firm and market, we may wish
to expand the detail in factors such as this one and represent various factors
individually. However, for our purpose, which is merely to examine some
underlying causal relationships in a company-market interaction and implications of feedback mechanisms and time lags, the simplification we have
employed will suffice.

**Capacity
Expansion
Loop**

Thus far we have considered the cases of unlimited exponential growth
without any capacity restriction and of company-market interaction with
a fixed production capacity. To complete examination of this growth system
we will add the negative feedback loop of capacity expansion as depicted
in Figure 13.27. In this sector of the model, capacity is expanded in
response to demand which rises above the capacity of the firm. A capital

expansion decision is a very complex decision dependent upon many factors, but in the interest of simplicity we will include only one aggregate variable which relates capacity expansion to pressures arising from increased demand. A more complete model would add such factors as return on investment, cost and availability of capital, and long-range market forecasts. To add these to the present model would require more space than we have available and would make the model much more complex and difficult to understand.

Expansion Decision. The basis for expansion in this model is the ratio of backlog to production capacity. The backlog-capacity ratio was computed in the production rate sector. In the capacity expansion sector, information about the backlog-capacity ratio available to company decision makers is delayed by a four-month first-order exponential delay, "backlog-capacity perceived by company." The rationale for the delay in the information flow is the same as for delivery delay: managers are not likely to be aware of instantaneous fluctuations in the information flow, and the delay serves to represent the time required for managers to respond to changes in backlog-capacity ratio. Demand would have to be above production capacity for some period of time before the company would decide to expand capacity.

Next we determine a desired ratio of backlog to capacity. The model provides for two different goal situations. One situation is for a fixed goal and the other is for a goal that changes over time to correspond to historical trends. The fixed goal is represented by a constant, backlog-capacity ratio fixed goal, and the goal based upon past performance is represented by a variable, the long-range average backlog-capacity ratio. Perceived backlog condition is compared with the desired condition by means of a backlog-capacity goal ratio, and is the ratio of perceived to desired system states. This goal ratio is used as the independent variable in the table in Figure 13.28 which relates goal ratio to capacity expansion rate. The expansion rate is expressed as the fraction per month by which capacity will be expanded. If the perceived system state is equal to the desired state, then the ratio is 1.0 and there will be no expansion.

As backlog rises relative to the desired level, expansion will occur. The rate rises to six per cent for a ratio of two to one. At this rate the company will just about double capacity in a year. As backlog falls, capacity will be reduced. Such reduction does not necessarily imply that capacity is sold or scrapped, but may represent the diversion of facilities to other products, or not performing necessary maintenance to keep equipment in operating condition. We include the capacity expansion switch to permit simulation runs with no capacity expansion.

Production capacity order rate is the product of current capacity and capacity expansion rate. A third-order delay of twelve months is used to represent the lead time required between orders for production capacity and its availability for use.

Figure 13.27   Growth Model: Capacity Expansion Loop

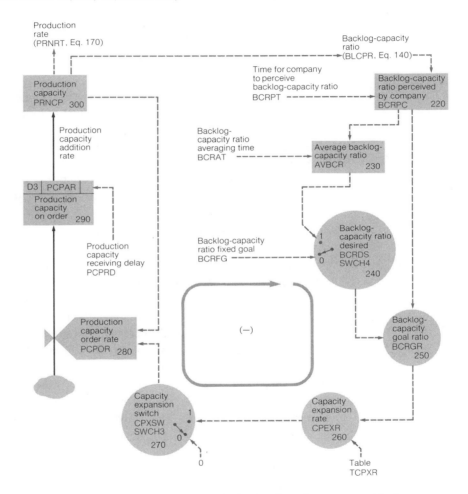

Fixed Backlog-Capacity Ratio Goal. To simulate the system with the capacity expansion decision function, we will consider first the case of the company adhering to a fixed backlog-capacity ratio goal. In this example, the simulation begins with an initial capacity of 1200 units per month and an initial production rate of 1000 units per month, approximately 83 per cent of capacity. We will assume that the company would like to maintain production at about 83 per cent of capacity, and that it would like to keep

Figure 13.28 Table for Capacity Expansion Rate

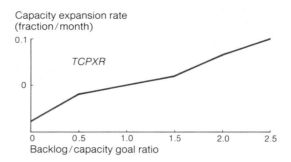

a backlog equal to 2 months' production, or 2000 units. Under these conditions, the backlog-capacity ratio goal would be $2000/1200 = 1.67$, and initial delivery delay would be 2 months. From the table in Figure 13.23 we see that for a two-month delivery delay the promotion multiplier is 0.92, which when multiplied by 0.2, the value of maximum promotion effectiveness, yields a promotion effectiveness of 0.184. Initial sales rate is 920 units per month, computed from initial promotional effort of $5000 multiplied by promotion effectiveness of 0.184.

Figure 13.29 illustrates the output from a simulation run of 100 months for the system. The sales rate increases at first because it is below production capacity, but levels off and declines at about the twentieth month due to a rising delivery delay. By the twentieth month the capacity expansion rate has increased to its maximum value in an effort to bring capacity into line with the high backlog. About six months later additional capacity becomes available and permits an increase in production rate. Since production is rising relative to sales, there is a reduction in delivery delay beginning in the thirty-sixth month. At this time the sales rate, which increases rapidly, turns around but remains below capacity. No further ordering of capacity occurs, and capacity levels off at about the fifty-sixth month, when sales again rise above capacity. The rapidly increasing sales rate cannot be sustained since capacity has fallen behind, and we see, beginning in the seventieth month, another decline in sales because of slow deliveries.

In this simulation run we observe an interesting form of growth instability. Sales decline at the same time that capacity is being expanded, because of slow deliveries. Sales and production grow and decay instead of continuing to grow at smooth rates. This instability is caused by an imbalance between the coupled feedback loops arising from time lags in the system.

Variable Backlog-Capacity Ratio Goal. However, growth is rapid as compared with the system in which management shifts its goal in response to relatively long-term historical trends. In Figure 13.30, we see an illustration of this latter situation. Initial conditions and parameters are the same as for

Figure 13.29 Growth Model: Expansion and Growth Resulting from Interaction of All
Feedback Loops

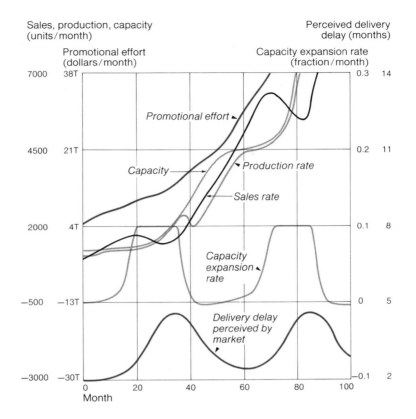

the previous simulation run, except that the goal relating to backlog-capacity
ratio is no longer fixed at 1.67, but is based upon past performance, as
determined from the long-run average backlog-capacity ratio. The averaging
time constant used here is twenty-four months. In this simulation sales
begin to grow slowly, as in the previous example, but, instead of continuing
to increase, reach a point of slow growth followed by stagnation and decay.
The backlog-capacity ratio begins at 1.67, but by the end of the simulation
run has risen to 4 and delivery delay is fluctuating between 4 and 6 months.
Slow deliveries depress the effectiveness of the firm's promotional efforts,
and ultimately result in a tapering off of promotional efforts.

In this example we have postulated a system which can grow with unlimited visible potential. Over a period of seven to eight years the growth
rate in the simulation of Figure 13.29 is about thirty per cent per year. This
is not unusual for many types of products, but there is some limit to demand
growth, and a more complete representation of the system would include
additional feedback loops representing the growth limiting mechanism.

Figure 13.30 Growth Model: Retardation of Growth Due to Variable Capacity Goal

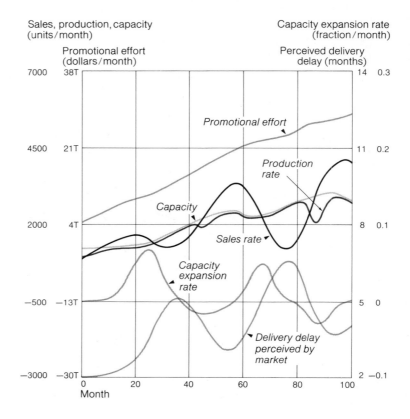

Although this is a relatively simple model of a hypothetical system, a great deal can be learned from analyzing the relationships among the several that no sector of the system can operate effectively independent from the other sectors. Managers of departments and divisions in an organization system sectors. One conclusion readily apparent from these experiments is must be continually aware of the implications of their decisions for other organizational units. It is also apparent that the nature of these relationships and feedback loops is not intuitively obvious, and their discovery requires careful analysis of the system.

Other Applications

Several applications of industrial dynamics models to actual situations have been reported in such diverse areas as production-employment systems, quality control systems, management of research and development firms, commercial salmon fishery regulation, and growth and stagnation of urban communities. The analysis of each of these systems was based upon the fundamental concepts of feedback system analysis developed in the models presented earlier. Discussion of these applications may be found in the references at the end of the chapter.

Production-Employment Study

One industrial dynamics study was undertaken to find the causes of excessive fluctuation in production and employment at Sprague Electric Company, a manufacturer of high-quality electronic components.[4] Figure 13.31 shows the basic structure of the customer-producer system that was analyzed. One product line was selected for detailed examination, and a simulation model was developed to study hypotheses about causes of the behavior patterns of the system. A review of the product revealed that customer usage rates did not fluctuate as widely as company sales and production. The flow diagram shows a feedback loop which relates delivery delay and the customers' ordering policy. In this system customers tended to order ahead as the company's delivery delay increased, and to cut back their ordering when delivery delay decreased. Tests of the simulation model showed amplification and fluctuation similar to that observed with the distribution system model in Figure 13.15. One reason for this similarity seemed to be that an attempt was made to adjust inventories rapidly whenever sales fluctuations caused inventories to rise and fall. Consequently, wide fluctuations occurred in production and employment, because inventories were not being used as a buffer to smooth sales fluctuations. One result of the study was a change in inventory replenishment and production scheduling policies which resulted in more stable production and employment rates.

Quality Control Systems

A commonly encountered management control situation which may be viewed in terms of its feedback structure is the control of quality of manufactured products. Edward B. Roberts has reported on an industrial dynamics models of such a system which demonstrates that the control system which is designed to regulate system performance may actually create rather than solve problems.[5] Figure 13.32 depicts the feedback structure of such systems. Following production, components are inspected, and rejects are discarded or reworked. Quality control reports are fed back to production to correct the process. When the reject rate indicates that the process is out of control, more time is required to adjust the production process and the production rate is lowered temporarily.

Now consider this quality control feedback process as part of a larger system which includes the flow of goods to customers, as portrayed in Figure 13.33. In this system, components which are accepted are sent to

---

[4] Jay W. Forrester, *Industrial Dynamics* (Cambridge, Mass.: The M.I.T. Press, 1961), Chapters 17 and 18.

[5] Edward B. Roberts, "Industrial Dynamics and the Design of Management Control Systems," *Management Technology* 3, no. 2 (December 1963): 100–118.

Figure 13.31 Basic Structure of Customer-Producer-Employment Model

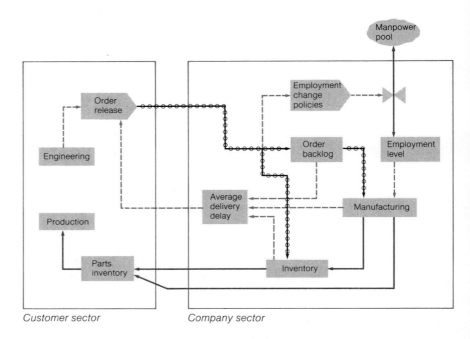

Customer sector   Company sector

Source: Adapted from Jay W. Forrester, *Industrial Dynamics* (Cambridge, Mass.: M.I.T. Press, 1961), p. 212. Copyright © 1961 by the Massachusetts Institute of Technology.

customers through the company's distribution system. If too many defective items get through inspection, customers will complain. Their complaints will be fed back to the quality control manager via' the company's sales-service department and top management. As complaints build up, pressure is put on the quality control manager, who, in turn, puts pressure on the inspectors to be more careful and detect more defective product. In response to this pressure inspectors reject more items.

Figure 13.32 Total Quality Control System

Source: Edward B. Roberts, "Industrial Dynamics and the Design of Management Control Systems," *Management Technology* 3, no. 2 (December 1963): 114.

This model was used to explore the impact of a system in which there is a significant subjective element in recognizing product quality, a situation

Figure 13.33 Feedback Structure of a Quality Control System

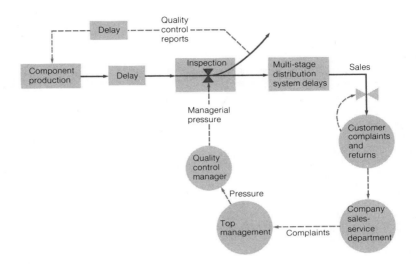

Source: Edward B. Roberts, "Industrial Dynamics and the Design of Management Control Systems," *Management Technology*, 3, no. 2 (December 1963): 116.

which exists for many products. Without objective measures of product quality, the inspectors' reject rate tends to be a function of subjective standards. With pressure from the quality control manager, inspectors' subjective standards rise and an increased proportion of actually acceptable quality products is rejected. As fewer defective products are delivered to customers, complaints about quality decrease and may then change to complaints about slow deliveries. This creates a counterpressure to increase output, and inspectors tend to gradually lower their standards. Eventually, the proportion of defective product coming through the system rises, and the cycle repeats.

The problem is further complicated by the long time delays around the feedback loops. Roberts found in his experiments with the model that these fluctuations could take on a seasonal appearance because top management pressures on the quality control manager may be a reflection of events which took place many months before. In this system the response of the quality control manager is a major factor in determining system performance, and he is a major aspect of the total system.

This feedback analysis demonstrates that effective control often lies outside traditional organizational boundaries. It also points out the important role of decision makers in the system, and that control system design often requires inclusion of the effects of intangibles such as managers' responses to pressure.

RUN				10
NOTE				11
NOTE	MULTI–STAGE PRODUCTION–DISTRIBUTION SYSTEM			12
NOTE	OPERATIONS MANAGEMENT BOOK			13
NOTE				14
NOTE	RETAIL INVENTORY FEEDBACK LOOP			20
NOTE				21
NOTE	RETAIL SALES INPUT FUNCTION			22
7R	RSLSR.KL=RSLST.K+RSLSN.K		RETAIL SALES	30
45A	RSLST.K=STEP(STPHT,STPTM)		RTL SALES STEP INPUT	40
31A	RSLSN.K=(SLAMP)SIN((2PI)(TIME.K)/PEROD)		RTL SLS SEASNL INPUT	50
NOTE	RETAIL INVENTORY/ORDER SECTOR			60
54R	RSHPR.KL=MIN(RSLSR.JK,RSHLM.K)		RETAIL SHIPPING RATE	70
20A	RSHLM.K=RTINV.K/DT		RTL SHIP RATE LIMIT	80
1L	RTINV.K=RTINV.J+(DT)(RGRCR.JK−RSHPR.JK)		RETAILERS INVENTORY	90
3L	RAVSL.K=RAVSL.J+(DT)(1/RSAVT)(RSLSR.JK−RAVSL.J)		RTL AVG SALES	100
12A	RINDS.K=(RAVSL.K)(RWIND)		RTL INV DESIRED	110
18A	RORDS.K=(RAVSL.K)(DTRND+DORFD)		RTL GDS ON ORDER DES	120
25R	RPRCR.KL=RAVSL.K+(1/RINAT)(RINDS.K+RORDS.K −RTINV.K−RGORD.K+0+0)			130
NOTE			RTL PURCHASE RATE	131
1L	RGORD.K=RGORD.J+(DT)(RPRCR.JK−RGRCR.JK)		RTL GOODS ON ORDER	140
1L	DUNOR.K=DUNOR.J+(DT)(RPRCR.JK−DSHPR.JK)		DST UNFILLED ORDERS	150
20A	DNSHR.K=DUNOR.K/DORFD		DST INDICATED SHP RT	160
20A	DSHLM.K=DSINV.K/DT		DST SHIP RATE LIMIT	170
54R	DSHPR.KL=MIN(DNSHR.K,DSHLM.K)		DST SHIPPING RATE	180
39R	RGRCR.KL=DELAY3(DSHPR.JK,DTRND)		RTL GOODS RECD RATE	190
NOTE				199
NOTE	PARAMETERS			200
C	STPHT=550	UNITS/WEEK	STEP HEIGHT	41
C	STPTM=3	WEEK	STEP TIME	42
C	SLAMP=0		SEASNL VARIATION AMPL	51
C	PEROD=52	WEEKS	SINE FTN PERIOD	52
C	RSAVT=4	WEEKS	RTL SLS AVG TIME	101
C	RINAT=4	WEEKS	RTL INV/ORDER ADJ TM	131
C	RWIND=8	WEEKS	RTL WKS INV DESIRED	111
C	DORFD=1	WEEKS	DST ORDER FILLING DEL	122
C	DTRND=1	WEEKS	DST TRANSIT DELAY	191
NOTE				209
NOTE	INITIAL VALUES			210
6N	RSLST=500	UNITS/WEEK		43
6N	RAVSL=RSLSR			102
6N	RTINV=RINDS			91
6N	RGORD=RORDS			141
6N	DUNOR=(RPRCR)(DORFD)			151
NOTE				299
NOTE	DISTRIBUTOR INVENTORY FEEDBACK LOOP			300
NOTE				301
1L	DSINV.K=DSINV.J+(DT)(DGRCR.JK−DSHPR.JK)		DSTR INVENTORY	310
25R	DPRCR.KL=DAVSL.K+(1/DINAT)(DINDS.K+DORDS.K−DSINV.K−DGORD.K+0+0)			320
NOTE			DST PURCHASE RATE	321
3L	DAVSL.K=DAVSL.J+(DT)(1/DSAVT)(RPRCR.JK−DAVSL.J)		DISTR AVG SALES	330
12A	DINDS.K=(DAVSL.K)(DWIND)		DST INV DESIRED	340
18A	DORDS.K=(DAVSL.K)(FTRND+FORFD)		DST GDS ON ORDER DES	350
1L	DGORD.K=DGORD.J+(DT)(DPRCR.JK−DGRCR.JK)		DST GOODS ON ORDER	360
1L	FUNOR.K=FUNOR.J+(DT)(DPRCR.JK−FSHPR.JK)		FACT UNFILLED ORDERS	370
20A	FNSHR.K=FUNOR.K/FORFD		FACT INDICATED SHP RT	380
20A	FSHLM.K=FGINV.K/DT		FACT SHIP RATE LIMIT	390
54R	FSHPR.KL=MIN(FNSHR.K,FSHLM.K)		FACT SHIPPING RATE	400

39R	DGRCR.KL=DELAY3(FSHPR.JK,FTRND)	DST GOODS RECD RATE	410
NOTE			419
NOTE	PARAMETERS		420
C	DSAVT=8 WEEKS	DST SLS AVG TIME	331
C	DINAT=8 WEEKS	DST INV/ORDER ADJ TM	322
C	DWIND=12 WEEKS	DST WKS INV DESIRED	341
C	FORFD=2 WEEKS	FACT ORDER FILLING DEL	351
C	FTRND=3 WEEKS	FACT TRANSIT DELAY	411
NOTE			419
NOTE	INITIAL VALUES		430
6N	DAVSL=RPRCR		332
6N	DSINV=DINDS		311
6N	DGORD=DORDS		361
6N	FUNOR=FUNDS		371
NOTE			499
NOTE	COMPANY PRODUCTION−INVENTORY FEEDBACK LOOP		500
NOTE			501
3L	FAVSL.K=FAVSL.J+(DT)(1/FSAVT)(DPRCR.JK−FAVSL.J)	FACT AVG SALES	510
12A	FINDS.K=(FAVSL.K)(FWIND)	FIN GDS INV DESIRED	520
12A	WIPDS.K=(FAVSL.K)(PRNTM)	WORK IN PROC DESIRED	530
12A	FUNDS.K=(FAVSL.K)(FORFD)	FACT UNF ORDERS DES	540
25A	DEPRN.K=FAVSL.K+(1/PNAJT)(FINDS.K+WIPDS.K+FUNOR.K−FGINV.K−WPINV.K−		550
X1	FUNDS.K)	DESIRED PRODN RATE	550
56A	PNMIN.K=MAX(DEPRN.K,O)	NON−NEGATIVE LIMIT	560
54R	PNSTR.KL=MIN(PNMIN.K,PNCAP)	PRODUCTION STARTED	570
39R	PNFNR.KL=DELAY3(PNSTR.JK,PRNTM)	PRODN FINISHED RATE	580
1L	WPINV.K=WPINV.J+(DT)(PNSTR.JK−PNFNR.JK)	WORK IN PROCESS INV	590
1L	FGINV.K=FGINV.J+(DT)(PNFNR.JK−FSHPR.JK)	FINISHED GOODS INV	600
NOTE			699
NOTE	PARAMETERS		700
C	FSAVT=8 WEEKS	FACT SLS AVG TIME	511
C	FWIND=4 WEEKS	FACT WKS INV DESIRED	521
C	PNAJT=4 WEEKS	PRODN ADJUSTMENT TIME	551
C	PRNTM=6 WEEKS	PRODUCTION TIME	581
C	PNCAP=10000 UNITS/WEEK	PRODN CAPACITY	571
NOTE			709
NOTE	INITIAL VALUES		710
6N	FAVSL=DPRCR		512
6N	FGINV=FINDS		601
6N	WPINV=WIPDS		591
NOTE			999
NOTE	CONTROL CARDS		1000
NOTE			1001
PLOT	RSLSR=S,RPRCR=R,DPRCR=D,PNFNR=P(250,750)/RTINV=I,DSINV=N,FGINV=F(1		1010
X1	400,11800)		1010
PRINT	1)RSLSR,RSHPR,RAVSL/2)RTINV,RINDS/3)RGORD,RORDS,DUNOR		1020
PRINT	4)RPRCR,RGRCR,DSHPR/5)DSINV,DINDS/6)DGORD,DORDS,FUNOR		1021
PRINT	7)DPRCR,DGRCR,FSHPR/8)DAVSL/9)FGINV,FINDS/10)WPINV,WIPDS		1022
PRINT	11)FAVSL/12)DEPRN/13)PNFNR,PNSTR		1023
SPEC	DT=0.1/LENGTH=52/PRTPER=1/PLTPER=1		1039
RUN	F15.18		1040
			1041
NOTE	RETAIL SALES SEASONAL VARIATION		1050
PLOT	RSLSR=S,RPRCR=R,DPRCR=D,PNFNR=P(−100,1100)		1051
SPEC	DT=0.1/LENGTH=104/PRTPER=2/PLTPER=2		1052
C	STPHT=500 UNITS/WEEK	STEP HEIGHT	1060
C	SLAMP=50 UNITS/WEEK	SEASNL VARIATION AMPL	1061

DYNAMO Program for Long-Term Growth Model of Figure 13.19

RUN	GRO01		10
NOTE			11
NOTE	GROWTH MODEL		12
NOTE	PRODUCTION–CAPACITY EXPANSION–MARKET INTERACTION		13
NOTE			14
NOTE	POSITIVE LOOP—PROMOTION EFFORT		20
12A	IPMB.K=(AVPRN.K)(PMSLS)	INDICATED PROM BUDGET	30
3L	PMEFR.K=PMEFR.J+(DT)(1/PMAT)(IPMB.J−PMEFR.J)	PROMOTIONAL EFFORT	40
49A	PMSW.K=SWITCH(PMCN,PMEFR.K,SWCH1)	LOOP CONTROL SWITCH	50
C	PMSLS=12 DOLLARS/UNIT/MONTH	PROMOTION/SALES RATIO	31
C	PMAT=24 MONTHS	PROMOTION ADJ TIME	47
C	PMCN=27000 DOLLARS/MONTH	PROMOTION CONSTANT	51
C	SWCH1=0	DEACTIVATE LOOP	52
6N	PMEFR=5000 DOLLARS/MONTH		42
NOTE			59
NOTE	NEGATIVE MARKET LOOP		60
NOTE			61
3L	DDLRM.K=DDLRM.J+(DT)(1/DDRMT)(DDLRC.J−DDLRM.J)	DLV DEL REC MKT	70
58A	PMMLT.K=TABHL(TPMML,DDLRM.K,0,10,1)	PROMOTION MULTIPLIER	80
49A	PMMLS.K=SWITCH(PMMLC,PMMLT.K,SWCH2)	LOOP CONTROL SWITCH	90
12A	PMEFC.KL=(PMMLS.K)(PMFMX)	PROM EFFECTIVENESS	100
12R	SLSRT.KL=(PMSW.K)(PMEFC.K)	SALES RATE	110
C	DDRMT=10 MONTHS	DLV DEL REC MKT TIME	71
C	TPMML*=1/.97/.92/.82/.67/.50/.33/.20/.12/.08/.05	TBL PROM MULT	81
C	PMMLC=1	PROM MULT CONSTANT	91
C	SWCH2=0	DEACTIVATE LOOP	92
C	PMFMX=.2 UNITS/DOLLAR/MONTH	PROM EFFECTIVENESS MAX	101
6N	DDLRM=DLVDL MONTHS		72
NOTE			119
NOTE	PRODUCTION LOOP		120
NOTE			121
1L	BKLOG.K=BKLOG.J+(DT)(SLSRT.JK−PRNRT.JK)	BACKLOG	130
20A	BLCPR.K=BKLOG.K/PRNCP.K	BKLOG/CAPACITY RATIO	140
58A	NPCPU.K=TABHL(TPNCU,BLCPR.K,0,5,.5)	INDICATED PRN CAP UTIL	150
3L	PNCPU.K=PNCPU.J+(DT)(1/PRNAJ)(NPCPU.J−PNCPU.J)	PRN CAP UTIL	160
12R	PRNRT.KL=(PRNCP.K)(PNCPU.K)	PRODUCTION RATE	170
3L	AVPRN.J=AVPRN.J+(DT)(1/PRNAT)(PRNRT.JK−AVPRN.J)	AVG PRODUCTION	180
20A	DLVDL.K=BKLOG.K/AVPRN.K	DELIVERY DELAY	190
3L	DDLRC.K=DDLRC.J+(DT)(1/DDRCT)(DLVDL.J−DDLRC.J)	DLV DEL REC CO	200
C	TPNCU*0/.25/.5/.75/1/1/1/1/1/1/1	TABLE PRODN CAP UTIL	151
C	PRNAJ=3 MONTHS	PRODN ADJUSTMENT TIME	161
C	PRNAT=1 MONTH	PRODN AVG TIME	181
C	DDRCT=4 MONTHS	DLV DEL REC CO TIME	201
6N	BKLOG=2000 UNITS		131
6N	PNCPU=NPCPU		162
6N	AVPRN=PRNRT		182
6N	DDLRC=DLVDL		202
NOTE			209
NOTE	CAPACITY LOOP		210
NOTE			211
3L	BCRRC.K=BCRRC.J+(DT)(1/BCRRT)(BLCPR.J−BCRRC.J)	BL/CAP REC CO	220
3L	AVBCR.K=AVBCR.J+(DT)(1/BCRAT)(BCRRC.J−AVBCR.J)	AV BL/CAP RATIO	230
49A	BCRDS.K=SWITCH(BCRFG,AVBCR.K,SWCH4)	BL/CAP RATIO DES	240

DYNAMO Program for Long-Term Growth Model of Figure 13.19

20A	BCRGR.K=BCRRC.K/BCRDS.K	BL/CAP GOAL RATIO	250
58A	CPEXF.K=TABHL(TCPXF,BCRGR.K,0,2.5,.5)	CAP EXPANSION FRACT	260
49A	CPXSW.K=SWITCH(0,CPEXF.K,SWCH3)	CAP EXPANSION SWITCH	270
12R	PCPOR.KL=(PRNCP.K)(CPXSW.K)	PRODN CAP ORDER RATE	280
39R	PCPAR.KL=DELAY3(PCPOR.JK,PCPRD)	PRODN CAP ADDN RATE	290
C	BCRFG=1.67　　　　MONTHS	BL/CAP FIXED GOAL	241
1L	PRNCP.K=PRNCP.J+(DT)(PCPAR.JK+0)	PRODUCTION CAPACITY	300
C	BCRRT=4　　　　MONTHS	BL/CAP CO REC TIME	221
C	BCRAT=24　　　　MONTHS	BL/CAP AVG TIME	231
C	SWCH4=0	FIXED DLV DEL GOAL	242
C	TCPXF*=−.08/−.02/0/.01/.06/.10	TBL CAP EXP RATE	261
C	SWCH3=0	DEACTIVATE EXP LOOP	277
C	PCPRD=12　　　　MONTHS	PRODN CAP RECV DELAY	291
6N	BCRRC=BLCPR		222
6N	AVBCR=BCRRC		232
6N	PRNCP=PCPIN		301
C	PCPIN=3000　　　UNITS/MONTH	INITIAL PRODN CAP	302
NOTE			309
NOTE	CONTROL CARDS		310
NOTE			311
PLOT	SLSRT=S,PRNRT=P(−2E3,6E3)/BKLOG=B(−10E3,30E3)/PMEFR=F(−15E3,45E3)		320
PRINT	1)SLSRT/2)PMSW,IPMB/3)PMEFC,PMMLS/4)PRNRT/5)PNCPU,NPCPU/6)AVPRN		330
PRINT	7)BKLOG,BLCPR/8)DLVDL,DDLRC/9)DDLRM/10)BCRRC,AVBCR/11)BCRDS,BCRGR		331
PRINT	12)CPXSW/13)PCPOR,PCPAR/14)PRNCP		332
RUN	GRO02		
NOTE	UNLIMITED EXPONENTIAL GROWTH—MARKET LOOP		351
SPEC	DT=0.1/LENGTH=100/PRTPER=2/PLTPER=2		
NOTE	FIG. 15.23—OPERATIONS MANAGEMENT TEXT		352
C	SWCH1=1	ACTIVATE LOOP	360
C	PCPIN=25000　　UNITS/MONTHS	INITIAL PRODN CAP	361
RUN	GRO03		370
NOTE	NEGATIVE MARKET LOOP OSCILLATION		371
NOTE	FIG. 15.28—OPERATIONS MANAGEMENT TEXT		372
C	SWCH2=1	ACTIVATE LOOP	380
PLOT	SLSRT=S,PRNRT=P(−3E3,5E3)/BKLOG=B(−15E3,25E3)/DDLRM=D(2,10)		381
RUN	GRO04		390
NOTE	CAPACITY EXPANSION—FIXED DELIVERY DELAY GOAL		391
NOTE	FIG. 15.31—OPERATIONS MANAGEMENT TEXT		392
PLOT	SLSRT=S,PRNRT=P,PRNCP=C(−3E3,7E3)/DDLRM=D(2,14)/PMEFR=F(−30E3,38E3		401
X1	)/CPEXF=X(−.1,.3)		401
C	SWCH1=1	ACTIVATE LOOP	402
C	SWCH2=1	ACTIVATE LOOP	403
C	SWCH3=1	ACTIVATE EXP LOOP	404
C	PCPIN=1200　　UNITS/MONTH	INITIAL PRODN CAP	405
RUN	GRO05		410
NOTE	CAPACITY EXPANSION—HISTORICAL DELIVERY DELAY GOAL		411
NOTE	FIG. 15.32—OPERATIONS MANAGEMENT TEXT		412
C	SWCH1=1	ACTIVATE LOOP	420
C	SWCH2=1	ACTIVATE LOOP	421
C	SWCH3=1	ACTIVATE EXP LOOP	422
C	SWCH4=1	HISTORICAL DL DL GOAL	423
C	PCPIN=1200　　UNITS/MONTH	INITIAL PRODN CAP	424

Summary

In order to analyze the dynamics of system behavior, it is necessary to understand the underlying causal relationships which are determinants of that behavior. Industrial dynamics is a methodology for the study of information feedback in socioeconomic systems. It involves analysis of interrelationships among components of complex systems, identification of feedback information flows and their associated time lags, and construction of dynamic simulation models. The perspective of industrial dynamics is one which permits viewing a system as continuous flows. Negative feedback is goal-seeking, and positive feedback is reinforcing and produces growth or decay in a system. The basic components of feedback system structure are state variables, called levels, and activity variables, called rates. Decision functions determine rates of flow and are generally based upon information about system state variables.

The complexity of system structure is a function of the order of feedback loops, which refers to the number of levels in a feedback loop, and the number of interconnected feedback loops in the system. Nonlinearities and time lags are important determinants of system behavior. A first-order system with a single feedback loop has goal-seeking behavior which gradually approaches a goal or desired system state. Second- and higher-order systems can exhibit oscillation. Time lags are often represented by exponential delays in continuous systems. Delay functions may be cascaded to shape response functions to correspond to actual conditions.

A multi-stage distribution system comprised of a series of interconnected negative feedback loops has a behavior pattern that amplifies variations in demand inputs. The degree of amplification is greatly affected by the number of sectors in the system and the rapidity of reaction times. Attempts to correct inventory fluctuations rapidly increases system amplification. A growth system is composed of interconnected positive and negative feedback loops. Time lags, nonlinearities, and interaction of feedback loops affect stability of growth rates.

Simulation of high level decision processes and system interactions in large systems is not an easy task. The rationality of decision functions in such systems may be difficult to determine and to represent in a simulation model. Validation of such models is difficult. A system analyst must determine appropriate measures of improved system performance. Improving stability, as suggested by the models discussed in this chapter, may not always be the most appropriate criteria. It may be necessary to include cost and profit considerations.

Selected References

Books

Forrester, Jay W. *Industrial Dynamics.* Cambridge, Mass.: M.I.T. Press, 1961.

Forrester, Jay W. *Urban Dynamics.* Cambridge, Mass.: M.I.T. Press, 1969, 285 pp.

Forrester, Jay W. *World Dynamics.* Cambridge, Mass.: Wright-Allen Press, 1971.

Meier, Robert C., Newell, William T., and Pazer, Harold L. *Simulation in Business and Economics.* Englewood Cliffs, N.J.: Prentice-Hall, Inc., 1969. Chapter 3: "Industrial Dynamics and Large System Simulation."

Nord, Ole C. *Growth of New Product: Effects of Capacity-Acquisition Policies.* Cambridge, Mass.: M.I.T. Press, 1963.

Jarmain, Edwin W. (ed.). *Problems in Industrial Dynamics.* Cambridge, Mass.: M.I.T. Press, 1963.

Pugh, Alexander L., III. *DYNAMO User's Manual.* 2nd ed. Cambridge, Mass.: M.I.T. Press, 1963.

Roberts, Edward B. *The Dynamics of Research and Development.* New York: Harper and Row, 1964.

Articles

Ansoff, H. Igor, and Slevin, Dennis P. "An Appreciation of Industrial Dynamics." *Management Science* 14 (March 1968): 383–397.

Carlson, Bruce R. "An Industrialist Views Industrial Dynamics." *Industrial Management Review*, Fall 1964, pp. 15–20.

Carlson, Bruce R. "Industrial Dynamics." *Management Services,* May-June 1964, pp. 32–39.

Fey, Willard R. "An Industrial Dynamics Case Study." *Industrial Management Review,* Fall 1962, pp. 79–99.

Forrester, Jay W. "Advertising: A Problem in Industrial Dynamics." *Harvard Business Review,* March-April 1959, pp. 100–110.

Forrester, Jay W. "Industrial Dynamics." In Carl Heyel (ed.), *The Encyclopedia of Management.* New York: Reinhold Publishing Company, 1963, pp. 313–319.

Forrester, Jay W. "Industrial Dynamics: After the First Decade." *Management Science* 14 (March 1968): 398–415.

Forrester, Jay W. "Industrial Dynamics: A Major Breakthrough for Decision Makers." *Harvard Business Review,* July-August 1958, pp. 37–66.

Forrester, Jay W. "Industrial Dynamics—A Reply to Ansoff and Slevin." *Management Science* 14 (May 1968): 601–618.

Forrester, Jay W. "Market Growth as Influenced by Capital Investment." *Industrial Management Review* 9 (Winter 1968): 83–105.

Newell, William T. "Simulation of Natural Resource Management and Sociological Systems: An Application of Industrial Dynamics." *Proceedings of Conference on Applications of Continuous System Simulation Languages.* San Francisco, California, June 30-July 1, 1969, pp. 97–103.

Roberts, Edward B. "A Systems Study of Policy Formulation in a Vertically-Integrated Firm." *Management Science* 14 (August 1968): B674–B694.

Roberts, Edward B. "Industrial Dynamics and the Design of Management Control Systems." *Management Technology,* December 1963, pp. 100–118.

Roberts, Edward B. "New Directions in Industrial Dynamics." *Industrial Management Review,* Fall 1964, pp. 5–14.

Roberts, Edward B. "Toward a New Theory for Research and Development." *Industrial Management Review,* Fall 1962, pp. 29–40.

Schlager, Kenneth J. "How Managers Use Industrial Dynamics." *Instrument Society of America Journal,* March 1964, pp. 59–64. Reprinted in *Industrial Management Review,* Fall 1964, pp. 21–29.

Sprague, Robert C. "Industrial Dynamics: Case Example." In Carl Heyel (ed.), *The Encyclopedia of Management.* New York: Reinhold Publishing Company, 1963, pp. 319–322.

Weymar, F. Helmut. "Industrial Dynamics: Interaction Between the Firm and Its Market." In Wroe Alderson and Stanley Shapiro, *Marketing and the Computer.* Englewood Cliffs, N.J.: Prentice-Hall, Inc., 1963, pp. 260–276.

Questions

1 Explain the industrial dynamics approach to systems analysis.

2 Distinguish between negative and positive feedback loops. Give an example of each.

3 Distinguish between state and activity variables in an information feedback system. Give an example of each.

4 How can state variables or accumulations introduce time lags in system flows?

5 How does a continuous flow model of an inventory replenishment system differ from a discrete event model, such as described in Chapter 10?

6 Give other examples of first-order negative feedback systems similar to those shown in Figures 13.1 and 13.2. Sketch a flow diagram for one of these examples and identify the state and activity variables and time lags.

7 Explain the characteristic behavior of a first-order negative feedback loop with a time lag.

8 If the inventory adjustment time in the system in Figure 13.2 were increased to eight weeks, how would this alter the system behavior?

9 What factors account for the amplification observed in the response of the multi-stage distribution system of Figure 13.11?

10 In the multi-stage distribution system of Figure 13.11, what is the effect of changing reaction time in the purchase rate decision?

11 What changes in the multi-stage distribution system of Figure 13.11 might be made to improve the stability of production rate?

12 In the growth system of Figure 13.19 what would be the effect of increasing the time to adjust promotional effort?

13 What factors account for the irregular growth pattern in the simulation run of Figure 13.29?

Problems

1 Refer to the first-order negative feedback system described in Figure 13.2 and equations 13.1 and 13.4. Simulate the system for 20 weeks using the same values as in the illustration in Table 13.1 and Figure 13.4, but change the inventory adjustment time to 10 weeks. Show the results of your simulation in table form and plot them on a graph. Compare your results with those in Table 13.1 and Figure 13.4.

2 Refer to the second-order feedback loop inventory replenishment decision system in Figure 13.9. Simulate the system for 30 weeks using the same input values and initial conditions as in Table 13.2 and Figure 13.10, but change the inventory adjustment time to 10 weeks. Show the results of your simulation in table form and plot them on a graph. Compare your results with those in Table 13.2 and Figure 13.10.

3 Simulate the system in Problem 2 for 30 weeks, but change the shipping delay to 2 weeks and return the inventory adjustment time to 4 weeks. Plot the results and compare them with those in Table 13.2 and Figure 13.10.

4 Simulate the system in Problem 2 for 30 weeks, but change the shipping delay to 2 weeks and the inventory adjustment time to 10 weeks. Plot the results and compare them with those in Table 13.2 and Figure 13.10.

5 Refer to the inventory replenishment decision system in Figure 13.9. Simulate the system for 30 weeks using the same input values and initial conditions as in Table 13.2 and Figure 13.10, but change the goods shipped rate to an increasing trend (a ramp function). Assume that the goods shipped rate is 100 units/weeks for three weeks, and beginning in the fourth week it increases at the rate of 20 units/week/week (120 units/week the fourth week, 140 units/week the fifth week, and so forth). Plot the results and explain the behavior of the system.

6 Refer to the inventory replenishment decision system in Figure 13.9. Simulate the system for 21 weeks using the same input values and initial conditions as in Table 13.2 and Figure 13.9, but change the goods shipped rate to seasonal fluctuation with the following values:

Week	Goods Shipped Rate	Week	Goods Shipped Rate	Week	Goods Shipped Rate
1	100	8	130	15	140
2	110	9	120	16	150
3	120	10	110	17	140
4	130	11	100	18	130
5	140	12	110	19	120
6	150	13	120	20	110
7	140	14	130	21	100

Plot the results and explain the behavior of the system.

7 a. Describe a management control situation in which negative feedback is used, and draw a flow diagram of the system. The situation may be taken from any area—industry, government, education, etc. The example should preferably be of a real situation as found in a periodical, paper, book, discussion with some person, or your personal experience.

b. Describe how a poorly designed control mechanism can create rather than solve problems in this situation. Be precise in identifying the specific elements that appear to create the problem.

c. Describe how the control mechanism should be designed, and draw a flow diagram of the revised system.

8 Dynamic Appliance Company has a production-inventory-distribution system like that described in the multi-stage distribution system, MSDS, in the chapter. The present scheduling and inventory policies of the company, and the inventory and purchasing policies of its distributors and retailers are represented in the simulation run of the MSDS model shown in Figure 13.11. Using the computer model listed at the end of the chapter, and using present situation and policies as a basis for comparison, analyze the impact on the dynamic behavior of the system of changing some of the parameter values in the system. Specifically, prepare a series of runs of the MSDS simulation model to explore two of the following questions. For this set of runs use a step increase in retail sales of 10 per cent.

a. What would be the effect of reducing (or increasing) the size of retail, distributor, and/or finished goods inventories?

b. What would be the effect of a slower (or faster) adjustment time on the part of retailers and distributors to changes in sales rate?

c. What would be the effect of a longer (or shorter) sales averaging time constant in the company, distributor, and/or retail sales forecast?

d. What would be the effect of longer (or shorter) transit delays?

e. What would be the effect if the company could respond more rapidly (or slowly) to changes in demand?

f. What would be the effect if the company's production time were longer (or shorter)?

g. What would be the combined effect if several of these changes were made simultaneously?

After completing the simulation runs of the model, write a brief report on the project. The report should focus upon three things: (1) a description of what you did, that is, the changes in parameter values you made; (2) an explanation of the results of the computer runs you made; (3) an explanation of the implications of these results for the management of the company.

9 Do the simulation project outlined in question 8, using a ± 10 per cent seasonal fluctuation in retail sales, instead of a step increase.

Chapter 14
The Systems
Approach—
An Integrative
Philosophy

The pressures of expanding populations, social unrest, the rising aspirations and needs of man, and the growing commitment by governmental units at all levels dramatize the need for the development of an integrative philosophy of management. Domestic problems are most acute in those urban centers having high densities of population. Transportation congestion, inadequate housing, crime, pollution, water shortages, and the struggle for economic and social equality by minority groups are examples of critical problems facing our cities.

Problems of such magnitude defy traditional approaches and solutions, and although the economic wealth of the United States has grown to record levels, we still face an absolute shortage of resources to do all that must be done. Consequently, we must organize and establish priorities for using our available resources to create a better economic world within a framework of social peace and adjustment.

The most promising philosophy and/or approach for organizing this mission centers around the systems approach. Lawrence Lessing, in a 1967 issue of *Fortune,* asserted that systems management is one of the two greatest inventions coming out of World War II. He commented that innovative industry had used this approach to achieve its goals in the shortest possible time.[1] If we organize and operate projects as systems, and improve the quality of decision making by adopting the appropriate techniques and tools, we will have an opportunity to make the kind of progress that is so essential. In this chapter we will attempt to summarize and integrate the contents of this book and suggest the wide range of potential applications for the concepts we have discussed.

Man tends to influence his future by what he thinks will happen, and then shapes his destiny by what he does. The most significant progress

---

[1] Lawrence Lessing, "Where the Industries of the Seventies Will Come From," *Fortune,* January 1967, p. 98.

occurs when there is a clear vision of what do do, followed by a substantial and sincere dedication toward goal achievement.

The Systems Approach

The term systems has been used in almost every conceivable way. Most people seem to accept this term as an everyday expression and to use it to describe what they do or how they live. They consider phrases like systems concepts, systems management, and systems analysis as synonymous terms. We have found it meaningful to categorize all aspects of systems under the general classification of the "systems approach," and to include under this classification the various uses of systems for example, systems theory and philosophy; systems management, or the design and operation of organizations as systems; and systems analysis. Table 14.1 depicts the relationship among these terms.

In systems theory, the viewpoint is conceptual; the method is cognitative (thinking or reflection); the management level is strategic;[2] and the task is to associate life phenomena as a unitary whole. In systems management, the viewpoint is pragmatic; the method is synthesis (the art of building an organization as a system through the assemblage or combination of parts); the management level is coordinate; and the task is to integrate operations and achieve objectives through design. In systems analysis, the viewpoint is planning or problem-solving; the method is through modeling (the abstraction of factors and identification of factors of the real world, manipulation of the variables, interpretation of analytical conclusions, and the relation of those conclusions to the real world); the management level is directed to operations, and the task is the achievement of objectives and utilization of resources.

Note that the items in Table 14.1 flow from the theoretical to the practical applications, from the conceptual to the techniques of analysis, and from the science to the day-to-day operations. The entire philosophy of the systems approach emphasizes the development of systematic ideas, that is, logical, thorough, and regular thinking.

Systems Theory

General systems theory is the development of a systematic, theoretical framework for explaining general relationships of the empirical world. Models have been developed which describe many physical, biological, behavioral, and social systems; and these are sometimes tied together to show the relationships among the various segments, and to illustrate a higher order of systems.

[2] See Thomas A. Pettit, "A Behavioral Theory of Management," *Academy of Management Journal,* December 1967, pp. 341–350.

A system is an organized or complex whole; an assemblage or combination of things or parts forming a complex whole. But each unitary whole, as described, must maintain some relationship with other systems. That is, each receives inputs and, after a transformation of some kind takes place, each produces output that will be input for other systems. Therein lies the basic concept of systems theory: the input, transformation, and output model. Once this general framework is established, the interesting task is to determine how these associations can be arranged, and how the transformation process of each contributes to the whole. It is a philosophical and conceptual way of thinking, a way of establishing hierarchies of relationships, a way of associating activities with other activities so that relationships can be identified and classified appropriately.

Table 14.1 The Systems Approach

	The systems approach		
	Systems theory	Systems management	Systems analysis
Viewpoint	Conceptual	Pragmatic	Problem solving
Method	Cogitative	Synthesis	Modeling
Managerial level	Strategic	Coordinative	Operating
Task	Association of life phenomena as a unitary whole	Integration of operations through design	Goal achievement and resource utilization

Systems theory is a vehicle for scientists and thinkers, but it also is a framework for doers. It is a way of making meaning out of chaos, and a means toward appreciation of the significance and contribution of various subsystems to the whole. For example, the delicate balance of some of our ecological systems has recently come to light. The need to understand these input-output relationships is, obviously, vital to the very existence of our world.

Systems Management

The theory of systems can be used as a framework to design and operate organizations. When this is accomplished, we refer to the viewpoint as pragmatic and the vehicle as systems management. There are four basic principles which apply: (1) it is goal-oriented, with continual emphasis on objective achievement (effectiveness); (2) it is total-system oriented, because decision-criteria stress optimization of the total system (as described) rather than that of the subsystems when a trade-off situation exists; (3) it is responsibility-oriented, because each manager is given a specific assignment with measureable inputs and outputs; and (4) it is people-oriented, because workers are given challenging assignments, and they are identified with output (achievement is recognized and rewarded). Although work assignments may be specific, the changing nature of systems encourages the intellectual growth and development of employees.

We use two models to illustrate the process of systems management through the four decision states—selection, design and creation, operation and control, and review and evaluation. The first model (Figure 14.1) outlines the systems structure for an entire organization; the second model (Figure 14.2) is a more detailed description of an operating system.

Illustrative Models. A single model cannot describe the detailed activities of every organization; each organization is unique. However, Figure 14.1 does show the major activities of an organization that applies the systems approach. How these activities would be grouped and detailed in a specific situation depends entirely upon the objectives and conditions associated with each case.

Figure 14.1 A Systems Model of an Organization

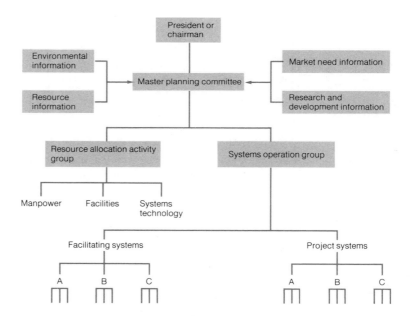

The Master Planning Committee considers inputs relating to the demand or need for the product or service, the present state of research and development technology, the resource capability of the organization, and other influences generated by the environment. At this level, decisions are made concerning the selection of new programs, and the expansion or discontinuation of existing programs.

Once such decisions are made the actual design and creation of the system are delegated to a resource allocation group. Specific inputs of manpower (energy), facilities (materials), and systems technology (information) are combined as necessary to plan and assemble new systems, or to make major revisions in existing systems.

Two types of operating systems can be created—project systems or facilitation systems. Project systems are the major programs of an organization and their output refers directly to organizational objectives. In contrast, facilitating systems are created to service project systems. Some may classify facilitating systems as subsystems of the major projects, but it is more meaningful to consider them as distinct systems since they usually serve more than one project. For example, a hospital organization may include major programs for maternity, heart, and elderly patients, and also have a facilitating system to provide drugs or medicines for all three programs. (Note that the objective of a hospital is not to dispense drugs.)

Generally, it is desirable to provide each program with all of the subsystems and components it needs to accomplish its goals. Such a strategy maintains closer responsibility, reduces problems of communication, transportation, and scheduling and simplifies the process of administration. There are times, however, when the service may be unique or specialized, or when the capital cost of operating a facility cannot be justified for each project system. In such instances, it is proper to create a facilitating system, but even in these cases the goals of the service system must be specified and inputs and outputs measured.

Figure 14.2 An Operating System

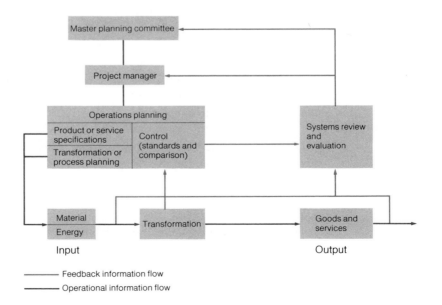

Figure 14.2 illustrates a detailed model of an operating system. The planning of operations may be of two types, namely, specifications planning or transformation planning. On the basis of the information released, material and energy inputs are introduced into the system and transformation occurs. The close relationship between planning and control is symbolized in the model by the union between the two. The feedback from input, transformation, and output is measured and compared with the plan, and new information is released to introduce corrective inputs as they are required.

Each project or program is responsible for meeting its objectives in the most efficient manner possible. Consequently, a periodic review and evaluation of operations is a common practice in progressive organizations. How effectively and efficiently is the system performing? What improvements in components or procedures could be incorporated in current design? How might operating decisions be improved? These are examples of questions which might be asked during the review and evaluation process.

The Relation to Functions

Managers are needed to convert the disorganized resources of men, machines, and money into a useful and effective enterprise. Essentially, management is the process whereby these unrelated resources are integrated into a total system for the accomplishment of objectives. A manager gets things done by working with people and physical resources in order to accomplish the objectives of the system. He coordinates and integrates the activities and work of others rather than performing operations himself.

Structuring an organization according to the systems approach does not eliminate the need for the basic functions of planning, organization, control, and communication. However, there is a definite change of emphasis, because the functions are performed in conjunction with the operation of the system and not as separate entities. In other words, everything revolves around the system and its objective, and each function is carried out only as a service to this end. We can clarify this point by reviewing each of the basic functions in terms of their relation to the models of systems management illustrated in this chapter.[3]

Planning. Figure 14.1 shows the three levels at which planning occurs. First, there is top level planning by the master planning committee. Second, the project and facilitating systems must be planned and resources allocated to them. Finally, the operation of each project and facilitating system must be planned.

The master planning committee establishes broad policies and goals and makes decisions about the products or services the organization produces. The committee decides upon general policy matters concerning the design

[3] Richard A. Johnson, et al., *The Theory and Management of Systems,* 2nd ed. (New York: McGraw-Hill Book Co., 1967), pp. 111–127.

of the operating systems and selects the director for each new program. It is the planning committee which receives informational inputs from the environmental and competitive systems. It combines these inputs with feedback information from the internal organizational system and serves as the key decision-making center within the company. Much of the decision making at this level is nonprogrammed, unstructured, but very significant. Although some of the new techniques of management science may be helpful, major reliance must be placed upon mature assessment of the entire situation by experienced, innovative top executives.

Once these broad decisions have been made, the planning function is transferred to the resource allocation and operating groups. They plan and allocate facilities and manpower for each new system and supply technical assistance for individual systems design. At this planning level it is possible to utilize programmed decision making, operations research analysis, and computer techniques.

The third level, planning the operations of each project or facilitating system, is concerned primarily with the optimum allocation of resources to meet the requirements established by the planning committee. This planning can be programmed most easily to automatic decision systems. However, the project director still must feed important nonquantifiable inputs into the system.

Under the systems approach to planning, a direct relationship exists between the planning performed at each of the three levels. The first planning level receives informational inputs from the environment and competitive system, and feedback information from within the organization. It translates this information into inputs for the next planning level which in turn moves to a more detailed level of planning and provides inputs for the third or project level. One of the major advantages of this systems model is to provide a clear-cut delineation of the responsibility for various types of planning.

This concept facilitates integrated planning on a systems basis at the project level within the organization. Given the inputs (premises, goals, and constraints) from the higher levels, the project managers are delegated the function of integrated planning for their project.

Organization. Traditional organization theory emphasized parts and segments of the structure and was concerned with the separation of activities into tasks or operational units. It did not give sufficient emphasis to the interrelationships and integration of activities. Adapting the business organization to systems management places emphasis upon the integration of all activities toward the accomplishment of overall objectives but also recognizes the importance of efficient subsystem performance.

The system basis of organization differs significantly from traditional organization structures such as line and staff; or line, staff, and functional relationships. As shown in Figure 14.1, there are three major organizational levels, each with clearly delineated functions. The master planning committee has broad planning, control, and integrative functions; the resource allocation group has the primary function of allocating manpower and facilities, and aids in systems design for the facilitating and operating systems. One of the major purposes of this type of organization is to provide an integration of activities at the most important level—the individual project or program.

Staff specialization of skills is provided for the master planning committee through such groups as financial, product research and development, and market research. Their activities, however, are integrated and coordinated by the planning committee. Specialists at the operating level are completely integrated into each project system. Thus, the activities of these specialists are geared to the effective and efficient performance of the individual project system. This type of organization minimizes a major problem associated with staff, scientific, and professional personnel, that is, their tendency to associate their activities with specialized areas rather than with the optimum performance of the overall operation. Yet, under the model the importance of initiative and innovation is recognized; in fact, the major function of the master planning committee is innovation. Specific provision for receiving information inputs from product and market research is given in this model.

There are other advantages to the systems concept. Business activities are dynamic, yet the typical organization is structured to perpetuate itself rather than change. There is generally resistance by the various specialized functions to change if the change is made to optimize organization performance. For example, Parkinson's law states that there is an ever increasing trend toward hierarchies of staff and functional personnel who are self-perpetuating and often do not contribute significantly to organizational effectiveness, and may stymie progress. In contrast, a system is designed to do a particular task. When the task is completed, the system is disbanded or redesigned to meet the needs of another project.

Systems are created from a central pool of resources. Facilities, machines, and manpower are assigned to specific projects or programs. The approach is to create and equip the project system with a complete arrangement of components to accomplish the job at hand. This may result in the duplication of certain activities in more than one operating system; however, this disadvantage is not as serious as it may seem. For example, it may be more efficient to have several typewriters assigned to each system rather than have a central pool of typewriters. In the first instance, the typewriters may be utilized less than 100 per cent of the time, but the problems of scheduling the work at the central pool, delays in work completion, accountability, and the proper measurement of the contribution would soon offset any advantage of centralizing the equipment. Too much effort may be spent in creating processing information which accomplishes no objective other than keeping the machines in use. A reasonable amount of redundancy or extra capacity will provide more flexibility to meet variations in demand, protect against breakdowns, reduce flow time, require less planning, eliminate many problems associated with interdepartmental communication, and reduce the amount of material handling required among the departments.

Obviously, there are situations when it is impractical to decentralize a particular facility, because individual systems cannot utilize it sufficiently to warrant its incorporation into each separate operation. In these instances, a facilitating system would be created to sell its services to any or all of the major project systems. These service systems should justify their existence by being effective and efficient and be expected to compete with outside vendors as a supplier for the major project systems.

The most significant advantage of systems management relates to the concept of accountability. Each system and subsystem has a specific job to do and is given measured resources to complete this task. When the assignment is accomplished efficiently, it is easy to determine whom to credit, and if the assignment is botched, there is no way to "pass the buck."

Control. Systems management features control as a means of gaining greater flexibility in operation, and, in addition, as a way of avoiding detailed planning of those operations when variables are not known or cannot be quantified. Control is designed to serve the operating system as a subsystem of the larger operation. Its effectiveness is measured by how accurately it identifies variations in systems operation from standard or plan, and by how quickly it reports the need for correction to the activating group.

We must conclude that error is inevitable in a system which is subject to variations in input. When the lag in time between input and output is great, more instability is introduced. Prompt feedback can reduce the time lag. However, corrective action which is out of phase will magnify rather than overcome the error. Every system should be designed to make its own corrections when necessary. That is, a means should be provided to reallocate resources if variation in transformation and output occur. When a change in requirements and/or operations exists which causes the system to operate outside of the established limits (out-of-control), the review and evaluation group should recognize this condition and redesign the system as necessary.

In controlling a system, it is important to measure inputs of information, energy, and materials and outputs of products and/or services. This will determine operating efficiency. In addition, it may be important to establish points of measurement during critical or significant stages of transformation.

Such measurements would be used principally to help management analyze and evaluate the operation and design of individual components. The best approach is to spotlight exceptions and significant changes so managers can focus their attention on these areas.

One important thing to remember is that control is not the objective of a processing system but is used to augment and serve the total system. For example, a cost control system is structured to furnish managers with information so that more efficient decisions can be made. When control does not result in more effective or efficient input decisions, or when the cost of control is greater than the marginal gain, the control system warrants review and evaluation.

Communication of Information. Communication plays a vital role in the implementation of the systems concept. It is the connecting and integrating link throughout the systems network. The flow of information, energy, and material—the elements of any processing system—is coordinated via communication systems. As shown in the model (Figure 14.2), the operating system requires information transmission to ensure control. Communication systems should be established to feedback information on the various flows of information, energy, and material. Information on the effectiveness of planning and scheduling activities (as an example of information flow) would be helpful in adjusting the nature of this activity for the future. Similarly, reports on absenteeism are examples of communication relating the energy flow (the people in the system) to the processing activity. Information on acceptance inspection illustrates information stemming from the material flow aspect of an operating system. All of these feedback communication systems provide for information flow to a sensor and a control unit. Comparison between the information received and the information stored (the master plan for this particular operating system) results in decisions concerning the transmission of corrective information to the appropriate points.

Relationships within and among various project systems and between the levels of the system as a whole are maintained by means of information flow which also can be visualized as a control device. Moreover, any operating system maintains contact with its environment through some sensory element. Referring to Figure 14.1, the sensory elements in this case are the groups reporting to the planning committee. This committee makes decisions about the product or service the organization will produce, based on information gained from market research, research and development, resource capability, and the environment in general. This information is consolidated and decisions are made about future courses of action. Here again, communication or information flow can be visualized as a necessary element in controlling the course of action for the enterprise as a whole. Based on the feedback of information about the environment in general, the nature of competition, and the performance of the enterprise itself, the committee can continue its current courses of activity or adjust in the light of developing circumstances. Thus, communication or information flow facilitates the accomplishments of the primary managerial functions of planning, organizing, and controlling.

Communication, by definition, is a system involving a sender and a receiver, with implications of feedback control. This concept is embodied in the lowest level projects of subsystems, in all larger systems, and in the system as a whole. Information-decision systems, regardless of formal charts or manuals, often flow across departmental boundaries and are structured for specific projects or programs. The systems approach focuses on this concept and makes explicit the information-decision system which might be implicit in many of today's organizations.

Systems management, therefore, does not eliminate the functions of management, that is, planning, organizing, control, and communication. Instead, it integrates these functions within a framework designed to emphasize their importance in creating more effective systems. Because of the great diversity of operations and environments, particular missions of organizations differ and each system must be unique or at least have some unique elements. Nevertheless, the illustrative models, and their application to the management functions can serve as a point of departure in systems design.

Systems Analysis

The analysis of systems is a significant part of the design process. Questions pertaining to the exact mission of the system, the kind or nature of facilities to use, and the arrangement of these facilities all involve detailed study. During the operation of a system, it is important to analyze the various units of input and to decide on the combination which will provide the most effective and efficient output. During this process, an analysis is made of the timing of inputs relative to outputs (scheduling); and material staging at the input, process, or output levels (inventory management). During operations, an analysis of the operation relative to predetermined standards of output (control) also is an important part of the operation. Finally, an analysis is made of the operation relative to determining why a system is not working properly (trouble shooting), or in evaluating the design of a system relative to its effectiveness and efficiency. During every stage of the process a study should be made about the nature and kind of information which must be provided to accomplish the kind of analysis which is required.

Decision Making. The process of systems analysis results in decision making, which is more than the final choice among alternative courses of action. It is necessary to outline the possible alternatives, determine the factors which pertain to each alternative, and establish value coefficients for the variables. The process can be illustrated by identifying the various elements, each of which involves a set of activities:

1. problem definition,
2. discovery of alternative courses of action,
3. evaluation of alternatives,
4. selection of course of action,
5. implementation of decision,
6. information feedback of results.

We discussed these elements in detail in Chapter 2.

The hierarchies of decisions have been illustrated in systems management by pointing out that some decisions involve organizational strategy, others involve design and construction of systems, still others relate to the operation and control, and finally some relate to the review and evaluation process whereby changes in design may be indicated. Some writers have referred to the classification relative to strategy and tactics, a classification used by military organizations.

Modeling. Modeling, a more or less abstract representation of a system, is one very important way to improve the quality of decision making. It is used to capture the essence, but not necessarily the detail of the system. It permits experimentation among the various decision strategies to test the results of different values of the variables involved. To the extent that models are a realistic representation of the system, they can be extremely valuable in analysis.

Figure 14.3 illustrates how problems from the real world can be abstracted in a form suitable for analysis, testing, and evaluation. Starting with the real world, the model builder abstracts those factors which represent the behavior of the system. The abstractions, to begin with, are of the major variables, with little or no attempt being made to detail or to

Figure 14.3 The Decision Process

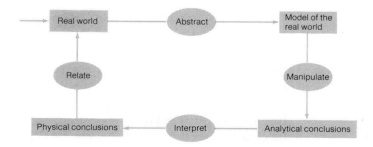

refine the model. Once the general model has been developed, it is much easier to expand the details to make the model a more realistic representation.

The model should be an accurate representation of the system, an outline of the various parts in relationship to the other parts. Building realistic models is probably the key to good decision making. A summary of some of the questions which must be asked include:

1. What is the general nature of the relationships among the variables in the system. If certain action is taken, how will this affect other variables?

2. How sensitive is an alternative solution to errors of measurement or changes in the general parameters which have been outlined?

3. If one does not or cannot adopt the optimal solution, how much will this change the effectiveness or efficiency of the system?

4. Does the analysis permit consideration of more variables than one could handle in an unstructured model?

Whether model building can extend beyond the theoretical and to the practical depends upon the analyst's ability to recognize that theoretical problems are vast simplifications, generally, of practical problems. Most practical problems are extremely complex, unique to a particular situation, and with consequences that are far reaching.[4]

The model can be manipulated by solving for unknowns based on known values, or hypothetical values can be given to the unknowns to test the reaction of different values on the total system (simulation). As a result of these kinds of exercises, certain analytical conclusions are drawn.

There are many instances when analytical solutions must be offered with concern for their realism. Such conclusions must be interpreted by managers who can add the dimension of experience, common sense, and good judgment to the analysis. All of this points to the inevitable fact that the model cannot capture the full complexity of reality. When the analyst realizes this, and is cautioned to respect the role that experienced managers can play in the total decision process, everyone benefits.

The actual decision, once it has been made and implemented, is related to the real world in a follow-up exercise to judge whether or not it was an optimal solution and how this evaluation reflects on the decision-making process. Obviously, the interpretation of what is optimal will depend upon the decision criteria which have been established. If the most important criterion is to maximize profit, then this will be the basis upon which to judge the merit of the particular decision. All of this presumes that the

---

[4] William T. Morris, *Analysis for Material Handling Management* (Homewood, Ill.: Richard D. Irwin, Inc., 1962), pp. 13–15.

analyst can measure the outcome of other alternative courses of action for a point of comparison.

Models may be grouped into three general categories: iconic, analog, and symbolic. The iconic model is a physical representation of a real world system, as a map represents the geography of a region. The analog model represents the real world by using a characteristic that behaves in direct relationship to that of the real world system; for example, it is possible to measure pressure and transfer this as a measure of temperature, or vice versa. Symbolic models represent the real world system in a different language; for example, mathematics can represent a system in the form of equations.

Table 14.2 illustrates the relationship among models, techniques, and tools. Techniques involve a methodology of analysis. Although they may be used at any stage of the decision process, most techniques are applied during the manipulation stage. Some techniques have application at all stages, however. For example, PERT is used as a method for abstracting the real world system in model form, for manipulating the various time/cost values to determine the critical path, to interpret these relationships to make decisions of resource allocation, and to relate the activities back to the real world when it is used as a control technique.

A tool is an instrument, a means of improving the process of data processing, manipulating, and testing. Tools will help the manager by providing more data, collating, manipulating, and testing it more quickly and accurately, and in freeing the manager from the routine decision-making process so that he can concentrate on more important issues.

The need to develop a communication link between the technician and the manager should be evident. Scientific methodology and tools can be of great value when used as an aid in the management process, rather than as an end in themselves. Management will appreciate the value of these tools and techniques when used properly; the technician has the responsibility to present useful information developed from sound analysis.

Table 14.2 The Relation of Models, Techniques, and Tools

MODELS (A Representation)	TECHNIQUES (A Methodology)	TOOLS (An Instrument)
Iconic Models (a physical representation)	PERT	Pencil
Analog Models (representing another characteristic)	Simulation	Slide Rule
Symbolic Models (represented by another language)	Queuing Theory	Computer

A Model for Systems Analysis. A general framework or model can be a valuable vehicle of analysis—a scientific methodology for planning and problem solving. As such, it becomes an orderly method which can be used to review and appraise alternative ways of using scarce resources to accomplish a particular objective. Considering the integrative nature of a problem (that is, the cause and effect relationships among the elements), the constantly changing environment in which planning must be formulated, and the limited resources and time available to complete a study, it becomes apparent why the logic of this approach can assist and refine the decision-making process.

Useful counsel for practitioners should include (1) determine, first of all, the boundaries of the defined system; (2) describe the system in detail; and (3) be completely objective, that is, do not make judgments or hazard solutions at the beginning of the study. Many studies are made to justify a predetermined decision to add a computer, rather than making an unbiased analysis of the system and its requirements.

In many ways, a model of systems analysis is very similar to the scientific method. It includes a phase where requirements and constraints are carefully outlined, alternative avenues of achieving the objectives are analyzed in detail, trade-off studies are made (within the selection criteria) to determine the best approach, and a decision plan developed which satisfies the specified objectives.[5]

The logic of the model follows the deductive-inductive sequence. In other words, the process starts with the objectives or general statement of the problem, and then develops those details or data relevant to the solution of the problem or an outline of a plan of action. The pattern of thinking produces a cycle to create, as nearly as possible, a closed loop for continuous feedback with periodic inputs. The process illustrated in Figure 14.4 goes through several stages of development, starting with a cluster which includes general objectives, translation of objectives, constraints, and analysis; and then proceeding through a second cluster which includes alternatives, criteria for selection, trade-off analysis, and synthesis. Figure 14.4 illustrates the close relationship between objectives and selection criteria, and also the need to relate the plan or decision back to the objectives in an evaluation procedure.

The broad objectives establish the initial format, but it is necessary to translate these objectives into more specific terms. The more specific the objectives can be, the easier it becomes to direct the systems analysis. It is not always possible to have a clear and precise definition of these objec-

[5] P. G. Thome and R. G. Willard, "The Systems Approach—A Unified Concept of Planning," *Aerospace Management,* General Electric Company, Missile and Space Division, Fall–Winter 1966, pp. 25–44.

Figure 14.4 A Model of Systems Analysis

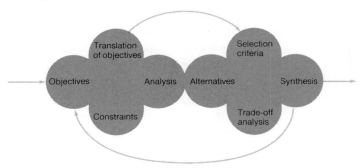

Source: Derived from P. G. Thome and R. G. Willard, *Aerospace Management*, General Electric Company, Missile and Space Division, Fall-Winter 1966, p. 31.

tives early in the study. Therefore, it is necessary to iterate and to refine the general definitions as more information becomes available. Often, for example, an analysis of the various factors will clarify the mission and permit the analyst to refine the objective in more precise terms.

The constraints represent those factors which limit the number of feasible solutions or alternative plans of action. They establish the boundary within which a solution must be found. Constraints may be technical, a limitation on the knowledge about the state-of-the-art; economical, the money available or the cost restrictions to a particular solution; political, legal restrictions resulting from laws or from a political subdivision; educational, the ability of the population to understand and/or initiate certain action; social, involving restrictions imposed by religious, work, or informal organzations; and time, the need to find a solution within a predetermined time which would obviously eliminate from consideration some long-range solutions.

The first cluster of the model is an organization and study cluster; the second grouping involves action. First a list of alternatives is prepared. Each alternative must be a feasible plan or solution to the problem. In other words, it must meet the objectives and not violate the constraints which have been outlined. Once the alternatives are developed, they are tested against the selection criteria. The selection criteria are really a list of priorities. It is an admission that each of the various alternatives will have certain characteristics which satisfy the original objectives better than others. It is necessary to decide which characteristics are the most important, assuming that it is not possible to satisfy all characteristics to the same degree. The listing and ranking of the selection criteria will determine the optimum solution. It will also establish for all parties the basis upon which the decision was made. If a manager disagrees with the selection criteria as listed, it is obvious that a different solution will be reached. On the other hand, if there is agreement at this point, and the logic and analysis are sound, most researchers should reach the same decision.

The trade off is the process of evaluating each alternative in terms of the selection criteria and, as the process occurs, to try to develop additional alternatives which may be either new or combinations of those already suggested. The creation of new alternatives is a logical development after the pros and cons of the first list of alternatives are evaluated.

The best alternative is synthesized into an action plan or decision. One of the significant features of this model is the feature of iteration, the process of continually refining the objectives, investigating the restrictiveness of certain constraints, the development of the analytical process, the investigation of other alternatives, and the refinement and synthesis of the actual plan or decision.

An Illustration of Systems Analysis—Paper Recycling

The following hypothetical example is presented to illustrate the systems analysis model. Obviously, a real example would be more comprehensive.

Objective

Initiate and implement a paper recycling program for the University.

Translation of Objectives

Design and create a system of paper recycling for the University that is capable of:

1. Efficiently collecting 75 to 90 per cent of all paper products used by the University that are now considered waste.
2. Effectively channeling collected waste to facilities capable of sorting paper into bio-degradable and non-bio-degradable categories for recycling waste into products that can be utilized by the community at large.

Constraints

1. Present technology—recycling facilities cost approximately $20 million to build.
2. Availability of water—adequate facilities use 10 million gallons of water daily and produce 2 million gallons of effluent, plus solid wastes from de-inking and other operations.
3. Only certain grades of paper can be recycled.
4. Paper can only be recycled a maximum of five or six times before fibers become too short for processing.
5. Legal constraint—the University is limited by law in the type of operations it can undertake.
6. Public support—it may be necessary to receive the support of the users before a feasible system can be outlined.

Analysis

1. Investigation of various collection schemes.
   a. Wastepaper containers
   b. Central disposal locations
   c. Conveyors
   d. Incinerators
   e. Compressor/Processors
2. Various removal schemes.
   a. Trucks
   b. Conveyors
   c. Incinerators
   d. Compressor/Processors
3. Investigation of future requirements and opportunities.
   a. Growth in paper consumption
   b. Pending disposal legislation
   c. Attitudes of paper suppliers, users, disposers, public
   d. Techniques of disposal and recovery
   e. List of agencies, organizations dealing with disposal and recovery
4. Investigate costs of various kinds of collection, sorting, and processing schemes.

Alternative Courses of Action

1. Collect, sort, and recycle the paper at a University plant.
2. Collect and sort, but sell the paper to an outside contractor for recycling.
3. Contract the collection, sorting, and processing of paper for recycling with outside organizations.
4. Same as 1, 2, 3, but purchasing for use only that paper which has been recycled.

Criteria for Selection

1. How effective is the program in utilizing the greatest percentage of waste paper for recycling?
2. What are the costs of the various alternatives to the University?
3. How acceptable is the system to the students, faculty, staff, and public?
4. How difficult will the program be to implement with respect to time and degree of change from present systems?

Trade Offs

The alternatives which have been suggested are all feasible in that they will achieve the objectives within the constraints which have been outlined. Now they need to be tested with regard to which of the alternatives rates highest relative to the selection criteria. That is, which will recycle the greatest amount of paper, at the lowest cost, with the least objection, and with the least difficulty of implementation. Each alternative may have certain advantages.

Synthesis   At the synthesis stage, it is necessary to develop a composite or program alternative which may include features of all alternatives, or, as the alternatives are reviewed in the trade-off/synthesis process, it may be possible to generate new alternatives or to refine some of those which have been suggested.

Systems Analysis and Social Problems

A newscaster many years ago started his program by saying, "There's good news tonight." In recent years there has been little in the news to encourage the listener, in fact, a general discouragement about conditions is common throughout the world. The phrase "stop the world, I want to get off" is too serious to be humorous. In 1968, the World Health Organization of the United Nations estimated that the number of people committing suicide throughout the world averaged 1,000 a day, or almost half a million a year. It may be that the very existence of this world depends on what we plan and do now.

Some people question the value of long-range planning with world conditions so unsettled and everything changing so rapidly. When we analyze the uncontrolled growth of the past and the problems this kind of growth has brought, the need for future planning appears to be too obvious to be discussed. Therefore, let us direct ourselves to the task. Before a plan can be outlined, however, some agreement must be reached concerning the kind of a world we wish to have. The first step, as always, is to determine the objectives; revolution without a vision of what change is necessary is meaningless.

The difficulty of setting goals is quite apparent; peoples' wants and needs are different. Man's physiological and psychological needs change in importance to him as he changes his pattern of living. Once his basic physiological needs of minimum shelter and food are satisfied, man not only attempts to improve or refine these needs, but he seeks other trappings which provide for him certain psychological satisfaction. As his standard of living improves, some amenities are regarded as a necessary way of life, but if something upsets this hierarchical need structure, his basic physiological needs again become of primary importance.

The level of need attainment of different nations varies, and the need attainment of social, economic, and geographic groupings of people within a nation may be very different. As a frame of reference for our discussion, let us assume that people in this country have the following requirements for a full and happy life:

Objectives   *1.* Adequate food and housing.

2. Opportunities to increase knowledge.

3. Adequate health care.

4. Freedom to speak, worship, own property, travel freely, and have privacy.

5. Adequate recreational facilities.

6. Protection against external forces, criminal action, persecution, and discrimination.

7. Employment in interesting and challenging work assignments.

8. A clean environment.

9. Sufficient goods and services.

The difference between the total requirements, as established by the objectives, and the resources available to satisfy these requirements, represents the need-gap. Figure 14.5 furnishes a hypothetical illustration of a situation where total needs are increasing more rapidly than available resources. Figure 14.6 depicts a more desirable condition where the increase of resources is greater than new requirements, and the need-gap is reduced.

Figure 14.5   An Increasing Need Gap

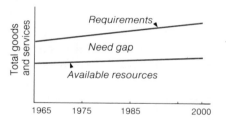

Figure 14.6   A Decreasing Need Gap

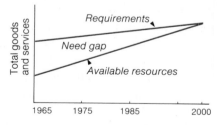

The requirement curve represents the totals needed to satisfy stated objectives of individuals multiplied by the number of people concerned. This analysis does not take into account the manner or equality of the distribution process among people; it assumes an average or equal sharing. Any unequal division will obviously create need-gap pockets among the population in excess of the figures shown in the macro analysis.

The resources available reflect the additions and development of new resources during the stated time period. The requirements are determined by need expectations (goals) and by the number of people whose needs must be satisfied. Goods and services can be increased by planned capital expansion and development, while increases in requirements must be restrained somewhat by stabilizing individual expectations, and by controlling the rate of population growth. A country like India finds it difficult to narrow its need-gap, because, although substantial progress is being made in expanding available goods and services, the growth in population causes the total requirements to grow at an even faster rate. The discouraging consequence is an increasing need-gap rather than the more desirable trend.

We can represent goods and services by gross national product (GNP), and needs by numbers of people (population). In Table 14.3 we list the past and projected world population, the GNP, and the GNP per capita for 1965, 1975, 1985, 2000, and 2020. This gives the reader some idea of the task ahead.

Expanding Resources

The resources of any nation occur in the form of information, material, and energy; of the three, information (knowledge) is by far the most important. Brainpower is the base by which materials and energy are developed, improved, and utilized. The harnessing and conversion of energy depends on the availability of material resources, namely, fuel, water, gas, oil, and uranium as well as information. The total resources of a nation can be expanded by discovering new resources, by expanding the use of resources presently available, and by utilizing resources more completely through better systems of conversion.

The increase of basic knowledge and its application toward better living has been accelerated by the productive partnership between theoreticians and practitioners, engineers and managers, and private and public employees. This resource can be expanded by identifying and utilizing the brainpower of all of the people in a nation, by developing talent through good programs of education, and through better utilization of known information as better systems for classifying and retrieving knowledge are designed.

The twentieth century has seen the introduction of many new materials; light alloys based on aluminum and magnesium, steel containing other metals as well as carbon, and plastics and other polymers. The expanded application of the basic elements with the countless combinations thereof has provided materials to design products that could not have been built before, has improved the quality and usefulness of existing products, and permitted the substitution of new materials for those already in short supply. Resources of edible materials are expanding as new sources are discovered such as new foods from the sea, and as better seeds and fertilizers increase the yield of planted crops.

Table 14.3 Population and Gross National Product Trends

	1965	1975	1985	2000	2020
Population, Continents[1]					
(Millions)					
Africa	310.7	398	520	779	1,320
Asia	1,889.0	2,343	2,863	3,701	5,100
Europe[2]	674.7	732	792	886	1,040
Oceania	14.0	16	20	25	35
North America	294.2	354	431	578	850
South America	166.2	221	291	420	680
World	3,348.8	4,064	4,917	6,389	9,025
GNP, Continents[1]					
(Billion 1965 United States dollars)					
Africa	43.9	69	109	216	537
Asia	287.4	501	883	2,137	7,317
Europe[2]	923.9	1,447	2,271	4,476	11,124
Oceania	28.0	41	60	107	232
North America	774.2	1,203	1,865	3,620	8,740
South America	59.4	91	144	292	761
World	2,116.8	3,352	5,332	10,848	28,711
GNP Per Capita, Continents[1]					
(1965 U.S. Dollars)					
Africa	141	174	209	277	407
Asia	152	214	308	577	1,436
Europe[2]	1,369	1,976	2,867	5,055	10,730
Oceania	2,000	2,510	3,080	4,310	6,600
North America	2,632	3,403	4,329	6,255	10,280
South America	357	413	496	695	1,112
World	632	825	1,085	1,700	3,180

[1] With minor omissions. For instance, Oceania is Australia plus New Zealand only, and Europe is European OECD plus Warsaw Pact.
[2] Includes all of U.S.S.R.
Sources: 1965: *China:* medium estimate—U.S. State Department, Bureau of Intelligence and Research, *Indicators of East-West Strength,* 1965 (Research Memo. REV-69, October 11, 1966), Table I. Low estimate—partly allows for a possible 5–15 per cent undercount in the 1953 census. G. E. Pearce, "Mainland China—Geographic Strength and Weaknesses," *Department of State Bulletin,* August 29, 1966, p. 298. High estimate—exceeds the medium by roughly the margin for the UN estimates. UN Department of Economic and Social Affairs, *World Population Prospects as Assessed in 1963,* Population Studies No. 41 (New York, 1966), p. 57. Projections presented by Herman Kahn and Anthony J. Wiener, *The Year 2000; A Framework for Speculation on the Next Thirty-Three Years,* New York: The Macmillan Company, 1967.

During the past century, a tremendous shift has occurred in the energy sources utilized by man. From wood to petroleum, and more recently a gradual shift toward the use of nuclear energy is occurring. It has been estimated that world energy consumption will be more than five times as great in 2000 A.D. as it was in 1960 if the current consumption trend continues. As we find and develop new energy sources, or discover means of improving the utilization of current forms of energy, the availability of low-cost energy will permit the introduction of a better life to people in the underdeveloped countries. In these countries, manpower is still serving as its most important energy source. Note the difference between the ability of developed countries and less developed countries to produce agricultural goods, for example (see Figure 14.7).

Figure 14.7   World Agricultural Production

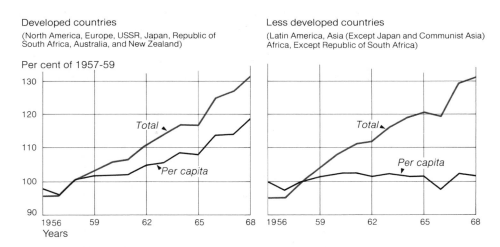

Developed countries
(North America, Europe, USSR, Japan, Republic of
South Africa, Australia, and New Zealand)

Less developed countries
(Latin America, Asia (Except Japan and Communist Asia)
Africa, Except Republic of South Africa)

Per cent of 1957-59

Source: U.S. Department of Agriculture.

Population Control

Even if the revolution in food production fulfills our maximum hopes, the world cannot feed an infinitely expanding population. Lord Snow envisions a "sea of hunger" flooding vast areas of the earth by the end of the century. "Many millions of people in the poor countries are going to starve to death before our eyes—or, to complete the domestic picture, we shall see them doing so upon television sets."[6] Lord Snow concludes that people in many nations will not control their population growth, and people in wealthier nations will show little interest in preventing the starvation which will follow.

[6] *Newsweek,* 25 November 1968, p. 25.

The population and population growth rates for the ten major countries of the world are projected by Herman Kahn and Anthony Wiener as illustrated in Table 14.4. Their figures are primarily an extrapolation of present trends with some allowance for probable developments. The data represent a gradual decrease in the rate of increase for these ten countries. Population totals for each country are determined by the birth rate, the death rate, and the net migration in or out of the country.

Table 14.4 shows the various rates of increase by country, but even within a country the growth will be much greater for certain economic and cultural groups. In America, for example, the increase is concentrated in urban areas; for example, ". . . the exploding growth of the slums, which are swelling so fast that some 500,000 Negroes would have to be dispersed from the central cities each year just to keep the ghetto population at its present size."[7]

A variety of measures may need to be introduced in order to control the population growth. Obviously, there must be some trade off between goal achievement for the macro system and freedom of choice for the individual. Some of the proposals which have been suggested include: (1) education programs for better family planning; (2) wide and free disbursement of birth control drugs and devices; (3) legalized abortion; and (4) programs of sterilization. All of these proposals are directed toward reducing the birth rate. It is interesting to note, however, that the dramatic increase in population has not resulted from an increase in fertility, but instead from a significant decrease in the death rate.

In 1798 Thomas Malthus proposed that population tends to increase geometrically whereas food supplies increase arithmetically. His dire predictions of disaster have not occurred, but this is not to say that they were wrong. Malthus could not foresee the impact of technology. Today we have more information about the complex phenomenon of population growth and the environment it affects. We know that energy, space, and food are finite, and that pollution has a close relationship to both population and energy consumption. Malthus's predictions of war, famine, disease, and a general breakdown of law and order may still occur if we fail to recognize the danger.

Programs of Study

Each of the objectives listed in this chapter can be organized as a distinct program for study and action. The reader should note the relationship among all of the goals, however, and consider that progress in one area will affect the amount of resources available for other programs. Analysis should be directed towards a determination of which objectives are the most important, which will serve the most people, and which can be

---

[7] *Newsweek,* 18 November 1968, p. 24.

Table 14.4   Population and Population Growth Rates, Ten Major Countries, in Millions

	1965	Rates	1975	Rates	1985	Rates 1985–2000	2000	2020
China[1]	700	1.3	793	1.0	872	.9	992	1160
	755	1.8	903	1.5	1052	1.3	1271	1610
	800	2.3	1004	2.1	1240	1.7	1600	2400
India	487	2.2	604	1.9	727	1.5	914	1170
		2.4	616	2.1	761	1.8	988	1280
		2.5	622	2.5	794	2.4	1128	1700
U.S.S.R.	231	1.0	255	1.0	282	.9	316	360
		1.3	260	1.3	296	1.2	352	450
		1.6	273	1.6	320	1.5	402	540
U.S.	195	1.2	219	1.2	246	1.1	290	370
		1.3	222	1.5	256	1.5	318	420
		1.7	230	1.7	274	1.9	362	500
Japan	98	.6	104	.6	111	.3	116	120
		.8	107	.8	116	.4	123	135
		1.1	110	1.1	123	.8	139	165
W. Germany	59	.2	60	.2	61	.0	61	61
(including		.4	61	.4	64	.3	67	72
W. Berlin		.5	62	.5	65	.5	70	78
U.K.	55	.1	55	.0	55	.0	55	55
		.3	57	.2	58	.2	60	63
		.5	57	.4	60	.5	64	71
Italy	52	.3	53	.1	54	.1	55	57
		.5	54	.3	56	.4	60	65
		.6	55	.4	57	.6	62	70
France	49	.8	53	.5	56	.4	59	64
		1.0	54	.7	58	.7	64	74
		1.1	55	.8	59	.9	68	81
Canada	20	1.7	23	1.6	27	1.6	34	46
		1.8	23	1.9	28	2.0	38	56
		2.2	24	2.1	30	2.4	43	68

[1] Estimates of 1965 population vary from 700 M to 800 M.
Source: See sources for Table 14.3.

achieved in the shortest time. Careful utilization of scarce resources will make it possible to provide a "good life" for many more people.

The future presents a challenge for young people. Not only a challenge but a real opportunity. Many forecasters have predicted a gloomy future because they have merely extrapolated present trends. There is no reason why a vision of the future needs to be undermined by conditions which prevail today—tomorrow can be a new ball game. It is far better to regroup our resources for a fresh attack aimed at solving every problem standing in the way of progress. We must provide a better standard of living for people, but only if we can maintain individual freedom, equality, and a good environment in which to live. As an Italian industrialist once said when a group was reviewing possible applications of the computer: "Let us never get the lights in the street so bright that we cannot see the stars."

Selected References

Eells, R., and Walton, C., eds. *Man in the City of the Future.* New York: Macmillan, 1968.

The book presents a series of reports by experts projecting changes which may occur in the structure and operation of future cities.

Ehrlich, P. R. *The Population Bomb.* New York: Ballantine Books, 1968.

The author reviews the population crisis with facts, projections, and analysis.

Fortune. Special Issue. "The Environment: A National Mission for the Seventies." February 1970.

This issue evaluates the problem of our environment, the kind of resources needed to change present trends, and the kind of priority this effort should have.

Johnson, Richard A., et al. *The Theory and Management of Systems.* 2nd ed. New York: McGraw-Hill Book Company, 1967, pp. 1–130.

The first section of this book presents the systems management concepts.

"The Markets of Change." Kaiser News. Oakland, California, 1970–71.

This series has six publications on ecology, shelter, energy, food, mobility, and communications.

Murdock, William W., ed. *Environment: Resources, Pollution & Society.* Stamford, Conn.: Sinauer Associates, 1971.

This book is a collection of papers, by authors representing a wide range of environmental disciplines, which analyzes the problems we face now and will face in the future.

Nowick, David, ed. *Program Analysis and the Federal Budget.* The Rand Corporation, 1965.

The book presents a series of articles on this subject, varying from a conceptual framework to limitations and risks.

Questions

1 What is systems management? What basic principles exemplify this philosophy? How does it relate to systems theory?

2 What is the relationship between project and facilitating systems? When should facilitating systems be created?

3 How would a model like the one illustrated in Figure 14.1 differ if you wish to describe a public organization?

4 What is the relationship between control and planning as demonstrated in Figure 14.2? Between control and review and evaluation?

5 To what extent would environmental inputs affect planning at the project level? Give an example.

6 What are the important functions of the master planning committee?

7 How does a control system provide more flexibility to planning?

8 How does the function of communication relate to information input in an operating system?

9 Distinguish between systems management and systems analysis. Which is the more useful for practitioners?

10 Determine the relationship between constraints and selection criteria as demonstrated in Figure 14.4. How does the translation of objectives affect the analytical process?

11 Give other examples of techniques and tools which would follow the categories of models illustrated in Table 14.2.

12 Explain the hierarchical needs of man. Which needs are the most important? Are all people alike in this regard?

13 List the alternatives of resource-need fulfillment which are available to every nation.

14 Would the need-gap vary with the level of economic activity achieved by a country? How? What other factors influence the need-gap?

Problems

1 Illustrate some system with which you are familiar. Describe it in terms of the model in Figure 14.1. Be specific in your distinction between the facilitating and project systems.

2 Outline a plan to redesign a specific system (for example, a registration system at a university) using the systems analysis model. Describe each step that you establish as you follow the model in Figure 14.4.

3 Review the objectives suggested for our society. Establish and then justify priorities for the objectives.

4 Use any one of the nine goals listed in the text and outline a comprehensive program for goal achievement.

Appendix: Tables

Table A Single Payment Present Worth Factors (Per Cent)

Year	1	2	4	6	8	10	12	14	15	16	18
1	.990	.980	.962	.943	.926	.909	.893	.877	.870	.862	.847
2	.980	.961	.915	.890	.857	.826	.797	.769	.756	.743	.718
3	.971	.942	.889	.840	.794	.751	.712	.675	.658	.641	.609
4	.961	.924	.855	.792	.735	.683	.636	.592	.572	.552	.516
5	.951	.906	.822	.747	.681	.621	.567	.519	.497	.476	.437
6	.942	.888	.790	.705	.630	.564	.507	.456	.432	.410	.370
7	.933	.871	.760	.665	.583	.513	.452	.400	.376	.354	.314
8	.923	.853	.731	.627	.540	.467	.404	.351	.327	.305	.266
9	.914	.837	.703	.592	.500	.424	.361	.308	.284	.263	.225
10	.905	.820	.676	.558	.463	.386	.322	.270	.247	.227	.191
11	.896	.804	.650	.527	.429	.350	.287	.237	.215	.195	.162
12	.887	.788	.625	.497	.397	.319	.257	.208	.187	.168	.137
13	.879	.773	.601	.469	.368	.290	.229	.182	.163	.145	.116
14	.870	.758	.577	.442	.340	.263	.205	.160	.141	.125	.099
15	.861	.743	.555	.417	.315	.239	.183	.140	.123	.108	.084
16	.853	.728	.534	.394	.292	.218	.163	.123	.107	.093	.071
17	.844	.714	.513	.371	.270	.198	.146	.108	.093	.080	.060
18	.836	.700	.494	.350	.250	.180	.130	.095	.081	.069	.051
19	.828	.686	.475	.331	.232	.164	.116	.083	.070	.060	.043
20	.820	.673	.456	.312	.215	.149	.104	.073	.061	.051	.037
21	.811	.660	.439	.294	.199	.135	.093	.064	.053	.044	.031
22	.803	.647	.422	.278	.184	.123	.083	.056	.046	.038	.026
23	.795	.634	.406	.262	.170	.112	.074	.049	.040	.033	.022
24	.788	.622	.390	.247	.158	.102	.066	.043	.035	.028	.019
25	.780	.610	.375	.233	.146	.092	.059	.038	.030	.024	.016
26	.772	.598	.361	.220	.135	.084	.053	.033	.026	.021	.014
27	.764	.586	.347	.207	.125	.076	.047	.029	.023	.018	.011
28	.757	.574	.333	.196	.116	.069	.042	.026	.020	.016	.010
29	.749	.563	.321	.185	.107	.063	.037	.022	.017	.014	.008
30	.742	.552	.308	.174	.099	.057	.033	.020	.015	.012	.007
31	.735	.541	.296	.164	.092	.052	.030	.017	.013	.010	.006
32	.727	.531	.285	.155	.085	.047	.027	.015	.011	.009	.005
33	.720	.520	.274	.146	.079	.043	.024	.013	.010	.007	.004
34	.713	.510	.264	.138	.073	.039	.021	.012	.009	.006	.004
35	.706	.500	.253	.130	.068	.036	.019	.010	.008	.006	.003
40	.672	.453	.208	.097	.046	.022	.011	.005	.004	.003	.001
45	.639	.410	.171	.073	.031	.014	.006	.003	.002	.001	.001
50	.608	.372	.141	.054	.021	.009	.003	.001	.001	.001	.000

Table A   Continued

Year	20	22	24	25	26	28	30	35	40	45	50
1	.833	.820	.806	.800	.794	.781	.769	.741	.714	.690	.667
2	.694	.672	.650	.640	.630	.610	.592	.549	.510	.476	.444
3	.579	.551	.524	.512	.500	.477	.455	.406	.364	.328	.296
4	.482	.451	.423	.410	.397	.373	.350	.301	.260	.226	.198
5	.402	.370	.341	.328	.315	.291	.269	.223	.186	.156	.132
6	.335	.303	.275	.262	.250	.227	.207	.165	.133	.108	.088
7	.279	.249	.222	.210	.198	.178	.159	.122	.095	.074	.059
8	.233	.204	.179	.168	.157	.139	.123	.091	.068	.051	.039
9	.194	.167	.144	.134	.125	.108	.094	.067	.048	.035	.026
10	.162	.137	.116	.107	.099	.085	.073	.050	.035	.024	.017
11	.135	.112	.094	.086	.079	.066	.056	.037	.025	.017	.012
12	.112	.092	.076	.069	.062	.052	.043	.027	.018	.012	.008
13	.093	.075	.061	.055	.050	.040	.033	.020	.013	.008	.005
14	.078	.062	.049	.044	.039	.032	.025	.015	.009	.006	.003
15	.065	.051	.040	.035	.031	.025	.020	.011	.006	.004	.002
16	.054	.042	.032	.028	.025	.019	.015	.008	.005	.003	.002
17	.045	.034	.026	.023	.020	.015	.012	.006	.003	.002	.001
18	.038	.028	.021	.018	.016	.012	.009	.005	.002	.001	.001
19	.031	.023	.017	.014	.012	.009	.007	.003	.002	.001	.000
20	.026	.019	.014	.012	.010	.007	.005	.002	.001	.001	.000
21	.022	.015	.011	.009	.008	.006	.004	.002	.001	.000	.000
22	.018	.013	.009	.007	.006	.004	.003	.001	.001	.000	.000
23	.015	.010	.007	.006	.005	.003	.002	.001	.000	.000	.000
24	.013	.008	.006	.005	.004	.003	.002	.001	.000	.000	.000
25	.010	.007	.005	.004	.003	.002	.001	.001	.000	.000	.000
26	.009	.006	.004	.003	.002	.002	.001	.000	.000	.000	.000
27	.007	.005	.003	.002	.002	.001	.001	.000	.000	.000	.000
28	.006	.004	.002	.002	.002	.001	.001	.000	.000	.000	.000
29	.005	.003	.002	.002	.001	.001	.000	.000	.000	.000	.000
30	.004	.003	.002	.001	.001	.001	.000	.000	.000	.000	.000
31	.004	.002	.001	.001	.001	.000	.000	.000	.000	.000	.000
32	.003	.002	.001	.001	.001	.000	.000	.000	.000	.000	.000
33	.002	.001	.001	.001	.000	.000	.000	.000	.000	.000	.000
34	.002	.001	.001	.001	.000	.000	.000	.000	.000	.000	.000
35	.002	.001	.001	.000	.000	.000	.000	.000	.000	.000	.000
40	.001	.000	.000	.000	.000	.000	.000	.000	.000	.000	.000
45	.000	.000	.000	.000	.000	.000	.000	.000	.000	.000	.000
50	.000	.000	.000	.000	.000	.000	.000	.000	.000	.000	.000

Table B Series Present Worth Factors (Per Cent)

Year	1	2	4	6	8	10	12	14	15	16	18
1	.990	.980	.962	.943	.926	.909	.893	.877	.870	.862	.847
2	1.970	1.942	1.886	1.833	1.783	1.736	1.690	1.647	1.626	1.605	1.566
3	2.941	2.884	2.775	2.673	2.577	2.487	2.402	2.322	2.283	2.246	2.174
4	3.902	3.808	3.630	3.465	3.312	3.170	3.037	2.914	2.855	2.798	2.690
5	4.853	4.713	4.452	4.212	3.993	3.791	3.605	3.433	3.352	3.274	3.127
6	5.795	5.601	5.242	4.917	4.623	4.355	4.111	3.889	3.784	3.685	3.498
7	6.728	6.472	6.002	5.582	5.206	4.868	4.564	4.288	4.160	4.039	3.812
8	7.652	7.325	6.733	6.210	5.747	5.335	4.968	4.639	4.487	4.344	4.078
9	8.566	8.162	7.435	6.802	6.247	5.759	5.328	4.946	4.772	4.607	4.303
10	9.471	8.983	8.111	7.360	6.710	6.145	5.650	5.216	5.019	4.833	4.494
11	10.368	9.787	8.760	7.887	7.139	6.495	5.938	5.453	5.234	5.029	4.656
12	11.255	10.575	9.385	8.384	7.536	6.814	6.194	5.660	5.421	5.197	4.793
13	12.134	11.348	9.986	8.853	7.904	7.103	6.424	5.842	5.583	5.342	4.910
14	13.004	12.106	10.563	9.295	8.244	7.367	6.628	6.002	5.724	5.468	5.008
15	13.865	12.849	11.118	9.712	8.559	7.606	6.811	6.142	5.847	5.575	5.092
16	14.718	13.578	11.652	10.106	8.851	7.824	6.974	6.265	5.954	5.668	5.162
17	15.562	14.292	12.166	10.477	9.122	8.022	7.120	6.373	6.047	5.749	5.222
18	16.398	14.992	12.659	10.828	9.372	8.201	7.250	6.467	6.128	5.818	5.273
19	17.226	15.678	13.134	11.158	9.604	8.365	7.366	6.550	6.198	5.877	5.316
20	18.046	16.351	13.590	11.470	9.818	8.514	7.469	6.623	6.259	5.929	5.353
21	18.857	17.011	14.029	11.764	10.017	8.649	7.562	6.687	6.312	5.973	5.384
22	19.660	17.658	14.451	12.042	10.201	8.772	7.645	6.743	6.359	6.011	5.410
23	20.456	18.292	14.857	12.303	10.371	8.883	7.718	6.792	6.399	6.044	5.432
24	21.243	18.914	15.247	12.550	10.529	8.985	7.784	6.835	6.434	6.073	5.451
25	22.023	19.523	15.622	12.783	10.675	9.077	7.843	6.873	6.464	6.097	5.467
26	22.795	20.121	15.983	13.003	10.810	9.161	7.896	6.906	6.491	6.118	5.480
27	23.560	20.707	16.330	13.211	10.935	9.237	7.943	6.935	6.514	6.136	5.492
28	24.316	21.281	16.663	13.406	11.051	9.307	7.984	6.961	6.534	6.152	5.502
29	25.066	21.844	16.984	13.591	11.158	9.370	8.022	6.983	6.551	6.166	5.510
30	25.808	22.396	17.292	13.765	11.258	9.427	8.055	7.003	6.566	6.177	5.517
31	26.542	22.938	17.588	13.929	11.350	9.479	8.085	7.020	6.579	6.187	5.523
32	27.270	23.468	17.874	14.084	11.435	9.526	8.112	7.035	6.591	6.196	5.528
33	27.990	23.989	18.148	14.230	11.514	9.569	8.135	7.048	6.600	6.203	5.532
34	28.703	24.499	18.411	14.368	11.587	9.609	8.157	7.060	6.609	6.210	5.536
35	29.409	24.999	18.665	14.498	11.655	9.644	8.176	7.070	6.617	6.215	5.539
40	32.835	27.355	19.793	15.046	11.925	9.779	8.244	7.105	6.642	6.233	5.548
45	36.095	29.490	20.720	15.456	12.108	9.863	8.283	7.123	6.654	6.242	5.552
50	39.196	31.424	21.482	15.762	12.233	9.915	8.304	7.133	6.661	6.246	5.554

Table B Continued

Year	20	22	24	25	26	28	30	35	40	45	50
1	.833	.820	.806	.800	.794	.781	.769	.741	.714	.690	.667
2	1.528	1.492	1.457	1.440	1.424	1.392	1.361	1.289	1.224	1.165	1.111
3	2.106	2.042	1.981	1.952	1.923	1.868	1.816	1.696	1.589	1.493	1.407
4	2.589	2.494	2.404	2.362	2.320	2.241	2.166	1.997	1.849	1.720	1.605
5	2.991	2.864	2.745	2.689	2.635	2.532	2.436	2.220	2.035	1.876	1.737
6	3.326	3.167	3.020	2.951	2.885	2.759	2.643	2.385	2.168	1.983	1.824
7	3.605	3.416	3.242	3.161	3.083	2.937	2.802	2.508	2.263	2.057	1.883
8	3.837	3.619	3.421	3.329	3.241	3.076	2.925	2.598	2.331	2.109	1.922
9	4.031	3.786	3.566	3.463	3.366	3.184	3.019	2.665	2.379	2.144	1.948
10	4.192	3.923	3.682	3.571	3.465	3.269	3.092	2.715	2.414	2.168	1.965
11	4.327	4.035	3.776	3.656	3.543	3.335	3.147	2.752	2.438	2.185	1.977
12	4.439	4.127	3.851	3.725	3.606	3.387	3.190	2.779	2.456	2.196	1.985
13	4.533	4.203	3.912	3.780	3.656	3.427	3.223	2.799	2.469	2.204	1.990
14	4.611	4.265	3.962	3.824	3.695	3.459	3.249	2.814	2.478	2.210	1.993
15	4.675	4.315	4.001	3.859	3.726	3.483	3.268	2.825	2.484	2.214	1.995
16	4.730	4.357	4.033	3.887	3.751	3.503	3.283	2.834	2.489	2.216	1.997
17	4.775	4.391	4.059	3.910	3.771	3.518	3.295	2.840	2.492	2.218	1.998
18	4.812	4.419	4.080	3.928	3.786	3.529	3.304	2.844	2.494	2.219	1.999
19	4.843	4.442	4.097	3.942	3.799	3.539	3.311	2.848	2.496	2.220	1.999
20	4.870	4.460	4.110	3.954	3.808	3.546	3.316	2.850	2.497	2.221	1.999
21	4.891	4.476	4.121	3.963	3.816	3.551	3.320	2.852	2.498	2.221	2.000
22	4.909	4.488	4.130	3.970	3.822	3.556	3.323	2.853	2.498	2.222	2.000
23	4.925	4.499	4.137	3.976	3.827	3.559	3.325	2.854	2.499	2.222	2.000
24	4.937	4.507	4.143	3.981	3.831	3.562	3.327	2.855	2.499	2.222	2.000
25	4.948	4.514	4.147	3.985	3.834	3.564	3.329	2.856	2.499	2.222	2.000
26	4.956	4.520	4.151	3.988	3.837	3.566	3.330	2.856	2.500	2.222	2.000
27	4.964	4.524	4.154	3.990	3.839	3.567	3.331	2.856	2.500	2.222	2.000
28	4.970	4.528	4.157	3.992	3.840	3.568	3.331	2.857	2.500	2.222	2.000
29	4.975	4.531	4.159	3.994	3.841	3.569	3.332	2.857	2.500	2.222	2.000
30	4.979	4.534	4.160	3.995	3.842	3.569	3.332	2.857	2.500	2.222	2.000
31	4.982	4.536	4.161	3.996	3.843	3.570	3.332	2.857	2.500	2.222	2.000
32	4.985	4.538	4.162	3.997	3.844	3.570	3.333	2.857	2.500	2.222	2.000
33	4.988	4.539	4.163	3.997	3.844	3.570	3.333	2.857	2.500	2.222	2.000
34	4.990	4.540	4.164	3.998	3.845	3.571	3.333	2.857	2.500	2.222	2.000
35	4.992	4.541	4.164	3.998	3.845	3.571	3.333	2.857	2.500	2.222	2.000
40	4.997	4.544	4.166	3.999	3.846	3.571	3.333	2.857	2.500	2.222	2.000
45	4.999	4.545	4.166	4.000	3.846	3.571	3.333	2.857	2.500	2.222	2.000
50	4.999	4.545	4.167	4.000	3.846	3.571	3.333	2.857	2.500	2.222	2.000

Table C Capital Recovery Factors (Per Cent)

Year	1	2	4	6	8	10	12	14	15	16	18
1	1.010	1.020	1.040	1.060	1.080	1.100	1.120	1.140	1.150	1.160	1.180
2	.508	.515	.530	.545	.561	.576	.592	.607	.615	.623	.639
3	.340	.347	.360	.374	.388	.402	.415	.431	.438	.445	.460
4	.256	.263	.275	.289	.302	.315	.329	.343	.350	.357	.372
5	.206	.212	.225	.237	.250	.264	.277	.291	.298	.305	.320
6	.173	.179	.191	.203	.216	.230	.243	.257	.264	.271	.286
7	.149	.155	.167	.179	.192	.205	.219	.233	.240	.248	.262
8	.131	.137	.149	.161	.174	.187	.201	.216	.223	.230	.245
9	.117	.123	.134	.147	.160	.174	.188	.202	.210	.217	.232
10	.106	.111	.123	.136	.149	.163	.177	.192	.199	.207	.223
11	.096	.102	.114	.127	.140	.154	.168	.183	.191	.199	.215
12	.089	.095	.107	.119	.133	.147	.161	.177	.184	.192	.209
13	.082	.088	.100	.113	.127	.141	.155	.171	.179	.187	.204
14	.077	.083	.095	.108	.121	.136	.151	.167	.175	.183	.200
15	.072	.078	.090	.103	.117	.131	.147	.163	.171	.179	.196
16	.068	.074	.086	.099	.113	.128	.143	.160	.168	.176	.194
17	.064	.070	.082	.095	.110	.125	.140	.157	.165	.174	.191
18	.061	.067	.079	.092	.107	.122	.138	.155	.163	.172	.190
19	.058	.064	.076	.090	.104	.120	.136	.153	.161	.170	.188
20	.055	.061	.074	.087	.102	.117	.134	.151	.160	.169	.187
21	.053	.059	.071	.085	.100	.116	.132	.150	.158	.167	.186
22	.051	.057	.069	.083	.098	.114	.131	.148	.157	.166	.185
23	.049	.055	.067	.081	.096	.113	.130	.147	.156	.165	.184
24	.047	.053	.066	.080	.095	.111	.128	.146	.155	.165	.183
25	.045	.051	.064	.078	.094	.110	.127	.145	.155	.164	.183
26	.044	.050	.063	.077	.093	.109	.127	.145	.154	.163	.182
27	.042	.048	.061	.076	.091	.108	.126	.144	.154	.163	.182
28	.041	.047	.060	.075	.090	.107	.125	.144	.153	.163	.182
29	.040	.046	.059	.074	.090	.107	.125	.143	.153	.162	.181
30	.039	.045	.058	.073	.089	.106	.124	.143	.152	.162	.181
31	.038	.044	.057	.072	.088	.105	.124	.142	.152	.162	.181
32	.037	.043	.056	.071	.087	.105	.123	.142	.152	.161	.181
33	.036	.042	.055	.070	.087	.104	.123	.142	.152	.161	.181
34	.035	.041	.054	.070	.086	.104	.123	.142	.151	.161	.181
35	.034	.040	.054	.069	.086	.104	.122	.141	.151	.161	.181
40	.030	.037	.051	.066	.084	.102	.121	.141	.151	.160	.180
45	.028	.034	.048	.065	.083	.101	.121	.140	.150	.160	.180
50	.026	.032	.047	.063	.082	.101	.120	.140	.150	.160	.180

Table C Continued

Year	20	22	24	25	26	28	30	35	40	45	50
1	1.200	1.220	1.240	1.250	1.260	1.280	1.300	1.350	1.400	1.450	1.500
2	.655	.670	.686	.694	.702	.719	.735	.776	.817	.858	.900
3	.475	.490	.505	.512	.520	.535	.551	.590	.629	.670	.711
4	.386	.401	.416	.423	.431	.446	.462	.501	.541	.582	.623
5	.334	.349	.364	.372	.379	.395	.411	.450	.491	.533	.576
6	.301	.316	.331	.339	.347	.362	.378	.419	.461	.504	.548
7	.277	.293	.308	.316	.324	.340	.357	.399	.442	.486	.531
8	.261	.276	.292	.300	.309	.325	.342	.385	.429	.474	.520
9	.248	.264	.280	.289	.297	.314	.331	.375	.420	.466	.513
10	.239	.255	.272	.280	.289	.306	.323	.368	.414	.461	.509
11	.231	.248	.265	.273	.282	.300	.318	.363	.410	.458	.506
12	.225	.242	.260	.268	.277	.295	.313	.360	.407	.455	.504
13	.221	.238	.256	.265	.274	.292	.310	.357	.405	.454	.503
14	.217	.234	.252	.262	.271	.289	.308	.355	.404	.452	.502
15	.214	.232	.250	.259	.268	.287	.306	.354	.403	.452	.501
16	.211	.230	.248	.257	.267	.285	.305	.353	.402	.451	.501
17	.209	.228	.246	.256	.265	.284	.304	.352	.401	.451	.501
18	.208	.226	.245	.255	.264	.283	.303	.352	.401	.451	.500
19	.206	.225	.244	.254	.263	.283	.302	.351	.401	.450	.500
20	.205	.224	.243	.253	.263	.282	.302	.351	.400	.450	.500
21	.204	.223	.243	.252	.262	.282	.301	.351	.400	.450	.500
22	.204	.223	.242	.252	.262	.281	.301	.350	.400	.450	.500
23	.203	.222	.242	.251	.261	.281	.301	.350	.400	.450	.500
24	.203	.222	.241	.251	.261	.281	.301	.350	.400	.450	.500
25	.202	.222	.241	.251	.261	.281	.300	.350	.400	.450	.500
26	.202	.221	.241	.251	.261	.280	.300	.350	.400	.450	.500
27	.201	.221	.241	.251	.261	.280	.300	.350	.400	.450	.500
28	.201	.221	.241	.250	.260	.280	.300	.350	.400	.450	.500
29	.201	.221	.240	.250	.260	.280	.300	.350	.400	.450	.500
30	.201	.221	.240	.250	.260	.280	.300	.350	.400	.450	.500
31	.201	.220	.240	.250	.260	.280	.300	.350	.400	.450	.500
32	.201	.220	.240	.250	.260	.280	.300	.350	.400	.450	.500
33	.200	.220	.240	.250	.260	.280	.300	.350	.400	.450	.500
34	.200	.220	.240	.250	.260	.280	.300	.350	.400	.450	.500
35	.200	.220	.240	.250	.260	.280	.300	.350	.400	.450	.500
40	.200	.220	.240	.250	.260	.280	.300	.350	.400	.450	.500
45	.200	.220	.240	.250	.260	.280	.300	.350	.400	.450	.500
50	.200	.220	.240	.250	.260	.280	.300	.350	.400	.450	.500

Table D Cumulative Probabilities of the Normal Probability Distribution
(Areas under the Normal Curve from − ∞ to z)

z	.00	.01	.02	.03	.04	.05	.06	.07	.08	.09
.0	.5000	.5040	.5080	.5120	.5160	.5199	.5239	.5279	.5319	.5359
.1	.5398	.5438	.5478	.5517	.5557	.5596	.5636	.5675	.5714	.5753
.2	.5793	.5832	.5871	.5910	.5948	.5987	.6026	.6064	.6103	.6141
.3	.6179	.6217	.6255	.6293	.6331	.6368	.6406	.6443	.6480	.6517
.4	.6554	.6591	.6628	.6664	.6700	.6736	.6772	.6808	.6844	.6879
.5	.6915	.6950	.6985	.7019	.7054	.7088	.7123	.7157	.7190	.7224
.6	.7257	.7291	.7324	.7357	.7389	.7422	.7454	.7486	.7517	.7549
.7	.7580	.7611	.7642	.7673	.7704	.7734	.7764	.7794	.7823	.7852
.8	.7881	.7910	.7939	.7967	.7995	.8023	.8051	.8078	.8106	.8133
.9	.8159	.8186	.8212	.8238	.8264	.8289	.8315	.8340	.8365	.8389
1.0	.8413	.8438	.8461	.8485	.8508	.8531	.8554	.8577	.8599	.8621
1.1	.8643	.8665	.8686	.8708	.8729	.8749	.8770	.8790	.8810	.8830
1.2	.8849	.8869	.8888	.8907	.8925	.8944	.8962	.8980	.8997	.9015
1.3	.9032	.9049	.9066	.9082	.9099	.9115	.9131	.9147	.9162	.9177
1.4	.9192	.9207	.9222	.9236	.9251	.9265	.9279	.9292	.9306	.9319
1.5	.9332	.9345	.9357	.9370	.9382	.9394	.9406	.9418	.9429	.9441
1.6	.9452	.9463	.9474	.9484	.9495	.9505	.9515	.9525	.9535	.9545
1.7	.9554	.9564	.9573	.9582	.9591	.9599	.9608	.9616	.9625	.9633
1.8	.9641	.9649	.9656	.9664	.9671	.9678	.9686	.9693	.9699	.9706
1.9	.9713	.9719	.9726	.9732	.9738	.9744	.9750	.9756	.9761	.9767
2.0	.9772	.9778	.9783	.9788	.9793	.9798	.9803	.9808	.9812	.9817
2.1	.9821	.9826	.9830	.9834	.9838	.9842	.9846	.9850	.9854	.9857
2.2	.9861	.9864	.9868	.9871	.9875	.9878	.9881	.9884	.9887	.9890
2.3	.9893	.9896	.9898	.9901	.9904	.9906	.9909	.9911	.9913	.9916
2.4	.9918	.9920	.9922	.9925	.9927	.9929	.9931	.9932	.9934	.9936
2.5	.9938	.9940	.9941	.9943	.9945	.9946	.9948	.9949	.9951	.9952
2.6	.9953	.9955	.9956	.9957	.9959	.9960	.9961	.9962	.9963	.9964
2.7	.9965	.9966	.9967	.9968	.9969	.9970	.9971	.9972	.9973	.9974
2.8	.9974	.9975	.9976	.9977	.9977	.9978	.9979	.9979	.9980	.9981
2.9	.9981	.9982	.9982	.9983	.9984	.9984	.9985	.9985	.9986	.9986
3.0	.9987	.9987	.9987	.9988	.9988	.9989	.9989	.9989	.9990	.9990
3.1	.9990	.9991	.9991	.9991	.9992	.9992	.9992	.9992	.9993	.9993
3.2	.9993	.9993	.9994	.9994	.9994	.9994	.9994	.9995	.9995	.9995
3.3	.9995	.9995	.9995	.9996	.9996	.9996	.9996	.9996	.9996	.9997
3.4	.9997	.9997	.9997	.9997	.9997	.9997	.9997	.9997	.9997	.9998

z	1.282	1.645	1.960	2.326	2.576	3.090	3.291	3.891	4.417
$F(z)$	.90	.95	.975	.99	.995	.999	.9995	.99995	.999995
$2[1 - F(z)]$	.20	.10	.05	.02	.01	.002	.001	.0001	.00001

Source: Reprinted with permission from A. M. Mood, *Introduction to the Theory of Statistics* (New York: McGraw-Hill Book Co., Inc., 1950), p. 423.

Table E Random Numbers Table

1581922396	2068577984	8262130892	8374856049	4637567488
0928105582	7295088579	9586111652	7055508767	6472382934
4112077556	3440672486	1882412963	0684012006	0933147914
7457477468	5435810788	9670852913	1291265730	4890031305
0099520858	3090908872	2039593181	5973470495	9776135501
7245174840	2275698645	8416549348	4676463101	2229367983
6749420382	4832630032	5670984959	5432114610	2966095680
5503161011	7413686599	1198757695	0414294470	0140121598
7164238934	7666127259	5263097712	5133648980	4011966963
3593969525	0272759769	0385998136	9999089966	7544056852
4192054466	0700014629	5169439659	8408705169	1074373131
9697426117	6488888550	4031652526	8123543276	0927534537
2007950579	9564268448	3457416988	1531027886	7016633739
4584768758	2389278610	3859431781	3643768456	4141314518
3840145867	9120831830	7228567652	1267173884	4020651657
0190453442	4800088084	1165628559	5407921254	3768932478
6766554338	5585265145	5089052204	9780623691	2195448096
6315116284	9172824179	5544814339	0016943666	3828538786
3908771938	4035554324	0840126299	4942059208	1475623997
5570024586	9324732596	1186563397	4425143189	3216653251
2999997185	0135968938	7678931194	1351031403	6002561840
7864375912	8383232768	1892857070	2323673751	3188881718
7065492027	6349104233	3382569662	4579426926	1513082455
0654683246	4765104877	8149224168	5468631609	6474393896
7830555058	5255147182	3519287786	2481675649	8907598697
7626984369	4725370390	9641916289	5049082870	7463807244
4785048453	3646121751	8436077768	2928794356	9956043516
4627791048	5765558107	8762592043	6185670830	6363845920
9376470693	0441608934	8749472723	2202271078	5897002653
1227991661	7936797054	9527542791	4711871173	8300978148
5582095589	5535798279	4764439855	6279247618	4446895088
4959397698	1056981450	8416606706	8234013222	6426813469
1824779358	1333750468	9434074212	5273692238	5902177065
7041092295	5726289716	3420847871	1820481234	0318831723
3555104281	0903099163	6827824899	6383872737	5901682626
9717595534	1634107293	8521057472	1471300754	3044151557
5571564123	7344613447	1129117244	3208461091	1699403490
4674262892	2809456764	5806554509	8224980942	5738031833
8461228715	0746980892	9285305274	6331989646	8764467686
1838538678	3049068967	6955157269	5482964330	2161984904
1834182305	6203476893	5937802079	3445280195	3694915658
1884227732	2923727501	8044389132	4611203081	6072112445
6791857341	6696243386	2219599137	3193884236	8224729718
3007929946	4031562749	5570757297	6273785046	1455349704
6085440624	2875556938	5496629750	4841817356	1443167141
7005051056	3496332071	5054070890	7303867953	6255181190
9846413446	8306646692	0661684251	8875127201	6251533454
0625457703	4229164694	7321363715	7051128285	1108468072
5457593922	9751489574	1799906380	1989141062	5595364247
4076486653	8950826528	4934582003	4071187742	1456207629

Source: Dudley J. Cowden and Mercedes S. Cowden, *Practical Problems in Business Statistics*, 2d ed, © 1960. Reprinted by permission of Prentice-Hall, Inc., Englewood Cliffs, N.J.

Table F Summation of Terms of the Poisson Formula*

μ or np' \ c	0	1	2	3	4	5	6	7	8	9
0.02	980	1,000								
0.04	961	999	1,000							
0.06	942	998	1,000							
0.08	923	997	1,000							
0.10	905	995	1,000							
0.15	861	990	999	1,000						
0.20	819	982	999	1,000						
0.25	779	974	998	1,000						
0.30	741	963	996	1,000						
0.35	705	951	994	1,000						
0.40	670	938	992	999	1,000					
0.45	638	925	989	999	1,000					
0.50	607	910	986	998	1,000					
0.55	577	894	982	998	1,000					
0.60	549	878	977	997	1,000					
0.65	522	861	972	996	999	1,000				
0.70	497	844	966	994	999	1,000				
0.75	472	827	959	993	999	1,000				
0.80	449	809	953	991	999	1,000				
0.85	427	791	945	989	998	1,000				
0.90	407	772	937	987	998	1,000				
0.95	387	754	929	984	997	1,000				
1.00	368	736	920	981	996	999	1,000			
1.1	333	699	900	974	995	999	1,000			
1.2	301	663	879	966	992	998	1,000			
1.3	273	627	857	957	989	998	1,000			
1.4	247	592	833	946	986	997	999	1,000		
1.5	223	558	809	934	981	996	999	1.000		
1.6	202	525	783	921	976	994	999	1,000		
1.7	183	493	757	907	970	992	998	1,000		
1.8	165	463	731	891	964	990	997	999	1,000	
1.9	150	434	704	875	956	987	997	999	1,000	
2.0	135	406	677	857	947	983	995	999	1,000	

$$*1{,}000 \times P(r \le c\,;\mu) = 1{,}000 \sum_{r=0}^{r=c} \frac{u^r e^{-\mu}}{r!}$$

1,000 × probability of c or less occurrences of event that has average number of occurrences equal to c' or np'.

Source: *Statistical Quality Control* by E. L. Grant. Copyright, 1964, by McGraw-Hill, Inc. Used by permission of McGraw-Hill Book Co.

Table F   Continued

μ or np'	c 0	1	2	3	4	5	6	7	8	9
2.2	111	355	623	819	928	975	993	998	1,000	
2.4	091	308	570	779	904	964	988	997	999	1,000
2.6	074	267	518	736	877	951	983	995	999	1,000
2.8	061	231	469	692	848	935	976	992	998	999
3.0	050	199	423	647	815	916	966	988	996	999
3.2	041	171	380	603	781	895	955	983	994	998
3.4	033	147	340	558	744	871	942	977	992	997
3.6	027	126	303	515	706	844	927	969	988	996
3.8	022	107	269	473	668	816	909	960	984	994
4.0	018	092	238	433	629	785	889	949	979	992
4.2	015	078	210	395	590	753	867	936	972	989
4.4	012	066	185	359	551	720	844	921	964	985
4.6	010	056	163	326	513	686	818	905	955	980
4.8	008	048	143	294	476	651	791	887	944	975
5.0	007	040	125	265	440	616	762	867	932	968
5.2	006	034	109	238	406	581	732	845	918	960
5.4	005	029	095	213	373	546	702	822	903	951
5.6	004	024	082	191	342	512	670	797	886	941
5.8	003	021	072	170	313	478	638	771	867	929
6.0	002	017	062	151	285	446	606	744	847	916

μ or np'	10	11	12	13	14	15	16
2.8	1,000						
3.0	1,000						
3.2	1,000						
3.4	999	1.000					
3.6	999	1,000					
3.8	998	999	1,000				
4.0	997	999	1,000				
4.2	996	999	1,000				
4.4	994	998	999	1,000			
4.6	992	997	999	1,000			
4.8	990	996	999	1,000			
5.0	986	995	998	999	1,000		
5.2	982	993	997	999	1,000		
5.4	977	990	996	999	1,000		
5.6	972	988	995	998	999	1,000	
5.8	965	984	993	997	999	1,000	
6.0	957	980	991	996	999	999	1,000

Table G Factors for Calculating Statistical Control Charts

Number of observations in subgroup n	Factors for $\overline{X}$ chart			Factors for R chart				Factor for estimate from R $d_2 = \overline{R}/\sigma'$	Factor for estimate from σ $c_2 = \overline{\sigma}/\sigma'$	Factors for σ chart			
	A	A_1	A_2	Lower control limit D_1	Upper control limit D_2	Lower control limit D_3	Upper control limit D_4			Lower control limit B_1	Upper control limit B_2	Lower control limit B_3	Upper control limit B_4
2	2.12	3.76	1.88	0	3.69	0	3.27	1.128	0.5642	0	1.84	0	3.27
3	1.73	2.39	1.02	0	4.36	0	2.57	1.693	0.7236	0	1.86	0	2.57
4	1.50	1.38	0.73	0	4.70	0	2.28	2.059	0.7979	0	1.81	0	2.27
5	1.34	1.60	0.58	0	4.92	0	2.11	2.326	0.8407	0	1.76	0	2.09
6	1.22	1.41	0.48	0	5.08	0	2.00	2.534	0.8686	0.03	1.71	0.03	1.97
7	1.13	1.28	0.42	0.20	5.20	0.08	1.92	2.704	0.8882	0.10	1.67	0.12	1.88
8	1.06	1.17	0.37	0.39	5.31	0.14	1.86	2.847	0.9027	0.17	1.64	0.19	1.81
9	1.00	1.09	0.34	0.55	5.39	0.18	1.82	2.970	0.9139	0.22	1.61	0.24	1.76
10	0.95	1.03	0.31	0.69	5.47	0.22	1.78	3.078	0.9227	0.26	1.58	0.28	1.72
11	0.90	0.97	0.29	0.81	5.53	0.26	1.74	3.173	0.9300	0.30	1.56	0.32	1.68
12	0.87	0.93	0.27	0.92	5.59	0.28	1.72	3.258	0.9359	0.36	1.54	0.35	1.65
13	0.83	0.88	0.25	1.03	5.65	0.31	1.69	3.336	0.9410	0.36	1.52	0.38	1.62
14	0.80	0.85	0.24	1.12	5.69	0.33	1.67	3.407	0.9453	0.38	1.51	0.41	1.59
15	0.77	0.82	0.22	1.21	5.74	0.35	1.65	3.472	0.9490	0.41	1.49	0.43	1.57
16	0.75	0.79	0.21	1.28	5.78	0.36	1.64	3.532	0.9523	0.43	1.48	0.45	1.55
17	0.73	0.76	0.20	1.36	5.82	0.38	1.62	3.588	0.9551	0.44	1.47	0.47	1.53
18	0.71	0.74	0.19	1.43	5.85	0.39	1.61	3.640	0.9576	0.46	1.45	0.48	1.52
19	0.69	0.72	0.19	1.49	5.89	0.40	1.60	3.689	0.9599	0.48	1.44	0.50	1.50
20	0.67	0.70	0.18	1.55	5.92	0.41	1.59	3.735	0.9619	0.49	1.43	0.51	1.49

Upper Control Limit for $\overline{X} = UCL_{\overline{X}} = \overline{\overline{X}} + A_2\overline{R}$
Lower Control Limit for $\overline{X} = LCL_{\overline{X}} = \overline{\overline{X}} - A_2\overline{R}$

$UCL_{\overline{X}} = \overline{X}' + A\sigma'$
$LCL_{\overline{X}} = \overline{X}' - A\sigma'$

$UCL_{\overline{X}} = \overline{X}' + A_1\overline{\sigma}$
$LCL_{\overline{X}} = \overline{X}' - A_1\overline{\sigma}$

Upper Control Limit for $R = UCL_R = D_4\overline{R}$
Lower Control Limit for $R = LCL_R = D_3\overline{R}$

$UCL_R = D_2\sigma'$
Central line$_R = d_2\sigma'$
$LCL_R = D_1\sigma'$

Upper Control Limit for $\sigma = UCL_\sigma = B_4\overline{\sigma}$
Lower Control Limit for $\sigma = LCL_\sigma = B_3\overline{\sigma}$

$UCL_\sigma = B_2\sigma'$
Central line$_\sigma = c_2\sigma'$
$LCL_\sigma = B_1\sigma'$

Estimate of $\sigma' = \overline{R}/d_2$ or $\overline{\sigma}/c_2$.

Source: E. L. Grant, *Statistical Quality Control*, 3rd ed. (New York: McGraw-Hill Book Co., 1964).

Index